PELICAN BOOKS

The Essentials of Psycho-Analysis

Sigmund Freud was born in 1856 in Moravia; between the ages of four and eighty-two his home was in Vienna; in 1938 Hitler's invasion of Austria forced him to seek asylum in London, where he died in the following year. His career began with several years of brilliant work on the anatomy and physiology of the nervous system. He was almost thirty when, after a period of study under Charcot in Paris, his interests first turned to psychology, and another ten years of clinical work in Vienna (at first in collaboration with Breuer, an older colleague) saw the birth of his creation, psycho-analysis. This began simply as a method of treating neurotic patients by investigating their minds, but it quickly grew into an accumulation of knowledge about the workings of the mind in general, whether sick or healthy. Freud was thus able to demonstrate the normal development of the sexual instinct in childhood and, largely on the basis of an examination of dreams, arrived at his fundamental discovery of the unconscious forces that influence our everyday thoughts and actions. Freud's life was uneventful, but his ideas have shaped not only many specialist disciplines, but the whole intellectual climate of the last half-century.

Anna Freud was one of Sigmund Freud's six children, born in Vienna. She wrote many books on psychology and psycho-analysis, some with a particular emphasis on the psychology of children. This definitive collection of her father's work was compiled shortly before her death.

D1353623

SIGMUND FREUD

The Essentials
of Psycho-Analysis

Selected, with an introduction and commentaries, by
ANNA FREUD

Translated from the German by
JAMES STRACHEY

PENGUIN BOOKS

Penguin Books Ltd, Harmondsworth, Middlesex, England
Viking Penguin Inc., 40 West 23rd Street, New York, New York 10010, U.S.A.
Penguin Books Australia Ltd, Ringwood, Victoria, Australia
Penguin Books Canada Limited, 2801 John Street, Markham, Ontario, Canada L3R 1B4
Penguin Books (N.Z.) Ltd, 182–190 Wairau Road, Auckland 10, New Zealand

This collection first published by the Hogarth Press 1986
Published in Pelican Books 1986

Made and printed in Great Britain by
Hazell Watson & Viney Limited,
Member of the BPCC Group,
Aylesbury, Bucks
Filmset in Linotron Baskerville

Contents

Foreword

CLIFFORD YORKE

Psycho-analysts are often asked to recommend a short introduction to the work of Sigmund Freud and, in particular, to his psycho-analytic psychology. Hitherto, that request has defied an easy answer. Freud's own expository introductions to, and summaries of, his work, for all their interest and value, do not meet the needs of those who wish to acquire a sound general grasp of his theoretical ideas, whether in furtherance of a broader knowledge of contemporary thought or as a framework within which to build a more comprehensive under-standing of psycho-analysis.

In her Introduction to this volume Anna Freud comments on some of these essays of her father's, but certain points may be emphasized here with advantage. The necessity for continual, and sometimes substantial, revision of his formulations, occasioned by his own major advances, has meant that Freud's summaries of his own work inevi-tably bore the stamp of their time and could not take account of future developments. Substantial changes in the theory of anxiety, of female sexual development, and of the concept of mental structure would each, for example, provide a case in point. Indeed, it was the recognition of this difficulty which led Freud to supplement his *Introductory Lectures* of 1916–17 with the *New Introductory Lectures* (1933*a*) some sixteen years later. It was this same logic which suggested that these works form the first two volumes of the Pelican Freud Library. And although *An Outline of Psycho-Analysis* (1940*a*), written shortly before Freud's death, is restricted to the compass of a single volume, it is in no sense a work for beginners. It is a condensed summary for the informed which makes its points with scant illustration and without frills or supporting argument.

Anna Freud had long held the view that the one work of her father's which could best introduce his work to a wide audience was *The Question of Lay Analysis* (1926*e*). She recognized, however, that its treatment of the various contributions which psycho-analysis had made to the understanding of mental functioning was insufficiently detailed for fuller expository purposes. In her view, these demanded that each idea outlined in Freud's discussion be elaborated through further expository writings by Freud, and it was the task of making an appropriate selection to which she then applied herself. Furthermore, she thought it necessary, from the first, to link these items with her own explanatory passages. A fruitful collaboration with Ilse Grubrich-Simitis resulted in a two-volume work published in German under the title *Sigmund Freud Werkausgabe in zwei Bänden* (1978), the first volume of which was devoted to major theoretical issues and the second to applied psycho-analysis.

Given the scope of *The Question of Lay Analysis*, it was natural that this valuable work, edited and annotated by Mrs Grubrich-Simitis, took the form it did. But it went beyond the requirements of a single-volume introduction to Freud's theoretical thinking. It was the continuing need for just such a volume which prompted Anna Freud to try to supply it, and she applied the principle she had adopted in the first part of the German work to this task.

Since, for the new purpose, it was unnecessary to enlarge at length on the arguments of *Lay Analysis*, she omitted those papers which would mainly be of interest to the practising analyst, such as the papers on technique, or which lent themselves to discussion by psycho-analytic institutes, such as papers on training. These contributions were in no way essential for the general exposition which Anna Freud had in mind for the immediate task in hand. At the suggestion of Mrs Juliet Mitchell Rossdale, she decided to illustrate Freud's developing views on female sexuality by the appropriate chapter of *New Introductory Lectures* (1933*a*) rather than the earlier paper, 'Female Sexuality' (1931*b*).

The work now presented is something more than a one-volume 'Freud by Freud'. For Anna Freud's selection is not only comprehensive within the limitations imposed by length, but is put together in a form made all the more valuable by her own coordinating passages. Anna Freud was uniquely equipped for such a task. For some years before she wrote her first published paper ('Beating Fantasies and Daydreams', 1922), and thereby gained admission to the Vienna Psycho-Analytic Society, she had acted as her father's secretary and amanuensis. She was at all times thoroughly conversant with his thinking, and with that of his colleagues in the Society, and she had unrivalled opportunities to discuss his thoughts with him in the very process of their development. Although her dedication to her father's ideas was never in doubt, her pursuit of them was never slavish. Indeed, it could be said that her wider devotion was to psycho-analysis and its development rather than to her father's thinking as such. Even though she did not actively criticize some of his ideas, there were areas of his thinking which she refused to follow. She never, for example, showed the least enthusiasm for the concept of the death instinct (*Beyond the Pleasure Principle*, 1920g), perhaps because she never regarded it as a basic requirement for psycho-analytic thinking. Throughout her long and productive life, in which she herself extended and enriched psycho-analysis, in particular through her contributions to the understanding of children and developmental psychology, she remained aware that there were certain irreducible concepts, the abnegation of which impoverished the entire discipline and rendered its arguments ineffective. It is those basic principles which are to be found in the present volume.

Earlier attempts to introduce the enquiring reader to Freud's work on the basis of his own writings have included the selection by Rickman (1937). This was an influential work but it was insufficiently comprehensive and has long been out of print. Expository works by others, such as Stafford-Clark's *What Freud Really Said* (1967), have been interpretative, and introductory works like Brenner's *Elementary Textbook of Psychoanalysis* (1973) tend to be influenced by the writer's own ideas – in this case, that the so-called 'topographical theory' was replaced by the 'structural theory'. It can at last be confidently asserted that the present volume fulfils a long-felt need for the very first time, and does so with authority. It is throughout informed by that lucidity which was a trademark of both father and daughter.

It is a pleasure to acknowledge the careful preparation of this volume for press by Albert Dickson, who also compiled the bibliography. Thanks are due to Messrs Allen & Unwin and W. W. Norton for permission to reprint the chapter on female sexuality from *Introductory Lectures on Psycho-Analysis*. The translation is throughout from that supervised by James Strachey in the *Standard Edition of the Complete Psychological Works of Sigmund Freud*, jointly published by The Hogarth Press and The Institute of Psycho-Analysis, and to which reference is made in the text by the abbreviation *Standard Ed.* Strachey's editorial notes, taken from the *Standard Edition*, are indicated by square brackets, other notes being by Freud himself. Throughout the book, the reference *P.F.L.* is to the Pelican Freud Library.

Clifford Yorke
Editor of Books,
International Psycho-Analytical Library

Introduction[1]

Introducing lay persons – whether students or readers with no prior knowledge – to the world of psycho-analytic thought is a difficult task, no matter how one goes about it. The mental processes of adults and children, whether in illness or health, have many meanings, and their infinite variations may produce a sense of estrangement. If the instructor wants to spare his student surprises and difficulties, he cannot help but falsify his material. If he wants to do justice to the facts, he runs the risk of demanding too much from his students and losing their interest and continuing attention.

Freud himself strove throughout his life to take a middle course between these two dangers. His efforts to present the results of psycho-analytic work clearly and as far as possible in generally comprehensible language began in the year 1904 with 'Freud's Psycho-Analytic Procedure' (1904a) and ended only in the last year of his life with the unfinished paper *An Outline of Psycho-Analysis* (1940a) and 'Some Elementary Lessons in Psycho-Analysis' (1940b). During the intervening years he wrote numerous other surveys that differ in length and range, and are directed to very different audiences; some of these were initiated by his own interest, others were the result of requests. Thus, *Introductory Lectures on Psycho-Analysis* (1916–17) and *New Introductory Lectures on Psycho-Analysis* (1933a) are directed primarily to an academic audience, the first having in fact been presented at the University of Vienna. 'The Claims of Psycho-Analysis to Scientific Interest' (1913j) and 'A Short Account of Psycho-Analysis' (1924f), and 'Psycho-Analysis' (1926f), on the other hand, are highly condensed summaries that were written as contributions to dictionaries and encyclopedias in Germany, Italy, England, and the United

[1] This introduction and the commentaries which precede each section of the present volume first appeared in English under the title 'A Study Guide to Freud's Writings' in Volume 8 of Miss Freud's Collected Writings, *Psychoanalytic Psychology of Normal Development*, published by The Hogarth Press (London).

States. 'On the History of the Psycho-Analytic movement' (1914*d*), in addition to describing the basic concepts of psycho-analysis, also serves the purpose of defining the boundaries separating psycho-analysis from the two movements that broke away from it, namely, Adler's individual psychology and Jung's analytic psychology. *An Autobiographical Study* (1925*d*) deals primarily with the life work of the author and barely touches on his personal biography.

In the middle of this series is the essay *The Question of Lay Analysis* (1926*e*), a publication that owes its existence to the need to defend the psycho-analytic treatment method against the claim by the medical profession that only physicians can carry it out. This claim, which based itself on the Austrian law against 'quackery', threatened all non-medical psycho-analysts with legal prosecution at that time. It was Freud's task to take up arms and to justify his view that 'the important question is not whether an analyst possesses a medical diploma but whether he has had the special training necessary for the practice of analysis'. In a postscript (1927*a*) to his extensive tract, Freud then wonders whether he has succeeded in sufficiently clarifying the problem of lay analysis. In fact, the issue of accepting non-medical persons for training in psycho-analysis still remains unsolved to this day. In Europe and other continents, Freud's exposition led to far-reaching acceptance of his point of view. This is not so in the United States where, however, it is not the official authorities that oppose lay analysis, as had been the case in Austria; rather, it is the psycho-analytic speciality itself that advocates the medical privilege and excludes non-physicians from the American Psychoanalytic Association.

Apart from possibly pointing the way to a solution of this dispute in the present and the future, Freud's treatise on this topic remains a publication of permanent value which is better suited than any of the above-mentioned introductions to make psycho-analytic teachings accessible to the interested student. In it Freud leads an imaginary 'Impartial Person', step by step, from the conscious surface of mental processes to the depth of the unconscious.

He starts with the meaning of dreams as evidence of the existence of an *unconscious mental life*, of which waking life has no knowledge. From there he leads over to the other elements which comprise that same psychic system and endow it with energy, i.e., the *instinctual drives*. The detailed description of man's *sexual life* from its infantile pre-stages to its definitive organization in the adult serves Freud as the basis for presenting the conflict between the individual's search for pleasure and the demands of reality opposed to it. He demonstrates how the battle between instinctual urges and the inhibiting external world, a battle that begins in childhood, changes its character with the progressive building up of the *psychic personality*. He divides the latter into an instinctual unconscious *id*, a rationally orientated *ego*, and an ethical-moral, critical agency, the *super-ego*, which develops on the basis of identifications. The circumstance that each of these inner agencies pursues its own goals leads to the insight into the *dynamic* aspect of mental life; i.e., to the psycho-analytic concept of *psychic conflict*: the ego mobilizes all methods available to it, in the first line, *repression*, to prevent the instinctual impulses from unrestrainedly gaining their goal. The knowledge of these defensive struggles opens the way to an understanding of those compromise formations between ego and id from which *neurotic symptoms* evolve.

Having described these complications of mental life, Freud returns to his original question concerning the practice of psycho-analysis and draws attention to the inherent difficulties of *therapeutic technique*: the patient's ever-present positive attachment to his symptoms, i.e., his need to remain ill; the resistance against the lifting of repressions and the undoing of the other defensive accomplishments as well as the fear of instinctual breakthroughs, an anxiety that led to the illness in the first place; the *transference of feelings* originally directed to persons in the patient's past to the treating analyst and the technical difficulties in their management. The obvious fact that there is nothing in the medical curriculum to prepare the physician for dealing with these psychic complications becomes the basis for Freud's demand that analysts be required to have special, lengthy, and careful *training* in specialized institutes which do not follow the traditional medical course of study.

In introducing the student to the elements of psycho-analysis, we cannot find a better arrangement than that adopted by Freud in *The Question of Lay Analysis*. On the one hand, we can presuppose that those wanting to learn about analysis bring to this task the same critical yet open-minded attitude that Freud accords to his partner in the conversations presented in this essay, and that they, like the Impartial Person, will welcome the interplay of questions and answers which encourages the participant in this discussion to voice his doubts and to seek further clarification of obscure points. For this reason I would suggest that the study of Freud's writings begin with *The Question of Lay Analysis*.

On the other hand, we would be convinced that a student of psycho-analysis wishes to learn more than the 'higher functionary', who wanted to use his newly acquired knowledge solely for deciding a legal question. Thus, we would use Freud's sequence of themes as a guiding principle for introducing students to the major elements of psycho-analysis: starting with the dream, we would proceed to the unconscious, the instinctual and sexual life, the structure of the personality, the defence mechanisms, and symptom-formation. Each of these elements is extensively treated in Freud's work. The selections from his writings outlined below constitute a reasonable course of study which will enable the student to penetrate the theoretical structure of psycho-analysis to a certain depth.

ANNA FREUD

One
LAY ANALYSIS

The Question of Lay Analysis

Conversations with an Impartial Person

(1926)*

INTRODUCTION

The title of this small work is not immediately intelligible. I will therefore explain it. 'Layman' = 'non-doctor'; and the question is whether non-doctors as well as doctors are to be allowed to practise analysis. This question has its limitations both in time and place. In *time*, because up to now no one has been concerned as to *who* practises analysis. Indeed, people have been much too little concerned about it – the one thing they were agreed on was a wish that *no one* should practise it. Various reasons were given for this, but they were based on the same underlying distaste. Thus the demand that only doctors should analyse corresponds to a new and apparently more friendly attitude to analysis – if, that is, it can escape the suspicion of being after all only a slightly modified derivative of the earlier attitude. It is conceded that in some circumstances an analytic treatment shall be undertaken; but, if so, only doctors are to undertake it. The reason for this restriction then becomes a matter for enquiry.

The question is limited in *place* because it does not arise in all countries with equal significance. In Germany and America it would be no more than an academic discussion; for in those countries every patient can have himself treated how and by whom he chooses, and anyone who chooses can, as a 'quack', handle any patients, provided only that he undertakes the responsibility for his actions. The law does not intervene until it is called in to expiate some injury done to the patient. But in Austria, in which and for which I am writing, there is a preventive law, which forbids non-doctors from undertaking the treatment of patients, without waiting for its outcome.[1] So here the question whether laymen (= non-doctors) may treat patients by

---

* First published as a pamphlet by Internationaler Psychoanalytischer Verlag (Leipzig, Vienna, Zurich). The present version is included in *Standard Ed.*, **20**, 183, and *P.F.L.*, **15**. The reasons for its publication are given in the preceding introduction, and discussed by Freud in the 'Postscript' which follows it.
[1] The same holds good in France.

psycho-analysis has a practical sense. As soon as it is raised, however, it appears to be settled by the wording of the law. Neurotics are patients, laymen are non-doctors, psycho-analysis is a procedure for curing or improving nervous disorders, and all such treatments are reserved to doctors. It follows that laymen are not permitted to practise analysis on neurotics, and are punishable if they nevertheless do so. The position being so simple, one hardly ventures to take up the question of lay analysis. All the same, there are some complications, which the law does not trouble about, but which nevertheless call for consideration. It may perhaps turn out that in this instance the patients are not like other patients, that the laymen are not really laymen, and that the doctors have not exactly the qualities which one has a right to expect of doctors and on which their claims should be based. If this can be proved, there will be justifiable grounds for demanding that the law shall not be applied without modification to the instance before us.

I

Whether this happens will depend on people who are not obliged to be familiar with the peculiarities of an analytic treatment. It is our task to give information on the subject to these impartial persons, whom we shall assume to be, at the moment, still in ignorance. It is to be regretted that we cannot let them be present as an audience at a treatment of this kind. But the 'analytic situation' allows of the presence of no third person. Moreover the different sessions are of very unequal value. An unauthorized listener who hit upon a chance one of them would as a rule form no useful impression; he would be in danger of not understanding what was passing between the analyst and the patient, or he would be bored. For good or ill, therefore, he must be content with our information, which we shall try to make as trustworthy as possible.

A patient, then, may be suffering from fluctuations in his moods which he cannot control, or from a sense of despondency by which his energy feels paralysed because he thinks he is incapable of doing anything properly, or from a nervous embarrassment among strangers. He may perceive, without understanding the reason for it, that he has difficulties in carrying out his professional work, or indeed any comparatively important decision or any undertaking. He may one day have suffered from a distressing attack – unknown in its origin – of feelings of anxiety, and since then have been unable; without a struggle, to walk along the street alone, or to travel by train; he may perhaps have had to give up both entirely. Or, a very remarkable thing, his thoughts may go their own way and refuse to be directed by his will. They pursue problems that are quite indifferent to him, but from which he cannot get free. Quite ludicrous tasks, too, are imposed on him, such as counting up the windows on the fronts of houses. And when he has performed simple actions such as posting a letter or turning off a gas-jet, he finds himself a moment later doubting whether he has really done so. This may be no more than an annoyance and a nuisance. But his state becomes intolerable if he suddenly finds he is unable to fend off the idea that he has pushed a child under the wheels of a car or has thrown a stranger off the bridge into the water, or if he has to ask himself whether he is not the murderer whom the police are looking for in connection with a crime that was discovered that day. It is obvious nonsense, as he himself knows; he has never done any harm to anyone; but if he were really the murderer who is being looked for, his feeling – his sense of guilt – could not be stronger.

Or again our patient – and this time let us make her a woman – may suffer in another way and in a different field. She is a pianist, but her fingers are overcome by cramp and refuse to serve her. Or when she thinks of going to a party she promptly becomes aware of a call of nature the satisfaction of which would be incompatible with a social gathering. She has therefore given up going to parties, dances, theatres or concerts. She is overcome by violent headaches or other painful sensations at times when they are most inconvenient. She may even be unable to keep down any meal she eats – which can become dangerous in the long run. And, finally, it is a lamentable fact that she cannot tolerate any agitations, which after all are inevitable in life. On such occasions she falls in a faint, often accompanied by muscular spasms that recall sinister pathological states.

Other patients, again, suffer from disturbances in a particular field in which emotional life converges with demands of a bodily sort. If they are men, they find they are incapable of giving physical express-ion to their tenderest feelings towards the opposite sex, while towards less loved objects they may perhaps have every reaction at their command. Or their sensual feelings attach them to people whom they despise and from whom they would like to get free; or those same feelings impose requirements on them whose fulfilment they them-selves find repulsive. If they are women, they feel prevented by anxiety or disgust or by unknown obstructions from meeting the demands of sexual life; or, if they have surrendered to love, they find themselves cheated of the enjoyment which nature has provided as a reward for such compliance.

All these people recognize that they are ill and go to doctors, by whom people expect nervous disorders like these to be removed. The doctors, too, lay down the categories into which these complaints are divided. They diagnose them, each according to his own standpoint, under different names: neurasthenia, psychasthenia, phobias, obsessional neurosis, hysteria. They examine the organs which produce the symptoms, the heart, the stomach, the bowels, the genitals, and find them healthy. They recommend interruptions in the patient's accustomed mode of life, holidays, strengthening exercises, tonics, and by these means bring about temporary improvements – or no result at all. Eventually the patients hear that there are people who are concerned quite specially with the treatment of such complaints and start an analysis with them.

During this disquisition on the symptoms of neurotics, the Impartial Person, whom I imagine as being present, has been showing signs of impatience. At this point, however, he becomes attentive and interested. 'So now', he says, 'we shall learn what the analyst does with the patient whom the doctor has not been able to help.'

Nothing takes place between them except that they talk to each other. The analyst makes use of no instruments – not even for examining the patient – nor does he prescribe any medicines. If it is at all possible, he even leaves the patient in his environment and in his usual mode of life during the treatment. This is not a necessary condition, of course, and may not always be practicable. The analyst agrees upon a fixed regular hour with the patient, gets him to talk, listens to him, talks to him in his turn and gets him to listen.

The Impartial Person's features now show signs of unmistakable relief and relaxation, but they also clearly betray some contempt. It is as though he were thinking: 'Nothing more than that? Words, words, words, as Prince Hamlet says.' And no doubt he is thinking too of Mephistopheles' mocking speech on how comfortably one can get along with words[1] – lines that no German will ever forget.

'So it is a kind of magic,' he comments: 'you talk, and blow away his ailments.'

[1] [In the scene with the student in *Faust*, Part I, Scene 4.]

Quite true. It *would* be magic if it worked rather quicker. An essential attribute of a magician is speed – one might say suddenness – of success. But analytic treatments take months and even years: magic that is so slow loses its miraculous character. And incidentally do not let us despise the *word*. After all it is a powerful instrument; it is the means by which we convey our feelings to one another, our method of influencing other people. Words can do unspeakable good and cause terrible wounds. No doubt 'in the beginning was the deed'[1] and the word came later; in some circumstances it meant an advance in civilization when deeds were softened into words. But originally the word was magic – a magical act; and it has retained much of its ancient power.

The Impartial Person proceeds: 'Let us suppose that the patient is no better prepared to understand analytic treatment than I am; then how are you going to make him believe in the magic of the word or of the speech that is to free him from his sufferings?'

Some preparation must of course be given to him; and there is a simple way of doing it. We call on him to be completely straightforward with his analyst, to keep nothing back intentionally that comes into his head, and then to put aside *every* reservation that might prevent his reporting certain thoughts or memories. Everyone is aware that there are some things in himself that he would be very unwilling to tell other people or that he considers it altogether out of the question to tell. These are his 'intimacies'. He has a notion too – and this represents a great advance in psychological self-knowledge – that there are other things that one would not care to admit *to oneself*: things that one likes to conceal from oneself and which for that reason one breaks off short and drives out of one's thoughts if, in spite of everything, they turn up. Perhaps he may himself notice that a very remarkable psychological problem begins to appear in this situation – of a thought of his own being kept secret from his own self. It looks as though his own self were no longer the unity which he had always considered it to be, as though there were something else as well in him that could confront that self. He may become obscurely aware of a contrast between a self and a mental life in the wider sense. If now he accepts the demand made by analysis that he shall say everything, he will easily become accessible to an expectation that to have relations

---

[1] [Goethe, *Faust*, Part I, Scene 3.]

and exchanges of thought with someone under such unusual conditions might also lead to peculiar results.

'I understand,' says our Impartial Person. 'You assume that every neurotic has something oppressing him, some secret. And by getting him to tell you about it you relieve his oppression and do him good. That, of course, is the principle of confession, which the Catholic Church has used from time immemorial in order to make secure its dominance over people's minds.'

We must reply: 'Yes and no!' Confession no doubt plays a part in analysis – as an introduction to it, we might say. But it is very far from constituting the essence of analysis or from explaining its effects. In confession the sinner tells what he knows; in analysis the neurotic has to tell more. Nor have we heard that confession has ever developed enough power to get rid of actual pathological symptoms.

'Then, after all, I do not understand,' comes the rejoinder. 'What can you possibly mean by "telling more than he knows"? But I can well believe that as an analyst you gain a stronger influence over your patients than a father confessor over his penitents, since your contacts with him are so much longer, more intensive and also more individual, and since you use this increased influence to divert him from his sick thoughts, to talk him out of his fears, and so on. It would certainly be strange if it were possible by such means to control purely physical phenomena as well, such as vomiting, diarrhoea, convulsions; but I know that influence like that is in fact quite possible if a person is put into a state of hypnosis. By the trouble you take with the patient you probably succeed in bringing about a hypnotic relation of that sort with him – a suggestive attachment to yourself – even though you may not intend to; and in that case the miraculous results of your treatment are the effect of hypnotic suggestion. But, so far as I know, hypnotic treatment works much faster than your analysis, which, as you tell me, lasts for months and years.'

Our Impartial Person cannot be either so ignorant or so perplexed as we thought to begin with. There are unmistakable signs that he is trying to understand psycho-analysis with the help of his previous knowledge, that he is trying to link it up with something he already knows. The difficult task now lies ahead of us of making it clear to him that he will not succeed in this: that analysis is a procedure *sui generis*, something novel and special, which can only be understood with the help of *new* insights – or hypotheses, if that sounds better. But he is still waiting for our answer to his last remarks.

What you say about the special personal influence of the analyst certainly deserves great attention. An influence of the kind exists and plays a large part in analysis – but not the same part as in hypnotism. It ought to be possible to convince you that the situations in the two cases are quite different. It may be enough to point out that we do not use this personal influence, the factor of 'suggestion', to suppress the symptoms of the illness, as happens with *hypnotic* suggestion. Further, it would be a mistake to believe that this factor is the vehicle and promoter of the treatment throughout its length. At its beginning, no doubt. But later on it opposes our analytic intentions and forces us to adopt the most far-reaching counter-measures. And I should like to show by an example how far diverting a patient's thoughts and talking him out of things are from the technique of analysis. If a patient of ours is suffering from a sense of guilt, as though he had committed a serious crime, we do not recommend him to disregard his qualms of conscience and do not emphasize his undoubted innocence; he himself has often tried to do so without success. What we do is to remind him that such a strong and persistent feeling must after all be based on something real, which it may perhaps be possible to discover.

'It would surprise me', comments the Impartial Person, 'if you were able to soothe your patients by agreeing with their sense of guilt in that way. But what *are* your analytic intentions? and what *do* you do with your patients?'

II

If I am to say anything intelligible to you, I shall no doubt have to tell you something of a psychological theory which is not known or not appreciated outside analytic circles. It will be easy to deduce from this theory what we want from our patients and how we obtain it. I shall expound it to you dogmatically, as though it were a complete theoretical structure. But do not suppose that it came into being as such a structure, like a philosophical system. We have developed it very slowly, we have wrestled over every small detail of it, we have unceasingly modified it, keeping a continuous contact with observation, till it has finally taken a shape in which it seems to suffice for our purposes. Only a few years ago I should have had to clothe this theory in other terms. Nor, of course, can I guarantee to you that the form in which it is expressed to-day will remain the final one. Science, as you know, is not a revelation; long after its beginnings it still lacks the attributes of definiteness, immutability and infallibility for which human thought so deeply longs. But such as it is, it is all that we can have. If you will further bear in mind that our science is very young, scarcely as old as the century, and that it is concerned with what is perhaps the most difficult material that can be the subject of human research, you will easily be able to adopt the correct attitude towards my exposition. But interrupt me whenever you feel inclined, if you cannot follow me or if you want further explanations.

'I will interrupt you before you have even begun. You say that you intend to expound a new psychology to me; but I should have thought that psychology was no new science. There have been psychologies and psychologists enough; and I heard of great achievements in that field while I was at college.'

I should not dream of disputing them. But if you look into the matter more closely you will have to class these great achievements as belonging rather to the physiology of the sense organs. The theory of mental life could not be developed, because it was inhibited by a single essential misunderstanding. What does it comprise to-day, as it is taught at college? Apart from those valuable discoveries in the physiology of the senses, a number of classifications and definitions of our mental processes which, thanks to linguistic usage, have become the common property of every educated person. That is clearly not enough to give a view of our mental life. Have you not noticed that every philosopher, every imaginative writer, every historian and every biographer makes up his own psychology for himself, brings forward his own particular hypotheses concerning the inter-connections and aims of mental acts – all more or less plausible and all equally untrustworthy? There is an evident lack of any common foundation. And it is for that reason too that in the field of psychology there is, so to speak, no respect and no authority. In that field everyone can 'run wild' as he chooses. If you raise a question in physics or chemistry, anyone who knows he possesses no 'technical knowledge' will hold his tongue. But if you venture upon a psycholo-gical assertion, you must be prepared to meet judgements and contradictions from every quarter. In this field, apparently, there is no 'technical knowledge'. Everyone has a mental life, so everyone regards himself as a psychologist. But that strikes me as an inadequ-ate legal title. The story is told of how someone who applied for a post as a children's nurse was asked if she knew how to look after babies. 'Of course,' she replied, 'why, after all, I was a baby once myself.'

'And you claim that you have discovered this "common foundation" of mental life, which has been overlooked by every psychologist, from observations on *sick people*?'

The source of our findings does not seem to me to deprive them of their value. Embryology, to take an example, would not deserve to be trusted if it could not give a plain explanation of the origin of innate malformations. I have told you of people whose thoughts go their own way, so that they are obliged to worry over problems to which they are perfectly indifferent. Do you think that academic psychology could ever make the smallest contribution towards explaining an abnormality such as that? And, after all, we all of us have the experience at night-time of our thoughts going their own way and creating things which we do not understand, which puzzle us, and which are suspiciously reminiscent of pathological products. Our dreams, I mean. The common people have always firmly believed that dreams have a sense and a value – that they mean something. Academic psychology has never been able to inform us what this meaning is. It could make nothing of dreams. If it attempted to produce explanations, they were non-psychological – such as tracing them to sensory stimuli, or to an unequal depth of sleep in different portions of the brain, and so on. But it is fair to say that a psychology which cannot explain dreams is also useless for an understanding of normal mental life, that it has no claim to be called a science.

'You are becoming aggressive; so you have evidently got on to a sensitive spot. I have heard, it is true, that in analysis great value is attached to dreams, that they are interpreted, and that memories of real events are looked for behind them, and so on. But I have heard as well that the interpretation of dreams is left to the caprice of analysts, and that they themselves have never ceased disputing over the way of interpreting dreams and the justification for drawing conclusions from them. If that is so, you ought not to underline so heavily the advantage that analysis has won over academic psychology.'

There is really a great deal of truth in what you say. It is true that the interpretation of dreams has come to have unequalled importance both for the theory and the practice of analysis. If I seem to be aggressive, that is only a way of defending myself. And when I think of all the mischief some analysts have done with the interpretation of dreams I might lose heart and echo the pessimistic pronouncement of our great satirist Nestroy[1] when he says that every step forward is

---

[1] [Johann Nestroy (1801–62), famous in Vienna as a writer of comedies and farces.]

only half as big as it looks at first. But have you ever found that men do anything but confuse and distort what they get hold of? By the help of a little foresight and self-discipline most of the dangers of dream-interpretation can be avoided with certainty. But you will agree that I shall never come to my exposition if we let ourselves be led aside like this.

'Yes. If I understood rightly, you wanted to tell me about the fundamental postulate of the new psychology.'

That was not what I wanted to begin with. My purpose is to let you hear what pictures we have formed of the structure of the mental apparatus in the course of our analytic studies.

'What do you mean by the "mental apparatus"? and what, may I ask, is it constructed of?'

It will soon be clear what the mental apparatus is; but I must beg you not to ask what material it is constructed of. That is not a subject of psychological interest. Psychology can be as indifferent to it as, for instance, optics can be to the question of whether the walls of a telescope are made of metal or cardboard. We shall leave entirely on one side the *material* line of approach,[1] but not so the *spatial* one. For we picture the unknown apparatus which serves the activities of the mind as being really like an instrument constructed of several parts (which we speak of as 'agencies'), each of which performs a particular function and which have a fixed spatial relation to one another: it being understood that by spatial relation – 'in front of' and 'behind', 'superficial' and 'deep' – we merely mean in the first instance a representation of the regular succession of the functions. Have I made myself clear?

'Scarcely. Perhaps I shall understand it later. But, in any case, here is a strange anatomy of the soul – a thing which, after all, no longer exists at all for the scientists.'

What do you expect? It is a hypothesis like so many others in the sciences: the very earliest ones have always been rather rough. 'Open to revision' we can say in such cases. It seems to me unnecessary for me to appeal here to the 'as if' which has become so popular. The value of a 'fiction' of this kind (as the philosopher Vaihinger[2] would call it) depends on how much one can achieve with its help.

---

[1] [The question of what *material* the mental apparatus is constructed of.]

[2] [Hans Vaihinger (1852–1933). His philosophical system was enunciated in *Die Philosophie des Als Ob* (1911).]

But to proceed. Putting ourselves on the footing of everyday knowledge, we recognize in human beings a mental organization which is interpolated between their sensory stimuli and the perception of their somatic needs on the one hand and their motor acts on the other, and which mediates between them for a particular purpose. We call this organization their '*Ich*' ['ego'; literally, 'I']. Now there is nothing new in this. Each one of us makes this assumption without being a philosopher, and some people even in spite of being philosophers. But this does not, in our opinion, exhaust the description of the mental apparatus. Besides this 'I', we recognize another mental region, more extensive, more imposing and more obscure than the 'I', and this we call the '*Es*' ['id'; literally, 'it']. The relation between the two must be our immediate concern.

You will probably protest at our having chosen simple pronouns to describe our two agencies or provinces instead of giving them orotund Greek names. In psycho-analysis, however, we like to keep in contact with the popular mode of thinking and prefer to make its concepts scientifically serviceable rather than to reject them. There is no merit in this; we are obliged to take this line; for our theories must be understood by our patients, who are often very intelligent, but not always learned. The impersonal 'it' is immediately connected with certain forms of expression used by normal people. 'It shot through me,' people say; 'there was something in me at that moment that was stronger than me.' '*C'était plus fort que moi.*'

In psychology we can only describe things by the help of analogies. There is nothing peculiar in this; it is the case elsewhere as well. But we have constantly to keep changing these analogies, for none of them lasts us long enough. Accordingly, in trying to make the relation between the ego and the id clear, I must ask you to picture the ego as a kind of façade of the id, as a frontage, like an external, cortical, layer of it. We can hold on to this last analogy. We know that cortical layers owe their peculiar characteristics to the modifying influence of the external medium on which they abut. Thus we suppose that the ego is the layer of the mental apparatus (of the id) which has been modified by the influence of the external world (of reality). This will show you how in psycho-analysis we take spatial ways of looking at things seriously. For us the ego is really something superficial and the id something deeper – looked at from outside, of course. The ego lies between reality and the id, which is what is truly mental.

'I will not ask any questions yet as to how all this can be known. But tell me first what you gain from this distinction between an ego and an id? What leads you to make it?'

Your question shows me the right way to proceed. For the important and valuable thing is to know that the ego and the id differ greatly from each other in several respects. The rules governing the course of mental acts are different in the ego and the id; the ego pursues different purposes and by other methods. A great deal could be said about this; but perhaps you will be content with a fresh analogy and an example. Think of the difference between 'the front' and 'behind the lines', as things were during the war. We were not surprised then that some things were different at the front from what they were behind the lines, and that many things were permitted behind the lines which had to be forbidden at the front. The determining influence was, of course, the proximity of the enemy; in the case of mental life it is the proximity of the external world. There was a time when 'outside', 'strange' and 'hostile' were identical concepts. And now we come to the example. In the id there are no conflicts; contradictions and antitheses persist side by side in it unconcernedly, and are often adjusted by the formation of compromises. In similar circumstances the ego feels a conflict which must be decided; and the decision lies in one urge being abandoned in favour of the other. The ego is an organization characterized by a very remarkable trend towards unification, towards synthesis. This characteristic is lacking in the id; it is, as we might say, 'all to pieces'; its different urges pursue their own purposes independently and regardless of one another.

'And if such an important mental region "behind the lines" exists, how can you explain its having been overlooked till the time of analysis?'

That brings us back to one of your earlier questions. Psychology had barred its own access to the region of the id by insisting on a postulate which is plausible enough but untenable: namely, that all mental acts are conscious to us – that being conscious[1] is the criterion of what is mental, and that, if there are processes in our brain which are not conscious, they do not deserve to be called mental acts and are no concern of psychology.

[1] [Here written '*Bewusst-sein*': literally, 'being conscioused'. This word (the ordinary word for 'consciousness') is of course normally written without a hyphen. The hyphen is inserted here to show that Freud is emphasizing the underlying passive sense of the word '*bewusst*'. Cf. the Editor's Note to Freud's paper on 'The Unconscious' (1915*e*), *Standard Ed.*, **14**, 165 *n.*; *P.F.L.*, **11**, 165 *n.*]

'But I should have thought that was obvious.'

Yes, and that is what psychologists think. Nevertheless it can easily be shown to be false – that is, to be a quite inexpedient distinction. The idlest self-observation shows that ideas may occur to us which cannot have come about without preparation. But you experience nothing of these preliminaries of your thought, though they too must certainly have been of a mental nature; all that enters your consciousness is the ready-made result. Occasionally you can make these preparatory thought-structures conscious *in retrospect*, as though in a reconstruction.

'Probably one's attention was distracted, so that one failed to notice the preparations.'

Evasions! You cannot in that way get around the fact that acts of a mental nature, and often very complicated ones, can take place in you, of which your consciousness learns nothing and of which you know nothing. Or are you prepared to suppose that a greater or smaller amount of your 'attention' is enough to transform a non-mental act into a mental one? But what is the use of disputing? There are hypnotic experiments in which the existence of such non-conscious thoughts are irrefutably demonstrated to anyone who cares to learn.

'I shall not retract; but I believe I understand you at last. What you call "ego" is consciousness; and your "id" is the so-called subconscious that people talk about so much nowadays. But why the masquerading with the new names?'

It is not masquerading. The other names are of no use. And do not try to give me literature instead of science. If someone talks of subconsciousness, I cannot tell whether he means the term topographically – to indicate something lying in the mind beneath consciousness – or qualitatively – to indicate another consciousness, a subterranean one, as it were. He is probably not clear about any of it. The only trustworthy antithesis is between conscious and unconscious. But it would be a serious mistake to think that this antithesis coincides with the distinction between ego and id. Of course it would be delightful if it were as simple as that: our theory would have a smooth passage. But things are not so simple. All that is true is that everything that happens in the id is and remains unconscious, and that processes in the ego, and they alone, *can* become conscious. But not all of them are, nor always, nor necessarily; and large portions of the ego can remain permanently unconscious.

The becoming conscious of a mental process is a complicated affair. I cannot resist telling you – once again, dogmatically – our hypotheses about it. The ego, as you will remember, is the external, peripheral layer of the id. Now, we believe that on the outermost surface of this ego there is a special agency directed immediately to the external world, a system, an organ, through the excitation of which alone the phenomenon that we call consciousness comes about. This organ can be equally well excited from outside – thus receiving (with the help of the sense-organs) the stimuli from the external world – and from inside – thus becoming aware, first, of the sensations in the id, and then also of the processes in the ego.

'This is getting worse and worse and I can understand it less and less. After all, what you invited me to was a discussion of the question whether laymen (= non-doctors) ought to undertake analytic treatments. What is the point, then, of all these disquisitions on daring and obscure theories which you cannot convince me are justified?'

I know I cannot convince you. That is beyond any possibility and for that reason beyond my purpose. When we give our pupils theoretical instruction in psycho-analysis, we can see how little impression we are making on them to begin with. They take in the theories of analysis as coolly as other abstractions with which they are nourished. A few of them may perhaps *wish* to be convinced, but there is not a trace of their being so. But we also require that everyone who wants to practise analysis on other people shall first himself submit to an analysis. It is only in the course of this 'self-analysis' (as it is misleadingly termed),[1] when they actually experience as affecting their own person – or rather, their own mind – the processes asserted by analysis, that they acquire the convictions by which they are later guided as analysts. How then could I expect to convince you, the Impartial Person, of the correctness of our theories, when I can only put before you an abbreviated and therefore unintelligible account of them, without confirming them from your own experiences?

I am acting with a different purpose. The question at issue between us is not in the least whether analysis is sensible or nonsensical, whether it is right in its hypotheses or has fallen into gross errors. I am unrolling our theories before you since that is the best way of making clear to you what the range of ideas is that analysis embraces, on the

---

[1] [This is now usually described as a 'training analysis'. 'Self-analysis', in the literal sense, is mentioned by Freud in 'On the History of the Psycho-Analytic Movement' (1914d), *Standard Ed.*, **14**, 20 n.; *P.F.L..*, **15**.]

basis of what hypotheses it approaches a patient and what it does with him. In this way a quite definite light will be thrown on the question of lay analysis. And do not be alarmed. If you have followed me so far you have got over the worst. Everything that follows will be easier for you. – But now, with your leave, I will pause to take breath.

III

'I expect you will want to tell me how, on the basis of the theories of psycho-analysis, the origin of a neurotic illness can be pictured.'

I will try to. But for that purpose we must study our ego and our id from a fresh angle, from the *dynamic* one – that is to say, having regard to the forces at work in them and between them. Hitherto we have been content with a *description* of the mental apparatus.

'My only fear is that it may become unintelligible again!'

I hope not. You will soon find your way about in it. Well then, we assume that the forces which drive the mental apparatus into activity are produced in the bodily organs as an expression of the major somatic needs. You will recollect the words of our poet-philosoper: 'Hunger and love [are what moves the world].'[1] Incidentally, quite a formidable pair of forces! We give these bodily needs, in so far as they represent an instigation to mental activity, the name of '*Triebe*' [instincts], a word for which we are envied by many modern languages.[2] Well, these instincts fill the id: all the energy in the id, as we may put it briefly, originates from them. Nor have the forces in the ego any other origin; they are derived from those in the id. What, then, do these instincts want? Satisfaction – that is, the establishment of situations in which the bodily needs can be extinguished. A lowering of the tension of need is felt by our organ of consciousness as pleasurable; an increase of it is soon felt as unpleasure. From these oscillations arises the series of feelings of pleasure-unpleasure, in accordance with which the whole mental apparatus regulates its activity. In this connection we speak of a 'dominance of the pleasure principle'.

If the id's instinctual demands meet with no satisfaction, intolerable conditions arise. Experience soon shows that these situations of satisfaction can only be established with the help of the external

---

[1] [Schiller, 'Die Weltweisen'.]

[2] [Various translations have been adopted for the word '*Trieb*', the most literal being 'drive'. The reasons for using 'instinct' in the *Standard Edition* are discussed in the General Preface in Volume I.]

world. At that point the portion of the id which is directed towards the external world – the ego – begins to function. If all the driving force that sets the vehicle in motion is derived from the id, the ego, as it were, undertakes the steering, without which no goal can be reached. The instincts in the id press for immediate satisfaction at all costs, and in that way they achieve nothing or even bring about appreciable damage. It is the task of the ego to guard against such mishaps, to mediate between the claims of the id and the objections of the external world. It carries on its activity in two directions. On the one hand, it observes the external world with the help of its sense-organ, the system of consciousness, so as to catch the favourable moment for harmless satisfaction; and on the other hand it influences the id, bridles its 'passions', induces its instincts to postpone their satisfaction, and indeed, if the necessity is recognized, to modify its aims, or, in return for some compensation, to give them up. In so far as it tames the id's impulses in this way, it replaces the pleasure principle, which was formerly alone decisive, by what is known as the 'reality principle', which, though it pursues the same ultimate aims, takes into account the conditions imposed by the real external world. Later, the ego learns that there is yet another way of securing satisfaction besides the *adaptation* to the external world which I have described. It is also possible to intervene in the external world by *changing* it, and to establish in it intentionally the conditions which make satisfaction possible. This activity then becomes the ego's highest function; decisions as to when it is more expedient to control one's passions and bow before reality, and when it is more expedient to side with them and to take arms against the external world – such decisions make up the whole essence of worldly wisdom.

'And does the id put up with being dominated like this by the ego, in spite of being, if I understand you aright, the stronger party?'

Yes, all will be well if the ego is in possession of its whole organization and efficiency, if it has access to all parts of the id and can exercise its influence on them. For there is no natural opposition between ego and id; they belong together, and under healthy conditions cannot in practice be distinguished from each other.

'That sounds very pretty; but I cannot see how in such an ideal relation there can be the smallest room for a pathological disturbance.'

You are right. So long as the ego and its relations to the id fulfil these ideal conditions, there will be no neurotic disturbance. The point at which the illness makes its breach is an unexpected one, though no one acquainted with general pathology will be surprised to find a confirmation of the principle that it is precisely the most important developments and differentiations that carry in them the seeds of illness, of failure of function.

'You are becoming too learned. I cannot follow you.'

I must go back a little bit further. A small living organism is a truly miserable, powerless thing, is it not? compared with the immensely powerful external world, full as it is of destructive influences. A primitive organism, which has not developed any adequate ego-organization, is at the mercy of all these 'traumas'. It lives by the 'blind' satisfaction of its instinctual wishes and often perishes in consequence. The differentiation of an ego is above all a step towards self-preservation. Nothing, it is true, can be learnt from being destroyed; but if one has luckily survived a trauma one takes notice of the approach of similar situations and signalizes the danger by an abbreviated repetition of the impressions one has experienced in connection with the trauma – by an *affect of anxiety*. This reaction to the perception of the danger now introduces an attempt at flight, which can have a life-saving effect till one has grown strong enough to meet the dangers of the external world in a more active fashion – even aggressively, perhaps.

'All this is very far away from what you promised to tell me.'

You have no notion how close I am to fulfilling my promise. Even in organisms which later develop an efficient ego-organization, their ego is feeble and little differentiated from their id to begin with, during their first years of childhood. Imagine now what will happen if this powerless ego experiences an instinctual demand from the id which it would already like to resist (because it senses that to satisfy it is dangerous and would conjure up a traumatic situation, a collision with the external world) but which it cannot control, because it does not yet possess enough strength to do so. In such a case the ego treats the instinctual danger as if it was an external one; it makes an attempt at flight, draws back from this portion of the id and leaves it to its fate, after withholding from it all the contributions which it usually makes to instinctual impulses. The ego, as we put it, institutes a *repression* of these instinctual impulses. For the moment this has the effect of fending off the danger; but one cannot confuse the inside and the outside with impunity. One cannot run away from oneself. In repression the ego is following the pleasure principle, which it is usually in the habit of correcting; and it is bound to suffer damage in revenge. This lies in the ego's having permanently narrowed its sphere of influence. The repressed instinctual impulse is now isolated, left to itself, inaccessible, but also uninfluenceable. It goes its own way. Even later, as a rule, when the ego has grown stronger, it still cannot lift the repression; its synthesis is impaired, a part of the id remains forbidden ground to the ego. Nor does the isolated instinctual impulse remain idle; it understands how to make up for being denied normal satisfaction; it produces psychical derivatives which take its place; it links itself to other processes which by its influence it likewise tears away from the ego; and finally it breaks through into the ego and into consciousness in the form of an unrecognizably distorted substitute, and creates what we call a symptom. All at once the nature of a neurotic disorder becomes clear to us: on the one hand an ego which is inhibited in its synthesis, which has no influence on parts of the id, which must renounce some of its activities in order to avoid a fresh collision with what has been repressed, and which exhausts itself in what are for the most part vain acts of defence against the symptoms, the derivatives of the repressed impulses; and on the other hand an id in which individual instincts have made themselves independent, pursue their aims regardless of the interests of the person as a whole and henceforth obey the laws only of the primitive psychology that rules in the depths of the id. If we survey the whole situation we arrive at a simple formula for the origin of a neurosis: the ego has made an attempt to suppress certain portions of the id *in an inappropriate manner*, this attempt has failed and the id has taken its revenge. A neurosis is thus the result of a conflict between the ego and the id, upon which the ego has embarked because, as careful investigation shows, it wishes at all costs to retain its adaptability in relation to the real external world. The disagreement is between the external world and the id; and it is because the ego, loyal to its inmost nature, takes sides with the external world that it becomes involved in a conflict with its id. But please observe that what creates the determinant for the illness is not the fact of this conflict – for disagreements of this kind between reality and the id are unavoidable and it is one of the ego's standing tasks to mediate in them – but the circumstance that the ego has made use of the inefficient instrument of repression for dealing with the conflict. But this in turn is due to the fact that the ego, at the time at which it was set the task, was undeveloped and powerless. The decisive repressions all take place in early childhood.

'What a remarkable business! I shall follow your advice and not make criticisms, since you only want to show me what psycho-analysis believes about the origin of neurosis so that you can go on to say how it sets about combating it. I should have various questions to ask and later on I shall raise some of them. But at the moment I myself feel tempted for once to carry your train of thought further and to venture upon a theory of my own. You have expounded the relation between external world, ego and id, and you have laid it down as the determinant of a neurosis that the ego in its dependence on the external world struggles against the id. Is not the opposite case conceivable of the ego in a conflict of this kind allowing itself to be dragged away by the id and disavowing its regard for the external world? What happens in a case like that? From my lay notions of the nature of insanity I should say that such a decision on the part of the ego might be the determinant of insanity. After all, a turning away of that kind from reality seems to be the essence of insanity.'

Yes. I myself have thought of that possibility,[1] and indeed I believe it meets the facts – though to prove the suspicion true would call for a discussion of some highly complicated considerations. Neuroses and psychoses are evidently intimately related, but they must nevertheless differ in some decisive respect. That might well be the side taken by the ego in a conflict of this kind. In both cases the id would retain its characteristic of blind inflexibility.

'Well, go on! What hints on the treatment of neurotic illnesses does your theory give?'

It is easy now to describe our therapeutic aim. We try to restore the ego, to free it from its restrictions, and to give it back the command over the id which it has lost owing to its early repressions. It is for this one purpose that we carry out analysis, our whole technique is directed to this aim. We have to seek out the repressions which have been set up and to urge the ego to correct them with our help and to deal with conflicts better than by an attempt at flight. Since these repressions belong to the very early years of childhood, the work of analysis leads us, too, back to that period. Our path to these situations of conflict, which have for the most part been forgotten and which we try to revive in the patient's memory, is pointed out to us by his symptoms, dreams and free associations. These must, however, first be interpreted – translated – for, under the influence of the psychology

[1] [Cf. 'Neurosis and Psychosis' in Chapter 10 below.]

of the id, they have assumed forms of expression that are strange to our comprehension. We may assume that whatever associations, thoughts and memories the patient is unable to communicate to us without internal struggles are in some way connected with the repressed material or are its derivatives. By encouraging the patient to disregard his resistances to telling us these things, we are educating his ego to overcome its inclination towards attempts at flight and to tolerate an approach to what is repressed. In the end, if the situation of the repression can be successfully reproduced in his memory, his compliance will be brilliantly rewarded. The whole difference between his age then and now works in his favour; and the thing from which his childish ego fled in terror will often seem to his adult and strengthened ego no more than child's play.

IV

'Everything you have told me so far has been psychology. It has often sounded strange, difficult, or obscure; but it has always been – if I may put it so – "pure". I have known very little hitherto, no doubt, about your psycho-analysis; but the rumour has nevertheless reached my ears that you are principally occupied with things that have no claim to that predicate. The fact that you have not yet touched on anything of the kind makes me feel that you are deliberately keeping something back. And there is another doubt that I cannot suppress. After all, as you yourself say, neuroses are disturbances of mental life. Is it possible, then, that such important things as our ethics, our conscience, our ideals, play no part at all in these profound disturbances?'

So you feel that a consideration both of what is lowest and of what is highest has been missing from our discussions up till now? The reason for that is that we have not yet considered the *contents* of mental life at all. But allow me now for once myself to play the part of an interrupter who holds up the progress of the conversation. I have talked so much psychology to you because I wanted you to get the impression that the work of analysis is a part of applied psychology – and, moreover, of a psychology that is unknown outside analysis. An analyst must therefore first and foremost have learnt this psychology, this depth-psychology or psychology of the unconscious, or as much of it at least as is known to-day. We shall need this as a basis for our later conclusions. But now, what was it you meant by your allusion to 'purity'?

'Well, it is generally reported that in analyses the most intimate –

and the nastiest – events in sexual life come up for discussion in every detail. If that is so – I have not been able to gather from your psychological discussions that it is necessarily so – it would be a strong argument in favour of restricting these treatments to doctors. How could one dream of allowing such dangerous liberties to people of whose discretion one was not sure and of whose character one had no guarantee?'

It is true that doctors enjoy certain privileges in the sphere of sex: they are even allowed to inspect people's genitals – though they were not allowed to in the East and though some idealistic reformers (you know whom I have in mind)[1] have disputed this privilege. But you want to know in the first place whether it is so in analysis and why it must be so. – Yes, it is so.

And it must be so, firstly, because analysis is entirely founded on complete candour. Financial circumstances, for instance, are discussed with equal detail and openness: things are said that are kept back from every fellow-citizen, even if he is not a competitor or a tax-collector. I will not dispute – indeed, I will myself insist with energy – that this obligation to candour puts a grave moral responsibility on the analyst as well. And it must be so, secondly, because factors from sexual life play an extremely important, a dominating, perhaps even a *specific* part among the causes and precipitating factors of neurotic illnesses. What else can analysis do but keep close to its subject-matter, to the material brought up by the patient? The analyst never entices his patient on to the ground of sex. He does not say to him in advance: 'We shall be dealing with the intimacies of your sexual life!' He allows him to begin what he has to say wherever he pleases, and quietly waits until the patient himself touches on sexual things. I used always to warn my pupils: 'Our opponents have told us that we shall come upon cases in which the factor of sex plays no part. Let us be careful not to introduce it into our analyses and so spoil our chance of finding such a case.' But so far none of us has had that good fortune.

I am aware, of course, that our recognition of sexuality has become – whether admittedly or not – the strongest motive for other people's hostility to analysis. Can that shake our confidence? It merely shows us how neurotic our whole civilized life is, since ostensibly normal people do not behave very differently from neurotics. At a time when

---

[1] [An allusion to Tolstoy.]

psycho-analysis was solemnly put on its trial before the learned
societies of Germany – to-day things have grown altogether quieter –
one of the speakers claimed to possess peculiar authority because, so
he said, he even allowed his patients to talk: for diagnostic purposes,
clearly, and to test the assertions of analysts. 'But', he added, 'if they
begin to talk about sexual matters I shut their mouths.' What do you
think of that as a method of demonstration? The learned society
applauded the speaker to the echo instead of feeling suitably ashamed
on his account. Only the triumphant certainty afforded by the
consciousness of prejudices held in common can explain this speaker's
want of logical thought. Years later a few of those who had at that time
been my followers gave in to the need to free human society from the
yoke of sexuality which psycho-analysis was seeking to impose on it.
One of them explained that what is sexual does not mean sexuality at
all, but something else, something abstract and mystical. And
another actually declared that sexual life is merely one of the spheres
in which human beings seek to put in action their driving need for
power and domination. They have met with much applause, for the
moment at least.

'I shall venture, for once in a way, to take sides on that point. It
strikes me as extremely bold to assert that sexuality is not a natural,
primitive need of living organisms, but an expression of something
else. One need only take the example of animals.'

That makes no difference. There is no mixture, however absurd,
that society will not willingly swallow down if it is advertised as an
antidote to the dreaded predominance of sexuality.

I confess, moreover, that the dislike that you yourself have betrayed
of assigning to the factor of sexuality so great a part in the causation of
neurosis – I confess that this scarcely seems to me consistent with your
task as an Impartial Person. Are you not afraid that this antipathy
may interfere with your passing a just judgement?

'I am sorry to hear you say that. Your reliance on me seems to be
shaken. But in that case why not have chosen someone else as your
Impartial Person?'

Because that someone else would not have thought any differently
from you. But if he had been prepared from the first to recognize the
importance of sexual life, everyone would have exclaimed: 'Why, that
is no Impartial Person, he is one of your supporters!' No, I am far from
abandoning the expectation of being able to influence your opinions. I
must admit, however, that from my point of view this situation is

different from the one we dealt with earlier. As regards our psychological discussions it is a matter of indifference to me whether you
believe me or not, provided only that you get an impression that what
we are concerned with are purely psychological problems. But here,
as regards the question of sexuality, I should nevertheless be glad if
you were accessible to the realization that your strongest motive for
contradiction is precisely the ingrained hostility which you share with
so many other people.

'But after all I am without the experience that has given you your
unshakable certainty.'

Very well. I can now proceed with my exposition. Sexual life is not
simply something spicy; it is also a serious scientific problem. There
was much that was novel to be learnt about it, many strange things to
be explained. I told you just now that analysis has to go back into the
early years of the patient's childhood, because the decisive repressions
have taken place then, while his ego was feeble. But surely in
childhood there is no sexual life? surely it only starts at puberty? On
the contrary. We have to learn that sexual instinctual impulses
accompany life from birth onwards, and that it is precisely in order to
fend off those instincts that the infantile ego institutes repressions. A
remarkable coincidence, is it not? that small children should already
be struggling against the power of sexuality, just as the speaker in the
learned society was to do later, and later still my followers who have
set up their own theories. How does that come about? The most general explanation would be that our civilization is built up entirely at the
expense of sexuality; but there is much more to be said on the subject.

The discovery of infantile sexuality is one of those of which we have
reason to feel ashamed [because of its obviousness]. A few paediatricians have, it seems, always known about it, and a few children's
nurses. Clever men, who call themselves child psychologists, have
thereupon spoken in tones of reproach of a 'desecration of the
innocence of childhood'. Once again, sentiment instead of argument!
Events of that kind are of daily occurrence in political bodies. A
member of the Opposition rises and denounces some piece of mal-
administration in the Civil Service, in the Army, in the Judiciary and
so on. Upon this another member, preferably one of the Government,
declares that such statements are an affront to the sense of honour of
the body politic, of the army, of the dynasty, or even of the nation. So
they are as good as untrue. Feelings such as these can tolerate no
affronts.

The sexual life of children is of course different from that of adults. The sexual function, from its beginnings to the definitive form in which it is so familiar to us, undergoes a complicated process of development. It grows together from numerous component instincts with different aims and passes through several phases of organization till at last it comes into the service of reproduction. Not all the component instincts are equally serviceable for the final outcome; they must be diverted, remodelled and in part suppressed. Such a far-reaching course of development is not always passed through without a flaw; inhibitions in development take place, partial fix-ations at early stages of development. If obstacles arise later on to the exercise of the sexual function, the sexual urge – the libido, as we call it – is apt to hark back to these earlier points of fixation. The study of the sexuality of children and its transformations up to maturity has also given us the key to an understanding of what are known as the sexual perversions, which people used always to describe with all the requisite indications of disgust but whose origin they were never able to explain. The whole topic is of uncommon interest, but for the purposes of our conversation there is not much sense in telling you more about it. To find one's way about in it one of course needs anatomical and physiological knowledge, all of which is unfortunately not to be acquired in medical schools. But a familiarity with the history of civilization and with mythology is equally indispensable.

'After all that, I still cannot form any picture of the sexual life of children.'

Then I will pursue the subject further; in any case it is not easy for me to get away from it. I will tell you, then, that the most remarkable thing about the sexual life of children seems to me that it passes through the whole of its very far-reaching development in the first five years of life. From then onwards until puberty there stretches what is known as the period of latency. During it sexuality normally advances no further; on the contrary, the sexual urges diminish in strength and many things are given up and forgotten which the child did and knew. During that period of life, after the early efflorescence of sexuality has withered, such attitudes of the ego as shame, disgust and morality arise, which are destined to stand up against the later tempest of puberty and to lay down the path of the freshly awakening sexual desires. This 'diphasic onset', as it is named, of sexual life has a great deal to do with the genesis of neurotic illnesses. It seems to occur only in human beings, and it is perhaps one of the determinants of the human privilege of becoming neurotic. The prehistory of sexual life was just as much overlooked before psycho-analysis as, in another department, the background to conscious mental life. You will rightly suspect that the two are intimately connected.

There is much to be told, for which our expectations have not prepared us, about the contents, manifestations and achievements of this early period of sexuality. For instance, you will no doubt be surprised to hear how often little boys are afraid of being eaten up by their father. (And you may also be surprised at my including this fear among the phenomena of sexual life.) But I may remind you of the mythological tale which you may still recall from your schooldays of how the god Kronos swallowed his children. How strange this must have sounded to you when you first heard it! But I suppose none of us thought about it at the time. To-day we can also call to mind a number of fairy tales in which some ravenous animal like a wolf appears, and we shall recognize it as a disguise of the father. And this is an opportunity of assuring you that it was only through the knowledge of infantile sexuality that it became possible to understand mythology and the world of fairy tales. Here then something has been gained as a by-product of analytic studies.

You will be no less surprised to hear that male children suffer from a fear of being robbed of their sexual organ by their father, so that this fear of being castrated has a most powerful influence on the development of their character and in deciding the direction to be followed by their sexuality. And here again mythology may give you the courage to believe psycho-analysis. The same Kronos who swallowed his children also emasculated his father Uranus, and was afterwards himself emasculated in revenge by his son Zeus, who had been rescued through his mother's cunning. If you have felt inclined to suppose that all that psycho-analysis reports about the early sexuality of children is derived from the disordered imagination of the analysts, you must at least admit that their imagination has created the same product as the imaginative activities of primitive man, of which myths and fairy tales are the precipitate. The alternative friendlier, and probably also the more pertinent view would be that in the mental life of children to-day we can still detect the same archaic factors which were once dominant generally in the primaeval days of human civilization. In his mental development the child would be repeating the history of his race in an abbreviated form, just as embryology long since recognized was the case with somatic development.

Another characteristic of early infantile sexuality is that the female sexual organ proper as yet plays no part in it: the child has not yet discovered it. Stress falls entirely on the male organ, all the child's interest is directed towards the question of whether it is present or not. We know less about the sexual life of little girls than of boys. But we need not feel ashamed of this distinction; after all, the sexual life of adult women is a 'dark continent' for psychology. But we have learnt that girls feel deeply their lack of a sexual organ that is equal in value to the male one; they regard themselves on that account as inferior, and this 'envy for the penis' is the origin of a whole number of characteristic feminine reactions.

It is also characteristic of children that their two excretory needs are cathected [charged] with sexual interest. Later on, education draws a sharp distinction here, which is once more obliterated in the practice of joking. It may seem to us an unsavoury fact, but it takes quite a long time for children to develop feelings of disgust. This is not disputed even by people who insist otherwise on the seraphic purity of the child's mind.

Nothing, however, deserves more notice than the fact that children regularly direct their sexual wishes towards their nearest relatives – in the first place, therefore, towards their father and mother, and afterwards towards their brothers and sisters. The first object of a boy's love is his mother, and of a girl's her father (except in so far as an innate bisexual disposition favours the simultaneous presence of the contrary attitude). The other parent is felt as a disturbing rival and not infrequently viewed with strong hostility. You must understand me aright. What I mean to say is not that the child wants to be treated by its favourite parent merely with the kind of affection which we adults like to regard as the essence of the parent-child relation. No, analysis leaves us in no doubt that the child's wishes extend beyond such affection to all that we understand by sensual satisfaction – so far, that is, as the child's powers of imagination allow. It is easy to see that the child never guesses the actual facts of sexual intercourse; he replaces them by other notions derived from his own experience and feelings. As a rule his wishes culminate in the intention to bear, or in some indefinable way, to procreate a baby. Boys, too, in their ignorance, do not exclude themselves from the wish to bear a baby. We give the whole of this mental structure the name of 'Oedipus complex', after the familiar Greek legend. With the end of the early sexual period it should normally be given up, should radically

disintegrate and become transformed; and the results of this transformation are destined for important functions in later mental life.
But as a rule this is not effected radically enough, in which case
puberty brings about a revival of the complex, which may have
serious consequences.

I am surprised that you are still silent. That can scarcely mean
consent. – In asserting that a child's first choice of an object is, to use
the technical term, an incestuous one, analysis no doubt once more
hurt the most sacred feelings of humanity, and might well be prepared
for a corresponding amount of disbelief, contradiction and attack.
And these it has received in abundance. Nothing has damaged it more
in the good opinion of its contemporaries than its hypothesis of the
Oedipus complex as a structure universally bound to human destiny.
The Greek myth, incidentally, must have had the same meaning; but
the majority of men to-day, learned and unlearned alike, prefer to
believe that Nature has laid down an innate abhorrence in us as a
guard against the possibility of incest.

But let us first summon history to our aid. When Caius Julius
Caesar landed in Egypt, he found the young Queen Cleopatra (who
was soon to become so important to him) married to her still younger
brother Ptolemy. In an Egyptian dynasty there was nothing peculiar
in this; the Ptolemies, who were of Greek origin, had merely carried on
the custom which had been practised by their predecessors, the
ancient Pharaohs, for a few thousand years. This, however, was
merely brother-and-sister incest, which even at the present time is not
judged so harshly. So let us turn to our chief witness in matters
concerning primaeval times – mythology. It informs us that the myths
of every people, and not only of the Greeks, are filled with examples of
love-affairs between fathers and daughters and even between mothers
and sons. Cosmology, no less than the genealogy of royal races, is
founded upon incest. For what purpose do you suppose these legends
were created? To brand gods and kings as criminals? to fasten on them
the abhorrence of the human race? Rather, surely, because incestuous
wishes are a primordial human heritage and have never been fully
overcome, so that their fulfilment was still granted to gods and their
descendants when the majority of common humans were already
obliged to renounce them. It is in complete harmony with these
lessons of history and mythology that we find incestuous wishes still
present and operative in the childhood of the individual.

'I might take it amiss that you tried to keep back all this about infantile sexuality from me. It seems to me most interesting, particularly on account of its connection with human prehistory.'

I was afraid it might take us too far from our purpose. But perhaps after all it will be of use.

'Now tell me, though, what certainty can you offer for your analytic findings on the sexual life of children? Is your conviction based solely on points of agreement with mythology and history?'

Oh, by no means. It is based on direct observation. What happened was this. We had begun by inferring the content of sexual childhood from the analysis of adults – that is to say, some twenty to forty years later. Afterwards, we undertook analyses on children themselves, and it was no small triumph when we were thus able to confirm in them everything that we had been able to divine, in spite of the amount to which it had been overlaid and distorted in the interval.

'What? You have had small children in analysis? children of less than six years? *Can* that be done? And is it not most risky for the children?'

It can be done very well. It is hardly to be believed what goes on in a child of four or five years old. Children are very active-minded at that age; their early sexual period is also a period of intellectual flowering. I have an impression that with the onset of the latency period they become mentally inhibited as well, stupider. From that time on, too, many children lose their physical charm. And, as regards the damage done by early analysis, I may inform you that the first child on whom the experiment was ventured, nearly twenty years ago, has since then grown into a healthy and capable young man, who has passed through his puberty irreproachably, in spite of some severe psychical traumas. It may be hoped that things will turn out no worse for the other 'victims' of early analysis. Much that is of interest attaches to these child analyses; it is possible that in the future they will become still more important. From the point of view of theory, their value is beyond question. They give unambiguous information on problems which remain unsolved in the analyses of adults; and they thus protect the analyst from errors that might have momentous consequences for him. One surprises the factors that lead to the formation of a neurosis while they are actually at work and one cannot then mistake them. In the child's interest, it is true, analytic influence must be combined with educational measures. The technique has still to receive its shaping. But practical interest is aroused by the observation that a very large number of our children pass through a plainly neurotic phase in the course of their development. Since we have learnt how to look more sharply, we are tempted to say that neurosis in children is not the exception but the rule, as though it could scarcely be avoided on the path from the innate disposition of infancy to civilized society. In most cases this neurotic phase in childhood is overcome spontaneously. But may it not also regularly leave its traces in the average healthy adult? On the other hand in those who are neurotics in later life we never fail to find links with the illness in childhood, though at the time it need not have been very noticeable. In a precisely analogous way physicians to-day, I believe, hold the view that each one of us has gone through an attack of tuberculosis in his childhood. It is true that in the case of the neuroses the factor of immunization does not operate, but only the factor of predisposition.

Let me return to your question about certainty. We have become quite generally convinced from the direct analytic examination of children that we were right in our interpretation of what adults told us about their childhood. In a number of cases, however, another sort of confirmation has become possible. The material of the analysis of some patients has enabled us to reconstruct certain external happenings, certain impressive events of their childhood years, of which they have preserved no conscious memory. Lucky accidents, information from parents or nurses, have afterwards provided irrefutable evidence that these occurrences which we had inferred really did take place. This, of course, has not happened often, but when it has it has made an overwhelming impression. The correct reconstruction, you must know, of such forgotten experiences of childhood always has a great therapeutic effect, whether they permit of objective confirmation or not.[1] These events owe their importance, of course, to their having occurred at such an early age, at a time when they could still produce a traumatic effect on the feeble ego.

'And what sort of events can these be, that have to be discovered by analysis?'

Various sorts. In the first place, impressions capable of permanently influencing the child's budding sexual life – such as observations of sexual activities between adults, or sexual experiences of his own with an adult or another child (no rare events); or, again, overhearing conversations, understood either at the time or retro-

---

[1] [Cf. Freud's later paper on this subject, 'Constructions in Analysis' (1937d), *Standard Ed.*, **23**, 257.]

spectively, from which the child thought it could draw conclusions about mysterious or uncanny matters; or again, remarks or actions by the child himself which give evidence of significant attitudes of affection or enmity towards other people. It is of special importance in an analysis to induce a memory of the patient's own forgotten sexual activity as a child and also of the intervention by the adults which brought it to an end.

'That gives me an opportunity of bringing up a question that I have long wanted to ask. What, then, is the nature of this "sexual activity" of children at an early age, which, as you say, was overlooked before the days of analysis?'

It is an odd thing that the regular and essential part of this sexual activity was *not* overlooked. Or rather, it is by no means odd; for it was impossible to overlook it. Children's sexual impulses find their main expressions in self-gratification by friction of their own genitals, or, more precisely, of the male portion of them. The extraordinarily wide distribution of this form of childish 'naughtiness' was always known to adults, and it was regarded as a grave sin and severely punished. But please do not ask me how people could reconcile these observations of the immoral inclinations of children – for children do it, as they themselves say, because it gives them pleasure – with the theory of their innate purity and non-sensuality. You must get our opponents to solve this riddle. *We* have a more important problem before us. What attitude should we adopt towards the sexual activity of early childhood? We know the responsibility we are incurring if we suppress it; but we do not venture to let it take its course without restriction. Among races at a low level of civilization, and among the lower strata of civilized races, the sexuality of children seems to be given free rein. This probably provides a powerful protection against the subsequent development of neuroses in the individual. But does it not at the same time involve an extraordinary loss of the aptitude for cultural achievements? There is a good deal to suggest that here we are faced by a new Scylla and Charybdis.

But whether the interests which are stimulated by the study of the sexual life of neurotics create an atmosphere favourable to the encouragement of lasciviousness – *that* is a question which I venture to leave to your own judgement.

V

'I believe I understand your purpose. You want to show me what kind of knowledge is needed in order to practise analysis, so that I may be able to judge whether only doctors should have a right to do so. Well, so far very little to do with medicine has turned up: a great deal of psychology and a little biology or sexual science. But perhaps we have not got to the end?'

Decidedly not. There are still gaps to be filled. May I make a request? Will you describe how you now picture an analytic treatment? – just as though you had to undertake one yourself.

'A fine idea, to be sure! No, I have not the least intention of settling our controversy by an experiment of that sort. But just to oblige, I will do what you ask – the responsibility will be yours. Very well. I will suppose that the patient comes to me and complains of his troubles. I promise him recovery or improvement if he will follow my directions. I call on him to tell me with perfect candour everything that he knows and that occurs to him, and not to be deterred from that intention even if some things are disagreeable to say. Have I taken in the rule properly?'

Yes. You should add: 'even if what occurs to him seems unimportant or senseless.'

'I will add that. Thereupon he begins to talk and I listen. And what then? I infer from what he tells me the kind of impressions, experiences and wishes which he has repressed because he came across them at a time when his ego was still feeble and was afraid of them instead of dealing with them. When he has learnt this from me, he puts himself back in the old situations and with my help he manages better. The limitations to which his ego was tied then disappear, and he is cured. Is that right?'

Bravo! bravo! I see that once again people will be able to accuse me of having made an analyst of someone who is not a doctor. You have mastered it all admirably.

'I have done no more than repeat what I have heard from you – as though it was something I had learnt by heart. All the same, I cannot form any picture of how I should do it, and I am quite at a loss to understand why a job like that should take an hour a day for so many months. After all, an ordinary person has not as a rule experienced such a lot, and what was repressed in childhood is probably in every case the same.'

When one really practises analysis one learns all kinds of things besides. For instance: you would not find it at all such a simple matter to deduce from what the patient tells you the experiences he has forgotten and the instinctual impulses he has repressed. He says something to you which at first means as little to you as it does to him. You will have to make up your mind to look at the material which he delivers to you in obedience to the rule in a quite special way: as though it were ore, perhaps, from which its content of precious metal has to be extracted by a particular process. You will be prepared, too, to work over many tons of ore which may contain but little of the valuable material you are in search of. Here we should have a first reason for the prolonged character of the treatment.

'But how does one work over this raw material – to keep to your simile?'

By assuming that the patient's remarks and associations are only distortions of what you are looking for – allusions, as it were, from which you have to guess what is hidden behind them. In a word, this material, whether it consists of memories, associations or dreams, has first to be *interpreted*. You will do this, of course, with an eye to the expectations you have formed as you listened, thanks to your special knowledge.

' "Interpret!" A nasty word! I dislike the sound of it; it robs me of all certainty. If everything depends on my interpretation who can guarantee that I interpret right? So after all everything *is* left to my caprice.'

Just a moment! Things are not quite as bad as that. Why do you choose to except your own mental processes from the rule of law which you recognize in other people's? When you have attained some degree of self-discipline and have certain knowledge at your disposal, your interpretations will be independent of your personal characteristics and will hit the mark. I am not saying that the analyst's personality is a matter of indifference for this portion of his task. A kind of sharpness of hearing for what is unconscious and repressed, which is not possessed equally by everyone, has a part to play. And here, above all, we are brought to the analyst's obligation to make himself capable, by a deep-going analysis of his own, of the unprejudiced reception of the analytic material. Something, it is true, still remains over: something comparable to the 'personal equation' in astronomical observations. This individual factor will always play a larger part in psycho-analysis than elsewhere. An abnormal person can become an accurate physicist; as an analyst he will be hampered by his own abnormality from seeing the pictures of mental life undistorted. Since it is impossible to demonstrate to anyone his own abnormality, general agreement in matters of depth-psychology will be particularly hard to reach. Some psychologists, indeed, think it is quite impossible and that every fool has an equal right to give out his folly as wisdom. I confess that I am more of an optimist about this. After all, our experiences show that fairly satisfactory agreements can be reached even in psychology. Every field of research has its particular difficulty which we must try to eliminate. And, moreover, even in the interpretative art of analysis there is much that can be learnt like any other material of study: for instance, in connection with the peculiar method of indirect representation through symbols.

'Well, I no longer have any desire to undertake an analytic treatment even in my imagination. Who can say what other surprises I might meet with?'

You are quite right to give up the notion. You see how much more training and practice would be needed. When you have found the right interpretation, another task lies ahead. You must wait for the right moment at which you can communicate your interpretation to the patient with some prospect of success.

'How can one always tell the right moment?'

That is a question of tact, which can become more refined with experience. You will be making a bad mistake if, in an effort, perhaps, at shortening the analysis, you throw your interpretations at the patient's head as soon as you have found them. In that way you will draw expressions of resistance, rejection and indignation from him; but you will not enable his ego to master his repressed material. The formula is: to wait till he has come so near to the repressed material that he has only a few more steps to take under the lead of the interpretation you propose.

'I believe I should never learn to do that. And if I carry out these precautions in making my interpretation, what next?'

It will then be your fate to make a discovery for which you were not prepared.

'And what may that be?'

That you have been deceived in your patient; that you cannot count in the slightest on his collaboration and compliance; that he is ready to place every possible difficulty in the way of your common work – in a word, that he has no wish whatever to be cured.

'Well! that is the craziest thing you have told me yet. And I do not believe it either. The patient who is suffering so much, who complains so movingly about his troubles, who is making so great a sacrifice for the treatment – you say he has no wish to be cured! But of course you do not mean what you say.'

Calm yourself! I *do* mean it. What I said was the truth – not the whole truth, no doubt, but a very noteworthy part of it. The patient wants to be cured – but he also wants not to be. His ego has lost its unity, and for that reason his will has no unity either. If that were not so, he would be no neurotic.

'"Were I sagacious, I should not be Tell!"'[1]

The derivatives of what is repressed have broken into his ego and established themselves there; and the ego has as little control over trends from that source as it has over what is actually repressed, and as a rule it knows nothing about them. These patients, indeed, are of a peculiar nature and raise difficulties with which we are not accustomed to reckon. All our social institutions are framed for people with a united and normal ego, which one can classify as good or bad, which either fulfils its function or is altogether eliminated by an overpowering influence. Hence the juridical alternative: responsible or irresponsible. None of these distinctions apply to neurotics. It must be admitted that there is difficulty in adapting social demands to their psychological condition. This was experienced on a large scale during the last war. Were the neurotics who evaded service malingerers or not? They were both. If they were treated as malingerers and if their illness was made highly uncomfortable, they recovered; if after being ostensibly restored they were sent back into service, they promptly took flight once more into illness. Nothing could be done with them. And the same is true of neurotics in civil life. They complain of their illness but exploit it with all their strength; and if someone tries to take it away from them they defend it like the proverbial lioness with her young. Yet there would be no sense in reproaching them for this contradiction.

'But would not the best plan be not to give these difficult people any treatment at all, but to leave them to themselves? I cannot think it is worth while to expend such great efforts over each of them as you lead me to suppose that you make.'

I cannot approve of your suggestion. It is undoubtedly a more

[1] [Schiller, *Wilhelm Tell*, Act III, Scene 3.]

proper line to accept the complications of life rather than struggle against them. It may be true that not every neurotic whom we treat is worth the expenditure of an analysis; but there are some very valuable individuals among them as well. We must set ourselves the goal of bringing it about that as few human beings as possible enter civilized life with such a defective mental equipment. And for that purpose we must collect much experience and learn to understand many things. Every analysis can be instructive and bring us a yield of new understanding quite apart from the personal value of the individual patient.

'But if a volitional impulse has been formed in the patient's ego which wishes to retain the illness, it too must have its reasons and motives and be able in some way to justify itself. But it is impossible to see why anyone should want to be ill or what he can get out of it.'

Oh, that is not so hard to understand. Think of the war neurotics, who do not have to serve, precisely because they are ill. In civil life illness can be used as a screen to gloss over incompetence in one's profession or in competition with other people; while in the family it can serve as a means for sacrificing the other members and extorting proofs of their love or for imposing one's will upon them. All of this lies fairly near the surface; we sum it up in the term 'gain from illness'. It is curious, however, that the patient – that is, his ego – nevertheless knows nothing of the whole concatenation of these motives and the actions which they involve. One combats the influence of these trends by compelling the ego to take cognizance of them. But there are other motives, that lie still deeper, for holding on to being ill, which are not so easily dealt with. But these cannot be understood without a fresh journey into psychological theory.

'Please go on. A little more theory will make no odds now.'

When I described the relation between the ego and the id to you, I suppressed an important part of the theory of the mental apparatus. For we have been obliged to assume that within the ego itself a particular agency has become differentiated, which we name the super-ego. This super-ego occupies a special position between the ego and the id. It belongs to the ego and shares its high degree of psychological organization; but it has a particularly intimate connection with the id. It is in fact a precipitate of the first object-cathexes of the id and is the heir to the Oedipus complex after its demise. This super-ego can confront the ego and treat it like an object; and it often treats it very harshly. It is as important for the ego to remain on good terms with the super-ego as with the id. Estrangements between the ego and the super-ego are of great significance in mental life. You will already have guessed that the super-ego is the vehicle of the phenomenon that we call conscience. Mental health very much depends on the super-ego's being normally developed – that is, on its having become sufficiently impersonal. And that is precisely what it is not in neurotics, whose Oedipus complex has not passed through the correct process of transformation. Their super-ego still confronts their ego as a strict father confronts a child; and their morality operates in a primitive fashion in that the ego gets itself punished by the super-ego. Illness is employed as an instrument for this 'self-punishment', and neurotics have to behave as though they were governed by a sense of guilt which, in order to be satisfied, needs to be punished by illness.

'That really sounds most mysterious. The strangest thing about it is that apparently even this mighty force of the patient's conscience does not reach his consciousness.'

Yes, we are only beginning to appreciate the significance of all these important circumstances. That is why my description was bound to turn out so obscure. But now I can proceed. We describe all the forces that oppose the work of recovery as the patient's 'resistances'. The gain from illness is one such resistance. The 'unconscious sense of guilt' represents the super-ego's resistance; it is the most powerful factor, and the one most dreaded by us. We meet with still other resistances during the treatment. If the ego during the early period has set up a repression out of fear, then the fear still persists and manifests itself as a resistance if the ego approaches the repressed material. And finally, as you can imagine, there are likely to be difficulties if an instinctual process which has been going along a particular path for whole decades is suddenly expected to take a new path that has just been made open for it. That might be called the id's resistance. The struggle against all these resistances is our main work during an analytic treatment; the task of making interpretations is nothing compared to it. But as a result of this struggle and of the overcoming of the resistances, the patient's ego is so much altered and strengthened that we can look forward calmly to his future behaviour when the treatment is over. On the other hand, you can understand now why we need such long treatments. The length of the path of development and the wealth of the material are not the decisive factors. It is more a question of whether the path is clear. An army can be held up for weeks on a stretch of country which in peace time an express train crosses in a couple of hours – if the army has to overcome the enemy's resistance there. Such battles call for time in mental life too. I am unfortunately obliged to tell you that every effort to hasten analytic treatment appreciably has hitherto failed. The best way of shortening it seems to be to carry it out according to the rules.

'If I ever felt any desire to poach on your preserves and try my hand at analysing someone else, what you tell me about the resistances would have cured me of it. But how about the special personal influence that you yourself have after all admitted? Does not that come into action against the resistances?'

It is a good thing you have asked me about that. This personal influence is our most powerful dynamic weapon. It is the new element which we introduce into the situation and by means of which we make it fluid. The intellectual content of our explanations cannot do it, for the patient, who shares all the prejudices of the world around him, need believe us as little as our scientific critics do. The neurotic sets to work because he has faith in the analyst, and he believes him because he acquires a special emotional attitude towards the figure of the analyst. Children, too, only believe people they are attached to. I have already told you what use we make of this particularly large 'suggestive' influence. Not for suppressing the symptoms – this distinguishes the analytic method from other psychotherapeutic procedures – but as a motive force to induce the patient to overcome his resistances.

'Well, and if that succeeds, does not everything then go smoothly?'

Yes, it ought to. But there turns out to be an unexpected complication. It was perhaps the greatest of the analyst's surprises to find that the emotional relation which the patient adopts towards him is of a quite peculiar nature. The very first doctor who attempted an analysis – it was not myself – came up against this phenomenon and did not know what to make of it. For this emotional relation is, to put it plainly, in the nature of falling in love. Strange, is it not? Especially when you take into account that the analyst does nothing to provoke it but on the contrary rather keeps at a distance from the patient, speaking humanly, and surrounds himself with some degree of reserve – when you learn besides that this odd love-relationship disregards anything else that is really propitious and every variation in personal attraction, age, sex or class. This love is of a positively compulsive kind. Not that that characteristic need be absent from spontaneous falling in love. As you know, the contrary is often the case. But in the analytic situation it makes its appearance with complete regularity without there being any rational explanation for it. One would have thought that the patient's relation to the analyst called for no more than a certain amount of respect, trust, gratitude and human sympathy. Instead, there is this falling in love, which itself gives the impression of being a pathological phenomenon.

'I should have thought all the same that it would be favourable for your analytic purposes. If someone is in love, he is amenable, and he will do anything in the world for the sake of the other person.'

Yes. It *is* favourable to start with. But when this falling in love has grown deeper, its whole nature comes to light, much of which is incompatible with the task of analysis. The patient's love is not satisfied with being obedient; it grows exacting, calls for affectionate and sensual satisfactions, it demands exclusiveness, it develops jealousy, and it shows more and more clearly its reverse side, its readiness to become hostile and revengeful if it cannot obtain its ends. At the same time, like all falling in love, it drives away all other mental material; it extinguishes interest in the treatment and in recovery – in short, there can be no doubt that it has taken the place of the neurosis and that our work has had the result of driving out one form of illness with another.

'That does sound hopeless! What can be done about it? The analysis would have to be given up. But if, as you say, the same thing happens in every case, it would be impossible to carry through any analyses at all.'

We will begin by using the situation in order to learn something from it. What we learn may then perhaps help us to master it. Is it not an extremely noteworthy fact that we succeed in transforming every neurosis, whatever its content, into a condition of pathological love?

Our conviction that a portion of erotic life that has been abnormally employed lies at the basis of neuroses must be unshakably strengthened by this experience. With this discovery we are once more on a firm footing and can venture to make this love itself the object of analysis. And we can make another observation. Analytic love is not manifested in every case as clearly and blatantly as I have tried to depict it. Why not? We can soon see. In proportion as the purely sensual and the hostile sides of his love try to show themselves, the patient's opposition to them is aroused. He struggles against them and tries to repress them before our very eyes. And now we understand what is happening. The patient is *repeating* in the form of falling in love with the analyst mental experiences which he has already been through once before; he has *transferred* on to the analyst mental attitudes that were lying ready in him and were intimately connected with his neurosis. He is also repeating before our eyes his old defensive actions; he would like best to repeat in his relation to the analyst *all* the history of that forgotten period of his life. So what he is showing us is the kernel of his intimate life history: *he is reproducing it tangibly, as though it were actually happening, instead of remembering it*. In this way the riddle of the transference-love is solved and the analysis can proceed on its way – with the *help* of the new situation which had seemed such a menace to it.

'That is very cunning. And is the patient so easy to convince that he is not in love but only obliged to stage a revival of an old piece?'

Everything now depends on that. And the whole skill in handling the 'transference' is devoted to bringing it about. As you see, the requirements of analytic technique reach their maximum at this point. Here the gravest mistakes can be made or the greatest successes be registered. It would be folly to attempt to evade the difficulties by suppressing or neglecting the transference; whatever else had been done in the treatment, it would not deserve the name of an analysis. To send the patient away as soon as the inconveniences of his transference-neurosis make their appearance would be no more sensible, and would moreover be cowardly. It would be as though one had conjured up spirits and run away from them as soon as they appeared. Sometimes, it is true, nothing else is possible. There are cases in which one cannot master the unleashed transference and the analysis has to be broken off; but one must at least have struggled with the evil spirits to the best of one's strength. To yield to the demands of the transference, to fulfil the patient's wishes for affectionate and sensual satisfaction, is not only justly forbidden by moral considerations but is also completely ineffective as a technical method for attaining the purpose of the analysis. A neurotic cannot be cured by being enabled to reproduce uncorrected an unconscious stereotype plate that is ready to hand in him. If one engages in compromises with him by offering him partial satisfactions in exchange for his further collaboration in the analysis, one must beware of falling into the ridiculous situation of the cleric who was supposed to convert a sick insurance agent. The sick man remained unconverted but the cleric took his leave insured. The only possible way out of the transference situation is to trace it back to the patient's past, as he really experienced it or as he pictured it through the wish-fulfilling activity of his imagination. And this demands from the analyst much skill, patience, calm and self-abnegation.

'And where do you suppose the neurotic experienced the prototype of his transference-love?'

In his childhood: as a rule in his relation with one of his parents. You will remember what importance we had to attribute to these earliest emotional ties. So here the circle closes.

'Have you finished at last? I am feeling just a little bewildered with all I have heard from you. Only tell me one thing more: how and where can one learn what is necessary for practising analysis?'

There are at the moment two Institutes at which instruction in psycho-analysis is given. The first has been founded in Berlin by Dr Max Eitingon, who is a member of the Society there. The second is maintained by the Vienna Psycho-Analytical Society at its own expense and at considerable sacrifice. The part played by the authorities is at present limited to the many difficulties which they put in the way of the young undertaking. A third training Institute is at this moment being opened in London by the Society there, under the direction of Dr Ernest Jones. At these Institutes the candidates themselves are taken into analysis, receive theoretical instruction by lectures on all the subjects that are important for them, and enjoy the supervision of older and more experienced analysts when they are allowed to make their first trials with comparatively slight cases. A period of some two years is calculated for this training. Even after this period, of course, the candidate is only a beginner and not yet a master. What is still needed must be acquired by practice and by an exchange of ideas in the psycho-analytical societies in which young and old members meet together. Preparation for analytic activity is by no means so easy and simple. The work is hard, the responsibility great. But anyone who has passed through such a course of instruction, who has been analysed himself, who has mastered what can be taught to-day of the psychology of the unconscious, who is at home in the science of sexual life, who has learnt the delicate technique of psycho-analysis, the art of interpretation, of fighting resistances and of handling the transference – anyone who has accomplished all this *is no longer a layman in the field of psycho-analysis*. He is capable of undertaking the treatment of neurotic disorders, and will be able in time to achieve in that field whatever can be required from this form of therapy.

VI

'You have expended a great deal of effort on showing me what psycho-analysis is and what sort of knowledge is needed in order to practise it with some prospect of success. Very well. Listening to you can have done me no harm. But I do not know what influence on my judgement you expect your explanations to have. I see before me a case which has nothing unusual about it. The neuroses are a particular kind of illness and analysis is a particular method of treating them – a specialized branch of medicine. It is the rule in other cases as well for a doctor who has chosen a special branch of medicine not to be satisfied with the education that is confirmed by his diploma: particularly if he intends to set up in a fairly large town, such as can alone offer a livelihood to specialists. Anyone who wants to be a surgeon tries to work for a few years at a surgical clinic, and similarly with oculists, laryngologists and so on – to say nothing of psychiatrists, who are perhaps never able to get away from a state institution or a sanatorium. And the same will happen in the case of psycho-analysts: anyone who decides in favour of this new specialized branch of medicine will, when his studies are completed, take on the two years' training you spoke of in a training institute, if it really requires so much time. He will realize afterwards, too, that it is to his advantage to keep up his contact with his colleagues in a psycho-analytical society, and everything will go along swimmingly. I cannot see where there is a place in this for the question of lay analysis.'

A doctor who does what you have promised on his behalf will be welcome to all of us. Four-fifths of those whom I recognize as my pupils are in any case doctors. But allow me to point out to you how the relations of doctors to analysis have really developed and how they will probably continue to develop. Doctors have no historical claim to the sole possession of analysis. On the contrary, until recently they have met it with everything possible that could damage it, from the shallowest ridicule to the gravest calumny. You will justly reply that that belongs to the past and need not affect the future. I agree, but I fear the future will be different from what you have foretold.

Permit me to give the word 'quack' the meaning it ought to have instead of the legal one. According to the law a quack is anyone who treats patients without possessing a state diploma to prove he is a doctor. I should prefer another definition: a quack is anyone who undertakes a treatment without possessing the knowledge and capacities necessary for it. Taking my stand on this definition, I venture to assert that – not only in European countries – doctors form a preponderating contingent of quacks in analysis. They very frequently practise analytic treatment without having learnt it and without understanding it.

It is no use your objecting that that is unconscientious and that you cannot believe doctors capable of it; that after all a doctor knows that a medical diploma is not a letter of marque[1] and that a patient is not an outlaw; and that one must always grant to a doctor that he is acting in good faith even if he may perhaps be in error.

The facts remain; we will hope that they can be accounted for as you think. I will try to explain to you how it becomes possible for a doctor to act in connection with psycho-analysis in a manner which he would carefully avoid in every other field.

The first consideration is that in his medical school a doctor receives a training which is more or less the opposite of what he would need as a preparation for psycho-analysis. His attention has been directed to objectively ascertainable facts of anatomy, physics and chemistry, on the correct appreciation and suitable influencing of which the success of medical treatment depends. The problem of life is brought into his field of vision so far as it has hitherto been explained to us by the play of forces which can also be observed in inanimate nature. His interest is not aroused in the mental side of vital phenomena; medicine is not concerned with the study of the higher intellectual functions, which lies in the sphere of another faculty. Only psychiatry is supposed to deal with the disturbances of mental functions; but we know in what manner and with what aims it does so. It looks for the somatic determinants of mental disorders and treats them like other causes of illness.

Psychiatry is right to do so and medical education is clearly excellent. If it is described as one-sided, one must first discover the standpoint from which one is making that characteristic into a reproach. In itself every science is one-sided. It must be so, since it restricts itself to particular subjects, points of view and methods. It is a piece of nonsense in which I would take no part to play off one science against another. After all, physics does not diminish the value of chemistry; it cannot take its place but on the other hand cannot be replaced by it. Psycho-analysis is certainly quite particularly one-

[1] [I.e. does not give him a privateer's licence.]

sided, as being the science of the mental unconscious. We must not therefore dispute to the medical sciences their right to be one-sided.

We shall only find the standpoint we are in search of if we turn from scientific medicine to practical therapeutics. A sick person is a complicated organism. He may remind us that even the mental phenomena which are so hard to grasp should not be effaced from the picture of life. Neurotics, indeed, are an undesired complication, an embarrassment as much to therapeutics as to jurisprudence and to military service. But they exist and are a particular concern of medicine. Medical education, however, does nothing, literally nothing, towards their understanding and treatment. In view of the intimate connection between the things that we distinguish as physical and mental, we may look forward to a day when paths of knowledge and, let us hope, of influence will be opened up, leading from organic biology and chemistry to the field of neurotic phenomena. That day still seems a distant one, and for the present these illnesses are inaccessible to us from the direction of medicine.

It would be tolerable if medical education merely failed to give doctors any orientation in the field of the neuroses. But it does more: it gives them a false and detrimental attitude. Doctors whose interest has not been aroused in the psychical factors of life are all too ready to form a low estimate of them and to ridicule them as unscientific. For that reason they are unable to take anything really seriously which has to do with them and do not recognize the obligations which derive from them. They therefore fall into the layman's lack of respect for psychological research and make their own task easy for themselves. – No doubt neurotics have to be treated, since they are sick people and come to the doctor; and one must always be ready to experiment with something new. But why burden oneself with a tedious preparation? We shall manage all right; who can tell if what they teach in the analytic institutes is any good? – The less such doctors understand about the matter, the more venturesome they become. Only a man who really knows is modest, for he knows how insufficient his knowledge is.

The comparison which you brought up to pacify me, between specialization in analysis and in other branches of medicine, is thus not applicable. For surgery, ophthalmology, and so on, the medical school itself offers an opportunity for further education. The analytic training institutes are few in number, young in years, and without authority. The medical schools have not recognized them and take no notice of them. The young doctor, who has had to take so much on trust from his teachers that he has had little occasion for educating his judgement, will gladly seize an occasion for playing the part of a critic for once in a field in which there is as yet no recognized authority.

There are other things too that favour his appearing as an analytic quack. If he tried to undertake eye-operations without sufficient preparation, the failure of his cataract extractions and iridectomies and the absence of patients would soon bring his hazardous enterprise to an end. The practice of analysis is comparatively safe for him. The public is spoilt by the average successful outcome of eye-operations and expects cure from the surgeon. But if a 'nerve-specialist' fails to restore his patients no one is surprised. People have not been spoilt by successes in the therapy of the neuroses; the nerve-specialist has at least 'taken a lot of trouble with them'. Indeed, there is not much that can be done; nature must help, or time. With women there is first menstruation, then marriage, and later on the menopause. Finally death is a real help. Moreover, what the medical analyst has done with his neurotic patient is so inconspicuous that no reproach can attach to it. He has made use of no instruments or medicines; he has merely conversed with him and tried to talk him into or out of something. Surely that can do no harm, especially if he avoids touching on distressing or agitating subjects. The medical analyst, who has avoided any strict teaching, will, no doubt, not have omitted an attempt to improve analysis, to pull out its poison fangs and make it pleasant for the patient. And it will be wise for him to stop there; for if he really ventures to call up resistances and then does not know how to meet them, he may in true earnest make himself unpopular.

Honesty compels me to admit that the activity of an untrained analyst does less harm to his patients than that of an unskilled surgeon. The possible damage is limited to the patient having been led into useless expenditure and having his chances of recovery removed or diminished. Furthermore, the reputation of analytic therapy has been lowered. All this is most undesirable, but it bears no comparison with the dangers that threaten from the knife of a surgical quack. In my judgement, severe or permanent aggravations of a pathological condition are not to be feared even with an unskilled use of analysis. The unwelcome reactions cease after a while. Compared with the traumas of life which have provoked the illness, a little mishandling by the doctor is of no account. It is simply that the unsuitable attempt at a cure has done the patient no good.

'I have listened to your account of the medical quack in analysis without interrupting you, though I formed an impression that you are dominated by a hostility against the medical profession to the historical explanation of which you yourself have pointed the way. But I will grant you one thing: if analyses are to be carried out, it should be by people who have been thoroughly trained for it. And do you not think that with time the doctors who turn to analysis will do everything to obtain that training?'

I fear not. So long as the attitude of the medical school to the analytic training institute remains unaltered, doctors will find the temptation to make things easier for themselves too great.

'But you seem to be consistently evading any direct pronouncement on the question of lay analysis. What I guess now is that, because it is impossible to keep a check on doctors who want to analyse, you are proposing, out of revenge, as it were, to punish them by depriving them of their monopoly in analysis and by throwing open this medical activity to laymen as well.'

I cannot say whether you have guessed my motives correctly. Perhaps I shall be able later on to put evidence before you of a less partial attitude. But I lay stress on the demand that *no one should practise analysis who has not acquired the right to do so by a particular training.* Whether such a person is a doctor or not seems to me immaterial.

'Then what definite proposals have you to make?'

I have not got so far as that yet; and I cannot tell whether I shall get there at all. I should like to discuss another question with you, and first of all to touch on one special point. It is said that the authorities, at the instigation of the medical profession, want to forbid the practice of analysis by laymen altogether. Such a prohibition would also affect the non-medical members of the Psycho-Analytical Society, who have enjoyed an excellent training and have perfected themselves greatly by practice. If the prohibition were enacted, we should find ourselves in a position in which a number of people are prevented from carrying out an activity which one can safely feel convinced they can perform very well, while the same activity is opened to other people for whom there is no question of a similar guarantee. That is not precisely the sort of result to which legislation should lead. However, this special problem is neither very important nor difficult to solve. Only a handful of people are concerned, who cannot be seriously damaged. They will probably emigrate to Germany where no legislation will prevent them from finding recognition for their proficiency. If it is desired to spare them this and to mitigate the law's severity, that can easily be done on the basis of some well-known precedents. Under the Austrian monarchy it repeatedly happened that permission was given to notorious quacks, *ad personam* [personally], to carry out medical activities in certain fields, because people were convinced of their real ability. Those concerned were for the most part peasant healers, and their recommendation seems regularly to have been made by one of the Archduchesses who were once so numerous; but it ought to be possible for it also to be done in the case of town-dwellers and on the basis of a different and merely expert guarantee. Such a prohibition would have more important effects on the Vienna analytic training institute, which would thenceforward be unable to accept any candidates for training from non-medical circles. Thus once again in our country a line of intellectual activity would be suppressed which is allowed to develop freely elsewhere. I am the last person to claim any competence in judging laws and regulations. But this much I can see: that to lay emphasis on our quackery law does not lead in the direction of the approach to conditions in Germany which is so much aimed at to-day,[1] and that the application of that law to the case of psycho-analysis has something of an anachronism about it, since at the time of its enactment there was as yet no such thing as analysis and the peculiar nature of neurotic illnesses was not yet recognized.

I come now to a question the discussion of which seems to me more important. Is the practice of psycho-analysis a matter which should in general be subject to official interference, or would it be more expedient to leave it to follow its natural development? I shall certainly not come to any decision on this point here and now, but I shall take the liberty of putting the problem before you for your consideration. In our country from of old a positive *furor prohibendi* [passion for prohibitions] has been the rule, a tendency to keep people under tutelage, to interfere and to forbid, which, as we all know, has not borne particularly good fruit. In our new republican Austria, it seems, things have not yet changed very much. I fancy you will have an important word to say in deciding the case of psycho-analysis which we are now considering; I do not know whether you have the wish or the influence with which to oppose these bureaucratic tendencies. At all events, I shall not spare you my unauthoritative thoughts on the subject. In my opinion a superabundance of regu-

---

[1] [This of course was in the days of the Weimar republic.]

lations and prohibitions injures the authority of the law. It can be observed that where only a few prohibitions exist they are carefully observed, but where one is accompanied by prohibitions at every step, one feels definitely tempted to disregard them. Moreover, it does not mean one is quite an anarchist if one is prepared to realize that laws and regulations cannot from their origin claim to possess the attribute of being sacred and untransgressable, that they are often inadequately framed and offend our sense of justice, or will do so after a time, and that, in view of the sluggishness of the authorities, there is often no other means of correcting such inexpedient laws than by boldly violating them. Furthermore, if one desires to maintain respect for laws and regulations it is advisable not to enact any where a watch cannot easily be kept on whether they are obeyed or transgressed. Much of what I have quoted above on the practice of analysis by doctors could be repeated here in regard to genuine analysis by laymen which the law is seeking to suppress. The course of an analysis is most inconspicuous, it employs neither medicines nor instruments and consists only in talking and an exchange of information; it will not be easy to prove that a layman is practising 'analysis', if he asserts that he is merely giving encouragement and explanations and trying to establish a healthy human influence on people who are in search of mental assistance. It would surely not be possible to forbid that merely because doctors sometimes do the same thing. In English-speaking countries the practices of Christian Science have become very widespread: a kind of dialectical denial of the evils in life, based on an appeal to the doctrines of the Christian religion. I do not hesitate to assert that that procedure represents a regrettable aberration of the human spirit; but who in America or England would dream of forbidding it and making it punishable? Are the authorities so certain of the right path to salvation that they venture to prevent each man from trying 'to be saved after his own fashion'.[1] And granted that many people if they are left to themselves run into danger and come to grief, would not the authorities do better carefully to mark the limits of the regions which are to be regarded as not to be trespassed upon, and for the rest, so far as possible, to allow human beings to be educated by experience and mutual influence? Psycho-analysis is something so new in the world, the mass of mankind is so

---

[1] [An allusion to a saying attributed to Frederick the Great: 'In my State every man can be saved after his own fashion'.]

little instructed about it, the attitude of official science to it is still so
vacillating, that it seems to me over-hasty to intervene in its development with legislative regulations. Let us allow patients themselves to
discover that it is damaging to them to look for mental assistance to
people who have not learnt how to give it. If we explain this to them
and warn them against it, we shall have spared ourselves the need to
forbid it. On the main roads of Italy the pylons that carry high-tension
cables bear the brief and impressive inscription: '*Chi tocca, muore* [He
who touches will die].' This is perfectly calculated to regulate the
behaviour of passers-by to any wires that may be hanging down. The
corresponding German notices exhibit an unnecessary and offensive
verbosity: '*Das Berühren der Leitungsdrähte ist, weil lebensgefährlich, streng-
stens verboten* [Touching the transmission cables is, since it is dangerous to life, most strictly prohibited].' Why the prohibition? Anyone
who holds his life dear will make the prohibition for himself; and
anyone who wants to kill himself in that way will not ask for
permission.

'But there are instances that can be quoted as legal precedents
against allowing lay analysis; I mean the prohibition against laymen
practising hypnotism and the recently enacted prohibition against
holding spiritualist séances or founding spiritualist societies.'

I cannot say that I am an admirer of these measures. The second
one is a quite undisguised encroachment of police supervision to the
detriment of intellectual freedom. I am beyond suspicion of having
much belief in what are known as 'occult phenomena' or of feeling any
desire that they should be recognized. But prohibitions like these will
not stifle people's interest in that supposedly mysterious world. They
may on the contrary have done much harm and have closed the door
to an impartial curiosity which might have arrived at a judgement
that would have set us free from these harassing possibilities. But once
again this only applies to Austria. In other countries 'parapsychical'
researches are not met by any legal obstacles. The case of hypnotism
is somewhat different from that of analysis. Hypnotism is the evoking
of an abnormal mental state and is used by laymen to-day only for the
purpose of public shows. If hypnotic therapy had maintained its very
promising beginnings, a position would have been arrived at similar
to that of analysis. And incidentally the history of hypnotism provides
a precedent for that of analysis in another direction. When I was a
young lecturer in neuropathology, the doctors inveighed passionately
against hypnotism, declared that it was a swindle, a deception of the

Devil's and a highly dangerous procedure. To-day they have mono-
polized this same hypnotism and they make use of it unhesitatingly as
a method of examination; for some nerve specialists it is still their chief
therapeutic instrument.

But I have already told you that I have no intention of making
proposals which are based on the decision as to whether legal control
or letting things go is to be preferred in the matter of analysis. I know
this is a question of principle on the reply to which the inclinations of
persons in authority will probably have more influence than arguments. I have already set out what seems to me to speak in favour of a
policy of *laissez faire*. If the other decision is taken – for a policy of
active intervention – then it seems to me that in any case a lame and
unjust measure of ruthlessly forbidding analysis by non-doctors will
be an insufficient outcome. More will have to be considered in that
case: the conditions will have to be laid down under which the
practice of analysis shall be permitted to all those who seek to make
use of it, an authority will have to be set up from whom one can learn
what analysis is and what sort of preparation is needed for it, and the
possibilities for instruction in analysis will have to be encouraged. We
must therefore either leave things alone or establish order and clarity;
we must not rush into a complicated situation with a single isolated
prohibition derived mechanically from a regulation that has become
inadequate.

VII

'Yes, but the doctors! the doctors! I cannot induce you to go into the
real subject of our conversations. You still keep on evading me. It is a
question of whether we should not give doctors the exclusive right of
practising analysis – for all I care, after they have fulfilled certain
conditions. The majority of doctors are certainly not quacks in
analysis as you have represented them. You say yourself that the great
majority of your pupils and followers are doctors. It has come to my
ears that they are far from sharing your point of view on the question
of lay analysis. I may no doubt assume that your pupils agree with
your demands for sufficient preparation and so on; and yet these
pupils think it consistent to close the practice of analysis to laymen. Is
that so? and if so, how do you explain it?'

I see you are well informed. Yes, it is so. Not all, it is true, but a good
proportion of my medical colleagues do not agree with me over this,
and are in favour of doctors having an exclusive right to the analytic

treatment of neurotics. This will show you that differences of opinion are allowed even in our camp. The side I take is well known and the contradiction on the subject of lay analysis does not interfere with our good understanding. How can I explain the attitude of these pupils of mine to you? I do not know for certain; I think it must be the power of professional feeling. The course of their development has been different from mine, they still feel uncomfortable in their isolation from their colleagues, they would like to be accepted by the 'profession' as having plenary rights, and are prepared, in exchange for that tolerance, to make a sacrifice at a point whose vital importance is not obvious to them. Perhaps it may be otherwise; to impute motives of competition to them would be not only to accuse them of base sentiments but also to attribute a strange shortsightedness to them. They are always ready to introduce other doctors into analysis, and from a material point of view it must be a matter of indifference to them whether they have to share the available patients with medical colleagues or with laymen. But something different probably plays a part. These pupils of mine may be influenced by certain factors which guarantee a doctor an undoubted advantage over a layman in analytic practice.

'Guarantee him an advantage? There we have it. So you are admitting the advantage at last? This should settle the question.'

The admission is not hard for me to make. It may show you that I am not so passionately prejudiced as you suppose. I have put off mentioning these things because their discussion will once again make theoretical considerations necessary.

'What are you thinking of now?'

First there is the question of diagnosis. When one takes into analysis a patient suffering from what are described as nervous disorders, one wishes beforehand to be certain – so far, of course, as certainty can be attained – that he is suited for this kind of treatment, that one can help him, that is to say, by this method. That, however, is only the case if he really has a neurosis.

'I should have thought that would be recognizable from the phenomena, the symptoms, of which he complains.'

This is where a fresh complication arises. It cannot always be recognized with complete certainty. The patient may exhibit the external picture of a neurosis, and yet it may be something else – the beginning of an incurable mental disease or the preliminary of a destructive process in the brain. The distinction – the differential diagnosis – is not always easy and cannot be made immediately in every phase. The responsibility for such a decision can of course only be undertaken by a doctor. As I have said, it is not always easy for him. The illness may have an innocent appearance for a considerable time, till in the end it after all displays its evil character. Indeed, it is one of the regular fears of neurotics that they may become insane. However, if a doctor has been mistaken for a time over a case of this sort or has been in uncertainty about it, no harm has been caused and nothing unnecessary has been done. Nor indeed would the analytic treatment of this case have done any harm, though it would have been exposed as an unnecessary waste. And moreover there would certainly be enough people who would blame the analysis for the unfortunate outcome. Unjustly, no doubt, but such occasions ought to be avoided.

'But that sounds hopeless. It strikes at the roots of everything you have told me about the nature and origin of a neurosis.'

Not at all. It merely confirms once again the fact that neurotics are a nuisance and an embarrassment for all concerned – including the analysts. But perhaps I shall clear up your confusion if I state my new information in more correct terms. It would probably be more correct to say of the cases we are now dealing with that they have really developed a neurosis, but that it is not psychogenic but somatogenic – that its causes are not mental but physical. Do you understand?

'Oh, yes, I understand. But I cannot bring it into harmony with the other side, the psychological one.'

That can be managed, though, if one bears in mind the complexities of living substance. In what did we find the essence of a neurosis? In the fact that the ego, the higher organization of the mental apparatus (elevated through the influence of the external world), is not able to fulfil its function of mediating between the id and reality, that in its feebleness it draws back from some instinctual portions of the id and, to make up for this, has to put up with the consequences of its renunciation in the form of restrictions, symptoms and unsuccessful reaction-formations.

A feebleness of the ego of this sort is to be found in all of us in childhood; and that is why the experiences of the earliest years of childhood are of such great importance for later life. Under the extraordinary burden of this period of childhood – we have in a few years to cover the enormous developmental distance between stone-age primitive men and the participants in contemporary civilization, and, at the same time and in particular, we have to fend off the instinctual impulses of the early sexual period – under this burden, then, our ego takes refuge in repression and lays itself open to a childhood neurosis, the precipitate of which it carries with it into maturity as a disposition to a later nervous illness. Everything now depends on how the growing organism is treated by fate. If life becomes too hard, if the gulf between instinctual claims and the demands of reality becomes too great, the ego may fail in its efforts to reconcile the two, and the more readily, the more it is inhibited by the disposition carried over by it from infancy. The process of repression is then repeated, the instincts tear themselves away from the ego's domination, find their substitutive satisfactions along the paths of regression, and the poor ego has become helplessly neurotic.

Only let us hold fast to this: the nodal point and pivot of the whole situation is the relative strength of the ego organization. We shall then find it easy to complete our aetiological survey. As what may be called the normal causes of neurotic illness we already know the feebleness of the childhood ego, the task of dealing with the early sexual impulses and the effects of the more or less chance experiences of childhood. Is it not possible, however, that yet other factors play a part, derived from the time before the beginning of the child's life? For instance, an innate strength and unruliness of the instinctual life in the id, which from the outset sets the ego tasks too hard for it? Or a special developmental feebleness of the ego due to unknown reasons? Such factors must of course acquire an aetiological importance, in some cases a transcendent one. We have invariably to reckon with the instinctual strength of the id; if it has developed to excess, the prospects of our therapy are poor. We still know too little of the causes of a developmental inhibition of the ego. These then would be the cases of neurosis with an essentially constitutional basis. Without some such constitutional, congenital favouring factors a neurosis can, no doubt, scarcely come about.

But if the relative feebleness of the ego is the decisive factor for the genesis of a neurosis, it must also be possible for a later physical illness to produce a neurosis, provided that it can bring about an enfeeblement of the ego. And that, once again, is very frequently found. A physical disorder of this kind can affect the instinctual life in the id and increase the strength of the instincts beyond the limit up to which the ego is capable of coping with them. The normal model of such processes is perhaps the alteration in women caused by the disturbances of menstruation and the menopause. Or again, a general somatic illness, indeed an organic disease of the nervous central organ, may attack the nutritional conditions of the mental apparatus and compel it to reduce its functioning and to bring to a halt its more delicate workings, one of which is the maintenance of the ego organization. In all these cases approximately the same picture of neurosis emerges; neurosis always has the same psychological mechanism, but, as we see, a most varied and often very complex aetiology.

'You please me better now. You have begun talking like a doctor at last. And now I expect you to admit that such a complicated medical affair as a neurosis can only be handled by a doctor.'

I fear you are overshooting the mark. What we have been discussing was a piece of pathology, what we are concerned with in analysis is a therapeutic procedure. I allow – no, I insist – that in every case which is under consideration for analysis the diagnosis shall be established first by a doctor. Far the greater number of neuroses which occupy us are fortunately of a psychogenic nature and give no grounds for pathological suspicions. Once the doctor has established this, he can confidently hand over the treatment to a lay analyst. In our analytical societies matters have always been arranged in that way. Thanks to the intimate contact between medical and non-medical members, mistakes such as might be feared have been as good as completely avoided. There is a further contingency, again, in which the analyst has to ask the doctor's help. In the course of an analytic treatment, symptoms – most often physical symptoms – may appear about which one is doubtful whether they should be regarded as belonging to the neurosis or whether they should be related to an independent organic illness that has intervened. The decision on this point must once again be left to a doctor.

'So that even during the course of an analysis a lay analyst cannot do without a doctor. A fresh argument against their fitness.'

No. No argument against lay analysts can be manufactured out of this possibility, for in such circumstances a medical analyst would not act differently.

'I do not understand that.'

There is a technical rule that an analyst, if dubious symptoms like this emerge during the treatment, shall not submit them to his own judgement but shall get them reported upon by a doctor who is not connected with analysis – a consultant physician, perhaps – even if the analyst himself is a doctor and still well versed in his medical knowledge.

'And why should a rule be made that seems to me so uncalled-for?'

It is not uncalled-for; in fact there are several reasons for it. In the first place it is not a good plan for a combination of organic and psychical treatment to be carried out by one and the same person. Secondly the relation in the transference may make it inadvisable for the analyst to examine the patient physically. And thirdly the analyst has every reason for doubting whether he is unprejudiced, since his interests are directed so intensely to the psychical factors.

'I now understand your attitude to lay analysis quite clearly. You are determined that there must be lay analysts. And since you cannot dispute their inadequacy for their task, you are scraping together everything you can to excuse them and make their existence easier. But I cannot in the least see why there should be lay analysts, who, after all, can only be therapists of the second class. I am ready, so far as I am concerned, to make an exception in the case of the few laymen who have already been trained as analysts; but no fresh ones should be created and the training institutes should be put under an obligation to take no more laymen into training.'

I am at one with you, if it can be shown that all the interests involved will be served by this restriction. You will agree that these interests are of three sorts: that of the patients, that of the doctors and – last not least – that of science, which indeed comprises the interests of all future patients. Shall we examine these three points together?

For the patient, then, it is a matter of indifference whether the analyst is a doctor or not, provided only that the danger of his condition being misunderstood is excluded by the necessary medical report before the treatment begins and on some possible occasions during the course of it. For him it is incomparably more important that the analyst should possess personal qualities that make him trustworthy, and that he should have acquired the knowledge and understanding as well as the experience which alone can make it possible for him to fulfil his task. It might be thought that it would damage an analyst's authority if the patient knows that he is not a doctor and cannot in some situations do without a doctor's support. We have, of course, never omitted to inform patients of their analyst's qualification, and we have been able to convince ourselves that professional prejudices find no echo in them and that they are ready to accept a cure from whatever direction it is offered them – which, incidentally, the medical profession discovered long ago to its deep mortification. Nor are the lay analysts who practise analysis to-day any chance collection of riff-raff, but people of academic education, doctors of philosophy, educationalists, together with a few women of great experience in life and outstanding personality. The analysis, to which all the candidates in an analytic training institute have to submit, is at the same time the best means of forming an opinion of their personal aptitude for carrying out their exacting occupation.

Now as to the interest of the doctors. I cannot think that it would gain by the incorporation of psycho-analysis into medicine. The medical curriculum already lasts for five years and the final examinations extend well into a sixth year. Every few years fresh demands are made on the student, without the fulfilment of which his equipment for the future would have to be declared insufficient. Access to the medical profession is very difficult and its practice neither very satisfying nor very remunerative. If one supports what is certainly a fully justified demand that doctors should also be familiar with the mental side of illness, and if on that account one extends medical education to include some preparation for analysis, that implies a further increase in the curriculum and a corresponding prolongation of the period of study. I do not know whether the doctors will be pleased by this consequence of their claim upon analysis. But it can scarcely be escaped. And this at a period in which the conditions of material existence have so greatly deteriorated for the classes from which doctors are recruited, a period in which the younger generation sees itself compelled to make itself self-supporting as early in life as possible.

But perhaps you will choose not to burden medical studies with the preparation for analytic practice but think it more expedient for future analysts to take up their necessary training only after the end of their medical studies. You may say the loss of time involved in this is of no practical account, since after all a young man of less than thirty will never enjoy his patients' confidence, which is a *sine qua non* of giving mental assistance. It might no doubt be said in reply that a newly-fledged physician for physical illnesses cannot count upon being treated by his patients with very great respect either, and that a young analyst might very well fill in his time by working in a psycho-analytic out-patient clinic under the supervision of experienced practitioners.

But what seems to me more important is that with this proposal of yours you are giving support to a waste of energy for which, in these difficult times, I can really find no economic justification. Analytic training, it is true, cuts across the field of medical education, but neither includes the other. If – which may sound fantastic to-day – one had to found a college of psycho-analysis, much would have to be taught in it which is also taught by the medical faculty: alongside of depth-psychology, which would always remain the principal subject, there would be an introduction to biology, as much as possible of the science of sexual life, and familiarity with the symptomatology of psychiatry. On the other hand, analytic instruction would include branches of knowledge which are remote from medicine and which the doctor does not come across in his practice: the history of civilization, mythology, the psychology of religion and the science of literature. Unless he is well at home in these subjects, an analyst can make nothing of a large amount of his material. By way of compensation, the great mass of what is taught in medical schools is of no use to him for his purposes. A knowledge of the anatomy of the tarsal bones, of the constitution of the carbohydrates, of the course of the cranial nerves, a grasp of all that medicine has brought to light on bacillary exciting causes of disease and the means of combating them, on serum reactions and on neoplasms – all of this knowledge, which is undoubtedly of the highest value in itself, is nevertheless of no consequence to him; it does not concern him; it neither helps him directly to understand a neurosis and to cure it nor does it contribute to a sharpening of those intellectual capacities on which his occupation makes the greatest demands. It cannot be objected that the case is much the same when a doctor takes up some other special branch of medicine – dentistry, for instance: in that case, too, he may not need some of what he has to pass examinations in, and he will have to learn much in addition, for which his schooling has not prepared him. But the two cases cannot be put on a par. In dentistry the great principles of pathology – the theories of inflammation, suppuration, necrosis, and of the metabolism of the bodily organs – still retain their importance. But the experience of an analyst lies in another world, with other phenomena and other laws. However much philosophy may ignore the gulf between the physical and the mental, it still exists for our immediate experience and still more for our practical endeavours.

It is unjust and inexpedient to try to compel a person who wants to set someone else free from the torment of a phobia or an obsession to take the roundabout road of the medical curriculum. Nor will such an endeavour have any success, unless it results in suppressing analysis entirely. Imagine a landscape in which two paths lead to a hilltop with a view – one short and straight, the other long, winding and circuitous. You try to stop up the short path by a prohibitory notice, perhaps because it passes by some flower-beds that you want to protect. The only chance you have of your prohibition being respected is if the short path is steep and difficult while the longer one leads gently up. If, however, that is not so, and the roundabout path is on the contrary the harder, you may imagine the use of your prohibition and the fate of your flower-beds! I fear you will succeed in compelling the laymen to study medicine just as little as I shall be able to induce doctors to learn analysis. For you know human nature as well as I do.

'If you are right, that analytic treatment cannot be carried out without special training, but that the medical curriculum cannot bear the further burden of a preparation for it, and that medical knowledge is to a great extent unnecessary for an analyst, how shall we achieve the ideal physician who shall be equal to all the tasks of his calling?'

I cannot foresee the way out of these difficulties, nor is it my business to point it out. I see only two things, first that analysis is an embarrassment to you and that the best thing would be for it not to exist – though neurotics, no doubt, are an embarrassment too; and secondly, that the interests of everyone concerned would for the time being be met if the doctors could make up their minds to tolerate a class of therapists which would relieve them of the tedium of treating the enormously common psychogenic neuroses while remaining in constant touch with them to the benefit of the patients.

'Is that your last word on the subject? or have you something more to say?'

Yes indeed. I wanted to bring up a third interest – the interest of science. What I have to say about that will concern you little; but, by comparison, it is of all the more importance to me.

For we do not consider it at all desirable for psycho-analysis to be swallowed up by medicine and to find its last resting-place in a text-book of psychiatry under the heading 'Methods of Treatment', alongside of procedures such as hypnotic suggestion, autosuggestion, and persuasion, which, born from our ignorance, have to thank the laziness and cowardice of mankind for their short-lived effects. It deserves a better fate and, it may be hoped, will meet with one. As a 'depth-psychology', a theory of the mental unconscious, it can become indispensable to all the sciences which are concerned with the evolution of human civilization and its major institutions such as art, religion and the social order. It has already, in my opinion, afforded these sciences considerable help in solving their problems. But these are only small contributions compared with what might be achieved if historians of civilization, psychologists of religion, philologists and so on would agree themselves to handle the new instrument of research which is at their service. The use of analysis for the treatment of the neuroses is only one of its applications; the future will perhaps show that it is not the most important one. In any case it would be wrong to sacrifice all the other applications to this single one, just because it touches on the circle of medical interests.

For here a further prospect stretches ahead, which cannot be encroached upon with impunity. If the representatives of the various mental sciences are to study psycho-analysis so as to be able to apply its methods and angles of approach to their own material, it will not be enough for them to stop short at the findings which are laid down in analytic literature. They must learn to understand analysis in the only way that is possible – by themselves undergoing an analysis. The neurotics who need analysis would thus be joined by a second class of persons, who accept analysis from intellectual motives, but who will no doubt also welcome the increase in their capacities which they will incidentally achieve. To carry out these analyses a number of analysts will be needed, for whom any medical knowledge will have particularly little importance. But these 'teaching analysts' – let us call them – will require to have had a particularly careful education. If this is not to be stunted, they must be given an opportunity of collecting experience from instructive and informative cases; and since healthy people who also lack the motive of curiosity do not present themselves for analysis, it is once more only upon neurotics that it will be possible for the teaching analysts – under careful supervision – to be educated for their subsequent non-medical activity. All this, however, requires a certain amount of freedom of movement, and is not compatible with petty restrictions.

Perhaps you do not believe in these purely theoretical interests of psycho-analysis or cannot allow them to affect the practical question of lay analysis. Then let me advise you that psycho-analysis has yet another sphere of application, which is outside the scope of the quackery law and to which the doctors will scarcely lay claim. Its application, I mean, to the bringing-up of children. If a child begins to show signs of an undesirable development, if it grows moody, refractory and inattentive, the paediatrician and even the school doctor can do nothing for it, even if the child produces clear neurotic symptoms, such as nervousness, loss of appetite, vomiting or insomnia. A treatment that combines analytic influence with educational measures, carried out by people who are not ashamed to concern themselves with the affairs in a child's world, and who understand how to find their way into a child's mental life, can bring about two things at once: the removal of the neurotic symptoms and the reversal of the change in character which had begun. Our recognition of the importance of these inconspicuous neuroses of children as laying down the disposition for serious illnesses in later life points to these child analyses as an excellent method of prophylaxis. Analysis undeniably still has its enemies. I do not know whether they have means at their command for stopping the activities of these educational analysts or analytic educationalists. I do not think it very likely; but one can never feel too secure.

Moreover, to return to our question of the analytic treatment of adult neurotics, even there we have not yet exhausted every line of approach. Our civilization imposes an almost intolerable pressure on us and it calls for a corrective. Is it too fantastic to expect that psycho-analysis in spite of its difficulties may be destined to the task of preparing mankind for such a corrective? Perhaps once more an American may hit on the idea of spending a little money to get the 'social workers' of his country trained analytically and to turn them into a band of helpers for combating the neuroses of civilization.

'Aha! a new kind of Salvation Army!'

Why not? Our imagination always follows patterns. The stream of eager learners who will then flow to Europe will be obliged to pass Vienna by, for here the development of analysis may have succumbed to a premature trauma of prohibition. You smile? I am not saying this as a bribe for your support. Not in the least. I know you do not believe me; nor can I guarantee that it will happen. But one thing I do know. It is by no means so important what decision you give on the question of lay analysis. It may have a local effect. But the things that really matter – the possibilities in psycho-analysis for *internal* development – can never be affected by regulations and prohibitions.

Postscript
(1927)*

The immediate occasion of my writing the small volume which was the starting-point of the present discussion was a charge of quackery brought against a non-medical member of our Society, Dr Theodor Reik, in the Vienna Courts. It is generally known, I think, that after all the preliminary proceedings had been completed and a number of expert opinions had been received, the charge was dropped. I do not believe that this was a result of my book. No doubt the prosecution's case was too weak, and the person who brought the charge as an aggrieved party proved an untrustworthy witness. So that the quashing of the proceedings against Dr Reik is probably not to be regarded as a considered judgement of the Vienna Courts on the general question of lay analysis. When I drew the figure of the 'Impartial Person' who was my interlocutor in my tract, I had before my mind one of our high officials. This was a man with a friendly attitude and a mind of unusual integrity, to whom I had myself talked about Reik's case and for whom I had, at his request, written a confidential opinion on the subject. I knew I had not succeeded in converting him to my views, and that was why I made my dialogue with the Impartial Person end without agreement too.

Nor did I expect that I should succeed in bringing about unanimity in the attitude of analysts themselves towards the problem of lay analysis. Anyone who compares the views expressed by the Hungarian Society in this discussion with those of the New York group will perhaps conclude that my book has produced no effect whatever and that everyone persists in his former opinion. But I do not believe this either. I think that many of my colleagues have modified their extreme *parti pris* and that the majority have accepted my view that the problem of lay analysis ought not to be decided along the lines of traditional usage but that it arises from a novel situation and therefore demands a fresh judgement.

Again, the turn which I gave to the whole discussion seems to have met with approval. My main thesis was that the important question is not whether an analyst possesses a medical diploma but whether he

---

* First published in *Int. Z. Psychoanal.* The present text is included in *Standard Ed.*, **20**, 251; P.F.L., **15**.

has had the special training necessary for the practice of analysis. This served as the starting-point for a discussion, which was eagerly embarked upon, as to what is the training most suitable for an analyst. My own view was and still remains that it is not the training prescribed by the University for future doctors. What is known as medical education appears to me to be an arduous and circuitous way of approaching the profession of analysis. No doubt it offers an analyst much that is indispensable to him. But it burdens him with too much else of which he can never make use, and there is a danger of its diverting his interest and his whole mode of thought from the understanding of psychical phenomena. A scheme of training for analysts has still to be created. It must include elements from the mental sciences, from psychology, the history of civilization and sociology, as well as from anatomy, biology and the study of evolution. There is so much to be taught in all this that it is justifiable to omit from the curriculum anything which has no direct bearing on the practice of analysis and only serves indirectly (like any other study) as a training for the intellect and for the powers of observation. It is easy to meet this suggestion by objecting that analytic colleges of this kind do not exist and that I am merely setting up an ideal. An ideal, no doubt. But an ideal which can and must be realized. And in our training institutes, in spite of all their youthful insufficiencies, that realization has already begun.

It will not have escaped my readers that in what I have said I have assumed as axiomatic something that is still violently disputed in the discussion. I have assumed, that is to say, that psycho-analysis is not a specialized branch of medicine. I cannot see how it is possible to dispute this. Psycho-analysis is a part of psychology; not of medical psychology in the old sense, not of the psychology of morbid processes, but simply of psychology. It is certainly not the whole of psychology, but its substructure and perhaps even its entire foundation. The possibility of its application to medical purposes must not lead us astray. Electricity and radiology also have their medical application, but the science to which they both belong is none the less physics. Nor can their situation be affected by historical arguments. The whole theory of electricity had its origin in an observation of a nerve-muscle preparation; yet no one would dream to-day of regarding it as a part of physiology. It is argued that psycho-analysis was after all discovered by a physician in the course of his efforts to assist his patients. But that is clearly neither here nor there. Moreover, the historical argument is double-edged. We might pursue the story and recall the unfriendliness and indeed the animosity with which the medical profession treated analysis from the very first. That would seem to imply that it can have no claims over analysis to-day. And though I do not accept that implication, I still feel some doubts as to whether the present wooing of psycho-analysis by the doctors is based, from the point of view of the libido theory, upon the first or upon the second of Abraham's sub-stages [cf. Abraham, 1924] – whether they wish to take possession of their object for the purpose of destroying or of preserving it.

I should like to consider the historical argument a moment longer. Since it is with me personally that we are concerned, I can throw a little light, for anyone who may be interested, on my own motives. After forty-one years of medical activity, my self-knowledge tells me that I have never really been a doctor in the proper sense. I became a doctor through being compelled to deviate from my original purpose; and the triumph of my life lies in my having, after a long and roundabout journey, found my way back to my earliest path. I have no knowledge of having had any craving in my early childhood to help suffering humanity. My innate sadistic disposition was not a very strong one, so that I had no need to develop this one of its derivatives. Nor did I ever play the 'doctor game'; my infantile curiosity evidently chose other paths. In my youth I felt an overpowering need to understand something of the riddles of the world in which we live and perhaps even to contribute something to their solution. The most hopeful means of achieving this end seemed to be to enrol myself in the medical faculty; but even after that I experimented – unsuccessfully – with zoology and chemistry, till at last, under the influence of Brücke,[1] who carried more weight with me than any one else in my whole life, I settled down to physiology, though in those days it was too narrowly restricted to histology. By that time I had already passed all my medical examinations; but I took no interest in anything to do with medicine till the teacher whom I so deeply respected warned me that in view of my impoverished material circumstances I could not possibly take up a theoretical career. Thus I passed from the histology of the nervous system to neuropathology and then, prompted by fresh influences, I began to be concerned with the neuroses. I scarcely

---

[1] [Ernst Wilhelm von Brücke (1819–92), Professor of Physiology at Vienna University, and head of the Physiological Institute, where Freud did his early neurological studies.]

think, however, that my lack of a genuine medical temperament has done much damage to my patients. For it is not greatly to the advantage of patients if their doctor's therapeutic interest has too marked an emotional emphasis. They are best helped if he carries out his task coolly and keeping as closely as possible to the rules.

No doubt what I have just said throws little light on the problem of lay analysis; it was only intended to exhibit my personal credentials as being myself a supporter of the inherent value of psycho-analysis and of its independence of its application to medicine. But it will be objected at this point that whether psycho-analysis, regarded as a science, is a subdivision of medicine or of psychology is a purely academic question and of no practical interest. The real point at issue, it will be said, is a different one, namely the application of analysis to the treatment of patients; in so far as it claims to do this it must be content, the argument will run, to be accepted as a specialized branch of medicine, like radiology, for instance, and to submit to the rules laid down for all therapeutic methods. I recognize that that is so; I admit it. I only want to feel assured that the therapy will not destroy the science. Unluckily analogies never carry one more than a certain distance; a point is soon reached at which the subjects of the comparison take divergent paths. The case of analysis differs from that of radiology. A physicist does not require to have a patient in order to study the laws that govern X-rays. But the only subject-matter of psycho-analysis is the mental processes of human beings and it is only in human beings that it can be studied. For reasons which can easily be understood, neurotic human beings offer far more instructive and accessible material than normal ones, and to withhold that material from anyone who wishes to study and apply analysis is to dock him of a good half of his training possibilities. I have, of course, no intention of asking that the interests of neurotic patients should be sacrificed to those of instruction and scientific research. The aim of my small volume on the question of lay analysis was precisely to show that, if certain precautions are observed, the two interests can quite easily be brought into harmony and that the interests of medicine, as rightly understood, will not be the last to profit by such a solution.

I myself brought forward all the necessary precautions and I can safely say that the discussion added nothing on this point. But I should like to remark that the emphasis was often placed in a manner which did not do justice to the facts. What was said about the difficulties of differential diagnosis and the uncertainty in many cases in deciding about somatic symptoms – situations, that is, in which medical knowledge and medical intervention are necessary – this is all of it perfectly true. Nevertheless, the number of cases in which doubts of this kind never arise at all and in which a doctor is *not* required is surely incomparably greater. These cases may be quite uninteresting scientifically, but they play an important enough part in life to justify the activity of lay analysts, who are perfectly competent to deal with them. Some time ago I analysed a colleague who gave evidence of a particularly strong dislike of the idea of anyone being allowed to engage in a medical activity who was not himself a medical man. I was in a position to say to him: 'We have now been working for more than three months. At what point in our analysis have I had occasion to make use of my medical knowledge?' He admitted that I had had no such occasion.

Again, I attach no great importance to the argument that a lay analyst, because he must be prepared to consult a doctor, will have no authority in the eyes of his patients and will be treated with no more respect than such people as bone-setters or masseurs. Once again, the analogy is an imperfect one – quite apart from the fact that what governs patients in their recognition of authority is usually their emotional transference and that the possession of a medical diploma does not impress them nearly so much as doctors believe. A professional lay analyst will have no difficulty in winning as much respect as is due to a secular pastoral worker. Indeed, the words, 'secular pastoral worker', might well serve as a general formula for describing the function which the analyst, whether he is a doctor or a layman, has to perform in his relation to the public. Our friends among the protestant clergy, and more recently among the catholic clergy as well, are often able to relieve their parishioners of the inhibitions of their daily life by confirming their faith – after having first offered them a little analytic information about the nature of their conflicts. Our opponents, the Adlerian 'individual psychologists', endeavour to produce a similar result in people who have become unstable and inefficient by arousing their interest in the social community – after having first thrown some light upon a single corner of their mental life and shown them the part played in their illness by their egoistic and distrustful impulses. Both of these procedures, which derive their power from being based on analysis, have their place in psychotherapy. We who are analysts set before us as our aim the most complete and profoundest possible analysis of whoever may be our patient. We do not seek to bring him relief by receiving him into the catholic, protestant or socialist community. We seek rather to enrich him from his own internal sources, by putting at the disposal of his ego those energies which, owing to repression, are inaccessibly confined in his unconscious, as well as those which his ego is obliged to squander in the fruitless task of maintaining these repressions. Such activity as this is pastoral work in the best sense of the words. Have we set ourselves too high an aim? Are the majority of our patients worth the pains that this work requires of us? Would it not be more economical to prop up their weaknesses from without rather than rebuild them from within? I cannot say; but there is something else that I *do* know. In psycho-analysis there has existed from the very first an inseparable bond between cure and research. Knowledge brought therapeutic success. It was impossible to treat a patient without learning something new; it was impossible to gain fresh insight without perceiving its beneficent results. Our analytic procedure is the only one in which this precious conjunction is assured. It is only by carrying on our analytic pastoral work that we can deepen our dawning comprehension of the human mind. This prospect of scientific gain has been the proudest and happiest feature of analytic work. Are we to sacrifice it for the sake of any considerations of a practical sort?

Some remarks that have been made in the course of this discussion have led me to suspect that, in spite of everything, my book on lay analysis has been misunderstood in one respect. The doctors have been defended against me, as though I had declared that they were in general incompetent to practise analysis and as though I had given it out as a password that medical reinforcements were to be rejected. That was not my intention. The idea probably arose from my having been led to declare in the course of my observations (which had a controversial end in view) that untrained medical analysts were even more dangerous than laymen. I might make my true opinion on this question clear by echoing a cynical remark about women that once appeared in *Simplicissimus*.[1] One man was complaining to another about the weaknesses and troublesome nature of the fair sex. 'All the same,' replied his companion, 'women are the best thing we have of the kind.' I am bound to admit that, so long as schools such as we desire for the training of analysts are not yet in existence, people who

---

[1] [The satirical Munich periodical.]

have had a preliminary education in medicine are the best material
for future analysts. We have a right to demand, however, that they
should not mistake their preliminary education for a complete training, that they should overcome the one-sidedness that is fostered by
instruction in medical schools and that they should resist the temptation to flirt with endocrinology and the autonomic nervous
system, when what is needed is an apprehension of psychological facts
with the help of a framework of psychological concepts. I also share
the view that all those problems which relate to the connection
between psychical phenomena and their organic, anatomical and
chemical foundations can be approached only by those who have
studied both, that is, by medical analysts. It should not be forgotten,
however, that this is not the whole of psycho-analysis, and that for its
other aspect we can never do without the co-operation of people who
have had a preliminary education in the *mental* sciences. For practical
reasons we have been in the habit – and this is true, incidentally, of
our publications as well – of distinguishing between medical and
applied analysis. But that is not a logical distinction. The true line of
division is between *scientific* analysis and its *applications* alike in medical
and in non-medical fields.

In these discussions the bluntest rejection of lay analysis has been
expressed by our American colleagues. A few words to them in reply
will, I think, not be out of place. I can scarcely be accused of making a
misuse of analysis for controversial purposes if I express an opinion
that their resistance is derived wholly from practical factors. They see
how in their own country lay analysts put analysis to all kinds of
mischievous and illegitimate purposes and in consequence cause
injury both to their patients and to the good name of analysis. It is
therefore not to be wondered at if in their indignation they give the
widest possible berth to such unscrupulous mischief-makers and try
to prevent any laymen from having a share in analysis. But these facts
are already enough to diminish the significance of the American
position; for the question of lay analysis must not be decided on
practical considerations alone, and local conditions in America
cannot be the sole determining influence on our views.

The resolution passed by our American colleagues against lay
analysts, based as it essentially is upon practical reasons, appears to
me nevertheless to be unpractical; for it cannot affect any of the factors
which govern the situation. It is more or less equivalent to an attempt
at repression. If it is impossible to prevent the lay analysts from

pursuing their activities and if the public does not support the campaign against them, would it not be more expedient to recognize the fact of their existence by offering them opportunities for training? Might it not be possible in this way to gain some influence over them? And, if they were offered as an inducement the possibility of receiving the approval of the medical profession and of being invited to co-operate, might they not have some interest in raising their own ethical and intellectual level?

Vienna, June 1927

Two

THE MEANING OF
DREAMS

Introduction

Some students may not be inclined to turn their attention to the meaning of dreams as long as the important problems of waking life have not yet been discussed. For what has since time immemorial directed men's interest to psychology is the hope that they will learn to understand what in the course of every life is determined by external forces and what the individual himself contributes to his fate by his faults and mistakes, his passions, his inclinations and aversions.

I would maintain that no psychological discipline can answer this question as long as it takes as the object of its study only what transpires at the surface of consciousness. Only when we learn what occurs – to quote Freud (1950a, p. 170) – 'behind the official consciousness' do we obtain a realistic picture of the influences that determine human behaviour.

Today it is no longer unknown that a large part of our mental life proceeds without our awareness, i.e., that our ego – to quote Freud again (1917a, p. 143) – 'is not master in its own house'. Gradually it has also become part of everyday knowledge that this unconscious includes the instinctual life whose derivatives in the form of wishes strive for satisfaction.

Another characteristic of the unconscious is less well known, however; namely, its predominant mode of thought which in many respects differs from our waking thought processes. While our conscious thinking and planning are subject to the rules of reason and logic and also take into account the conditions in the external world, the mode inherent in the unconscious follows its own paths that are directed solely to the gain of pleasure. It uses a picture language that has no words at its disposal; it does not distinguish between past, present, and future; it treats opposites as though they were one and the same; it does not hesitate to displace affects such as anger and rage from one target to another; it creates mixed figures from a number of single individuals; and so forth.

This mode of expression is strange to us and, in order to understand it, we must laboriously translate it into our own, much as we would the language of some primitive tribe. Mothers who observe the language development of their young children are familiar with at least some of these phenomena. They know that in the young child laughter and tears are close together; that anger and rage at one person can easily flow over to another; that at this age cause and effect are not yet being connected with each other; that the gain of pleasure and the avoidance of unpleasure are the paramount motives of all actions.

We understand that this form of thinking is age-appropriate and primary and that only with increasing maturation will it be overlaid by a secondary, logical and rational thought process. This does not imply that the primary mode then becomes extinguished. It continues to exist, but hidden, and can again gain dominance over the psychic life whenever the reasonable ego is for some reason weakened. The phantasies of feverish patients and the deliria of the mentally ill provide evidence of such reversion. Only the healthy adult steadfastly adheres to the secondary mode of thinking as long as he is awake and in full control of his mental forces. For him, it is only sleep that nightly turns him back to the primary process. It is the function of sleep to inactivate conscious thinking; to abolish, for its duration, the moral censor whose task it is to guard the access of the unconscious to consciousness; to let wishful impulses deriving from the earliest infantile period rise to the surface again – in short, that the sleeper returns to a primary state and attempts to experience in the dream that which during the day he kept under strict control for the sake of reality considerations.

Viewed from this perspective, the preoccupation with the dream is far from an idle intellectual pursuit. At the beginning of his psycho-analytic work, the dream represented for Freud the most important road to the subterranean forces which determine the parapraxes in everyday life, the choice of one's partner in love, and symptom-formation in neurosis and psychosis in mental illness. His *Interpretation of Dreams*, published in 1900, proved to be a trail-blazing study of the role of dreaming in the mental life of the healthy; the infantile and actual sources of the dream; the language of the dream; the thought processes prevalent in the unconscious; the distortion of wishes in the dream, which is necessary to disguise the inadmissible and for-bidden aspects characteristic of these wishes and to hide them from the sleeper's critical judgement, which never entirely ceases to operate.

The Interpretation of Dreams itself, which in view of its length may not be feasible in an introductory course of study, can in part be replaced by Freud's own summary of it, *On Dreams* (1901*a*). But even in this necessarily abbreviated form, the section on 'The Meaning of Dreams' offers the student the main ideas that should serve to introduce him to this important area of his mental life; without a thorough knowledge of it everything that can be observed on the surface must remain unintelligible.

Not all of Freud's followers share his high estimation of the dream as an aid in psycho-analytic treatment. Today the patient's behaviour in the psycho-analytic hour and, above all, the revival, in the psycho-analytic relationship, of repressed childhood conflicts in connection with long-vanished persons compete for the outstanding position of the dream. Important as this emotional transference by the patient to the analyst is and much as it can contribute to the reconstruction of the patient's past, however, the dream retains *one* prerogative that no other measure of psycho-analytic technique can even remotely attain to: only the penetration into the nature of the dream is capable of clearly bringing into our view the language of the unconscious; that is to say, to convince us of the existence of a primitive mode of thought which all men have in common, which continues to live on in the unconscious long after our conscious mind has learned to acknowledge the supremacy of reason and logic.

Freud only touches on the relationship between sleep and dreaming, which since then has attracted the attention of many investigators. Without contributing to the problems or the content of the dream, the language of the dream, of dream distortion, these mostly physiological studies carried out under laboratory conditions have nevertheless yielded numerous results of interest to psycho-analysis. We now know that there exist two types of sleep, which are scarcely less different from each other than they are from the waking state. The first type, which occurs in periods of roughly ninety minutes, is characterized by rapid eye movements; experiments have established that in this the eyes follow the movements of the objects hallucinated in the dream. Paradoxically, this relatively light sleep is otherwise accompanied only by weak body movements, which is to say that in this respect the sleep state is 'deep'. Dreaming is confined to this type of sleep which is called 'paradoxical' and which, on the basis of its wish-fulfilling hallucinatory activity, is in fact the 'guardian' of sleep.

The second type of sleep, called 'orthodox', has physiologically entirely different characteristics, and the thought activity associated with it is much closer to waking thought. In this phase, problems of the previous day can be dealt with logically, though the path leading to their solution cannot be remembered after awakening. In this respect every thought activity that occurs in orthodox sleep is more evanescent than the content of dreams during the paradoxical period.

Physiological research into the nature of sleep continues, but we can already say that it has led to far-reaching agreements with Freud's work on the interpretation of dreams. One example is the role played by day residues in the content of the dream, a role which in the meantime has been demonstrated experimentally. Most significant, however, is the experimental confirmation of Freud's hypothesis that the dream serves the important function of relieving tension in the psychic apparatus and thereby ensures the continuation of undisturbed sleep.

On Dreams

(1901)*

I

During the epoch which may be described as pre-scientific, men had no difficulty in finding an explanation of dreams. When they remembered a dream after waking up, they regarded it as either a favourable or a hostile manifestation by higher powers, daemonic and divine. When modes of thought belonging to natural science began to flourish, all this ingenious mythology was transformed into psychology, and to-day only a small minority of educated people doubt that dreams are a product of the dreamer's own mind.

Since the rejection of the mythological hypothesis, however, dreams have stood in need of explanation. The conditions of their origin, their relation to waking mental life, their dependence upon stimuli which force their way upon perception during the state of sleep, the many peculiarities of their content which are repugnant to waking thought, the inconsistency between their ideational images and the affects attaching to them, and lastly their transitory character, the manner in which waking thought pushes them on one side as something alien to it, and mutilates or extinguishes them in memory – all of these and other problems besides have been awaiting clarification for many hundreds of years, and till now no satisfactory solution of them has been advanced. But what stands in the foreground of our interest is the question of the *significance* of dreams, a question which bears a double sense. It inquires in the first place as to the psychical significance of dreaming, as to the relation of dreams to other mental processes, and as to any biological function that they may have; in the second place it seeks to discover whether dreams can be interpreted, whether the content of individual dreams has a 'meaning', such as we are accustomed to find in other psychical structures.

---

* The German original appeared in the series *Grundfragen des Nerven- und Seelenlebens*, published by Bergmann (Wiesbaden). The present translation is included in *Standard Ed.*, 5, 633.

In the assessment of the significance of dreams three lines of
thought can be distinguished. One of these, which echoes, as it were,
the ancient overvaluation of dreams, is expressed in the writings of
certain philosophers. They consider that the basis of dream-life is a
peculiar state of mental activity, and even go so far as to acclaim that
state as an elevation to a higher level. For instance, Schubert [1814]
declares that dreams are a liberation of the spirit from the power of
external nature, and a freeing of the soul from the bonds of the senses.
Other thinkers, without going so far as this, insist nevertheless that
dreams arise essentially from mental impulses and represent
manifestations of mental forces which have been prevented from
expanding freely during the daytime. (Cf. the 'dream imagination'
of Scherner [1861, 97 f.] and Volkelt [1875, 28 f.].) A large
number of observers agree in attributing to dream-life a capacity
for superior functioning in certain departments at least (e.g. in
memory).

In sharp contrast to this, the majority of medical writers adopt a
view according to which dreams scarcely reach the level of being
psychical phenomena at all. On their theory, the sole instigators of
dreams are the sensory and somatic stimuli which either impinge
upon the sleeper from outside or become active accidentally in his
internal organs. What is dreamt, they contend, has no more claim to
sense and meaning than, for instance, the sounds which would be
produced if 'the ten fingers of a man who knows nothing of music were
wandering over the keys of a piano'. [Strümpell, 1877, 84.] Dreams
are described by Binz [1878, 35] as being no more than 'somatic
processes which are in every case useless and in many cases positively
pathological'. All the characteristics of dream-life would thus be
explained as being due to the disconnected activity of separate organs
or groups of cells in an otherwise sleeping brain, an activity forced
upon them by physiological stimuli.

Popular opinion is but little affected by this scientific judgement,
and is not concerned as to the sources of dreams; it seems to persist in
the belief that nevertheless dreams have a meaning, which relates to
the prediction of the future and which can be discovered by some
process of interpretation of a content which is often confused and
puzzling. The methods of interpretation employed consist in transforming the content of the dream as it is remembered, either by
replacing it piecemeal in accordance with a fixed key, or by replacing
the dream as a whole by another whole to which it stands in a

symbolic relation. Serious-minded people smile at these efforts: '*Träume sind Schäume*' – 'dreams are froth'.

II

One day I discovered to my great astonishment that the view of dreams which came nearest to the truth was not the medical but the popular one, half involved though it still was in superstition. For I had been led to fresh conclusions on the subject of dreams by applying to them a new method of psychological investigation which had done excellent service in the solution of phobias, obsessions and delusions, etc. Since then, under the name of 'psycho-analysis', it has found acceptance by a whole school of research workers. The numerous analogies that exist between dream-life and a great variety of conditions of psychical illness in waking life have indeed been correctly observed by many medical investigators. There seemed, therefore, good ground for hoping that a method of investigation which had given satisfactory results in the case of psychopathic structures would also be of use in throwing light upon dreams. Phobias and obsessions are as alien to normal consciousness as dreams are to waking consciousness; their origin is as unknown to consciousness as that of dreams. In the case of these psychopathic structures practical considerations led to an investigation of their origin and mode of development; for experience had shown that the discovery of the trains of thought which, concealed from consciousness, connect the pathological ideas with the remaining contents of the mind is equivalent to a resolution of the symptoms and has as its consequence the mastering of ideas which till then could not be inhibited. Thus psychotherapy was the starting-point of the procedure of which I made use for the explanation of dreams.

This procedure is easily described, although instruction and practice would be necessary before it could be put into effect. If we make use of it on someone else, let us say on a patient with a phobia, we require him to direct his attention on to the idea in question, not, however, to reflect upon it as he has done so often already, but to take notice of *whatever occurs to his mind without any exception* and report it to the physician. If he should then assert that his attention is unable to grasp anything at all, we dismiss this with an energetic assurance that a complete absence of any ideational subject-matter is quite impossible. And in fact very soon numerous ideas will occur to him and will lead on to others; but they will invariably be prefaced by a judgement on the part of the self-observer to the effect that they are senseless or unimportant, that they are irrelevant, and that they occurred to him by chance and without any connection with the topic under consideration. We perceive at once that it was this critical attitude which prevented the subject from reporting any of these ideas, and which indeed had previously prevented them from becoming conscious. If we can induce him to abandon his criticism of the ideas that occur to him, and to continue pursuing the trains of thought which will emerge so long as he keeps his attention turned upon them', we find ourselves in possession of a quantity of psychical material, which we soon find is clearly connected with the pathological idea which was our starting-point; this material will soon reveal connections between the pathological idea and other ideas, and will eventually enable us to replace the pathological idea by a new one which fits into the nexus of thought in an intelligible fashion.

This is not the place in which to give a detailed account of the premises upon which this experiment was based, or the consequences which follow from its invariable success. It will therefore be enough to say that we obtain material that enables us to resolve any pathological idea if we turn our attention precisely to those associations which are 'involuntary', which 'interfere with our reflection', and which are normally dismissed by our critical faculty as worthless rubbish.

If we make use of this procedure upon *ourselves*, we can best assist the investigation by at once writing down what are at first unintelligible associations.

I will now show what results follow if I apply this method of investigation to dreams. Any example of a dream should in fact be equally appropriate for the purpose; but for particular reasons I will choose some dream of my own, one which seems obscure and meaningless as I remember it, and one which has the advantage of brevity. A dream which I actually had last night will perhaps meet these requirements. Its content, as I noted it down immediately after waking up, was as follows:

'Company at table or table d'hôte . . . spinach was being eaten . . . Frau E. L. was sitting beside me; she was turning her whole attention to me and laid her hand on my knee in an intimate manner. I removed her hand unresponsively. She then said: "But you've always had such beautiful eyes." . . . I then had an indistinct picture of two eyes, as though it were a drawing or like the outline of a pair of spectacles. . .'

This was the whole of the dream, or at least all that I could remember of it. It seemed to me obscure and meaningless, but above all surprising. Frau E. L. is a person with whom I have hardly at any time been on friendly terms, nor, so far as I know, have I ever wished to have any closer relations with her. I have not seen her for a long time, and her name has not, I believe, been mentioned during the last few days. The dream-process was not accompanied by affects of any kind.

Reflecting over this dream brought me no nearer to understanding it. I determined, however, to set down without any premeditation or criticism the associations which presented themselves to my self-observation. As I have found, it is advisable for this purpose to divide a dream into its elements and to find the associations attaching to each of these fragments separately.

Company at table or table d'hôte. This at once reminded me of an episode which occurred late yesterday evening. I came away from a small party in the company of a friend who offered to take a cab and drive me home in it. 'I prefer taking a cab with a taximeter,' he said, 'it occupies one's mind so agreeably; one always has something to look at.' When we had taken our places in the cab and the driver had set the dial, so that the first charge of sixty hellers became visible, I carried the joke further. 'We've only just got in,' I said, 'and already we owe him sixty hellers. A cab with a taximeter always reminds me of a table d'hôte. It makes me avaricious and selfish, because it keeps on reminding me of what I owe. My debt seems to be growing too fast, and I'm afraid of getting the worst of the bargain; and in just the same way at a table d'hôte I can't avoid feeling in a comic way that I'm getting too little, and must keep an eye on my own interests.' I went on to quote, somewhat discursively:

> Ihr führt ins Leben uns hinein,
> Ihr lasst den Armen *schuldig* werden.[1]

And now a second association to 'table d'hôte'. A few weeks ago, while we were at table in a hotel at a mountain resort in the Tyrol, I was very much annoyed because I thought my wife was not being

---

[1] [These lines are from one of the Harp-player's songs in Goethe's *Wilhelm Meister*. In the original the words are addressed to the Heavenly Powers and may be translated literally: 'You lead us into life, you make the poor creature guilty.' But the words '*Armen*' and '*schuldig*' are both capable of bearing another meaning. '*Armen*' might mean 'poor' in the financial sense and '*schuldig*' might mean 'in debt'. So in the present context the last line could be rendered: 'You make the poor man fall into debt.']

sufficiently reserved towards some people sitting near us whose acquaintance I had no desire at all to make. I asked her to concern herself more with me than with these strangers. This was again *as though I were getting the worst of the bargain at the table d'hôte*. I was struck too by the contrast between my wife's behaviour at table and that of Frau E. L. in the dream, who 'turned her whole attention to me'.

To proceed. I now saw that the events in the dream were a reproduction of a small episode of a precisely similar kind which occurred between my wife and me at the time at which I was secretly courting her. The caress which she gave me under the table-cloth was her reply to a pressing love letter. In the dream, however, my wife was replaced by a comparative stranger – E. L.

Frau E. L. is the daughter of a man to whom I was once *in debt*. I could not help noticing that this revealed an unsuspected connection between parts of the content of the dream and my associations. If one follows the train of association starting out from one element of a dream's content, one is soon brought back to another of its elements. My associations to the dream were bringing to light connections which were not visible in the dream itself.

If a person expects one to keep an eye on his interests without any advantage to oneself, his artlessness is apt to provoke the scornful question: 'Do you suppose I'm going to do this or that for the sake of your *beaux yeux* [*beautiful eyes*]?' That being so, Frau E. L.'s speech in the dream, 'You've always had such beautiful eyes', can only have meant: 'People have always done everything for you for love; you have always had everything *without paying for it*.' The truth is, of course, just the contrary: I have always paid dearly for whatever advantage I have had from other people. The fact that my friend took me home yesterday in a cab *without my paying for it* must, after all, have made an impression on me.

Incidentally, the friend whose guests we were yesterday has often put me in his debt. Only recently I allowed an opportunity of repaying him to slip by. He has had only one present from me – an antique bowl, round which there are *eyes* painted: what is known as an '*occhiale*', to avert the *evil eye*. Moreover he is an *eye surgeon*. The same evening I asked him after a woman patient, whom I had sent on to him for a consultation to fit her with *spectacles*.

As I now perceived, almost all the elements of the dream's content had been brought into the new context. For the sake of consistency, however, the further question might be asked of why *spinach*, of all things, was being served in the dream. The answer was that *spinach* reminded me of an episode which occurred not long ago at our family table, when one of the children – and precisely the one who really deserves to be admired for his *beautiful eyes* – refused to eat any spinach. I myself behaved in just the same way when I was a child; for a long time I detested spinach, till eventually my taste changed and promoted that vegetable into one of my favourite foods. My own early life and my child's were thus brought together by the mention of this dish. 'You ought to be glad to have spinach,' the little *gourmet's* mother exclaimed; 'there are children who would be only too pleased to have spinach.' Thus I was reminded of the duties of parents to their children. Goethe's words

> Ihr führt ins Leben uns hinein,
> Ihr lasst den Armen schuldig werden.

gained a fresh meaning in this connection.[1]

I will pause here to survey the results I had so far reached in my dream-analysis. By following the associations which arose from the separate elements of the dream divorced from their context, I arrived at a number of thoughts and recollections, which I could not fail to recognize as important products of my mental life. This material revealed by the analysis of the dream was intimately connected with the dream's content, yet the connection was of such a kind that I could never have inferred the fresh material from that content. The dream was unemotional, disconnected and unintelligible; but while I was producing the thoughts behind the dream, I was aware of intense and well-founded affective impulses; the thoughts themselves fell at once into logical chains, in which certain ideas made their appearance more than once. Thus, the contrast between 'selfish' and 'unselfish', and the elements 'being in debt' and 'without paying for it' were central ideas of this kind, not represented in the dream itself. I might draw closer together the threads in the material revealed by the analysis, and I might then show that they converge upon a single nodal point, but considerations of a personal and not of a scientific nature prevent my doing so in public. I should be obliged to betray many things which had better remain my secret, for on my way to discovering the solution of the dream all kinds of things were revealed

---

[1] [The first line of the couplet might now be taken to mean that the verses are addressed to parents.]

which I was unwilling to admit even to myself. Why then, it will be asked, have I not chosen some other dream, whose analysis is better suited for reporting, so that I could produce more convincing evidence of the meaning and connectedness of the material uncovered by analysis? The answer is that *every* dream with which I might try to deal would lead to things equally hard to report and would impose an equal discretion upon me. Nor should I avoid this difficulty by bringing up someone else's dream for analysis, unless circumstances enabled me to drop all disguise without damage to the person who had confided in me.

At the point which I have now reached, I am led to regard the dream as a sort of *substitute* for the thought-processes, full of meaning and emotion, at which I arrived after the completion of the analysis. We do not yet know the nature of the process which has caused the dream to be generated from these thoughts, but we can see that it is wrong to regard it as purely physical and without psychical meaning, as a process which has arisen from the isolated activity of separate groups of brain cells aroused from sleep.

Two other things are already clear. The content of the dream is very much shorter than the thoughts for which I regard it as a substitute; and analysis has revealed that the instigator of the dream was an unimportant event of the evening before I dreamt it.

I should, of course, not draw such far-reaching conclusions if only a single dream-analysis was at my disposal. If experience shows me, however, that by uncritically pursuing the associations arising from *any* dream I can arrive at a similar train of thoughts, among the elements of which the constituents of the dream re-appear and which are interconnected in a rational and intelligible manner, then it will be safe to disregard the slight possibility that the connections observed in a first experiment might be due to chance. I think I am justified, therefore, in adopting a terminology which will crystallize our new discovery. In order to contrast the dream as it is retained in my memory with the relevant material discovered by analysing it, I shall speak of the former as the '*manifest* content of the dream' and the latter – without, in the first instance, making any further distinction – as the '*latent* content of the dream'. I am now faced by two new problems which have not hitherto been formulated. (1) What is the psychical process which has transformed the latent content of the dream into the manifest one which is known to me from my memory? (2) What are the motive or motives which have necessitated this transformation? I shall describe the process which transforms the latent into the manifest content of dreams as the 'dream-work'. The counterpart to this activity – one which brings about a transformation in the opposite direction – is already known to us as the work of analysis. The remaining problems arising out of dreams – questions as to the instigators of dreams, as to the origin of their material, as to their possible meaning, as to the possible function of dreaming, and as to the reasons for dreams being forgotten – all these problems will be discussed by me on the basis, not of the manifest, but of the newly discovered latent dream-content. Since I attribute all the contradictory and incorrect views upon dream-life which appear in the literature of the subject to ignorance of the latent content of dreams as revealed by analysis, I shall be at the greatest pains henceforward to avoid confusing the *manifest dream* with the *latent dream-thoughts*.

III

The transformation of the latent dream-thoughts into the manifest dream-content deserves all our attention, since it is the first instance known to us of psychical material being changed over from one mode of expression to another, from a mode of expression which is immediately intelligible to us to another which we can only come to understand with the help of guidance and effort, though it too must be recognized as a function of our mental activity.

Dreams can be divided into three categories in respect of the relation between their latent and manifest content. In the first place, we may distinguish those dreams which *make sense* and are at the same time *intelligible*, which, that is to say, can be inserted without further difficulty into the context of our mental life. We have numbers of such dreams. They are for the most part short and appear to us in general to deserve little attention, since there is nothing astonishing or strange about them. Incidentally, their occurrence constitutes a powerful argument against the theory according to which dreams originate from the isolated activity of separate groups of brain cells. They give no indication of reduced or fragmentary psychical activity, but nevertheless we never question the fact of their being dreams, and do not confuse them with the products of waking life. A second group is formed by those dreams which, though they are connected in themselves and have a clear sense, nevertheless have a *bewildering* effect, because we cannot see how to fit that sense into our mental life. Such would be the case if we were to dream, for instance, that a relative of whom we were fond had died of the plague, when we had no reason for expecting, fearing or assuming any such thing; we should ask in astonishment: 'How did I get hold of such an idea?' The third group, finally, contains those dreams which are without either sense or intelligibility, which seem *disconnected*, *confused* and *meaningless*. The preponderant majority of the products of our dreaming exhibit these characteristics, which are the basis of the low opinion in which dreams are held and of the medical theory that they are the outcome of a restricted mental activity. The most evident signs of incoherence are seldom absent, especially in dream-compositions of any considerable length and complexity.

The contrast between the manifest and latent content of dreams is clearly of significance only for dreams of the second and more particularly of the third category. It is there that we are faced by riddles which only disappear after we have replaced the manifest dream by the latent thoughts behind it; and it was on a specimen of the last category – a confused and unintelligible dream – that the analysis which I have just recorded was carried out. Contrary to our expectation, however, we came up against motives which prevented us from becoming fully acquainted with the latent dream-thoughts. A repetition of similar experiences may lead us to suspect that *there is an intimate and regular relation between the unintelligible and confused nature of dreams and the difficulty of reporting the thoughts behind them.* Before enquiring into the nature of this relation, we may with advantage turn our attention to the more easily intelligible dreams of the first category, in which the manifest and latent content coincide, and there appears to be a consequent saving in dream-work.

Moreover, an examination of these dreams offers advantages from another standpoint. For *children's* dreams are of that kind – significant and not puzzling. Here, incidentally, we have a further argument against tracing the origin of dreams to dissociated cerebral activity during sleep. For why should a reduction in psychical functioning of this kind be a characteristic of the state of sleep in the case of adults but not in that of children? On the other hand, we shall be fully justified in expecting that an explanation of psychical processes in children, in whom they may well be greatly simplified, may turn out to be an indispensable prelude to the investigation of the psychology of adults.

I will therefore record a few instances of dreams which I have collected from children. A little girl nineteen months old had been kept without food all day because she had had an attack of vomiting in the morning; her nurse declared that she had been upset by eating strawberries. During the night after this day of starvation she was heard saying her own name in her sleep and adding: '*Stwawbewwies, wild stwawbewwies, omblet, pudden!*' She was thus dreaming of eating a meal, and she laid special stress in her menu on the particular delicacy of which, as she had reason to expect, she would only be allowed scanty quantities in the near future. – A little boy of twenty-two months had a similar dream of a feast which he had been denied. The day before, he had been obliged to present his uncle with a gift of a basket of fresh cherries, of which he himself, of course, had only been allowed to taste a single sample. He awoke with this cheerful news: '*Hermann eaten all the chewwies!*' – One day a girl of three and a quarter made a trip across a lake. The voyage was evidently not long enough for her, for she cried when she had to get off the boat. Next morning she reported that during the night she had been for a trip on the lake: she had been continuing her interrupted voyage. – A boy of five and a quarter showed signs of dissatisfaction in the course of a walk in the neighbourhood of the Dachstein. Each time a new mountain came into view he asked if it was the Dachstein and finally refused to visit a waterfall with the rest of the company. His behaviour was attributed to fatigue; but it found a better explanation when next morning he reported that he had dreamt that *he had climbed up the Dachstein*. He had evidently had the idea that the expedition would end in a climb up the Dachstein, and had become depressed when the promised mountain never came in view. He made up in his dream for what the previous day had failed to give him. – A six-year-old girl had an exactly similar dream. In the course of a walk her father had stopped short of their intended goal as the hour was getting late. On their way back she had noticed a signpost bearing the name of another landmark; and her father had promised to take her there as well another time. Next morning she met her father with the news that she had dreamt that *he had been with her to both places*.

The common element in all these children's dreams is obvious. All of them fulfilled wishes which were active during the day but had remained unfulfilled. The dreams were simple and undisguised *wish-fulfilments*.

Here is another child's dream, which, though at first sight it is not quite easy to understand, is also nothing more than a wish-fulfilment. A little girl not quite four years old had been brought to town from the country because she was suffering from an attack of poliomyelitis. She spent the night with an aunt who had no children, and was put to sleep in a large bed – much too large for her, of course. Next morning she said she had had a dream that *the bed had been far too small for her, and that there had been no room for her in it*. It is easy to recognize this dream as a wishful dream if we remember that children very often express a wish '*to be big*'. The size of the bed was a disagreeable reminder of her smallness to the would-be big child; she therefore corrected the unwelcome relation in her dream, and grew so big that even the large bed was too small for her.

Even when the content of children's dreams becomes complicated and subtle, there is never any difficulty in recognizing them as wish-fulfilments. An eight-year-old boy had a dream that he was driving in a chariot with Achilles and that Diomede was the charioteer. It was shown that the day before he had been deep in a book of legends about the Greek heroes; and it was easy to see that he had taken the heroes as his models and was sorry not to be living in their days.[1]

This small collection throws a direct light on a further characteristic of children's dreams: their connection with daytime life. The wishes which are fulfilled in them are carried over from daytime and as a rule from the day before, and in waking life they have been accompanied by intense emotion. Nothing unimportant or indifferent, or nothing which would strike a child as such, finds its way into the content of their dreams.

Numerous examples of dreams of this infantile type can be found occurring in adults as well, though, as I have said, they are usually brief in content. Thus a number of people regularly respond to a stimulus of thirst during the night with dreams of drinking, which thus endeavour to get rid of the stimulus and enable sleep to continue. In some people 'dreams of convenience' of this kind often occur before waking, when the necessity for getting up presents itself. They dream that they are already up and at the washing-stand, or that they are already at the school or office where they are due at some particular time. During the night before a journey we not infrequently dream of having arrived at our destination; so too, before a visit to the theatre or a party, a dream will often anticipate the pleasure that lies ahead – out

---

[1] [Most of these dreams are reported in greater detail in *The Interpretation of Dreams* (1900a), *Standard Ed.*, **4**, 122 ff.; *P.F.L.*, **4**, 200 ff.; and in Lecture 8 of the *Introductory Lectures* (1916–17), *Standard Ed.*, **15**, 126 ff; *P.F.L.*, **1**, 157 ff.]

of impatience, as it were. In other dreams the wish-fulfilment is expressed a stage more indirectly: some connection or implication must be established – that is, the work of interpretation must be begun – before the wish-fulfilment can be recognized. A man told me, for instance, that his young wife had had a dream that her period had started. I reflected that if this young woman had missed her period she must have known that she was faced with a pregnancy. Thus when she reported her dream she was announcing her pregnancy, and the meaning of the dream was to represent as fulfilled her wish that the pregnancy might be postponed for a while. Under unusual or extreme conditions dreams of this infantile character are particularly common. Thus the leader of a polar expedition has recorded that the members of his expedition, while they were wintering in the ice-field and living on a monotonous diet and short rations, regularly dreamt like children of large meals, of mountains of tobacco, and of being back at home.

It by no means rarely happens that in the course of a comparatively long, complicated and on the whole confused dream one particularly clear portion stands out, which contains an unmistakable wish-fulfilment, but which is bound up with some other, unintelligible material. But in the case of adults, anyone with some experience in analysing their dreams will find to his surprise that even those dreams which have an appearance of being transparently clear are seldom as simple as those of children, and that behind the obvious wish-fulfilment some other meaning may lie concealed.

It would indeed be a simple and satisfactory solution of the riddle of dreams if the work of analysis were to enable us to trace even the meaningless and confused dreams of adults back to the infantile type of fulfilment of an intensely felt wish of the previous day. There can be no doubt, however, that appearances do not speak in favour of such an expectation. Dreams are usually full of the most indifferent and strangest material, and there is no sign in their content of the fulfilment of any wish.

But before taking leave of infantile dreams with their undisguised wish-fulfilments, I must not omit to mention one principal feature of dreams, which has long been evident and which emerges particularly clearly precisely in this group. Every one of these dreams can be replaced by an optative clause: 'Oh, if only the trip on the lake had lasted longer!' – 'If only I were already washed and dressed!' – 'If only I could have kept the cherries instead of giving them to Uncle!' But dreams give us more than such optative clauses. They show us the wish as already fulfilled; they represent its fulfilment as real and present; and the material employed in dream-representation consists principally, though not exclusively, of situations and of sensory images, mostly of a visual character. Thus, even in this infantile group, a species of transformation, which deserves to be described as dream-work, is not completely absent: *a thought expressed in the optative has been replaced by a representation in the present tense*.

IV

We shall be inclined to suppose that a transformation of some such kind has occurred even in confused dreams, though we cannot tell whether what has been transformed was an optative in their case too. There are, however, two passages in the specimen dream which I have reported, and with whose analysis we have made some headway, that give us reason to suspect something of the kind. The analysis showed that my wife had concerned herself with some other people at table, and that I had found this disagreeable; the dream contained precisely the opposite of this – the person who took the place of my wife was turning her whole attention to me. But a disagreeable experience can give rise to no more suitable wish than that its opposite might have occurred – which was what the dream represented as fulfilled. There was an exactly similar relation between the bitter thought revealed in the analysis that I had never had anything free of cost and the remark made by the woman in the dream – 'You've always had such beautiful eyes'. Some part of the opposition between the manifest and latent content of dreams is thus attributable to wish-fulfilment.

But another achievement of the dream-work, tending as it does to produce incoherent dreams, is even more striking. If in any particular instance we compare the number of ideational elements or the space taken up in writing them down in the case of the dream and of the dream-thoughts to which the analysis leads us and of which traces are to be found in the dream itself, we shall be left in no doubt that the dream-work has carried out a work of compression or *condensation* on a large scale. It is impossible at first to form any judgement of the degree of this condensation; but the deeper we plunge into a dream-analysis the more impressive it seems. From every element in a dream's content associative threads branch out in two or more directions; every situation in a dream seems to be put together out of two or more impressions or experiences. For instance, I once had a dream of a sort of swimming-pool, in which the bathers were scattering in all directions; at one point on the edge of the pool someone was standing and bending towards one of the people bathing, as though to help her out of the water. The situation was put together from a memory of an experience I had had at puberty and from two paintings, one of which I had seen shortly before the dream. One was a picture from Schwind's series illustrating the legend of Mélusine, which showed the water-nymphs surprised in their pool (cf. the scattering bathers in the dream); the other was a picture of the Deluge by an Italian Master; while the little experience remembered from my puberty was of having seen the instructor at a swimming-school helping a lady out of the water who had stopped in until after the time set aside for men bathers. – In the case of the example which I chose for interpretation, an analysis of the situation led me to a small series of recollections each of which contributed something to the content of the dream. In the first place, there was the episode from the time of my engagement of which I have already spoken. The pressure upon my hand under the table, which was a part of that episode, provided the dream with the detail 'under the table' – a detail which I had to add as an afterthought to my memory of the dream. In the episode itself there was of course no question of 'turning to me'; the analysis showed that this element was the fulfilment of a wish by presenting the opposite of an actual event, and that it related to my wife's behaviour at the table d'hôte. But behind this recent recollection there lay concealed an exactly similar and far more important scene from the time of our engagement, which estranged us for a whole day: The intimate laying of a hand on my knee belonged to a quite different context and was concerned with quite other people. This element in the dream was in turn the starting-point of two separate sets of memories – and so on.

The material in the dream-thoughts which is packed together for the purpose of constructing a dream-situation must of course in itself be adaptable for that purpose. There must be one or more *common elements* in all the components. The dream-work then proceeds just as Francis Galton did in constructing his family photographs. It superimposes, as it were, the different components upon one another. The common element in them then stands out clearly in the composite picture, while contradictory details more or less wipe one another out. This method of production also explains to some extent the varying degrees of characteristic vagueness shown by so many elements in the content of dreams. Basing itself on this discovery, dream-interpretation has laid down the following rule: in analysing a dream, if an uncertainty can be resolved into an 'either–or', we must replace it for purposes of interpretation by an 'and', and take each of the apparent alternatives as an independent starting-point for a series of associations.

If a common element of this kind between the dream-thoughts is not present, the dream-work sets about *creating* one, so that it may be possible for the thoughts to be given a common representation in the dream. The most convenient way of bringing together two dream-thoughts which, to start with, have nothing in common, is to alter the verbal form of one of them, and thus bring it half-way to meet the other, which may be similarly clothed in a new form of words. A parallel process is involved in hammering out a rhyme, where a similar sound has to be sought for in the same way as a common element is in our present case. A large part of the dream-work consists in the creation of intermediate thoughts of this kind which are often highly ingenious, though they frequently appear far-fetched; these then form a link between the composite picture in the manifest content of the dream and the dream-thoughts, which are themselves diverse both in form and essence and have been determined by the exciting factors of the dream. The analysis of our sample dream affords us an instance of this kind in which a thought has been given a new form in order to bring it into contact with another which is essentially foreign to it. In carrying out the analysis I came upon the following thought: '*I should like to get something sometimes without paying for it.*' But in that form the thought could not be employed in the dream-content. It was therefore given a fresh form: '*I should like to get some enjoyment without cost* ["Kosten"].'[1] Now the word '*Kosten*' in its second sense fits into the 'table d'hôte' circle of ideas, and could thus be represented in the '*spinach*' which was served in the dream. When a dish appears at our table and the children refuse it, their mother begins by trying persuasion, and urges them '*just to taste* ["*kosten*"] *a bit of it*'. It may seem strange that the dream-work should make such free use of verbal ambiguity, but further experience will teach us that the occurrence is quite a common one.

The process of condensation further explains certain constituents of the content of dreams which are peculiar to them and are not found in

---

[1] [The German word '*Kosten*' means both 'cost' and 'to taste'.]

waking ideation. What I have in mind are 'collective' and 'composite figures' and the strange 'composite structures', which are creations not unlike the composite animals invented by the folk-imagination of the Orient. The latter, however, have already assumed stereotyped shapes in our thought, whereas in dreams fresh composite forms are being perpetually constructed in an inexhaustible variety. We are all of us familiar with such structures from our own dreams.

There are many sorts of ways in which figures of this kind can be put together. I may build up a figure by giving it the features of two people; or I may give it the *form* of one person but think of it in the dream as having the *name* of another person; or I may have a visual picture of one person, but put it in a situation which is appropriate to another. In all these cases the combination of different persons into a single representative in the content of the dream has a meaning; it is intended to indicate an 'and' or 'just as', or to compare the original persons with each other in some particular respect, which may even be specified in the dream itself. As a rule, however, this common element between the combined persons can only be discovered by analysis, and is only indicated in the contents of the dream by the formation of the collective figure.

The composite structures which occur in dreams in such immense numbers are put together in an equal variety of ways, and the same rules apply to their resolution. There is no need for me to quote any instances. Their strangeness disappears completely when once we have made up our minds not to class them with the objects of our waking perception, but to remember that they are products of dream-condensation and are emphasizing in an effectively abbreviated form some common characteristic of the objects which they are thus combining. Here again the common element has as a rule to be discovered by analysis. The content of the dream merely says as it were: 'All these things have an element *x* in common.' The dissection of these composite structures by means of analysis is often the shortest way to finding the meaning of a dream. – Thus, I dreamt on one occasion that I was sitting on a bench with one of my former university teachers, and that the bench, which was surrounded by other benches, was moving forward at a rapid pace. This was a combination of a lecture theatre and a *trottoir roulant*.[1] I will not pursue

---

[1] [The '*trottoir roulant*' was a moving roadway installed at the Paris Exhibition of 1900.]

this train of ideas further. – Another time I was sitting in a railway carriage and holding on my lap an object in the shape of a top-hat ['*Zylinderhut*', literally 'cylinder-hat'], which however was made of transparent glass. The situation made me think at once of the proverb: '*Mit dem Hute in der Hand kommt man durchs ganze Land.*'[1] The glass cylinder led me by a short *détour* to think of an incandescent gas-mantle; and I soon saw that I should like to make a discovery which would make me as rich and independent as my fellow-countryman Dr Auer von Welsbach was made by his, and that I should like to travel instead of stopping in Vienna. In the dream I was travelling with my discovery, the hat in the shape of a glass cylinder – a discovery which, it is true, was not as yet of any great practical use. – The dream-work is particularly fond of representing two *contrary* ideas by the same composite structure. Thus, for instance, a woman had a dream in which she saw herself carrying a tall spray of flowers, such as the angel is represented as holding in pictures of the Annunciation. (This stood for innocence; incidentally, her own name was Maria.) On the other hand, the spray was covered with large white[2] flowers like camellias. (This stood for the opposite of innocence; it was associated with *La dame aux camélias*.)

A good proportion of what we have learnt about condensation in dreams may be summarized in this formula: each element in the content of a dream is 'overdetermined' by material in the dream-thoughts; it is not derived from a *single* element in the dream-thoughts, but may be traced back to a whole number. These elements need not necessarily be closely related to each other in the dream-thoughts themselves; they may belong to the most widely separated regions of the fabric of those thoughts. A dream-element is, in the strictest sense of the word, the 'representative' of all this disparate material in the content of the dream. But analysis reveals yet another side of the complicated relation between the content of the dream and the dream-thoughts. Just as connections lead from each element of the dream to several dream-thoughts, so as a rule a single dream-thought is represented by more than one dream-element; the threads of association do not simply converge from the dream-thoughts to the

---

[1] ['If you go hat in hand, you can cross the whole land.']
[2] [This should probably be 'red'. The flowers are so described in the much fuller account of the dream given in *The Interpretation of Dreams* (*Standard Ed.*, 5, 347, P.F.L., 4, 463f.).]

dream-content, they cross and interweave with each other many times over in the course of their journey.

Condensation, together with the transformation of thoughts into situations ('dramatization'), is the most important and peculiar characteristic of the dream-work. So far, however, nothing has transpired as to any *motive* necessitating this compression of the material.

V

In the case of the complicated and confused dreams with which we are now concerned, condensation and dramatization alone are not enough to account for the whole of the impression that we gain of the dissimilarity between the content of the dream and the dream-thoughts. We have evidence of the operation of a third factor, and this evidence deserves careful sifting.

First and foremost, when by means of analysis we have arrived at a knowledge of the dream-thoughts, we observe that the manifest dream-content deals with quite different material from the latent thoughts. This, to be sure, is no more than an appearance, which evaporates under closer examination, for we find ultimately that the whole of the dream-content is derived from the dream-thoughts, and that almost all the dream-throughts are represented in the dream-content. Nevertheless, something of the distinction still remains. What stands out boldly and clearly in the dream as its essential content must, after analysis, be satisfied with playing an extremely subordinate role among the dream-thoughts; and what, on the evidence of our feelings, can claim to be the most prominent among the dream-thoughts is either not present at all as ideational material in the content of the dream or is only remotely alluded to in some obscure region of it. We may put it in this way: *in the course of the dream-work the psychical intensity passes over from the thoughts and ideas to which it properly belongs on to others which in our judgement have no claim to any such emphasis*. No other process contributes so much to concealing the meaning of a dream and to making the connection between the dream-content and the dream-thoughts unrecognizable. In the course of this process, which I shall describe as 'dream-displacement', the psychical intensity, significance or affective potentiality of the thoughts is, as we further find, transformed into sensory vividness. We assume as a matter of course that the most distinct element in the manifest content of a dream is the most important one; but in fact [owing to the displacement that has occurred] it is often an *indistinct* element which turns out to be the most direct derivative of the essential dream-thought.

What I have called dream-displacement might equally be described [in Nietzsche's phrase] as 'a transvaluation of psychical values'. I shall not have given an exhaustive estimate of this phenomenon, however, unless I add that this work of displacement or transvaluation is performed to a very varying degree in different dreams. There are dreams which come about almost without any displacement. These are the ones which make sense and are intelligible, such, for instance, as those which we have recognized as undisguised wishful dreams. On the other hand, there are dreams in which not a single piece of the dream-thoughts has retained its own psychical value, or in which everything that is essential in the dream-thoughts has been replaced by something trivial. And we can find a complete series of transitional cases between these two extremes. The more obscure and confused a dream appears to be, the greater the share in its construction which may be attributed to the factor of displacement.

Our specimen dream exhibits displacement to this extent at least, that its content seems to have a different *centre* from its dream-thoughts. In the foreground of the dream-content a prominent place is taken by a situation in which a woman seems to be making advances to me; while in the dream-thoughts the chief emphasis is laid on a wish for once to enjoy unselfish love, love which 'costs nothing' – an idea concealed behind the phrase about 'beautiful eyes' and the far-fetched allusion to 'spinach'.

If we undo dream-displacement by means of analysis, we obtain what seems to be completely trustworthy information on two much-disputed problems concerning dreams: as to their instigators and as to their connection with waking life. There are dreams which immediately reveal their derivation from events of the day; there are others in which no trace of any such derivation is to be discovered. If we seek the help of analysis, we find that every dream without any possible exception goes back to an impression of the past few days, or, it is probably more correct to say, of the day immediately preceding the dream, of the 'dream-day'. The impression which plays the part of dream-instigator may be such an important one that we feel no surprise at being concerned with it in the daytime, and in that case we rightly speak of the dream as carrying on with the significant interests of our waking life. As a rule, however, if a connection is to be found in the content of the dream with any impression of the previous day, that impression is so trivial, insignificant and unmemorable, that it is only with difficulty that we ourselves can recall it. And in such cases the content of the dream itself, even if it is connected and intelligible, seems to be concerned with the most indifferent trivialities, which would be unworthy of our interest if we were awake. A good deal of the contempt in which dreams are held is due to the preference thus shown in their content for what is indifferent and trivial.

Analysis does away with the misleading appearance upon which this derogatory judgement is founded. If the content of a dream puts forward some indifferent impression as being its instigator, analysis invariably brings to light a significant experience, and one by which the dreamer has good reason to be stirred. This experience has been replaced by the indifferent one, with which it is connected by copious associative links. Where the content of the dream treats of insignificant and uninteresting ideational material, analysis uncovers the numerous associative paths connecting these trivialities with things that are of the highest psychical importance in the dreamer's estimation. *If what make their way into the content of dreams are impressions and material which are indifferent and trivial rather than justifiably stirring and interesting, that is only the effect of the process of displacement.* If we answer our questions about dream-instigators and the connection between dreaming and daily affairs on the basis of the new insight we have gained from replacing the manifest by the latent content of dreams, we arrive at these conclusions: *dreams are never concerned with things which we should not think it worth while to be concerned with during the day, and trivialities which do not affect us during the day are unable to pursue us in our sleep.*

What was the dream-instigator in the specimen that we have chosen for analysis? It was the definitely insignificant event of my friend giving me *a drive in a cab free of cost*. The situation in the dream at the table d'hôte contained an allusion to this insignificant precipitating cause, for in my conversation I had compared the taximeter cab with a table d'hôte. But I can also point to the important experience which was represented by this trivial one. A few days earlier I had paid out a considerable sum of money on behalf of a member of my family of whom I am fond. No wonder, said the dream-thoughts, if this person were to feel grateful to me: love of that sort would not be 'free of cost'. Love that is free of cost, however, stood in the forefront of the dream-thoughts. The fact that not long before I had had several *cab-drives* with the relative in question, made it possible for the cab-drive with my friend to remind me of my connections with this other person.

The indifferent impression which becomes a dream-instigator owing to associations of this kind is subject to a further condition which does not apply to the true source of the dream: it must always be a *recent* impression, derived from the dream-day.

I cannot leave the subject of dream-displacement without drawing attention to a remarkable process which occurs in the formation of dreams and in which condensation and displacement *combine* to produce the result. In considering condensation we have already seen the way in which two ideas in the dream-thoughts which have something in common, some point of contact, are replaced in the dream-content by a composite idea, in which a relatively distinct nucleus represents what they have in common, while indistinct subordinate details correspond to the respects in which they differ from each other. If displacement takes place in addition to condensation, what is constructed is not a composite idea but an 'intermediate common entity', which stands in a relation to the two different elements similar to that in which the resultant in a parallelogram of forces stands to its components. For instance, in the content of one of my dreams there was a question of an injection with *propyl*. To begin with, the analysis only led me to an indifferent experience which had acted as dream-instigator, and in which a part was played by *amyl*. I was not yet able to justify the confusion between amyl and propyl. In the group of ideas behind this same dream, however, there was also a recollection of my first visit to Munich, where I had been struck by the *Propylaea*.[1] The details of the analysis made it plausible to suppose that it was the influence of this second group of ideas upon the first one that was responsible for the displacement from amyl to propyl. *Propyl* is as it were an intermediate idea between *amyl* and *Propylaea*, and found its way into the content of the dream as a kind of *compromise*, by means of simultaneous condensation and displacement.

There is a still more urgent necessity in the case of the process of displacement than in that of condensation to discover the motive for these puzzling efforts on the part of the dream-work.

[1] [A ceremonial portico on the Athenian model.]

VI

It is the process of displacement which is chiefly responsible for our being unable to discover or recognize the dream-thoughts in the dream-content, unless we understand the reason for their distortion. Nevertheless, the dream-thoughts are also submitted to another and milder sort of transformation, which leads to our discovering a new achievement on the part of the dream-work – one, however, which is easily intelligible. The dream-thoughts which we first come across as we proceed with our analysis often strike us by the unusual form in which they are expressed; they are not clothed in the prosaic language usually employed by our thoughts, but are on the contrary represented symbolically by means of similes and metaphors, in images resembling those of poetic speech. There is no difficulty in accounting for the constraint imposed upon the form in which the dream-thoughts are expressed. The manifest content of dreams consists for the most part in pictorial situations; and the dream-thoughts must accordingly be submitted in the first place to a treatment which will make them suitable for a representation of this kind. If we imagine ourselves faced by the problem of representing the arguments in a political leading article or the speeches of counsel before a court of law in a series of pictures, we shall easily understand the modifications which must necessarily be carried out by the dream-work owing to *considerations of representability in the content of the dream.*

The psychical material of the dream-thoughts habitually includes recollections of impressive experiences – not infrequently dating back to early childhood – which are thus themselves perceived as a rule as situations having a visual subject-matter. Wherever the possibility arises, this portion of the dream-thoughts exercises a determining influence upon the form taken by the content of the dream; it constitutes, as it were, a nucleus of crystallization, attracting the material of the dream-thoughts to itself and thus affecting their distribution. The situation in a dream is often nothing other than a modified repetition, complicated by interpolations, of an impressive experience of this kind; on the other hand, faithful and straightforward reproductions of real scenes only rarely appear in dreams.

The content of dreams, however, does not consist entirely of situations, but also includes disconnected fragments of visual images, speeches and even bits of unmodified thoughts. It may therefore perhaps be of interest to enumerate very briefly the modes of representation available to the dream-work for reproducing the dream-thoughts in the peculiar form of expression necessary in dreams.

The dream-thoughts which we arrive at by means of analysis reveal themselves as a psychical complex of the most intricate possible structure. Its portions stand in the most manifold logical relations to one another: they represent foreground and background, conditions, digressions and illustrations, chains of evidence and counter-arguments. Each train of thought is almost invariably accompanied by its contradictory counterpart. This material lacks none of the characteristics that are familiar to us from our waking thinking. If now all of this is to be turned into a dream, the psychical material will be submitted to a pressure which will condense it greatly, to an internal fragmentation and displacement which will, as it were, create new surfaces, and to a selective operation in favour of those portions of it which are the most appropriate for the construction of situations. If we take into account the genesis of the material, a process of this sort deserves to be described as a 'regression'. In the course of this transformation, however, the logical links which have hitherto held the psychical material together are lost. It is only, as it were, the substantive content of the dream-thoughts that the dream-work takes over and manipulates. The restoration of the connections which the dream-work has destroyed is a task which has to be performed by the work of analysis.

The modes of expression open to a dream may therefore be qualified as meagre by comparison with those of our intellectual speech; nevertheless a dream need not wholly abandon the possibility of reproducing the logical relations present in the dream-thoughts. On the contrary, it succeeds often enough in replacing them by formal characteristics in its own texture.

In the first place, dreams take into account the connection which undeniably exists between all the portions of the dream-thoughts by combining the whole material into a single situation. They reproduce *logical connection* by *approximation in time and space*, just as a painter will represent all the poets in a single group in a picture of Parnassus. It is true that they were never in fact assembled on a single mountain-top; but they certainly form a conceptual group. Dreams carry this method of reproduction down to details; and often when they show us two elements in the dream-content close together, this indicates that there is some specially intimate connection between what correspond to them among the dream-thoughts. Incidentally, it is to be observed that all dreams produced during a single night will be found on analysis to be derived from the same circle of thoughts.

A *casual relation* between two thoughts is either left unrepresented or is replaced by a *sequence* of two pieces of dream of different lengths. Here the representation is often reversed, the beginning of the dream standing for the consequence and its conclusion for the premise. An immediate *transformation* of one thing into another in a dream seems to represent the relation of *cause and effect*.

The alternative '*either–or*' is never expressed in dreams, both of the alternatives being inserted in the text of the dream as though they were equally valid. I have already mentioned that an 'either–or' used in *recording* a dream is to be translated by 'and'.

Ideas which are contraries are by preference expressed in dreams by one and the same element.[1] 'No' seems not to exist so far as dreams are concerned. Opposition between two thoughts, the relation of *reversal*, may be represented in dreams in a most remarkable way. It may be represented by some *other* piece of the dream-content being turned into its opposite – as it were by an afterthought. We shall hear presently of a further method of expressing contradiction. The sensation of *inhibition of movement* which is so common in dreams also serves to express a contradiction between two impulses, a *conflict of will*.

One and one only of these logical relations – that of *similarity, consonance, the possession of common attributes* – is very highly favoured by the mechanism of dream-formation. The dream-work makes use of such cases as a foundation for dream-condensation, by bringing together everything that shows an agreement of this kind into a new unity.

This short series of rough comments is of course inadequate to deal with the full extent of the formal means employed by dreams for the expression of logical relations in the dream-thoughts. Different dreams are more or less carefully constructed in this respect; they keep more or less closely to the text presented to them; they make more or less use of the expedients that are open to the dream-work. In the second case they appear obscure, confused and disconnected. If,

---

[1] [*Footnote added* 1911:] It deserves to be remarked that well-known philologists have asserted that the most ancient human languages tended in general to express contradictory opposites by the same word. (E.g. 'strong–weak', 'inside–outside'. This has been described as 'the antithetical meaning of primal words'.) [Cf. Freud, 1910*e*.]

however, a dream strikes one as *obviously* absurd, if its content includes a piece of palpable nonsense, this is intentionally so; its apparent disregard of all the requirements of logic is expressing a piece of the intellectual content of the dream-thoughts. Absurdity in a dream signifies the presence in the dream-thoughts of *contradiction, ridicule and derision*. Since this statement is in the most marked opposition to the view that dreams are the product of a dissociated and uncritical mental activity, I will emphasize it by means of an example.

One of my acquaintances, Herr M., had been attacked in an essay with an unjustifiable degree of violence, as we all thought – by no less a person than Goethe. Herr M. was naturally crushed by the attack. He complained of it bitterly to some company at table; his veneration for Goethe had not been affected, however, by this personal experience. I now tried to throw a little light on the chronological data, which seemed to me improbable. Goethe died in 1832. Since his attack on Herr M. must naturally have been made earlier than that, Herr M. must have been quite a young man at the time. It seemed to be a plausible notion that he was eighteen. I was not quite sure, however, what year we were actually in, so that my whole calculation melted into obscurity. Incidentally, the attack was contained in Goethe's well-known essay on 'Nature'.

The nonsensical character of this dream will be even more glaringly obvious, if I explain that Herr M. is a youngish business man, who is far removed from any poetical and literary interests. I have no doubt, however, that when I have entered into the analysis of the dream I shall succeed in showing how much 'method' there is in its nonsense.

The material of the dream was derived from three sources:

(1) Herr M., whom I had got to know among some *company at table*, asked me one day to examine his elder brother, who was showing signs of [general paralysis]. In the course of my conversation with the patient an awkward episode occurred, for he gave his brother away for no accountable reason by talking of his *youthful follies*. I had asked the patient the *year of his birth* (cf. the *year of* Goethe's *death* in the dream) and had made him carry out a number of calculations in order to test the weakness of his memory.

(2) A medical journal, which bore my name among others on its title-page, had published a positively '*crushing*' criticism by a *youthful* reviewer of a book by my friend F.[1] in Berlin. I took the editor to task over this; but, though he expressed his regret, he would not undertake

---

[1] [A reference to Wilhelm Fliess (1858–1928), an otolaryngologist with whom Freud, early in his career, conducted an extensive correspondence (Freud, 1950a). Cf. Fliess (1892).]

to offer any redress. I therefore severed my connection with the journal, but in my letter of resignation expressed a hope that *our personal relations would not be affected by the event*. This was the true source of the dream. The unfavourable reception of my friend's work had made a profound impression on me. It contained, in my opinion, a fundamental biological discovery, which is only now – many years later – beginning to find favour with the experts.

(3) A woman patient of mine had given me an account a short time before of her brother's illness, and how he had broken out in a frenzy with cries of '*Nature! Nature!*' The doctors believed that his exclamation came from his having read *Goethe*'s striking essay on that subject and that it showed he had been overworking at his studies. I had remarked that *it seemed to me more plausible* that his exclamation of the word 'Nature' should be taken in the sexual sense in which it is used by the less educated people here. This idea of mine was at least not disproved by the fact that the unfortunate young man subsequently mutilated his own genitals. He was *eighteen* at the time of his outbreak.

Behind my own ego in the dream-content there lay concealed, in the first instance, my friend who had been so badly treated by the critic. '*I tried to throw a little light on the chronological data.*' My friend's book dealt with the *chronological data* of life and among other things showed that the length of *Goethe*'s life was a multiple of a number of days that has a significance in biology. But this ego was compared with a paralytic: '*I was not quite sure what year we were in.*' Thus the dream made out that my friend was behaving like a paralytic, and in this respect it was a mass of absurdities. The dream-thoughts, however, were saying ironically: 'Naturally, it's *he* [my friend F.] who is the crazy fool and it's *you* [the critics] who are the men of genius and know better. Surely it couldn't be the *reverse?*' There were plenty of examples of this *reversal* in the dream. For instance, Goethe attacked the young man, which is absurd, whereas it is still easy for quite a young man to attack the great Goethe.

I should like to lay it down that no dream is prompted by motives other than egoistic ones.[1] In fact, the ego in the present dream does not stand only for my friend but for myself as well. I was identifying myself with him, because the fate of his discovery seemed to fore-

---

[1] [Freud has, however, qualified this statement in an additional footnote written in 1925, which will be found near the end of Chapter V of *The Interpretation of Dreams* (*Standard Ed.*, 4, 270); *P.F.L.*, 4, 374n.).]

shadow the reception of my own findings. If I were to bring forward my theory emphasizing the part played by sexuality in the aetiology of psychoneurotic disorders (cf. the allusion to the eighteen-year-old patient's cry of 'Nature! Nature!'), I should come across the same criticisms; and I was already preparing to meet them with the same derision.

If we pursue the dream-thoughts further, we shall keep on finding ridicule and derision as correlates of the absurdities of the manifest dream. It is well known that it was the discovery of the split skull of a sheep on the Lido of Venice that gave Goethe the idea of the so-called 'vertebral' theory of the skull. My friend boasts that, when he was a student, he released a storm which led to the resignation of an old professor who, though he had once been distinguished (among other things in connection precisely with the same branch of comparative anatomy), had become incapable of teaching owing to *senile dementia*. Thus the agitation which my friend promoted served to combat the mischievous system according to which there is no *age limit* for academic workers in German universities – for *age is proverbially no defence against folly*. – In the hospital here I had the honour of serving for years under a chief who had long been a *fossil* and had for decades been notoriously *feeble-minded*, but who was allowed to continue carrying on his responsible duties. At this point I thought of a descriptive term based upon the discovery on the lido.[1] Some of my young contemporaries at the hospital concocted, in connection with this man, a version of what was then a popular song: '*Das hat kein Goethe g'schrieben, das hat kein Schiller g'dicht . . .*'[2]

VII

We have not yet come to the end of our consideration of the dream-work. In addition to condensation, displacement and pictorial arrangement of the psychical material, we are obliged to assign it yet another activity, though this is not to be found in operation in *every* dream. I shall not deal exhaustively with this part of the dream-work, and will therefore merely remark that the easiest way of forming an idea of its nature is to suppose – though the supposition probably does not meet the facts – that *it only comes into operation* AFTER *the dream-content has already been constructed*. Its function would then consist in

---

[1] ['*Schafkopf*', literally 'sheep's head' = 'silly ass'.]
[2] ['This was written by no Goethe, this was composed by no Schiller.']

arranging the constituents of the dream in such a way that they form an approximately connected whole, a dream-composition. In this way the dream is given a kind of façade (though this does not, it is true, hide its content at every point), and thus receives a first, preliminary interpretation, which is supported by interpolations and slight modifications. Incidentally, this revision of the dream-content is only possible if it is not too punctiliously carried out; nor does it present us with anything more than a glaring misunderstanding of the dream-thoughts. Before we start upon the analysis of a dream we have to clear the ground of this attempt at an interpretation.

The motive for this part of the dream-work is particularly obvious. *Considerations of intelligibility* are what lead to this final revision of a dream; and this reveals the origin of the activity. It behaves towards the dream-content lying before it just as our normal psychical activity behaves in general towards any perceptual content that may be presented to it. It understands that content on the basis of certain anticipatory ideas, and arranges it, even at the moment of perceiving it, on the presupposition of its being intelligible; in so doing it runs a risk of falsifying it, and in fact, if it cannot bring it into line with anything familiar, is a prey to the strangest misunderstandings. As is well known, we are incapable of seeing a series of unfamiliar signs or of hearing a succession of unknown words, without at once falsifying the perception from considerations of intelligibility, on the basis of something already known to us.

Dreams which have undergone a revision of this kind at the hands of a psychical activity completely analogous to waking thought may be described as 'well-constructed'. In the case of other dreams this activity has completely broken down; no attempt even has been made to arrange or interpret the material, and, since after we have woken up we feel ourselves identical with this last part of the dream-work, we make a judgement that the dream was 'hopelessly confused'. From the point of view of analysis, however, a dream that resembles a disordered heap of disconnected fragments is just as valuable as one that has been beautifully polished and provided with a surface. In the former case, indeed, we are saved the trouble of demolishing what has been superimposed upon the dream-content.

It would be a mistake, however, to suppose that these dream-façades are nothing other than mistaken and somewhat arbitrary revisions of the dream-content by the conscious agency of our mental life. In the erection of a dream-façade use is not infrequently made of wishful phantasies which are present in the dream-thoughts in a pre-constructed form, and are of the same character as the appro-priately named 'day-dreams' familiar to us in waking life. The wishful phantasies revealed by analysis in night-dreams often turn out to be repetitions or modified versions of scenes from infancy; thus in some cases the façade of the dream directly reveals the dream's actual nucleus, distorted by an admixture of other material.

The dream-work exhibits no activities other than the four that have already been mentioned. If we keep to the definition of 'dream-work' as the process of transforming the dream-thoughts into the dream-content, it follows that the dream-work is not creative, that it develops no phantasies of its own, that it makes no judgements and draws no conclusions; it has no functions whatever other than condensation and displacement of the material and its modification into pictorial form, to which must be added as a variable factor the final bit of interpretative revision. It is true that we find various things in the dream-content which we should be inclined to regard as a product of some other and higher intellectual function; but in every case analysis shows convincingly that *these intellectual operations have already been performed in the dream-thoughts and have only been* TAKEN OVER *by the dream-content*. A conclusion drawn in a dream is nothing other than the repetition of a conclusion in the dream-thoughts; if the conclusion is taken over into the dream unmodified, it will appear impeccable; if the dream-work has displaced it on to some other material, it will appear nonsensical. A calculation in the dream-content signifies nothing more than that there is a calculation in the dream-thoughts; but while the latter is always rational, a dream-calculation may produce the wildest results if its factors are condensed or if its mathematical operations are displaced on to other material. Not even the speeches that occur in the dream-content are original compo-sitions; they turn out to be a hotchpotch of speeches made, heard or read, which have been revived in the dream-thoughts and whose wording is exactly reproduced, while their origin is entirely disregarded and their meaning is violently changed.

It will perhaps be as well to support these last assertions by a few examples.

(1) Here is an innocent-sounding, well-constructed dream dreamt by a woman patient:

She dreamt she was going to the market with her cook, who was carrying the basket. After she had asked for something, the butcher said to her: 'That's not

obtainable any longer,' and offered her something else, adding: 'This is good too.'
She rejected it and went on to the woman who sells vegetables, who tried to get her
to buy a peculiar vegetable that was tied up in bundles but was of a black colour.
She said: 'I don't recognize that: I won't take it.'

The remark 'That's not obtainable any longer' originated from the treatment itself. A few days earlier I had explained to the patient in those very words that the earliest memories of childhood were 'not obtainable any longer as such', but were replaced in analysis by 'transferences' and dreams. So *I* was the butcher.

The second speech – 'I don't recognize that' – occurred in an entirely different connection. On the previous day she had reproved her cook, who incidentally also appeared in the dream, with the words: 'Behave yourself properly! I don't recognize that!' meaning, no doubt, that she did not understand such behaviour and would not put up with it. As the result of a displacement, it was the more innocent part of this speech which made its way into the content of the dream; but in the dream-thoughts it was only the other part of the speech that played a part. For the dream-work had reduced to complete unintelligibility and extreme innocence an imaginary situation in which *I* was *behaving improperly* to the lady in a particular way. But this situation which the patient was expecting in her imagination was itself only a new edition of something she had once actually experienced.

(11) Here is an apparently quite meaningless dream containing figures. *She was going to pay for something. Her daughter took 3 florins and 65 kreuzers from her (the mother's) purse. The dreamer said to her: 'What are you doing? It only costs 21 kreuzers.'*

The dreamer came from abroad and her daughter was at school here. She was in a position to carry on her treatment with me as long as her daughter remained in Vienna. The day before the dream the headmistress had suggested to her that she should leave her daughter at school for another year. In that case she could also have continued her treatment for a year. The figures in the dream become significant if we remember that 'time is money'. One year is equal to 365 days, or, expressed in money, 365 kreuzers or 3 florins 65 kreuzers. The 21 kreuzers corresponded to the 3 weeks which had still to run between the dream-day and the end of the school term and also to the end of the patient's treatment. It was clearly financial considerations which had induced the lady to refuse the headmistress's proposal, and which were responsible for the smallness of the sums mentioned in the dream.

(III) A lady who, though she was still young, had been married for a number of years, received news that an acquaintance of hers, Fräulein Elise L., who was almost exactly her contemporary, had become engaged. This was the precipitating cause of the following dream:

She was at the theatre with her husband. One side of the stalls was completely empty. Her husband told her that Elise L. and her fiancé had wanted to go too, but had only been able to get bad seats – three for 1 florin 50 kreuzers – and of course they could not take those. She thought it would not really have done any harm if they had.

What interests us here is the source of the figures in the material of the dream-thoughts and the transformations which they underwent. What was the origin of the 1 florin 50 kreuzers? It came from what was in fact an indifferent event of the previous day. Her sister-in-law had been given a present of 150 florins by her husband and had *been in a hurry* to get rid of them by buying a piece of jewellery. It is to be noticed that 150 florins is a *hundred* times as much as 1 florin 50 kreuzers. The only connection with the 'three', which was the number of the theatre tickets, was that her newly engaged friend was that number of months – three – her junior. The situation in the dream was a repetition of a small incident which her husband often teased her about. On one occasion she had been in a great hurry to buy tickets for a play in advance, and when she got to the theatre she had found that one side of the stalls was almost completely empty. There had been *no need for her to be in such a hurry*. Finally, we must not overlook the *absurdity* in the dream of two people taking three tickets for a play.

Now for the dream-thoughts: 'It was *absurd* to marry so early. There was *no need for me to be in such a hurry*. I see from Elise L.'s example that I should have got a husband in the end. Indeed, I should have got one *a hundred times* better' (a treasure) 'if I had only waited. My money' (or dowry) 'could have bought *three* men just as good.'

VIII

Having been made acquainted with the dream-work by the foregoing discussion, we shall no doubt be inclined to pronounce it a quite peculiar psychical process, the like of which, so far as we are aware, does not exist elsewhere. It is as though we were carrying over on to the dream-work all the astonishment which used formerly to be aroused in us by its product, the dream. In fact, however, the dream-work is only the first to be discovered of a whole series of psychical processes, responsible for the generation of hysterical symptoms, of phobias, obsessions and delusions. Condensation and, above all, displacement are invariable characteristics of these other processes as well. Modification into a pictorial form, on the other hand, remains a peculiarity of the dream-work. If this explanation places dreams in a single series alongside the structures produced by psychical illness, this makes it all the more important for us to discover the essential determining conditions of such processes as those of dream-formation. We shall probably be surprised to hear that neither the state of sleep nor illness is among these indispensable conditions. A whole number of the phenomena of the everyday life of healthy people – such as forgetting, slips of the tongue, bungled actions and a particular class of errors – owe their origin to a psychical mechanism analogous to that of dreams and of the other members of the series.

The heart of the problem lies in displacement, which is by far the most striking of the special achievements of the dream-work. If we enter deeply into the subject, we come to realize that the essential determining condition of displacement is a purely psychological one: something in the nature of a *motive*. One comes upon its track if one takes into consideration certain experiences which one cannot escape in analysing dreams. In analysing my specimen dream I was obliged to break off my report of the dream-thoughts on page 87, because, as I confessed, there were some among them which I should prefer to conceal from strangers and which I could not communicate to other people without doing serious mischief in important directions. I added that nothing would be gained if I were to choose another dream instead of that particular one with a view to reporting its analysis: I should come upon dream-thoughts which required to be kept secret in the case of *every* dream with an obscure or confused content. If, however, I were to continue the analysis on my own account, without any reference to other people (whom, indeed, an experience so personal as my dream cannot possibly have been intended to reach), I should eventually arrive at thoughts which would surprise me, whose presence in me I was unaware of, which were not only *alien* but also *disagreeable* to me, and which I should therefore feel inclined to dispute energetically, although the chain of thoughts running through the analysis insisted upon them remorselessly. There is only one way of accounting for this state of affairs, which is of quite universal occurrence; and that is to suppose that these thoughts really were present in my mind, and in possession of a certain amount of psychical intensity or energy, but that they were in a peculiar psychological situation, as a consequence of which they *could not become conscious* to me. (I describe this particular condition as one of 'repression'.) We cannot help concluding, then, that there is a causal connection between the obscurity of the dream-content and the state of repression (inadmissibility to consciousness) of certain of the dream-thoughts, and that the dream had to be obscure so as not to betray the proscribed dream-thoughts. Thus we are led to the concept of a 'dream-distortion', which is the product of the dream-work and serves the purpose of dissimulation, that is, of disguise.

I will test this on the specimen dream which I chose for analysis, and enquire what the thought was which made its way into that dream in a distorted form, and which I should be inclined to repudiate if it were undistorted. I recall that my free cab-drive reminded me of my recent expensive drive with a member of my family, that the interpretation of the dream was 'I wish I might for once experience love that cost me nothing', and that a short time before the dream I had been obliged to spend a considerable sum of money on this same person's account. Bearing this context in mind, I cannot escape the conclusion that *I regret having made that expenditure.* Not until I have recognized this impulse does my wish in the dream for the love which would call for *no* expenditure acquire a meaning. Yet I can honestly say that when I decided to spend this sum of money I did not hesitate for a moment. My regret at having to do so – the contrary current of feeling – did not become conscious to me. *Why* it did not, is another and a far-reaching question, the answer to which is known to me but belongs in another connection.

If the dream that I analyse is not my own, but someone else's, the conclusion will be the same, though the grounds for believing it will be different. If the dreamer is a healthy person, there is no other means open to me of obliging him to recognize the repressed ideas that have been discovered than by pointing out the context of the dream-thoughts; and I cannot help it if he refuses to recognize them. If, however, I am dealing with a neurotic patient, with a hysteric for instance, he will find the acceptance of the repressed thought forced upon him, owing to its connection with the symptoms of his illness, and owing to the improvement he experiences when he exchanges those symptoms for the repressed ideas. In the case, for instance, of the woman patient who had the dream I have just quoted about the three theatre tickets which cost 1 florin 50 kreuzers, the analysis led to the inevitable conclusion that she had a low estimate of her husband (cf. her idea that she could have got one 'a hundred times better'), that she regretted having married him, and that she would have liked to exchange him for another one. It is true that she asserted that she loved her husband, and that her emotional life knew nothing of any such low estimate of him, but all her symptoms led to the same conclusion as the dream. And after her repressed memories had been revived of a particular period during which she had consciously not loved her husband, her symptoms cleared up and her resistance against the interpretation of the dream disappeared.

IX

Now that we have established the concept of repression and have brought dream-distortion into relation with repressed psychical material, we can express in general terms the principal finding to which we have been led by the analysis of dreams. In the case of dreams which are intelligible and have a meaning, we have found that they are undisguised wish-fulfilments; that is, that in their case the dream-situation represents as fulfilled a wish which is known to consciousness, which is left over from daytime life, and which is deservedly of interest. Analysis has taught us something entirely analogous in the case of obscure and confused dreams: once again the dream-situation represents a wish as fulfilled – a wish which invariably arises from the dream-thoughts, but one which is represented in an unrecognizable form and can only be explained when it has been traced back in analysis. The wish in such cases is either itself a repressed one and alien to consciousness, or it is intimately connected with repressed thoughts and is based upon them. Thus the formula for such dreams is as follows: *they are disguised fulfilments of repressed wishes*. It is interesting in this connection to observe that the popular belief that dreams always foretell the future is confirmed. Actually the future which the dream shows us is not the one which *will* occur but the one which we should *like* to occur. The popular mind is behaving here as it usually does: what it wishes, it believes.

Dreams fall into three classes according to their attitude to wish-fulfilment. The first class consists of those which represent an un-repressed wish undisguisedly; these are the dreams of an infantile type which become ever rarer in adults. Secondly there are the dreams which express a repressed wish disguisedly; these no doubt form the overwhelming majority of all our dreams, and require analysis before they can be understood. In the third place there are the dreams which represent a repressed wish, but do so with insufficient or no disguise. These last dreams are invariably accompanied by anxiety, which interrupts them. In their case anxiety takes the place of dream-distortion; and in dreams of the second class anxiety is only avoided owing to the dream-work. There is no great difficulty in proving that the ideational content which produces anxiety in us in dreams was once a wish but has since undergone repression.

There are also clear dreams with a distressing content, which, however, is not felt as distressing in the dream itself. For this reason they cannot be counted as anxiety-dreams; but they have always been taken as evidence of the fact that dreams are without meaning and have no psychical value. An analysis of a dream of this kind will show that we are dealing with well-disguised fulfilments of repressed wishes, that is to say with a dream of the second class; it will also show how admirably the process of displacement is adapted for disguising wishes.

A girl had a dream of seeing her sister's only surviving child lying dead in the same surroundings in which a few years earlier she had in fact seen the dead body of her sister's *first* child. She felt no pain over this; but she naturally rejected the idea that this situation represented any wish of hers. Nor was there any need to suppose this. It had been beside the first child's coffin, however, that, years before, she had seen and spoken to the man she was in love with; if the second child died, she would no doubt meet the man again in her sister's house. She longed for such a meeting, but fought against the feeling. On the dream-day she had bought a ticket for a lecture which was to be given by this same man, to whom she was still devoted. Her dream was a simple dream of impatience of the kind that often occurs before journeys, visits to the theatre, and similar enjoyments that lie ahead. But in order to disguise this longing from her, the situation was displaced on to an event of a kind most unsuitable for producing a feeling of enjoyment, though it had in fact done so in the past. It is to be observed that the emotional behaviour in the dream was appropriate to the real content which lay in the background and not to what was pushed into the foreground. The dream-situation anticipated the meeting she had so long desired; it offered no basis for any painful feelings.

X

Hitherto philosophers have had no occasion to concern themselves with a psychology of repression. We may therefore be permitted to make a first approach to this hitherto unknown topic by constructing a pictorial image of the course of events in dream-formation. It is true that the schematic picture we have arrived at – not only from the study of dreams – is a fairly complicated one; but we cannot manage with anything simpler. Our hypothesis is that in our mental apparatus there are two thought-constructing agencies, of which the second enjoys the privilege of having free access to consciousness for its products, whereas the activity of the first is in itself unconscious and can only reach consciousness by way of the second. On the frontier between the two agencies, where the first passes over to the second, there is a censorship, which only allows what is agreeable to it to pass through and holds back everything else. According to our definition, then, what is rejected by the censorship is in a state of repression. Under certain conditions, of which the state of sleep is one, the relation between the strength of the two agencies is modified in such a way that what is repressed can no longer be held back. In the state of sleep this probably occurs owing to a relaxation of the censorship; when this happens it becomes possible for what has hitherto been repressed to make a path for itself to consciousness. Since, however, the censorship is never completely eliminated but merely reduced, the repressed material must submit to certain alterations which mitigate its offensive features. What becomes conscious in such cases is a compromise between the intentions of one agency and the demands of the other. *Repression – relaxation of the censorship – the formation of a compromise*, this is the fundamental pattern for the generation not only of dreams but of many other psychopathological structures; and in the latter cases too we may observe that the formation of compromises is accompanied by processes of condensation and displacement and by the employment of superficial associations, which we have become familiar with in the dream-work.

We have no reason to disguise the fact that in the hypothesis which we have set up in order to explain the dream-work a part is played by what might be described as a 'daemonic' element. We have gathered an impression that the formation of obscure dreams occurs *as though* one person who was dependent upon a second person had to make a remark which was bound to be disagreeable in the ears of this second one; and it is on the basis of this simile that we have arrived at the concepts of dream-distortion and censorship, and have endeavoured to translate our impression into a psychological theory which is no doubt crude but is at least lucid. Whatever it may be with which a further investigation of the subject may enable us to identify our first and second agencies, we may safely expect to find a confirmation of some correlate of our hypothesis that the second agency controls access to consciousness and can bar the first agency from such access.

When the state of sleep is over, the censorship quickly recovers its full strength; and it can now wipe out all that was won from it during the period of its weakness. This must be one part at least of the explanation of the forgetting of dreams, as is shown by an observation which has been confirmed on countless occasions. It not infrequently happens that during the narration of a dream or during its analysis a fragment of the dream-content which had seemed to be forgotten re-emerges. This fragment which has been rescued from oblivion invariably affords us the best and most direct access to the meaning of the dream. And that, in all probability, must have been the only reason for its having been forgotten, that is, for its having been once more suppressed.

XI

When once we have recognized that the content of a dream is the representation of a fulfilled wish and that its obscurity is due to alterations in repressed material made by the censorship, we shall no longer have any difficulty in discovering the *function* of dreams. It is commonly said that sleep is disturbed by dreams; strangely enough, we are led to a contrary view and must regard dreams as *the guardians of sleep*.

In the case of children's dreams there should be no difficulty in accepting this statement. The state of sleep or the psychical modification involved in sleep, whatever that may be, is brought about by a resolve to sleep which is either imposed upon the child or is reached on the basis of sensations of fatigue; and it is only made possible by the withholding of stimuli which might suggest to the psychical apparatus aims other than that of sleeping. The means by which *external* stimuli can be kept off are familiar to us; but what are the means available for controlling *internal* mental stimuli which set themselves against falling asleep? Let us observe a mother putting her child to sleep. The child gives vent to an unceasing stream of desires: he wants one more kiss, he wants to go on playing. His mother satisfies some of these desires, but uses her authority to postpone others of them to the next day. It is clear that any wishes or needs that may arise have an inhibiting effect upon falling asleep. We all know the amusing story told by Balduin Groller [a popular nineteenth-century Austrian novelist] of the bad little boy who woke up in the middle of the night and shouted across the night-nursery: 'I want the rhino!' A better behaved child, instead of shouting, would have *dreamt* that he was playing with the rhino. Since a dream that shows a wish as fulfilled is *believed* during sleep, it does away with the wish and makes sleep possible. It cannot be disputed that dream-images are believed in in this way, for they are clothed in the psychical appearance of perceptions, and children have not yet acquired the later faculty of distinguishing hallucinations or phantasies from reality.

Adults have learnt to make this distinction; they have also grasped the uselessness of wishing, and after lengthy practice know how to postpone their desires until they can find satisfaction by the long and roundabout path of altering the external world. In their case, accordingly, wish-fulfilments along the short psychical path are rare in sleep too; it is even possible, indeed, that they never occur at all, and that anything that may seem to us to be constructed on the pattern of a child's dream in fact requires a far more complicated solution. On the other hand, in the case of adults – and this no doubt applies without exception to everyone in full possession of his senses – a differentiation has occurred in the psychical material, which was not present in children. A psychical agency has come into being, which, taught by experience of life, exercises a dominating and inhibiting influence upon mental impulses and maintains that influence with jealous severity, and which, owing to its relation to consciousness and to voluntary movement, is armed with the strongest instruments of psychical power. A portion of the impulses of childhood has been suppressed by this agency as being useless to life, and any thought-material derived from those impulses is in a state of repression.

Now while this agency, in which we recognize our normal ego, is concentrated on the wish to sleep, it appears to be compelled by the psycho-physiological conditions of sleep to relax the energy with which it is accustomed to hold down the repressed material during the day. In itself, no doubt, this relaxation does no harm; however much the suppressed impulses of the childish mind may prance around, their access to consciousness is still difficult and their access to movement is barred, as the result of this same state of sleep. The danger of sleep being disturbed by them must, however, be guarded against. We must in any case suppose that even during deep sleep a certain amount of free attention is on duty as a guard against sensory stimuli, and that this guard may sometimes consider waking more advisable than a continuation of sleep. Otherwise there would be no explanation of how it is that we can be woken up at any moment by sensory stimuli of some particular *quality*. As the physiologist Burdach [1838, 486] insisted long ago, a mother, for instance, will be roused by the whimpering of her baby, or a miller if his mill comes to a stop, or most people if they are called softly by their own name. Now the attention which is thus on guard is also directed towards internal wishful stimuli arising from the repressed material, and combines with them to form the dream which, as a compromise, simultaneously satisfies both of the two agencies. The dream provides a kind of psychical consummation for the wish that has been suppressed (or formed with the help of repressed material) by representing it as fulfilled; but it also satisfies the other agency by allowing sleep to continue. In this respect our ego is ready to behave like a child; it gives credence to the dream-images, as though what it wanted to say was: 'Yes, yes! you're quite right, but let me go on sleeping!' The low estimate which we form of dreams when we are awake, and which we relate to their confused and apparently illogical character, is probably nothing other than the judgement passed by our sleeping ego upon the repressed impulses, a judgement based, with better right, upon the motor impotence of these disturbers of sleep. We are sometimes aware in our sleep of this contemptuous judgement. If the content of a dream goes too far in overstepping the censorship, we think: 'After all, it's only a dream!' – and go on sleeping.

This view is not traversed by the fact that there are marginal cases in which the dream – as happens with anxiety-dreams – can no longer perform its function of preventing an interruption of sleep, but assumes instead the other function of promptly bringing sleep to an end. In doing so it is merely behaving like a conscientious night-watchman, who first carries out his duty by suppressing disturbances so that the townsmen may not be woken up, but afterwards continues to do his duty by himself waking the townsmen up, if the causes of the disturbance seem to him serious and of a kind that he cannot cope with alone.

The function of the dream as a guardian of sleep becomes particularly evident when an external stimulus impinges upon the senses of a sleeper. It is generally recognized that sensory stimuli arising during sleep influence the content of dreams; this can be proved experimentally and is among the few certain (but, incidentally, greatly overvalued) findings of medical investigation into dreams. But this finding involves a puzzle which has hitherto proved insoluble. For the sensory stimulus which the experimenter causes to impinge upon the sleeper is not correctly recognized in the dream; it is subjected to one of an indefinite number of possible interpretations, the choice being apparently left to an arbitrary psychical determination. But there is, of course, no such thing as arbitrary determination in the mind. There are several ways in which a sleeper may react to an external sensory stimulus. He may wake up or he may succeed in continuing his sleep in spite of it. In the latter case he may make use of a dream in order to get rid of the external stimulus, and here again there is more than one method open to him. For instance, he may get rid of the stimulus by dreaming that he is in a situation which is absolutely incompatible with the stimulus. Such was the line taken by a sleeper who was subject to disturbance by a painful abscess on the perineum. He dreamt that he was riding on a horse, making use of the poultice that was intended to mitigate his pain as a saddle, and in this way he avoided being disturbed. Or, as happens more frequently, the external stimulus is given an interpretation which brings it into the context of a repressed wish which is at the moment awaiting fulfilment; in this way the external stimulus is robbed of its reality and is treated as though it were a portion of the psychical material. Thus someone dreamt that he had written a comedy with a particular plot; it was produced in a theatre, the first act was over, and there were thunders of applause; the clapping was terrific ... The dreamer must have succeeded in prolonging his sleep till after the interference had ceased; for when he woke up he no longer heard the noise, but rightly concluded that someone must have been beating a carpet or mattress. Every dream which occurs immediately before the sleeper is woken by a loud noise has made an attempt at explaining away the arousing stimulus by providing another explanation of it and has thus sought to prolong sleep, even if only for a moment.

XII

No one who accepts the view that the censorship is the chief reason for dream-distortion will be surprised to learn from the results of dream-interpretation that most of the dreams of adults are traced back by analysis to *erotic wishes*. This assertion is not aimed at dreams with an *undisguised* sexual content, which are no doubt familiar to all dreamers from their own experience and are as a rule the only ones to be described as 'sexual dreams'. Even dreams of this latter kind offer enough surprises in their choice of the people whom they make into sexual objects, in their disregard of all the limitations which the dreamer imposes in his waking life upon his sexual desires, and by their many strange details, hinting at what are commonly known as 'perversions'. A great many other dreams, however, which show no sign of being erotic in their manifest content, are revealed by the work of interpretation in analysis as sexual wish-fulfilments; and, on the other hand, analysis proves that a great many of the thoughts left over from the activity of waking life as 'residues of the previous day' only find their way to representation in dreams through the assistance of repressed erotic wishes.

There is no theoretical necessity why this should be so; but to explain the fact it may be pointed out that no other group of instincts has been submitted to such far-reaching suppression by the demands of cultural education, while at the same time the sexual instincts are also the ones which, in most people, find it easiest to escape from the control of the highest mental agencies. Since we have become acquainted with infantile sexuality, which is often so unobtrusive in its manifestations and is always overlooked and misunderstood, we are justified in saying that almost every civilized man retains the infantile forms of sexual life in some respect or other. We can thus understand how it is that repressed infantile sexual wishes provide the most frequent and strongest motive-forces for the construction of dreams.[1]

There is only one method by which a dream which expresses erotic wishes can succeed in appearing innocently non-sexual in its manifest content. The material of the sexual ideas must not be represented as such, but must be replaced in the content of the dream by hints, allusions and similar forms of indirect representation. But, unlike other forms of indirect representation, that which is employed in dreams must not be immediately intelligible. The modes of representation which fulfil these conditions are usually described as 'symbols' of the things which they represent. Particular interest has been directed to them since it has been noticed that dreamers

[1] See my *Three Essays on the Theory of Sexuality* (1905*d*). [Chapter 5 in this volume.]

speaking the same language make use of the same symbols, and that in some cases, indeed, the use of the same symbols extends beyond the use of the same language. Since dreamers themselves are unaware of the meaning of the symbols they use, it is difficult at first sight to discover the source of the connection between the symbols and what they replace and represent. The fact itself, however, is beyond doubt, and it is important for the technique of dream-interpretation. For, with the help of a knowledge of dream-symbolism, it is possible to understand the meaning of separate elements of the content of a dream or separate pieces of a dream or in some cases even whole dreams, without having to ask the dreamer for his associations.[1] Here we are approaching the popular ideal of translating dreams and on the other hand are returning to the technique of interpretation used by the ancients, to whom dream-interpretation was identical with interpretation by means of symbols.

Although the study of dream-symbols is far from being complete, we are in a position to lay down with certainty a number of general statements and a quantity of special information on the subject. There are some symbols which bear a single meaning almost universally: thus the Emperor and Empress (or the King and Queen) stand for the parents, rooms represent women[2] and their entrances and exits the openings of the body. The majority of dream-symbols serve to represent persons, parts of the body and activities invested with erotic interest; in particular, the genitals are represented by a number of often very surprising symbols, and the greatest variety of objects are employed to denote them symbolically. Sharp weapons, long and stiff objects, such as tree-trunks and sticks, stand for the male genital; while cupboards, boxes, carriages or ovens may represent the uterus. In such cases as these the *tertium comparationis*, the common element in these substitutions, is immediately intelligible; but there are other symbols in which it is not so easy to grasp the connection. Symbols such as a staircase or going upstairs to represent sexual intercourse, a tie or cravat for the male organ, or wood for the female one, provoke our unbelief until we can arrive at an understanding of the symbolic relation underlying them by some other means. Moreover a whole number of dream-symbols are bisexual and can relate to the male or female genitals according to the context.

---

[1] [See, however, the qualification three paragraphs lower down.]

[2] Cf. '*Frauenzimmer*' [literally 'women's apartment,' commonly used in German as a slightly derogatory word for 'woman'].

Some symbols are universally disseminated and can be met with in all dreamers belonging to a single linguistic or cultural group; there are others which occur only within the most restricted and individual limits, symbols constructed by an individual out of his own ideational material. Of the former class we can distinguish some whose claim to represent sexual ideas is immediately justified by linguistic usage (such, for instance, as those derived from agriculture, e.g. 'fertilization' or 'seed') and others whose relation to sexual ideas appears to reach back into the very earliest ages and to the most obscure depths of our conceptual functioning. The power of constructing symbols has not been exhausted in our own days in the case of either of the two sorts of symbols which I have distinguished at the beginning of this paragraph. Newly discovered objects (such as airships) are, as we may observe, at once adopted as universally available sexual symbols.

It would, incidentally, be a mistake to expect that if we had a still profounder knowledge of dream-symbolism (of the 'language of dreams') we could do without asking the dreamer for his associations to the dream and go back entirely to the technique of dream-interpretation of antiquity. Quite apart from individual symbols and oscillations in the use of universal ones, one can never tell whether any particular element in the content of a dream is to be interpreted symbolically or in its proper sense, and one can be certain that the *whole* content of a dream is not to be interpreted symbolically. A knowledge of dream-symbolism will never do more than enable us to translate certain constituents of the dream-content, and will not relieve us of the necessity for applying the technical rules which I gave earlier. It will, however, afford the most valuable assistance to interpretation precisely at points at which the dreamer's associations are insufficient or fail altogether.

Dream-symbolism is also indispensable to an understanding of what are known as 'typical' dreams, which are common to everyone, and of 'recurrent' dreams in individuals.

If the account I have given in this short discussion of the symbolic mode of expression in dreams appears incomplete, I can justify my neglect by drawing attention to one of the most important pieces of knowledge that we possess on this subject. Dream-symbolism extends far beyond dreams: it is not peculiar to dreams, but exercises a similar dominating influence on representation in fairy-tales, myths and legends, in jokes and in folk-lore. It enables us to trace the intimate connections between dreams and these latter productions. We must not suppose that dream-symbolism is a creation of the dream-work; it is in all probability a characteristic of the unconscious thinking which provides the dream-work with the material for condensation, displacement and dramatization.[1]

XIII

I lay no claim to have thrown light in these pages upon *all* the problems of dreams, nor to having dealt in a convincing way with those that I *have* discussed. Anyone who is interested in the whole extent of the literature of dreams may be referred to a work by Sante de Sanctis (*I sogni*, 1899); and anyone who wishes to hear more detailed arguments in favour of the view of dreams which I myself have put forward should turn to my volume *The Interpretation of Dreams*, 1900. It only remains for me now to indicate the direction in which my exposition of the subject of the dream-work calls for pursuit.

I have laid it down as the task of dream-interpretation to replace the dream by the latent dream-thoughts, that is, to unravel what the dream-work has woven. In so doing I have raised a number of new psychological problems dealing with the mechanism of this dream-work itself, as well as with the nature and conditions of what is described as repression; on the other hand I have asserted the existence of the dream-thoughts – a copious store of psychical structures of the highest order, which is characterized by all the signs of normal intellectual functioning, but is nevertheless withdrawn from consciousness till it emerges in distorted form in the dream-content. I cannot but assume that thoughts of this kind are present in everyone, since almost everyone, including the most normal people, is capable of dreaming. The unconscious material of the dream-thoughts and its relation to consciousness and to repression raise further questions of significance to psychology, the answers to which must no doubt be postponed until analysis has clarified the origin of other psychopathological structures, such as hysterical symptoms and obsessional ideas.

---

[1] Further information on dream-symbolism may be found in the works of early writers on dream-interpretation, e.g. Artemidorus of Daldis and Scherner (1861), and also in my own *Interpretation of Dreams* (1900a) [Chapter VI, Section E], in the mythological studies of the psycho-analytic school, as well as in some of W. Stekel's writings (e.g. 1911).

Three

THE CONCEPT OF
THE UNCONSCIOUS

Introduction

Students who were ready to be introduced to the previously enigmatic realm of the dream now confront the task of penetrating deeper into the complexities of human thought activities.

Psycho-analysis has frequently been reproached, though without justification, for incorrectly claiming priority for its assumption of *unconscious* mental activities. In its defence, I refer to words which Freud wrote in the last year of his life: 'The concept of the unconscious has long been knocking at the gates of psychology and asking to be let in. Philosophy and literature have often toyed with it, but science could find no use for it. Psycho-analysis has seized upon the concept, has taken it seriously and has given it a fresh content' (1940*b*, p. 189 below).

Those who make the effort to pursue psycho-analytic teachings can themselves gain an impression of the characteristics of this new content. It does not in any way consist of a low estimation of conscious psychic activities and their role in mastering the tasks of life. On the contrary, it is the task and the goal of psycho-analytic work to enlarge the domain of conscious thinking, to fill gaps in it, to uncover and dissolve resistances against permitting psychic contents to gain consciousness. It is a triumph for every analyst when he succeeds in making unconscious processes conscious.

The historian who immerses himself in the prehistory and early history of psycho-analysis is impressed by the contrast in attitudes to the mentally ill before and after the assumption of unconscious thinking. Cold water packs and faradization, in the past the only aids in the fight against psychic suffering, simultaneously were evidence of the physician's lack of understanding hysterics, obsessional neurotics, and hypochondriacs. Nothing that occurs in conscious thinking opens up a path to the irrational and abnormal thought processes which underlie psychic symptoms.

It was this, for Freud unbearable, darkness which was illuminated for him by the work of three men. The first was, in 1885–86, Jean-Martin Charcot in Paris, who succeeded in uncovering the meaning of hysterical attacks. Next Freud was influenced, in 1889, by Hippolyte Bernheim in Nancy, who in his demonstrations with hypnosis proved that human behaviour and action can be motivated by thought processes of which the person is unaware. The decisive step, finally, is linked to the name of Josef Breuer, a respected Viennese physician, who, in painstaking work with his patient Anna O., was able to trace back her numerous hysterical symptoms to their origins in psychic experiences that had become unconscious.

Breuer and Freud (1893–95) both realized that an individual's hysterical illness was triggered by a return to the past, a finding that was succinctly put in the formulation: 'Hysterics suffer mainly from reminiscences' (1893a, p. 7). In his earliest works, Freud attributed this 'reminiscence' to sexual seduction in childhood, a view which he already abandoned in 1897. He replaced it with the realization that the recollection to which the hysteric is tied is not of real events but goes back to phantasies. We can say that the hysteric regresses to infantile wish-phantasies.

In their pioneering efforts Freud and Breuer also shared the discovery that what occurs in consciousness constitutes only a part of human mental life and that the logical mode of thinking with which we are familiar extends no further than the surface of consciousness. What transpires behind it and rises to the surface in the form of pathological symptoms is as irrational, distorted, and compressed as the phenomena of dream-life. It is not 'nonsensical' in the usual sense of this word; rather, it follows its own sense, which is alien to us, in its own form of expression, which is alien to consciousness. The psychoanalytic interpreter of dreams who can unravel the dream distortion and translate the latent content of the dream into manifest thoughts is the model for the psycho-analytic therapist who understands the language of symptoms and traces the pathological manifestations back to their actual origins.

The first person who, following Breuer's example, took this path was Freud. The *Studies on Hysteria* by Breuer and Freud (1895d) document the painstaking work involved in proceeding from consciousness to the thoughts lying behind it. At that time it was still hypnosis which was called upon to remove the obstacles in this path. Soon, however, hypnosis proved to be an unreliable aid; its therapeutic effect was tied too closely to the person of the hypnotist and his suggestions; therefore, it always carried with it the danger that the therapeutic effect would be extinguished with the resolution of the patient's emotional tie to the therapist. A new method to reach the unconscious had to be found – a method, moreover, which was in keeping with Freud's rationality and non-authoritarian attitude. The commands of the hypnotist who autocratically intrudes into the patient's inner world were to be replaced by the patient himself who by his own act of will and free decision resolved to put his conscious, logical, and goal-directed thinking out of action and to give his thoughts free rein, which soon leads them away from the rational exigencies of everyday life and subjects them to the pressing urges of instinctual wishes and phantasies with which we have become familiar in the theory of dreams. Today we regard the replacement of hypnosis by so-called 'free association' as the real birth of psycho-analysis. Free association is, next to the interpretation of dreams, the second *via regia* to insight into the unconscious.

For the serious student of psycho-analysis the assumption of unconscious thought processes represents only a first step. Four further steps serve to lead him into a world of hard-won clinical insights and theories derived from them.

The first fundamental insight of this kind concerns the contrast between psycho-analysis and all earlier psychological theories. For the latter, it was axiomatic that consciousness equalled psychic activity, an assumption that was in full accord with the popular opinion that people knew what went on in their ideational world, were aware of the origins of their emotional attitudes and phantasies, and were informed about the motives of their actions. It is this familiar notion, lulling man into deceptive security, which decisively contrasts with psycho-analysis. Its findings, as described above, not only aim at psychic processes occurring *outside* of the conscious realm; they also change the proportion between awareness and unawareness of one's own self. They teach that our psychic activity proceeds for the most part unconsciously; that only fragments of this activity emerge temporarily into consciousness; that we, far from controlling our inner life, are in many respects subject to domination by it – in short, to use Freud's formulation again, that psychologically we are 'not master in [our] own house' (1917a, p. 143). On several occasions Freud compared the injury which he inflicted upon man with his findings with the effect of the unwelcome realization (by Darwin) that man descended from the apes and the no less unwelcome discovery (by Copernicus) that the earth is not the centre of the universe (e.g., 1925*e*, p. 221). No other finding of psycho-analysis, with the exception of the revelation of infantile sexuality, earned it more enemies and elicited more resistances.

A second insight further complicates matters for the student: there is not one but two kinds of unconscious. It is possible to demonstrate thought processes which temporarily disappear from the surface of consciousness and which descriptively are therefore unconscious, though they do not change their character by disappearing. They merely make room for other, at the moment more relevant thought processes, but for this purpose they leave the realm of consciousness only temporarily; they can at any time without difficulties again return to it. In psycho-analysis they are called *preconscious*, a term that is meant to characterize their position of waiting in the forecourt of consciousness. We distinguish the preconscious thought processes from the unconscious ones – *unconscious* in the real sense of the word – which lead their existence in a different realm of mental life and which are cut off from consciousness by strong counterforces, i.e., resistances that can be overcome only with the aid of dream interpretation or free association. This classification of psychic processes into conscious, preconscious and unconscious proved to be an important advance in a new orientation to the mental life of man.

A third insight concerns the characteristics of the mode of thought dominant in the realm of the unconscious – an insight for which our students have already been prepared by the discussion of dream processes. I repeat: we are dealing here with modes of expression that are closer to hallucination than they are to thinking in words; opposites become one and the same thing; temporal relationships and sequences are disregarded; logical thinking and consequential cause-effect connections are missing; emotions are easily displaced from their real object to another; mixed figures are formed as the result of condensation of several single figures. Altogether this mode of thinking characteristic of the unconscious strikes one as extraordinarily primitive; it is not different from what we assume to prevail in the infant before the acquisition of language. In psycho-analytic terminology, we call it the *primary process*, in contrast to the later evolving conscious thought process, the *secondary process*. The differences between these two thought processes are decisive for man's inner life and cannot be overestimated.

The fourth, necessary advance is the interest in the mutual relations between conscious, preconscious and unconscious processes, especially the interchange between these two different systems. While the preconscious and the conscious can without difficulty pass over into each other and exchange their elements, there are at the border between the system conscious (system *Cs.*) and the system unconscious (system *Ucs.*) guardians which examine and censor the elements emerging from the depth with regard to their admissibility and turn back everything that is objectionable to consciousness. In the personifying language of psycho-analysis, these guarding forces are in fact compared with a political censor; the method employed to keep objectionable elements away from consciousness is called *repression*. Whenever elements from the system unconscious circumvent the censors and undefended penetrate into the system conscious, anxiety arises, not different from what happens in the anxiety dream in which a forbidden instinct derivative without being distorted succeeded in entering the manifest content of the dream. Much psychic suffering of man derives from nothing other than the continuous struggle between the instinct derivatives that are held in check but strive to rise to the surface and the system conscious that wards off these invaders or, when the defence miscarries, attempts by one or another means of disguise at least to minimize their harm. A person who – like the analyst – once has learned to follow such a defensive struggle in all its details will forever remain fascinated by the never-ending variations and complications of man's psychic life.

The student who has followed us thus far should now be in a position to undertake the study of Freud's 'A Note on the Unconscious in Psycho-Analysis' (1912*g*), 'The Unconscious' (1915*e*), and 'Some Elementary Lessons in Psycho-Analysis' (1940*b*).

A Note on the Unconscious in Psycho-Analysis

(1912)*

I wish to expound in a few words and as plainly as possible what the term 'unconscious' has come to mean in psycho-analysis and in psycho-analysis alone.

A conception – or any other psychical element – which is now *present* to my consciousness may become *absent* the next moment, and may become *present again*, after an interval, unchanged, and, as we say, from memory, not as a result of a fresh perception by our senses. It is this fact which we are accustomed to account for by the supposition that during the interval the conception has been present in our mind, although *latent* in consciousness. In what shape it may have existed while present in the mind and latent in consciousness we have no means of guessing.

At this very point we may be prepared to meet with the philosophical objection that the latent conception did not exist as an object of psychology, but as a physical disposition for the recurrence of the same psychical phenomenon, i.e. of the said conception. But we may reply that this is a theory far overstepping the domain of psychology proper; that it simply begs the question by asserting 'conscious' to be an identical term with 'psychical', and that it is clearly at fault in denying psychology the right to account for its most common facts, such as memory, by its own means.

Now let us call 'conscious' the conception which is present to our consciousness and of which we are aware, and let this be the only meaning of the term 'conscious'. As for latent conceptions, if we have any reason to suppose that they exist in the mind – as we had in the case of memory – let them be denoted by the term 'unconscious'.

Thus an unconscious conception is one of which we are not aware,

* First published in English in the *Proceedings* of the Society for Psychical Research. The present text is an amended version of the original, taken from *Standard Ed.*, 12, 260; *P.F.L.*, 11, 50.

but the existence of which we are nevertheless ready to admit on account of other proofs or signs.

This might be considered an uninteresting piece of descriptive or classificatory work if no experience appealed to our judgement other than the facts of memory, or the cases of association by unconscious links. The well-known experiment, however, of the 'post-hypnotic suggestion' teaches us to insist upon the importance of the distinction between *conscious* and *unconscious* and seems to increase its value.

In this experiment, as performed by Bernheim, a person is put into a hypnotic state and is subsequently aroused. While he was in the hypnotic state, under the influence of the physician, he was ordered to execute a certain action at a certain fixed moment after his awakening, say half an hour later. He awakes, and seems fully conscious and in his ordinary condition; he has no recollection of his hypnotic state, and yet at the prearranged moment there rushes into his mind the impulse to do such and such a thing, and he does it consciously, though not knowing why. It seems impossible to give any other description of the phenomenon than to say that the order had been present in the mind of the person in a condition of latency, or had been present unconsciously, until the given moment came, and then had become conscious. But not the whole of it emerged into consciousness: only the conception of the act to be executed. All the other ideas associated with this conception – the order, the influence of the physician, the recollection of the hypnotic state, remained unconscious even then. [Cf. Bernheim, 1886, 1891.]

But we have more to learn from such an experiment. We are led from the purely descriptive to a *dynamic* view of the phenomenon. The idea of the action ordered in hypnosis not only became an object of consciousness at a certain moment, but the more striking aspect of the fact is that this idea grew *active*: it was translated into action as soon as consciousness became aware of its presence. The real stimulus to the action being the order of the physician, it is hard not to concede that the idea of the physician's order became active too. Yet this last idea did not reveal itself to consciousness, as did its outcome, the idea of the action; it remained unconscious, and so it was *active and unconscious* at the same time.

A post-hypnotic suggestion is a laboratory production, an artificial fact. But if we adopt the theory of hysterical phenomena first put forward by P. Janet and elaborated by Breuer and myself, we shall not be at a loss for plenty of natural facts showing the psychological character of the post-hypnotic suggestion even more clearly and distinctly.

The mind of the hysterical patient is full of active yet unconscious ideas; all her symptoms proceed from such ideas. It is in fact the most striking character of the hysterical mind to be ruled by them. If the hysterical woman vomits, she may do so from the idea of being pregnant. She has, however, no knowledge of this idea, although it can easily be detected in her mind, and made conscious to her, by one of the technical procedures of psycho-analysis. If she is executing the jerks and movements constituting her 'fit', she does not even consciously represent to herself the intended actions, and she may perceive those actions with the detached feelings of an onlooker. Nevertheless analysis will show that she was acting her part in the dramatic reproduction of some incident in her life, the memory of which was unconsciously active during the attack. The same preponderance of active unconscious ideas is revealed by analysis as the essential fact in the psychology of all other forms of neurosis.

We learn therefore by the analysis of neurotic phenomena that a latent or unconscious idea is not necessarily a weak one, and that the presence of such an idea in the mind admits of indirect proofs of the most cogent kind, which are equivalent to the direct proof furnished by consciousness. We feel justified in making our classification agree with this addition to our knowledge by introducing a fundamental distinction between different kinds of latent or unconscious ideas. We were accustomed to think that every latent idea was so because it was weak and that it grew conscious as soon as it became strong. We have now gained the conviction that there are some latent ideas which do not penetrate into consciousness, however strong they may have become. Therefore we may call the latent ideas of the first type *foreconscious*,[1] while we reserve the term *unconscious* (proper) for the latter type which we came to study in the neuroses. The term *unconscious*, which was used in the purely descriptive sense before, now comes to imply something more. It designates not only latent ideas in general, but especially ideas with a certain dynamic character, ideas keeping apart from consciousness in spite of their intensity and activity.

Before continuing my exposition I will refer to two objections which

[1] [In the 1925 English version, throughout the paper, 'foreconscious' was altered to 'preconscious', which has, of course, become the regular translation of the German '*vorbewusst*'.]

are likely to be raised at this point. The first of these may be stated thus: instead of subscribing to the hypothesis of unconscious ideas of which we know nothing, we had better assume that consciousness can be split up, so that certain ideas or other psychical acts may constitute a consciousness apart, which has become detached and estranged from the bulk of conscious psychical activity. Well-known pathological cases like that of Dr Azam[1] seem to go far to show that the splitting up of consciousness is no fanciful imagination.

I venture to urge against this theory that it is a gratuitous assumption, based on the abuse of the word 'conscious'. We have no right to extend the meaning of this word so far as to make it include a consciousness of which its owner himself is not aware. If philosophers find difficulty in accepting the existence of unconscious ideas, the existence of an unconscious consciousness seems to me even more objectionable. The cases described as splitting of consciousness, like Dr Azam's, might better be denoted as shifting of consciousness, – that function – or whatever it be – oscillating between two different psychical complexes which become conscious and unconscious in alternation.

The other objection that may probably be raised would be that we apply to normal psychology conclusions which are drawn chiefly from the study of pathological conditions. We are enabled to answer it by another fact, the knowledge of which we owe to psycho-analysis. Certain deficiencies of function of most frequent occurrence among healthy people, e.g. *lapsus linguae*, errors in memory and speech, forgetting of names, etc., may easily be shown to depend on the action of strong unconscious ideas in the same way as neurotic symptoms. We shall meet with another still more convincing argument at a later stage of this discussion.

By the differentiation of foreconscious and unconscious ideas, we are led on to leave the field of classification and to form an opinion about functional and dynamical relations in psychical action. We have found a *foreconscious activity* passing into consciousness with no difficulty, and an *unconscious activity* which remains so and seems to be cut off from consciousness.

Now we do not know whether these two modes of psychical activity are identical or essentially divergent from their beginning, but we

[1] The reference is to the case of Félida X., a striking example of alternating or double personality, first described by Azam (1876, 1887).

may ask why they should become different in the course of psychical action. To this last question psycho-analysis gives a clear and unhesitating answer. It is by no means impossible for the product of unconscious activity to pierce into consciousness, but a certain amount of exertion is needed for this task. When we try to do it in ourselves, we become aware of a distinct feeling of *repulsion* which must be overcome, and when we produce it in a patient we get the most unquestionable signs of what we call his *resistance* to it. So we learn that the unconscious idea is excluded from consciousness by living forces which oppose themselves to its reception, while they do not object to other ideas, the foreconscious ones. Psycho-analysis leaves no room for doubt that the repulsion from unconscious ideas is only provoked by the tendencies embodied in their contents. The next and most probable theory which can be formulated at this stage of our knowledge is the following. Unconsciousness is a regular and inevitable phase in the processes constituting our psychical activity; every psychical act begins as an unconscious one, and it may either remain so or go on developing into consciousness, according as it meets with resistance or not. The distinction between foreconscious and unconscious activity is not a primary one, but comes to be established after repulsion has sprung up. Only then the difference between foreconscious ideas, which can appear in consciousness and reappear at any moment, and unconscious ideas which cannot do so gains a theoretical as well as a practical value. A rough but not inadequate analogy to this supposed relation of conscious to unconscious activity might be drawn from the field of ordinary photography. The first stage of the photograph is the 'negative'; every photographic picture has to pass through the 'negative process', and some of these negatives which have held good in examination are admitted to the 'positive process' ending in the picture.

But the distinction between foreconscious and unconscious activity, and the recognition of the barrier which keeps them asunder, is not the last or the most important result of the psycho-analytic investigation of psychical life. There is one psychical product to be met with in the most normal persons, which yet presents a very striking analogy to the wildest productions of insanity, and was no more intelligible to philosophers than insanity itself. I refer to dreams. Psycho-analysis is founded upon the analysis of dreams; the interpretation of dreams is the most complete piece of work the young science has done up to the present. One of the most common types of

dream-formation may be described as follows: a train of thoughts has
been aroused by the working of the mind in the daytime, and retained
some of its activity, escaping from the general inhibition of interests
which introduces sleep and constitutes the psychical preparation for
sleeping. During the night this train of thoughts succeeds in finding
connections with one of the unconscious tendencies present ever since
his childhood in the mind of the dreamer, but ordinarily *repressed* and
excluded from his conscious life. By the borrowed force of this
unconscious help, the thoughts, the residue of the day's work, now
become active again, and emerge into consciousness in the shape of
the dream. Now three things have happened:

(1) The thoughts have undergone a change, a disguise and a
distortion, which represents the part of the unconscious helpmate.

(2) The thoughts have occupied consciousness at a time when they
ought not.

(3) Some part of the unconscious, which could not otherwise have
done so, has emerged into consciousness.

We have learnt the art of finding out the 'residual thoughts', the
latent thoughts of the dream, and, by comparing them with the apparent
dream, we are able to form a judgement on the changes they underwent
and the manner in which these were brought about.

The latent thoughts of the dream differ in no respect from the
products of our regular conscious activity; they deserve the name of
foreconscious thoughts, and may indeed have been conscious at some
moment of waking life. But by entering into connection with the
unconscious tendencies during the night they have become assimi-
lated to the latter, degraded as it were to the condition of unconscious
thoughts, and subjected to the laws by which unconscious activity is
governed. And here is the opportunity to learn what we could not
have guessed from speculation, or from another source of empirical
information – that the laws of unconscious activity differ widely from
those of the conscious. We gather in detail what the peculiarities of the
Unconscious are, and we may hope to learn still more about them by a
profounder investigation of the processes of dream-formation.

This inquiry is not yet half finished, and an exposition of the results
obtained hitherto is scarcely possible without entering into the most
intricate problems of dream-analysis. But I would not break off this
discussion without indicating the change and progress in our comprehension of the Unconscious which are due to our psycho-analytic
study of dreams.

Unconsciousness seemed to us at first only an enigmatical characteristic of a definite psychical act. Now it means more for us. It is a sign that this act partakes of the nature of a certain psychical category known to us by other and more important characters and that it belongs to a system of psychical activity which is deserving of our fullest attention. The index-value of the unconscious has far outgrown its importance as a property. The system revealed by the sign that the single acts forming parts of it are unconscious we designate by the name 'The Unconscious', for want of a better and less ambiguous term. In German, I propose to denote this system by the letters *Ubw*, an abbreviation of the German word 'Unbewusst'.[1] And this is the third and most significant sense which the term 'unconscious' has acquired in psycho-analysis.

---

[1] [The equivalent English abbreviation is, of course, '*Ucs.*'.]

The Unconscious

(1915)*

We have learnt from psycho-analysis that the essence of the process of repression lies, not in putting an end to, in annihilating, the idea which represents an instinct, but in preventing it from becoming conscious. When this happens we say of the idea that it is in a state of being 'unconscious', and we can produce good evidence to show that even when it is unconscious it can produce effects, even including some which finally reach consciousness. Everything that is repressed must remain unconscious; but let us state at the very outset that the repressed does not cover everything that is unconscious. The unconscious has the wider compass: the repressed is a part of the unconscious.

How are we to arrive at a knowledge of the unconscious? It is of course only as something conscious that we know it, after it has undergone transformation or translation into something conscious. Psycho-analytic work shows us every day that translation of this kind is possible. In order that this should come about, the person under analysis must overcome certain resistances – the same resistances as those which, earlier, made the material concerned into something repressed by rejecting it from the conscious.

I. JUSTIFICATION FOR THE CONCEPT OF THE UNCONSCIOUS

Our right to assume the existence of something mental that is unconscious and to employ that assumption for the purposes of scientific work is disputed in many quarters. To this we can reply that our assumption of the unconscious is *necessary* and *legitimate*, and that we possess numerous proofs of its existence.

It is *necessary* because the data of consciousness have a very large

* First published in *Int. Z. Psychoanal.* The present English version is included in *Standard Ed.*, **14**, 166; *P.F.L.*, **11**, 167. Together with the papers 'Instincts and their Vicissitudes' and 'Repression' (see Chapters 4 and 8 in this volume), it belongs to Freud's series of papers on metapsychology. Cf. p. 155 and *n*.

number of gaps in them; both in healthy and in sick people psychical acts often occur which can be explained only by presupposing other acts, of which, nevertheless, consciousness affords no evidence. These not only include parapraxes and dreams in healthy people, and everything described as a psychical symptom or an obsession in the sick; our most personal daily experience acquaints us with ideas that come into our head we do not know from where, and with intellectual conclusions arrived at we do not know how. All these conscious acts remain disconnected and unintelligible if we insist upon claiming that every mental act that occurs in us must also necessarily be experienced by us through consciousness; on the other hand, they fall into a demonstrable connection if we interpolate between them the unconscious acts which we have inferred. A gain in meaning is a perfectly justifiable ground for going beyond the limits of direct experience. When, in addition, it turns out that the assumption of there being an unconscious enables us to construct a successful procedure by which we can exert an effective influence upon the course of conscious processes, this success will have given us an incontrovertible proof of the existence of what we have assumed. This being so, we must adopt the position that to require that whatever goes on in the mind must also be known to consciousness is to make an untenable claim.

We can go further and argue, in support of there being an unconscious psychical state, that at any given moment consciousness includes only a small content, so that the greater part of what we call conscious knowledge must in any case be for very considerable periods of time in a state of latency, that is to say, of being psychically unconscious. When all our latent memories are taken into consideration it becomes totally incomprehensible how the existence of the unconscious can be denied. But here we encounter the objection that these latent recollections can no longer be described as psychical, but that they correspond to residues of somatic processes from which what is psychical can once more arise. The obvious answer to this is that a latent memory is, on the contrary, an unquestionable residuum of a *psychical* process. But it is more important to realize clearly that this objection is based on the equation – not, it is true, explicitly stated but taken as axiomatic – of what is conscious with what is mental. This equation is either a *petitio principii* which begs the question whether everything that is psychical is also necessarily conscious; or else it is a matter of convention, of nomenclature. In this latter case it is, of course, like any other convention, not open to refutation. The question remains, however, whether the convention is so expedient that we are bound to adopt it. To this we may reply that the conventional equation of the psychical with the conscious is totally inexpedient. It disrupts psychical continuities, plunges us into the insoluble difficulties of psycho-physical parallelism,[1] is open to the reproach that for no obvious reason it over-estimates the part played by consciousness, and that it forces us prematurely to abandon the field of psychological research without being able to offer us any compensation from other fields.

It is clear in any case that this question – whether the latent states of mental life, whose existence is undeniable, are to be conceived of as conscious mental states or as physical ones – threatens to resolve itself into a verbal dispute. We shall therefore be better advised to focus our attention on what we know with certainty of the nature of these debatable states. As far as their physical characteristics are concerned, they are totally inaccessible to us: no physiological concept or chemical process can give us any notion of their nature. On the other hand, we know for certain that they have abundant points of contact with conscious mental processes; with the help of a certain amount of work they can be transformed into, or replaced by, conscious mental processes, and all the categories which we employ to describe conscious mental acts, such as ideas, purposes, resolutions and so on, can be applied to them. Indeed, we are obliged to say of some of these latent states that the only respect in which they differ from conscious ones is precisely in the absence of consciousness. Thus we shall not hesitate to treat them as objects of psychological research, and to deal with them in the most intimate connection with conscious mental acts.

The stubborn denial of a psychical character to latent mental acts is accounted for by the circumstance that most of the phenomena concerned have not been the subject of study outside psycho-analysis. Anyone who is ignorant of pathological facts, who regards the parapraxes of normal people as accidental, and who is content with the old saw that dreams are froth ['*Träume sind Schäume*'] has only to ignore a few more problems of the psychology of consciousness in order to spare himself any need to assume an unconscious mental activity. Incidentally, even before the time of psycho-analysis, hyp-

---

[1] [Freud seems himself at one time to have been inclined to accept this theory, as is suggested by a passage in his book on aphasia (1891*b*, 56 ff.). This will be found translated below in Appendix B.]

notic experiments, and especially post-hypnotic suggestion, had tangibly demonstrated the existence and mode of operation of the mental unconscious.[1]

The assumption of an unconscious is, moreover, a perfectly *legitimate* one, inasmuch as in postulating it we are not departing a single step from our customary and generally accepted mode of thinking. Consciousness makes each of us aware only of his own states of mind; that other people, too, possess a consciousness is an inference which we draw by analogy from their observable utterances and actions, in order to make this behaviour of theirs intelligible to us. (It would no doubt be psychologically more correct to put it in this way: that without any special reflection we attribute to everyone else our own constitution and therefore our consciousness as well, and that this identification is a *sine qua non* of our understanding.) This inference (or this identification) was formerly extended by the ego to other human beings, to animals, plants, inanimate objects and to the world at large, and proved serviceable so long as their similarity to the individual ego was overwhelmingly great; but it became more untrustworthy in proportion as the difference between the ego and these 'others' widened. To-day, our critical judgement is already in doubt on the question of consciousness in animals; we refuse to admit it in plants and we regard the assumption of its existence in inanimate matter as mysticism. But even where the original inclination to identification has withstood criticism – that is, when the 'others' are our fellow-men – the assumption of a consciousness in them rests upon an inference and cannot share the immediate certainty which we have of our own consciousness.

Psycho-analysis demands nothing more than that we should apply this process of inference to ourselves also – a proceeding to which, it is true, we are not constitutionally inclined. If we do this, we must say: all the acts and manifestations which I notice in myself and do not know how to link up with the rest of my mental life must be judged as if they belonged to someone else: they are to be explained by a mental life ascribed to this other person. Furthermore, experience shows that we understand very well how to interpret in other people (that is, how to fit into their chain of mental events) the same acts which we refuse to acknowledge as being mental in ourselves. Here some special

[1] [In his very last discussion of the subject, 'Some Elementary Lessons in Psycho-Analysis' (1940*b*), Freud entered at some length into the evidence afforded by post-hypnotic suggestion. See p. 188 below.]

hindrance evidently deflects our investigations from our own self and prevents our obtaining a true knowledge of it.

This process of inference, when applied to oneself in spite of internal opposition, does not, however, lead to the disclosure of an unconscious; it leads logically to the assumption of another, second consciousness which is united in one's self with the consciousness one knows. But at this point, certain criticisms may fairly be made. In the first place, a consciousness of which its own possessor knows nothing is something very different from a consciousness belonging to another person, and it is questionable whether such a consciousness, lacking, as it does, its most important characteristic, deserves any discussion at all. Those who have resisted the assumption of an unconscious *psychical* are not likely to be ready to exchange it for an unconscious *consciousness*. In the second place, analysis shows that the different latent mental processes inferred by us enjoy a high degree of mutual independence, as though they had no connection with one another, and knew nothing of one another. We must be prepared, if so, to assume the existence in us not only of a second consciousness, but of a third, fourth, perhaps of an unlimited number of states of consciousness, all unknown to us and to one another. In the third place – and this is the most weighty argument of all – we have to take into account the fact that analytic investigation reveals some of these latent processes as having characteristics and peculiarities which seem alien to us, or even incredible, and which run directly counter to the attributes of consciousness with which we are familiar. Thus we have grounds for modifying our inference about ourselves and saying that what is proved is not the existence of a second consciousness in us, but the existence of psychical acts which lack consciousness. We shall also be right in rejecting the term 'subconsciousness' as incorrect and misleading.[1] The well-known cases of '*double conscience*'[2] (splitting of consciousness) prove nothing against our view. We may most aptly describe them as cases of a splitting of the mental activities into two groups, and say that the same consciousness turns to one or the other of these groups alternately.

---

[1] [In some of his very early writings, Freud himself used the term 'subconscious', e.g. *Studies on Hysteria* (1895*d*), *Standard Ed.*, **2**, 69*n*.; *P.F.L.*, **3**, 126*n*. But he disrecommends the term as early as in *The Interpretation of Dreams* (1900*a*), *Standard Ed.*, **5**, 615; *P.F.L.*, **4**, 776. He argues it a little more fully in *The Question of Lay Analysis* (1926*e*), Chapter 1 above.]

[2] [The French term for 'dual consciousness'.]

In psycho-analysis there is no choice for us but to assert that mental processes are in themselves unconscious, and to liken the perception of them by means of consciousness to the perception of the external world by means of the sense-organs.[1] We can even hope to gain fresh knowledge from the comparison. The psycho-analytic assumption of unconscious mental activity appears to us, on the one hand, as a further expansion of the primitive animism which caused us to see copies of our own consciousness all around us, and, on the other hand, as an extension of the corrections undertaken by Kant of our views on external perception. Just as Kant warned us not to overlook the fact that our perceptions are subjectively conditioned and must not be regarded as identical with what is perceived though unknowable, so psycho-analysis warns us not to equate perceptions by means of consciousness with the unconscious mental processes which are their object. Like the physical, the psychical is not necessarily in reality what it appears to us to be. We shall be glad to learn, however, that the correction of internal perception will turn out not to offer such great difficulties as the correction of external perception – that internal objects are less unknowable than the external world.

II. VARIOUS MEANINGS OF 'THE UNCONSCIOUS' –
THE TOPOGRAPHICAL POINT OF VIEW

Before going any further, let us state the important, though inconvenient, fact that the attribute of being unconscious is only one feature that is found in the psychical and is by no means sufficient fully to characterize it. There are psychical acts of very varying value which yet agree in possessing the characteristic of being unconscious. The unconscious comprises, on the one hand, acts which are merely latent, temporarily unconscious, but which differ in no other respect from conscious ones and, on the other hand, processes such as repressed ones, which if they were to become conscious would be bound to stand out in the crudest contrast to the rest of the conscious processes. It would put an end to all misunderstandings if, from now on, in describing the various kinds of psychical acts we were to disregard the question of whether they were conscious or unconscious, and were to classify and correlate them only according to their relation to instincts and aims, according to their composition and

[1] [This idea had already been dealt with at some length in Chapter VII (F) of *The Interpretation of Dreams* (1900a), *Standard Ed.*, **5**, 615–17; *P.F.L.*, **4**, 776 ff.]

according to which of the hierarchy of psychical systems they belong to. This, however, is for various reasons impracticable, so that we cannot escape the ambiguity of using the words 'conscious' and 'unconscious' sometimes in a descriptive and sometimes in a systematic sense, in which latter they signify inclusion in particular systems and possession of certain characteristics. We might attempt to avoid confusion by giving the psychical systems which we have distinguished certain arbitrarily chosen names which have no reference to the attribute of being conscious. Only we should first have to specify what the grounds are on which we distinguish the systems, and in doing this we should not be able to evade the attribute of being conscious, seeing that it forms the point of departure for all our investigations. Perhaps we may look for some assistance from the proposal to employ, at any rate in writing, the abbreviation *Cs.* for consciousness and *Ucs.* for what is unconscious, when we are using the two words in the systematic sense.[1]

Proceeding now to an account of the positive findings of psychoanalysis, we may say that in general a psychical act goes through two phases as regards its state, between which is interposed a kind of testing (censorship). In the first phase the psychical act is unconscious and belongs to the system *Ucs.*; if, on testing, it is rejected by the censorship, it is not allowed to pass into the second phase; it is then said to be 'repressed' and must remain unconscious. If, however, it passes this testing, it enters the second phase and thenceforth belongs to the second system, which we will call the system *Cs.* But the fact that it belongs to that system does not yet unequivocally determine its relation to consciousness. It is not yet conscious, but it is certainly *capable of becoming conscious* (to use Breuer's expression)[2] – that is, it can now, given certain conditions, become an object of consciousness without any special resistance. In consideration of this capacity for becoming conscious we also call the system *Cs.* the 'preconscious'. If it should turn out that a certain censorship also plays a part in determining whether the preconscious becomes conscious, we shall discriminate more sharply between the systems *Pcs.* and *Cs.* For the present let it suffice us to bear in mind that the system *Pcs.* shares the

[1] [Freud had already introduced these abbreviations in *The Interpretation of Dreams* (1900a), *Standard Ed.*, **5**, 540 ff. *P.F.L.*, **4**, 689 ff.]

[2] [See *Studies on Hysteria*, Breuer and Freud (1895d), *Standard Ed.*, **2**, 225; *P.F.L.*, **3**, 304.]

characteristics of the system *Cs.* and that the rigorous censorship exercises its office at the point of transition from the *Ucs.* to the *Pcs.* (or *Cs.*).

By accepting the existence of these two (or three) psychical systems, psycho-analysis has departed a step further from the descriptive 'psychology of consciousness' and has raised new problems and acquired a new content. Up till now, it has differed from that psychology mainly by reason of its *dynamic* view of mental processes; now in addition it seems to take account of psychical *topography* as well, and to indicate in respect of any given mental act within what system or between what systems it takes place. On account of this attempt, too, it has been given the name of 'depth psychology'.[1] We shall hear that it can be further enriched by taking yet another point of view into account.

If we are to take the topography of mental acts seriously we must direct our interest to a doubt which arises at this point. When a psychical act (let us confine ourselves here to one which is in the nature of an idea[2]) is transposed from the system *Ucs.* into the system *Cs.* (or *Pcs.*), are we to suppose that this transposition involves a fresh record – as it were, a second registration – of the idea in question, which may thus be situated as well in a fresh psychical locality, and alongside of which the original unconscious registration continues to exist?[3] Or are we rather to believe that the transposition consists in a change in the state of the idea, a change involving the same material and occurring in the same locality? This question may appear abstruse, but it must be raised if we wish to form a more definite conception of psychical topography, of the dimension of depth in the mind. It is a difficult one because it goes beyond pure psychology and touches on the relations of the mental apparatus to anatomy. We know that in the very roughest sense such relations exist. Research has given irrefutable proof that mental activity is bound up with the function of the brain as it is with no other organ. We are taken a step further – we do not know how much – by the discovery of the unequal importance of the different parts of the brain and their special

[1] [By Bleuler (1914).]

[2] [The German word here is '*Vorstellung*', which covers the English terms 'idea', 'image' and 'presentation'.]

[3] [The conception of an idea being present in the mind in more than one 'registration' is used in connection with the theory of memory in *The Interpretation of Dreams* (1900*a*), *Standard Ed.*, **5**, 539; *P.F.L.*, **4**, 688.]

relations to particular parts of the body and to particular mental activities. But every attempt to go on from there to discover a localization of mental processes, every endeavour to think of ideas as stored up in nerve-cells and of excitations as travelling along nerve-fibres, has miscarried completely. The same fate would await any theory which attempted to recognize, let us say, the anatomical position of the system *Cs.* – conscious mental activity – as being in the cortex, and to localize the unconscious processes in the subcortical parts of the brain. There is a hiatus here which at present cannot be filled, nor is it one of the tasks of psychology to fill it. Our psychical topography has *for the present* nothing to do with anatomy; it has reference not to anatomical localities, but to regions in the mental apparatus, wherever they may be situated in the body.

In this respect, then, our work is untrammelled and may proceed according to its own requirements. It will, however, be useful to remind ourselves that as things stand our hypotheses set out to be no more than graphic illustrations. The first of the two possibilities which we considered – namely, that the *Cs.* phase of an idea implies a fresh registration of it, which is situated in another place – is doubtless the cruder but also the more convenient. The second hypothesis – that of a merely *functional* change of state – is *a priori* more probable, but it is less plastic, less easy to manipulate. With the first, or topographical, hypothesis is bound up that of a topographical separation of the systems *Ucs.* and *Cs.* and also the possibility that an idea may exist simultaneously in two places in the mental apparatus – indeed, that if it is not inhibited by the censorship, it regularly advances from the one position to the other, possibly without losing its first location or registration.

This view many seem odd, but it can be supported by observations from psycho-analytic practice. If we communicate to a patient some idea which he has at one time repressed but which we have discovered in him, our telling him makes at first no change in his mental condition. Above all, it does not remove the repression nor undo its effects, as might perhaps be expected from the fact that the previously unconscious idea has now become conscious. On the contrary, all that we shall achieve at first will be a fresh rejection of the repressed idea. But now the patient has in actual fact the same idea in two forms in different places in his mental apparatus: first, he has the conscious memory of the auditory trace of the idea, conveyed in what we told him; and secondly, he also has – as we know for certain – the unconscious memory of his experience as it was in its earlier form.[1] Actually there is no lifting of the repression until the conscious idea, after the resistances have been overcome, has entered into connection with the unconscious memory-trace. It is only through the making conscious of the latter itself that success is achieved. On superficial consideration this would seem to show that conscious and unconscious ideas are distinct registrations, topographically separated, of the same content. But a moment's reflection shows that the identity of the information given to the patient with his repressed memory is only apparent. To have heard something and to have experienced something are in their psychological nature two quite different things, even though the content of both is the same.

So for the moment we are not in a position to decide between the two possibilities that we have discussed. Perhaps later on we shall come upon factors which may turn the balance in favour of one or the other. Perhaps we shall make the discovery that our question was inadequately framed and that the difference between an unconscious and a conscious idea has to be defined in quite another way.

III. UNCONSCIOUS FEELINGS

We have limited the foregoing discussion to ideas; we may now raise a new question, the answer to which is bound to contribute to the elucidation of our theoretical views. We have said that there are conscious and unconscious ideas; but are there also unconscious instinctual impulses, emotions and feelings, or is it in this instance meaningless to form combinations of the kind?

I am in fact of the opinion that the antithesis of conscious and unconscious is not applicable to instincts. An instinct can never become an object of consciousness – only the idea that represents the instinct can. Even in the unconscious, moreover, an instinct cannot be represented otherwise than by an idea. If the instinct did not attach itself to an idea or manifest itself as an affective state, we could know nothing about it. When we nevertheless speak of an unconscious instinctual impulse or of a repressed instinctual impulse, the looseness of phraseology is a harmless one. We can only mean an instinctual

---

[1] [The topographical picture of the distinction between conscious and unconscious ideas is presented in Freud's discussion of the case of 'Little Hans' (1909*b*), *Standard Ed.*, **10**, 120 f.; *P.F.L.*, **8**, 278–9.]

impulse the ideational representative of which is unconscious, for nothing else comes into consideration.[1]

We should expect the answer to the question about unconscious feelings, emotions and affects to be just as easily given. It is surely of the essence of an emotion that we should be aware of it, i.e. that it should become known to consciousness. Thus the possibility of the attribute of unconsciousness would be completely excluded as far as emotions, feelings and affects are concerned. But in psycho-analytic practice we are accustomed to speak of unconscious love, hate, anger, etc., and find it impossible to avoid even the strange conjunction, 'unconscious consciousness of guilt', or a paradoxical 'unconscious anxiety'. Is there more meaning in the use of these terms than there is in speaking of 'unconscious instincts'?

The two cases are in fact not on all fours. In the first place, it may happen that an affective or emotional impulse is perceived but misconstrued. Owing to the repression of its proper representative it has been forced to become connected with another idea, and is now regarded by consciousness as the manifestation of that idea. If we restore the true connection, we call the original affective impulse an 'unconscious' one. Yet its affect was never unconscious; all that had happened was that its *idea* had undergone repression. In general, the use of the terms 'unconscious affect' and 'unconscious emotion' has reference to the vicissitudes undergone, in consequence of repression, by the quantitative factor in the instinctual impulse. We know that three such vicissitudes are possible:[2] either the affect remains, wholly or in part, as it is; or it is transformed into a qualitatively different quota of affect, above all into anxiety; or it is suppressed, i.e. it is prevented from developing at all. (These possibilities may perhaps be studied even more easily in the dream-work than in neuroses.) We know, too, that to suppress the development of affect is the true aim of repression and that its work is incomplete if this aim is not achieved. In every instance where repression has succeeded in inhibiting the development of affects, we term those affects (which we restore when we undo the work of repression) 'unconscious'. Thus it cannot be denied that the use of the terms in question is consistent; but in comparison with unconscious ideas there is the important difference that unconscious ideas continue to exist after repression as actual

---

[1] [Cf. 'Instincts and their Vicissitudes' in Chapter 4 below.]
[2] [Cf. the paper on 'Repression' in Chapter 8 below.]

structures in the system *Ucs.*, whereas all that corresponds in that system to unconscious affects is a potential beginning which is prevented from developing. Strictly speaking, then, and although no fault can be found with the linguistic usage, there are no unconscious affects as there are unconscious ideas. But there may very well be in the system *Ucs.* affective structures which, like others, become conscious. The whole difference arises from the fact that ideas are cathexes – basically of memory-traces – whilst affects and emotions correspond to processes of discharge, the final manifestations of which are perceived as feelings. In the present state of our knowledge of affects and emotions we cannot express this difference more clearly.[1]

It is of especial interest to us to have established the fact that repression can succeed in inhibiting an instinctual impulse from being turned into a manifestation of affect. This shows us that the system *Cs.* normally controls affectivity as well as access to motility; and it enhances the importance of repression, since it shows that repression results not only in withholding things from consciousness, but also in preventing the development of affect and the setting-off of muscular activity. Conversely, too, we may say that as long as the system *Cs.* controls affectivity and motility, the mental condition of the person in question is spoken of as normal. Nevertheless, there is an unmistakable difference in the relation of the controlling system to the two contiguous processes of discharge.[2] Whereas the control by the *Cs.* over voluntary motility is firmly rooted, regularly withstands the onslaught of neurosis and only breaks down in psychosis, control by the *Cs.* over the development of affects is less secure. Even within the limits of normal life we can recognize that a constant struggle for primacy over affectivity goes on between the two systems *Cs.* and *Ucs.*, that certain spheres of influence are marked off from one another and that intermixtures between the operative forces occur.

The importance of the system *Cs.* (*Pcs.*) as regards access to the release of affect and to action enables us also to understand the part played by substitutive ideas in determining the form taken by illness. It is possible for the development of affect to proceed directly from the system *Ucs.*; in that case the affect always has the character of anxiety, for which all 'repressed' affects are exchanged. Often, however, the

[1] [This question is discussed again in the second part of *The Ego and the Id* in Chapter 6 below.]

[2] Affectivity manifests itself essentially in motor (secretory and vasomotor) discharge resulting in an (internal) alteration of the subject's own body without reference to the external world; motility, in actions designed to effect changes in the external world.

instinctual impulse has to wait until it has found a substitutive idea in the system *Cs.* The development of affect can then proceed from this conscious substitute, and the nature of that substitute determines the qualitative character of the affect. We have asserted that in repression a severance takes place between the affect and the idea to which it belongs, and that each then undergoes its separate vicissitudes. Descriptively, this is incontrovertible; in actuality, however, the affect does not as a rule arise till the break-through to a new representation in the system *Cs.* has been successfully achieved.

IV. TOPOGRAPHY AND DYNAMICS OF REPRESSION

We have arrived at the conclusion that repression is essentially a process affecting ideas on the border between the systems *Ucs.* and *Pcs.* (*Cs.*), and we can now make a fresh attempt to describe the process in greater detail.

It must be a matter of a *withdrawal* of cathexis; but the question is, in which system does the withdrawl take place and to which system does the cathexis that is withdrawn belong? The repressed idea remains capable of action in the *Ucs.*, and it must therefore have retained its cathexis. What has been withdrawn must be something else. Let us take the case of repression proper ('after-pressure')[1] as it affects an idea which is preconscious or even actually conscious. Here repression can only consist in withdrawing from the idea the (pre)conscious cathexis which belongs to the system *Pcs.* The idea then either remains uncathected, or receives cathexis from the *Ucs.*, or retains the *Ucs.* cathexis which it already had. Thus there is a withdrawal of the preconscious cathexis, retention of the unconscious cathexis, or replacement of the preconscious cathexis by an unconscious one. We notice, moreover, that we have based these reflections (as it were, without meaning to) on the assumption that the transition from the system *Ucs.* to the system next to it is not effected through the making of a new registration but through a change in its state, an alteration in its cathexis. The functional hypothesis has here easily defeated the topographical one.

But this process of withdrawal of libido[2] is not adequate to make another characteristic of repression comprehensible to us. It is not clear why the idea which has remained cathected or has received cathexis from the *Ucs.* should not, in virtue of its cathexis, renew the

---

[1] [Cf. p. 525 below.]
[2] [For the use of 'libido' here see four paragraphs lower down.]

attempt to penetrate into the system *Pcs.* If it could do so, the withdrawal of libido from it would have to be repeated, and the same performance would go on endlessly; but the outcome would not be repression. So, too, when it comes to describing *primal* repression, the mechanism just discussed of withdrawal of preconscious cathexis would fail to meet the case; for here we are dealing with an uncon-scious idea which has as yet received *no* cathexis from the *Pcs.* and therefore cannot have that cathexis withdrawn from it.

What we require, therefore, is another process which maintains the repression in the first case [i.e. the case of after-pressure] and, in the second [i.e. that of primal repression], ensures its being established as well as continued. This other process can only be found in the assumption of an *anticathexis*, by means of which the system *Pcs.* protects itself from the pressure upon it of the unconscious idea. We shall see from clinical examples how such an anticathexis, operating in the system *Pcs.*, manifests itself. It is this which represents the permanent expenditure [of energy] of a primal repression, and which also guarantees the permanence of that repression. Anticathexis is the sole mechanism of primal repression; in the case of repression proper ('after-pressure') there is in addition withdrawal of the *Pcs.* cathexis. It is very possible that it is precisely the cathexis which is withdrawn from the idea that is used for anticathexis.

We see how we have gradually been led into adopting a third point of view in our account of psychical phenomena. Besides the dynamic and the topographical points of view we have adopted the *economic* one. This endeavours to follow out the vicissitudes of amounts of excitation and to arrive at least at some *relative* estimate of their magnitude.

It will not be unreasonable to give a special name to this whole way of regarding our subject-matter, for it is the consummation of psycho-analytic research. I propose that when we have succeeded in describ-ing a psychical process in its dynamic, topographical and economic aspects, we should speak of it as a *metapsychological* [1] presentation. We must say at once that in the present state of our knowledge there are only a few points at which we shall succeed in this.

Let us make a tentative effort to give a metapsychological description of the process of repression in the three transference neuroses which

---

[1] [Freud had first used this term some twenty years earlier in a letter to Fliess of February 13, 1896. (Freud, 1950a, Letter 41.)]

are familiar to us. Here we may replace 'cathexis' by 'libido', because, as we know, it is the vicissitudes of *sexual* impulses with which we shall be dealing.

In anxiety hysteria a first phase of the process is frequently overlooked, and may perhaps be in fact missed out; on careful observation, however, it can be clearly discerned. It consists in anxiety appearing without the subject knowing what he is afraid of. We must suppose that there was present in the *Ucs.* some love-impulse demanding to be transposed into the system *Pcs.*; but the cathexis directed to it from the latter system has drawn back from the impulse (as though in an attempt at flight) and the unconscious libidinal cathexis of the rejected idea has been discharged in the form of anxiety.

On the occasion of a repetition (if there should be one) of this process, a first step is taken in the direction of mastering the unwelcome development of anxiety. The [*Pcs.*] cathexis that has taken flight attaches itself to a substitutive idea which, on the one hand, is connected by association with the rejected idea, and, on the other, has escaped repression by reason of its remoteness from that idea. This substitutive idea – a 'substitute by displacement' – permits the still uninhibitable development of anxiety to be rationalized. It now plays the part of an anticathexis for the system *Cs.* (*Pcs.*), by securing it against an emergence in the *Cs.* of the repressed idea. On the other hand it is, or acts as if it were, the point of departure for the release of the anxiety-affect, which has now really become quite uninhibitable. Clinical observation shows, for instance, that a child suffering from an animal phobia experiences anxiety under two kinds of conditions: in the first place, when his repressed love-impulse becomes intensified, and, in the second, when he perceives the animal he is afraid of. The substitutive idea acts in the one instance as a point at which there is a passage across from the system *Ucs.* to the system *Cs.*, and, in the other instance, as a self-sufficing source for the release of anxiety. The extending dominance of the system *Cs.* usually manifests itself in the fact that the first of these two modes of excitation of the substitutive idea gives place more and more to the second. The child may perhaps end by behaving as though he had no predilection whatever towards his father but had become quite free from him, and as though his fear of the animal was a real fear – except that this fear of the animal, fed as such a fear is from an unconscious instinctual source, proves obdurate and exaggerated in the face of all influences brought to bear from the system *Cs.*, and thereby betrays its derivation from the system *Ucs.* – In the second phase of anxiety hysteria, therefore, the anticathexis from the system *Cs.* has led to substitute-formation.

Soon the same mechanism finds a fresh application. The process of repression, as we know, is not yet completed, and it finds a further aim in the task of inhibiting the development of the anxiety which arises from the substitute. This is achieved by the whole of the associated environment of the substitutive idea being cathected with special intensity, so that it can display a high degree of sensibility to excitation. Excitation of any point in this outer structure must inevitably, on account of its connection with the substitutive idea, give rise to a slight development of anxiety; and this is now used as a signal to inhibit, by means of a fresh flight on the part of the [*Pcs.*] cathexis, the further progress of the development of anxiety.[1] The further away the sensitive and vigilant anticathexes are situated from the feared substitute, the more precisely can the mechanism function which is designed to isolate the substitutive idea and to protect it from fresh excitations. These precautions naturally only guard against excitations which approach the substitutive idea from outside, through perception; they never guard against instinctual excitation, which reaches the substitutive idea from the direction of its link with the repressed idea. Thus the precautions do not begin to operate till the substitute has satisfactorily taken over representation of the repressed, and they can never operate with complete reliability. With each increase of instinctual excitation the protecting rampart round the substitutive idea must be shifted a little further outwards. The whole construction, which is set up in an analogous way in the other neuroses, is termed a *phobia*. The flight from a conscious cathexis of the substitutive idea is manifested in the avoidances, renunciations and prohibitions by which we recognize anxiety hysteria.

Surveying the whole process, we may say that the third phase repeats the work of the second on an ampler scale. The system *Cs.* now protects itself against the activation of the substitutive idea by an anticathexis of its environment, just as previously it had secured itself against the emergence of the repressed idea by a cathexis of the substitutive idea. In this way the formation of substitutes by displacement has been further continued. We must also add that the system

---

[1] [The notion of a small release of unpleasure acting as a 'signal' to prevent a much larger release is developed further in *Inhibitions, Symptoms and Anxiety* (1926*d*), *Standard Ed.*, **20**, 160–3; *P.F.L.*, **10**, 320–22.]

Cs. had earlier only one small area at which the repressed instinctual impulse could break through, namely, the substitutive idea; but that ultimately this *enclave* of unconscious influence extends to the whole phobic outer structure. Further, we may lay stress on the interesting consideration that by means of the whole defensive mechanism thus set in action a projection outward of the instinctual danger has been achieved. The ego behaves as if the danger of a development of anxiety threatened it not from the direction of an instinctual impulse but from the direction of a perception, and it is thus enabled to react against this external danger with the attempts at flight represented by phobic avoidances. In this process repression is successful in one particular: the release of anxiety can to some extent be dammed up, but only at a heavy sacrifice of personal freedom. Attempts at flight from the demands of instinct are, however, in general useless, and, in spite of everything, the result of phobic flight remains unsatisfactory.

A great deal of what we have found in anxiety hysteria also holds good for the other two neuroses, so that we can confine our discussion to their points of difference and to the part played by anticathexis. In conversion hysteria the instinctual cathexis of the repressed idea is changed into the innervation of the symptom. How far and in what circumstances the unconscious idea is drained empty by this discharge into innervation, so that it can relinquish its pressure upon the system *Cs.* – these and similar questions had better be reserved for a special investigation of hysteria.[1] In conversion hysteria the part played by the anticathexis proceeding from the system *Cs.* (*Pcs.*) is clear and becomes manifest in the formation of the symptom. It is the anticathexis that decides upon what portion of the instinctual representative the whole cathexis of the latter is able to be concentrated. The portion thus selected to be a symptom fulfils the condition of expressing the wishful aim of the instinctual impulse no less than the defensive or punitive efforts of the system *Cs.*; thus it becomes hypercathected, and it is maintained from both directions like the substitutive idea in anxiety hysteria. From this circumstance we may conclude without hesitation that the amount of energy expended by the system *Cs.* on repression need not be so great as the cathectic energy of the symptom; for the strength of the repression is measured by the amount of anticathexis expended, whereas the symptom is

---

[1] [Freud had already touched on the question in *Studies on Hysteria* (1895*d*), *Standard Ed.*, **2**, 166–7; *P.F.L.*, **3**, 237 f.]

supported not only by this anticathexis but also by the instinctual cathexis from the system *Ucs.* which is condensed in the symptom.

As regards obsessional neurosis, we need only add to the observations brought forward in the preceding[1] paper that it is here that the anticathexis from the system *Cs.* comes most noticeably into the foreground. It is this which, organized as a reaction-formation, brings about the first repression, and which is later the point at which the repressed idea breaks through. We may venture the supposition that it is because of the predominance of the anticathexis and the absence of discharge that the work of repression seems far less successful in anxiety hysteria and in obsessional neurosis than in conversion hysteria.

V. THE SPECIAL CHARACTERISTICS OF THE SYSTEM *Ucs.*

The distinction we have made between the two psychical systems receives fresh significance when we observe that processes in the one system, the *Ucs.*, show characteristics which are not met with again in the system immediately above it.

The nucleus of the *Ucs.* consists of instinctual representatives which seek to discharge their cathexis; that is to say, it consists of wishful impulses. These instinctual impulses are co-ordinate with one another, exist side by side without being influenced by one another, and are exempt from mutual contradiction. When two wishful impulses whose aims must appear to us incompatible become simultaneously active, the two impulses do not diminish each other or cancel each other out, but combine to form an intermediate aim, a compromise.

There are in this system no negation, no doubt, no degrees of certainty: all this is only introduced by the work of the censorship between the *Ucs.* and the *Pcs.* Negation is a substitute, at a higher level, for repression.[2] In the *Ucs.* there are only contents, cathected with greater or lesser strength.

The cathectic intensities [in the *Ucs.*] are much more mobile. By the process of *displacement* one idea may surrender to another its whole quota of cathexis; by the process of *condensation* it may appropriate the whole cathexis of several other ideas. I have proposed to regard these two processes as distinguishing marks of the so-called *primary psychical*

---

[1] [This refers to Freud's paper 'Repression', which is included in Chapter 8.]

[2] [Cf. the similar statement in 'Formulations on the Two Principles of Mental Functioning' in Chapter 7, p. 511 below.]

process. In the system *Pcs.* the *secondary process*[1] is dominant. When a primary process is allowed to take its course in connection with elements belonging to the system *Pcs.*, it appears 'comic' and excites laughter.[2]

The processes of the system *Ucs.* are *timeless*; i.e. they are not ordered temporally, are not altered by the passage of time; they have no reference to time at all. Reference to time is bound up, once again, with the work of the system *Cs.*[3]

The *Ucs.* processes pay just as little regard to *reality*. They are subject to the pleasure principle; their fate depends only on how strong they are and on whether they fulfil the demands of the pleasure-unpleasure regulation.[4]

To sum up: *exemption from mutual contradiction, primary process* (mobility of cathexes), *timelessness*, and *replacement of external by psychical reality* – these are the characteristics which we may expect to find in processes belonging to the system *Ucs.*[5]

Unconscious processes only become cognizable by us under the conditions of dreaming and of neurosis – that is to say, when processes of the higher, *Pcs.*, system are set back to an earlier stage by being lowered (by regression). In themselves they cannot be cognized, indeed are even incapable of carrying on their existence; for the system *Ucs.* is at a very early moment overlaid by the *Pcs.* which has taken over access to consciousness and to motility. Discharge from the system *Ucs.* passes into somatic innervation that leads to development of affect; but even this path of discharge is, as we have seen, contested by the *Pcs.* By itself, the system *Ucs.* would not in normal conditions be

---

[1] Cf. the discussion in Chapter VII of *The Interpretation of Dreams* [Section E. *Standard Ed.*, **5**, 588 ff.; *P.F.L.*, **4**, 745 ff.], based on ideas developed by Breuer in *Studies on Hysteria* (Breuer and Freud, 1895).

[2] [The point is dealt with more fully in Freud's book on jokes (1905*c*), *Standard Ed.*, **8**, 199 ff.; *P.F.L.*, **6**, 260 ff.]

[3] [Mentions of the 'timelessness' of the unconscious will be found scattered throughout Freud's writings. The earliest is perhaps a sentence dating from 1897 (Freud, 1950*a*, Draft M) in which he declares that 'disregard of the characteristic of time is no doubt an essential distinction between activity in the preconscious and unconscious', but the first explicit published mention of it seems to have been in a footnote added in 1907 to *The Psychopathology of Everyday Life* (1901*b*), *Standard Ed.*, **6**, 274*n*.; *P.F.L.*, **5**, 399*n*. Cf. also pp. 237 and 499 below.]

[4] [Cf. Section 8 of 'The Two Principles of Mental Functioning' (1911*b*), in Chapter 7 below.]

[5] We are reserving for a different context the mention of another notable privilege of the *Ucs.* [Cf. Freud's letter to Groddeck (Freud, 1960*a*, p. 323).]

able to bring about any expedient muscular acts, with the exception of those already organized as reflexes.

The full significance of the characteristics of the system *Ucs.* described above could only be appreciated by us if we were to contrast and compare them with those of the system *Pcs.* But this would take us so far afield that I propose that we should once more call a halt and not undertake the comparison of the two till we can do so in connection with our discussion of the higher system. Only the most pressing points of all will be mentioned at this stage.

The processes of the system *Pcs.* display – no matter whether they are already conscious or only capable of becoming conscious – an inhibition of the tendency of cathected ideas towards discharge. When a process passes from one idea to another, the first idea retains a part of its cathexis and only a small portion undergoes displacement. Displacements and condensations such as happen in the primary process are excluded or very much restricted. This circumstance caused Breuer to assume the existence of two different states of cathectic energy in mental life: one in which the energy is tonically 'bound' and the other in which it is freely mobile and presses towards discharge.[1] In my opinion this distinction represents the deepest insight we have gained up to the present into the nature of nervous energy, and I do not see how we can avoid making it. A metapsychological presentation would most urgently call for further discussion at this point, though perhaps that would be too daring an undertaking as yet.

Further, it devolves upon the system *Pcs.* to make communication possible between the different ideational contents so that they can influence one another, to give them an order in time, and to set up a censorship or several censorships; 'reality-testing' too, and the reality principle, are in its province. Conscious memory, moreover, seems to depend wholly on the *Pcs.*[2] This should be clearly distinguished from the memory-traces in which the experiences of the *Ucs.* are fixed, and probably corresponds to a special registration such as we proposed (but later rejected) to account for the relation of conscious to unconscious ideas. In this connection, also, we shall find means for putting an end to our oscillations in regard to the naming of the higher system – which we have hitherto spoken of indifferently, sometimes as the *Pcs.* and sometimes as the *Cs.*

[1] [Cf. Breuer and Freud (1895*d*).]
[2] [See Freud's paper 'On Narcissism' (1914*c*), *Standard Ed.*, **14**, 67 ff.; *P.F.L.*, **11**, 65.]

Nor will it be out of place here to utter a warning against any over-hasty generalization of what we have brought to light concerning the distribution of the various mental functions between the two systems. We are describing the state of affairs as it appears in the adult human being, in whom the system *Ucs.* operates, strictly speaking, only as a preliminary stage of the higher organization. The question of what the content and connections of that system are during the development of the individual, and of what significance it possesses in animals – these are points on which no conclusion can be deduced from our description: they must be investigated independently. Moreover, in human beings we must be prepared to find possible pathological conditions under which the two systems alter, or even exchange, both their content and their characteristics.

VI. COMMUNICATION BETWEEN THE TWO SYSTEMS

It would nevertheless be wrong to imagine that the *Ucs.* remains at rest while the whole work of the mind is performed by the *Pcs.* – that the *Ucs.* is something finished with, a vestigial organ, a residuum from the process of development. It is wrong also to suppose that communication between the two systems is confined to the act of repression, with the *Pcs.* casting everything that seems disturbing to it into the abyss of the *Ucs.* On the contrary, the *Ucs.* is alive and capable of development and maintains a number of other relations with the *Pcs.*, amongst them that of co-operation. In brief, it must be said that the *Ucs.* is continued into what are known as derivatives,[1] that it is accessible to the impressions of life, that it constantly influences the *Pcs.*, and is even, for its part, subjected to influences from the *Pcs.*

Study of the derivatives of the *Ucs.* will completely disappoint our expectations of a schematically clear-cut distinction between the two psychical systems. This will no doubt give rise to dissatisfaction with our results and will probably be used to cast doubts on the value of the way in which we have divided up the psychical processes. Our answer is, however, that we have no other aim but that of translating into theory the results of observation, and we deny that there is any obligation on us to achieve at our first attempt a well-rounded theory which will commend itself by its simplicity. We shall defend the complications of our theory so long as we find that they meet the

---

[1] [See the paper on 'Repression' in Chapter 8.]

results of observation, and we shall not abandon our expectations of being led in the end by those very complications to the discovery of a state of affairs which, while simple in itself, can account for all the complications of reality.

Among the derivatives of the *Ucs.* instinctual impulses, of the sort we have described, there are some which unite in themselves characters of an opposite kind. On the one hand, they are highly organized, free from self-contradiction, have made use of every acquisition of the system *Cs.* and would hardly be distinguished in our judgement from the formations of that system. On the other hand they are unconscious and are incapable of becoming conscious. Thus *qualitatively* they belong to the system *Pcs.*, but *factually* to the *Ucs.* Their origin is what decides their fate. We may compare them with individuals of mixed race who, taken all round, resemble white men, but who betray their coloured descent by some striking feature or other, and on that account are excluded from society and enjoy none of the privileges of white people. Of such a nature are those phantasies of normal people as well as of neurotics which we have recognized as preliminary stages in the formation both of dreams and of symptoms and which, in spite of their high degree of organization, remain repressed and therefore cannot become conscious.[1] They draw near to consciousness and remain undisturbed so long as they do not have an intense cathexis, but as soon as they exceed a certain height of cathexis they are thrust back. Substitutive formations, too, are highly organized derivatives of the *Ucs.* of this kind; but these succeed in breaking through into consciousness, when circumstances are favourable – for example, if they happen to join forces with an anticathexis from the *Pcs.*

When, elsewhere, we come to examine more closely the preconditions for becoming conscious, we shall be able to find a solution of some of the difficulties that arise at this juncture. Here it seems a good plan to look at things from the angle of consciousness, in contrast to our previous approach, which was upwards from the *Ucs.* To consciousness the whole sum of psychical processes presents itself as the realm of the preconscious. A very great part of this preconscious originates in the unconscious, has the character of its derivatives and is subjected to a censorship before it can become conscious. Another part of the *Pcs.* is capable of becoming conscious without any censorship. Here we come upon a contradiction of an earlier assump-

---

[1] [See p. 360*n*. 3 below.]

tion. In discussing the subject of repression we were obliged to place the censorship which is decisive for becoming conscious between the systems *Ucs.* and *Pcs.* Now it becomes probable that there is a censorship between the *Pcs.* and the *Cs.*[1] Nevertheless we shall do well not to regard this complication as a difficulty, but to assume that to every transition from one system to that immediately above it (that is, every advance to a higher stage of psychical organization) there corresponds a new censorship. This, it may be remarked, does away with the assumption of a continuous laying down of new registrations.

The reason for all these difficulties is to be found in the circumstance that the attribute of being conscious, which is the only characteristic of psychical processes that is directly presented to us, is in no way suited to serve as a criterion for the differentiation of systems. Apart from the fact that the conscious is not always conscious but also at times latent, observation has shown that much that shares the characteristics of the system *Pcs.* does not become conscious; and we learn in addition that the act of becoming conscious is dependent on the attention of the *Pcs.* being turned in certain directions. Hence consciousness stands in no simple relation either to the different systems or to repression. The truth is that it is not only the psychically repressed that remains alien to consciousness, but also some of the impulses which dominate our ego – something, therefore, that forms the strongest functional antithesis to the repressed. The more we seek to win our way to a metapsychological view of mental life, the more we must learn to emancipate ourselves from the importance of the symptom of 'being conscious'.[2]

So long as we still cling to this belief we see our generalizations regularly broken through by exceptions. On the one hand we find that derivatives of the *Ucs.* become conscious as substitutive formations and symptoms – generally, it is true, after having undergone great distortion as compared with the unconscious, though often retaining many characteristics which call for repression. On the other hand, we find that many preconscious formations remain unconscious, though we should have expected that, from their nature, they might very well have become conscious. Probably in the latter case the stronger

---

[1] [This point is discussed at greater length in Chapter 6.]

[2] [The complication discussed in this paragraph was reinforced by Freud in *The Ego and the Id* (1923*b*), Section I, p. 444 below, and in Section II he propounded his new structural picture of the mind, which so greatly simplified his whole description of its workings.]

attraction of the *Ucs.* is asserting itself. We are led to look for the more important distinction as lying, not between the conscious and the preconscious, but between the preconscious and the unconscious. The *Ucs.* is turned back on the frontier of the *Pcs.* by the censorship, but derivatives of the *Ucs.* can circumvent this censorship, achieve a high degree of organization and reach a certain intensity of cathexis in the *Pcs.* When, however, this intensity is exceeded and they try to force themselves into consciousness, they are recognized as derivatives of the *Ucs.* and are repressed afresh at the new frontier of censorship, between the *Pcs.* and the *Cs.* Thus the first of these censorships is exercised against the *Ucs.* itself, and the second against its *Pcs.* derivatives. One might suppose that in the course of individual development the censorship had taken a step forward.

In psycho-analytic treatment the existence of the second censorship, located between the systems *Pcs.* and *Cs.*, is proved beyond question. We require the patient to form numerous derivatives of the *Ucs.*, we make him pledge himself to overcome the objections of the censorship to these preconscious formations becoming conscious, and by overthrowing *this* censorship, we open up the way to abrogating the repression accomplished by the *earlier* one. To this let us add that the existence of the censorship between the *Pcs.* and the *Cs.* teaches us that becoming conscious is no mere act of perception, but is probably also a *hypercathexis*,[1] a further advance in the psychical organization.

Let us turn to the communications between the *Ucs.* and the other systems, less in order to establish anything new than in order to avoid omitting what is most prominent. At the roots of instinctual activity the systems communicate with one another most extensively. One portion of the processes which are there excited passes through the *Ucs.*, as through a preparatory stage, and reaches the highest psychical development in the *Cs.*; another portion is retained as *Ucs.* But the *Ucs.* is also affected by experiences originating from external perception. Normally all the paths from perception to the *Ucs.* remain open, and only those leading on from the *Ucs.* are subject to blocking by repression.

It is a very remarkable thing that the *Ucs.* of one human being can react upon that of another, without passing through the *Cs.* This deserves closer investigation, especially with a view to finding out

---

[1] [Cf. p. 172 below.]

whether preconscious activity can be excluded as playing a part in it; but, descriptively speaking, the fact is incontestable.

The content of the system *Pcs.* (or *Cs.*) is derived partly from instinctual life (through the medium of the *Ucs.*), and partly from perception. It is doubtful how far the processes of this system can exert a direct influence on the *Ucs.*; examination of pathological cases often reveals an almost incredible independence and lack of susceptibility to influence on the part of the *Ucs.* A complete divergence of their trends, a total severance of the two systems, is what above all characterizes a condition of illness. Nevertheless, psycho-analytic treatment is based upon an influencing of the *Ucs.* from the direction of the *Cs.*, and at any rate shows that this, though a laborious task, is not impossible. The derivatives of the *Ucs.* which act as intermediaries between the two systems open the way, as we have already said, towards accomplishing this. But we may safely assume that a spontaneously effected alteration in the *Ucs.* from the direction of the *Cs.* is a difficult and slow process.

Co-operation between a preconscious and an unconscious impulse, even when the latter is intensely repressed, may come about if there is a situation in which the unconscious impulse can act in the same sense as one of the dominant trends. The repression is removed in this instance, and the repressed activity is admitted as a reinforcement of the one intended by the ego. The unconscious becomes ego-syntonic in respect of this single conjunction without any change taking place in its repression apart from this. In this co-operation the influence of the *Ucs.* is unmistakable: the reinforced tendencies reveal themselves as being nevertheless different from the normal; they make specially perfect functioning possible, and they manifest a resistance in the face of opposition which is similar to that offered, for instance, by obsessional symptoms.

The content of the *Ucs.* may be compared with an aboriginal population in the mind. If inherited mental formations exist in the human being – something analogous to instinct in animals – these constitute the nucleus of the *Ucs.* Later there is added to them what is discarded during childhood development as unserviceable; and this need not differ in its nature from what is inherited. A sharp and final division between the content of the two systems does not, as a rule, take place till puberty.

VII. ASSESSMENT OF THE UNCONSCIOUS

What we have put together in the preceding discussions is probably as much as we can say about the *Ucs.* so long as we only draw upon our knowledge of dream-life and the transference neuroses. It is certainly not much, and at some points it gives an impression of obscurity and confusion; and above all it offers us no possibility of co-ordinating or subsuming the *Ucs.* into any context with which we are already familiar. It is only the analysis of one of the affections which we call narcissistic psychoneuroses that promises to furnish us with conceptions through which the enigmatic *Ucs.* will be brought more within our reach and, as it were, made tangible.

Since the publication of a work by Abraham (1908) – which that conscientious author has attributed to my instigation – we have tried to base our characterization of Kraepelin's 'dementia praecox' (Bleuler's 'schizophrenia') on its position with reference to the antithesis between ego and object. In the transference neuroses (anxiety hysteria, conversion hysteria and obsessional neurosis) there was nothing to give special prominence to this antithesis. We knew, indeed, that frustration in regard to the object brings on the outbreak of the neurosis and that the neurosis involves a renunciation of the real object; we knew too that the libido that is withdrawn from the real object reverts first to a phantasied object and then to one that had been repressed (introversion).[1] But in these disorders object-cathexis in general is retained with great energy, and more detailed examination of the process of repression has obliged us to assume that object-cathexis persists in the system *Ucs.* in spite of – or rather in consequence of – repression. Indeed, the capacity for transference, of which we make use for therapeutic purposes in these affections, presupposes an unimpaired object-cathexis.

In the case of schizophrenia, on the other hand, we have been driven to the assumption that after the process of repression the libido that has been withdrawn does not seek a new object, but retreats into the ego; that is to say, that here the object-cathexes are given up and a primitive objectless condition of narcissism is re-established. The incapacity of these patients for transference (so far as the pathological process extends), their consequent inaccessibility to therapeutic

---

[1] [The process is described in detail in Section (*a*) of Freud's paper on 'Types of Onset of Neurosis' (1912*c*), *Standard Ed.*, **12**, 232; *P.F.L.*, **10**, 120.]

efforts, their characteristic repudiation of the external world, the appearance of signs of a hypercathexis of their own ego, the final outcome in complete apathy – all these clinical features seem to agree excellently with the assumption that their object-cathexes have been given up. As regards the relation of the two psychical systems to each other, all observers have been struck by the fact that in schizophrenia a great deal is expressed as being conscious which in the transference neuroses can only be shown to be present in the *Ucs.* by psycho-analysis. But to begin with we were not able to establish any intelligible connection between the ego-object relation and the relationships of consciousness.

What we are seeking seems to present itself in the following unexpected way. In schizophrenics we observe – especially in the initial stages, which are so instructive – a number of changes in *speech*, some of which deserve to be regarded from a particular point of view. The patient often devotes peculiar care to his way of expressing himself, which becomes 'stilted' and 'precious'. The construction of his sentences undergoes a peculiar disorganization, making them so incomprehensible to us that his remarks seem nonsensical. Some reference to bodily organs or innervations is often given prominence in the content of these remarks. To this may be added the fact that in such symptoms of schizophrenia as are comparable with the substi-tutive formations of hysteria or obsessional neurosis, the relation between the substitute and the repressed material nevertheless dis-plays peculiarities which would surprise us in these two forms of neurosis.

Dr V. Tausk of Vienna has placed at my disposal some obser-vations he has made in the initial stages of schizophrenia in a female patient, which are particularly valuable, as the patient was ready to explain her utterances herself. I will take two of his examples to illustrate the view I wish to put forward, and I have no doubt that every observer could easily produce plenty of such material.

A patient of Tausk's, a girl who was brought to the clinic after a quarrel with her lover, complained that *her eyes were not right, they were twisted.* This she herself explained by bringing forward a series of reproaches against her lover in coherent language. 'She could not understand him at all, he looked different every time; he was a hypocrite, an eye-twister,[1] he had twisted her eyes; now she had

---

[1] [The German '*Augenverdreher*' has the figurative meaning of 'deceiver'.]

twisted eyes; they were not her eyes any more; now she saw the world with different eyes.'

The patient's comments on her unintelligible remark have the value of an analysis, for they contain the equivalent of the remark expressed in a generally comprehensible form. They throw light at the same time on the meaning and the genesis of schizophrenic word-formation. I agree with Tausk in stressing in this example the point that the patient's relation to a bodily organ (the eye) has arrogated to itself the representation of the whole content [of her thoughts]. Here the schizophrenic utterance exhibits a hypochondriac trait: it has become '*organ-speech*'.[1]

A second communication by the same patient was as follows: 'She was standing in church. Suddenly she felt a jerk; she had to *change her position, as though somebody was putting her into a position, as though she was being put in a certain position.*'

Now came the analysis of this through a fresh series of reproaches against her lover. 'He was common, he had made her common, too, though she was naturally refined. He had made her like himself by making her think that he was superior to her; now she had become like him, because she thought she would be better if she were like him. He had *given a false impression of his position*; now she was just like him' (by identification), 'he had *put her in a false position*'.

The physical movement of 'changing her position', Tausk remarks, depicted the words 'putting her in a false position' and her identification with her lover. I would call attention once more to the fact that the whole train of thought is dominated by the element which has for its content a bodily innervation (or, rather, the sensation of it). Furthermore, a hysterical woman would, in the first example, have *in fact* convulsively twisted her eyes, and, in the second, have given actual jerks, instead of having the *impulse* to do so or the *sensation* of doing so: and in neither example would she have any accompanying conscious thoughts, nor would she have been able to express any such thoughts afterwards.

These two observations, then, argue in favour of what we have called hypochondriacal speech or 'organ-speech'. But, what seems to us more important, they also point to something else, of which we

---

[1] [Cf. Freud's discussion of hypochondria in his paper on narcissism (1914*c*), *Standard Ed.*, **14**, 83 ff.; *P.F.L.*, **11**, 76 ff.]

have innumerable instances (for example, in the cases collected in Bleuler's monograph [1911]) and which may be reduced to a definite formula. In schizophrenia *words* are subjected to the same process as that which makes the dream-images out of latent dream-thoughts – to what we have called the primary psychical process. They undergo condensation, and by means of displacement transfer their cathexes to one another in their entirety. The process may go so far that a single word, if it is specially suitable on account of its numerous connections, takes over the representation of a whole train of thought.[1] The works of Bleuler, Jung and their pupils offer a quantity of material which particularly supports this assertion.[2]

Before we draw any conclusion from impressions such as these, let us consider further the distinctions between the formation of substitutes in schizophrenia on the one hand, and in hysteria and obsessional neurosis on the other – subtle distinctions which nevertheless make a strange impression. A patient whom I have at present under observation has allowed himself to be withdrawn from all the interests of life on account of a bad condition of the skin of his face. He declares that he has blackheads and deep holes in his face which everyone notices. Analysis shows that he is playing out his castration complex upon his skin. At first he worked at these blackheads remorselessly; and it gave him great satisfaction to squeeze them out, because, as he said, something spurted out when he did so. Then he began to think that a deep cavity appeared wherever he had got rid of a blackhead, and he reproached himself most vehemently with having ruined his skin for ever by 'constantly fiddling about with his hand'. Pressing out the content of the blackheads is clearly to him a substitute for masturbation. The cavity which then appears owing to his fault is the female genital, i.e. the fulfilment of the threat of castration (or the phantasy representing that threat) provoked by his masturbating. This substitutive formation has, in spite of its hypochondriacal character, considerable resemblance to a hysterical conversion; and yet we have a feeling that something different must be going on here, that a substitutive formation such as this cannot be attributed to hysteria, even before we can say in what the difference

---

[1] [*The Interpretation of Dreams* (1900a), *Standard Ed.*, 5, 595; *P.F.L.*, 4, 753.]

[2] The dream-work, too, occasionally treats words like things, and so creates very similar 'schizophrenic' utterances or neologisms. [See *The Interpretation of Dreams* (1900a), *Standard Ed.*, 4, 295 ff.; *P.F.L.*, 4, 401 ff.]

consists. A tiny little cavity such as a pore of the skin would hardly be used by a hysteric as a symbol for the vagina, which he is otherwise ready to compare with every imaginable object that encloses a hollow space. Besides, we should expect the multiplicity of these little cavities to prevent him from using them as a substitute for the female genital. The same applies to the case of a young patient reported by Tausk some years ago to the Vienna Psycho-Analytical Society. This patient behaved in other respects exactly as though he were suffering from an obsessional neurosis; he took hours to wash and dress, and so on. It was noticeable, however, that he was able to give the meaning of his inhibitions without any resistance. In putting on his stockings, for instance, he was disturbed by the idea that he must pull apart the stitches in the knitting, i.e. the holes, and to him every hole was a symbol of the female genital aperture. This again is a thing which we cannot attribute to an obsessional neurotic. Reitler observed a patient of the latter sort, who also suffered from having to take a long time over putting on his stockings; this man, after overcoming his resistances, found as the explanation that his foot symbolized a penis, that putting on the stocking stood for a masturbatory act, and that he had to keep on pulling the stocking on and off, partly in order to complete the picture of masturbation, and partly in order to undo that act.

If we ask ourselves what it is that gives the character of strangeness to the substitutive formation and the symptom in schizophrenia, we eventually come to realize that it is the predominance of what has to do with words over what has to do with things. As far as the thing goes, there is only a very slight similarity between squeezing out a blackhead and an emission from the penis, and still less similarity between the innumerable shallow pores of the skin and the vagina; but in the former case there is, in both instances, a 'spurting out', while in the latter the cynical saying, 'a hole is a hole', is true verbally. What has dictated the substitution is not the resemblance between the things denoted but the sameness of the words used to express them. Where the two – word and thing – do not coincide, the formation of substitutes in schizophrenia deviates from that in the transference neuroses.

If now we put this finding alongside the hypothesis that in schizophrenia object-cathexes are given up, we shall be obliged to modify the hypothesis by adding that the cathexis of the *word*-presentations of objects is retained. What we have permissibly called the conscious presentation[1] of the object can now be split up into the presentation of the *word* and the presentation of the *thing*; the latter consists in the cathexis, if not of the direct memory-images of the thing, at least of remoter memory-traces derived from these. We now seem to know all at once what the difference is between a conscious and an unconscious presentation. The two are not, as we supposed, different registrations of the same content in different psychical localities, nor yet different functional states of cathexis in the same locality; but the conscious presentation comprises the presentation of the thing plus the presentation of the word belonging to it, while the unconscious presentation is the presentation of the thing alone. The system *Ucs.* contains the thing-cathexes of the objects, the first and true object-cathexes; the system *Pcs.* comes about by this thing-presentation being hypercathected through being linked with the word-presentations corresponding to it. It is these hypercathexes, we may suppose, that bring about a higher psychical organization and make it possible for the primary process to be succeeded by the secondary process which is dominant in the *Pcs.* Now, too, we are in a position to state precisely what it is that repression denies to the rejected presentation in the transference neuroses [p. 154]: what it denies to the presentation is translation into words which shall remain attached to the object. A presentation which is not put into words, or a psychical act which is not hypercathected, remains thereafter in the *Ucs.* in a state of repression.

I should like to point out at what an early date we already possessed the insight which to-day enables us to understand one of the most striking characteristics of schizophrenia. In the last few pages of *The Interpretation of Dreams*, which was published in 1900, the view was developed that thought-processes, i.e. those acts of cathexis which are comparatively remote from perception, are in themselves without quality and unconscious, and that they attain their capacity to become conscious only through being linked with the residues of

---

[1] ['*Vorstellung.*' This word has as a rule been translated above by 'idea'. From this point till the end of the paper, '*Vorstellung*' is uniformly translated by 'presentation', as are the cognate terms 'word-presentation' and 'thing-presentation'. The distinction between 'word-presentations' and 'thing-presentations' was already in his mind when Freud wrote his earlier works, and it no doubt derives from his studies on the aphasias. The matter was discussed at some length in his monograph on the subject (1891*b*), though in somewhat different terminology. The relevant passage in that work has been translated below in Appendix C.]

perceptions of *words*.[1] But word-presentations, for their part too, are derived from sense-perceptions, in the same way as thing-presentations are; the question might therefore be raised why presentations of objects cannot become conscious through the medium of their *own* perceptual residues. Probably, however, thought proceeds in systems so far remote from the original perceptual residues that they have no longer retained anything of the qualities of those residues, and, in order to become conscious, need to be reinforced by new qualities. Moreover, by being linked with words, cathexes can be provided with quality even when they represent only *relations* between presentations of objects and are thus unable to derive any quality from perceptions. Such relations, which become comprehensible only through words, form a major part of our thought-processes. As we can see, being linked with word-presentations is not yet the same thing as becoming conscious, but only makes it possible to become so; it is therefore characteristic of the system *Pcs.* and of that system alone.[2] With these discussions, however, we have evidently departed from our subject proper and find ourselves plunged into problems concerning the preconscious and the conscious, which for good reasons we are reserving for separate treatment.

As regards schizophrenia, which we only touch on here so far as seems indispensable for a general understanding of the *Ucs.*, a doubt must occur to us whether the process here termed repression has anything at all in common with the repression which takes place in the transference neuroses. The formula that repression is a process which occurs between the systems *Ucs.* and *Pcs.* (or *Cs.*), and results in keeping something at a distance from consciousness, must in any event be modified, in order that it may also be able to include the case of dementia praecox and other narcissistic affections. But the ego's attempt at flight, which expresses itself in the withdrawal of the conscious cathexis, nevertheless remains a factor common [to the two classes of neurosis]. The most superficial reflection shows us how much more radically and profoundly this attempt at flight, this flight of the ego, is put into operation in the narcissistic neuroses.

If, in schizophrenia, this flight consists in withdrawal of instinctual cathexis from the points which represent the *unconscious* presentation

---

[1] [*The Interpretation of Dreams* (1900a), *Standard Ed.*, 5, 617; *P.F.L.*, 4, 778 ff. This hypothesis is also mentioned in 'Formulations on the Two Principles of Mental Functioning' (1911b), Chapter 7 below.]

[2] [Freud took up this subject again in *The Ego and the Id* (1923b), Chapter 6 below.]

of the object, it may seem strange that the part of the presentation of this object which belongs to the system *Pcs.* – namely, the word-presentations corresponding to it – should, on the contrary, receive a more intense cathexis. We might rather expect that the word-presentation, being the preconscious part, would have to sustain the first impact of repression and that it would be totally uncathectable after repression had proceeded as far as the unconscious thing-presentations. This, it is true, is difficult to understand. It turns out that the cathexis of the word-presentation is not part of the act of repression, but represents the first of the attempts at recovery or cure which so conspicuously dominate the clinical picture of schizophrenia.[1] These endeavours are directed towards regaining the lost object, and it may well be that to achieve this purpose they set off on a path that leads to the object *via* the verbal part of it, but then find themselves obliged to be content with words instead of things. It is a general truth that our mental activity moves in two opposite directions: either it starts from the instincts and passes through the system *Ucs.* to conscious thought-activity; or, beginning with an instigation from outside, it passes through the system *Cs.* and *Pcs.* till it reaches the *Ucs.* cathexes of the ego and objects. This second path must, in spite of the repression which has taken place, remain traversable, and it lies open to some extent to the endeavours made by the neurosis to regain its objects. When we think in abstractions there is a danger that we may neglect the relations of words to unconscious thing-presentations, and it must be confessed that the expression and content of our philosophizing then begins to acquire an unwelcome resemblance to the mode of operation of schizophrenics. We may, on the other hand, attempt a characterization of the schizophrenic's mode of thought by saying that he treats concrete things as though they were abstract.

If we have made a true assessment of the nature of the *Ucs.* and have correctly defined the difference between an unconscious and a preconscious presentation, then our researches will inevitably bring us back from many other points to this same piece of insight.

---

[1] [See Part III of Freud's Schreber analysis (1911*c*).]

APPENDIX A
Freud and Ewald Hering

Among Freud's seniors in Vienna was the physiologist Ewald Hering (1834–1918), who, as we learn from Dr Jones (1953, 244), offered the young man a post as his assistant at Prague; this was probably while Freud was still working at Brücke's Physiological Institute, most likely in 1882; Hering went to Prague as Professor Ordinarius in 1870. An episode some forty years later seems to suggest, as Ernst Kris (1956) pointed out, that Hering's influence may have contributed to Freud's views on the unconscious. In 1880 Samuel Butler published his *Unconscious Memory*. This included a translation of a lecture delivered by Hering in 1870, 'Über das Gedächtnis als eine allgemeine Funktion der organisierten Materie' ('On Memory as a Universal Function of Organized Matter'), with which Butler found himself in general agreement. A book with the title *The Unconscious*, by Israel Levine, was published in England in 1923; and a German translation of it by Anna Freud appeared in 1926. One section of it, however (Part I, Section 13), which deals with Samuel Butler, was translated by Freud himself. The author, Levine, though he mentioned Hering's lecture, was more concerned with Butler than with Hering, and in that connection (on page 34 of the German translation) Freud added a footnote as follows:

'German readers, familiar with this lecture of Hering's and regarding it as a masterpiece, would not, of course, be inclined to bring into the foreground the considerations based on it by Butler. Moreover, some pertinent remarks are to be found in Hering which allow psychology the right to assume the existence of unconscious mental activity: "Who could hope to disentangle the fabric of our inner life with its thousandfold complexities, if we were willing to pursue its threads only so far as they traverse consciousness? . . . Chains such as these of unconscious material nerve-processes, which end in a link accompanied by a conscious perception, have been described as 'unconscious trains of ideas' and 'unconscious inferences'; and from the standpoint of psychology this can be justified. For the mind would often slip through the fingers of psychology, if psychology refused to keep a hold on the mind's unconscious states." [Hering, 1870, 11 and 13.]'

APPENDIX B
Psycho-Physical Parallelism

[It has been pointed out above that Freud's earlier views on the relation between the mind and the nervous system were greatly influenced by Hughlings Jackson. This is particularly shown by the following passage extracted from his monograph on aphasia (1891*b*, 56–8). It is especially instructive to compare the last sentences on the subject of latent memories with Freud's later position. In order to preserve a uniform terminology, a new translation has been made.]

After this digression we return to the consideration of aphasia. We may recall that on the basis of Meynert's teachings the theory has grown up that the speech apparatus consists of distinct cortical centres in whose cells the word-presentations are contained, these centres being separated by a functionless cortical region, and linked together by white fibres (associative fasciculi). The question may at once be raised whether a hypothesis of this kind, which encloses presentations in nerve cells, can possibly be correct and permissible. I think not.

The tendency of earlier periods in medicine was to localize whole mental faculties, as they are defined by psychological nomenclature, in certain regions of the brain. By contrast, therefore, it was bound to seem a great advance when Wernicke declared that only the simplest psychical elements, the different sensory presentations, could legitimately be localized – localized at the central termination of the peripheral nerve which has received the impression. But shall we not be making the same mistake in principle, whether what we are trying to localize is a complicated concept, a whole mental activity, or a psychical element? Is it justifiable to take a nerve fibre, which for the whole length of its course has been a purely physiological structure and has been subject to purely physiological modifications, and to plunge its end into the sphere of the mind and to fit this end out with a presentation or a mnemic image? If 'will', 'intelligence', and so on, are recognized as being psychological technical terms to which very complicated states of affairs correspond in the physiological world, can we feel any more sure that a 'simple sensory presentation' is anything other than a technical term of the same kind?

It is probable that the chain of physiological events in the nervous system does not stand in a causal connection with the psychical events. The physiological events do not cease as soon as the psychical ones begin; on the contrary, the physiological chain continues. What happens is simply that, after a certain point of time, each (or some) of its links has a psychical phenomenon corresponding to it. Accordingly, the psychical is a process parallel to the physiological – 'a dependent concomitant'.[1]

I know quite well that I cannot accuse the people whose views I am here disputing of having executed this jump and change in their scientific angle of approach [i.e. from the physiological to the psychological] without consideration. They obviously mean nothing else than that the physiological modification of the nerve fibres which accompanies sensory excitation produces another modification in the central nerve cell, and that this latter modification becomes the physiological correlate of the 'presentation'. Since they can say a great deal more about presentations than about the modifications, of which no physiological characterization whatever has yet been reached and which are unknown, they make use of the elliptical statement that the presentation is localized in the nerve cell. This way of putting matters, however, at once leads to a confusion between the two things, which need have no resemblance to each other. In psychology a simple presentation is something elementary for us, which we can sharply distinguish from its connections with other presentations. This leads us to suppose that the physiological correlate of the presentation – i.e. the modification that originates from the excited nerve fibre with its termination at the centre – is something simple too, which can be localized at a particular point. To draw a parallel of this kind is of course entirely unjustifiable; the characteristics of the modification must be established on their own account and independently of their psychological counterpart.[2]

What, then, is the physiological correlate of a simple presentation or of the same presentation when it recurs? Clearly nothing static, but something in the nature of a process. This process admits of localiza-

---

[1] [In English in the original. The phrase is from Hughlings Jackson.]

[2] Hughlings Jackson has given the most emphatic warning against confusions of this kind between the physical and the psychical in the process of speech: 'in all our studies of diseases of the nervous system we must be on our guard against the fallacy that what are physical states in lower centres fine away into psychical states in higher centres; that, for example, vibrations of sensory nerves become sensations, or that somehow or another an idea produces a movement.' (1878, 306.)

tion. It starts from a particular point in the cortex and spreads from there over the whole cortex or along certain tracts. When this process is completed, it leaves a modification behind in the cortex that has been affected by it – the possibility of remembering. It is highly doubtful whether there is anything psychical that corresponds to this modification either. Our consciousness shows nothing of a sort to justify, from the psychical point of view, the name of a 'latent mnemic image'. But whenever the same state of the cortex is provoked again, the psychical aspect comes into being once more as a mnemic image . . .

APPENDIX C

Words and Things

[The final section of Freud's paper on 'The Unconscious' seems to have roots in his early monograph on aphasia (1891*b*). It may be of interest, therefore, to reproduce here a passage from that work which, though not particularly easy to follow in itself, nevertheless throws light on the assumptions that underlay some of Freud's later views. The passage has the further incidental interest of presenting Freud in the very unusual position of talking in the technical language of the 'academic' psychology of the later nineteenth century. The passage here quoted follows after a train of destructive and constructive anatomical and physiological argument which has led Freud to a hypothetical scheme of neurological functioning which he describes as the 'speech apparatus'. It must be noted, however, that there is an important and perhaps confusing difference between the terminology Freud uses here and in 'The Unconscious'. What he here calls the 'object-presentation' is what in 'The Unconscious' he calls the 'thing-presentation'; while what in 'The Unconscious' he calls the 'object-presentation' denotes a complex made up of the combined 'thing-presentation' and 'word-presentation' – a complex which has no name given to it in the *Aphasia* passage. The translation has been made specially for this occasion, since, for terminological reasons, the published one was not entirely adapted to the present purpose. As in the last section of 'The Unconscious', we have here always used the word 'presentation' to render the German '*Vorstellung*', while 'image' stands for the German '*Bild*'.]

I now propose to consider what hypotheses are required to explain disturbances of speech on the basis of a speech apparatus constructed in this manner – in other words, what the study of disturbance of speech teaches us about the function of this apparatus. In doing so I shall keep the psychological and anatomical sides of the question as separate as possible.

From the point of view of psychology the unit of the function of speech is the 'word', a complex presentation, which proves to be a combination put together from auditory, visual and kinaesthetic elements. We owe our knowledge of this combination to pathology, which shows us that in organic lesions of the apparatus of speech a disintegration of speech takes place along the lines on which the combination is put together. We shall thus expect to find that the absence of one of these elements of the word-presentation will prove to be the most important indication for enabling us to arrive at a localization of the disease. Four components of the word-presentation are usually distinguished: the 'sound-image', the 'visual letter-image', the 'motor speech-image' and the 'motor writing-image'. This combination, however, turns out to be more complicated when one enters into the probable process of association that takes place in each of the various activities of speech:

(1) We learn to *speak* by associating a 'sound-image of a word' with a 'sense of the innervation of a word'.[1] After we have spoken, we are also in possession of a 'motor speech-presentation' (centripetal sensations from the organs of speech); so that, in a motor respect, the 'word' is doubly determined for us. Of the two determining elements, the first – the innervatory word-presentation – seems to have the least value from a psychological point of view; indeed its appearance at all as a psychical factor may be disputed. In addition to this, after speaking, we receive a 'sound-image' of the spoken word. So long as we have not developed our power of speech very far, this second sound-image need not be the same as the first one, but only associated with it.[2] At this stage of speech-development – that of early childhood – we make use

---

[1] ['It was once supposed that actively initiated movements involved a peculiar sort of sensation connected directly with the discharge of nervous impulses from the motor areas of the brain to the muscles. . . . The existence of this "innervation-sense", or sense of energy put forth, is now generally denied.' Stout (1938, 258). This last remark is confirmed by Freud a few lines lower down.]

[2] [The second sound-image is the sound-image of the word spoken by ourselves, and the first one is that of the word we are imitating (the sound-image mentioned at the beginning of the paragraph).]

of a language constructed by ourselves. We behave in this like motor aphasics, for we associate a variety of extraneous verbal sounds with a single one produced by ourselves.

(2) We learn to speak the language of other people by endeavouring to make the sound-image produced by ourselves as like as possible to the one which gave rise to our speech-innervation. We learn in this way to 'repeat' – to 'say after' another person. When we juxtapose words in connected speech, we hold back the innervation of the next word till the sound-image or the motor speech-presentation (or both) of the preceding word has reached us. The security of our speech is thus overdetermined, and can easily stand the loss of one or other of the determining factors. On the other hand, a loss of the correction exercised by the second sound-image and by the motor speech-image explains some of the peculiarities of paraphasia, both physiological and pathological.

(3) We learn to *spell* by linking the visual images of the letters with new sound-images, which, for their part, must remind us of verbal sounds which we already know. We at once 'repeat' the sound-image that denotes the letter; so that letters, too, are seen to be determined by two sound-images which coincide, and two motor presentations which correspond to each other.

(4) We learn to *read* by linking up in accordance with certain rules the succession of innervatory and motor word-presentations which we receive when we speak separate letters, so that new motor word-presentations arise. As soon as we have spoken these new word-presentations aloud, we discover from their sound-images that the two motor images and sound-images which we have received in this way have long been familiar to us and are identical with the images used in speaking. We then associate the meaning which was attached to the primary verbal sounds with the speech-images which have been acquired by spelling. We now read with understanding. If what was spoken primarily was a dialect and not a literary language, the motor and sound-images of the words acquired through spelling have to be super-associated with the old images; thus we have to learn a new language – a task which is facilitated by the similarity between the dialect and the literary language.

It will be seen from this description of learning to read that it is a very complicated process, in which the course of the associations must repeatedly move backwards and forwards. We shall also be prepared to find that disturbances of reading in aphasia are bound to occur in a great variety of ways. The only thing that decisively indicates a lesion in the *visual* element of reading is a disturbance in the reading of *separate letters*. The *combination* of letters into a word takes place during transmission to the speech-tract and will thus be abolished in *motor* aphasia. An *understanding* of what is read is arrived at only through the medium of the sound-images produced by the words that have been spoken, or through the medium of the motor word-images that arose in speaking. It is therefore seen to be a function that is extinguished not only where there are motor lesions, but also where there are *acoustic* ones. Understanding what is read is further seen to be a function independent of the actual performance of reading. Anyone can discover from self-observation that there are several kinds of reading, in some of which we do without an understanding of what is read. When I am reading proofs with a view to paying special attention to the visual images of the letters and other typographical signs, the sense of what I read escapes me so completely that I have to read the proofs through again specially, if I want to correct the style. When, on the other hand, I am reading a book that interests me, a novel, for instance, I overlook all the misprints; and it may happen that the names of the characters in it leave only a confused impression on my mind – a recollection, perhaps, that they are long or short, or contain some unusual letter, such as an 'x' or a 'z'. When I have to read aloud, and have to pay particular attention to the sound-images of my words and the intervals between them, I am once more in danger of concerning myself too little with the meaning of the words; and as soon as I get tired I read in such a way that, though other people can still understand what I am reading, I myself no longer know what I have read. These are phenomena of divided attention, which arise precisely here because an understanding of what is read only comes about in such a very circuitous way. If the process of reading itself offers difficulties, there is no longer any question of understanding. This is made clear by analogy with our behaviour when we are learning to read; and we must be careful not to regard the absence of understanding as evidence of the interruption of a tract. Reading aloud is not to be regarded as a process in any way different from reading to oneself, apart from the fact that it helps to divert attention from the sensory part of the process of reading.

(5) We learn to *write* by reproducing the visual images of the letters by means of innervatory images of the hand, till the same or similar visual images appear. As a rule, the writing images are only similar to,

and super-associated with, the reading images, since what we learn to read is *print* and what we learn to write is *hand-writing*. Writing proves to be a comparatively simple process and one that is not so easily disturbed as reading.

(6) It is to be assumed that later on, too, we carry out these different functions of speech along the same associative paths as those along which we learnt them. At this later stage, abbreviations and substitutions may occur, but it is not always easy to say what their nature is. Their importance is diminished by the consideration that in cases of organic lesion the apparatus of speech will probably be damaged to some extent as a whole and be compelled to return to the modes of association which are primary, well-established and lengthier. As regards reading, the 'visual word-image' undoubtedly makes its influence felt with practised readers, so that individual words (particularly proper names) can be read even without spelling them.

A word is thus a complex presentation consisting of the images enumerated above; or, to put it in another way, there corresponds to the word a complicated associative process into which the elements of visual, acoustic and kinaesthetic origin enumerated above enter together.

A word, however, acquires its *meaning* by being linked to an 'object-presentation',[1] at all events if we restrict ourselves to a consideration of substantives. The object-presentation itself is once again a complex of associations made up of the greatest variety of visual, acoustic, tactile, kinaesthetic and other presentations. Philosophy tells us that an object-presentation consists in nothing more than this – that the appearance of there being a 'thing' to whose various 'attributes' these sense-impressions bear witness is merely due to the fact that, in enumerating the sense-impressions which we have received from an object, we also assume the possibility of there being a large number of further impressions in the same chain of associations (J. S. Mill).[2] The object-presentation is thus seen to be one which is not closed and almost one which cannot be closed, while the word-presentation is seen to be something closed, even though capable of extension.

---

[1] [The 'thing-presentation' of the paper on 'The Unconscious'.]

[2] Cf. J. S. Mill, *A System of Logic* (1843), **1**, Book I, Chapter III, also *An Examination of Sir William Hamilton's Philosophy* (1865).

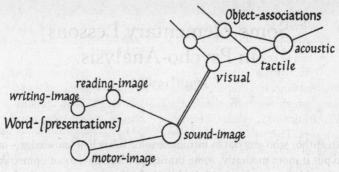

Psychological Diagram of a Word-Presentation

The word-presentation is shown as a closed complex of presentations, whereas the object-presentation is shown as an open one. The word-presentation is not linked to the object-presentation by *all* its constituent elements, but only by its sound-image. Among the object-associations, it is the visual ones which stand for the object, in the same kind of way as the sound-image stands for the word. The connections linking the sound-image of the word with object-associations other than the visual ones are not indicated.

The pathology of disorders of speech leads us to assert that *the word-presentation is linked at its sensory end (by its sound-images) with the object-presentation*. We thus arrive at the existence of two classes of disturbance of speech: (1) A first-order aphasia, *verbal aphasia*, in which only the associations between the separate elements of the word-presentation are disturbed; and (2) a second-order aphasia, *asymbolic aphasia*, in which the association between the word-presentation and the object-presentation is disturbed.

I use the term 'asymbolia' in a sense other than that in which it has been ordinarily used since Finkelnburg [1870],[1] because the relation between word [-presentation] and object-presentation rather than that between object and object-presentation seems to me to deserve to be described as a 'symbolic' one. For disturbances in the recognition of objects, which Finkelnburg classes as asymbolia, I should like to propose the term 'agnosia'. It is possible that 'agnostic' disturbances (which can only occur in cases of bilateral and extensive cortical lesions) may also entail a disturbance of speech, since all incitements to spontaneous speaking arise from the field of object-associations. I should call such disturbances of speech third-order aphasias or *agnostic aphasias*. Clinical observation has in fact brought to our knowledge a few cases which require to be viewed in this way . . .

[1] Quoted by Spamer (1876).

Some Elementary Lessons
in Psycho-Analysis
(1940 [1938])*

An author who sets out to introduce some branch of knowledge – or, to put it more modestly, some branch of research – to an uninstructed public must clearly make his choice between two methods or techniques.

It is possible to start off from what every reader knows (or think he knows) and regards as self-evident, without in the first instance contradicting him. An opportunity will soon occur for drawing his attention to facts in the same field, which, though they are known to him, he has so far neglected or insufficiently appreciated. Beginning from these, one can introduce further facts to him of which he has *no* knowledge and so prepare him for the necessity of going beyond his earlier judgements, of seeking new points of view and of taking new hypotheses into consideration. In this way one can get him to take a part in building up a new theory about the subject and one can deal with his objections to it during the actual course of the joint work. A method of this kind might well be called *genetic*. It follows the path along which the investigator himself has travelled earlier. In spite of all its advantages, it has the defect of not making a sufficiently striking effect upon the learner. He will not be nearly so much impressed by something which he has watched coming into existence and passing through a slow and difficult period of growth as he would be by something that is presented to him ready-made as an apparently self-contained whole.

It is precisely this last effect which is produced by the alternative method of presentation. This other method, the *dogmatic* one, begins straight away by stating its conclusions. Its premises make demands upon the audience's attention and belief and very little is adduced in support of them. And there is then a danger that a critical hearer may

* First published in *Int. Z. Psychoanal.* (in part). The English text is included in *Standard Ed.*, **23**, 281.

shake his head and say: 'All this sounds most peculiar: where does the fellow get it from?'

In what follows I shall not rely exclusively upon either of the two methods of presentation: I shall make use now of one and now of the other. I am under no delusion about the difficulty of my task. Psycho-analysis has little prospect of becoming liked or popular. It is not merely that much of what it has to say offends people's feelings. Almost as much difficulty is created by the fact that our science involves a number of hypotheses – it is hard to say whether they should be regarded as postulates[1] or as products of our researches – which are bound to seem very strange to ordinary modes of thought and which fundamentally contradict current views. But there is no help for it. We must begin our brief study with two of these hazardous hypotheses.

THE NATURE OF THE PSYCHICAL

Psycho-analysis is a part of the mental science of psychology. It is also described as 'depth psychology' – we shall later discover why. If someone asks what 'the psychical' really means, it is easy to reply by enumerating its constituents: our perceptions, ideas, memories, feelings and acts of volition – all these form part of what is psychical. But if the questioner goes further and asks whether there is not some common quality possessed by all these processes which makes it possible to get nearer to the *nature*, or, as people sometimes say, the *essence* of the psychical, then it is harder to give an answer.

If an analogous question had been put to a physicist (as to the nature of electricity, for instance), his reply, until quite recently, would have been: 'For the purpose of explaining certain phenomena, we assume the existence of electrical forces which are present in things and which emanate from them. We study these phenomena, discover the laws that govern them and even put them to practical use. This satisfies us provisionally. We do not know the *nature* of electricity. Perhaps we may discover it later, as our work goes on. It must be admitted that what we are ignorant of is precisely the most important and interesting part of the whole business, but for the moment that does not worry us. It is simply how things happen in the natural sciences.'

---

[1] [In the only German edition in which this passage appears, this word, '*Voraussetzungen*', is inexplicably misprinted '*Moralbesetzungen*' ('moral cathexes').]

Psychology, too, is a natural science. What else can it be? But its case is different. Not everyone is bold enough to make judgements about physical matters; but everyone – the philosopher and the man in the street alike – has his opinion on psychological questions and behaves as if he were at least an *amateur* psychologist. And now comes the remarkable thing. Everyone – or almost everyone – was agreed that what is psychical really *has* a common quality in which its essence is expressed: namely the quality of *being conscious* – unique, indescribable, but needing no description. All that is conscious, they said, is psychical, and conversely all that is psychical is conscious: that is self-evident and to contradict it is nonsense. It cannot be said that this decision threw much light upon the nature of the psychical, for consciousness is one of the fundamental facts of our life and our researches come up against it like a blank wall and can find no path beyond it. Moreover the equation of what is mental with what is conscious had the unwelcome result of divorcing psychical processes from the general context of events in the universe and of setting them in complete contrast to all others. But this would not do, since the fact could not long be overlooked that psychical phenomena are to a high degree dependent upon somatic influences and on their side have the most powerful effects upon somatic processes. If ever human thought found itself in an *impasse* it was here. To find a way out, the philosophers at least were obliged to assume that there were organic processes parallel to the conscious psychical ones, related to them in a manner that was hard to explain, which acted as intermediaries in the reciprocal relations between 'body and mind', and which served to re-insert the psychical into the texture of life. But this solution remained unsatisfactory.

Psycho-analysis escaped such difficulties as these by energetically denying the equation between what is psychical and what is conscious. No; being conscious cannot be the essence of what is psychical. It is only a *quality* of what is psychical, and an inconstant quality at that – one that is far oftener absent than present. The psychical, whatever its nature may be, is in itself unconscious and probably similar in kind to all the other natural processes of which we have obtained knowledge.

Psycho-analysis bases this assertion on a number of facts, of which I shall now proceed to give a selection.

We know what is meant by ideas 'occurring' to one – thoughts that suddenly come into consciousness without one's being aware of the steps that led up to them, though they, too, must have been psychical acts. It can even happen that one arrives in this way at the solution of some difficult intellectual problem which has previously for a time baffled one's efforts. All the complicated processes of selection, rejection and decision which occupied the interval were withdrawn from consciousness. We shall not be putting forward any new theory in saying that they were unconscious and perhaps, too, remained so.

In the second place, I shall pick a single instance to represent an immensely large class of phenomena.[1] The President of a public body (the Lower House of the Austrian Parliament) on one occasion opened a sitting with the following words: 'I take notice that a full quorum of members is present and herewith declare the sitting *closed*.' It was a slip of the tongue – for there can be no doubt that what the President intended to say was 'opened'. Why, then, did he say the opposite? We shall expect to be told it was an accidental mistake, a failure in carrying out an intention such as may easily happen for various reasons: it had no meaning – and in any case contraries are particularly easily substituted for each other. If, however, we bear in mind the situation in which the slip of the tongue occurred, we shall be inclined to prefer another explanation. Many of the previous sittings of the House had been disagreeably stormy and had accomplished nothing, so that it would be only too natural for the President to think at the moment of making his opening statement: 'If only the sitting that's just beginning were finished! I would much rather be closing than opening it!' When he began to speak he was probably not aware of this wish – it was not conscious to him – but it was certainly present and it succeeded in making itself effective, against the speaker's will, in his apparent mistake. A single instance can scarcely enable us to decide between two such different explanations. But what if every other instance of a slip of the tongue could be explained in the same way, and similarly every slip of the pen, every case of mis-reading or mis-hearing, and every faulty action? What if in all those instances (one might actually say, without a single exception) it was possible to demonstrate the presence of a psychical act – a thought, a wish or an intention – which would account for the apparent mistake and which was unconscious at the moment at which it became effective, even though it may have been conscious previously? If that were so, it

---

[1] Cf. *The Psychopathology of Everyday Life*. [1901*b*, Chapter V, *Standard Ed.*, **6**, 59–60; *P.F.L.*, **5**, 101.]

would really no longer be possible to dispute the fact that psychical acts which are unconscious do exist and that they are even sometimes active while they are unconscious and that in that case they can even sometimes get the better of conscious intentions. The person concerned in a mistake of this kind can react to it in various ways. He may overlook it completely or he may notice it himself and become embarrassed and ashamed. He cannot as a rule find the explanation of it himself without outside help; and he often refuses to accept the solution when it is put before him – for a time, at all events.

In the third place, finally, it is possible in the case of persons in a state of hypnosis to prove experimentally that there are such things as unconscious psychical acts and that consciousness is not an indispensable condition of [psychical] activity. Anyone who has witnessed such an experiment will receive an unforgettable impression and a conviction that can never be shaken. Here is more or less what happens. The doctor enters the hospital ward, puts his umbrella in the corner, hypnotizes one of the patients and says to him: 'I'm going out now. When I come in again, you will come to meet me with my umbrella open and hold it over my head.' The doctor and his assistants then leave the ward. As soon as they come back, the patient, who is no longer under hypnosis, carries out exactly the instructions that were given him while he was hypnotized. The doctor questions him: 'What's this you're doing? What's the meaning of all this?' The patient is clearly embarrassed. He makes some lame remark such as 'I only thought, doctor, as it's raining outside you'd open your umbrella in the room before you went out.' The explanation is obviously quite inadequate and made up on the spur of the moment to offer some sort of motive for his senseless behaviour. It is clear to us spectators that he is in ignorance of his real motive. We, however, know what it is, for we were present when the suggestion was made to him which he is now carrying out, while he himself knows nothing of the fact that it is at work in him.[1]

The question of the relation of the conscious to the psychical may now be regarded as settled: consciousness is only a *quality* or attribute of what is psychical, and moreover an inconstant one. But there is one further objection with which we have to deal. We are told that, in spite of the facts that have been mentioned, there is no necessity to abandon

---

[1] I am describing experiments made by Bernheim at Nancy in 1889 which I myself witnessed. In these days there is no need for me to discuss any doubts as to the genuineness of hypnotic phenomena of this kind. [Cf. p. 136 above.]

the identity between what is conscious and what is psychical: the so-called unconscious psychical processes are the organic processes which have long been recognized as running parallel to the mental ones. This, of course, would reduce our problem to an apparently indifferent matter of definition. Our reply is that it would be unjustifiable and inexpedient to make a breach in the unity of mental life for the sake of propping up a definition, since it is clear in any case that consciousness can only offer us an incomplete and broken chain of phenomena. And it can scarcely be a matter of chance that it was not until the change had been made in the definition of the psychical that it became possible to construct a comprehensive and coherent theory of mental life.

Nor need it be supposed that this alternative view of the psychical is an innovation due to psycho-analysis. A German philosopher, Theodor Lipps,[1] asserted with the greatest explicitness that the psychical is in itself unconscious and that the unconscious is the truly psychical. The concept of the unconscious has long been knocking at the gates of psychology and asking to be let in. Philosophy and literature have often toyed with it, but science could find no use for it. Psycho-analysis has seized upon the concept, has taken it seriously and has given it a fresh content. By its researches it has led to a knowledge of characteristics of the unconscious psychical which have hitherto been unsuspected, and it has discovered some of the laws which govern it. But none of this implies that the quality of being conscious has lost its importance for us. It remains the one light which illuminates our path and leads us through the darkness of mental life. In consequence of the special character of our discoveries, our scientific work in psychology will consist in translating unconscious processes into conscious ones, and thus filling in the gaps in conscious perception . . .

[1] [1851–1914. Professor of Philosophy at Munich. Some notes on Freud's relation to his writings will be found in the Editor's Preface to his book on jokes (1905c), *Standard Ed.*, **8**, 4–5; *P.F.L.*, **6**, 32.]

Four

THE INSTINCTUAL
DRIVES

Introduction

We assume that our students have by now become convinced of the existence of an unconscious mental life and have gradually approached four further pieces of knowledge: insight into the overwhelming range of the unconscious processes which is in no way comparable to that of conscious experience; the difference between what is genuinely unconscious and what is only descriptively and temporarily separated from consciousness; an understanding of the extraordinarily primitive mode of thinking dominant in the unconscious, one which is suggestive of the psychic processes in very early childhood; a first impression of the disharmony between the different psychic agencies which as 'inner conflicts' aggravate and burden human life. What we now expect of the student thus prepared is a fifth step: a look at the *content* of the unconscious, i.e., at the elements comprising this system, because it is only an understanding of their characteristics which explains why they must be barred from consciousness and why man must be continually on the alert against their emergence.

In seminars of our training institutes the candidates are frequently told that psycho-analysis is essentially a drive psychology. But this does not mean that psycho-analysis also claims to have formulated a theory of instinctual drives which in comprehensiveness, specificity, and usefulness surpasses all previous attempts aiming in that direction. On the contrary, Freud repeatedly stressed that he regarded the state of the psycho-analytic instinct theory as unsatisfactory. He referred to the drives themselves as 'mythical entities, magnificent in their indefiniteness', their description being not much more than 'so to say our mythology'. At the same time, however, he asserted that the analyst in his work 'cannot for a moment disregard them' (1933*a*, p. 95). It is precisely this constant preoccupation with the existence and workings of the instinctual drives that gives psycho-analytic work and theory their special character. The investigation of the unconscious by means of the dream, free association and interpretation of the transference behaviour in the analytic situation is at the same time research work aimed at the understanding of the drives. It goes beyond the realm of psychology to the extent that the sources of the instinctual drives lie in the biological and somatic sphere from which the instinctual drives merely send out their derivatives into the psychic realm. In their search for satisfaction these derivatives reach the unconscious, the system closest to them, and from there attempt to force an entry into conscious thinking and action. The above-mentioned 'inner conflict', which causes trouble for the individual and his analyst, is accordingly the incompatibility between the demands made by the instinctual drives and the moral, ethical and social side of the human personality that opposes them.

Freud's lifelong, persistent and tentative attempts to create his own drive theory led him far away from his predecessors. He regarded the single instincts described by other authors, such as the instinct for power, imitation, play, or the sociable instinct, as too unimportant to explain the outstandingly significant occurrences dominating human mental life. His search was directed to a dualism, to two supreme opposing forces with the demands of which the psychic processes had to contend: self-preservation versus preservation of the species, ego instincts versus sexual instincts, life instinct versus death instinct. Freud's view was directed to biology, the area lying behind the psychic sphere, i.e., to the vital processes themselves which are only reflected in the psychic processes.

Each of these attempts to solve the riddle of the instinctual drives dominated whole phases of Freud's life work and productivity. At times these were close to clinical observations, supported and re-quired by them; at others, they were far removed and more akin to biological speculations than descriptions of clinical facts. It was the fate of these different advances to evoke as much agreement as disagreement, not only in wider circles but especially among Freud's immediate followers. In particular, the dualism between life and death instincts postulated by him became a matter of dispute; many psycho-analytic clinicians regard the hypothesis of a death instinct as a foreign body; others welcome it and consider it to be the basis of all psychic conflicts. Be that as it may, Freud felt that with his last formulation of instinct theory he had come closer to a factor which, extending far beyond individual psychic life, was responsible for the life processes in their widest sense.

For the general student it would be too difficult to follow in detail the sequence of instinctual drive concepts in analysis. I would therefore assign first 'Instincts and Their Vicissitudes' (1915c), drawing attention to the fact that this paper is a relatively early attempt of Freud's to treat the topic comprehensively. It has remained a fundamental work, not least for an understanding of the subsequent changes in the classification of instinctual drives. Freud's last formulation, expressed in the contrasting pair of Eros and Thanatos, can then be studied in *Beyond the Pleasure Principle* (1920g).

Instincts and their Vicissitudes

(1915)*

We have often heard it maintained that sciences should be built up on clear and sharply defined basic concepts. In actual fact no science, not even the most exact, begins with such definitions. The true beginning of scientific activity consists rather in describing phenomena and then in proceeding to group, classify and correlate them. Even at the stage of description it is not possible to avoid applying certain abstract ideas to the material in hand, ideas derived from somewhere or other but certainly not from the new observations alone. Such ideas – which will later become the basic concepts of the science – are still more indispensable as the material is further worked over. They must at first necessarily possess some degree of indefiniteness; there can be no question of any clear delimitation of their content. So long as they remain in this condition, we come to an understanding about their meaning by making repeated references to the material of observation from which they appear to have been derived, but upon which, in fact, they have been imposed. Thus, strictly speaking, they are in the nature of conventions – although everything depends on their not being arbitrarily chosen but determined by their having significant relations to the empirical material, relations that we seem to sense before we can clearly recognize and demonstrate them. It is only after more thorough investigation of the field of observation that we are able to formulate its basic scientific concepts with increased precision, and progressively so to modify them that they become serviceable and consistent over a wide area. Then, indeed, the time may have come to confine them in definitions. The advance of knowledge, however, does not tolerate any rigidity even in definitions. Physics furnishes an excellent illustration of the way in which even 'basic concepts' that have been established in the form of definitions are constantly being altered in their content.

* First published in *Int. Z. Psychoanal.* The present text is included in *Standard Ed.*, 14, 117; *P.F.L.*, 11, 113.

A conventional basic concept of this kind, which at the moment is still somewhat obscure but which is indispensable to us in psychology, is that of an 'instinct'. Let us try to give a content to it by approaching it from different angles.

First, from the angle of *physiology*. This has given us the concept of a 'stimulus' and the pattern of the reflex arc, according to which a stimulus applied to living tissue (nervous substance) *from* the outside is discharged by action *to* the outside. This action is expedient in so far as it withdraws the stimulated substance from the influence of the stimulus, removes it out of its range of operation.

What is the relation of 'instinct' to 'stimulus'? There is nothing to prevent our subsuming the concept of 'instinct' under that of 'stimulus' and saying that an instinct is a stimulus applied to the mind. But we are immediately set on our guard against *equating* instinct and mental stimulus. There are obviously other stimuli to the mind besides those of an instinctual kind, stimuli which behave far more like physiological ones. For example, when a strong light falls on the eye, it is not an instinctual stimulus; it *is* one, however, when a dryness of the mucous membrane of the pharynx or an irritation of the mucous membrane of the stomach makes itself felt.[1]

We have now obtained the material necessary for distinguishing between instinctual stimuli and other (physiological) stimuli that operate on the mind. In the first place, an instinctual stimulus does not arise from the external world but from within the organism itself. For this reason it operates differently upon the mind and different actions are necessary in order to remove it. Further, all that is essential in a stimulus is covered if we assume that it operates with a single impact, so that it can be disposed of by a single expedient action. A typical instance of this is motor flight from the source of stimulation. These impacts may, of course, be repeated and summated, but that makes no difference to our notion of the process and to the conditions for the removal of the stimulus. An instinct, on the other hand, never operates as a force giving a *momentary* impact but always as a *constant* one. Moreover, since it impinges not from without but from within the organism, no flight can avail against it. A better term for an instinctual stimulus is a 'need'. What does away with a need is 'satisfaction'. This can be attained only by an appropriate ('adequate') alteration of the internal source of stimulation.

[1] Assuming, of course, that these internal processes are the organic basis of the respective needs of thirst and hunger.

Let us imagine ourselves in the situation of an almost entirely helpless living organism, as yet unorientated in the world, which is receiving stimuli in its nervous substance.[1] This organism will very soon be in a position to make a first distinction and a first orientation. On the one hand, it will be aware of stimuli which can be avoided by muscular action (flight); these it ascribes to an external world. On the other hand, it will also be aware of stimuli against which such action is of no avail and whose character of constant pressure persists in spite of it; these stimuli are the signs of an internal world, the evidence of instinctual needs. The perceptual substance of the living organism will thus have found in the efficacy of its muscular activity a basis for distinguishing between an 'outside' and an 'inside'.[2]

We thus arrive at the essential nature of instincts in the first place by considering their main characteristics – their origin in sources of stimulation within the organism and their appearance as a constant force – and from this we deduce one of their further features, namely, that no actions of flight avail against them. In the course of this discussion, however, we cannot fail to be struck by something that obliges us to make a further admission. In order to guide us in dealing with the field of psychological phenomena, we do not merely apply certain conventions to our empirical material as basic *concepts*; we also make use of a number of complicated *postulates*. We have already alluded to the most important of these, and all we need now do is to state it expressly. This postulate is of a biological nature, and makes use of the concept of 'purpose' (or perhaps of expediency) and runs as follows: the nervous system is an apparatus which has the function of getting rid of the stimuli that reach it, or of reducing them to the lowest possible level; or which, if it were feasible, would maintain itself in an altogether unstimulated condition.[3] Let us for the present

---

[1] [The hypothesis which follows concerning the behaviour of a primitive living organism, and the postulation of a fundamental 'principle of constancy', had been stated in similar terms in some of the very earliest of Freud's psychological works. See, for instance, Chapter VII, Sections C and E, of *The Interpretation of Dreams* (1900a), *Standard Ed.*, 5, 565 ff. and 598 ff. But it had been expressed still earlier in *neurological* terms in his posthumously published 'Project' of 1895 (1950a, Part I, Section 1), as well as, more briefly, in his lecture on the Breuer and Freud 'Preliminary Communication' (1893h) and in the penultimate paragraph of his French paper on hysterical paralyses (1893c). Freud returned to the hypothesis once more, in *Beyond the Pleasure Principle* (1920g). See pp. 219–20 and 234–6 below.]

[2] [Freud dealt with the subject later in his paper on 'Negation' (1925h) and in Chapter I of *Civilization and its Discontents* (1930a).]

[3] [This is the 'principle of constancy'.]

not take exception to the indefiniteness of this idea and let us assign to the nervous system the task – speaking in general terms – of *mastering stimuli*. We then see how greatly the simple pattern of the physiological reflex is complicated by the introduction of instincts. External stimuli impose only the single task of withdrawing from them; this is accomplished by muscular movements, one of which eventually achieves that aim and thereafter, being the expedient movement, becomes a hereditary disposition. Instinctual stimuli, which originate from within the organism, cannot be dealt with by this mechanism. Thus they make far higher demands on the nervous system and cause it to undertake involved and interconnected activities by which the external world is so changed as to afford satisfaction to the internal source of stimulation. Above all, they oblige the nervous system to renounce its ideal intention of keeping off stimuli, for they maintain an incessant and unavoidable afflux of stimulation. We may therefore well conclude that instincts and not external stimuli are the true motive forces behind the advances that have led the nervous system, with its unlimited capacities, to its present high level of development. There is naturally nothing to prevent our supposing that the instincts themselves are, at least in part, precipitates of the effects of external stimulation, which in the course of phylogenesis have brought about modifications in the living substance.

When we further find that the activity of even the most highly developed mental apparatus is subject to the pleasure principle, i.e. is automatically regulated by feelings belonging to the pleasure-unpleasure series, we can hardly reject the further hypothesis that these feelings reflect the manner in which the process of mastering stimuli takes place – certainly in the sense that unpleasurable feelings are connected with an increase and pleasurable feelings with a decrease of stimulus. We will, however, carefully preserve this assumption in its present highly indefinite form, until we succeed, if that is possible, in discovering what sort of relation exists between pleasure and unpleasure, on the one hand, and fluctuations in the amounts of stimulus affecting mental life, on the other. It is certain that many very various relations of this kind, and not very simple ones, are possible.[1]

[1] [It will be seen that two principles are here involved: the 'principle of constancy' and the 'pleasure principle', which Freud assumed, to begin with, were closely correlated (cf. p. 218 ff. below). A similar view is taken in *The Interpretation of Dreams* (1900a), *Standard Ed.*, **5**, 598; *P.F.L.*, **4**, 755. In the passage above, however, a doubt appears to be expressed as to the completeness of the correlation between the two

If now we apply ourselves to considering mental life from a *biological* point of view, an 'instinct' appears to us as a concept on the frontier between the mental and the somatic, as the psychical representative of the stimuli originating from within the organism and reaching the mind, as a measure of the demand made upon the mind for work in consequence of its connection with the body.

We are now in a position to discuss certain terms which are used in reference to the concept of an instinct – for example, its 'pressure', its 'aim', its 'object' and its 'source'.

By the pressure [*Drang*] of an instinct we understand its motor factor, the amount of force or the measure of the demand for work which it represents. The characteristic of exercising pressure is common to all instincts; it is in fact their very essence. Every instinct is a piece of activity; if we speak loosely of passive instincts, we can only mean instincts whose *aim* is passive.[1]

The aim [*Ziel*] of an instinct is in every instance satisfaction, which can only be obtained by removing the state of stimulation at the source of the instinct. But although the ultimate aim of each instinct remains unchangeable, there may yet be differnet paths leading to the same ultimate aim; so that an instinct may be found to have various nearer or intermediate aims, which are combined or interchanged with one another. Experience permits us also to speak of instincts which are 'inhibited in their aim', in the case of processes which are allowed to make some advance towards instinctual satisfaction but are then inhibited or deflected. We may suppose that even processes of this kind involve a partial satisfaction.

---

principles. This doubt is carried farther in *Beyond the Pleasure Principle* (pp. 219 and 267 below) and is discussed at some length in 'The Economic Problem of Masochism' (1924*c*). Freud there argues that the two principles cannot be identical, since there are unquestionably states of increasing tension which are pleasurable (e.g. sexual excitement), and he goes on to suggest (what had already been hinted at in the two passages in *Beyond the Pleasure Principle* just referred to) that the pleasurable or unpleasurable quality of a state may be related to a *temporal* characteristic (or rhythm) of the changes in the quantity of excitation present. He concludes that in any case the two principles must not be regarded as identical: the pleasure principle is a *modification* of the Nirvana principle. The Nirvana principle, he maintains, is to be attributed to the 'death instinct', and its modification into the pleasure principle is due to the influence of the 'life instinct' or libido.]

[1] [Some remarks on the active nature of instincts will be found in a footnote added in 1915 to Section 4 of the third of Freud's *Three Essays* (1905*d*), p. 355 below. – A criticism of Adler for misunderstanding this 'pressing' characteristic of instincts appears at the end of the second Section of Part III of the 'Little Hans' analysis (1909*b*), *Standard Ed.*, **10**, 140–1; *P.F.L.*, **8**, 296–7.]

The object [*Objekt*] of an instinct is the thing in regard to which or through which the instinct is able to achieve its aim. It is what is most variable about an instinct and is not originally connected with it, but becomes assigned to it only in consequence of being peculiarly fitted to make satisfaction possible. The object is not necessarily something extraneous: it may equally well be a part of the subject's own body. It may be changed any number of times in the course of the vicissitudes which the instinct undergoes during its existence; and highly import-ant parts are played by this displacement of instinct. It may happen that the same object serves for the satisfaction of several instincts simultaneously, a phenomenon which Adler [1908] has called a 'confluence' of instincts [*Triebverschränkung*].[1] A particularly close attachment of the instinct to its object is distinguished by the term 'fixation'. This frequently occurs at very early periods of the develop-ment of an instinct and puts an end to its mobility through its intense opposition to detachment.

By the source [*Quelle*] of an instinct is meant the somatic process which occurs in an organ or part of the body and whose stimulus is represented in mental life by an instinct. We do not know whether this process is invariably of a chemical nature or whether it may also correspond to the release of other, e.g. mechanical, forces. The study of the sources of instincts lies outside the scope of psychology. Although instincts are wholly determined by their origin in a somatic source, in mental life we know them only by their aims. An exact knowledge of the sources of an instinct is not invariably necessary for purposes of psychological investigation; sometimes its source may be inferred from its aim.

Are we to suppose that the different instincts which originate in the body and operate on the mind are also distinguished by different *qualities*, and that is why they behave in qualitatively different ways in mental life? This supposition does not seem to be justified; we are much more likely to find the simpler assumption sufficient – that the instincts are all qualitatively alike and owe the effect they make only to the amount of excitation they carry, or perhaps, in addition, to certain functions of that quantity. What distinguishes from one another the mental effects produced by the various instincts may be traced to the difference in their sources. In any event, it is only in a

---

[1] [Two instances of this are given by Freud in the analysis of 'Little Hans' (1909*b*), *Standard Ed.*, **10**, 106 and 127; *P.F.L.*, **8**, 265 and 284.]

later connection that we shall be able to make plain what the problem of the quality of instincts signifies.

What instincts should we suppose there are, and how many? There is obviously a wide opportunity here for arbitrary choice. No objection can be made to anyone's employing the concept of an instinct of play or of destruction or of gregariousness, when the subject-matter demands it and the limitations of psychological analysis allow of it. Nevertheless, we should not neglect to ask ourselves whether instinctual motives like these, which are so highly specialized on the one hand, do not admit of further dissection in accordance with the *sources* of the instinct, so that only primal instincts – those which cannot be further dissected – can lay claim to importance.

I have proposed that two groups of such primal instincts should be distinguished: the *ego*, or *self-preservative*, instincts and the *sexual* instincts. But this supposition has not the status of a necessary postulate, as has, for instance, our assumption about the biological purpose of the mental apparatus; it is merely a working hypothesis, to be retained only so long as it proves useful, and it will make little difference to the results of our work of description and classification if it is replaced by another. The occasion for this hypothesis arose in the course of the evolution of psycho-analysis, which was first employed upon the psychoneuroses, or, more precisely, upon the group described as 'transference neuroses' (hysteria and obsessional neurosis); these showed that at the root of all such affections there is to be found a conflict between the claims of sexuality and those of the ego. It is always possible that an exhaustive study of the other neurotic affections (especially of the narcissistic psychoneuroses, the schizophrenias) may oblige us to alter this formula and to make a different classification of the primal instincts. But for the present we do not know of any such formula, nor have we met with any argument unfavourable to drawing this contrast between sexual and ego instincts.

I am altogether doubtful whether any decisive pointers for the differentiation and classification of the instincts can be arrived at on the basis of working over the psychological material. This working-over seems rather itself to call for the application to the material of definite assumptions concerning instinctual life, and it would be a desirable thing if those assumptions could be taken from some other branch of knowledge and carried over to psychology. The contribution which biology has to make here certainly does not run counter to the distinction between sexual and ego instincts. Biology teaches that sexuality is not to be put on a par with other functions of the individual; for its purposes go beyond the individual and have as their content the production of new individuals – that is, the preservation of the species. It shows, further, that two views, seemingly equally well-founded, may be taken of the relation between the ego and sexuality. On the one view, the individual is the principal thing, sexuality is one of its activities and sexual satisfaction one of its needs; while on the other view the individual is a temporary and transient appendage to the quasi-immortal germ-plasm, which is entrusted to him by the process of generation. The hypothesis that the sexual function differs from other bodily processes in virtue of a special chemistry is, I understand, also a postulate of the Ehrlich school of biological research.[1]

Since a study of instinctual life from the direction of consciousness presents almost insuperable difficulties, the principal source of our knowledge remains the psycho-analytic investigation of mental disturbances. Psycho-analysis, however, in consequence of the course taken by its development, has hitherto been able to give us information of a fairly satisfactory nature only about the *sexual* instincts; for it is precisely that group which alone can be observed in isolation, as it were, in the psychoneuroses. With the extension of psycho-analysis to the other neurotic affections, we shall no doubt find a basis for our knowledge of the ego instincts as well, though it would be rash to expect equally favourable conditions for observation in this further field of research.

This much can be said by way of a general characterization of the sexual instincts. They are numerous, emanate from a great variety of organic sources, act in the first instance independently of one another and only achieve a more or less complete synthesis at a late stage. The aim which each of them strives for is the attainment of 'organ-pleasure';[2] only when synthesis is achieved do they enter the service of

---

[1] [Cf. p. 352 below.]

[2] ['Organ-pleasure' (i.e. pleasure attached to one particular bodily organ) seems to be used here for the first time by Freud. The term is discussed at greater length in the early part of Lecture 21 of the *Introductory Lectures* (1916–17). The underlying idea, of course, goes back much earlier. See, for instance, the opening passage of the third of the *Three Essays* (1905*d*), p. 344f. below.]

the reproductive function and thereupon become generally recognizable as sexual instincts. At their first appearance they are attached to the instincts of self-preservation, from which they only gradually become separated; in their choice of object, too, they follow the paths that are indicated to them by the ego instincts. A portion of them remains associated with the ego instincts throughout life and furnishes them with libidinal components, which in normal functioning easily escape notice and are revealed clearly only by the onset of illness. They are distinguished by possessing the capacity to act vicariously for one another to a wide extent and by being able to change their objects readily. In consequence of the latter properties they are capable of functions which are far removed from their original purposive actions – capable, that is, of 'sublimation'.

Our inquiry into the various vicissitudes which instincts undergo in the process of development and in the course of life must be confined to the sexual instincts, which are the more familiar to us. Observation shows us that an instinct may undergo the following vicissitudes:

> Reversal into its opposite.
> Turning round upon the subject's own self.
> Repression.
> Sublimation.

Since I do not intend to treat of sublimation here and since repression requires a special chapter to itself, it only remains for us to describe and discuss the two first points. Bearing in mind that there are motive forces which work against an instinct's being carried through in an unmodified form, we may also regard these vicissitudes as modes of *defence* against the instincts.

Reversal of an instinct into its opposite resolves on closer examination into two different processes: a change from activity to passivity, and a reversal of its content. The two processes, being different in their nature, must be treated separately.

Examples of the first process are met with the two pairs of opposites: sadism – masochism and scopophilia – exhibitionism. The reversal affects only the *aims* of the instincts. The active aim (to torture, to look at) is replaced by the passive aim (to be tortured, to be looked at). Reversal of *content* is found in the single instance of the transformation of love into hate.

The turning round of an instinct upon the subject's own self is made plausible by the reflection that masochism is actually sadism turned round upon the subject's own ego, and that exhibitionism includes looking at his own body. Analytic observation, indeed, leaves us in no doubt that the masochist shares in the enjoyment of the assault upon himself, and that the exhibitionist shares in the enjoyment of [the sight of] his exposure. The essence of the process is thus the change of the *object*, while the aim remains unchanged. We cannot fail to notice, however, that in these examples the turning round upon the subject's self and transformation from activity to passivity converge or coincide.

To elucidate the situation, a more thorough investigation is essential.

In the case of the pair of opposites sadism – masochism, the process may be represented as follows:

(*a*) Sadism consists in the exercise of violence or power upon some other person as object.

(*b*) This object is given up and replaced by the subject's self. With the turning round upon the self the change from an active to a passive instinctual aim is also effected.

(*c*) An extraneous person is once more sought as object; this person, in consequence of the alteration which has taken place in the instinctual aim, has to take over the role of the subject.[1]

Case (*c*) is what is commonly termed masochism. Here, too, satisfaction follows along the path of the original sadism, the passive ego placing itself back in phantasy in its first role, which has now in fact been taken over by the extraneous subject. Whether there is, besides this, a more direct masochistic satisfaction is highly doubtful. A primary masochism, not derived from sadism in the manner I have described, seems not to be met with.[2] That it is not superfluous to assume the existence of stage (*b*) is to be seen from the behaviour of the sadistic instinct in obsessional neurosis. There there is a turning round upon the subject's self *without* an attitude of passivity towards another person: the change has only got as far as stage (*b*). The desire to torture has turned into self-torture and self-punishment, not into

---

[1] [Though the general sense of these passages is clear, there may be some confusion in the use of the word 'subject'. As a rule 'subject' and 'object' are used respectively for the person in whom an instinct (or other state of mind) originates, and the person or thing to which it is directed. Here, however, 'subject' seems to be used for the person who plays the active part in the relationship – the agent.

[2] [*Footnote added* 1924:] In later works (cf. 'The Economic Problem of Masochism', 1924*c*) relating to problems of instinctual life I have expressed an opposite view.

masochism. The active voice is changed, not into the passive, but into the reflexive, middle voice.

Our view of sadism is further prejudiced by the circumstance that this instinct, side by side with its general aim (or perhaps, rather, within it), seems to strive towards the accomplishment of a quite special aim – not only to humiliate and master, but, in addition, to inflict pains. Psycho-analysis would appear to show that the infliction of pain plays no part among the original purposive actions of the instinct. A sadistic child takes no account of whether or not he inflicts pains, nor does he intend to do so. But when once the transformation into masochism has taken place, the pains are very well fitted to provide a passive masochistic aim; for we have every reason to believe that sensations of pain, like other unpleasurable sensations, trench upon sexual excitation and produce a pleasurable condition, for the sake of which the subject will even willingly experience the unpleasure of pain.[1] When once feeling pains has become a masochistic aim, the sadistic aim of *causing* pains can arise also, retrogressively; for while these pains are being inflicted on other people, they are enjoyed masochistically by the subject through his identification of himself with the suffering object. In both cases, of course, it is not the pain itself which is enjoyed, but the accompanying sexual excitation – so that this can be done especially conveniently from the sadistic position. The enjoyment of pain would thus be an aim which was originally masochistic, but which can only become an instinctual aim in someone who was originally sadistic.

For the sake of completeness I may add that feelings of pity cannot be described as a result of a transformation of instinct occurring in sadism, but necessitate the notion of a *reaction-formation* against that instinct. (For the difference, see later.)[2]

Rather different and simpler findings are afforded by the investigation of another pair of opposites – the instincts whose respective aim is to look and to display oneself (scopophilia and exhibitionism, in the

---

[1] [See p. 342 below.]

[2] [It is not clear to what passage this is intended to refer, unless, again, it was included in a missing paper on sublimation. There is in fact some discussion of the subject in 'Thoughts for the Times on War and Death' (1915*b*). But this cannot have been what Freud had in mind, for it was originally published in a different volume. In a footnote added in 1915 to the *Three Essays* (1905*d*), Freud insists that sublimation and reaction-formation are to be regarded as distinct processes (p. 319 *n.* 2 below). Another view of the origin of the feeling is expressed in the 'Wolf Man' analysis (1918*b*); *Standard Ed.*, **17**, 88; *P.F.L.*, **9**, 327.]

language of the perversions). Here again we may postulate the same stages as in the previous instance: (a) Looking as an *activity* directed towards an extraneous object. (b) Giving up of the object and turning of the scopophilic instinct towards a part of the subject's own body; with this, transformation to passivity and setting up of a new aim – that of being looked at. (c) Introduction of a new subject[1] to whom one displays oneself in order to be looked at by him. Here, too, it can hardly be doubted that the active aim appears before the passive, that looking precedes being looked at. But there is an important divergence from what happens in the case of sadism, in that we can recognize in the case of the scopophilic instinct a yet earlier stage than that described as (a). For the beginning of its activity the scopophilic instinct is auto-erotic: it has indeed an object, but that object is part of the subject's own body. It is only later that the instinct is led, by a process of comparison, to exchange this object for an analogous part of someone else's body – stage (a). This preliminary stage is interesting because it is the source of *both* the situations represented in the resulting pair of opposites, the one or the other according to which element in the original situation is changed. The following might serve as a diagrammatic picture of the scopophilic instinct:

(α) Oneself looking at a sexual = A sexual organ being looked
      organ   at by oneself

(β) Oneself looking at an   (γ) An object which is oneself or
      extraneous object   part of oneself being looked
      (active scopophilia)   at by an extraneous person
                                         (exhibitionism)

A preliminary stage of this kind is absent in sadism, which from the outset is directed upon an extraneous object, although it might not be altogether unreasonable to construct such a stage out of the child's efforts to gain control over his own limbs.[2]

With regard to both the instincts which we have just taken as examples, it should be remarked that their transformation by a reversal from activity to passivity and by a turning round upon the subject never in fact involves the whole quota of the instinctual

[1] [I.e. agent.]
[2] [*Footnote added* 1924:] Cf. footnote 2 on p. 206.

impulse. The earlier active direction of the instinct persists to some degree side by side with its later passive direction, even when the process of its transformation has been very extensive. The only correct statement to make about the scopophilic instinct would be that all the stages of its development, its auto-erotic, preliminary stage as well as its final active or passive form, co-exist alongside one another; and the truth of this becomes obvious if we base our opinion, not on the actions to which the instinct leads, but on the mechanism of its satisfaction. Perhaps, however, it is permissible to look at the matter and represent it in yet another way. We can dvide the life of each instinct into a series of separate successive waves, each of which is homogeneous during whatever period of time it may last, and whose relation to one another is comparable to that of successive eruptions of lava. We can then perhaps picture the first, original eruption of the instinct as proceeding in an unchanged form and undergoing no development at all. The next wave would be modified from the outset – being turned, for instance, from active to passive – and would then, with this new characteristic, be added to the earlier wave, and so on. If we were then to take a survey of the instinctual impulse from its beginning up to a given point, the succession of waves which we have described would inevitably present the picture of a definite development of the instinct.

The fact that, at this later period of development of an instinctual impulse, its (passive) opposite may be observed alongside of it deserves to be marked by the very apt term introduced by Bleuler – 'ambivalence'.[1]

This reference to the developmental history of instincts and the permanence of their intermediate stages should make the development of instincts fairly intelligible to us. Experience shows that the amount of demonstrable ambivalence varies greatly between individuals, groups and races. Marked instinctual ambivalence in a human being living at the present day may be regarded as an archaic inheritance, for we have reason to suppose that the part played in instinctual life by the active impulses in their unmodified form was greater in primaeval times than it is on an average to-day.

[1] [The term 'ambivalence', coined by Bleuler (1910, and 1911, 43 and 305), seems not to have been used by him in this sense. He distinguished three kinds of ambivalence: (1) emotional, i.e. oscillation between love and hate, (2) volitional, i.e. inability to decide on an action, and (3) intellectual, i.e. belief in contradictory propositions. Freud generally uses the term in the first of these senses. The passage in the text is one of the few in which he has applied the term to activity and passivity.]

We have become accustomed to call the early phase of the development of the ego, during which its sexual instincts find auto-erotic satisfaction, 'narcissism', without at once entering on any discussion of the relation between auto-erotism and narcissism. It follows that the preliminary stage of the scopophilic instinct, in which the subject's own body is the object of the scopophilia, must be classed under narcissism, and that we must describe it as a narcissistic formation. The active scopophilic instinct develops from this, by leaving narcissism behind. The passive scopophilic instinct, on the contrary, holds fast to the narcissistic object. Similarly, the transformation of sadism into masochism implies a return to the narcissistic object. And in both these cases [i.e. in passive scopophilia and masochism] the narcissistic *subject* is, through identification, replaced by another, extraneous ego. If we take into account our constructed preliminary narcissistic stage of sadism, we shall be approaching a more general realization – namely, that the instinctual vicissitudes which consist in the instinct's being turned round upon the subject's own ego and undergoing reversal from activity to passivity are dependent on the narcissistic organization of the ego and bear the stamp of that phase. They perhaps correspond to the attempts at defence which at higher stages of the development of the ego are effected by other means.

At this point we may call to mind that so far we have considered only two pairs of opposite instincts: sadism – masochism and scopophilia – exhibitionism. These are the best-known sexual instincts that appear in an ambivalent manner. The other components of the later sexual function are not yet sufficiently accessible to analysis for us to be able to discuss them in a similar way. In general we can assert of them that their activities are *auto-erotic*; that is to say, their object is negligible in comparison with the organ which is their source, and as a rule coincides with that organ. The object of the scopophilic instinct, however, though it too is in the first instance a part of the subject's own body, is not the eye itself; and in sadism the organic source, which is probably the muscular apparatus with its capacity for action, points unequivocally at an object other than itself, even though that object is part of the subject's own body. In the auto-erotic instincts, the part played by the organic source is so decisive that, according to a plausible suggestion of Federn (1913) and Jekels (1913), the form and function of the organ determine the activity or passivity of the instinctual aim.

The change of the *content* of an instinct into its opposite is observed in a single instance only – the transformation of *love into hate*.[1] Since it is particularly common to find both these directed simultaneously towards the same object, their co-existence furnishes the most important example of ambivalence of feeling.

The case of love and hate acquires a special interest from the circumstance that it refuses to be fitted into our scheme of the instincts. It is impossible to doubt that there is the most intimate relation between these two opposite feelings and sexual life, but we are naturally unwilling to think of love as being some kind of special component instinct of sexuality in the same way as the others we have been discussing. We should prefer to regard loving as the expression of the *whole* sexual current of feeling; but this idea does not clear up our difficulties, and we cannot see what meaning to attach to an opposite content of this current.

Loving admits not merely of one, but of three opposites. In addition to the antithesis 'loving–hating', there is the other one of 'loving–being loved'; and, in addition to these, loving and hating taken together are the opposite of the condition of unconcern or indifference. The second of these three antitheses, loving–being loved, corresponds exactly to the transformation from activity to passivity and may be traced to an underlying situation in the same way as in the case of the scopophilic instinct. This situation is that of *loving oneself*, which we regard as the characteristic feature of narcissism. Then, according as the object or the subject is replaced by an extraneous one, what results is the active aim of loving or the passive one of being loved – the latter remaining near to narcissism.

Perhaps we shall come to a better understanding of the several opposites of loving if we reflect that our mental life as a whole is governed by *three polarities*, the antitheses

Subject (ego) – Object (external world),
Pleasure – Unpleasure, and
Active – Passive.

The antithesis ego–non-ego (external), i.e. subject–object, is, as we have already said, thrust upon the individual organism at an early stage, by the experience that it can silence *external* stimuli by means of muscular action but is defenceless against *instinctual* stimuli. This

[1] [In the German editions previous to 1924 this reads 'the transformation of *love and hate*'.]

antithesis remains, above all, sovereign in our intellectual activity and creates for research the basic situation which no efforts can alter. The polarity of pleasure–unpleasure is attached to a scale of feelings, whose paramount importance in determining our actions (our will) has already been emphasized. The antithesis active–passive must not be confused with the antithesis ego-subject–external world-object. The relation of the ego to the external world is passive in so far as it receives stimuli from it and active when it reacts to these. It is forced by its instincts into a quite special degree of activity towards the external world, so that we might bring out the essential point if we say that that the ego-subject is passive in respect of external stimuli but active through its own instincts. The antithesis active–passive coalesces later with the antithesis masculine–feminine, which, until this has taken place, has no psychological meaning. The coupling of activity with masculinity and of passivity with femininity meets us, indeed, as a biological fact; but it is by no means so invariably complete and exclusive as we are inclined to assume.[1]

The three polarities of the mind are connected with one another in various highly significant ways. There is a primal psychical situation in which two of them coincide. Originally, at the very beginning of mental life, the ego is cathected with instincts and is to some extent capable of satisfying them on itself. We call this condition 'narcissism' and this way of obtaining satisfaction 'auto-erotic'.[2] At this time the external world is not cathected with interest (in a general sense) and is indifferent for purposes of satisfaction. During this period, therefore, the ego-subject coincides with what is pleasurable and the external world with what is indifferent (or possibly unpleasurable, as being a source of stimulation). If for the moment we define loving as the relation of the ego to its sources of pleasure, the situation in which the

---

[1] [See p. 355 and n. below for a fuller discussion of this point.]
[2] Some of the sexual instincts are, as we know, capable of this auto-erotic satisfaction, and so are adapted to being the vehicle for the development under the dominance of the pleasure principle [from the original 'reality-ego' into the 'pleasure-ego'] which we are about to describe [in the next paragraphs of the text]. Those sexual instincts which from the outset require an object, and the needs of the ego instincts, which are never capable of auto-erotic satisfaction, naturally disturb this state [of primal narcissism] and so pave the way for an advance from it. Indeed, the primal narcissistic state would not be able to follow the development [that is to be described] if it were not for the fact that every individual passes through a period during which he is helpless and has to be looked after and during which his pressing needs are satisfied by an external agency and are thus prevented from becoming greater.

ego loves itself only and is indifferent to the external world illustrates the first of the opposites which we found to 'loving'.[1]

In so far as the ego is auto-erotic, it has no need of the external world, but, in consequence of experiences undergone by the instincts of self-preservation, it acquires objects from that world, and, in spite of everything, it cannot avoid feeling internal instinctual stimuli for a time as unpleasurable. Under the dominance of the pleasure principle a further development now takes place in the ego. In so far as the objects which are presented to it are sources of pleasure, it takes them into itself, 'introjects' them (to use Ferenczi's [1909] term); and, on the other hand, it expels whatever within itself becomes a cause of unpleasure. (See below, the mechanism of projection.)

Thus the original 'reality-ego', which distinguished internal and external by means of a sound objective criterion,[2] changes into a purified 'pleasure-ego', which places the characteristic of pleasure above all others. For the pleasure-ego the external world is divided into a part that is pleasurable, which it has incorporated into itself, and a remainder that is extraneous to it. It has separated off a part of its own self, which it projects into the external world and feels as hostile. After this new arrangement, the two polarities coincide once more: the ego-subject coincides with pleasure, and the external world with unpleasure (with what was earlier indifference).

When, during the stage of primary narcissism, the object makes its appearance, the second opposite to loving, namely hating, also attains its development.

As we have seen, the object is brought to the ego from the external world in the first instance by the instincts of self-preservation; and it cannot be denied that hating, too, originally characterized the relation of the ego to the alien external world with the stimuli it introduces. Indifference falls into place as a special case of hate or dislike, after having first appeared as their forerunner. At the very beginning, it seems, the external world, objects, and what is hated are identical. If later on an object turns out to be a source of pleasure, it is loved, but it is also incorporated into the ego; so that for the purified pleasure-

---

[1] [Freud enumerates the opposites of loving in the following order: (1) hating, (2) being loved and (3) indifference. In the present passage, and below on pp. 214 and 216, he adopts a different order: (1) indifference, (2) hating and (3) being loved. It seems probable that in this second arrangement he gives indifference the first place as being the first to appear in the course of development.]

[2] [The 'reality-ego' and the 'pleasure-ego' had already been introduced in the paper on the two principles of mental functioning (1911*b*), Chapter 7 below.]

ego once again objects coincide with what is extraneous and hated.

Now, however, we may note that just as the pair of opposites love–indifference reflects the polarity ego–external world, so the second antithesis love–hate reproduces the polarity pleasure–unpleasure, which is linked to the first polarity. When the purely narcissistic stage has given place to the object-stage, pleasure and unpleasure signify relations of the ego to the object. If the object becomes a source of pleasurable feelings, a motor urge is set up which seeks to bring the object closer to the ego and to incorporate it into the ego. We then speak of the 'attraction' exercised by the pleasure-giving object, and say that we 'love' that object. Conversely, if the object is a source of unpleasurable feelings, there is an urge which endeavours to increase the distance between the object and the ego and to repeat in relation to the object the original attempt at flight from the external world with its emission of stimuli. We feel the 'repulsion' of the object, and hate it; this hate can afterwards be intensified to the point of an aggressive inclination against the object – an intention to destroy it.

We might at a pinch say of an instinct that it 'loves' the objects towards which it strives for purposes of satisfaction; but to say that an instinct 'hates' an object strikes us as odd. Thus we become aware that the attitudes[1] of love and hate cannot be made use of for the relations of *instincts* to their objects, but are reserved for the relations of the *total ego* to objects. But if we consider linguistic usage, which is certainly not without significance, we shall see that there is a further limitation to the meaning of love and hate. We do not say of objects which serve the interests of self-preservation that we *love* them; we emphasize the fact that we *need* them, and perhaps express an additional, different kind of relation to them by using words that denote a much reduced degree of love – such as, for example, 'being fond of', 'liking' or 'finding agreeable'.

Thus the word 'to love' moves further and further into the sphere of the pure pleasure-relation of the ego to the object and finally becomes fixed to sexual objects in the narrower sense and to those which satisfy the needs of sublimated sexual instincts. The distinction between the ego instincts and the sexual instincts which we have imposed upon our psychology is thus seen to be in conformity with the spirit of our

---

[1] [German '*Beziehungen*', literally 'relations'. In the first edition this word is printed '*Bezeichnungen*', 'descriptions' or 'terms' – which seems to make better sense.]

language. The fact that we are not in the habit of saying of a single sexual instinct that it loves its object, but regard the relation of the ego to its sexual object as the most appropriate case in which to employ the word 'love' – this fact teaches us that the word can only begin to be applied in this relation after there has been a synthesis of all the component instincts of sexuality under the primacy of the genitals and in the service of the reproductive function.

It is noteworthy that in the use of the word 'hate' no such intimate connection with sexual pleasure and the sexual function appears. The relation of *unpleasure* seems to be the sole decisive one. The ego hates, abhors and pursues with intent to destroy all objects which are a source of unpleasurable feeling for it, without taking into account whether they mean a frustration of sexual satisfaction or of the satisfaction of self-preservative needs. Indeed, it may be asserted that the true prototypes of the relation of hate are derived not from sexual life, but from the ego's struggle to preserve and maintain itself.

So we see that love and hate, which present themselves to us as complete opposites in their content, do not after all stand in any simple relation to each other. They did not arise from the cleavage of any originally common entity, but sprang from different sources, and had each its own development before the influence of the pleasure– unpleasure relation made them into opposites.

It now remains for us to put together what we know of the genesis of love and hate. Love is derived from the capacity of the ego to satisfy some of its instinctual impulses auto-erotically by obtaining organ-pleasure. It is originally narcissistic, then passes over on to objects, which have been incorporated into the extended ego, and expresses the motor efforts of the ego towards these objects as sources of pleasure. It becomes intimately linked with the activity of the later sexual instincts and, when these have been completely synthesized, coincides with the sexual impulsion as a whole. Preliminary stages of love emerge as provisional sexual aims while the sexual instincts are passing through their complicated development. As the first of these aims we recognize the phase of incorporating or devouring – a type of love which is consistent with abolishing the object's separate exist-ence and which may therefore be described as ambivalent.[1] At the higher stage of the pregenital sadistic-anal organization,[2] the striving

[1] [See Chapter 5, p. 337 below.]
[2] [See 'The Disposition to Obsessional Neurosis' (1913*i*).]

for the object appears in the form of an urge for mastery, to which injury or annihilation of the object is a matter of indifference. Love in this form and at this preliminary stage is hardly to be distinguished from hate in its attitude towards the object. Not until the genital organization is established does love become the opposite of hate.

Hate, as a relation to objects, is older than love. It derives from the narcissistic ego's primordial repudiation of the external world with its outpouring of stimuli. As an expression of the reaction of unpleasure evoked by objects, it always remains in an intimate relation with the self-preservative instincts; so that sexual and ego instincts can readily develop an antithesis which repeats that of love and hate. When the ego instincts dominate the sexual function, as is the case at the stage of the sadistic-anal organization, they impart the qualities of hate to the instinctual aim as well.

The history of the origins and relations of love makes us understand how it is that love so frequently manifests itself as 'ambivalent' – i.e. as accompanied by impulses of hate against the same object. The hate which is admixed with the love is in part derived from the preliminary stages of loving which have not been wholly surmounted; it is also in part based on reactions of repudiation by the ego instincts, which, in view of the frequent conflicts between the interests of the ego and those of love, can find grounds in real and contemporary motives. In both cases, therefore, the admixed hate has as its source the self-preservative instincts. If a love-relation with a given object is broken off, hate not infrequently emerges in its place, so that we get the impression of a transformation of love into hate. This account of what happens leads on to the view that the hate, which has its real motives, is here reinforced by a regression of the love to the sadistic preliminary stage; so that the hate acquires an erotic character and the continuity of a love-relation is ensured.

The third antithesis of loving, the transformation of loving into being loved, corresponds to the operation of the polarity of activity and passivity, and is to be judged in the same way as the cases of scopophilia and sadism.[1]

We may sum up by saying that the essential feature in the vicissitudes undergone by instincts lies in *the subjection of the instinctual impulses to the*

---

[1] [The relation between love and hate was further discussed by Freud, in the light of his hypothesis of a death instinct, in *The Ego and the Id* (1923*b*), p. 462 ff. below.]

influences of the three great polarities that dominate mental life. Of these three polarities we might describe that of activity–passivity as the *biological*, that of ego–external world as the *real*, and finally that of pleasure–unpleasure as the *economic* polarity.

The instinctual vicissitude of *repression* will form the subject of an inquiry which follows. [See p. 523 ff. below.]

Beyond the Pleasure Principle

(1920)*

I

In the theory of psycho-analysis we have no hesitation in assuming that the course taken by mental events is automatically regulated by the pleasure principle. We believe, that is to say, that the course of those events is invariably set in motion by an unpleasurable tension, and that it takes a direction such that its final outcome coincides with a lowering of that tension – that is, with an avoidance of unpleasure or a production of pleasure. In taking that course into account in our consideration of the mental processes which are the subject of our study, we are introducing an 'economic' point of view into our work; and if, in describing those processes, we try to estimate this 'economic' factor in addition to the 'topographical' and 'dynamic' ones, we shall, I think, be giving the most complete description of them of which we can at present conceive, and one which deserves to be distinguished by the term 'metapsychological'.[1]

It is of no concern to us in this connection to enquire how far, with this hypothesis of the pleasure principle, we have approached or adopted any particular, historically established, philosophical system. We have arrived at these speculative assumptions in an attempt to describe and to account for the facts of daily observation in our field of study. Priority and originality are not among the aims that psycho-analytic work sets itself; and the impressions that underlie the hypothesis of the pleasure principle are so obvious that they can scarcely be overlooked. On the other hand we would readily express our gratitude to any philosophical or psychological theory which was able to inform us of the meaning of the feelings of pleasure and unpleasure which act so imperatively upon us. But on this point we are, alas, offered nothing to our purpose. This is the most obscure and

---

* First published by Internationaler Psychoanalytischer Verlag (Leipzig, Vienna, Zurich). The present English translation is included in *Standard Ed.*, 18, 7; *P.F.L.*, 11, 275.
[1] [See Section IV of 'The Unconscious' (1915*e*) in Chapter 3 above.]

inaccessible region of the mind, and, since we cannot avoid contact with it, the least rigid hypothesis, it seems to me, will be the best. We have decided to relate pleasure and unpleasure to the quantity of excitation that is present in the mind but is not in any way 'bound';[1] and to relate them in such a manner that unpleasure corresponds to an *increase* in the quantity of excitation and pleasure to a *diminution*. What we are implying by this is not a simple relation between the strength of the feelings of pleasure and unpleasure and the corresponding modifications in the quantity of excitation; least of all – in view of all we have been taught by psycho-physiology – are we suggesting any directly proportional ratio: the factor that determines the feeling is probably the amount of increase or diminution in the quantity of excitation *in a given period of time*. Experiment might possibly play a part here; but it is not advisable for us analysts to go into the problem further so long as our way is not pointed by quite definite observations.[2]

We cannot, however, remain indifferent to the discovery that an investigator of such penetration as G. T. Fechner held a view on the subject of pleasure and unpleasure which coincides in all essentials with the one that has been forced upon us by psycho-analytic work. Fechner's statement is to be found contained in a small work, *Einige Ideen zur Schöpfungs- und Entwicklungsgeschichte der Organismen*, 1873 (Part XI, Supplement, 94), and reads as follows: 'In so far as conscious impulses always have some relation to pleasure or unpleasure, pleasure and unpleasure too can be regarded as having a psycho-physical relation to conditions of stability and instability. This provides a basis for a hypothesis into which I propose to enter in greater detail elsewhere. According to this hypothesis, every psycho-physical motion rising above the threshold of consciousness is attended by pleasure in proportion as, beyond a certain limit, it approximates to complete stability, and is attended by unpleasure in proportion as, beyond a certain limit, it deviates from complete stability; while between the two limits, which may be described as qualitative thresholds of pleasure and unpleasure, there is a certain margin of aesthetic indifference. . . .'

The facts which have caused us to believe in the dominance of the pleasure principle in mental life also find expression in the hypothesis

---

[1] [Cf. p. 161 above.]

[2] [This point is further developed in 'The Economic Problem of Masochism' (1924c).]

that the mental apparatus endeavours to keep the quantity of excitation present in it as low as possible or at least to keep it constant.
This latter hypothesis is only another way of stating the pleasure
principle; for if the work of the mental apparatus is directed towards
keeping the quantity of excitation low, then anything that is calculated to increase that quantity is bound to be felt as adverse to the
functioning of the apparatus, that is as unpleasurable. The pleasure
principle follows from the principle of constancy: actually the latter
principle was inferred from the facts which forced us to adopt the
pleasure principle.[1] Moreover, a more detailed discussion will show
that the tendency which we thus attribute to the mental apparatus is
subsumed as a special case under Fechner's principle of the 'tendency
towards stability', to which he has brought the feelings of pleasure
and unpleasure into relation.

It must be pointed out, however, that strictly speaking it is
incorrect to talk of the dominance of the pleasure principle over the
course of mental processes. If such a dominance existed, the immense
majority of our mental processes would have to be accompanied by
pleasure or to lead to pleasure, whereas universal experience completely contradicts any such conclusion. The most that can be said,
therefore, is that there exists in the mind a strong *tendency* towards the
pleasure principle, but that that tendency is opposed by certain other
forces or circumstances, so that the final outcome cannot always be in
harmony with the tendency towards pleasure. We may compare what
Fechner (1873, 90) remarks on a similar point: 'Since however a
tendency towards an aim does not imply that the aim is attained, and
since in general the aim is attainable only by approximations. . . .'

If we turn now to the question of what circumstances are able to
prevent the pleasure principle from being carried into effect, we find
ourselves once more on secure and well-trodden ground and, in
framing our answer, we have at our disposal a rich fund of analytic
experience.

The first example of the pleasure principle being inhibited in this
way is a familiar one which occurs with regularity. We know that the
pleasure principle is proper to a *primary* method of working on the part
of the mental apparatus, but that, from the point of view of the
self-preservation of the organism among the difficulties of the external
world, it is from the very outset inefficient and even highly dangerous.

[1] [Cf. p. 191 above.]

Under the influence of the ego's instincts of self-preservation, the pleasure principle is replaced by the *reality principle*.[1] This latter principle does not abandon the intention of ultimately obtaining pleasure, but it nevertheless demands and carries into effect the postponement of satisfaction, the abandonment of a number of possibilities of gaining satisfaction and the temporary toleration of unpleasure as a step on the long indirect road to pleasure The pleasure principle long persists, however, as the method of working employed by the sexual instincts, which are so hard to 'educate', and, starting from those instincts, or in the ego itself, it often succeeds in overcoming the reality principle, to the detriment of the organism as a whole.

There can be no doubt, however, that the replacement of the pleasure principle by the reality principle can only be made responsible for a small number, and by no means the most intense, of unpleasurable experiences. Another occasion of the release of unpleasure, which occurs with no less regularity, is to be found in the conflicts and dissensions that take place in the mental apparatus while the ego is passing through its development into more highly composite organizations. Almost all the energy with which the apparatus is filled arises from its innate instinctual impulses. But these are not all allowed to reach the same phases of development. In the course of things it happens again and again that individual instincts or parts of instincts turn out to be incompatible in their aims or demands with the remaining ones, which are able to combine into the inclusive unity of the ego. The former are then split off from this unity by the process of repression, held back at lower levels of psychical development and cut off, to begin with, from the possibility of satisfaction. If they succeed subsequently, as can so easily happen with repressed sexual instincts, in struggling through, by roundabout paths, to a direct or to a substitutive satisfaction, that event, which would in other cases have been an opportunity for pleasure, is felt by the ego as unpleasure. As a consequence of the old conflict which ended in repression, a new breach has occurred in the pleasure principle at the very time when certain instincts were endeavouring, in accordance with the principle, to obtain fresh pleasure. The details of the process by which repression turns a possibility of pleasure into a source of unpleasure are not yet clearly understood or cannot be clearly represented; but there is

[1] [Cf. Chapter 7.]

no doubt that all neurotic unpleasure is of that kind – pleasure that cannot be felt as such.[1]

The two sources of unpleasure which I have just indicated are very far from covering the majority of our unpleasurable experiences. But as regards the remainder it can be asserted with some show of justification that their presence does not contradict the dominance of the pleasure principle. Most of the unpleasure that we experience is *perceptual* unpleasure. It may be perception of pressure by unsatisfied instincts; or it may be external perception which is either distressing in itself or which excites unpleasurable expectations in the mental apparatus – that is, which is recognized by it as a 'danger'. The reaction to these instinctual demands and threats of danger, a reaction which constitutes the proper activity of the mental apparatus, can then be directed in a correct manner by the pleasure principle or the reality principle by which the former is modified. This does not seem to necessitate any far-reaching limitation of the pleasure principle. Nevertheless the investigation of the mental reaction to external danger is precisely in a position to produce new material and raise fresh questions bearing upon our present problem.

II

A condition has long been known and described which occurs after severe mechanical concussions, railway disasters and other accidents involving a risk to life; it has been given the name of 'traumatic neurosis'. The terrible war which has just ended gave rise to a great number of illnesses of this kind, but it at least put an end to the temptation to attribute the cause of the disorder to organic lesions of the nervous system brought about by mechanical force.[2] The symptomatic picture presented by traumatic neurosis approaches that of hysteria in the wealth of its similar motor symptoms, but surpasses it as a rule in its strongly marked signs of subjective ailment (in which it resembles hypochondria or melancholia) as well as in the evidence it gives of a far more comprehensive general enfeeblement and disturbance of the mental capacities. No complete explanation has yet been reached either of war neuroses or of the traumatic neuroses of peace.

[1] [*Footnote added* 1925:] No doubt the essential point is that pleasure and unpleasure, being conscious feelings, are attached to the ego.

[2] Cf. the discussion on the psycho-analysis of war neuroses by Freud, Ferenczi, Abraham, Simmel and Jones (1919) [to which Freud provided the introduction (1919*d*).]

In the case of the war neuroses, the fact that the same symptoms sometimes came about without the intervention of any gross mechanical force seemed at once enlightening and bewildering. In the case of the ordinary traumatic neuroses two characteristics emerge prominently: first, that the chief weight in their causation seems to rest upon the factor of surprise, of fright; and secondly, that a wound or injury inflicted simultaneously works as a rule *against* the development of a neurosis. 'Fright', 'fear' and 'anxiety' are improperly used as synonymous expressions; they are in fact capable of clear distinction in their relation to danger. 'Anxiety' describes a particular state of expecting the danger or preparing for it, even though it may be an unknown one. 'Fear' requires a definite object of which to be afraid. 'Fright', however, is the name we give to the state a person gets into when he has run into danger without being prepared for it; it emphasizes the factor of surprise. I do not believe anxiety can produce a traumatic neurosis. There is something about anxiety that protects its subject against fright and so against fright-neuroses. We shall return to this point later.[1]

The study of dreams may be considered the most trustworthy method of investigating deep mental processes. Now dreams occurring in traumatic neuroses have the characteristic of repeatedly bringing the patient back into the situation of his accident, a situation from which he wakes up in another fright. This astonishes people far too little. They think the fact that the traumatic experience is constantly forcing itself upon the patient even in his sleep is a proof of the strength of that experience: the patient is, as one might say, fixated to his trauma. Fixations to the experience which started the illness have long been familiar to us in hysteria. Breuer and Freud declared in 1893[2] that 'hysterics suffer mainly from reminiscences'. In the war neuroses, too, observers like Ferenczi and Simmel have been able to explain certain motor symptoms by fixation to the moment at which the trauma occurred.

I am not aware, however, that patients suffering from traumatic neurosis are much occupied in their waking lives with memories of

[1] [Freud is very far indeed from always carrying out the distinction he makes here. More often than not he uses the word '*Angst*' to denote a state of fear without any reference to the future. It seems not unlikely that in this passage he is beginning to adumbrate the distinction drawn in *Inhibitions, Symptoms and Anxiety* (1926d) between anxiety as a reaction to a traumatic situation – probably equivalent to what is here called *Schreck* – and anxiety as a warning signal of the approach of such an event.]

[2] ['On the Psychical Mechanism of Hysterical Phenomena', end of Section I.]

their accident. Perhaps they are more concerned with *not* thinking of it. Anyone who accepts it as something self-evident that their dreams should put them back at night into the situation that caused them to fall ill has misunderstood the nature of dreams. It would be more in harmony with their nature if they showed the patient pictures from his healthy past or of the cure for which he hopes. If we are not to be shaken in our belief in the wish-fulfilling tenor of dreams by the dreams of traumatic neurotics, we still have one resource open to us: we may argue that the function of dreaming, like so much else, is upset in this condition and diverted from its purposes, or we may be driven to reflect on the mysterious masochistic trends of the ego.

At this point I propose to leave the dark and dismal subject of the traumatic neurosis and pass on to examine the method of working employed by the mental apparatus in one of its earliest *normal* activities – I mean in children's play.

The different theories of children's play have only recently been summarized and discussed from the psycho-analytic point of view by Pfeifer (1919), to whose paper I would refer my readers. These theories attempt to discover the motives which lead children to play, but they fail to bring into the foreground the *economic* motive, the consideration of the yield of pleasure involved. Without wishing to include the whole field covered by these phenomena, I have been able, through a chance opportunity which presented itself, to throw some light upon the first game played by a little boy of one and a half and invented by himself. It was more than a mere fleeting observation, for I lived under the same roof as the child and his parents for some weeks, and it was some time before I discovered the meaning of the puzzling activity which he constantly repeated.

The child was not at all precocious in his intellectual development. At the age of one and a half he could say only a few comprehensible words; he could also make use of a number of sounds which expressed a meaning intelligible to those around him. He was, however, on good terms with his parents and their one servant-girl, and tributes were paid to his being a 'good boy'. He did not disturb his parents at night, he conscientiously obeyed orders not to touch certain things or go into certain rooms, and above all he never cried when his mother left him for a few hours. At the same time, he was greatly attached to his mother, who had not only fed him herself but had also looked after him without any outside help. This good little boy, however, had an occasional disturbing habit of taking any small objects he could get hold of and throwing them away from him into a corner, under the bed, and so on, so that hunting for his toys and picking them up was often quite a business. As he did this he gave vent to a loud, long-drawn-out 'o-o-o-o', accompanied by an expression of interest and satisfaction. His mother and the writer of the present account were agreed in thinking that this was not a mere interjection but represented the German word '*fort*' ['gone']. I eventually realized that it was a game and that the only use he made of any of his toys was to play 'gone' with them. One day I made an observation which confirmed my view. The child had a wooden reel with a piece of string tied round it. It never occurred to him to pull it along the floor behind him, for instance, and play at its being a carriage. What he did was to hold the reel by the string and very skilfully throw it over the edge of his curtained cot, so that it disappeared into it, at the same time uttering his expressive 'o-o-o-o'. He then pulled the reel out of the cot again by the string and hailed its reappearance with a joyful '*da*' ['there']. This, then, was the complete game – disappearance and return. As a rule one only witnessed its first act, which was repeated untiringly as a game in itself, though there is no doubt that the greater pleasure was attached to the second act.[1]

The interpretation of the game then became obvious. It was related to the child's great cultural achievement – the instinctual renunciation (that is, the renunciation of instinctual satisfaction) which he had made in allowing his mother to go away without protesting. He compensated himself for this, as it were, by himself staging the disappearance and retun of the objects within his reach. It is of course a matter of indifference from the point of view of judging the effective nature of the game whether the child invented it himself or took it over on some outside suggestion. Our interest is directed to another point. The child cannot possibly have felt his mother's departure as something agreeable or even indifferent. How then does his repetition of this distressing experience as a game fit in with the pleasure principle? It may perhaps be said in reply that her departure had to be enacted

---

[1] A further observation subsequently confirmed this interpretation fully. One day the child's mother had been away for several hours and on her return was met with the words 'Baby o-o-o-o!' which was at first incomprehensible. It soon turned out, however, that during this long period of solitude the child had found a method of making *himself* disappear. He had discovered his reflection in a full-length mirror which did not quite reach to the ground, so that by crouching down he could make his mirror-image 'gone'.

as a necessary preliminary to her joyful return, and that it was in the latter that lay the true purpose of the game. But against this must be counted the observed fact that the first act, that of departure, was staged as a game in itself and far more frequently than the episode in its entirety, with its pleasurable ending.

No certain decision can be reached from the analysis of a single case like this. On an unprejudiced view one gets an impression that the child turned his experience into a game from another motive. At the outset he was in a *passive* situation – he was overpowered by the experience; but, by repeating it, unpleasurable though it was, as a game, he took on an *active* part. These efforts might be put down to an instinct for mastery that was acting independently of whether the memory was in itself pleasurable or not. But still another interpretation may be attempted. Throwing away the object so that it was 'gone' might satisfy an impulse of the child's, which was suppressed in his actual life, to revenge himself on his mother for going away from him. In that case it would have a defiant meaning: 'All right, then, go away! I don't need you. I'm sending you away myself.' A year later, the same boy whom I had observed at his first game used to take a toy, if he was angry with it, and throw it on the floor, exclaiming: 'Go to the fwont!' He had heard at that time that his absent father was 'at the front', and was far from regretting his absence; on the contrary he made it quite clear that he had no desire to be disturbed in his sole possession of his mother.[1] We know of other children who liked to express similar hostile impulses by throwing away objects instead of persons.[2] We are therefore left in doubt as to whether the impulse to work over in the mind some overpowering experience so as to make oneself master of it can find expression as a primary event, and independently of the pleasure principle. For, in the case we have been discussing, the child may, after all, only have been able to repeat his unpleasant experience in play because the repetition carried along with it a yield of pleasure of another sort but none the less a direct one.

Nor shall we be helped in our hesitation between these two views by further considering children's play. It is clear that in their play children repeat everything that has made a great impression on them in real life, and that in doing so they abreact the strength of the

[1] When this child was five and three-quarters, his mother died. Now that she was really 'gone' ('o-o-o'), the little boy showed no signs of grief. It is true that in the interval a second child had been born and had roused him to violent jealousy.

[2] Cf. my note on a childhood memory of Goethe's (1917*b*).

impression and, as one might put it, make themseves master of the situation. But on the other hand it is obvious that all their play is influenced by a wish that dominates them the whole time – the wish to be grown-up and to be able to do what grown-up people do. It can also be observed that the unpleasurable nature of an experience does not always unsuit it for play. If the doctor looks down a child's throat or carries out some small operation on him, we may be quite sure that these frightening experiences will be the subject of the next game; but we must not in that connection overlook the fact that there is a yield of pleasure from another source. As the child passes over from the passivity of the experience to the activity of the game, he hands on the disagreeable experience to one of his playmates and in this way revenges himself on a substitute.

Nevertheless, it emerges from this discussion that there is no need to assume the existence of a special imitative instinct in order to provide a motive for play. Finally, a reminder may be added that the artistic play and artistic imitation carried out by adults, which, unlike children's, are aimed at an audience, do not spare the spectators (for instance, in tragedy) the most painful experiences and can yet be felt by them as highly enjoyable.[1] This is convincing proof that, even under the dominance of the pleasure principle, there are ways and means enough of making what is in itself unpleasurable into a subject to be recollected and worked over in the mind. The consideration of these cases and situations, which have a yield of pleasure as their final outcome, should be undertaken by some system of aesthetics with an economic approach to its subject-matter. They are of no use for *our* purposes, since they presuppose the existence and dominance of the pleasure principle; they give no evidence of the operation of tendencies *beyond* the pleasure principle, that is, of tendencies more primitive than it and independent of it.

III

Twenty-five years of intense work have had as their result that the immediate aims of psycho-analytic technique are quite other to-day than they were at the outset. At first the analysing physician could do no more than discover the unconscious material that was concealed from the patient, put it together, and, at the right moment, communi-

---

[1] [Freud had made a tentative study of this point in his posthumously published paper on 'Psychopathic Characters on the Stage' (1942a [1905–6]), *Standard Ed.*, 7, 305; *P.F.L.*, **14.**, 121.]

cate it to him. Psychoanalysis was then first and foremost an art of interpreting. Since this did not solve the therapeutic problem, a further aim quickly came in view: to oblige the patient to confirm the analyst's construction from his own memory. In that endeavour the chief emphasis lay upon the patient's resistances: the art consisted now in uncovering these as quickly as possible, in pointing them out to the patient and in inducing him by human influence – this was where suggestion operating as 'transference' played its part – to abandon his resistances.

But it became ever clearer that the aim which had been set up – the aim that what was unconscious should become conscious – is not completely attainable by that method. The patient cannot remember the whole of what is repressed in him, and what he cannot remember may be precisely the essential part of it. Thus he acquires no sense of conviction of the correctness of the construction that has been communicated to him. He is obliged to *repeat* the repressed material as a contemporary experience instead of, as the physician would prefer to see, *remembering* it as something belonging to the past.[1] These reproductions, which emerge with such unwished-for exactitude, always have as their subject some portion of infantile sexual life – of the Oedipus complex, that is, and its derivatives; and they are invariably acted out in the sphere of the transference, of the patient's relation to the physician. When things have reached this stage, it may be said that the earlier neurosis has now been replaced by a fresh, 'transference neurosis'. It has been the physician's endeavour to keep this transference neurosis within the narrowest limits: to force as much as possible into the channel of memory and to allow as little as possible to emerge as repetition. The ratio between what is remembered and what is reproduced varies from case to case. The physician cannot as a rule spare his patient this phase of the treatment. He must get him to re-experience some portion of his forgotten life, but must see to it, on the other hand, that the patient retains some degree of aloofness, which will enable him, in spite of everything, to recognize that what appears to be reality is in fact only a reflection of a forgotten past. If this can be successfully achieved, the patient's sense of conviction is

---

[1] See my paper on 'Recollecting, Repeating and Working Through' (1914g). [An early reference will be found in this same paper to the 'compulsion to repeat', which is one of the principal topics discussed in the present work. The term 'transference neurosis' in the special sense in which it is used a few lines lower down also appears in that paper.]

won, together with the therapeutic success that is dependent on it.

In order to make it easier to understand this 'compulsion to repeat', which emerges during the psycho-analytic treatment of neurotics, we must above all get rid of the mistaken notion that what we are dealing with in our struggle against resistances is resistance on the part of the *unconscious*. The unconscious – that is to say, the 'repressed' – offers no resistance whatever to the efforts of the treatment. Indeed, it itself has no other endeavour than to break through the pressure weighing down on it and force its way either to consciousness or to a discharge through some real action. Resistance during treatment arises from the same higher strata and systems of the mind which originally carried out repression. But the fact that, as we know from experience, the motives of the resistances, and indeed the resistances themselves, are unconscious at first during the treatment, is a hint to us that we should correct a shortcoming in our terminology. We shall avoid a lack of clarity if we make our contrast not between the conscious and the unconscious but between the coherent *ego* and the *repressed*. It is certain that much of the ego is itself unconscious, and notably what we may describe as its nucleus;[1] only a small part of it is covered by the term 'preconscious'. Having replaced a purely descriptive terminology by one which is systematic or dynamic, we can say that the patient's resistance arises from his ego,[2] and we then at once perceive that the compulsion to repeat must be ascribed to the unconscious repressed. It seems probable that the compulsion can only express itself after the work of treatment has gone half-way to meet it and has loosened the repression.[3]

There is no doubt that the resistance of the conscious and unconscious ego operates under the sway of the pleasure principle: it seeks to avoid the unpleasure which would be produced by the liberation of the repressed. *Our* efforts, on the other hand, are directed towards procuring the toleration of that unpleasure by an appeal to the reality principle. But how is the compulsion to repeat – the manifestation of the power of the repressed – related to the pleasure principle? It is

[1] [Cf. p. 452 *n.* 3 below.]

[2] [A fuller and somewhat different account of the sources of resistance will be found in Chap. XI of *Inhibitions, Symptoms and Anxiety* (1962d).]

[3] [*Footnote added* 1923:] I have argued elsewhere [1923c] that what thus comes to the help of the compulsion to repeat is the factor of 'suggestion' in the treatment – that is, the patient's submissiveness to the physician, which has its roots deep in his unconscious parental complex.

clear that the great part of what is re-experienced under the compulsion to repeat must cause the ego unpleasure, since it brings to light activities of repressed instinctual impulses. That, however, is unpleasure of a kind we have already considered and does not contradict the pleasure principle: unpleasure for one system and simultaneously satisfaction for the other. But we came now to a new and remarkable fact, namely that the compulsion to repeat also recalls from the past experiences which include no possibility of pleasure, and which can never, even long ago, have brought satisfaction even to instinctual impulses which have since been repressed.

The early efflorescence of infantile sexual life is doomed to extinction because its wishes are incompatible with reality and with the inadequate stage of development which the child has reached. That efflorescence comes to an end in the most distressing circumstances and to the accompaniment of the most painful feelings. Loss of love and failure leave behind them a permanent injury to self-regard in the form of a narcissistic scar, which in my opinion, as well as in Marcinowski's (1918), contributes more than anything to the 'sense of inferiority' which is so common in neurotics. The child's sexual researches, on which limits are imposed by his physical development, lead to no satisfactory conclusion; hence such later complaints as 'I can't accomplish anything; I can't succeed in anything'. The tie of affection, which binds the child as a rule to the parent of the opposite sex, succumbs to disappointment, to a vain expectation of satisfaction or to jealousy over the birth of a new baby – unmistakable proof of the infidelity of the object of the child's affections. His own attempt to make a baby himself, carried out with tragic seriousness, fails shamefully. The lessening amount of affection he receives, the increasing demands of education, hard words and an occasional punishment – these show him at last the full extent to which he has been scorned. These are a few typical and constantly recurring instances of the ways in which the love characteristic of the age of childhood is brought to a conclusion.

Patients repeat all of these unwanted situations and painful emotions in the transference and revive them with the greatest ingenuity. They seek to bring about the interruption of the treatment while it is still incomplete; they contrive once more to feel themselves scorned, to oblige the physician to speak severely to them and treat them coldly; they discover appropriate objects for their jealousy; instead of the passionately desired baby of their childhood, they produce a plan or a promise of some grand present – which turns out as a rule to be no less unreal. None of these things can have produced pleasure in the past, and it might be supposed that they would cause less unpleasure to-day if they emerged as memories or dreams instead of taking the form of fresh experiences. They are of course the activities of instincts intended to lead to satisfaction; but no lesson has been learnt from the old experience of these activities having led instead only to unpleasure. In spite of that, they are repeated, under pressure of a compulsion.

What psycho-analysis reveals in the transference phenomena of neurotics can also be observed in the lives of some normal people. The impression they give is of being pursued by a malignant fate or possessed by some 'daemonic' power; but psycho-analysis has always taken the view that their fate is for the most part arranged by themselves and determined by early infantile influences. The compulsion which is here in evidence differs in no way from the compulsion to repeat which we have found in neurotics, even though the people we are now considering have never shown any signs of dealing with a neurotic conflict by producing symptoms. Thus we have come across people all of whose human relationships have the same outcome: such as the benefactor who is abandoned in anger after a time by each of his *protégés*, however much they may otherwise differ from one another, and who thus seems doomed to taste all the bitterness of ingratitude; or the man whose friendships all end in betrayal by his friend; or the man who time after time in the course of his life raises someone else into a position of great private or public authority and then, after a certain interval, himself upsets that authority and replaces him by a new one; or, again, the lover each of whose love affairs with a woman passes through the same phases and reaches the same conclusion. This 'perpetual recurrence of the same thing' causes us no astonishment when it relates to *active* behaviour on the part of the person concerned and when we can discern in him an essential character-trait which always remains the same and which is compelled to find expression in a repetition of the same experiences. We are much more impressed by cases where the subject appears to have a *passive* experience, over which he has no influence, but in which he meets with a repetition of the same fatality. There is the case, for instance, of the woman who married three successive husbands each of whom fell ill soon afterwards and had to be nursed by her on their deathbeds.[1] The most moving poetic picture of a fate such as this is given by Tasso in his romantic epic *Gerusalemme Liberata*. Its hero, Tancred, unwittingly kills his beloved Clorinda in a duel while she is disguised in the armour of an enemy knight. After her burial he makes his way into a strange magic forest which strikes the Crusaders' army with terror. He slashes with his sword at a tall tree; but blood streams from the cut and the voice of Clorinda, whose soul is imprisoned in the tree, is heard complaining that he has wounded his beloved once again.

If we take into account observations such as these, based upon behaviour in the transference and upon the life-histories of men and women, we shall find courage to assume that there really does exist in the mind a compulsion to repeat which overrides the pleasure principle. Now too we shall be inclined to relate to this compulsion the dreams which occur in traumatic neuroses and the impulse which leads children to play.

But it is to be noted that only in rare instances can we observe the pure effects of the compulsion to repeat, unsupported by other motives. In the case of children's play we have already laid stress on the other ways in which the emergence of the compulsion may be interpreted; the compulsion to repeat and instinctual satisfaction which is immediately pleasurable seem to converge here into an intimate partnership. The phenomena of transference are obviously exploited by the resistance which the ego maintains in its pertinacious insistence upon repression; the compulsion to repeat, which the treatment tries to bring into its service is, as it were, drawn over by the ego to *its* side (clinging as the ego does to the pleasure principle). A great deal of what might be described as the compulsion of destiny seems intelligible on a rational basis; so that we are under no necessity to call in a new and mysterious motive force to explain it.

The least dubious instance [of such a motive force] is perhaps that of traumatic dreams. But on maturer reflection we shall be forced to admit that even in the other instances the whole ground is not covered by the operation of the familiar motive forces. Enough is left unexplained to justify the hypothesis of a compulsion to repeat – something that seems more primitive, more elementary, more instinctual than the pleasure principle which it over-rides. But if a compulsion to repeat *does* operate in the mind, we should be glad to know something about it, to learn what function it corresponds to, under what

---

[1] Cf. the apt remarks on this subject by C. G. Jung (1909).

conditions it can emerge and what its relation is to the pleasure principle – to which, after all, we have hitherto ascribed dominance over the course of the processes of excitation in mental life.

IV

What follows is speculation, often far-fetched speculation, which the reader will consider or dismiss according to his individual predilection. It is further an attempt to follow out an idea consistently, out of curiosity to see where it will lead.

Psycho-analytic speculation takes as its point of departure the impression, derived from examining unconscious processes, that consciousness may be, not the most universal attribute of mental processes, but only a particular function of them. Speaking in metapsychological terms, it asserts that consciousness is a function of a particular system which it describes as $Cs.$[1] What consciousness yields consists essentially of perceptions of excitations coming from the external world and of feelings of pleasure and unpleasure which can only arise from within the mental apparatus; it is therefore possible to assign to the system $Pcpt.$-$Cs.$[2] a position in space. It must lie on the borderline between outside and inside; it must be turned towards the external world and must envelop the other psychical systems. It will be seen that there is nothing daringly new in these assumptions; we have merely adopted the views on localization held by cerebral anatomy, which locates the 'seat' of consciousness in the cerebral cortex – the outermost, enveloping layer of the central organ. Cerebral anatomy has no need to consider why, speaking anatomically, consciousness should be lodged on the surface of the brain instead of being safely housed somewhere in its inmost interior. Perhaps *we* shall be more successful in accounting for this situation in the case of our system $Pcpt.$-$Cs.$

Consciousness is not the only distinctive character which we ascribe to the processes in that system. On the basis of impressions derived from our psycho-analytic experience, we assume that all excitatory processes that occur in the *other* systems leave permanent traces behind in them which form the foundation of memory. Such

---

[1] [See *The Interpretation of Dreams* (1900a), *Standard Ed.*, 5, 610 ff.; *P.F.L.*, 4, 770 ff. See also 'The Unconscious' (1915e), Section II, in Chapter 3 above.]

[2] [The system *Pcpt.* (the perceptual system) was first described by Freud in *The Interpretation of Dreams*, *Standard Ed.*, 5, 536 ff., *P.F.L.*, 4, 685 ff. In a later paper (1917d) he argued that the system *Pcpt.* coincided with the system *Cs.*]

memory-traces, then, have nothing to do with the fact of becoming conscious; indeed they are often most powerful and most enduring when the process which left them behind was one which never entered consciousness. We find it hard to believe, however, that permanent traces of excitation such as these are also left in the system *Pcpt.-Cs.* If they remained constantly conscious, they would very soon set limits to the system's aptitude for receiving fresh excitations.[1] If, on the other hand, they were unconscious, we should be faced with the problem of explaining the existence of unconscious processes in a system whose functioning was otherwise accompanied by the phenomenon of consciousness. We should, so to say, have altered nothing and gained nothing by our hypothesis relegating the process of becoming conscious to a special system. Though this consideration is not absolutely conclusive, it nevertheless leads us to suspect that becoming conscious and leaving behind a memory-trace are processes incompatible with each other within one and the same system. Thus we should be able to say that the excitatory process becomes conscious in the system *Cs.* but leaves no permanent trace behind there; but that the excitation is transmitted to the systems lying next within and that it is in *them* that its traces are left. I followed these same lines in the schematic picture which I included in the speculative section of my *Interpretation of Dreams.*[2] It must be borne in mind that little enough is known from other sources of the origin of consciousness; when, therefore, we lay down the proposition that *consciousness arises instead of a memory-trace*, the assertion deserves consideration, at all events on the ground of its being framed in fairly precise terms.

If this is so, then, the system *Cs.* is characterized by the peculiarity that in it (in contrast to what happens in the other psychical systems) excitatory processes do not leave behind any permanent change in its elements but expire, as it were, in the phenomenon of becoming conscious. An exception of this sort to the general rule requires to be explained by some factor that applies exclusively to that one system. Such a factor, which is absent in the other systems, might well be the exposed situation of the system *Cs.*, immediately abutting as it does on the external world.

Let us picture a living organism in its most simplified possible form as an undifferentiated vesicle of a substance that is susceptible to

---

[1] What follows is based throughout on Breuer's views in [the second section of his theoretical contribution to] *Studies on Hysteria* (Breuer and Freud, 1895d).

[2] [*Standard Ed.*, 5, 538; *P.F.L.*, 4, 687.]

stimulation. Then the surface turned towards the external world will from its very situation be differentiated and will serve as an organ for receiving stimuli. Indeed embryology, in its capacity as a recapitulation of developmental history, actually shows us that the central nervous system originates from the ectoderm; the grey matter of the cortex remains a derivative of the primitive superficial layer of the organism and may have inherited some of its essential properties. It would be easy to suppose, then, that as a result of the ceaseless impact of external stimuli on the surface of the vesicle, its substance to a certain depth may have become permanently modified, so that excitatory processes run a different course in it from what they run in the deeper layers. A crust would thus be formed which would at last have been so thoroughly 'baked through' by stimulation that it would present the most favourable possible conditions for the reception of stimuli and become incapable of any further modification. In terms of the system Cs., this would mean that its elements could undergo no further permanent modification from the passage of excitation, because they had already been modified in the respect in question to the greatest possible extent: now, however, they would have become capable of giving rise to consciousness. Various ideas may be formed which cannot at present be verified as to the nature of this modification of the substance and of the excitatory process. It may be supposed that, in passing from one element to another, an excitation has to overcome a resistance, and that the diminution of resistance thus effected is what lays down a permanent trace of the excitation, that is, a facilitation. In the system Cs., then, resistance of this kind to passage from one element to another would no longer exist. This picture can be brought into relation with Breuer's distinction between quiescent (or bound) and mobile cathectic energy in the elements of the psychical systems;[1] the elements of the system Cs. would carry no bound energy but only energy capable of free discharge. It seems best, however, to express oneself as cautiously as possible on these points. None the less, this speculation will have enabled us to bring the origin of consciousness into some sort of connection with the situation of the system Cs. and with the peculiarities that must be ascribed to the excitatory processes taking place in it.

But we have more to say of the living vesicle with its receptive

---

[1] Breuer and Freud, 1895. [See Section 2 of Breuer's theoretical contribution, and in particular the footnote at the beginning of that section.]

cortical layer. This little fragment of living substance is suspended in the middle of an external world charged with the most powerful energies; and it would be killed by the stimulation emanating from these if it were not provided with a protective shield against stimuli. It acquires the shield in this way: its outermost surface ceases to have the structure proper to living matter, becomes to some degree inorganic and thenceforward functions as a special envelope or membrane resistant to stimuli. In consequence, the energies of the external world are able to pass into the next underlying layers, which have remained living, with only a fragment of their original intensity; and these layers can devote themselves, behind the protective shield, to the reception of the amounts of stimulus which have been allowed through it. By its death, the outer layer has saved all the deeper ones from a similar fate – unless, that is to say, stimuli reach it which are so strong that they break through the protective shield. *Protection against* stimuli is an almost more important function for the living organism than *reception of* stimuli. The protective shield is supplied with its own store of energy and must above all endeavour to preserve the special modes of transformation of energy operating in it against the effects threatened by the enormous energies at work in the external world – effects which tend towards a levelling out of them and hence towards destruction. The main purpose of the *reception* of stimuli is to discover the direction and nature of the external stimuli; and for that it is enough to take small specimens of the external world, to sample it in small quantities. In highly developed organisms the receptive cortical layer of the former vesicle has long been withdrawn into the depths of the interior of the body, though portions of it have been left behind on the surface immediately beneath the general shield against stimuli. These are the sense organs, which consist essentially of apparatus for the reception of certain specific effects of stimulation, but which also include special arrangements for further protection against excessive amounts of stimulation and for excluding unsuitable kinds of stimuli. It is characteristic of them that they deal only with very small quantities of external stimulation and only take in *samples* of the external world. They may perhaps be compared with feelers which are all the time making tentative advances towards the external world and then drawing back from it.

At this point I shall venture to touch for a moment upon a subject which would merit the most exhaustive treatment. As a result of certain psycho-analytic discoveries, we are to-day in a position to embark on a discussion of the Kantian theorem that time and space are 'necessary forms of thought'. We have learnt that unconscious mental processes are in themselves 'timeless'.[1] This means in the first place that they are not ordered temporally, that time does not change them in any way and that the idea of time cannot be applied to them. These are negative characteristics which can only be clearly understood if a comparison is made with *conscious* mental processes. On the other hand, our abstract idea of time seems to be wholly derived from the method of working of the system *Pcpt.-Cs.* and to correspond to a perception on its own part of that method of working. This mode of functioning may perhaps constitute another way of providing a shield against stimuli. I know that these remarks must sound very obscure, but I must limit myself to these hints.

We have pointed out how the living vesicle is provided with a shield against stimuli from the external world; and we had previously shown that the cortical layer next to that shield must be differentiated as an organ for receiving stimuli from without. This sensitive cortex, however, which is later to become the system *Cs.*, also receives excitations from *within*. The situation of the system between the outside and the inside and the difference between the conditions governing the reception of excitations in the two cases have a decisive effect on the functioning of the system and of the whole mental apparatus. Towards the outside it is shielded against stimuli, and the amounts of excitation impinging on it have only a reduced effect. Towards the inside there can be no such shield; the excitations in the deeper layers extend into the system directly and in undiminished amount, in so far as certain of their characteristics give rise to feelings in the pleasure-unpleasure series. The excitations coming from within are, however, in their intensity and in other, qualitative, respects – in their amplitude, perhaps – more commensurate with the system's method of working than the stimuli which stream in from the external world. This state of things produces two definite results. First, the feelings of pleasure and unpleasure (which are an index to what is happening in the interior of the apparatus) predominate over all external stimuli. And secondly, a particular way is adopted of dealing with any internal excitations which produce too great an increase of unpleasure: there is a tendency to treat them as though they were acting, not from the inside, but from the outside, so that it may be

___
[1] [See p. 160 and *n.* 3 above.]

possible to bring the shield against stimuli into operation as a means of defence against them. This is the origin of *projection*, which is destined to play such a large part in the causation of pathological processes.

I have an impression that these last considerations have brought us to a better understanding of the dominance of the pleasure principle; but no light has yet been thrown on the cases that contradict that dominance. Let us therefore go a step further. We describe as 'traumatic' any excitations from outside which are powerful enough to break through the protective shield. It seems to me that the concept of trauma necessarily implies a connection of this kind with a breach in an otherwise efficacious barrier against stimuli. Such an event as an external trauma is bound to provoke a disturbance on a large scale in the functioning of the organism's energy and to set in motion every possible defensive measure. At the same time, the pleasure principle is for the moment put out of action. There is no longer any possibility of preventing the mental apparatus from being flooded with large amounts of stimulus, and another problem arises instead – the problem of mastering the amounts of stimulus which have broken in and of binding them, in the psychical sense, so that they can then be disposed of.

The specific unpleasure of physical pain is probably the result of the protective shield having been broken through in a limited area. There is then a continuous stream of excitations from the part of the periphery concerned to the central apparatus of the mind, such as could normally arise only from *within* the apparatus.[1] And how shall we expect the mind to react to this invasion? Cathectic energy is summoned from all sides to provide sufficiently high cathexes of energy in the environs of the breach. An 'anticathexis' on a grand scale is set up, for whose benefit all the other psychical systems are impoverished, so that the remaining psychical functions are extensively paralysed or reduced. We must endeavour to draw a lesson from examples such as this and use them as a basis for our meta-psychological speculations. From the present case, then, we infer that a system which is itself highly cathected is capable of taking up an additional stream of fresh inflowing energy and of converting it into quiescent cathexis, that is of binding it psychically. The higher the system's own quiescent cathexis, the greater seems to be its binding

---

[1] Cf. 'Instincts and their Vicissitudes' (1915c) [p. 198 above].

force; conversely, therefore, the lower its cathexis, the less capacity will it have for taking up inflowing energy[1] and the more violent must be the consequences of such a breach in the protective shield against stimuli. To this view it cannot be justly objected that the increase of cathexis round the breach can be explained far more simply as the direct result of the inflowing masses of excitation. If that were so, the mental apparatus would merely receive an increase in its cathexes of energy, and the paralysing character of pain and the impoverishment of all the other systems would remain unexplained. Nor do the very violent phenomena of discharge to which pain gives rise affect our explanation, for they occur in a reflex manner – that is, they follow without the intervention of the mental apparatus. The indefiniteness of all our discussions on what we describe as metapsychology is of course due to the fact that we know nothing of the nature of the excitatory process that takes place in the elements of the psychical systems, and that we do not feel justified in framing any hypothesis on the subject. We are consequently operating all the time with a large unknown factor, which we are obliged to carry over into every new formula. It may be reasonably supposed that this excitatory process can be carried out with energies that vary *quantitatively*; it may also seem probable that it has more than one *quality* (in the nature of amplitude, for instance). As a new factor we have taken into consideration Breuer's hypothesis that charges of energy occur in two forms; so that we have to distinguish between two kinds of cathexis of the psychical systems or their elements – a freely flowing cathexis that presses on towards discharge and a quiescent cathexis. We may perhaps suspect that the binding of the energy that streams into the mental apparatus consists in its change from a freely flowing into a quiescent state.

We may, I think, tentatively venture to regard the common traumatic neurosis as a consequence of an extensive breach being made in the protective shield against stimuli. This would seem to reinstate the old, naive theory of shock, in apparent contrast to the later and psychologically more ambitious theory which attributes aetiological importance not to the effects of mechanical violence but to fright and the threat to life. These opposing views are not, however, irreconcilable; nor is the psycho-analytic view of the traumatic

[1] [Cf. the 'principle of the insusceptibility to excitation of uncathected systems' in a footnote near the end of Freud, 1917*d*.]

neurosis identical with the shock theory in its crudest form. The latter regards the essence of the shock as being the direct damage to the molecular structure or even to the histological structure of the elements of the nervous system; whereas what *we* seek to understand are the effects produced on the organ of the mind by the breach in the shield against stimuli and by the problems that follow in its train. And we still attribute importance to the element of fright. It is caused by lack of any preparedness for anxiety,[1] including lack of hypercathexis of the systems that would be the first to receive the stimulus. Owing to their low cathexis those systems are not in a good position for binding the inflowing amounts of excitation and the consequences of the breach in the protective shield follow all the more easily. It will be seen, then, that preparedness for anxiety and the hypercathexis of the receptive systems constitute the last line of defence of the shield against stimuli. In the case of quite a number of traumas, the difference between systems that are unprepared and systems that are well prepared through being hypercathected may be a decisive factor in determining the outcome; though where the strength of a trauma exceeds a certain limit this factor will no doubt cease to carry weight. The fulfilment of wishes is, as we know, brought about in a hallucinatory manner by dreams, and under the dominance of the pleasure principle this has become their function. But it is not in the service of that principle that the dreams of patients suffering from traumatic neuroses lead them back with such regularity to the situation in which the trauma occurred. We may assume, rather, that dreams are here helping to carry out another task, which must be accomplished before the dominance of the pleasure principle can even begin. These dreams are endeavouring to master the stimulus retrospectively, by developing the anxiety whose omission was the cause of the traumatic neurosis. They thus afford us a view of a function of the mental apparatus which, though it does not contradict the pleasure principle, is nevertheless independent of it and seems to be more primitive than the purpose of gaining pleasure and avoiding unpleasure.

This would seem to be the place, then, at which to admit for the first time an exception to the proposition that dreams are fulfilments of wishes. Anxiety dreams, as I have shown repeatedly and in detail, offer no such exception. Nor do 'punishment dreams', for they merely replace the forbidden wish-fulfilment by the appropriate punishment

---

[1] [Cf. p. 223 *n*.1 above.]

for it; that is to say, they fulfil the wish of the sense of guilt which is the reaction to the repudiated impulse. But it is impossible to classify as wish-fulfilments the dreams we have been discussing which occur in traumatic neuroses, or the dreams during psycho-analyses which bring to memory the psychical traumas of childhood. They arise, rather, in obedience to the compulsion to repeat, though it is true that in analysis that compulsion is supported by the wish (which is encouraged by 'suggestion') to conjure up what has been forgotten and repressed. Thus it would seem that the function of dreams, which consists in setting aside any motives that might interrupt sleep, by fulfilling the wishes of the disturbing impulses, is not their *original* function. It would not be possible for them to perform that function until the whole of mental life had accepted the dominance of the pleasure principle. If there is a 'beyond the pleasure principle', it is only consistent to grant that there was also a time before the purpose of dreams was the fulfilment of wishes. This would imply no denial of their later function. But if once this general rule has been broken, a further question arises. May not dreams which, with a view to the psychical binding of traumatic impressions, obey the compulsion to repeat – may not such dreams occur *outside* analysis as well? And the reply can only be a decided affirmative.

I have argued elsewhere[1] that 'war neuroses' (in so far as that term implies something more than a reference to the circumstances of the illness's onset) may very well be traumatic neuroses which have been facilitated by a conflict in the ego. The fact to which I have referred on p. 222, that a gross physical injury caused simultaneously by the trauma diminishes the chances that a neurosis will develop, becomes intelligible if one bears in mind two facts which have been stressed by psycho-analytic research: firstly, that mechanical agitation must be recognized as one of the sources of sexual excitation,[2] and secondly, that painful and feverish illnesses exercise a powerful effect, so long as they last, on the distribution of libido. Thus, on the one hand, the mechanical violence of the trauma would liberate a quantity of sexual excitation which, owing to the lack of preparation for anxiety, would have a traumatic effect; but, on the other hand, the simultaneous physical injury, by calling for a narcissistic hypercathexis of the

---

[1] See my introduction (1919*d*) to *Psycho-Analysis and the War Neuroses*.
[2] Cf. my remarks elsewhere (*Three Essays* [p. 340 below]) on the effect of swinging and railway-travel.

injured organ,[1] would bind the excess of excitation. It is also well known, though the libido theory has not yet made sufficient use of the fact, that such severe disorders in the distribution of libido as melancholia are temporarily brought to an end by intercurrent organic illness, and indeed that even a fully developed condition of dementia praecox is capable of a temporary remission in these same circumstances.

V

The fact that the cortical layer which receives stimuli is without any protective shield against excitations from within must have as its result that these latter transmissions of stimulus have a preponderance in economic importance and often occasion economic disturbances comparable with traumatic neuroses. The most abundant sources of this internal excitation are what are described as the organism's 'instincts' – the representatives of all the forces originating in the interior of the body and transmitted to the mental apparatus – at once the most important and the most obscure element of psychological research.

It will perhaps not be thought too rash to suppose that the impulses arising from the instincts do not belong to the type of *bound* nervous processes but of *freely mobile* processes which press towards discharge. The best part of what we know of these processes is derived from our study of the dream-work. We there discovered that the processes in the unconscious systems were fundamentally different from those in the preconscious (or conscious) systems. In the unconscious, cathexes can easily be completely transferred, displaced and condensed. Such treatment, however, could produce only invalid results if it were applied to preconscious material; and this accounts for the familiar peculiarities exhibited by manifest dreams after the preconscious residues of the preceding day have been worked over in accordance with the laws operating in the unconscious. I described the type of process found in the unconscious as the 'primary' psychical process, in contradistinction to the 'secondary' process which is the one obtaining in our normal waking life. Since all instinctual impulses have the unconscious systems as their point of impact, it is hardly an innovation to say that they obey the primary process. Again, it is easy to identify the primary psychical process with Breuer's freely mobile

[1] See my paper on narcissism (1914c) [*Standard Ed.*, 14, 82 ff.; *P.F.L.*, 11, 75.]

cathexis and the secondary process with changes in his bound or tonic cathexis.[1] If so, it would be the task of the higher strata of the mental apparatus to bind the instinctual excitation reaching the primary process. A failure to effect this binding would provoke a disturbance analogous to a traumatic neurosis; and only after the binding has been accomplished would it be possible for the dominance of the pleasure principle (and of its modification, the reality principle) to proceed unhindered. Till then the other task of the mental apparatus, the task of mastering or binding excitations, would have precedence – not, indeed, in *opposition* to the pleasure principle, but independently of it and to some extent in disregard of it.

The manifestations of a compulsion to repeat (which we have described as occurring in the early activities of infantile mental life as well as among the events of psycho-analytic treatment) exhibit to a high degree an instinctual character and, when they act in opposition to the pleasure principle, give the appearance of some 'daemonic' force at work. In the case of children's play we seemed to see that children repeat unpleasurable experiences for the additional reason that they can master a powerful impression far more thoroughly by being active than they could by merely experiencing it passively. Each fresh repetition seems to strengthen the mastery they are in search of. Nor can children have their *pleasurable* experiences repeated often enough, and they are inexorable in their insistence that the repetition shall be an identical one. This character trait disappears later on. If a joke is heard for a second time it produces almost no effect; a theatrical production never creates so great an impression the second time as the first; indeed, it is hardly possible to persuade an adult who has very much enjoyed reading a book to re-read it immediately. Novelty is always the condition of enjoyment. But children will never tire of asking an adult to repeat a game that he has shown them or played with them, till he is too exhausted to go on. And if a child has been told a nice story, he will insist on hearing it over and over again rather than a new one; and he will remorselessly stipulate that the repetition shall be an identical one and will correct any alterations of which the narrator may be guilty – though they may actually have been made in the hope of gaining fresh approval. None of this contradicts the pleasure principle; repetition, the re-experiencing of something

---

[1] Cf. my *Interpretation of Dreams*, Chapter VII [*Standard Ed.*, **5**, 588 ff.; *P.F.L.*, **4**, 375 ff. Cf. also Breuer and Freud, 1895 (Section 2 of Breuer's theoretical contribution)].

identical, is clearly in itself a source of pleasure. In the case of a person in analysis, on the contrary, the compulsion to repeat the events of his childhood in the transference evidently disregards the pleasure principle in every way. The patient behaves in a purely infantile fashion and thus shows us that the repressed memory-traces of his primaeval experiences are not present in him in a bound state and are indeed in a sense incapable of obeying the secondary process. It is to this fact of not being bound, moreover, that they owe their capacity for forming, in conjunction with the residues of the previous day, a wishful phantasy that emerges in a dream. This same compulsion to repeat frequently meets us as an obstacle to our treatment when at the end of an analysis we try to induce the patient to detach himself completely from his physician. It may be presumed, too, that when people unfamiliar with analysis feel an obscure fear – a dread of rousing something that, so they feel, is better left sleeping – what they are afraid of at bottom is the emergence of this compulsion with its hint of possession by some 'daemonic' power.

But how is the predicate of being 'instinctual' related to the compulsion to repeat? At this point we cannot escape a suspicion that we may have come upon the track of a universal attribute of instincts and perhaps of organic life in general which has not hitherto been clearly recognized or at least not explicitly stressed. *It seems, then, that an instinct is an urge inherent in organic life to restore an earlier state of things* which the living entity has been obliged to abandon under the pressure of external disturbing forces; that is, it is a kind of organic elasticity, or, to put it another way, the expression of the inertia inherent in organic life.[1]

This view of instincts strikes us as strange because we have become used to see in them a factor impelling towards change and development, whereas we are now asked to recognize in them the precise contrary – an expression of the *conservative* nature of living substance. On the other hand we soon call to mind examples from animal life which seem to confirm the view that instincts are historically determined. Certain fishes, for instance, undertake laborious migrations at spawning-time in order to deposit their spawn in particular waters far removed from their customary haunts. In the opinion of many biologists what they are doing is merely to seek out the localities in which their species formerly resided but which in the course of time

---

[1] I have no doubt that similar notions as to the nature of 'instincts' have already been put forward repeatedly.

they have exchanged for others. The same explanation is believed to apply to the migratory flights of birds of passage – but we are quickly relieved of the necessity for seeking for further examples by the reflection that the most impressive proofs of there being an organic compulsion to repeat lie in the phenomena of heredity and the facts of embryology. We see how the germ of a living animal is obliged in the course of its development to recapitulate (even if only in a transient and abbreviated fashion) the structures of all the forms from which it is sprung, instead of proceeding quickly by the shortest path to its final shape. This behaviour is only to a very slight degree attributable to mechanical causes, and the historical explanation cannot accordingly be neglected. So too the power of regenerating a lost organ by growing afresh a precisely similar one extends far up into the animal kingdom.

We shall be met by the plausible objection that it may very well be that, in addition to the conservative instincts which impel towards repetition, there may be others which push forward towards progress and the production of new forms. This argument must certainly not be overlooked, and it will be taken into account at a later stage. But for the moment it is tempting to pursue to its logical conclusion the hypothesis that all instincts tend towards the restoration of an earlier state of things. The outcome may give an impression of mysticism or of sham profundity; but we can feel quite innocent of having had any such purpose in view. We seek only for the sober results of research or of reflection based on it; and we have no wish to find in those results any quality other than certainty.[1]

Let us suppose, then, that all the organic instincts are conservative, are acquired historically and tend towards the restoration of an earlier state of things. It follows that the phenomena of organic development must be attributed to external disturbing and diverting influences. The elementary living entity would from its very beginning have had no wish to change; if conditions remained the same, it would do no more than constantly repeat the same course of life. In the last resort, what has left its mark on the development of organisms must be the history of the earth we live in and of its relation to the sun. Every modification which is thus imposed upon the course of the organism's

---

[1] [*Footnote added* 1925:] The reader should not overlook the fact that what follows is the development of an extreme line of thought. Later on, when account is taken of the sexual instincts, it will be found that the necessary limitations and corrections are applied to it.

life is accepted by the conservative organic instincts and stored up for further repetition. Those instincts are therefore bound to give a deceptive appearance of being forces tending towards change and progress, whilst in fact they are merely seeking to reach an ancient goal by paths alike old and new. Moreover it is possible to specify this final goal of all organic striving. It would be in contradiction to the conservative nature of the instincts if the goal of life were a state of things which had never yet been attained. On the contrary, it must be an *old* state of things, an initial state from which the living entity has at one time or other departed and to which it is striving to return by the circuitous paths along which its development leads. If we are to take it as a truth that knows no exception that everything living dies for *internal* reasons – becomes inorganic once again – then we shall be compelled to say that '*the aim of all life is death*' and, looking backwards, that '*inanimate things existed before living ones*'.

The attributes of life were at some time evoked in inanimate matter by the action of a force of whose nature we can form no conception. It may perhaps have been a process similar in type to that which later caused the development of consciousness in a particular stratum of living matter. The tension which then arose in what had hitherto been an inanimate substance endeavoured to cancel itself out. In this way the first instinct came into being: the instinct to return to the inanimate state. It was still an easy matter at that time for a living substance to die; the course of its life was probably only a brief one, whose direction was determined by the chemical structure of the young life. For a long time, perhaps, living substance was thus being constantly created afresh and easily dying, till decisive external influences altered in such a way as to oblige the still surviving substance to diverge ever more widely from its original course of life and to make ever more complicated *détours* before reaching its aim of death. These circuitous paths to death, faithfully kept to by the conservative instincts, would thus present us to-day with the picture of the phenomena of life. If we firmly maintain the exclusively conservative nature of instincts, we cannot arrive at any other notions as to the origin and aim of life.

The implications in regard to the great groups of instincts which, as we believe, lie behind the phenomena of life in organisms must appear no less bewildering. The hypothesis of self-preservative instincts, such as we attribute to all living beings, stands in marked opposition to the idea that instinctual life as a whole serves to bring about death. Seen in this light, the theoretical importance of the instincts of self-preservation, of self-assertion and of mastery greatly diminishes. They are component instincts whose function it is to assure that the organism shall follow its own path to death, and to ward off any possible ways of returning to inorganic existence other than those which are immanent in the organism itself. We have no longer to reckon with the organism's puzzling determination (so hard to fit into any context) to maintain its own existence in the face of every obstacle. What we are left with is the fact that the organism wishes to die only in its own fashion. Thus these guardians of life, too, were originally the myrmidons of death. Hence arises the paradoxical situation that the living organism struggles most energetically against events (dangers, in fact) which might help it to attain its life's aim rapidly – by a kind of short-circuit. Such behaviour is, however, precisely what characterizes purely instinctual as contrasted with intelligent efforts.

But let us pause for a moment and reflect. It cannot be so. The sexual instincts, to which the theory of the neuroses gives a quite special place, appear under a very different aspect.

The external pressure which provokes a constantly increasing extent of development has not imposed itself upon *every* organism. Many have succeeded in remaining up to the present time at their lowly level. Many, though not all, such creatures, which must resemble the earliest stages of the higher animals and plants, are, indeed, living to-day. In the same way, the whole path of development to natural death is not trodden by *all* the elementary entities which compose the complicated body of one of the higher organisms. Some of them, the germ-cells, probably retain the original structure of living matter and, after a certain time, with their full complement of inherited and freshly acquired instinctual dispositions, separate themselves from the organism as a whole. These two characteristics may be precisely what enables them to have an independent existence. Under favourable conditions, they begin to develop – that is, to repeat the performance to which they owe their existence; and in the end once again one portion of their substance pursues its development to a finish, while another portion harks back once again as a fresh residual germ to the beginning of the process of development. These germ-cells, therefore, work against the death of the living substance and succeed in winning for it what we can only regard as potential immortality, though that may mean no more than a lengthening of the road to death. We must regard as in the highest degree significant the fact that this function of the germ-cell is reinforced, or only made possible, if it coalesces with another cell similar to itself and yet differing from it.

The instincts which watch over the destinies of these elementary organisms that survive the whole individual, which provide them with a safe shelter while they are defenceless against the stimuli of the external world, which bring about their meeting with other germ-cells, and so on – these constitute the group of the sexual instincts. They are conservative in the same sense as the other instincts in that they bring back earlier states of living substance; but they are conservative to a higher degree in that they are peculiarly resistant to external influences; and they are conservative too in another sense in that they preserve life itself for a comparatively long period.[1] They are the true life instincts. They operate against the purpose of the other instincts, which leads, by reason of their function, to death; and this fact indicates that there is an opposition between them and the other instincts, an opposition whose importance was long ago recognized by the theory of the neuroses. It is as though the life of the organism moved with a vacillating rhythm. One group of instincts rushes forward so as to reach the final aim of life as swiftly as possible; but when a particular stage in the advance has been reached, the other group jerks back to a certain point to make a fresh start and so prolong the journey. And even though it is certain that sexuality and the distinction between the sexes did not exist when life began, the possibility remains that the instincts which were later to be described as sexual may have been in operation from the very first, and it may not be true that it was only at a later time that they started upon their work of opposing the activities of the 'ego instincts'.[2]

Let us now hark back for a moment ourselves and consider whether there is any basis at all for these speculations. Is it really the case that, *apart from the sexual instincts*, there are no instincts that do not seek to restore an earlier state of things? that there are none that aim at a state of things which has never yet been attained? I know of no certain example from the organic world that would contradict the character-

---

[1] [*Footnote added* 1923:] Yet it is to them alone that we can attribute an internal impulse towards 'progress' and towards higher development! (See below.)

[2] [*Footnote added* 1925:] It should be understood from the context that the term 'ego instincts' is used here as a provisional description and derives from the earliest psycho-analytical terminology.

ization I have thus proposed. There is unquestionably no universal instinct towards higher development observable in the animal or plant world, even though it is undeniable that development does in fact occur in that direction. But on the one hand it is often merely a matter of opinion when we declare that one stage of development is higher than another, and on the other hand biology teaches us that higher development in one respect is very frequently balanced or outweighed by involution in another. Moreover there are plenty of animal forms from whose early stages we can infer that their development has, on the contrary, assumed a retrograde character. Both higher development and involution might well be the consequences of adaptation to the pressure of external forces; and in both cases the part played by instincts might be limited to the retention (in the form of an internal source of pleasure) of an obligatory modification.[1]

It may be difficult, too, for many of us, to abandon the belief that there is an instinct towards perfection at work in human beings, which has brought them to their present high level of intellectual achievement and ethical sublimation and which may be expected to watch over their development into supermen. I have no faith, however, in the existence of any such internal instinct and I cannot see how this benevolent illusion is to be preserved. The present development of human beings requires, as it seems to me, no different explanation from that of animals. What appears in a minority of human individuals as an untiring impulsion towards further perfection can easily be understood as a result of the instinctual repression upon which is based all that is most precious in human civilization. The repressed instinct never ceases to strive for complete satisfaction, which would consist in the repetition of a primary experience of satisfaction. No substitutive or reactive formations and no sublimations will suffice to remove the repressed instinct's persisting tension; and it is the difference in amount between the pleasure of satisfaction which is *demanded* and that which is actually *achieved* that provides the driving factor which will permit of no halting at any position attained, but, in the poet's words, *'ungebändigt immer vorwärts dringt'*.[2] The backward path that leads to complete satisfaction is as a rule obstructed by the

[1] Ferenczi (1913, 137) has reached the same conclusion along different lines: 'If this thought is pursued to its logical conclusion, one must make oneself familiar with the idea of a tendency to perseveration or regression dominating organic life as well, while the tendency to further development, to adaptation, etc., would become active only as a result of external stimuli.'

[2] ['Presses ever forward unsubdued.'] Mephistopheles in *Faust*, Part I [Scene 4].

resistances which maintain the repressions. So there is no alternative but to advance in the direction in which growth is still free – though with no prospect of bringing the process to a conclusion or of being able to reach the goal. The processes involved in the formation of a neurotic phobia, which is nothing else than an attempt at flight from the satisfaction of an instinct, present us with a model of the manner of origin of this supposititious 'instinct towards perfection' – an instinct which cannot possibly be attributed to *every* human being. The *dynamic* conditions for its development are, indeed, universally present; but it is only in rare cases that the *economic* situation appears to favour the production of the phenomenon.

I will add only a word to suggest that the efforts of Eros to combine organic substances into ever larger unities probably provide a substitute for this 'instinct towards perfection' whose existence we cannot admit. The phenomena that are attributed to it seem capable of explanation by these efforts of Eros taken in conjunction with the results of repression.[1]

VI

The upshot of our enquiry so far has been the drawing of a sharp distinction between the 'ego instincts' and the sexual instincts, and the view that the former exercise pressure towards death and the latter towards a prolongation of life. But this conclusion is bound to be unsatisfactory in many respects even to ourselves. Moreover, it is actually only of the former group of instincts that we can predicate a conservative, or rather retrograde, character corresponding to a compulsion to repeat. For on our hypothesis the ego instincts arise from the coming to life of inanimate matter and seek to restore the inanimate state; whereas as regards the sexual instincts, though it is true that they reproduce primitive states of the organism, what they are clearly aiming at by every possible means is the coalescence of two germ-cells which are differentiated in a particular way. If this union is not effected, the germ-cells dies along with all the other elements of the multicellular organism. It is only on this condition that the sexual function can prolong the cell's life and lend it the appearance of immortality. But what is the important event in the development of living substance which is being repeated in sexual reproduction, or in

---

[1] [This paragraph, added in 1923, anticipates the account of Eros given on pp. 256 ff. below.]

its fore-runner, the conjugation of two protista? We cannot say; and we should consequently feel relieved if the whole structure of our argument turned out to be mistaken. The opposition between the ego or death instincts and the sexual or life instincts would then cease to hold and the compulsion to repeat would no longer possess the importance we have ascribed to it.

Let us turn back, then, to one of the assumptions that we have already made, with the expectation that we shall be able to give it a categorical denial. We have drawn far-reaching conclusions from the hypothesis that all living substance is bound to die from internal causes. We made this assumption thus carelessly because it does not seem to us to *be* an assumption. We are accustomed to think that such is the fact, and we are strengthened in our thought by the writings of our poets. Perhaps we have adopted the belief because there is some comfort in it. If we are to die ourselves, and first to lose in death those who are dearest to us, it is easier to submit to a remorseless law of nature, to the sublime 'Ανάγκη [Necessity], than to a chance which might perhaps have been escaped. It may be, however, that this belief in the internal necessity of dying is only another of those illusions which we have created '*um die Schwere des Daseins zu ertragen*'.[1] It is certainly not a primaeval belief. The notion of 'natural death' is quite foreign to primitive races; they attribute every death that occurs among them to the influence of an enemy or of an evil spirit. We must therefore turn to biology in order to test the validity of the belief.

If we do so, we may be astonished to find how little agreement there is among biologists on the subject of natural death and in fact that the whole concept of death melts away under their hands. The fact that there is a fixed average duration of life at least among the higher animals naturally argues in favour of there being such a thing as death from natural causes. But this impression is countered when we consider that certain large animals and certain gigantic arboreal growths reach a very advanced age and one which cannot at present be computed. In the large-scale conception of Wilhelm Fliess [1906], all the phenomena of life exhibited by organisms – and also, no doubt, their death – are linked with the completion of fixed periods, which express the dependence of two kinds of living substance (one male and the other female) upon the solar year. When we see, however, how easily and how extensively the influence of external forces is able to

---

[1] ['To bear the burden of existence.' (Schiller, *Die Braut von Messina*, I, 8.]

modify the date of the appearance of vital phenomena (especially in the plant world) – to precipitate them or hold them back – doubts must be cast upon the rigidity of Fliess's formulas or at least upon whether the laws laid down by him are the sole determining factors.

The greatest interest attaches from our point of view to the treatment given to the subject of the duration of life and the death of organisms in the writings of Weismann (1882, 1884, 1892, etc.) It was he who introduced the division of living substance into mortal and immortal parts. The mortal part is the body in the narrower sense – the 'soma' – which alone is subject to natural death. The germ-cells, on the other hand, are potentially immortal, in so far as they are able, under certain favourable conditions, to develop into a new individual, or, in other words, to surround themselves with a new soma. (Weismann, 1884).

What strikes us in this is the unexpected analogy with our own view, which was arrived at along such a different path. Weismann, regarding living substance morphologically, sees in it one portion which is destined to die – the soma, the body apart from the substance concerned with sex and inheritance – and an immortal portion – the germ-plasm, which is concerned with the survival of the species, with reproduction. We, on the other hand, dealing not with the living substance but with the forces operating in it, have been led to distinguish two kinds of instincts: those which seek to lead what is living to death, and others, the sexual instincts, which are perpetually attempting and achieving a renewal of life. This sounds like a dynamic corollary to Weismann's morphological theory.

But the appearance of a significant correspondence is dissipated as soon as we discover Weismann's views on the problem of death. For he only relates the distinction between the mortal soma and the immortal germ-plasm to *multicellular* organisms; in unicellular organisms the individual and the reproductive cell are still one and the same (Weismann, 1882, 38). Thus he considers that unicellular organisms are potentially immortal, and that death only makes its appearance with the multicellular metazoa. It is true that this death of the higher organisms is a natural one, a death from internal causes; but it is not founded on any primal characteristic of living substance (Weismann, 1884, 84) and cannot be regarded as an absolute necessity with its basis in the very nature of life (Weismann, 1882, 33). Death is rather a matter of expediency, a manifestation of adaptation to the external conditions of life; for, when once the cells of the body have been

divided into soma and germ-plasm, an unlimited duration of individual life would become a quite pointless luxury. When this differentiation had been made in the multicellular organisms, death
became possible and expedient. Since then, the soma of the higher
organisms has died at fixed periods for internal reasons, while the
protista have remained immortal. It is not the case, on the other hand,
that reproduction was only introduced at the same time as death. On
the contrary, it is a primal characteristic of living matter, like growth
(from which it originated), and life has been continuous from its first
beginning upon earth. (Weismann, 1884, 84 f.)

It will be seen at once that to concede in this way that higher
organisms have a natural death is of very little help to us. For if death
is a *late* acquisition of organisms, then there can be no question of
there having been death instincts from the very beginning of life on
this earth. Multicellular organisms may die for internal reasons,
owing to defective differentiation or to imperfections in their metabolism, but the matter is of no interest from the point of view of our
problem. An account of the origin of death such as this is moreover far
less at variance with our habitual modes of thought than the strange
assumption of 'death instincts'.

The discussion which followed upon Weismann's suggestions led,
so far as I can see, to no conclusive results in any direction.[1] Some
writers returned to the views of Goette (1883), who regarded death as
a direct result of reproduction. Hartmann (1906, 29) does not regard
the appearance of a 'dead body' – a dead portion of the living
substance – as the criterion of death, but defines death as 'the
termination of individual development'. In this sense protozoa too are
mortal; in their case death always coincides with reproduction, but is
to some extent obscured by it, since the whole substance of the parent
animal may be transmitted directly into the young offspring.

Soon afterwards research was directed to the experimental testing
on unicellular organisms of the alleged immortality of living substance. An American biologist, Woodruff, experimenting with a
ciliate infusorian, the 'slipper-animalcule', which reproduces by
fission into two individuals, persisted until the 3029th generation (at
which point he broke off the experiment), isolating one of the part-
products on each occasion and placing it in fresh water [Woodruff,
1914]. This remote descendant of the first slipper-animalcule was just

[1] Cf. Hartmann (1906), Lipschütz (1914) and Doflein (1919).

as lively as its ancestor and showed no signs of ageing or degeneration. Thus, in so far as figures of this kind prove anything, the immortality of the protista seemed to be experimentally demonstrable.[1]

Other experimenters arrived at different results. Maupas [1888], Calkins [1902] and others, in contrast to Woodruff, found that after a certain number of divisions these infusoria become weaker, diminish in size, suffer the loss of some part of their organization and eventually die, unless certain recuperative measures are applied to them. If this is so, protozoa would appear to die after a phase of senescence exactly like the higher animals – thus completely contradicting Weismann's assertion that death is a late acquisition of living organisms.

From the aggregate of these experiments two facts emerge which seem to offer us a firm footing.

First: If two of the animalculae, at the moment before they show signs of senescence, are able to coalesce with each other, that is to 'conjugate' (soon after which they once more separate), they are saved from growing old and become 'rejuvenated'. Conjugation is no doubt the fore-runner of the sexual reproduction of higher creatures; it is as yet unconnected with propagation and is limited to the mixing of the substances of the two individuals. (Weismann's 'amphimixis'.) The recuperative effects of conjugation can, however, be replaced by certain stimulating agents, by alterations in the composition of the fluid which provides their nourishment, by raising their temperature or by shaking them. We are reminded of the celebrated experiment made by J. Loeb [1909], in which, by means of certain chemical stimuli, he induced segmentation in sea-urchins' eggs – a process which can normally occur only after fertilization.

Secondly: It is probable nevertheless that infusoria die a natural death as a result of their own vital processes. For the contradiction between Woodruff's findings and the others is due to his having provided each generation with fresh nutrient fluid. If he omitted to do so, he observed the same signs of senescence as the other experimenters. He concluded that the animalculae were injured by the products of metabolism which they extruded into the surrounding fluid. He was then able to prove conclusively that it was only the products of its *own* metabolism which had fatal results for the particular kind of animalcule. For the same animalculae which inevitably perished if they were crowded together in their own

[1] For this and what follows see Lipschütz (1914, 26 and 52 ff.).

nutrient fluid flourished in a solution which was over-saturated with the waste products of a distantly related species. An infusorian, therefore, if it is left to itself, dies a natural death owing to its incomplete voidance of the products of its own metabolism. (It may be that the same incapacity is the ultimate cause of the death of all higher animals as well.)

At this point the question may well arise in our minds whether any object whatever is served by trying to solve the problem of natural death from a study of the protozoa. The primitive organization of these creatures may conceal from our eyes important conditions which, though in fact present in them too, only become *visible* in higher animals where they are able to find morphological expression. And if we abandon the morphological point of view and adopt the dynamic one, it becomes a matter of complete indifference to us whether natural death can be shown to occur in protozoa or not. The substance which is later recognized as being immortal has not yet become separated in them from the mortal one. The instinctual forces which seek to conduct life into death may also be operating in protozoa from the first, and yet their effects may be so completely concealed by the life-preserving forces that it may be very hard to find any direct evidence of their presence. We have seen, moreover, that the observations made by biologists allow us to assume that internal processes of this kind leading to death do occur also in protista. But even if protista turned out to be immortal in Weismann's sense, his assertion that death is a late acquisition would apply only to its *manifest* phenomena and would not make impossible the assumption of processes *tending* towards it.

Thus our expectation that biology would flatly contradict the recognition of death instincts has not been fulfilled. We are at liberty to continue concerning ourselves with their possibility, if we have other reasons for doing so. The striking similarity between Weismann's distinction of soma and germ-plasm and our separation of the death instincts from the life instincts persists and retains its significance.

We may pause for a moment over this pre-eminently dualistic view of instinctual life. According to E. Hering's [1878] theory, two kinds of processes are constantly at work in living substance, operating in contrary directions, one constructive or assimilatory and the other destructive or dissimilatory. May we venture to recognize in these two directions taken by the vital processes the activity of our two instinctual impulses, the life instincts and death instincts? There is something else, at any rate, that we cannot remain blind to. We have unwittingly steered our course into the harbour of Schopenhauer's philosophy. For him death is the 'true result and to that extent the purpose of life',[1] while the sexual instinct is the embodiment of the will to live.

Let us make a bold attempt at another step forward. It is generally considered that the union of a number of cells into a vital association – the multicellular character of organisms – has become a means of prolonging their life. One cell helps to preserve the life of another, and the community of cells can survive even if individual cells have to die. We have already heard that conjugation, too, the temporary co-alescence of two unicellular organisms, has a life-preserving and rejuvenating effect on both of them. Accordingly, we might attempt to apply the libido theory which has been arrived at in psycho-analysis to the mutual relationship of cells. We might suppose that the life instincts or sexual instincts which are active in each cell take the other cells as their object, that they partly neutralize the death instincts (that is, the processes set up by them) in those cells and thus preserve their life; while the other cells do the same for *them*, and still others sacrifice themselves in the performance of this libidinal function. The germ-cells themselves would behave in a completely 'narcissistic' fashion – to use the phrase that we are accustomed to use in the theory of the neuroses to describe a whole individual who retains his libido in his ego and pays none of it out in object-cathexes. The germ-cells require their libido, the activity of their life instincts, for themselves, as a reserve against their later momentous constructive activity. (The cells of the malignant neoplasms which destroy the organism should also perhaps be described as narcissistic in this same sense: pathology is prepared to regard their germs as innate and to ascribe embryonic attributes to them.) In this way the libido of our sexual instincts would coincide with the Eros of the poets and philosophers which holds all living things together.

Here then is an opportunity for looking back over the slow develop-ment of our libido theory. In the first instance the analysis of the transference neuroses forced upon our notice the opposition between the 'sexual instincts', which are directed towards an object, and certain other instincts, with which we were very insufficiently ac-

[1] Schopenhauer (1851; *Sämtliche Werke*, ed. Hübscher, 1938, 5, 236).

quainted and which we described provisionally as the 'ego-instincts'.[1] A foremost place among these was necessarily given to the instincts serving the self-preservation of the individual. It was impossible to say what other distinctions were to be drawn among them. No knowledge would have been more valuable as a foundation for true psychological science than an approximate grasp of the common characteristics and possible distinctive features of the instincts. But in no region of psychology were we groping more in the dark. Everyone assumed the existence of as many instincts or 'basic instincts' as he chose, and juggled with them like the ancient Greek natural philosophers with their four elements – earth, air, fire and water. Psychoanalysis, which could not escape making *some* assumption about the instincts, kept at first to the popular division of instincts typified in the phrase 'hunger and love'. At least there was nothing arbitrary in this; and by its help the analysis of the psychoneuroses was carried forward quite a distance. The concept of 'sexuality', and at the same time of the sexual instinct, had, it is true, to be extended so as to cover many things which could not be classed under the reproductive function; and this caused no little hubbub in an austere, respectable or merely hypocritical world.

The next step was taken when psycho-analysis felt its way closer towards the psychological ego, which it had first come to know only as a repressive, censoring agency, capable of erecting protective structures and reactive formations. Critical and far-seeing minds had, it is true, long since objected to the concept of libido being restricted to the energy of the sexual instincts directed towards an object. But they failed to explain how they had arrived at their better knowledge or to derive from it anything of which analysis could make use. Advancing more cautiously, psycho-analysis observed the regularity with which libido is withdrawn from the object and directed on to the ego (the process of introversion); and, by studying the libidinal development of children in its earliest phases, came to the conclusion that the ego is the true and original reservoir of libido,[2] and that it is only from that reservoir that libido is extended on to objects. The ego now found its position among sexual objects and was at once given the foremost place among them. Libido which was in this way lodged in the ego was described as 'narcissistic'.[3] This narcissistic libido was of course

---

[1] [Cf. footnote 1 on p. 265 below.]
[2] [See Freud (1914c), and a correction on p. 454 *n.* 1 below.]
[3] See my paper on narcissism (1914c) [Section I].

also a manifestation of the force of the sexual instinct in the analytical sense of those words, and it had necessarily to be identified with the 'self-preservative instincts' whose existence had been recognized from the first. Thus the original opposition between the ego instincts and the sexual instincts proved to be inadequate. A portion of the ego instincts was seen to be libidinal; sexual instincts – probably along-side others – operated in the ego. Nevertheless we are justified in saying that the old formula which lays it down that psychoneuroses are based on a conflict between ego-instincts and sexual instincts contains nothing that we need reject to-day. It is merely that the distinction between the two kinds of instinct, which was originally regarded as in some sort of way *qualitative*, must now be characterized differently – namely as being *topographical*. And in particular it is still true that the transference neuroses, the essential subject of psycho-analytic study, are the result of a conflict between the ego and the libidinal cathexis of objects.

But it is all the more necessary for us to lay stress upon the libidinal character of the self-preservative instincts now that we are venturing upon the further step of recognizing the sexual instinct as Eros, the preserver of all things, and of deriving the narcissistic libido of the ego from the stores of libido by means of which the cells of the soma are attached to one another. But we now find ourselves suddenly faced by another question. If the self-preservative instincts too are of a libidinal nature, are there perhaps no other instincts whatever but the libidinal ones? At all events there are none other visible. But in that case we shall after all be driven to agree with the critics who suspected from the first that psycho-analysis explains *everything* by sexuality, or with innovators like Jung who, making a hasty judgement, have used the word 'libido' to mean instinctual force in general. Must not this be so?

It was not our *intention* at all events to produce such a result. Our argument had as its point of departure a sharp distinction between ego instincts, which we equated with death instincts, and sexual instincts, which we equated with life instincts. (We were prepared at one stage to include the so-called self-preservative instincts of the ego among the death instincts; but we subsequently corrected ourselves on this point and withdrew it.) Our views have from the very first been *dualistic*, and to-day they are even more definitely dualistic than before – now that we describe the opposition as being, not between ego instincts and sexual instincts but between life instincts and death instincts. Jung's libido theory is on the contrary *monistic*; the fact that he has called his one instinctual force 'libido' is bound to cause confusion, but need not affect us otherwise. We suspect that instincts other than those of self-preservation operate in the ego, and it ought to be possible for us to point to them. Unfortunately, however, the analysis of the ego has made so little headway that it is very difficult for us to do so. It is possible, indeed, that the libidinal instincts in the ego may be linked in a peculiar manner[1] with these other ego instincts which are still strange to us. Even before we had any clear under-standing of narcissism, psycho-analysts had a suspicion that the 'ego instincts' had libidinal components attached to them. But these are very uncertain possibilities, to which our opponents will pay very little attention. The difficulty remains that psycho-analysis has not enabled us hitherto to point to any [ego] instincts other than the libidinal ones. That, however, is no reason for our falling in with the conclusion that no others in fact exist.

In the obscurity that reigns at present in the theory of the instincts, it would be unwise to reject any idea that promises to throw light on it. We started out from the great opposition between the life and death instincts. Now object-love itself presents us with a second example of a similar polarity – that between love (or affection) and hate (or aggressiveness). If only we could succeed in relating these two polarities to each other and in deriving one from the other! From the very first we recognized the presence of a sadistic component in the sexual instinct.[2] As we know, it can make itself independent and can, in the form of a perversion, dominate an individual's entire sexual activity. It also emerges as a predominant component instinct in one of the 'pregenital organizations', as I have named them. But how can the sadistic instinct, whose aim it is to injure the object, be derived from Eros, the preserver of life? Is it not plausible to suppose that this sadism is in fact a death instinct which, under the influence of the narcissistic libido, has been forced away from the ego and has consequently only emerged in relation to the object? It now enters the service of the sexual function. During the oral stage of organization of the libido, the act of obtaining erotic mastery over an object coincides with that object's destruction; later, the sadistic instinct separates off, and finally, at the stage of genital primacy, it takes on, for the

---

[1] [In the first edition only: '– by instinctual "confluence", to borrow a term used by Adler [1908] –'.]

[2] This was already so in the first edition of *Three Essays on the Theory of Sexuality* in 1905. [See pp. 301–3 below.]

purposes of reproduction, the function of overpowering the sexual object to the extent necessary for carrying out the sexual act. It might indeed be said that the sadism which has been forced out of the ego has pointed the way for the libidinal components of the sexual instinct, and that these follow after it to the object. Wherever the original sadism has undergone no mitigation or intermixture, we find the familiar ambivalence of love and hate in erotic life.[1]

If such an assumption as this is permissible, then we have met the demand that we should produce an example of a death instinct – though, it is true, a displaced one. But this way of looking at things is very far from being easy to grasp and creates a positively mystical impression. It looks suspiciously as though we were trying to find a way out of a highly embarrassing situation at any price. We may recall, however, that there is nothing new in an assumption of this kind. We put one forward on an earlier occasion, before there was any question of an embarrassing situation. Clinical observations led us at that time to the view that masochism, the component instinct which is complementary to sadism, must be regarded as sadism that has been turned round upon the subject's own ego.[2] But there is no difference in principle between an instinct turning from an object to the ego and its turning from the ego to an object – which is the new point now under discussion. Masochism, the turning round of the instinct upon the subject's own ego, would in that case be a return to an earlier phase of the instinct's history, a regression. The account that was formerly given of masochism requires emendation as being too sweeping in one respect: there *might* be such a thing as primary masochism – a possibility which I had contested at that time.[3]

Let us, however, return to the self-preservative sexual instincts. The experiments upon protista have already shown us that conjugation – that is, the coalescence of two individuals which separate soon

---

[1] [This foreshadows Freud's discussion of instinctual 'fusion' in *The Ego and the Id* (1923b), Chapter 6 below.]

[2] See my *Three Essays* (1905d) [p. 302 n.1 below]; and 'Instincts and their Vicissitudes' (1915c) [p. 206 above].

[3] A considerable portion of these speculations have been anticipated by Sabina Spielrein (1912) in an instructive and interesting paper which, however, is unfortunately not entirely clear to me. She there describes the sadistic components of the sexual instinct as 'destructive'. A. Stärcke (1914), again, has attempted to identify the concept of libido itself with the biological concept (assumed on theoretical grounds) of an impetus towards death. See also Rank (1907). All these discussions, like that in the text, give evidence of the demand for a clarification of the theory of the instincts such as has not yet been achieved.

afterwards without any subsequent cell-division occurring – has a strengthening and rejuvenating effect upon both of them.[1] In later generations they show no signs of degenerating and seem able to put up a longer resistance to the injurious effects of their own metabolism. This single observation may, I think, be taken as typical of the effect produced by sexual union as well. But how is it that the coalescence of two only slightly different cells can bring about this renewal of life? The experiment which replaces the conjugation of protozoa by the application of chemical or even of mechanical stimuli (cf. Lipschütz, 1914) enables us to give what is no doubt a conclusive reply to this question. The result is brought about by the influx of fresh amounts of stimulus. This tallies well with the hypothesis that the life process of the individual leads for internal reasons to an abolition of chemical tensions, that is to say, to death, whereas union with the living substance of a different individual increases those tensions, introducing what may be described as fresh 'vital differences' which must then be lived off. As regards this dissimilarity there must of course be one or more optima. The dominating tendency of mental life, and perhaps of nervous life in general, is the effort to reduce, to keep constant or to remove internal tension due to stimuli (the 'Nirvana principle', to borrow a term from Barbara Low [1920, 73]) – a tendency which finds expression in the pleasure principle;[2] and our recognition of that fact is one of our strongest reasons for believing in the existence of death instincts.

But we still feel our line of thought appreciably hampered by the fact that we cannot ascribe to the sexual instinct the characteristic of a compulsion to repeat which first put us on the track of the death instincts. The sphere of embryonic developmental processes is no doubt extremely rich in such phenomena of repetition; the two germ-cells that are involved in sexual reproduction and their life history are themselves only repetitions of the beginnings of organic life. But the essence of the processes to which sexual life is directed is the coalescence of two cell-bodies. That alone is what guarantees the immortality of the living substance in the higher organisms.

In other words, we need more information on the origin of sexual reproduction and of the sexual instincts in general. This is a problem which is calculated to daunt an outsider and which the specialists

---

[1] See the account quoted above, p. 254 from Lipschütz (1914).
[2] [The whole topic is further considered in 'The Economic Problem of Masochism' (1924c).]

themselves have not yet been able to solve. We shall therefore give only the briefest summary of whatever seems relevant to our line of thought from among the many discordant assertions and opinions.

One of these views deprives the problem of reproduction of its mysterious fascination by representing it as a part manifestation of growth. (Cf. multiplication by fission, sprouting or gemmation.) The origin of reproduction by sexually differentiated germ-cells might be pictured along sober Darwinian lines by supposing that the advantage of amphimixis, arrived at on some occasion by the chance conjugation of two protista, was retained and further exploited in later development.[1] On this view 'sex' would not be anything very ancient; and the extraordinarily violent instincts whose aim it is to bring about sexual union would be repeating something that had once occurred by chance and had since become established as being advantageous.

The question arises here, as in the case of death, whether we do right in ascribing to protista those characteristics alone which they actually exhibit, and whether it is correct to assume that forces and processes which become visible only in the higher organisms originated in those organisms for the first time. The view of sexuality we have just mentioned is of little help for our purposes. The objection may be raised against it that it postulates the existence of life instincts already operating in the simplest organisms; for otherwise conjugation, which works counter to the course of life and makes the task of ceasing to live more difficult, would not be retained and elaborated but would be avoided. If, therefore, we are not to abandon the hypothesis of death instincts, we must suppose them to be associated from the very first with life instincts. But it must be admitted that in that case we shall be working upon an equation with two unknown quantities.

Apart from this, science has so little to tell us about the origin of sexuality that we can liken the problem to a darkness into which not so much as a ray of a hypothesis has penetrated. In quite a different region, it is true, we *do* meet with such a hypothesis; but it is of so fantastic a kind – a myth rather than a scientific explanation – that I

[1] Though Weismann (1892) denies this advantage as well: 'In no case does fertilization correspond to a rejuvenescence or renewal of life, nor is its occurrence necessary in order that life may endure: it is merely an arrangement which renders possible the intermingling of two different hereditary tendencies.' He nevertheless believes that an intermingling of this kind leads to an increase in the variability of the organism concerned.

should not venture to produce it here, were it not that it fulfils precisely the one condition whose fulfilment we desire. For it traces the origin of an instinct to *a need to restore an earlier state of things*.

What I have in mind is, of course, the theory which Plato put into the mouth of Aristophanes in the *Symposium*, and which deals not only with the *origin* of the sexual instinct but also with the most important of its variations in relation to its object. 'The original human nature was not like the present, but different. In the first place, the sexes were originally three in number, not two as they are now; there was man, woman, and the union of the two . . .' Everything about these primaeval men was double: they had four hands and four feet, two faces, two privy parts, and so on. Eventually Zeus decided to cut these men in two, 'like a sorb-apple which is halved for pickling'. After the division had been made, 'the two parts of man, each desiring his other half, came together, and threw their arms about one another eager to grow into one'.[1]

Shall we follow the hint given us by the poet-philosopher, and venture upon the hypothesis that living substance at the time of its coming to life was torn apart into small particles, which have ever since endeavoured to reunite through the sexual instincts? that these instincts, in which the chemical affinity of inanimate matter persisted, gradually succeeded, as they developed through the kingdom of the

[1] [Jowett's translation. *Footnote added* 1921:] I have to thank Professor Heinrich Gomperz, of Vienna, for the following discussion on the origin of the Platonic myth, which I give partly in his own words. It is to be remarked that what is essentially the same theory is already to be found in the Upanishads. For we find the following passage in the *Brihadâranyaka-upanishad*, 1, 4, 3 [Max-Müller's translation, 2, 85 f.], where the origin of the world from the Atman (the Self or Ego) is described: 'But he felt no delight. Therefore a man who is lonely feels no delight. He wished for a second. He was so large as man and wife together. He then made this his Self to fall in two, and then arose husband and wife. Therefore Yagñavalkya said: "We two are thus (each of us) like half a shell." Therefore the void which was there, is filled by the wife.'

The *Brihadâranyaka-upanishad* is the most ancient of all the Upanishads, and no competent authority dates it later than about the year 800 BC. In contradiction to the prevailing opinion, I should hesitate to give an unqualified denial to the possibility of Plato's myth being derived, even if it were only indirectly, from the Indian source, since a similar possibility cannot be excluded in the case of the doctrine of transmigration. But even if a derivation of this kind (through the Pythagoreans in the first instance) were established, the significance of the coincidence between the two trains of thought would scarcely be diminished. For Plato would not have adopted a story of this kind which had somehow reached him through some oriental tradition – to say nothing of giving it so important a place – unless it had struck him as containing an element of truth.

In a paper devoted to a systematic examination of this line of thought before the time of Plato, Ziegler (1913) traces it back to Babylonian origins.

protista, in overcoming the difficulties put in the way of that endeavour by an environment charged with dangerous stimuli – stimuli which compelled them to form a protective cortical layer? that these splintered fragments of living substance in this way attained a multicellular condition and finally transferred the instinct for reuniting, in the most highly concentrated form, to the germ-cells? – But here, I think, the moment has come for breaking off.

Not, however, without the addition of a few words of critical reflection. It may be asked whether and how far I am myself convinced of the truth of the hypotheses that have been set out in these pages. My answer would be that I am not convinced myself and that I do not seek to persuade other people to believe in them. Or, more precisely, that I do not know how far I believe in them. There is no reason, as it seems to me, why the emotional factor of conviction should enter into this question at all. It is surely possible to throw oneself into a line of thought and to follow it wherever it leads out of simple scientific curiosity, or, if the reader prefers, as an *advocatus diaboli*, who is not on that account himself sold to the devil. I do not dispute the fact that the third step in the theory of the instincts, which I have taken here, cannot lay claim to the same degree of certainty as the two earlier ones – the extension of the concept of sexuality and the hypothesis of narcissism. These two innovations were a direct translation of observation into theory and were no more open to sources of error than is inevitable in all such cases. It is true that my assertion of the regressive character of instincts also rests upon observed material – namely on the facts of the compulsion to repeat. It may be, however, that I have overestimated their significance. And in any case it is impossible to pursue an idea of this kind except by repeatedly combining factual material with what is purely speculative and thus diverging widely from empirical observation. The more frequently this is done in the course of constructing a theory, the more untrustworthy, as we know, must be the final result. But the degree of uncertainty is not assignable. One may have made a lucky hit or one may have gone shamefully astray. I do not think a large part is played by what is called 'intuition' in work of this kind. From what I have seen of intuition, it seems to me to be the product of a kind of intellectual impartiality. Unfortunately, however, people are seldom impartial where ultimate things, the great problems of science and life, are concerned. Each of us is governed in such cases by deep-rooted internal prejudices, into whose hands our speculation unwittingly plays. Since we have such good grounds for being distrustful, our attitude towards the results of our own deliberations cannot well be other than one of cool benevolence. I hasten to add, however, that self-criticism such as this is far from binding one to any special tolerance towards dissentient opinions. It is perfectly legitimate to reject remorselessly theories which are contradicted by the very first steps in the analysis of observed facts, while yet being aware at the same time that the validity of one's own theory is only a provisional one.

We need not feel greatly disturbed in judging our speculation upon the life and death instincts by the fact that so many bewildering and obscure processes occur in it – such as one instinct being driven out by another or an instinct turning from the ego to an object, and so on. This is merely due to our being obliged to operate with the scientific terms, that is to say with the figurative language, peculiar to psychology (or, more precisely, to depth psychology). We could not otherwise describe the processes in question at all, and indeed we could not have become aware of them. The deficiencies in our description would probably vanish if we were already in a position to replace the psychological terms by physiological or chemical ones. It is true that they too are only part of a figurative language; but it is one with which we have long been familiar and which is perhaps a simpler one as well.

On the other hand it should be made quite clear that the uncertainty of our speculation has been greatly increased by the necessity for borrowing from the science of biology. Biology is truly a land of unlimited possibilities. We may expect it to give us the most surprising information and we cannot guess what answers it will return in a few dozen years to the questions we have put to it. They may be of a kind which will blow away the whole of our artificial structure of hypotheses. If so, it may be asked why I have embarked upon such a line of thought as the present one, and in particular why I have decided to make it public. Well – I cannot deny that some of the analogies, correlations and connections which it contains seemed to me to deserve consideration.[1]

---

[1] I will add a few words to clarify our terminology, which has undergone some development in the course of the present work. We came to know what the 'sexual instincts' were from their relation to the sexes and to the reproductive function. We retained this name after we had been obliged by the findings of psycho-analysis to connect them less closely with reproduction. With the hypothesis of narcissistic libido

VII

If it is really the case that seeking to restore an earlier state of things is such a universal characteristic of instincts, we need not be surprised that so many processes take place in mental life independently of the pleasure principle. This characteristic would be shared by all the component instincts and in their case would aim at returning once more to a particular stage in the course of development. These are matters over which the pleasure principle has as yet no control; but it does not follow that any of them are necessarily opposed to it, and we have still to solve the problem of the relation of the instinctual processes of repetition to the dominance of the pleasure principle.

We have found that one of the earliest and most important functions of the mental apparatus is to bind the instinctual impulses which impinge on it, to replace the primary process prevailing in them by the secondary process and convert their freely mobile cathectic energy into a mainly quiescent (tonic) cathexis. While this transformation is taking place no attention can be paid to the development of un-pleasure; but this does not imply the suspension of the pleasure principle. On the contrary, the transformation occurs on *behalf* of the

---

footnote continued

and the extension of the concept of libido to the individual cells, the sexual instinct was transformed for us into Eros, which seeks to force together and hold together the portions of living substance. What are commonly called the sexual instincts are looked upon by us as the part of Eros which is directed towards objects. Our speculations have suggested that Eros operates from the beginning of life and appears as a 'life instinct' in opposition to the 'death instinct' which was brought into being by the coming to life of inorganic substance. These speculations seek to solve the riddle of life by supposing that these two instincts were struggling with each other from the very first. [*Added* 1921:] It is not so easy, perhaps, to follow the transformations through which the concept of the 'ego instincts' has passed. To begin with we applied that name to all the instinctual trends (of which we had no closer knowledge) which could be distinguished from the sexual instincts directed towards an object; and we opposed the ego instincts to the sexual instincts of which the libido is the manifestation. Subsequently we came to closer grips with the analysis of the ego and recognized that a portion of the 'ego instincts' is also of a libidinal character and has taken the subject's own ego as its object. These narcissistic self-preservative instincts had thenceforward to be counted among the libidinal sexual instincts. The opposition between the ego instincts and the sexual instincts was transformed into one between the ego instincts and the object-instincts, both of a libidinal nature. But in its place a fresh opposition appeared between the libidinal (ego and object) instincts and others, which must be presumed to be present in the ego and which may perhaps actually be observed in the destructive instincts. Our speculations have transformed this opposition into one between the life instincts (Eros) and the death instincts.

pleasure principle; the binding is a preparatory act which introduces and assures the dominance of the pleasure principle.

Let us make a sharper distinction than we have hitherto made between function and tendency. The pleasure principle, then, is a tendency operating in the service of a function whose business it is to free the mental apparatus entirely from excitation or to keep the amount of excitation in it constant or to keep it as low as possible. We cannot yet decide with certainty in favour of any of these ways of putting it; but it is clear that the function thus described would be concerned with the most universal endeavour of all living substance – namely to return to the quiescence of the inorganic world. We have all experienced how the greatest pleasure attainable by us, that of the sexual act, is associated with a momentary extinction of a highly intensified excitation. The binding of an instinctual impulse would be a preliminary function designed to prepare the excitation for its final elimination in the pleasure of discharge.

This raises the question of whether feelings of pleasure and un-pleasure can be produced equally from bound and from unbound excitatory processes. And there seems to be no doubt whatever that the unbound or primary processes give rise to far more intense feelings in both directions than the bound or secondary ones. Moreover the primary processes are the earlier in time; at the beginning of mental life there are no others, and we may infer that if the pleasure principle had not already been operative in *them* it could never have been established for the later ones. We thus reach what is at bottom no very simple conclusion, namely that at the beginning of mental life the struggle for pleasure was far more intense than later but not so unrestricted: it had to submit to frequent interruptions. In later times the dominance of the pleasure principle is very much more secure, but it itself has no more escaped the process of taming than the other instincts in general. In any case, whatever it is that causes the appearance of feelings of pleasure and unpleasure in processes of excitation must be present in the secondary process just as it is in the primary one.

Here might be the starting-point for fresh investigations. Our consciousness communicates to us feelings from within not only of pleasure and unpleasure but also of a peculiar tension which in its turn can be either pleasurable or unpleasurable. Should the difference between these feelings enable us to distinguish between bound and unbound processes of energy? or is the feeling of tension to be related to the absolute magnitude, or perhaps to the level, of the cathexis, while the pleasure and unpleasure series indicates a change in the magnitude of the cathexis *within a given unit of time*? Another striking fact is that the life instincts have so much more contact with our internal perception – emerging as breakers of the peace and constantly producing tensions whose release is felt as pleasure – while the death instincts seem to do their work unobtrusively. The pleasure principle seems actually to serve the death instincts. It is true that it keeps watch upon stimuli from without, which are regarded as dangers by both kinds of instincts; but it is more especially on guard against increases of stimulation from within, which would make the task of living more difficult. This in turn raises a host of other questions to which we can at present find no answer. We must be patient and await fresh methods and occasions of research. We must be ready, too, to abandon a path that we have followed for a time, if it seems to be leading to no good end. Only believers, who demand that science shall be a substitute for the catechism they have given up, will blame an investigator for developing or even transforming his views. We may take comfort, too, for the slow advances of our scientific knowledge in the words of the poet:

> Was man nicht erfliegen kann, muss man erhinken.
> . . . .
> Die Schrift sagt, es ist keine Sünde zu hinken.[1]

---

[1] ['What we cannot reach flying we must reach limping. . . . The Book tells us it is no sin to limp.' The last lines of 'Die beiden Gulden', a version by Rückert of one of the *Maqâmât* of al-Hariri.]

Five

HUMAN SEXUALITY

Introduction

The scientific readers in Freud's times may have been put off by his assumption of an unconscious psychic life and his supposition of a dualistic instinct theory. But these reactions were far from evoking the hostilities that, beginning with the investigation of human sexuality, decided the fate of psycho-analysis.

Even the first surmises that sexual impulses might be at the bottom of hysterical symptoms cost Freud the collaboration and friendship of Josef Breuer, who in the pioneering treatment of his patient Anna O. uncovered the previously unrecognized relationship between suppressed memories and pathogenic manifestations. That Freud questioned his neurotic patients about the details of their sexual life offended the conventions of the bourgeois world in which he lived and worked, without sharing its hypocritical denials. What he himself regarded as resolute exploration others construed to be perverse pruriency. The situation grew worse with the publication of *Three Essays on the Theory of Sexuality* (1905*d*). This work contributed considerably to Freud's social and scientific isolation from his environment.

Today readers can scarcely imagine the outbursts of indignation aroused by this book. What in our days is counted as everyday knowledge of the instinctual side of human nature was then a shocking and prohibited attack on human dignity. It made no difference that the data presented in this book did not stem from the author's phantasies but were derived from laboriously won and painstakingly assembled clinical facts. The topic of sexuality itself was taboo, and the sufferings caused by the sexual difficulties and abstinences were to remain barred to all physicians.

Conceivably, the situation might gradually have been changed in view of the relief which Freud brought about in his patients by requesting that they speak openly about their sexuality. But it was the details he described in the *Three Essays* which had the opposite effect on his adversaries. Apparently, the most offending factor was the extension of the concept of sexuality, which was most important to Freud and which he himself described as follows: 'That extension is of a twofold kind. In the first place sexuality is divorced from its too close connection with the genitals and is regarded as a more comprehensive bodily function, having pleasure as its goal and only secondarily coming to serve the ends of reproduction. In the second place the sexual impulses are regarded as including all of those merely affectionate and friendly impulses to which usage applies the exceedingly ambiguous word "love"' (1925d, p. 38). Since then Freud was repeatedly implored, by well-meaning adherents as well as strangers, to drop this 'extension' or at least to substitute a harmless term for the word 'sexual'. But he remained firm. For him, the restriction of sexuality to the genital function constituted 'inexpedient limitations of the concept' (p. 38), which glossed over the fact that the feelings and relations named above have their roots in the very same sexual impulses that manifest themselves in various forms and degrees. He was convinced that large areas of human life become intelligible only when this common instinctual foundation is recognized, an insight that was to be illuminated and not obscured by the terminology.

Another thesis, however, carried even more weight. The detaching of sexuality from the genitals enabled Freud to trace the development of sexual functioning from its manifestations in the adult to its first beginnings in early childhood. What had until then been deemed infantile demeanours or misdemeanours – thumb-sucking, interest in excrement, masturbation – appeared in this new light as the search for sexual pleasure, though not connected with the genitals but dependent upon specific bodily zones which in the course of childhood development successively gain significance in view of their excitability; these are, at first, the mouth, then the anus, and later the penis. Oral, anal and phallic strivings, together comprising infantile sexuality, were characterized as physical accompaniments of the child's affectionate tie to his parents; this allowed for including the concept of sexual excitation in the early relationship to the mother and later in the triangular relationship to mother and father.

The world as it was then could not accept the statement that the child's love for his differently sexed parent resembles in many respects the adult's love for his sexual partner. This assertion contradicted the widely held popular view of the 'innocence of the child' – i.e., of a prestage which is devoid of any sexual knowledge and feeling and which comes to an end only with the stirrings in puberty; all sexual activities that could be observed in the preceding phase, especially masturbation, were taken as signs of moral depravity. The notion of infantile sexuality found its most stubborn opponents among the official German psychiatrists, who outdid each other in heaping accusations on Freud. Especially the concept of the so-called Oedipus complex (love for the mother and jealous and hostile impulses to the father, in the case of the male child) represented for them 'a poisoning of one of the few human relationships which mankind still regards as sacred'. They rejected psycho-analytic theories as a degenerate form of 'European nihilism, as dissolution of all accepted values', and called for its boycott and denunciation, i.e., a call to arms for a bitter and fierce fight against psycho-analysis (Editorial, 1931).[1]

Even the publication of 'Analysis of a Phobia in a Five-Year-Old Boy' (1909b), which appeared about four years after the *Three Essays*, contributed little to convince Freud's opponents and to take the edge off their enmity. This description of the illness and treatment of Little Hans for the first time opens up a path to the otherwise inaccessible world of feelings and thoughts of a young child, to his phantasies, anxieties, passions and death wishes, with all their bizarre entanglements, displacements and compromise formations. Anyone who has the slightest readiness to look at something so entirely novel will find here the picture of an infantile neurosis – not as a theoretical construction deduced retroactively from a neurosis in the adult, but as an individual, immediate, actually occurring event. The ideational world of Little Hans, though drastically accentuated at the height of his illness, is essentially not different from that of other – perhaps of all – children of his age. Since the publication of this case history, psycho-analytically informed parents have learned to observe their own children carefully, to understand the pregenital sexual manifestations as indications of a prescribed developmental course, and to connect the frequent anxieties, inhibitions and developmental disturbances with the conflicts to which they give rise. Within the psycho-analytic movement, the analysis of Little Hans thus became the starting-point for two important branches of the discipline: on the one hand, for child analysis, which steadily gained in importance; on the other, for psycho-analytically orientated direct observation of infants. But for the psychiatric world, hostile before and after, even

[1] *Süddeutsche Monatshefte*, Heft 2, Vol. 28, 1931.

this clinical advance in the understanding and treatment of childhood disturbances was just another grave reason for defamation.

The opposition to including childhood in the study of sexuality was so violent that it could be equalled only by the rejection of another thesis contained in the *Three Essays*. The detachment of the concept of sexuality from the genital zone and the study of its infantile prestages enabled Freud to gain a better understanding of perverse sexual activities as well. From the viewpoint of conventional genitality in the adult, all pregenital sexual pleasure was after all perverse; i.e., the entire infantile sexuality was polymorphously perverse. Seen in this light, the adult pervert was nothing other than a sexually disturbed person who failed to attain the sexual aim and who in its place was condemned to seek his orgastic satisfaction in the pregenital sphere. As convincing as this insight was for the psycho-analytic clinician, and as often as it was confirmed in analytic treatments, however, the psychiatric world persisted in its moral repudiation of the perversions as well as of psycho-analysis. Freud, who in general paid little or no attention to polemics and accepted even determined rejection with equanimity, once characterized this attitude by saying: 'German science will not have cause to be proud of those who represented it.' While the fact that they rejected psycho-analysis was understandable to him, there could be no excuse 'for the degree of arrogance which they displayed, for their conscienceless contempt of logic, and for the coarseness and bad taste of their attack' (1925*d*, p. 49).

It is characteristic of the resistances to and attacks on psycho-analysis that in the course of time their rationalizations and place of origin change, while the intensity and passionateness of the antagonism remain more or less the same. In the academic world of to-day the combative attitude to psycho-analysis has given way to peaceful coexistence, occasional collaboration, or some degree of indifference. The fact of infantile sexuality and the consequences it has for the normality and abnormality of adult sexuality has been widely recognized by the medical, psychiatric, and lay world. Homosexuals struggle with more or less success for public toleration and freedom from legal persecution. Such perversions as fetishism, transvestitism, and compulsive exhibitionism and voyeurism are regarded as symptoms of an illness and no longer as signs of moral depravity. One can no longer imagine the absence of descriptions of even crass or daring forms of sexuality in the literature, the theatre, and the mass media. Disbelief and indignation now come from a new side and are directed

to different aims: the side of the modern women's liberation movement which disputes Freud's theory of female sexuality and its
development. Representatives of this movement experience this
theory as an affront and depreciation, very similar to how formerly the
representatives of the ideal of 'innocent childhood' reacted to the
theory of infantile sexuality.

In fact, psycho-analysis and the women's movement differ in their
essential presuppositions. On the one hand, Freud stressed the
bisexual disposition of all human beings; on the other, he was
convinced that anatomy determined whether predominantly male or
female qualities would be developed and prepare the individual for
his or her differing future life tasks. As little as the sexual manifestations of boys and girls differ from each other in the oral and anal
phases, as significant is the marked dissimilarity in the phallic phase
during which the anatomical equipment of the female child puts her
at a disadvantage in relation to the possessor of the phallus, as far as
masturbatory and exhibitionistic pleasures are concerned. While the
boy who highly values his sexual organ is exposed to castration
anxiety, the girl in turn develops penis envy and the wish for a
substitute for what has been withheld from her, a wish that ultimately
culminates in the wish to have a child.

The prestages of female sexuality which Freud reconstructed, piece
by piece, on the basis of data gained in the analysis of female patients,
are simply brushed aside by liberated women as the result of male
chauvinistic prejudice. They deny the existence of any inherited
difference between man and woman and explain the appearance of
early unlikeness as the exclusive result of social influences on upbringing which push the girl to play with dolls and propel the boy toward
interest in motors, soldiers and war games. The anatomical difference
between penis and vagina, between impregnation and giving birth,
and its decisive impact on psychic development are pushed aside in
the passionate efforts to free women from the subjugation in which
they have in fact been held for centuries and to put women in a
position that in every respect equals that of their male partners.

Some of Freud's remarks relating to the attitude of women to
cultural tasks are a consequence of the exclusion of women from the
professional life of men in his times and as a description are no longer
valid in our times when all possible professional activities, in business,
medicine, the law, or as a head of state, are open to women.

The feminist battle, much like the early attacks on psycho-analysis, is being fought out by means of rigorous and wholesale condemnation. Thus, in the arguments of the women's movement, there is, for example, not a single appreciative reference to the facts that the equality of the sexes for which they strive existed in the analytic movement from the beginning, that analytic training institutes do not discriminate between male and female applicants, that at all times women played an important role as authors contributing to the psycho-analytic literature and as respected collaborators of Freud. The data that psycho-analysis laboriously won in order to throw some light on the difficulties and frequent disturbances of female sexual functioning are taken out of their narrow sexual context by its enemies and blindly applied to the general significance of woman as a social being and professional worker.

Today modern research into sex has resulted in further opposition. It was Freud's effort and merit that in the creation of his libido concept he welded together somatic and psychic processes into an inseparable unit. In contrast, Masters and Johnson (1970), for example, attempt to demonstrate that physical processes in isolation are amenable to therapeutic interventions. Thus, they once again divorce the sexual and the love life from each other and put the stamp of a purely physical process on the former.

In this way they undo what Freud accomplished with his *Three Essays*, which is still the central work in this area. After studying it, the student might proceed to some of the briefer writings (1908c, 1923e, 1924d, 1925j, 1933a) as variations on the theme and as evidence for the fact that Freud continued until the end of his life to work out and elaborate on specific elements of his theory of sexuality.

Three Essays on the Theory of Sexuality

(1905)*

Preface to the Second Edition

The author is under no illusion as to the deficiencies and obscurities of this little work. Nevertheless he has resisted the temptation of introducing into it the results of the researches of the last five years, since this would have destroyed its unity and documentary character. He is, therefore, reprinting the original text with only slight alterations, and has contented himself with adding a few footnotes which are distinguished from the older ones by an asterisk. It is, moreover, his earnest wish that the book may age rapidly – that what was once new in it may become generally accepted, and that what is imperfect in it may be replaced by something better.

VIENNA, *December 1909*

Preface to the Third Edition

I have now been watching for more than ten years the effects produced by this work and the reception accorded to it; and I take the opportunity offered by the publication of its third edition to preface it with a few remarks intended to prevent misunderstandings and expectations that cannot be fulfilled. It must above all be emphasized that the exposition to be found in the following pages is based entirely upon everyday medical observation, to which the findings of psychoanalytic research should lend additional depth and scientific significance. It is impossible that these *Three Essays on the Theory of Sexuality*

---

* The first edition of these *Essays* was published by Deuticke (Leipzig, Vienna). The present text is included in *Standard Ed.*, **7**, 130; *P.F.L.*, **7**, 39.

should contain anything but what psycho-analysis makes it necessary to assume or possible to establish. It is, therefore, out of the question that they could ever be extended into a complete 'theory of sexuality', and it is natural that there should be a number of important problems of sexual life with which they do not deal at all. But the reader should not conclude from this that the branches of this large subject which have been thus passed over are unknown to the author or have been neglected by him as of small importance.

The fact that this book is based upon the psycho-analytic observations which led to its composition is shown, however, not only in the choice of the topics dealt with, but also in their arrangement. Throughout the entire work the various factors are placed in a particular order of precedence: preference is given to the accidental factors, while disposition is left in the background, and more weight is attached to ontogenesis than to phylogenesis. For it is the accidental factors that play the principal part in analysis: they are almost entirely subject to its influence. The dispositional ones only come to light after them, as something stirred into activity by experience: adequate consideration of them would lead far beyond the sphere of psycho-analysis.

The relation between ontogenesis and phylogenesis is a similar one. Ontogenesis may be regarded as a recapitulation of phylogenesis, in so far as the latter has not been modified by more recent experience. The phylogenetic disposition can be seen at work behind the ontogenetic process. But disposition is ultimately the precipitate of earlier experience of the species to which the more recent experience of the individual, as the sum of the accidental factors, is super-added.

I must, however, emphasize that the present work is characterized not only by being completely based upon psycho-analytic research, but also by being deliberately independent of the findings of biology. I have carefully avoided introducing any preconceptions, whether derived from general sexual biology or from that of particular animal species, into this study – a study which is concerned with the sexual functions of human beings and which is made possible through the technique of psycho-analysis. Indeed, my aim has rather been to discover how far psychological investigation can throw light upon the biology of the sexual life of man. It was legitimate for me to indicate points of contact and agreement which came to light during my investigation, but there was no need for me to be diverted from my course if the psycho-analytic method led in a number of important respects to opinions and findings which differed largely from those based on biological considerations.

In this third edition I have introduced a considerable amount of fresh matter, but have not indicated it in any special way, as I did in the previous edition. Progress in our field of scientific work is at present less rapid; nevertheless it was essential to make a certain number of additions to this volume if it was to be kept in touch with recent psycho-analytic literature.[1]

VIENNA, *October* 1914

Preface to the Fourth Edition

Now the flood-waters of war have subsided, it is satisfactory to be able to record the fact that interest in psycho-analytic research remains unimpaired in the world at large. But the different parts of the theory have not all had the same history. The purely psychological theses and findings of psycho-analysis on the unconscious, repression, conflict as a cause of illness, the advantage accruing from illness, the mechanisms of the formation of symptoms, etc., have come to enjoy increasing recognition and have won notice even from those who are in general opposed to our views. That part of the theory, however, which lies on the frontiers of biology and the foundations of which are contained in this little work is still faced with undiminished contradiction. It has even led some who for a time took a very active interest in psycho-analysis to abandon it and to adopt fresh views which were intended to restrict once more the part played by the factor of sexuality in normal and pathological mental life.

Nevertheless I cannot bring myself to accept the idea that this part of psycho-analytic theory can be very much more distant than the rest from the reality which it is its business to discover. My recollections, as well as a constant re-examination of the material, assure me that this part of the theory is based upon equally careful and impartial observation. There is, moreover, no difficulty in finding an explanation of this discrepancy in the general acceptance of my views. In

[1] [The following footnote appeared at this point in 1915 only:] In 1910, after the publication of the second edition, an English translation by A. A. Brill was published in New York; and in 1911 a Russian one by N. Ossipow in Moscow.

the first place, the beginnings of human sexual life which are here described can only be confirmed by investigators who have enough patience and technical skill to trace back an analysis to the first years of a patient's childhood. And there is often no possibility of doing this, since medical treatment demands that an illness should, at least in appearance, be dealt with more rapidly. None, however, but physicians who practise psycho-analysis can have any access whatever to this sphere of knowledge or any possibility of forming a judgement that is uninfluenced by their own dislikes and prejudices. If mankind had been able to learn from a direct observation of children, these three essays could have remained unwritten.

It must also be remembered, however, that some of what this book contains – its insistence on the importance of sexuality in all human achievements and the attempt that it makes at enlarging the concept of sexuality – has from the first provided the strongest motives for the resistance against psycho-analysis. People have gone so far in their search for high-sounding catchwords as to talk of the 'pan-sexualism' of psycho-analysis and to raise the senseless charge against it of explaining 'everything' by sex. We might be astonished at this, if we ourselves could forget the way in which emotional factors make people confused and forgetful. For it is some time since Arthur Schopenhauer, the philosopher, showed mankind the extent to which their activities are determined by sexual impulses – in the ordinary sense of the word. It should surely have been impossible for a whole world of readers to banish such a startling piece of information so completely from their minds. And as for the 'stretching' of the concept of sexuality which has been necessitated by the analysis of children and what are called perverts, anyone who looks down with contempt upon psycho-analysis from a superior vantage-point should remember how closely the enlarged sexuality of psycho-analysis coincides with the Eros of the divine Plato. (Cf. Nachmansohn, 1915.)

VIENNA, *May* 1920

I

The Sexual Aberrations[1]

The fact of the existence of sexual needs in human beings and animals is expressed in biology by the assumption of a 'sexual instinct', on the analogy of the instinct of nutrition, that is of hunger. Everyday language possesses no counterpart to the word 'hunger', but science makes use of the word 'libido' for that purpose.[2]

Popular opinion has quite definite ideas about the nature and characteristics of this sexual instinct. It is generally understood to be absent in childhood, to set in at the time of puberty in connection with the process of coming to maturity and to be revealed in the manifestations of an irresistible attraction exercised by one sex upon the other; while its aim is presumed to be sexual union, or at all events actions leading in that direction. We have every reason to believe, however, that these views give a very false picture of the true situation. If we look into them more closely we shall find that they contain a number of errors, inaccuracies and hasty conclusions.

I shall at this point introduce two technical terms. Let us call the person from whom sexual attraction proceeds the *sexual object* and the act towards which the instinct tends the *sexual aim*. Scientifically sifted observation, then, shows that numerous deviations occur in respect of both of these – the sexual object and the sexual aim. The relation between these deviations and what is assumed to be normal requires thorough investigation.

(I) DEVIATIONS IN RESPECT OF THE SEXUAL OBJECT

The popular view of the sexual instinct is beautifully reflected in the poetic fable which tells how the original human beings were cut up into two halves – man and woman – and how these are always striving

---

[1] The information contained in this first essay is derived from the well-known writings of Krafft-Ebing, Moll, Moebius, Havelock Ellis, Schrenck-Notzing, Löwenfeld, Eulenburg, Bloch and Hirschfeld, and from the *Jahrbuch für sexuelle Zwischenstufen*, published under the direction of the last-named author. Since full bibliographies of the remaining literature of the subject will be found in the works of these writers, I have been able to spare myself the necessity for giving detailed references. [*Added* 1910:] The data obtained from the psycho-analytic investigation of inverts are based upon material supplied to me by I. Sadger [e.g. 1908] and upon my own findings.

[2] [*Footnote added* 1910:] The only appropriate word in the German language, '*Lust*', is unfortunately ambiguous, and is used to denote the experience both of a need and of a gratification.

to unite again in love.[1] It comes as a great surprise therefore to learn that there are men whose sexual object is a man and not a woman, and women whose sexual object is a woman and not a man. People of this kind are described as having 'contrary sexual feelings', or better, as being 'inverts', and the fact is described as 'inversion'. The number of such people is very considerable, though there are difficulties in establishing it precisely.[2]

(A) INVERSION

Behaviour of Inverts

Such people vary greatly in their behaviour in several respects.

(*a*) They may be *absolute* inverts. In that case their sexual objects are exclusively of their own sex. Persons of the opposite sex are never the object of their sexual desire, but leave them cold, or even arouse sexual aversion in them. As a consequence of this aversion, they are incapable, if they are men, of carrying out the sexual act, or else they derive no enjoyment from it.

(*b*) They may be *amphigenic* inverts, that is psychosexual hermaphrodites. In that case their sexual objects may equally well be of their own or of the opposite sex. This kind of inversion thus lacks the characteristic of exclusiveness.

(*c*) They may be *contingent* inverts. In that case, under certain external conditions – of which inaccessibility of any normal sexual object and imitation are the chief – they are capable of taking as their sexual object someone of their own sex and of deriving satisfaction from sexual intercourse with him.

Again, inverts vary in their views as to the peculiarity of their sexual instinct. Some of them accept their inversion as something in the natural course of things, just as a normal person accepts the direction of *his* libido, and insist energetically that inversion is as legitimate as the normal attitude; others rebel against their inversion and feel it as a pathological compulsion.[3]

Other variations occur which relate to questions of time. The trait

[1] [This is no doubt an allusion to the theory expounded by Aristophanes in Plato's *Symposium*. Freud recurred to this much later, at the end of Section VI of *Beyond the Pleasure Principle* (1920g) in Chapter 4 above.]

[2] On these difficulties and on the attempts which have been made to arrive at the proportional number of inverts, see Hirschfeld (1904).

[3] The fact of a person struggling in this way against a compulsion towards inversion may perhaps determine the possibility of his being influenced by suggestion [*added* 1910:] or psycho-analysis.

of inversion may either date back to the very beginning, as far back as the subject's memory reaches, or it may not have become noticeable till some particular time before or after puberty.[1] It may either persist throughout life, or it may go into temporary abeyance, or again it may constitute an episode on the way to a normal development. It may even make its first appearance late in life after a long period of normal sexual activity. A periodic oscillation between a normal and an inverted sexual object has also sometimes been observed. Those cases are of particular interest in which the libido changes over to an inverted sexual object after a distressing experience with a normal one.

As a rule these different kinds of variations are found side by side independently of one another. It is, however, safe to assume that the most extreme form of inversion will have been present from a very early age and that the person concerned will feel at one with his peculiarity.

Many authorities would be unwilling to class together all the various cases which I have enumerated and would prefer to lay stress upon their differences rather than their resemblances, in accordance with their own preferred view of inversion. Nevertheless, though the distinctions cannot be disputed, it is impossible to overlook the existence of numerous intermediate examples of every type, so that we are driven to conclude that we are dealing with a connected series.

Nature of Inversion

The earliest assessments regarded inversion as an innate indication of nervous degeneracy. This corresponded to the fact that medical observers first came across it in persons suffering, or appearing to suffer, from nervous diseases. This characterization of inversion involves two suppositions, which must be considered separately: that it is innate and that it is degenerate.

Degeneracy

The attribution of degeneracy in this connection is open to the objections which can be raised against the indiscriminate use of the word in general. It has become the fashion to regard any symptom

---

[1] Many writers have insisted with justice that the dates assigned by inverts themselves for the appearance of their tendency to inversion are untrustworthy, since they may have repressed the evidence of their heterosexual feelings from their memory. [Added 1910:] These suspicions have been confirmed by psycho-analysis in those cases of inversion to which it has had access; it has produced decisive alterations in their anamnesis by filling in their infantile amnesia.

which is not obviously due to trauma or infection as a sign of degeneracy. Magnan's classification of degenerates is indeed of such a kind as not to exclude the possibility of the concept of degeneracy being applied to a nervous system whose general functioning is excellent. This being so, it may well be asked whether an attribution of 'degeneracy' is of any value or adds anything to our knowledge. It seems wiser only to speak of it where (1) several serious deviations from the normal are found together, and (2) the capacity for efficient functioning and survival seem to be severely impaired.[1]

Several facts go to show that in this legitimate sense of the word inverts cannot be regarded as degenerate:

(1) Inversion is found in people who exhibit no other serious deviations from the normal.

(2) It is similarly found in people whose efficiency is unimpaired, and who are indeed distinguished by specially high intellectual development and ethical culture.[2]

(3) If we disregard the patients we come across in our medical practice, and cast our eyes round a wider horizon, we shall come in two directions upon facts which make it impossible to regard inversion as a sign of degeneracy:

(a) Account must be taken of the fact that inversion was a frequent phenomenon – one might almost say an institution charged with important functions – among the peoples of antiquity at the height of their civilization.

(b) It is remarkably widespread among many savage and primitive races, whereas the concept of degeneracy is usually restricted to states of high civilization (cf. Bloch); and, even amongst the civilized peoples of Europe, climate and race exercise the most powerful influence on the prevalence of inversion and upon the attitude adopted towards it.[3]

---

[1] Moebius (1900) confirms the view that we should be chary in making a diagnosis of degeneracy and that it has very little practical value: 'If we survey the wide field of degeneracy upon which some glimpses of revealing light have been thrown in these pages, it will at once be clear that there is small value in ever making a diagnosis of degeneracy.'

[2] It must be allowed that the spokesmen of 'Uranism' are justified in asserting that some of the most prominent men in all recorded history were inverts and perhaps even absolute inverts.

[3] The pathological approach to the study of inversion has been displaced by the anthropological. The merit for bringing about this change is due to Bloch (1902–3),

Innate Character

As may be supposed, innateness is only attributed to the first, most extreme, class of inverts, and the evidence for it rests upon assurances given by them that at no time in their lives has their sexual instinct shown any sign of taking another course. The very existence of the two other classes, and especially the third [the 'contingent' inverts], is difficult to reconcile with the hypothesis of the innateness of inversion. This explains why those who support this view tend to separate out the group of absolute inverts from all the rest, thus abandoning any attempt at giving an account of inversion which shall have universal application. In the view of these authorities inversion is innate in one group of cases, while in others it may have come about in other ways.

The reverse of this view is represented by the alternative one that inversion is an acquired character of the sexual instinct. This second view is based on the following considerations:

(1) In the case of many inverts, even absolute ones, it is possible to show that very early in their lives a sexual impression occurred which left a permanent after-effect in the shape of a tendency to homosexuality.

(2) In the case of many others, it is possible to point to external influences in their lives, whether of a favourable or inhibiting character, which have led sooner or later to a fixation of their inversion. (Such influences are exclusive relations with persons of their own sex, comradeship in war, detention in prison, the dangers of heterosexual intercourse, celibacy, sexual weakness, etc.)

(3) Inversion can be removed by hypnotic suggestion, which would be astonishing in an innate characteristic.

In view of these considerations it is even possible to doubt the very existence of such a thing as innate inversion. It can be argued (cf. Havelock Ellis [1897]) that, if the cases of allegedly innate inversion were more closely examined, some experience of their early childhood would probably come to light which had a determining effect upon the direction taken by their libido. This experience would simply have passed out of the subject's conscious recollection, but could be recalled to his memory under appropriate influence. In the opinion of

---

who has also laid stress on the occurrence of inversion among the civilizations of antiquity.

these writers inversion can only be described as a frequent variation of the sexual instinct, which can be determined by a number of external circumstances in the subject's life.

The apparent certainty of this conclusion is, however, completely countered by the reflection that many people are subjected to the same sexual influences (e.g. to seduction or mutual masturbation, which may occur in early youth) without becoming inverted or without remaining so permanently. We are therefore forced to a suspicion that the choice between 'innate' and 'acquired' is not an exclusive one or that it does not cover all the issues involved in inversion.

Explanation of Inversion

The nature of inversion is explained neither by the hypothesis that it is innate nor by the alternative hypothesis that it is acquired. In the former case we must ask in what respect it is innate, unless we are to accept the crude explanation that everyone is born with his sexual instinct attached to a particular sexual object. In the latter case it may be questioned whether the various accidental influences would be sufficient to explain the acquisition of inversion without the co-operation of something in the subject himself. As we have already shown, the existence of this last factor is not to be denied.

Bisexuality

A fresh contradiction of popular views is involved in the considerations put forward by Lydston (1889), Kiernan [1888] and Chevalier [1893] in an endeavour to account for the possibility of sexual inversion. It is popularly believed that a human being is either a man or a woman. Science, however, knows of cases in which the sexual characters are obscured, and in which it is consequently difficult to determine the sex. This arises in the first instance in the field of anatomy. The genitals of the individuals concerned combine male and female characteristics. (This condition is known as hermaphroditism.) In rare cases both kinds of sexual apparatus are found side by side fully developed (true hermaphroditism); but far more frequently both sets of organs are found in an atrophied condition.[1]

---

[1] For the most recent descriptions of somatic hermaphroditism, see Taruffi (1903), and numerous papers by Neugebauer in various volumes of the *Jahrbuch für sexuelle Zwischenstufen.*

The importance of these abnormalities lies in the unexpected fact that they facilitate our understanding of normal development. For it appears that a certain degree of anatomical hermaphroditism occurs normally. In every normal male or female individual, traces are found of the apparatus of the opposite sex. These either persist without function as rudimentary organs or become modified and take on other functions.

These long-familiar facts of anatomy lead us to suppose that an originally bisexual physical disposition has, in the course of evolution, become modified into a unisexual one, leaving behind only a few traces of the sex that has become atrophied.

It was tempting to extend this hypothesis to the mental sphere and to explain inversion in all its varieties as the expression of a psychical hermaphroditism. All that was required further in order to settle the question was that inversion should be regularly accompanied by the mental and somatic signs of hermaphroditism.

But this expectation was disappointed. It is impossible to demonstrate so close a connection between the hypothetical psychical hermaphroditism and the established anatomical one. A general lowering of the sexual instinct and a slight anatomical atrophy of the organs is found frequently in inverts (cf. Havelock Ellis, [1897]). Frequently, but by no means regularly or even usually. The truth must therefore be recognized that inversion and somatic hermaphroditism are on the whole independent of each other.

A great deal of importance, too, has been attached to what are called the secondary and tertiary sexual characters and to the great frequency of the occurrence of those of the opposite sex in inverts (cf. Havelock Ellis, [1897]). Much of this, again, is correct; but it should never be forgotten that in general the secondary and tertiary sexual characters of one sex occur very frequently in the opposite one. They are indications of hermaphroditism, but are not attended by any change of sexual object in the direction of inversion.

Psychical hermaphroditism would gain substance if the inversion of the sexual object were at least accompanied by a parallel changeover of the subject's other mental qualities, instincts and character traits into those marking the opposite sex. But it is only in inverted women that character-inversion of this kind can be looked for with any regularity. In men the most complete mental masculinity can be combined with inversion. If the belief in psychical hermaphroditism is to be persisted in, it will be necessary to add that its manifestations in various spheres show only slight signs of being mutually determined. Moreover the same is true of somatic hermaphroditism: according to Halban (1903),[1] occurrences of individual atrophied organs and of secondary sexual characters are to a considerable extent independent of one another.

The theory of bisexuality has been expressed in its crudest form by a spokesman of the male inverts: 'a feminine brain in a masculine body'. But we are ignorant of what characterizes a feminine brain. There is neither need nor justification for replacing the psychological problem by the anatomical one. Krafft-Ebing's attempted explanation seems to be more exactly framed than that of Ulrichs but does not differ from it in essentials. According to Krafft-Ebing (1895, 5), every individual's bisexual disposition endows him with masculine and feminine brain centres as well as with somatic organs of sex; these centres develop only at puberty, for the most part under the influence of the sex-gland, which is independent of them in the original disposition. But what has just been said of masculine and feminine brains applies equally to masculine and feminine 'centres'; and incidentally we have not even any grounds for assuming that certain areas of the brain ('centres') are set aside for the functions of sex, as is the case, for instance, with those of speech.[2]

[1] His paper includes a bibliography of the subject.

[2] It appears (from a bibliography given in the sixth volume of the *Jahrbuch für sexuelle Zwischenstufen*) that E. Gley was the first writer to suggest bisexuality as an explanation of inversion. As long ago as in January, 1884, he published a paper, 'Les aberrations de l'instinct sexuel', in the *Revue Philosophique*. It is moreover, noteworthy that the majority of authors who derive inversion from bisexuality bring forward that factor not only in the case of inverts, but also for all those who have grown up to be normal, and that, as a logical consequence, they regard inversion as the result of a disturbance in development. Chevalier (1893) already writes in this sense. Krafft-Ebing (1895, 10) remarks that there are a great number of observations 'which prove at least the virtual persistence of this second centre (that of the subordinated sex)'. A Dr. Arduin (1900) asserts that 'there are masculine and feminine elements in every human being (cf. Hirschfeld, 1899); but one set of these – according to the sex of the person in question – is incomparably more strongly developed than the other, so far as heterosexual individuals are concerned . . .' Herman (1903) is convinced that 'masculine elements and characteristics are present in every woman and feminine ones in every man', etc. [*Added* 1910:] Fliess (1906) subsequently claimed the idea of bisexuality (in the sense of *duality of sex*) as his own. [*Added* 1924:] In lay circles the hypothesis of human bisexuality is regarded as being due to O. Weininger, the philosopher, who died at an early age, and who made the idea the basis of a somewhat unbalanced book (1903). The particulars which I have enumerated above will be sufficient to show how little justification there is for the claim. [*Continued on next page.*]

Nevertheless, two things emerge from these discussions. In the first place, a bisexual disposition is somehow concerned in inversion, though we do not know in what that disposition consists, beyond anatomical structure. And secondly, we have to deal with disturbances that affect the sexual instinct in the course of its development.

Sexual Object of Inverts

The theory of psychical hermaphroditism presupposes that the sexual object of an invert is the opposite of that of a normal person. An inverted man, it holds, is like a woman in being subject to the charm that proceeds from masculine attributes both physical and mental: he feels he is a woman in search of a man.

But however well this applies to quite a number of inverts, it is, nevertheless, far from revealing a universal characteristic of inversion. There can be no doubt that a large proportion of male inverts retain the mental quality of masculinity, that they possess relatively few of the secondary characters of the opposite sex and that what they look for in their sexual object are in fact feminine mental traits. If this were not so, how would it be possible to explain the fact that male prostitutes who offer themselves to inverts – to-day just as they did in ancient times – imitate women in all the externals of their clothing and behaviour? Such imitation would otherwise inevitably clash with the ideal of the inverts. It is clear that in Greece, where the most masculine men were numbered among the inverts, what excited a man's love was not the *masculine* character of a boy, but his physical resemblance to a woman as well as his feminine mental qualities – his shyness, his modesty and his need for instruction and assistance. As soon as the boy became a man he ceased to be a sexual object for men and himself, perhaps, became a lover of boys. In this instance, therefore, as in many others, the sexual object is not someone of the same sex but someone who combines the characters of both sexes; there is as, it were, a compromise between an impulse that seeks for a man and one that seeks for a woman, while it remains a paramount condition that the object's body (i.e. genitals) shall be masculine.

[Freud's own realization of the importance of bisexuality owed much to Fliess, and his forgetfulness of this fact on one occasion provided him with an example in his *Psychopathology of Everyday Life*, 1901*b*, Chapter VII (II). He did not, however, accept Fliess's view that bisexuality provided the explanation of repression. See Freud's discussion of this in 'A Child is Being Beaten' (1919*e*)', *Standard Ed.*, **17**, 200–02; *P.F.L.*, **10**, 188–91).]

Thus the sexual object is a kind of reflection of the subject's own bisexual nature.[1]

The position in the case of women is less ambiguous; for among them the active inverts exhibit masculine characteristics, both physical and mental, with peculiar frequency and look for femininity in their sexual objects – though here again a closer knowledge of the facts might reveal greater variety.

---

[1] [*Footnote added* 1910:] It is true that psycho-analysis has not yet produced a complete explanation of the origin of inversion; nevertheless, it has discovered the psychical mechanism of its development, and has made essential contributions to the statement of the problems involved. In all the cases we have examined we have established the fact that the future inverts, in the earliest years of their childhood, pass through a phase of very intense but short-lived fixation to a woman (usually their mother), and that, after leaving this behind, they identify themselves with a woman and take *themselves* as their sexual object. That is to say, they proceed from a narcissistic basis, and look for a young man who resembles themselves and whom *they* may love as their mother loved *them*. Moreover, we have frequently found that alleged inverts have been by no means insusceptible to the charms of women, but have continually transposed the excitation aroused by women on to a male object. They have thus repeated all through their lives the mechanism by which their inversion arose. Their compulsive longing for men has turned out to be determined by their ceaseless flight from women.

[At this point the footnote proceeded as follows in the 1910 edition only: 'It must, however, be borne in mind that hitherto only a single type of invert has been submitted to psycho-analysis – persons whose sexual activity is in general stunted and the residue of which is manifested as inversion. The problem of inversion is a highly complex one and includes very various types of sexual activity and development. A strict conceptual distinction should be drawn between different cases of inversion according to whether the sexual character of the *object* or that of the *subject* has been inverted.']

[*Added* 1915:] Psycho-analytic research is most decidedly opposed to any attempt at separating off homosexuals from the rest of mankind as a group of a special character. By studying sexual excitations other than those that are manifestly displayed, it has found that all human beings are capable of making a homosexual object-choice and have in fact made one in their unconscious. Indeed, libidinal attachments to persons of the same sex play no less a part as factors in normal mental life, and a greater part as a motive force for illness, than do similar attachments to the opposite sex. On the contrary, psycho-analysis considers that a choice of an object independently of its sex – freedom to range equally over male and female objects – as it is found in childhood, in primitive states of society and early periods of history, is the original basis from which, as a result of restriction in one direction or the other, both the normal and the inverted types develop. Thus from the point of view of psycho-analysis the exclusive sexual interest felt by men for women is also a problem that needs elucidating and is not a self-evident fact based upon an attraction that is ultimately of a chemical nature. A person's final sexual attitude is not decided until after puberty and is the result of a number of factors, not all of which are yet known; some are of a constitutional nature but others are accidental. No doubt a few of these factors may happen to carry so much weight that they influence the result in their sense. But in general the multiplicity of determining factors is reflected in the variety of manifest sexual attitudes in which they find their issue in mankind. In inverted types, a predominance of archaic constitutions and primitive psychical mechanisms is regularly to be found. Their most essential

Sexual Aim of Inverts

The important fact to bear in mind is that no one single aim can be laid down as applying in cases of inversion. Among men, intercourse *per anum* by no means coincides with inversion; masturbation is quite as frequently their exclusive aim, and it is even true that restrictions of sexual aim – to the point of its being limited to simple outpourings of emotion – are commoner among them than among heterosexual lovers. Among women, too, the sexual aims of inverts are various: there seems to be a special preference for contact with the mucous membrane of the mouth.

---

characteristics seem to be a coming into operation of narcissistic object-choice and a retention of the erotic significance of the anal zone. There is nothing to be gained, however, by separating the most extreme types of inversion from the rest on the basis of constitutional peculiarities of that kind. What we find as an apparently sufficient explanation of these types can be equally shown to be present, though less strongly, in the constitution of transitional types and of those whose manifest attitude is normal. The differences in the end-products may be of a qualitative nature, but analysis shows that the differences between their determinants are only quantitative. Among the accidental factors that influence object-choice we have found that frustration (in the form of an early deterrence, by fear, from sexual activity) deserves attention, and we have observed that the presence of both parents plays an important part. The absence of a strong father in childhood not infrequently favours the occurrence of inversion. Finally, it may be insisted that the concept of inversion in respect of the sexual object should be sharply distinguished from that of the occurrence in the subject of a mixture of sexual characters. In the relation between these two factors, too, a certain degree of reciprocal independence is unmistakably present.

[*Added* 1920:] Ferenczi (1914) has brought forward a number of interesting points on the subject of inversion. He rightly protests that, because they have in common the symptom of inversion, a large number of conditions, which are very different from one another and which are of unequal importance both in organic and psychical respects, have been thrown together under the name of 'homosexuality' (or, to follow him in giving it a better name, 'homo-erotism'). He insists that a sharp distinction should at least be made between two types: 'subject homo-erotics', who feel and behave like women, and 'object homo-erotics', who are completely masculine and who have merely exchanged a female for a male object. The first of these two types he recognizes as true 'sexual intermediates' in Hirschfeld's sense of the word; the second he describes, less happily, as obsessional neurotics. According to him, it is only in the case of object homo-erotics that there is any question of their struggling against their inclination to inversion or of the possibility of their being influenced psychologically. While granting the existence of these two types, we may add that there are many people in whom a certain quantity of subject homo-erotism is found in combination with a proportion of object homo-erotism.

During the last few years work carried out by biologists, notably by Steinach, has thrown a strong light on the organic determinants of homo-erotism and of sexual characters in general. By carrying out experimental castration and subsequently grafting the sex-glands of the opposite sex, it was possible in the case of various species of mammals to transform a male into a female and vice versa. The transformation

Conclusion

It will be seen that we are not in a position to base a satisfactory explanation of the origin of inversion upon the material at present before us. Nevertheless our investigation has put us in possession of a piece of knowledge which may turn out to be of greater importance to us than the solution of that problem. It has been brought to our notice that we have been in the habit of regarding the connection between the sexual instinct and the sexual object as more intimate than it in fact is. Experience of the cases that are considered abnormal has shown us that in them the sexual instinct and the sexual object are merely soldered together – a fact which we have been in danger of overlooking in consequence of the uniformity of the normal picture, where the object appears to form part and parcel of the instinct. We are thus warned to loosen the bond that exists in our thoughts between instinct and object. It seems probable that the sexual instinct is in the first instance independent of its object; nor is its origin likely to be due to its object's attractions.

(B) SEXUALLY IMMATURE PERSONS AND ANIMALS AS SEXUAL OBJECTS

People whose sexual objects belong to the normally inappropriate sex – that is, inverts – strike the observer as a collection of individuals who may be quite sound in other respects. On the other hand, cases in

---

footnote continued

affected more or less completely both the somatic sexual characters and the psychosexual attitude (that is, both subject and object erotism). It appeared that the vehicle of the force which thus acted as a sex-determinant was not the part of the sex-gland which forms the sex-cells but what is known as its interstitial tissue (the 'puberty-gland'). In one case this transformation of sex was actually effected in a man who had lost his testes owing to tuberculosis. In his sexual life he behaved in a feminine manner, as a passive homosexual, and exhibited very clearly-marked feminine sexual characters of a secondary kind (e.g. in regard to growth of hair and beard and deposits of fat on the breasts and hips). After an undescended testis from another male patient had been grafted into him, he began to behave in a masculine manner and to direct his libido towards women in a normal way. Simultaneously his somatic feminine characters disappeared. (Lipschütz, 1919, 356–7.)

It would be unjustifiable to assert that these interesting experiments put the theory of inversion on a new basis, and it would be hasty to expect them to offer a universal means of 'curing' homosexuality. Fliess has rightly insisted that these experimental findings do not invalidate the theory of the general bisexual disposition of the higher animals. On the contrary, it seems to me probable that further research of a similar kind will produce a direct confirmation of this presumption of bisexuality.

which sexually immature persons (children) are chosen as sexual objects are instantly judged as sporadic aberrations. It is only exceptionally that children are the exclusive sexual objects in such a case. They usually come to play that part when someone who is cowardly or has become impotent adopts them as a substitute, or when an urgent instinct (one which will not allow of postponement) cannot at the moment get possession of any more appropriate object. Nevertheless, a light is thrown on the nature of the sexual instinct by the fact that it permits of so much variation in its objects and such a cheapening of them – which hunger, with its far more energetic retention of its objects, would only permit in the most extreme instances. A similar consideration applies to sexual intercourse with animals, which is by no means rare, especially among country people, and in which sexual attraction seems to override the barriers of species.

One would be glad on aesthetic grounds to be able to ascribe these and other severe aberrations of the sexual instinct to insanity; but that cannot be done. Experience shows that disturbances of the sexual instinct among the insane do not differ from those that occur among the healthy and in whole races or occupations. Thus the sexual abuse of children is found with uncanny frequency among school teachers and child attendants, simply because they have the best opportunity for it. The insane merely exhibit any such aberration to an intensified degree; or, what is particularly significant, it may become exclusive and replace normal sexual satisfaction entirely.

The very remarkable relation which thus holds between sexual variations and the descending scale from health to insanity gives us plenty of material for thought. I am inclined to believe that it may be explained by the fact that the impulses of sexual life are among those which, even normally, are the least controlled by the higher activities of the mind. In my experience anyone who is in any way, whether socially or ethically, abnormal mentally is invariably abnormal also in his sexual life. But many people are abnormal in their sexual life who in every other respect approximate to the average, and have, along with the rest, passed through the process of human cultural development, in which sexuality remains the weak spot.

The most general conclusion that follows from all these discussions seems, however, to be this. Under a great number of conditions and in surprisingly numerous individuals, the nature and importance of the sexual object recedes into the background. What is essential and constant in the sexual instinct is something else.[1]

(2) DEVIATIONS IN RESPECT OF THE SEXUAL AIM

The normal sexual aim is regarded as being the union of the genitals in the act known as copulation, which leads to a release of the sexual tension and a temporary extinction of the sexual instinct – a satisfaction analogous to the sating of hunger. But even in the most normal sexual process we may detect rudiments which, if they had developed, would have led to the deviations described as 'perversions'. For there are certain intermediate relations to the sexual object, such as touching and looking at it, which lie on the road towards copulation and are recognized as being preliminary sexual aims. On the one hand these activities are themselves accompanied by pleasure, and on the other hand they intensify the excitation, which should persist until the final sexual aim is attained. Moreover, the kiss, one particular contact of this kind, between the mucous membrane of the lips of the two people concerned, is held in high sexual esteem among many nations (including the most highly civilized ones), in spite of the fact that the parts of the body involved do not form part of the sexual apparatus but constitute the entrance to the digestive tract. Here, then, are factors which provide a point of contact between the perversions and normal sexual life and which can also serve as a basis for their classification. Perversions are sexual activities which either (a) extend, in an anatomical sense, beyond the regions of the body that are designed for sexual union, or (b) linger over the intermediate relations to the sexual object which should normally be traversed rapidly on the path towards the final sexual aim.

(A) ANATOMICAL EXTENSIONS

Overvaluation of the Sexual Object

It is only in the rarest instances that the psychical valuation that is set on the sexual object, as being the goal of the sexual instinct, stops short at its genitals. The appreciation extends to the whole body of the

---

[1] [*Footnote added* 1910:] The most striking distinction between the erotic life of antiquity and our own no doubt lies in the fact that the ancients laid the stress upon the instinct itself, whereas we emphasize its object. The ancients glorified the instinct and were prepared on its account to honour even an inferior object; while we despise the instinctual activity in itself, and find excuses for it only in the merits of the object.

sexual object and tends to involve every sensation derived from it. The same over-valuation spreads over into the psychological sphere: the subject becomes, as it were, intellectually infatuated (that is, his powers of judgement are weakened) by the mental achievements and perfections of the sexual object and he submits to the latter's judgements with credulity. Thus the credulity of love becomes an important, if not the most fundamental, source of *authority*.[1]

This sexual overvaluation is something that cannot be easily reconciled with a restriction of the sexual aim to union of the actual genitals and it helps to turn activities connected with other parts of the body into sexual aims.[2]

The significance of the factor of sexual overvaluation can be best studied in men, for their erotic life alone has become accessible to research. That of women – partly owing to the stunting effect of civilized conditions and partly owing to their conventional secretiveness and insincerity – is still veiled in an impenetrable obscurity.[3]

Sexual Use of the Mucous Membrane of the Lips and Mouth

The use of the mouth as a sexual organ is regarded as a perversion if the lips (or tongue) of one person are brought into contact with the

---

[1] In this connection I cannot help recalling the credulous submissiveness shown by a hypnotized subject towards his hypnotist. This leads me to suspect that the essence of hypnosis lies in an unconscious fixation of the subject's libido to the figure of the hypnotist, through the medium of the masochistic components of the sexual instinct. [*Added* 1910:] Ferenczi (1909) has brought this characteristic of suggestibility into relation with the 'parental complex'.

[2] [In the editions earlier than 1920 this paragraph ended with the further sentence: 'The emergence of these extremely various anatomical extensions clearly implies a need for variation, and this has been described by Hoche as "craving for stimulation".' The first two sentences of the footnote which follows were added in 1915, before which date it had begun with the sentence: 'Further consideration leads me to conclude that I. Bloch has over-estimated the theoretical importance of the factor of craving for stimulation.' The whole footnote and the paragraph in the text above were recast in their present form in 1920:] It must be pointed out, however, that sexual overvaluation is not developed in the case of *every* mechanism of object-choice. We shall become acquainted later on with another and more direct explanation of the sexual role assumed by the other parts of the body. The factor of 'craving for stimulation' has been put forward by Hoche and Bloch as an explanation of the extension of sexual interest to parts of the body other than the genitals; but it does not seem to me to deserve such an important place. The various channels along which the libido passes are related to each other from the very first like inter-communicating pipes, and we must take the phenomenon of collateral flow into account.

[3] [*Footnote added* 1920:] In typical cases women fail to exhibit any sexual overvaluation towards men; but they scarcely ever fail to do so towards their own children.

genitals of another, but not if the mucous membranes of the lips of both of them come together. This exception is the point of contact with what is normal. Those who condemn the other practices (which have no doubt been common among mankind from primaeval times) as being perversions, are giving way to an unmistakable feeling of *disgust*, which protects them from accepting sexual aims of the kind. The limits of such disgust are, however, often purely conventional: a man who will kiss a pretty girl's lips passionately, may perhaps be disgusted at the idea of using her tooth-brush, though there are no grounds for supposing that his own oral cavity, for which he feels no disgust, is any cleaner than the girl's. Here, then, our attention is drawn to the factor of disgust, which interferes with the libidinal over-valuation of the sexual object but can in turn be overridden by libido. Disgust seems to be one of the forces which have led to a restriction of the sexual aim. These forces do not as a rule extend to the genitals themselves. But there is no doubt that the genitals of the opposite sex can in themselves be an object of disgust and that such an attitude is one of the characteristics of all hysterics, and especially of hysterical women. The sexual instinct in its strength enjoys over-riding this disgust. (See below.)

Sexual Use of the Anal Orifice

Where the anus is concerned it becomes still clearer that it is disgust which stamps that sexual aim as a perversion. I hope, however, I shall not be accused of partisanship when I assert that people who try to account for this disgust by saying that the organ in question serves the function of excretion and comes in contact with excrement – a thing which is disgusting in itself – are not much more to the point than hysterical girls who account for their disgust at the male genital by saying that it serves to void urine.

The playing of a sexual part by the mucous membrane of the anus is by no means limited to intercourse between men: preference for it is in no way characteristic of inverted feeling. On the contrary, it seems that *paedicatio* with a male owes its origin to an analogy with a similar act performed with a woman; while mutual masturbation is the sexual aim most often found in intercourse between inverts.

Significance of Other Regions of the Body

The extension of sexual interest to other regions of the body, with all its variations, offers us nothing that is new in principle; it adds nothing to our knowledge of the sexual instinct, which merely proclaims its intention in this way of getting possession of the sexual object in every possible direction. But these anatomical extensions inform us that, besides sexual overvaluation, there is a second factor at work which is strange to popular knowledge. Certain regions of the body, such as the mucous membrane of the mouth and anus, which are constantly appearing in these practices, seem, as it were, to be claiming that they should themselves be regarded and treated as genitals. We shall learn later that this claim is justified by the history of the development of the sexual instinct and that it is fulfilled in the symptomatology of certain pathological states.

Unsuitable Substitutes for the Sexual Object – Fetishism

There are some cases which are quite specially remarkable – those in which the normal sexual object is replaced by another which bears some relation to it, but is entirely unsuited to serve the normal sexual aim. From the point of view of classification, we should no doubt have done better to have mentioned this highly interesting group of aberrations of the sexual instinct among the deviations in respect of the sexual *object*. But we have postponed their mention till we could become acquainted with the factor of sexual overvaluation, on which these phenomena, being connected with an abandonment of the sexual aim, are dependent.

What is substituted for the sexual object is some part of the body (such as the foot or hair) which is in general very inappropriate for sexual purposes, or some inanimate object which bears an assignable relation to the person whom it replaces and preferably to that person's sexuality (e.g. a piece of clothing or underlinen). Such substitutes are with some justice likened to the fetishes in which savages believe that their gods are embodied.

A transition to those cases of fetishism in which the sexual aim, whether normal or perverse, is entirely abandoned is afforded by other cases in which the sexual object is required to fulfil a fetishistic condition – such as the possession of some particular hair-colouring or clothing, or even some bodily defect – if the sexual aim is to be attained. No other variation of the sexual instinct that borders on the pathological can lay so much claim to our interest as this one, such is the peculiarity of the phenomena to which it gives rise. Some degree of diminution in the urge towards the normal sexual aim (an executive weakness of the sexual apparatus) seems to be a necessary precondition in every case.[1] The point of contact with the normal is provided by the psychologically essential overvaluation of the sexual object, which inevitably extends to everything that is associated with it. A certain degree of fetishism is thus habitually present in normal love, especially in those stages of it in which the normal sexual aim seems unattainable or its fulfilment prevented:

> Schaff' mir ein Halstuch von ihrer Brust,
> Ein Strumpfband meiner Liebeslust![2]

The situation only becomes pathological when the longing for the fetish passes beyond the point of being merely a necessary condition attached to the sexual object and actually *takes the place* of the normal aim, and, further, when the fetish becomes detached from a particular individual and becomes the *sole* sexual object. These are, indeed, the general conditions under which mere variations of the sexual instinct pass over into pathological aberrations.

Binet (1888) was the first to maintain (what has since been confirmed by a quantity of evidence) that the choice of a fetish is an after-effect of some sexual impression, received as a rule in early childhood. (This may be brought into line with the proverbial durability of first loves: *on revient toujours à ses premiers amours*.) This derivation is particularly obvious in cases where there is merely a fetishistic condition attached to the sexual object. We shall come across the importance of early sexual impressions again in another connection.[3]

---

[1] [*Footnote added* 1915:] This weakness would represent the *constitutional* precondition. Psycho-analysis has found that the phenomenon can also be *accidentally* determined, by the occurrence of an early deterrence from sexual activity owing to fear, which may divert the subject from the normal sexual aim and encourage him to seek a substitute for it.

[2] [Get me a kerchief from her breast,
A garter that her knee has pressed.

Goethe, *Faust*, Part I, Scene 7. (*Trans.* Bayard Taylor.)]

[3] [*Footnote added* 1920:] Deeper-going psycho-analytic research has raised a just criticism of Binet's assertion. All the observations dealing with this point have recorded a first meeting with the fetish at which it already aroused sexual interest without there being anything in the accompanying circumstances to explain the fact. Moreover, all of these 'early' sexual impressions relate to a time after the age of five or six, whereas psycho-analysis makes it doubtful whether fresh pathological fixations can occur so late as this. The true explanation is that behind the first recollection of the fetish's appearance there lies a submerged and forgotten phase of sexual development. The fetish, like a 'screen-memory', represents this phase and is thus a remnant and precipitate of it. The fact that this early infantile phase turns in the direction of fetishism, as well as the choice of the fetish itself, are constitutionally determined.

In other cases the replacement of the object by a fetish is determined by a symbolic connection of thought, of which the person concerned is usually not conscious. It is not always possible to trace the course of these connections with certainty. (The foot, for instance, is an age-old sexual symbol which occurs even in mythology;[1] no doubt the part played by fur as a fetish owes its origin to an association with the hair of the *mons Veneris*.) None the less even symbolism such as this is not always unrelated to sexual experiences in childhood.[2]

(B) FIXATIONS OF PRELIMINARY SEXUAL AIMS

Appearance of New Aims

Every external or internal factor that hinders or postpones the attainment of the normal sexual aim (such as impotence, the high price of the sexual object or the danger of the sexual act) will evidently lend support to the tendency to linger over the preparatory activities and to turn them into new sexual aims that can take the place of the normal one. Attentive examination always shows that even what seem to be the strangest of these new aims are already hinted at in the normal sexual process.

Touching and Looking

A certain amount of touching is indispensable (at all events among human beings) before the normal sexual aim can be attained. And

---

[1] [*Footnote added* 1910:] The shoe or slipper is a corresponding symbol of the *female* genitals.

[2] [*Footnote added* 1910:] Psycho-analysis has cleared up one of the remaining gaps in our understanding of fetishism. It has shown the importance, as regards the choice of a fetish, of a coprophilic pleasure in smelling which has disappeared owing to repression. Both the feet and the hair are objects with a strong smell which have been exalted into fetishes after the olfactory sensation has become unpleasurable and been abandoned. Accordingly, in the perversion that corresponds to foot-fetishism, it is only dirty and evil-smelling feet that become sexual objects. Another factor that helps towards explaining the fetishistic preference for the foot is to be found among the sexual theories of children (see below): the foot represents a woman's penis, the absence of which is deeply felt. [*Added* 1915:] In a number of cases of foot-fetishism it has been possible to show that the scopophilic instinct, seeking to reach its object (originally the genitals) from underneath, was brought to a halt in its pathway by prohibition and repression. For that reason it became attached to a fetish in the form of a foot or shoe, the female genitals (in accordance with the expectations of childhood) being imagined as male ones. – [The importance of the repression of pleasure in smell had been indicated by Freud in two letters to Fliess (Freud, 1950*a*, Letters 55 and 75). He returned to the subject at the end of his analysis of the 'Rat Man' (Freud, 1909*d*), and discussed it at considerable length in Chapter IV of *Civilization and its Discontents* (1930*a*).]

everyone knows what a source of pleasure on the one hand and what an influx of fresh excitation on the other is afforded by tactile sensations of the skin of the sexual object. So that lingering over the stage of touching can scarcely be counted a perversion, provided that in the long run the sexual act is carried further.

The same holds true of seeing – an activity that is ultimately derived from touching. Visual impressions remain the most frequent pathway along which libidinal excitation is aroused; indeed, natural selection counts upon the accessibility of this pathway – if such a teleological form of statement is permissible[1] – when it encourages the development of beauty in the sexual object. The progressive conceal-ment of the body which goes along with civilization keeps sexual curiosity awake. This curiosity seeks to complete the sexual object by revealing its hidden parts. It can, however, be diverted ('sublimated') in the direction of art, if its interest can be shifted away from the genitals on to the shape of the body as a whole.[2] It is usual for most normal people to linger to some extent over the intermediate sexual aim of a looking that has a sexual tinge to it; indeed, this offers them a possibility of directing some proportion of their libido on to higher artistic aims. On the other hand, this pleasure in looking [scopo-philia] becomes a perversion (a) if it is restricted exclusively to the genitals, or (b) if it is connected with the overriding of disgust (as in the case of *voyeurs* or people who look on at excretory functions), or (c) if, instead of being *preparatory* to the normal sexual aim, it supplants it. This last is markedly true of exhibitionists, who, if I may trust the findings of several analyses, exhibit their own genitals in order to obtain a reciprocal view of the genitals of the other person.[3]

In the perversions which are directed towards looking and being looked at, we come across a very remarkable characteristic with

---

[1] [The words in this parenthesis were added in 1915.]

[2] [*Footnote added* 1915:] There is to my mind no doubt that the concept of 'beautiful' has its roots in sexual excitation and that its original meaning was 'sexually stimulat-ing'. [There is an allusion in the original to the fact that the German word '*Reiz*' is commonly used both as the technical term for 'stimulus' and, in ordinary language, as an equivalent to the English 'charm' or 'attraction'.] This is related the fact that we never regard the genitals themselves, which produce the strongest sexual excitation, as really 'beautiful'.

[3] [*Footnote added* 1920:] Under analysis, these perversions – and indeed most others – reveal a surprising variety of motives and determinants. The compulsion to exhibit, for instance, is also closely dependent on the castration complex: it is a means of constantly insisting upon the integrity of the subject's own (male) genitals and it reiterates his infantile satisfaction at the absence of a penis in those of women.

which we shall be still more intensely concerned in the aberration that we shall consider next: in these perversions the sexual aim occurs in two forms, an *active* and a *passive* one.

The force which opposes scopophilia, but which may be overridden by it (in a manner parallel to what we have previously seen in the case of disgust), is *shame*.

Sadism and Masochism

The most common and the most significant of all the perversions – the desire to inflict pain upon the sexual object, and its reverse – received from Krafft-Ebing the names of 'sadism' and 'masochism' for its active and passive forms respectively. Other writers [e.g. Schrenck-Notzing (1899)] have preferred the narrower term 'algolagnia'. This emphasizes the pleasure in *pain*, the cruelty; whereas the names chosen by Krafft-Ebing bring into prominence the pleasure in any form of humiliation or subjection.

As regards active algolagnia, sadism, the roots are easy to detect in the normal. The sexuality of most male human beings contains an element of *aggressiveness* – a desire to subjugate; the biological significance of it seems to lie in the need for overcoming the resistance of the sexual object by means other than the process of wooing. Thus sadism would correspond to an aggressive component of the sexual instinct which has become independent and exaggerated and, by displacement, has usurped the leading position.[1]

In ordinary speech the connotation of sadism oscillates between, on the one hand, cases merely characterized by an active or violent attitude to the sexual object, and, on the other hand, cases in which satisfaction is entirely conditional on the humiliation and maltreatment of the object. Strictly speaking, it is only this last extreme instance which deserves to be described as a perversion.

Similarly, the term masochism comprises any passive attitude towards sexual life and the sexual object, the extreme instance of which appears to be that in which satisfaction is conditional upon suffering physical or mental pain at the hands of the sexual object. Masochism, in the form of a perversion, seems to be further removed

---

[1] [In the editions of 1905 and 1910 the following two sentences appeared in the text at this point: 'One at least of the roots of masochism can be inferred with equal certainty. It arises from sexual overvaluation as a necessary psychical consequence of the choice of a sexual object.' From 1915 onwards these sentences were omitted and the next two paragraphs were inserted in their place.]

from the normal sexual aim than its counterpart; it may be doubted at first whether it can ever occur as a primary phenomenon or whether, on the contrary, it may not invariably arise from a transformation of sadism.[1] It can often be shown that masochism is nothing more than an extension of sadism turned round upon the subject's own self, which thus, to begin with, takes the place of the sexual object. Clinical analysis of extreme cases of masochistic perversion show that a great number of factors (such as the castration complex and the sense of guilt) have combined to exaggerate and fixate the original passive sexual attitude.

Pain, which is overriden in such case, thus falls into line with disgust and shame as a force that stands in oppostion and resistance to the libido.

Sadism and masochism occupy a special position among the perversions, since the contrast between activity and passivity which lies behind them is among the universal characteristics of sexual life.

The history of human civilization shows beyond any doubt that there is an intimate connection between cruelty and the sexual instinct; but nothing has been done towards explaining the connection, apart from laying emphasis on the aggressive factor in the libido. According to some authorities this aggressive element of the sexual instinct is in reality a relic of cannibalistic desires – that is, it is a contribution derived from the apparatus for obtaining mastery, which is concerned with the satisfaction of the other and, ontogenetically, the older of the great instinctual needs.[2] It has also been maintained that every pain contains in itself the possibility of a feeling of pleasure. All that need be said is that no satisfactory explanation of this perversion has been put forward and that it seems possible that a number of mental impulses are combined in it to produce a single resultant.[3]

---

[1] [*Footnote added* 1924:] My opinion of masochism has been to a large extent altered by later reflection, based upon certain hypotheses as to the structure of the apparatus of the mind and the classes of instincts operating in it. I have been led to distinguish a primary or *erotogenic* masochism, out of which two later forms, *feminine* and *moral* masochism, have developed. Sadism which cannot find employment in actual life is turned round upon the subject's own self and so produces a *secondary* masochism, which is superadded to the primary kind. (Cf. Freud, 1924c.)

[2] [*Footnote added* 1915:] Cf. my remarks below [p. 336] on the pregenital phases of sexual development, which confirm this view.

[3] [*Footnote added* 1924:] The enquiry mentioned above [in footnote 1] has led me to assign a peculiar position, based upon the origin of the instincts, to the pair of opposites constituted by sadism and masochism, and to place them outside the class of the remaining 'perversions'.

But the most remarkable feature of this perversion is that its active and passive forms are habitually found to occur together in the same individual. A person who feels pleasure in producing pain in someone else in a sexual relationship is also capable of enjoying as pleasure any pain which he may himself derive from sexual relations. A sadist is always at the same time a masochist, although the active or the passive aspect of the perversion may be the more strongly developed in him and may represent his predominant sexual activity.[1]

We find, then, that certain among the impulses to perversion occur regularly as pairs of opposites; and this, taken in conjunction with material which will be brought forward later, has a high theoretical significance.[2] It is, moreover, a suggestive fact that the existence of the pair of opposites formed by sadism and masochism cannot be attributed merely to the element of aggressiveness. We should rather be inclined to connect the simultaneous presence of these opposites with the opposing masculinity and femininity which are combined in bisexuality – a contrast which often has to be replaced in psycho-analysis by that between activity and passivity.[3]

(3) THE PERVERSIONS IN GENERAL

Variation and Disease

It is natural that medical men, who first studied perversions in outstanding examples and under special conditions, should have been inclined to regard them, like inversion, as indications of degeneracy or disease. Nevertheless, it is even easier to dispose of that view in this case than in that of inversion. Everyday experience has shown that most of these extensions, or at any rate the less severe of them, are constituents which are rarely absent from the sexual life of healthy people, and are judged by them no differently from other intimate events. If circumstances favour such an occurrence, normal people too can substitute a perversion of this kind for the normal sexual aim

---

[1] Instead of multiplying the evidence for this statement, I will quote a passage from Havelock Ellis ([1913, 119; 1st ed.:] 1903): 'The investigation of histories of sadism and masochism, even those given by Krafft-Ebing (as indeed Colin Scott and Féré have already pointed out), constantly reveals traces of both groups of phenomena in the same individual.'

[2] [*Footnote added* 1915:] Cf. my discussion of 'ambivalence' below [p. 338].

[3] [The last clause did not occur in the 1905 or 1910 editions. In 1915 the following clause was added: 'a contrast whose significance is reduced in psycho-analysis to that between activity and passivity.' This was replaced in 1924 by the words now appearing in the text.]

for quite a time, or can find place for the one alongside the other. No healthy person, it appears, can fail to make some addition that might be called perverse to the normal sexual aim; and the universality of this finding is in itself enough to show how inappropriate it is to use the word perversion as a term of reproach. In the sphere of sexual life we are brought up against peculiar and, indeed, insoluble difficulties as soon as we try to draw a sharp line to distinguish mere variations within the range of what is physiological from pathological symptoms.

Nevertheless, in some of these perversions the quality of the new sexual aim is of a kind to demand special examination. Certain of them are so far removed from the normal in their content that we cannot avoid pronouncing them 'pathological'. This is especially so where (as, for instance, in cases of licking excrement or of intercourse with dead bodies) the sexual instinct goes to astonishing lengths in successfully overriding the resistances of shame, disgust, horror or pain. But even in such cases we should not be too ready to assume that people who act in this way will necessarily turn out to be insane or subject to grave abnormalities of other kinds. Here again we cannot escape from the fact that people whose behaviour is in other respects normal can, under the domination of the most unruly of all the instincts, put themselves in the category of sick persons in the single sphere of sexual life. On the other hand, manifest abnormality in the other relations of life can invariably be shown to have a background of abnormal sexual conduct.

In the majority of instances the pathological character in a perversion is found to lie not in the *content* of the new sexual aim but in its relation to the normal. If a perversion, instead of appearing merely *alongside* the normal sexual aim and object, and only when circumstances are unfavourable to *them* and favourable to *it* – if, instead of this, it ousts them completely and takes their place in *all* circumstances – if, in short, a perversion has the characteristics of exclusiveness and fixation – then we shall usually be justified in regarding it as a pathological symptom.

The Mental Factor in the Perversions

It is perhaps in connection precisely with the most repulsive perversions that the mental factor must be regarded as playing its largest part in the transformation of the sexual instinct. It is impossible to deny that in their case a piece of mental work has been performed which, in spite of its horrifying result, is the equivalent of an idealization of the instinct. The omnipotence of love is perhaps never more strongly proved than in such of its aberrations as these. The highest and the lowest are always closest to each other in the sphere of sexuality: 'vom Himmel durch die Welt zur Hölle.'[1]

Two Conclusions

Our study of the perversions has shown us that the sexual instinct has to struggle against certain mental forces which act as resistances, and of which shame and disgust are the most prominent. It is permissible to suppose that these forces play a part in restraining that instinct within the limits that are regarded as normal; and if they develop in the individual before the sexual instinct has reached its full strength, it is no doubt they that will determine the course of its development.[2]

In the second place we have found that some of the perversions which we have examined are only made intelligible if we assume the convergence of several motive forces. If such perversions admit of analysis, that is, if they can be taken to pieces, then they must be of a composite nature. This gives us a hint that perhaps the sexual instinct itself may be no simple thing, but put together from components which have come apart again in the perversions. If this is so, the clinical observation of these abnormalities will have drawn our attention to amalgamations which have been lost to view in the uniform behaviour of normal people.[3]

---

[1] ['From Heaven, across the world, to Hell.'
Goethe, *Faust*, Prelude in the Theatre.]
[2] [*Footnote added* 1915:] On the other hand, these forces which act like dams upon sexual development – disgust, shame and morality – must also be regarded as historical precipitates of the external inhibitions to which the sexual instinct has been subjected during the psychogenesis of the human race. We can observe the way in which, in the development of individuals, they arise at the appropriate moment, as though spontaneously, when upbringing and external influence give the signal.
[3] [*Footnote added* 1920:] As regards the origin of the perversions, I will add a word in anticipation of what is to come. There is reason to suppose that, just as in the case of fetishism, abortive beginnings of normal sexual development occur before the perversions become fixated. Analytic investigation has already been able to show in a few cases that perversions are a residue of development towards the Oedipus complex and that after the repression of that complex the components of the sexual instinct which are strongest in the disposition of the individual concerned emerge once more.

(4) THE SEXUAL INSTINCT IN NEUROTICS

Psycho-Analysis

An important addition to our knowledge of the sexual instinct in certain people who at least approximate to the normal can be obtained from a source which can only be reached in one particular way. There is only one means of obtaining exhaustive information that will not be misleading about the sexual life of the persons known as 'psychoneurotics' – sufferers from hysteria, from obsessional neurosis, from what is wrongly described as neurasthenia, and, undoubtedly, from dementia praecox and paranoia was well. They must be subject to psycho-analytic investigation, which is employed in the therapeutic procedure introduced by Josef Breuer and myself in 1893 and known at that time as 'catharsis'.

I must first explain – as I have already done in other writings – that all my experience shows that these psychoneuroses are based on sexual instinctual forces. By this I do not merely mean that the energy of the sexual instinct makes a contribution to the forces that maintain the pathological manifestations (the symptoms). I mean expressly to assert that that contribution is the most important and only constant source of energy of the neurosis and that in consequence the sexual life of the persons in question is expressed – whether exclusively or principally or only partly – in these symptoms. As I have put it elsewhere [1905e, Postscript], the symptoms constitute the sexual activity of the patient. The evidence for this assertion is derived from the ever-increasing number of psycho-analyses of hysterical and other neurotics which I have carried out during the last 25 years and of whose findings I have given (and shall continue to give) a detailed account in other publications.[1]

The removal of the symptoms of hysterical patients by psycho-analysis proceeds on the supposition that those symptoms are substitutes – transcriptions as it were – for a number of emotionally cathected mental processes, wishes and desires, which, by the operation of a special psychical procedure (repression), have been prevented from obtaining discharge in psychical activity that is admissible to consciousness. These mental processes, therefore, being held

[1] [*Footnote added* 1920:] It implies no qualification of the above assertion, but rather an amplification of it, if I restate it as follows: neurotic symptoms are based on the one hand on the demands of the libidinal instincts and on the other hand on those made by the ego by way of reaction to them.

back in a state of unconsciousness, strive to obtain an expression that shall be appropriate to their emotional importance – to obtain discharge; and in the case of hysteria they find such an expression (by means of the process of 'conversion') in somatic phenomena, that is, in hysterical symptoms. By systematically turning these symptoms back (with the help of a special technique) into emotionally cathected ideas – ideas that will now have become conscious – it is possible to obtain that most accurate knowledge of the nature and origin of these formerly unconscious psychical structures.

Findings of Psycho-Analysis

In this manner the fact has emerged that symptoms represent a substitute for impulses the source of whose strength is derived from the sexual instinct. What we know about the nature of hysterics before they fall ill – and they may be regarded as typical of all psychoneurotics – and about the occasions which precipitate their falling ill, is in complete harmony with this view. The character of hysterics shows a degree of sexual repression in excess of the normal quantity, an intensification of resistance against the sexual instinct (which we have already met with in the form of shame, disgust and morality), and what seems like an instinctive aversion on their part to any intellectual consideration of sexual problems. As a result of this, in especially marked cases, the patients remain in complete ignorance of sexual matters right into the period of sexual maturity.[1]

On a cursory view, this trait, which is so characteristic of hysteria, is not uncommonly screened by the existence of a second constitutional character present in hysteria, namely the predominant development of the sexual instinct. Psycho-analysis, however, can invariably bring the first of these factors to light and clear up the enigmatic contradiction which hysteria presents, by revealing the pair of opposites by which it is characterized – exaggerated sexual craving and excessive aversion to sexuality.

In the case of anyone who is predisposed to hysteria, the onset of his illness is precipitated when, either as a result of his own progressive maturity or of the external circumstances of his life, he finds himself faced by the demands of a real sexual situation. Between the pressure

---

[1] Breuer [in the second paragraph of the first case history, Breuer and Freud, 1895*d*] writes of the patient in connection with whom he first adopted the cathartic method: 'The factor of sexuality was astonishingly undeveloped in her.'

of the instinct and his antagonism to sexuality, illness offers him a way of escape. It does not solve his conflict, but seeks to evade it by transforming his libidinal impulses into symptoms.[1] The exception is only an *apparent* one when a hysteric – a male patient it may be – falls ill as a result of some trivial emotion, some conflict which does not centre around any sexual interest. In such cases psycho-analysis is regularly able to show that the illness has been made possible by the sexual component of the conflict, which has prevented the mental processes from reaching a normal issue.

Neurosis and Perversion

There is no doubt that a large part of the opposition to these views of mine is due to the fact that sexuality, to which I trace back psycho-neurotic symptoms, is regarded as though it coincided with the normal sexual instinct. But psycho-analytic teaching goes further than this. It shows that it is by no means only at the cost of the so-called *normal* sexual instinct that these symptoms originate – at any rate such is not exclusively or mainly the case; they also give expression (by conversion) to instincts which would be described as *perverse* in the widest sense of the word if they could be expressed directly in phantasy and action without being diverted from consciousness. Thus symptoms are formed in part at the cost of *abnormal* sexuality; *neuroses are, so to say, the negative of perversions*.[2]

The sexual instinct of psychoneurotics exhibits all the aberrations which we have studied as variations of normal, and as manifestations of abnormal, sexual life.

(*a*) The unconscious mental life of all neurotics (without exception) shows inverted impulses, fixation of their libido upon persons of their own sex. It would be impossible without deep discussion to give any adequate appreciation of the importance of this factor in determining the form taken by the symptoms of the illness. I can only insist that an unconscious tendency to inversion is never absent

---

[1] [This theme was elaborated by Freud in his paper on the different types of onset of neurosis (1912c).]

[2] [Cf. the case history of 'Dora' (1905e).] The contents of the clearly conscious phantasies of perverts (which in favourable circumstances can be transformed into manifest behaviour), of the delusional fears of paranoics (which are projected in a hostile sense on to other people) and of the unconscious phantasies of hysterics (which psycho-analysis reveals behind their symptoms) – all of these coincide with one another even down to their details.

and is of particular value in throwing light upon hysteria in men.[1]

(*b*) It is possible to trace in the unconscious of psychoneurotics tendencies to every kind of anatomical extension of sexual activity and to show that those tendencies are factors in the formation of symptoms. Among them we find occurring with particular frequency those in which the mucous membrane of the mouth and anus are assigned the role of genitals.

(*c*) An especially prominent part is played as factors in the formation of symptoms in psychoneuroses by the component instincts, which emerge for the most part as pairs of opposites and which we have met with as introducing new sexual aims – the scopophilic instinct and exhibitionism and the active and passive forms of the instinct for cruelty. The contribution made by the last of these is essential to the understanding of the fact that symptoms involve *suffering*, and it almost invariably dominates a part of the patient's social behaviour. It is also through the medium of this connection between libido and cruelty that the transformation of love into hate takes place, the transformation of affectionate into hostile impulses, which is characteristic of a great number of cases of neurosis, and indeed, it would seem, of paranoia in general.

The interest of these findings is still further increased by certain special facts.[2]

(α) Whenever we find in the unconscious an instinct of this sort which is capable of being paired off with an opposite one, this second instinct will regularly be found in operation as well. Every active perversion is thus accompanied by its passive counterpart: anyone who is an exhibitionist in his unconscious is at the same time a *voyeur*; in anyone who suffers from the consequences of repressed sadistic impulses there is sure to be another determinant of his symptoms which has its source in masochistic inclinations. The complete

[1] Psychoneuroses are also very often associated with *manifest* inversion. In such cases the heterosexual current of feeling has undergone complete suppression. It is only fair to say that my attention was first drawn to the necessary universality of the tendency to inversion in psychoneurotics by Wilhelm Fliess of Berlin, after I had discussed its presence in individual cases. – [*Added* 1920:] This fact, which has not been sufficiently appreciated, cannot fail to have a decisive influence on any theory of homosexuality.

[2] [In the editions before 1920 *three* such 'special facts' were enumerated. The first, which was subsequently omitted, ran as follows: 'Among the unconscious trains of thought found in neuroses there is nothing corresponding to a tendency to fetishism – a circumstance which throws light on the psychological peculiarity of this well-understood perversion.']

agreement which is here shown with what we have found to exist in the corresponding 'positive' perversions is most remarkable, though in the actual symptoms one or other of the opposing tendencies plays the predominant part.

(β) In any fairly marked case of psychoneurosis it is unusual for only a single one of these perverse instincts to be developed. We usually find a considerable number and as a rule traces of them all. The degree of development of each particular instinct is, however, independent of that of the others. Here, too, the study of the 'positive' perversions provides an exact counterpart.

(5) COMPONENT INSTINCTS AND EROTOGENIC ZONES

If we put together what we have learned from our investigation of positive and negative perversions, it seems plausible to trace them back to a number of 'component instincts', which, however, are not of a primary nature, but are susceptible to further analysis.[1] By an 'instinct' is provisionally to be understood the psychical representative of an endosomatic, continuously flowing source of stimulation, as contrasted with a 'stimulus', which is set up by *single* excitations coming from *without*. The concept of instinct is thus one of those lying on the frontier between the mental and the physical. The simplest and likeliest assumption as to the nature of instincts would seem to be that in itself an instinct is without quality, and, so far as mental life is concerned, is only to be regarded as a measure of the demand made upon the mind for work. What distinguishes the instincts from one another and endows them with specific qualities is their relation to their somatic sources and to their aims. The source of an instinct is a process of excitation occurring in an organ and the immediate aim of the instinct lies in the removal of this organic stimulus.[2]

[1] [The passage from this point till the end of the paragraph dates from 1915. In the first two editions (1905 and 1910) the following sentences appeared instead: 'We can distinguish in them [the component instincts] (in addition to an 'instinct' which is not itself sexual and which has its source in motor impulses) a contribution from an organ capable of receiving stimuli (e.g. the skin, the mucous membrane or a sense organ). An organ of this kind will be described in this connection as an "erotogenic zone" – as being the organ whose excitation lends the instinct a sexual character.' – The revised version dates from the period of Freud's paper on 'Instincts and their Vicissitudes' (1915c), where the whole topic is examined at length. Cf. Chapter 4.]

[2] [*Footnote added* 1924:] The theory of the instincts is the most important but at the same time the least complete portion of psycho-analytic theory. I have made further contributions to it in my later works *Beyond the Pleasure Principle* (1920g) and *The Ego and the Id* (1923b). [Cf. Chapters 4 and 6.]

There is a further provisional assumption that we cannot escape in the theory of the instincts. It is to the effect that excitations of two kinds arise from the somatic organs, based upon differences of a chemical nature. One of these kinds of excitation we describe as being specifically sexual, and we speak of the organ concerned as the 'erotogenic zone' of the sexual component instinct arising from it.[1]

The part played by the erotogenic zones is immediately obvious in the case of those perversions which assign a sexual significance to the oral and anal orifices. These behave in every respect like a portion of the sexual apparatus. In hysteria these parts of the body and the neighbouring tracts of mucous membrane become the seat of new sensations and of changes in innervation – indeed, of processes that can be compared to erection – in just the same way as do the actual genitalia under the excitations of the normal sexual processes.

The significance of the erotogenic zones as apparatuses subordinate to the genitals and as substitutes for them is, among all the psychoneuroses, most clearly to be seen in hysteria; but this does not imply that that significance is any the less in the other forms of illness. It is only that in them it is less recognizable, because in their case (obsessional neurosis and paranoia) the formation of the symptoms takes place in regions of the mental apparatus which are more remote from the particular centres concerned with somatic control. In obsessional neurosis what is more striking is the significance of those impulses which create new sexual aims and seem independent of erotogenic zones. Nevertheless, in scopophilia and exhibitionism the eye corresponds to an erotogenic zone; while in the case of those components of the sexual instinct which involve pain and cruelty the same role is assumed by the skin – the skin, which in particular parts of the body has become differentiated into sense organs or modified into mucous membrane, and is thus the erotogenic zone *par excellence*.[2]

[1] [*Footnote added* 1915:] It is not easy in the present place to justify these assumptions, derived as they are from the study of a particular class of neurotic illness. But on the other hand, if I omitted all mention of them, it would be impossible to say anything of substance about the instincts.

[2] We are reminded at this point of Moll's analysis of the sexual instinct into an instinct of 'contrectation' and an instinct of 'detumescence'. Contrectation represents a need for contact with the skin. [The instinct of detumescence was described by Moll (1898) as an impulse for the spasmodic relief of tension of the sexual organs, and the instinct of contrectation as an impulse to come into contact with another person. He believed that the latter impulse arose later than the first in the individual's development. – The following additional sentence appeared at the end of this footnote in 1905 and 1910, but was afterwards omitted: 'Strohmayer has very rightly inferred from a case under his observation that obsessive self-reproaches originate from suppressed sadistic impulses.']

(6) REASONS FOR THE APPARENT PREPONDERANCE OF
PERVERSE SEXUALITY IN THE PSYCHONEUROSES

The preceding discussion may perhaps have placed the sexuality of psychoneurotics in a false light. It may have given the impression that, owing to their disposition, psychoneurotics approximate closely to perverts in their sexual behaviour and are proportionately remote from normal people. It may indeed very well be that the constitutional disposition of these patients (apart from their exaggerated degree of sexual repression and the excessive intensity of their sexual instinct) includes an unusual tendency to perversion, using that word in its widest sense. Nevertheless, investigation of comparatively slight cases shows that this last assumption is not absolutely necessary, or at least that in forming a judgement on these pathological developments there is a factor to be considered which weighs in the other direction. Most psychoneurotics only fall ill after the age of puberty as a result of the demands made upon them by normal sexual life. (It is most particularly against the latter that repression is directed.) Or else illnesses of this kind set in later, when the libido fails to obtain satisfaction along normal lines. In both these cases the libido behaves like a stream whose main bed has become blocked. It proceeds to fill up collateral channels which may hitherto have been empty. Thus, in the same way, what appears to be the strong tendency (though, it is true, a negative one) of psychoneurotics to perversion may be collaterally determined, and must, in any case, be collaterally intensified. The fact is that we must put sexual repression as an internal factor alongside such external factors as limitation of freedom, inaccessibility of a normal sexual object, the dangers of the normal sexual act, etc., which bring about perversions in persons who might perhaps otherwise have remained normal.

In this respect different cases of neurosis may behave differently: in one case the preponderating factor may be the innate strength of the tendency to perversion, in another it may be the collateral increase of that tendency owing to the libido being forced away from a normal sexual aim and sexual object. It would be wrong to represent as opposition what is in fact a co-operative relation. Neurosis will always produce its greatest effects when constitution and experience work together in the same direction. Where the constitution is a marked one it will perhaps not require the support of actual experiences; while a great shock in real life will perhaps bring about a neurosis even in an average constitution. (Incidentally, this view of the relative aetiological importance of what is innate and what is accidentally experienced applies equally in other fields.)

If we prefer to suppose, nevertheless, that a particularly strongly developed tendency to perversion is among the characteristics of psychoneurotic constitutions, we have before us the prospect of being able to distinguish a number of such constitutions according to the innate preponderance of one or the other of the erotogenic zones or of one or the other of the component instincts. The question whether a special relation holds between the perverse disposition and the particular form of illness adopted, has, like so much else in this field, not yet been investigated.

(7) INTIMATION OF THE INFANTILE CHARACTER OF SEXUALITY

By demonstrating the part played by perverse impulses in the formation of symptoms in the psychoneuroses, we have quite remarkably increased the number of people who might be regarded as perverts. It is not only that neurotics in themselves constitute a very numerous class, but it must also be considered that an unbroken chain bridges the gap between the neuroses in all their manifestations and normality. After all, Moebius could say with justice that we are all to some extent hysterics. Thus the extraordinarily wide dissemination of the perversions forces us to suppose that the disposition to perversions is itself of no great rarity but must form a part of what passes as the normal constitution.

It is, as we have seen, debatable whether the perversions go back to innate determinants or arise, as Binet assumed was the case with fetishism, owing to chance experiences. The conclusion now presents itself to us that there is indeed something innate lying behind the perversions but that it is something innate in *everyone*, though as a disposition it may vary in its intensity and may be increased by the influences of actual life. What is in question are the innate constitutional roots of the sexual instinct. In one class of cases (the perversions) these roots may grow into the actual vehicles of sexual activity; in others they may be submitted to an insufficient suppression (repression) and thus be able in a roundabout way to attract a considerable proportion of sexual energy to themselves as symptoms; while in the most favourable cases, which lie between these two extremes, they may by means of effective restriction and other kinds of modification bring about what is known as normal sexual life.

We have, however a further reflection to make. This postulated constitution, containing the germs of all the perversions, will only be demonstrable in *children*, even though in them it is only with modest degrees of intensity that any of the instincts can emerge. A formula begins to take shape which lays it down that the sexuality of neurotics has remained in, or been brought back to, an infantile state. Thus our interest turns to the sexual life of children, and we will now proceed to trace the play of influences which govern the evolution of infantile sexuality till its outcome in perversion, neurosis or normal sexual life.

II
Infantile Sexuality

Neglect of the Infantile Factor

One feature of the popular view of the sexual instinct is that it is absent in childhood and only awakens in the period of life described as puberty. This, however, is not merely a simple error but one that has had grave consequences, for it is mainly to this idea that we owe our present ignorance of the fundamental conditions of sexual life. A thorough study of the sexual manifestations of childhood would probably reveal the essential characters of the sexual instinct and would show us the course of its development and the way in which it is put together from various sources.

It is noticeable that writers who concern themselves with explaining the characteristics and reactions of the adult have devoted much more attention to the primaeval period which is comprised in the life of the individual's ancestors – have, that is, ascribed much more influence to heredity – than to the other primaeval period, which falls within the lifetime of the individual himself—that is, to childhood. One would surely have supposed that the influence of this latter period would be easier to understand and could claim to be considered before that of heredity.[1] It is true that in the literature of the subject one occasionally comes across remarks upon precocious sexual activity in small children – upon erections, masturbation and

---

[1] [*Footnote added* 1915:] Nor is it possible to estimate correctly the part played by heredity until the part played by childhood has been assessed.

even activities resembling coitus. But these are always quoted only as exceptional events, as oddities or as horrifying instances of precocious depravity. So far as I know, not a single author has clearly recognized the regular existence of a sexual instinct in childhood; and in the writings that have become so numerous on the development of children, the chapter on 'Sexual Development' is as a rule omitted.[1]

Infantile Amnesia

The reason for this strange neglect is to be sought, I think, partly in considerations of propriety, which the authors obey as a result of their own upbringing, and partly in a psychological phenomenon which has itself hitherto eluded explanation. What I have in mind is the peculiar amnesia which, in the case of most people, though by no means all, hides the earliest beginnings of their childhood up to their sixth or eighth year. Hitherto it has not occurred to us to feel any astonishment at the fact of this amnesia, though we might have had good grounds for doing so. For we learn from other people that during these years, of which at a later date we retain nothing in our memory but a few unintelligible and fragmentary recollections, we reacted in a lively manner to impressions, that we were capable of expressing pain

[1] The assertion made in the text has since struck me myself as being so bold that I have undertaken the task of testing its validity by looking through the literature once more. The outcome of this is that I have allowed my statement to stand unaltered. The scientific examination of both the physical and mental phenomena of sexuality in childhood is still in its earliest beginnings. One writer, Bell (1902, 327), remarks: 'I know of no scientist who has given a careful analysis of the emotion as it is seen in the adolescent.' Somatic sexual manifestations from the period before puberty have only attracted attention in connection with phenomena of degeneracy and as indications of degeneracy. In none of the accounts which I have read of the psychology of this period of life is a chapter to be found on the erotic life of children; and this applies to the well-known works of Preyer [1882], Baldwin (1895), Pérez (1886), Strümpell (1899), Groos (1904), Heller (1904), Sully (1895) and others. We can obtain the clearest impression of the state of things in this field to-day from the periodical *Die Kinderfehler* from 1896 onwards. Nevertheless the conviction is borne in upon us that the existence of love in childhood stands in no need of discovery. Pérez (1886, 272 ff.) argues in favour of its existence. Groos (1899, 326) mentions as a generally recognized fact that 'some children are already accessible to sexual impulses at a very early age and feel an urge to have contact with the opposite sex'. The earliest instance of the appearance of 'sex-love' recorded by Bell (1902, 330) concerns a child in the middle of his third year. On this point compare further Havelock Ellis (1903, Appendix B).

[*Added* 1910:] This judgement upon the literature of infantile sexuality need no longer be maintained since the appearance of Stanley Hall's exhaustive work (1904) by Moll's recent book (1909). See, on the other hand, Bleuler (1908). [*Added* 1915:] Since this was written, a book by Hug-Hellmuth (1913) has taken the neglected sexual factor fully into account.

and joy in a human fashion, that we gave evidence of love, jealousy and other passionate feelings by which we were strongly moved at the time, and even that we gave utterance to remarks which were regarded by adults as good evidence of our possessing insight and the beginnings of a capacity for judgement. And of all this we, when we are grown up, have no knowledge of our own! Why should our memory lag so far behind the other activities of our minds? We have, on the contrary, good reason to believe that there is no period at which the capacity for receiving and reproducing impressions is greater than precisely during the years of childhood.[1]

On the other hand we must assume, or we can convince ourselves by a psychological examination of other people, that the very same impressions that we have forgotten have none the less left the deepest traces on our minds and have had a determining effect upon the whole of our later development. There can, therefore, be no question of any real abolition of the impressions of childhood, but rather of an amnesia similar to that which neurotics exhibit for later events, and of which the essence consists in a simple withholding of these impressions from consciousness, viz., in their repression. But what are the forces which bring about this repression of the impressions of childhood? Whoever could solve this riddle would, I think, have explained *hysterical* amnesia as well.

Meanwhile we must not fail to observe that the existence of infantile amnesia provides a new point of comparison between the mental states of children and psychoneurotics. We have already come across another such point in the formula to which we were led, to the effect that the sexuality of psychoneurotics has remained at, or been carried back to, an infantile stage. Can it be, after all, that infantile amnesia, too, is to be brought into relation with the sexual impulses of childhood?

Moreover, the connection between infantile and hysterical amnesia is more than a mere play upon words. Hysterical amnesia, which occurs at the bidding of repression, is only explicable by the fact that the subject is already in possession of a store of memory-traces which have been withdrawn from conscious disposal, and which are now, by

---

[1] I have attempted to solve one of the problems connected with the earliest memories of childhood in a paper on 'Screen Memories' (1899a). [*Added* 1924:] See also Chapter IV of my *Psychopathology of Everyday Life* (1901b).

an associative link, attracting to themselves the material which the forces of repression are engaged in repelling from consciousness.[1] It may be said that without infantile amnesia there would be no hysterical amnesia.

I believe, then, that infantile amnesia, which turns everyone's childhood into something like a prehistoric epoch and conceals from him the beginnings of his own sexual life, is responsible for the fact that in general no importance is attached to childhood in the development of sexual life. The gaps in our knowledge which have arisen in this way cannot be bridged by a single observer. As long ago as in the year 1896[2] I insisted on the significance of the years of childhood in the origin of certain important phenomena connected with sexual life, and since then I have never ceased to emphasize the part played in sexuality by the infantile factor.

[1] THE PERIOD OF SEXUAL LATENCY IN CHILDHOOD AND ITS INTERRUPTIONS

The remarkably frequent reports of what are described as irregular and exceptional sexual impulses in childhood, as well as the uncovering in neurotics of what have hitherto been unconscious memories of childhood, allow us to sketch out the sexual occurrences of that period in some such way as this.[3]

There seems no doubt that germs of sexual impulses are already present in the new-born child and that these continue to develop for a time, but are then overtaken by a progressive process of suppression; this in turn is itself interrupted by periodical advances in sexual development or may be held up by individual peculiarities. Nothing is known for certain concerning the regularity and periodicity of this oscillating course of development. It seems, however, that the sexual

---

[1] [*Footnote added* 1915:] The mechanism of repression cannot be understood unless account is taken of *both* of these two concurrent processes. They may be compared with the manner in which tourists are conducted to the top of the Great Pyramid of Giza by being pushed from one direction and pulled from the other. [Cf. Freud's paper on 'Repression' (1915*d*), Chapter 8 below.]

[2] [E.g. in the last paragraph of Section I of his paper on the aetiology of hysteria (1896*c*).]

[3] We are able to make use of the second of these two sources of material since we are justified in expecting that the early years of children who are later to become neurotic are not likely in this respect to differ *essentially* from those of children who are to grow up into normal adults, [*added* 1915:] but only in the intensity and clarity of the phenomena involved.

life of children usually emerges in a form accessible to observation round about the third or fourth year of life.[1]

Sexual Inhibitions

It is during this period of total or only partial latency that are built up the mental forces which are later to impede the course of the sexual instinct and, like dams, restrict its flow – disgust, feelings of shame and the claims of aesthetic and moral ideals. One gets an impression from civilized children that the construction of these dams is a product of education, and no doubt education has much to do with it. But in reality this development is organically determined and fixed by heredity, and it can occasionally occur without any help at all from education. Education will not be trespassing beyond its appropriate domain if it limits itself to following the lines which have already been laid down organically and to impressing them somewhat more clearly and deeply.

[1] There is a possible anatomical analogy to what I believe to be the course of development of the infantile sexual function in Bayer's discovery (1902) that the internal sexual organs (i.e. the uterus) are as a rule larger in new-born children than in older ones. It is not certain, however, what view we should take of this involution that occurs after birth (which has been shown by Halban to apply also to other portions of the genital apparatus). According to Halban (1904) the process of involution comes to an end after a few weeks of extra-uterine life. [*Added* 1920:] Those authorities who regard the interstitial portion of the sex-gland as the organ that determines sex have on their side been led by anatomical researches to speak of infantile sexuality and a period of sexual latency. I quote a passage from Lipschütz's book (1919, 168), which I mentioned on p. 292 *n*.: 'We shall be doing more justice to the facts if we say that the maturation of the sexual characters which is accomplished at puberty is only due to a great acceleration which occurs at that time of processes which began much earlier – in my view as early as during intra-uterine life.' 'What has hitherto been described in a summary way as puberty is probably only a second major phase of puberty which sets in about the middle of the second decade of life ... Childhood, from birth until the beginning of this second major phase, might be described as "the intermediate phase of puberty"' (ibid., 170). Attention was drawn to this coincidence between anatomical findings and psychological observation in a review [of Lipschütz's book] by Ferenczi (1920). The agreement is marred only by the fact that the 'first peak' in the development of the sexual organ occurs during the early intra-uterine period, whereas the early efflorescence of infantile sexual life must be ascribed to the third and fourth years of life. There is, of course, no need to expect that anatomical growth and psychical development must be exactly simultaneous. The researches in question were made on the sex-glands of human beings. Since a period of latency in the psychological sense does not occur in animals, it would be very interesting to know whether the anatomical findings which have led these writers to assume the occurrence of two peaks in sexual development are also demonstrable in the higher animals.

Reaction-Formation and Sublimation

What is it that goes to the making of these constructions which are so important for the growth of a civilized and normal individual? They probably emerge at the cost of the infantile sexual impulses themselves. Thus the activity of those impulses does not cease even during this period of latency, though their energy is diverted, wholly or in great part, from their sexual use and directed to other ends. Historians of civilization appear to be at one in assuming that powerful components are acquired for every kind of cultural achievement by this diversion of sexual instinctual forces from sexual aims and their direction to new ones – a process which deserves the name of 'sublimation'. To this we would add, accordingly, that the same process plays a part in the development of the individual and we would place its beginning in the period of sexual latency of childhood.[1]

It is possible further to form some idea of the mechanism of this process of sublimation. On the one hand, it would seem, the sexual impulses cannot be utilized during these years of childhood, since the reproductive functions have been deferred – a fact which constitutes the main feature of the period of latency. On the other hand, these impulses would seem in themselves to be perverse – that is, to arise from erotogenic zones and to derive their activity from instincts which, in view of the direction of the subject's development, can only arouse unpleasurable feelings. They consequently evoke opposing mental forces (reacting impulses) which, in order to suppress this unpleasure effectively, build up the mental dams that I have already mentioned – disgust, shame and morality.[2]

Interruptions of the Latency Period

We must not deceive ourselves as to the hypothetical nature and insufficient clarity of our knowledge concerning the processes of the infantile period of latency or deferment; but we shall be no firmer

[1] Once again, it is from Fliess that I have borrowed the term 'period of sexual latency'.

[2] [*Footnote added* 1915:] In the case which I am here discussing, the sublimation of sexual instinctual forces takes place along the path of reaction-formation. But in general it is possible to distinguish the concepts of sublimation and reaction-formation from each other as two different processes. Sublimation can also take place by other and simpler mechanisms. [Further theoretical discussions of sublimation will be found in Section III of Freud's paper on narcissism (1914c) and at several points in *The Ego and the Id*, pp. 454, 467–8 and 475–7 below.]

ground in pointing out that such an application of infantile sexuality represents an educational ideal from which individual development usually diverges at some point and often to a considerable degree. From time to time a fragmentary manifestation of sexuality which has evaded sublimation may break through; or some sexual activity may persist through the whole duration of the latency period until the sexual instinct emerges with greater intensity at puberty. In so far as educators pay any attention at all to infantile sexuality, they behave exactly as though they shared our views as to the construction of the moral defensive forces at the cost of sexuality, and as though they knew that sexual activity makes a child ineducable: for they stigmatize every sexual manifestation by children as a 'vice', without being able to do much against it. We, on the other hand, have every reason for turning our attention to these phenomena which are so much dreaded by education, for we may expect them to help us to discover the original configuration of the sexual instincts.

[2] THE MANIFESTATIONS OF
INFANTILE SEXUALITY

Thumb-sucking

For reasons which will appear later, I shall take thumb-sucking (or sensual sucking) as a sample of the sexual manifestations of childhood. (An excellent study of this subject has been made by the Hungarian paediatrician, Lindner, 1879.)[1]

Thumb-sucking appears already in early infancy and may continue into maturity, or even persist all through life. It consists in the rhythmic repetition of a sucking contact by the mouth (or lips). There is no question of the purpose of this procedure being the taking of nourishment. A portion of the lip itself, the tongue, or any other part of the skin within reach – even the big toe – may be taken as the object upon which this sucking is carried out. In this connection a grasping-instinct may appear and may manifest itself as a simultaneous rhythmic tugging at the lobes of the ears or a catching hold of some part of another person (as a rule the ear) for the same purpose. Sensual sucking involves a complete absorption of the attention and

---

[1] [There seems to be no nursery word in English equivalent to the German '*lutschen*' and '*ludeln*', used by Freud alongside '*wonnesaugen*' ('sensual sucking'). Conrad in *Struwwelpeter* was a '*Lutscher*'; but, as will be seen from the context, 'suck-a-thumbs' and 'thumb-sucking' have in fact too narrow a connotation for the present purpose.]

leads either to sleep or even to a motor reaction in the nature of an orgasm.[1] It is not infrequently combined with rubbing some sensitive part of the body such as the breast or the external genitalia. Many children proceed by this path from sucking to masturbation.

Lindner himself[2] clearly recognized the sexual nature of this activity and emphasized it without qualification. In the nursery, sucking is often classed along with the other kinds of sexual 'naughtiness' of children. This view has been most energetically repudiated by numbers of paediatricians and nerve-specialists, though this is no doubt partly due to a confusion between 'sexual' and 'genital'. Their objection raises a difficult question and one which cannot be evaded: what is the general characteristic which enables us to recognize the sexual manifestations of children? The concatenation of phenomena into which we have been given an insight by psycho-analytic investigation justifies us, in my opinion, in regarding thumb-sucking as a sexual manifestation and in choosing it for our study of the essential features of infantile sexual activity.[3]

Auto-Erotism

We are in duty bound to make a thorough examination of this example. It must be insisted that the most striking feature of this

[1] Thus we find at this early stage, what holds good all through life, that sexual satisfaction is the best soporific. Most cases of nervous insomnia can be traced back to lack of sexual satisfaction. It is well known that unscrupulous nurses put crying children to sleep by stroking their genitals.

[2] [This paragraph was added in 1915. In its place the following paragraph appears in the editions of 1905 and 1910 only: 'No observer has felt any doubt as to the sexual nature of this activity. Nevertheless, the best theories formed by adults in regard to this example of the sexual behaviour of children leave us in the lurch. Consider Moll's [1898] analysis of the sexual instinct into an instinct of detumescence and an instinct of contrectation. The first of these factors cannot be concerned in our present instance, and the second one can only be recognized with difficulty, since, according to Moll, it emerges later than the instinct of detumescence and is directed towards other people.' – In 1910 the following footnote was attached to the first sentence of this cancelled paragraph: 'With the exception of Moll (1909).']

[3] [*Footnote added* 1920:] In 1919, a Dr Galant published, under the title of 'Das Lutscherli', the confession of a grown-up girl who had never given up this infantile sexual activity and who represents the satisfaction to be gained from sucking as something completely analogous to sexual satisfaction, particularly when this is obtained from a lover's kiss: 'Not every kiss is equal to a "*Lutscherli*" – no, no, not by any means! It is impossible to describe what a lovely feeling goes through your whole body when you suck; you are right away from this world. You are absolutely satisfied, and happy beyond desire. It is a wonderful feeling; you long for nothing but peace – uninterrupted peace. It is just unspeakably lovely: you feel no pain and no sorrow, and ah! you are carried into another world.'

sexual activity is that the instinct is not directed towards other people, but obtains satisfaction from the subject's own body. It is 'auto-erotic', to call it by a happily chosen term introduced by Havelock Ellis [1898].[1]

Furthermore, it is clear that the behaviour of a child who indulges in thumb-sucking is determined by a search for some pleasure which has already been experienced and is now remembered. In the simplest case he proceeds to find this satisfaction by sucking rhythmically at some part of the skin or mucous membrane. It is also easy to guess the occasions on which the child had his first experiences of the pleasure which he is now striving to renew. It was the child's first and most vital activity, his sucking at his mother's breast, or at substitutes for it, that must have familiarized him with this pleasure. The child's lips, in our view, behave like an erotogenic zone, and no doubt stimulation by the warm flow of milk is the cause of the pleasurable sensation. The satisfaction of the erotogenic zone is associated, in the first instance, with the satisfaction of the need for nourishment. To begin with, sexual activity attaches itself to functions serving the purpose of self-preservation and does not become independent of them until later.[2] No one who has seen a baby sinking back satiated from the breast and falling asleep with flushed cheeks and a blissful smile can escape the reflection that this picture persists as a prototype of the expression of sexual satisfaction in later life. The need for repeating the sexual satisfaction now becomes detached from the need for taking nourishment – a separation which becomes inevitable when the teeth appear and food is no longer taken in only by sucking, but is also chewed up. The child does not make use of an extraneous body for his sucking, but prefers a part of his own skin because it is more convenient, because it makes him independent of the external world, which he is not yet able to control, and because in that way he provides himself, as it were, with a second erotogenic zone, though one of an inferior kind. The inferiority of this second region is among

---

[1] [*Footnote added* 1920:] Havelock Ellis, it is true, uses the word 'auto-erotic' in a somewhat different sense, to describe an excitation which is not provoked from outside but arises internally. What psycho-analysis regards as the essential point is not the genesis of the excitation, but the question of its relation to an object. – [In all editions before 1920 this footnote read as follows: 'Havelock Ellis, however, has spoilt the meaning of the term he invented by including the whole of hysteria and all the manifestations of masturbation among the phenomena of auto-erotism.']

[2] [This sentence was added in 1915. Cf. Section II of Freud's paper on narcissism (1914c).]

the reasons why at a later date he seeks the corresponding part – the lips – of another person. ('It's a pity I can't kiss myself', he seems to be saying.)

It is not every child who sucks in this way. It may be assumed that those children do so in whom there is a constitutional intensification of the erotogenic significance of the labial region. If that significance persists, these same children when they are grown up will become epicures in kissing, will be inclined to perverse kissing, or, if males, will have a powerful motive for drinking and smoking. If, however, repression ensues, they will feel disgust at food and will produce hysterical vomiting. The repression extends to the nutritional instinct owing to the dual purpose served by the labial zone. Many of my women patients who suffer from disturbances of eating, *globus hystericus*, constriction of the throat and vomiting, have indulged energetically in sucking during their childhood.

Our study of thumb-sucking or sensual sucking has already given us the three essential characteristics of an infantile sexual manifestation. At its origin it attaches itself to one of the vital somatic functions;[1] it has as yet no sexual object, and is thus auto-erotic; and its sexual aim is dominated by an erotogenic zone. It is to be anticipated that these characteristics will be found to apply equally to most of the other activities of the infantile sexual instincts.

[3] THE SEXUAL AIM OF INFANTILE SEXUALITY

Characteristics of Erotogenic Zones

The example of thumb-sucking shows us still more about what constitutes an erotogenic zone. It is a part of the skin or mucoumembrane in which stimuli of a certain sort evoke a feeling of pleasure possessing a particular quality. There can be no doubt that the stimuli which produce the pleasure are governed by special conditions, though we do not know what those are. A rhythmic character must play a part among them and the analogy of tickling is forced upon our notice. It seems less certain whether the character of the pleasurable feeling evoked by the stimulus should be described as a 'specific' one – a 'specific' quality in which the sexual factor would precisely lie. Psychology is still so much in the dark in questions of pleasure and

---

[1] [This clause was added in 1915; and in the earlier editions the word 'three' in the last sentence is replaced by 'two'.]

unpleasure that the most cautious assumption is the one most to be recommended. We may later come upon reasons which seem to support the idea that the pleasurable feeling does in fact possess a specific quality.

The character of erotogenicity can be attached to some parts of the body in a particularly marked way. There are predestined erotogenic zones, as is shown by the example of sucking. The same example, however, also shows us that any other part of the skin or mucous membrane can take over the functions of an erotogenic zone, and must therefore have some aptitude in that direction. Thus the quality of the stimulus has more to do with producing the pleasurable feeling than has the nature of the part of the body concerned. A child who is indulging in sensual sucking searches about his body and chooses some part of it to suck – a part which is afterwards preferred by him from force of habit; if he happens to hit upon one of the predestined regions (such as the nipples or genitals) no doubt it retains the preference. A precisely analogous tendency to displacement is also found in the symptomatology of hysteria. In that neurosis repression affects most of all the actual genital zones and these transmit their susceptibility to stimulation to other erotogenic zones (normally neglected in adult life), which then behave exactly like genitals. But besides this, precisely as in the case of sucking, any other part of the body can acquire the same susceptibility to simulation as is possessed by the genitals and can become an erotogenic zone. Erotogenic and hysterogenic zones show the same characteristics.[1]

The Infantile Sexual Aim

The sexual aim of the infantile instinct consists in obtaining satisfaction by means of an appropriate stimulation of the erotogenic zone which has been selected in one way or another. This satisfaction must have been previously experienced in order to have left behind a need for its repetition; and we may expect that Nature will have made safe provisions so that this experience of satisfaction shall not be left to

---

[1] [Footnote added 1915:] After further reflection and after taking other observations into account, I have been led to ascribe the quality of erotogenicity to all parts of the body and to all the internal organs. Cf. also in this connection what is said below on narcissism [p. 353 f.]. [In the 1910 edition only, the following footnote appeared at this point: 'The biological problems relating to the hypothesis of erotogenic zones have been discussed by Alfred Adler (1907).']

chance.[1] We have already learnt what the contrivance is that fulfils this purpose in the case of the labial zone: it is the simultaneous connection which links this part of the body with the taking in of food. We shall come across other, similar contrivances as sources of sexuality. The state of being in need of a repetition of the satisfaction reveals itself in two ways: by a peculiar feeling of tension, possessing, rather, the character of unpleasure, and by a sensation of itching or stimulation which is centrally conditioned and projected on to the peripheral erotogenic zone. We can therefore formulate a sexual aim in another way: it consists in replacing the projected sensation of stimulation in the erotogenic zone by an external stimulus which removes that sensation by producing a feeling of satisfaction. This external stimulus will usually consist in some kind of manipulation that is analogous to the sucking.

The fact that the need can also be evoked peripherally, by a real modification of the erotogenic zone, is in complete harmony with our physiological knowledge. This strikes us as somewhat strange only because, in order to remove one stimulus, it seems necessary to adduce a second one at the same spot.

[4] MASTURBATORY SEXUAL MANIFESTATIONS[2]

It must come as a great relief to find that, when once we have understood the nature of the instinct arising from a single one of the erotogenic zones, we shall have very little more to learn of the sexual activity of children. The clearest distinctions as between one zone and another concern the nature of the contrivance necessary for satisfying the instinct; in the case of the labial zone it consisted of sucking, and this has to be replaced by other muscular actions according to the position and nature of the other zones.

Activity of the Anal Zone

Like the labial zone, the anal zone is well suited by its position to act as a medium through which sexuality may attach itself to other somatic functions. It is to be presumed that the erotogenic significance of this

[1] [*Footnote added* 1920:] In biological discussions it is scarcely possible to avoid a teleological way of thinking, even though one is aware that in any particular instance one is not secure against error.

[2] Cf. the very copious literature on the subject of masturbation, which for the most part, however, is at sea upon the main issues, e.g. Rohleder (1899). [*Added* 1915:] See also the report of the discussion on the subject in the Vienna Psycho-Analytical Society (*Diskussionen*, 1912) – [and especially Freud's own contributions to it (1912*f*)].

part of the body is very great from the first. We learn with some astonishment from psycho-analysis of the transmutations normally undergone by the sexual excitations arising from this zone and of the frequency with which it retains a considerable amount of susceptibility to genital stimulation throughout life.[1] The intestinal disturbances which are so common in childhood see to it that the zone shall not lack intense excitations. Intestinal catarrhs at the tenderest age make children 'nervy', as people say, and in cases of later neurotic illness they have a determining influence on the symptoms in which the neurosis is expressed, and they put at its disposal the whole range of intestinal disturbances. If we bear in mind the erotogenic significance of the outlet of the intestinal canal, which persists, at all events in a modified form, we shall not be inclined to scoff at the influence of haemorrhoids, to which old-fashioned medicine used to attach so much importance in explaining neurotic conditions.

Children who are making use of the susceptibility to erotogenic stimulation of the anal zone betray themselves by holding back their stool till its accumulation brings about violent muscular contractions and, as it passes through the anus, is able to produce powerful stimulation of the mucous membrane. In so doing it must no doubt cause not only painful but also highly pleasurable sensations. One of the clearest signs of subsequent eccentricity or nervousness is to be seen when a baby obstinately refuses to empty his bowels when he is put on the pot – that is, when his nurse wants him to – and holds back that function till he himself chooses to exercise it. He is naturally not concerned with dirtying the bed, he is only anxious not to miss the subsidiary pleasure attached to defaecating. Educators are once more right when they describe children who keep the process back as 'naughty'.

The contents of the bowels,[2] which act as a stimulating mass upon a sexually sensitive portion of mucous membrane, behave like forerunners of another organ, which is destined to come into action after the phase of childhood. But they have other important meanings for the infant. They are clearly treated as a part of the infant's own body and represent his first 'gift': by producing them he can express his active compliance with his environment and, by withholding them,

---

[1] [*Footnote added* 1910:] Cf. my papers on 'Character and Anal Erotism' (1908*b*) [*added* 1920:] and 'On Transformations of Instinct as Exemplified in Anal Erotism' (1917*c*).

[2] [This paragraph was added in 1915. Its contents were expanded in one of the papers (1917*c*) mentioned in the last footnote.]

his disobedience. From being a 'gift' they later come to acquire the meaning of 'baby' – for babies, according to one of the sexual theories of children [see below, p. 335], are acquired by eating and are born through the bowels.

The retention of the faecal mass, which is thus carried out intentionally by the child to begin with, in order to serve, as it were, as a masturbatory stimulus upon the anal zone or to be employed in his relation to the people looking after him, is also one of the roots of the constipation which is so common among neuropaths. Further, the whole significance of the anal zone is reflected in the fact that few neurotics are to be found without their special scatological practices, ceremonies, and so on, which they carefully keep secret.[1]

Actual masturbatory stimulation of the anal zone by means of the finger, provoked by a centrally determined or peripherally maintained sensation of itching, is by no means rare among older children.

Activity of the Genital Zones

Among the erotogenic zones that form part of the child's body there is one which certainly does not play the opening part, and which cannot be the vehicle of the oldest sexual impulses, but which is destined to great things in the future. In both male and female children it is brought into connection with micturition (in the glans and clitoris) and in the former is enclosed in a pouch of mucous membrane, so that there can be no lack of stimulation of it by secretions which may give an early start to sexual excitation. The sexual activities of this erotogenic zone, which forms part of the sexual organs proper, are the beginning of what is later to become 'normal' sexual life. The anatomical situation of this region, the secretions in which it is bathed, the washing and rubbing to which it is subjected in the course

---

[1] [Footnote added 1920:] Lou Andreas-Salomé (1916), in a paper which has given us a very much deeper understanding of the significance of anal erotism, has shown how the history of the first prohibition which a child comes across – the prohibition against getting pleasure from anal activity and its products – has a decisive effect on his whole development. This must be the first occasion on which the infant has a glimpse of an environment hostile to his instinctual impulses, on which he learns to separate his own entity from this alien one and on which he carries out the first 'repression' of his possibilities for pleasure. From that time on, what is 'anal' remains the symbol of everything that is to be repudiated and excluded from life. The clear-cut distinction between anal and genital processes which is later insisted upon is contradicted by the close anatomical and functional analogies and relations which hold between them. The genital apparatus remains the neighbour of the cloaca, and actually [to quote Lou Andreas-Salomé] 'in the case of women is only taken from it on lease'.

of a child's toilet, as well as accidental stimulation (such as the movement of intestinal worms in the case of girls), make it inevitable that the pleasurable feeling which this part of the body is capable of producing should be noticed by children even during their earliest infancy, and should give rise to a need for its repetition. If we consider this whole range of contrivances and bear in mind that both making a mess and measures for keeping clean are bound to operate in much the same way, it is scarcely possible to avoid the conclusion that the foundations for the future primacy over sexual activity exercised by this erotogenic zone are established by early infantile masturbation, which scarcely a single individual escapes.[1] The action which disposes of the stimulus and brings about satisfaction consists in a rubbing movement with the hand or in the application of pressure (no doubt in the lines of a pre-existing reflex) either from the hand or by bringing the thighs together. This last method is by far the more common in the case of girls. The preference for the hand which is shown by boys is already evidence of the important contribution which the instinct for mastery is destined to make to masculine sexual activity.[2]

It will be in the interests of clarity[3] if I say at once that three phases of infantile masturbation are to be distinguished. The first of these belongs to early infancy, and the second to the brief efflorescence of

[1] [In the editions of 1905 and 1910 the last part of this sentence read: 'it is difficult to overlook Nature's purpose of establishing the future primacy over sexual activity exercised by this erotogenic zone by means of early infantile masturbation, which scarcely a single individual escapes.' The teleological nature of this argument in favour of the universality of infantile masturbation was sharply criticized by Rudolf Reitler in the course of the discussions on that topic in the Vienna Psycho-Analytical Society in 1912 (*Diskussionen*, 1912, 92 f.). In his own contribution to the discussion (ibid., 134; = Freud, 1912*f*), Freud agreed that the phrasing he had used was unfortunate, and undertook to alter it in later reprints. The present version of the sentence was accordingly substituted in 1915.]

[2] [*Footnote added* 1915:] Unusual techniques in carrying out masturbation in later years seem to point to the influence of a prohibition against masturbation which has been overcome.

[3] [This paragraph was added in 1915. In the edition of that year there were also added the title of the next paragraph and the parenthesis 'as a rule before the fourth year' in its second sentence. Moreover, in the first sentence of the same paragraph the words 'after a short time' were substituted for the words 'at the onset of the latency period' which had appeared in 1905 and 1910. Finally, in those first two editions, the *following* paragraph began with the words 'During the years of childhood (it has not yet been possible to generalize as to the chronology) the sexual excitation of early infancy returns . . .' The motive for all these changes made in 1915 was evidently to distinguish more sharply between the second and first phases of infantile sexual activity and to assign a more precise date – 'about the fourth year' – to the second phase.]

sexual activity about the fourth year of life; only the third phase corresponds to pubertal masturbation, which is often the only kind taken into account.

Second Phase of Infantile Masturbation

The masturbation of early infancy seems to disappear after a short time; but it may persist uninterruptedly until puberty, and this would constitute the first great deviation from the course of development laid down for civilized men. At some point of childhood after early infancy, as a rule before the fourth year, the sexual instinct belonging to the genital zone usually revives and persists again for a time until it is once more suppressed, or it may continue without interruption. This second phase of infantile sexual activity may assume a variety of different forms which can only be determined by a precise analysis of individual cases. But all its details leave behind the deepest (unconscious) impressions in the subject's memory, determine the development of his character, if he is to remain healthy, and the symptomatology of his neurosis, if he is to fall ill after puberty.[1] In the latter case we find that this sexual period has been forgotten and that the conscious memories that bear witness to it have been displaced. (I have already mentioned that I am also inclined to relate normal infantile amnesia to this infantile sexual activity.) Psycho-analytic investigation enables us to make what has been forgotten conscious and thus do away with a compulsion that arises from the unconscious psychical material.

Return of Early Infantile Masturbation

During the years of childhood with which I am now dealing, the sexual excitation of early infancy returns, either as a centrally determined tickling stimulus which seeks satisfaction in masturbation, or as a process in the nature of a nocturnal emission which, like the nocturnal emissions of adult years, achieves satisfaction without the help of any action by the subject. The latter case is the more frequent with girls and in the second half of childhood; its determinants are not

---

[1] [*Footnote added* 1915:] The problem of why the sense of guilt of neurotics is, as Bleuler [1913] recently recognized, regularly attached to the memory of some masturbatory activity, usually at puberty, still awaits an exhaustive analytic explanation. [*Added* 1920:] The most general and most important factor concerned must no doubt be that masturbation represents the executive agency of the whole of infantile sexuality and is, therefore, able to take over the sense of guilt attaching to it.

entirely intelligible and often, though not invariably, it seems to be conditioned by a period of earlier *active* masturbation. The symptoms of these sexual manifestations are scanty; they are mostly displayed on behalf of the still undeveloped sexual apparatus by the *urinary* apparatus, which thus acts, as it were, as the former's trustee. Most of the so-called bladder disorders of this period are sexual disturbances: nocturnal enuresis, unless it represents an epileptic fit, corresponds to a nocturnal emission.

The reappearance of sexual activity is determined by internal causes and external contingencies, both of which can be guessed in cases of neurotic illness from the form taken by their symptoms and can be discovered with certainty by psycho-analytic investigation. I shall have to speak presently of the internal causes; great and lasting importance attaches at this period to the accidental *external* contingencies. In the foreground we find the effects of seduction, which treats a child as a sexual object prematurely and teaches him, in highly emotional circumstances, how to obtain satisfaction from his genital zones, a satisfaction which he is then usually obliged to repeat again and again by masturbation. An influence of this kind may originate either from adults or from other children. I cannot admit that in my paper on 'The Aetiology of Hysteria' (1896c) I exaggerated the frequency or importance of that influence, though I did not then know that persons who remain normal may have had the same experiences in their childhood, and though I consequently overrated the importance of seduction in comparison with the factors of sexual constitution and development.[1] Obviously seduction is not required in order to arouse a child's sexual life; that can also come about spontaneously from internal causes.

Polymorphously Perverse Disposition

It is an instructive fact that under the influence of seduction children can become polymorphously perverse, and can be led into all possible

---

[1] [See Freud's detailed discussion of this in his second paper on the part played by sexuality in the neuroses (1906a).] Havelock Ellis [1903, Appendix B] has published a number of autobiographical narratives written by people who remained predominantly normal in later life and describing the first sexual impulses of their childhood and the occasions which gave rise to them. These reports naturally suffer from the fact that they omit the prehistoric period of the writers' sexual lives, which is veiled by infantile amnesia and which can only be filled in by psycho-analysis in the case of an individual who has developed a neurosis. In more than one respect, nevertheless, the statements are valuable, and similar narratives were what led me to make the modification in my aetiological hypotheses which I have mentioned in the text.

kinds of sexual irregularities. This shows that an aptitude for them is innately present in their disposition. There is consequently little resistance towards carrying them out, since the mental dams against sexual excesses – shame, disgust and morality – have either not yet been constructed at all or are only in course of construction, according to the age of the child. In this respect children behave in the same kind of way as an average uncultivated woman in whom the same poly-morphously perverse disposition persists. Under ordinary conditions she may remain normal sexually, but if she is led on by a clever seducer she will find every sort of perversion to her taste, and will retain them as part of her own sexual activities. Prostitutes exploit the same polymorphous, that is, infantile, disposition for the purposes of their profession; and, considering the immense number of women who are prostitutes or who must be supposed to have an aptitude for prostitution without becoming engaged in it, it becomes impossible not to recognize that this same disposition to perversions of every kind is a general and fundamental human characteristic.

Component Instincts

Moreover, the effects of seduction do not help to reveal the early history of the sexual instinct; they rather confuse our view of it by presenting children prematurely with a sexual object for which the infantile sexual instinct at first shows no need. It must, however, be admitted that infantile sexual life, in spite of the preponderating dominance of erotogenic zones, exhibits components which from the very first involve other people as sexual objects. Such are the instincts of scopophilia, exhibitionism and cruelty, which appear in a sense independently of erotogenic zones; these instincts do not enter into intimate relations with genital life until later, but are already to be observed in childhood as independent impulses, distinct in the first instance from erotogenic sexual activity. Small children are essen-tially without shame, and at some periods of their earliest years show an unmistakable satisfaction in exposing their bodies, with especial emphasis on the sexual parts. The counterpart of this supposedly perverse inclination, curiosity to see other people's genitals, probably does not become manifest until somewhat later in childhood, when the obstacle set up by a sense of shame has already reached a certain degree of development.[1] Under the influence of seduction the scopo-

[1] [In the first (1905) edition this sentence read: 'The counterpart . . . does not join in until later in childhood, when . . .' In 1910 the word 'probably' was inserted; in 1915 'join in' was replaced by 'become manifest'; in 1920 'somewhat' was inserted before 'later'.]

philic perversion can attain great importance in the sexual life of a child. But my researches into the early years of normal people, as well as of neurotic patients, force me to the conclusion that scopophilia can also appear in children as a spontaneous manifestation. Small children whose attention has once been drawn – as a rule by masturbation – to their own genitals usually take the further step without help from outside and develop a lively interest in the genitals of their playmates. Since opportunities for satisfying curiosity of this kind usually occur only in the course of satisfying the two kinds of need for excretion, children of this kind turn into *voyeurs*, eager spectators of the processes of micturition and defaecation. When repression of these inclinations sets in, the desire to see other people's genitals (whether of their own or the opposite sex) persists as a tormenting compulsion, which in some cases of neurosis later affords the strongest motive force for the formation of symptoms.

The cruel component of the sexual instinct develops in childhood even more independently of the sexual activities that are attached to erotogenic zones. Cruelty in general comes easily to the childish nature, since the obstacle that brings the instinct for mastery to a halt at another person's pain – namely a capacity for pity – is developed relatively late. The fundamental psychological analysis of this instinct has, as we know, not yet been satisfactorily achieved. It may be assumed that the impulse of cruelty arises from the instinct for mastery and appears at a period of sexual life at which the genitals have not yet taken over their later role. It then dominates a phase of sexual life which we shall later describe as a pregenital organization.[1] Children who distinguish themselves by special cruelty towards animals and playmates usually give rise to a just suspicion of an intense and precocious sexual activity arising from erotogenic zones; and, though all the sexual instincts may display simultaneous precocity, *erotogenic* sexual activity seems, nevertheless, to be the primary one. The absence of the barrier of pity brings with it a danger that the connection between the cruel and the erotogenic instincts, thus established in childhood, may prove unbreakable in later life. Ever

[1] [The last two sentences were given their present form in 1915. In 1905 and 1910 they read as follows: 'It may be assumed that the impulses of cruelty arise from sources which are in fact independent of sexuality, but may become united with it at an early stage owing to an anastomosis [cross-connection] near their points of origin. Observation teaches us, however, that sexual development and the development of the instinct of scopophilia and cruelty are subject to mutual influences which limit this presumed independence of the two sets of instincts.']

since Jean Jacques Rousseau's *Confessions*, it has been well known to all educationalists that the painful stimulation of the skin of the buttocks is one of the erotogenic roots of the *passive* instinct of cruelty (masochism). The conclusion has rightly been drawn by them that corporal punishment, which is usually applied to this part of the body, should not be inflicted upon any children whose libido is liable to be forced into collateral channels by the later demands of cultural education.[1]

[5] THE SEXUAL RESEARCHES OF CHILDHOOD

The Instinct for Knowledge

At about the same time as the sexual life of children reaches its first peak, between the ages of three and five, they also begin to show signs of the activity which may be ascribed to the instinct for knowledge or research. This instinct cannot be counted among the elementary instinctual components, nor can it be classed as exclusively belonging to sexuality. Its activity corresponds on the one hand to a sublimated manner of obtaining mastery, while on the other hand it makes use of the energy of scopophilia. Its relations to sexual life, however, are of particular importance, since we have learnt from psycho-analysis that the instinct for knowledge in children is attracted unexpectedly early and intensively to sexual problems and is in fact possibly first aroused by them.

---

[1] [*Footnote added* 1910:] When the account which I have given above of infantile sexuality was first published in 1905, it was founded for the most part on the results of psycho-analytic research upon adults. At that time it was impossible to make full use of direct observation on children: only isolated hints and some valuable pieces of confirmation came from that source. Since then it has become possible to gain direct insight into infantile psycho-sexuality by the analysis of some cases of neurotic illness during the early years of childhood. It is gratifying to be able to report that direct observation has fully confirmed the conclusions arrived at by psycho-analysis – which is incidentally good evidence of the trustworthiness of that method of research. In addition to this, the 'Analysis of a Phobia in a Five-Year-Old Boy' (1909*b*) has taught us much that is new for which we have not been prepared by psycho-analysis: for instance, the fact that sexual symbolism – the representation of what is sexual by non-sexual objects and relations – extends back into the first years of possession of the power of speech. I was further made aware of a defect in the account I have given in the text, which, in the interests of lucidity, describes the conceptual distinction between the two phases of auto-erotism and object-love as though it were also a separation in time. But the analyses that I have just mentioned, as well as the findings of Bell quoted above, show that children between the ages of three and five are capable of very clear object-choice, accompanied by strong affects.

The Riddle of the Sphinx

It is not by theoretical interests but by practical ones that activities of research are set going in children. The threat to the bases of a child's existence offered by the discovery or the suspicion of the arrival of a new baby and the fear that he may, as a result of it, cease to be cared for and loved, make him thoughtful and clear-sighted. And this history of the instinct's origin is in line with the fact that the first problem with which it deals is not the question of the distinction between the sexes but the riddle of where babies come from.[1] (This, in a distorted form which can easily be rectified, is the same riddle that was propounded by the Theban Sphinx.) On the contrary, the existence of two sexes does not to begin with arouse any difficulties or doubts in children. It is self-evident to a male child that a genital like his own is to be attributed to everyone he knows, and he cannot make its absence tally with his picture of these other people.

Castration Complex and Penis Envy

This conviction is energetically maintained by boys, is obstinately defended against the contradictions which soon result from observation, and is only abandoned after severe internal struggles (the castration complex). The substitutes for this penis which they feel is missing in women play a great part in determining the form taken by many perversions.[2]

The assumption that all human beings have the same (male) form of genital is the first of the many remarkable and momentous sexual theories of children. It is of little use to a child that the science of biology justifies his prejudice and has been obliged to recognize the female clitoris as a true substitute for the penis.

Little girls do not resort to denial of this kind when they see that boys' genitals are formed differently from their own. They are ready to recognize them immediately and are overcome by envy for the penis – an envy culminating in the wish, which is so important in its consequences, to be boys themselves.

---

[1] [In a later work, Freud (1925*j*) corrected this statement, saying that it is not true of girls, and not always true of boys. Cf. p. 406 *n.* 2 below.]

[2] [*Footnote added* 1920:] We are justified in speaking of a castration complex in women as well. Both male and female children form a theory that women no less than men originally had a penis, but that they have lost it by castration. The conviction which is finally reached by males that women have no penis often leads them to an enduringly low opinion of the other sex.

Theories of Birth

Many people can remember clearly what an intense interest they took during the prepubertal period in the question of where babies come from. The anatomical answers to the question were at the time very various: babies come out of the breast, or are cut out of the body, or the navel opens to let them through.[1] Outside analysis, there are very seldom memories of any similar researches having been carried out in the *early* years of childhood. These earlier researches fell a victim to repression long since, but all their findings were of a uniform nature: people get babies by eating some particular thing (as they do in fairy tales) and babies are born through the bowel like a discharge of faeces. These infantile theories remind us of conditions that exist in the animal kingdom – and especially of the cloaca in types of animals lower than mammals.

Sadistic View of Sexual Intercourse

If children at this early age witness sexual intercourse between adults – for which an opportunity is provided by the conviction of grown-up people that small children cannot understand anything sexual – they inevitably regard the sexual act as a sort of ill-treatment or act of subjugation: they view it, that is, in a sadistic sense. Psycho-analysis also shows us that an impression of this kind in early childhood contributes a great deal towards a predisposition to a subsequent sadistic displacement of the sexual aim. Furthermore, children are much concerned with the problem of what sexual intercourse – or, as they put it, being married – consists in: and they usually seek a solution of the mystery in some common activity concerned with the function of micturition or defaecation.

Typical Failure of Infantile Sexual Researches

We can say in general of the sexual theories of children that they are reflections of their own sexual constitution, and that in spite of their grotesque errors the theories show more understanding of sexual processes than one would have given their creators credit for. Children also perceive the alterations that take place in their mother owing to pregnancy and are able to interpret them correctly. The fable of the stork is often told to an audience that receives it with deep,

---

[1] [*Footnote added* 1924:] In these later years of childhood there is a great wealth of sexual theories, of which only a few examples are given in the text.

though mostly silent, mistrust. There are, however, two elements that remain undiscovered by the sexual researches of children: the fertilizing role of semen and the existence of the female sexual orifice – the same elements, incidentally, in which the infantile organization is itself undeveloped. It therefore follows that the efforts of the childish investigator are habitually fruitless, and end in a renunciation which not infrequently leaves behind it a permanent injury to the instinct for knowledge. The sexual researches of these early years of childhood are always carried out in solitude. They constitute a first step towards taking an independent attitude in the world, and imply a high degree of alienation of the child from the people in his environment who formerly enjoyed his complete confidence.

[6] THE PHASES OF DEVELOPMENT OF THE SEXUAL ORGANIZATION[1]

The characteristics of infantile sexual life which we have hitherto emphasized are the facts that it is essentially auto-erotic (i.e. that it finds its object in the infant's own body) and that its individual component instincts are upon the whole disconnected and independent of one another in their search for pleasure. The final outcome of sexual development lies in what is known as the normal sexual life of the adult, in which the pursuit of pleasure comes under the sway of the reproductive function and in which the component instincts, under the primacy of a single erotogenic zone, form a firm organization directed towards a sexual aim attached to some extraneous sexual object.

Pregenital Organizations

The study, with the help of psycho-analysis, of the inhibitions and disturbances of this process of development enables us to recognize abortive beginnings and preliminary stages of a firm organization of the component instincts such as this – preliminary stages which themselves constitute a sexual régime of a sort. These phases of sexual organization are normally passed through smoothly, without giving more than a hint of their existence. It is only in pathological

[1] [The whole of this section, too, first appeared in 1915. The concept of a 'pregenital organization' of sexual life seems to have been first introduced by Freud in his paper on 'The Predisposition to Obsessional Neurosis' (1913i), which, however, deals only with the sadistic-anal organization. The oral organization was apparently recognized as such for the first time in the present passage.]

cases that they become active and recognizable to superficial observation.

We shall give the name of 'pregenital' to organizations of sexual life in which the genital zones have not yet taken over their predominant part. We have hitherto identified two such organizations, which almost seem as though they were harking back to early animal forms of life.

The first of these is the oral or, as it might be called, cannibalistic pregenital sexual organization. Here sexual activity has not yet been separated from the ingestion of food; nor are opposite currents within the activity differentiated. The *object* of both activities is the same; the sexual *aim* consists in the incorporation of the object – the prototype of a process which, in the form of identification, is later to play such an important psychological part. A relic of this constructed phase of organization, which is forced upon our notice by pathology, may be seen in thumb-sucking, in which the sexual activity, detached from the nutritive activity, has substituted for the extraneous object one situated in the subject's own body.[1]

A second pregenital phase is that of the sadistic-anal organization. Here the opposition between two currents, which runs through all sexual life, is already developed: they cannot yet, however, be described as 'masculine' and 'feminine', but only as 'active' and 'passive'. The *activity* is put into operation by the instinct for mastery through the agency of the somatic musculature; the organ which, more than any other, represents the *passive* sexual aim is the erotogenic mucous membrane of the anus. Both of these currents have objects, which, however, are not identical. Alongside these, other component instincts operate in an auto-erotic manner. In this phase, therefore, sexual polarity and an extraneous object are already observable. But organization and subordination to the reproductive function are still absent.[2]

---

[1] [*Footnote added* 1920:] For remnants of this phase in adult neurotics, cf. Abraham (1916). [*Added* 1924:] In another, later work (1924) the same writer has divided both this oral phase, and also the later sadisticanal one, into two sub-divisions, which are characterized by differing attitudes towards the object.

[2] [*Footnote added* 1924:] Abraham, in the paper last quoted (1924), points out that the anus is developed from the embryonic blastopore – a fact which seems like a biological prototype of psychosexual development.

Ambivalence

This form of sexual organization can persist throughout life and can permanently attract a large portion of sexual activity to itself. The predominance in it of sadism and the cloacal part played by the anal zone give it a quite peculiarly archaic colouring. It is further characterized by the fact that in it the opposing pairs of instincts are developed to an approximately equal extent, a state of affairs described by Bleuler's [1910] happily chosen term 'ambivalence'.

The assumption of the existence of pregenital organizations of sexual life is based on the analysis of the neuroses, and without a knowledge of them can scarcely be appreciated. Further analytic investigation may be expected to provide us with far more information on the structure and development of the normal sexual function.

In order to complete our picture of infantile sexual life, we must also suppose that the choice of an object, such as we have shown to be characteristic of the pubertal phase of development, has already frequently or habitually been effected during the years of childhood: that is to say, the whole of the sexual currents have become directed towards a single person in relation to whom they seek to achieve their aims. This then is the closest approximation possible in childhood to the final form taken by sexual life after puberty. The only difference lies in the fact that in childhood the combination of the component instincts and their subordination under the primacy of the genitals have been effected only very incompletely or not at all. Thus the establishment of that primacy in the service of reproduction is the last phase through which the organization of sexuality passes.[1]

Diphasic Choice of Object

It may be regarded as typical of the choice of an object that the process is diphasic, that is, that it occurs in two waves. The first of these begins between the ages of two and five, and is brought to a halt or to a retreat by the latency period; it is characterized by the infantile nature of the

[1] [*Footnote added* 1924:] At a later date (1923), I myself modified this account by inserting a third phase in the development of childhood, subsequent to the two pregenital organizations. This phase, which already deserves to be described as genital, presents a sexual object and some degree of convergence of the sexual impulses upon that object; but it is differentiated from the final organization of sexual maturity in one essential respect. For it knows only one kind of genital: the male one. For that reason I have named it the 'phallic' stage of organization. (Freud, 1923e.) According to Abraham [1924], it has a biological prototype in the embryo's undifferentiated genital disposition, which is the same for both sexes.

sexual aims. The second wave sets in with puberty and determines the final outcome of sexual life.

Although the diphasic nature of object-choice comes down in essentials to no more than the operation of the latency period, it is of the highest importance in regard to disturbances of that final outcome. The resultants of infantile object-choice are carried over into the later period. They either persist as such or are revived at the actual time of puberty. But as a consequence of the repression which has developed between the two phases they prove unutilizable. Their sexual aims have become mitigated and they now represent what may be described as the 'affectionate current' of sexual life. Only psycho-analytic investigation can show that behind this affection, admiration and respect there lie concealed the old sexual longings of the infantile component instincts which have now become unserviceable. The object-choice of the pubertal period is obliged to dispense with the objects of childhood and to start afresh as a 'sensual current'. Should these two currents fail to converge, the result is often that one of the ideals of sexual life, the focusing of all desires upon a single object, will be unattainable.

[7] THE SOURCES OF INFANTILE SEXUALITY

Our efforts to trace the origins of the sexual instinct have shown us so far that sexual excitation arises (a) as a reproduction of a satisfaction experienced in connection with other organic processes, (b) through appropriate peripheral stimulation of erotogenic zones and (c) as an expression of certain 'instincts' (such as the scopophilic instinct and the instinct of cruelty) of which the origin is not yet completely intelligible. Psycho-analytic investigation, reaching back into childhood from a later time, and contemporary observation of children combine to indicate to us still other regularly active sources of sexual excitation. The direct observation of children has the disadvantage of working upon data which are easily misunderstandable; psycho-analysis is made difficult by the fact that it can only reach its data, as well as its conclusions, after long détours. But by co-operation the two methods can attain a satisfactory degree of certainty in their findings.

We have already discovered in examining the erotogenic zones that these regions of the skin merely show a special intensification of a kind of susceptibility to stimulus which is possessed in a certain degree by the whole cutaneous surface. We shall therefore not be surprised to find that very definite erotogenic effects are to be ascribed to certain kinds of general stimulation of the skin. Among these we may especially mention thermal stimuli, whose importance may help us to understand the therapeutic effects of warm baths.

Mechanical Excitations

At this point we must also mention the production of sexual excitation by rhythmic mechanical agitation of the body. Stimuli of this kind operate in three different ways: on the sensory apparatus of the vestibular nerves, on the skin, and on the deeper parts (e.g. the muscles and articular structures). The existence of these pleasurable sensations – and it is worth emphasizing the fact that in this connection the concepts of 'sexual excitation' and 'satisfaction' can to a great extent be used without distinction, a circumstance which we must later endeavour to explain – the existence, then, of these pleasurable sensations, caused by forms of mechanical agitation of the body, is confirmed by the fact that children are so fond of games of passive movement, such as swinging and being thrown up into the air, and insist on such games being incessantly repeated.[1] It is well known that rocking is habitually used to induce sleep in restless children. The shaking produced by driving in carriages and later by railway-travel exercises such a fascinating effect upon older children that every boy, at any rate, has at one time or other in his life wanted to be an engine driver or a coachman. It is a puzzling fact that boys take such an extraordinarily intense interest in things connected with railways, and, at the age at which the production of phantasies is most active (shortly before puberty), use those things as the nucleus of a symbolism that is peculiarly sexual. A compulsive link of this kind between railway-travel and sexuality is clearly derived from the pleasureable character of the sensations of movement. In the event of repression, which turns so many childish preferences into their opposite, these same individuals, when they are adolescents or adults, will react to rocking or swinging with a feeling of nausea, will be terribly exhausted by a railway journey, or will be subject to attacks of anxiety on the journey and will protect themselves against a repetition of the painful experience by a dread of railway-travel.

Here again we must mention the fact, which is not yet understood, that the combination of fright and mechanical agitation produces the severe, hysteriform, traumatic neurosis. It may at least be assumed

---

[1] Some people can remember that in swinging they felt the impact of moving air upon their genitals as an immediate sexual pleasure.

that these influences, which, when they are of small intensity, become sources of sexual excitation, lead to a profound disorder in the sexual mechanism or chemistry if they operate with exaggerated force.

Muscular Activity

We are all familiar with the fact that children feel a need for a large amount of active muscular exercise and derive extraordinary pleasure from satisfying it. Whether this pleasure has any connection with sexuality, whether it itself comprises sexual satisfaction or whether it can become the occasion of sexual excitation – all of this is open to critical questioning, which may indeed also be directed against the view maintained in the previous paragraphs that the pleasure derived from sensations of *passive* movement is of a sexual nature or may produce sexual excitation. It is, however, a fact that a number of people report that they experienced the first signs of excitement in their genitals while they were romping or wrestling with playmates – a situation in which, apart from general muscular exertion, there is a large amount of contact with the skin of the opponent. An inclination to physical struggles with some one particular person, just as in later years an inclination to *verbal* disputes,[1] is a convincing sign that object-choice has fallen on him. One of the roots of the sadistic instinct would seem to lie in the encouragement of sexual excitation by muscular activity. In many people the infantile connection between romping and sexual excitation is among the determinants of the direction subsequently taken by their sexual instinct.[2]

Affective Processes

The further sources of sexual excitation in children are open to less doubt. It is easy to establish, whether by contemporary observation or by subsequent research, that all comparatively intense affective processes, including even terrifying ones, trench upon sexuality – a fact which may incidentally help to explain the pathogenic effect of emotions of that kind. In schoolchildren dread of going in for an examination or tension over a difficult piece of work can be important

---

[1] 'Was sich liebt, das neckt sich.' [Lovers' quarrels are proverbial.]

[2] [*Footnote added* 1910:] The analysis of cases of neurotic abasia and agoraphobia removes all doubt as to the sexual nature of pleasure in movement. Modern education, as we know, makes great use of games in order to divert young people from sexual activity. It would be more correct to say that in these young people it replaces sexual enjoyment by pleasure in movement – and forces sexual activity back to one of its auto-erotic components.

not only in affecting the child's relations at school but also in bringing
about an irruption of sexual manifestations. For quite often in such
circumstances a stimulus may be felt which urges the child to touch
his genitals, or something may take place akin to a nocturnal emission
with all its bewildering consequences. The behaviour of children at
school, which confronts a teacher with plenty of puzzles, deserves in
general to be brought into relation with their budding sexuality. The
sexually exciting effect of many emotions which are in themselves
unpleasurable, such as feelings of apprehension, fright or horror,
persists in a great number of people throughout their adult life. There
is no doubt that this is the explanation of why so many people seek
opportunities for sensations of this kind, subject to the proviso that the
seriousness of the unpleasurable feeling is damped down by certain
qualifying facts, such as its occurring in an imaginary world, in a book
or in a play.

If we assume that a similar erotogenic effect attaches even to
intensely painful feelings, especially when the pain is toned down or
kept at a distance by some accompanying condition, we should here
have one of the main roots of the masochistic-sadistic instinct, into
whose numerous complexities we are very gradually gaining some
insight.[1]

Intellectual Work
Finally, it is an unmistakable fact that concentration of the attention
upon an intellectual task and intellectual strain in general produce a
concomitant sexual excitation in many young people as well as
adults. This is no doubt the only justifiable basis for what is in other
respects the questionable practice of ascribing nervous disorders to
intellectual 'overwork'.[2]

If we now cast our eyes over the tentative suggestions which I have
made as to the sources of infantile sexual excitation, though I have not
described them completely nor enumerated them fully, the following
conclusions emerge with more or less certainty. It seems that the
fullest provisions are made for setting in motion the process of sexual
excitation – a process the nature of which has, it must be confessed,

[1] [*Footnote added* 1924:] I am here referring to what is known as 'erotogenic' masochism. [See footnote 1, p. 302.]
[2] [Some earlier remarks by Freud on this subject will be found in the middle of his
first paper on 'Sexuality in the Aetiology of the Neuroses' (1898a), and some later ones
in a footnote to Section III of 'Analysis Terminable and Interminable' (1937c).]

become highly obscure to us. The setting in motion of this process is first and foremost provided for in a more or less direct fashion by the excitations of the sensory surfaces – the skin and the sense organs – and, most directly of all, by the operation of stimuli on certain areas known as erotogenic zones. The decisive element in these sources of sexual excitation is no doubt the *quality* of the stimuli, though the factor of intensity, in the case of pain, is not a matter of complete indifference. But apart from these sources there are present in the organism contrivances which bring it about that in the case of a great number of internal processes sexual excitation arises as a concomitant effect, as soon as the intensity of those processes passes beyond certain quantitative limits. What we have called the component instincts of sexuality are either derived directly from these internal sources or are composed of elements both from those sources and from the erotogenic zones. It may well be that nothing of considerable importance can occur in the organism without contributing some component to the excitation of the sexual instinct.

It does not seem to me possible at present to state these general conclusions with any greater clarity or certainty. For this I think two factors are responsible: first, the novelty of the whole method of approach to the subject, and secondly, the fact that the whole nature of sexual excitation is completely unknown to us. Nevertheless I am tempted to make two observations which promise to open out wide future prospects:

Varieties of Sexual Constitution

(*a*) Just as we saw previously that it was possible to derive a multiplicity of innate sexual constitutions from variety in the development of the erotogenic zones, so we can now make a similar attempt by including the *indirect* sources of sexual excitation. It may be assumed that, although contributions are made from these sources in the case of everyone, they are not in all cases of equal strength, and that further help towards the differentiation of sexual constitutions may be found in the varying development of the individual sources of sexual excitation.[1]

---

[1] [*Footnote added* 1920:] An inevitable consequence of these considerations is that we must regard each individual as possessing an oral erotism, an anal erotism, a urethral erotism, etc., and that the existence of mental complexes corresponding to these implies no judgement of abnormality or neurosis. The differences separating the normal from the abnormal can lie only in the relative strength of the individual components of the sexual instinct and in the use to which they are put in the course of development.

Pathways of Mutual Influence

(*b*) If we now drop the figurative expression that we have so long adopted in speaking of the 'sources' of sexual excitation, we are led to the suspicion that all the connecting pathways that lead from other functions to sexuality must also be traversable in the reverse direction. If, for instance, the common possession of the labial zone by the two functions is the reason why sexual satisfaction arises during the taking of nourishment, then the same factor also enables us to understand why there should be disorders of nutrition if the erotogenic functions of the common zone are disturbed. Or again, if we know that concentration of attention may give rise to sexual excitation, it seems plausible to assume that by making use of the same path, but in a contrary direction, the condition of sexual excitation may influence the possibility of directing the attention. A good portion of the symptomatology of the neuroses, which I have traced to disturbances of the sexual processes, is expressed in disturbances of other, non-sexual, somatic functions; and this circumstance, which has hitherto been unintelligible, becomes less puzzling if it is only the counterpart of the influences which bring about the production of sexual excitation.

The same pathways, however, along which sexual disturbances trench upon the other somatic functions must also perform another important function in normal health. They must serve as paths for the attraction of sexual instinctual forces to aims that are other than sexual, that is to say, for the sublimation of sexuality. But we must end with a confession that very little is as yet known with certainty of these pathways though they certainly exist and can probably be traversed in both directions.

III
The Transformations of Puberty

With the arrival of puberty, changes set in which are destined to give infantile sexual life its final, normal shape. The sexual instinct has hitherto been predominantly auto-erotic; it now finds a sexual object. Its activity has hitherto been derived from a number of separate instincts and erotogenic zones, which, independently of one another, have pursued a certain sort of pleasure as their sole sexual aim. Now, however, a new sexual aim appears, and all the component instincts combine to attain it, while the erotogenic zones become subordinated to the primacy of the genital zone.[1] Since the new sexual aim assigns very different functions to the two sexes, their sexual development now diverges greatly. That of males is the more straightforward and the more understandable, while that of females actually enters upon a kind of involution. A normal sexual life is only assured by an exact convergence of the two currents directed towards the sexual object and the sexual aim, the affectionate current and the sensual one.[2] (The former, the affectionate current, comprises what remains over of the infantile efflorescence of sexuality.) It is like the completion of a tunnel which has been driven through a hill from both directions.

The new sexual aim in men consists in the discharge of the sexual products. The earlier one, the attainment of pleasure, is by no means alien to it; on the contrary, the highest degree of pleasure is attached to this final act of the sexual process. The sexual instinct is now subordinated to the reproductive function; it becomes, so to say, altruistic. If this transformation is to succeed, the original dispositions and all the other characteristics of the instincts must be taken into account in the process. Just as on any other occasion on which the organism should by rights make new combinations and adjustments leading to complicated mechanisms, here too there are possibilities of pathological disorders if these new arrangements are not carried out. Every pathological disorder if sexual life is rightly to be regarded as an inhibition in development

[1] THE PRIMACY OF THE GENITAL ZONES
AND FORE-PLEASURE

The starting-point and the final aim of the process which I have described are clearly visible. The intermediate steps are still in many ways obscure to us. We shall have to leave more than one of them as an unsolved riddle.

The most striking of the processes at puberty has been picked upon as constituting its essence: the manifest growth of the external

---

[1] [*Footnote added* 1915:] The schematic picture which I have given in the text aims at emphasizing differences. I have already shown on p. 338 the extent to which infantile sexuality approximates to the final sexual organization, owing to its choice of object [*added* 1924:] and to the development of the phallic phase.

[2] [The last seven words were added in 1915.]

genitalia. (The latency period of childhood is, on the other hand, characterized by a relative cessation of their growth.) In the meantime the development of the internal genitalia has advanced far enough for them to be able to discharge the sexual products or, as the case may be, to bring about the formation of a new living organism. Thus a highly complicated apparatus has been made ready and awaits the moment of being put into operation.

This apparatus is to be set in motion by stimuli, and observation shows us that stimuli can impinge on it from three directions: from the external world by means of the excitation of the erotogenic zones with which we are already familiar, from the organic interior by ways which we have still to explore, and from mental life, which is itself a storehouse for external impressions and a receiving-post for internal excitations. All three kinds of stimuli produce the same effect, namely a condition described as 'sexual excitement', which shows itself by two sorts of indication, mental and somatic. The mental indications consist in a peculiar feeling of tension of an extremely compelling character; and among the numerous somatic ones are first and foremost a number of changes in the genitals, which have the obvious sense of being preparations for the sexual act – the erection of the male organ and the lubrication of the vagina.

Sexual Tension

The fact that sexual excitement possesses the character of tension raises a problem the solution of which is no less difficult than it would be important in helping us to understand the sexual processes. In spite of all the differences of opinion that reign on the subject among psychologists, I must insist that a feeling of tension necessarily involves unpleasure. What seems to me decisive is the fact that a feeling of this kind is accompanied by an impulsion to make a change in the psychological situation, that it operates in an urgent way which is wholly alien to the nature of the feeling of pleasure. If, however, the tension of sexual excitement is counted as an unpleasurable feeling, we are at once brought up against the fact that it is also undoubtedly felt as pleasurable. In every case in which tension is produced by sexual processes it is accompanied by pleasure; even in the preparatory changes in the genitals a feeling of satisfaction of some kind is plainly to be observed. How, then, are this unpleasurable tension and this feeling of pleasure to be reconciled?

Everything relating to the problem of pleasure and unpleasure touches upon one of the sorest spots of present-day psychology. It will be my aim to learn as much as possible from the circumstances of the instance with which we are at present dealing, but I shall avoid any approach to the problem as a whole.[1]

Let us begin by casting a glance at the way in which the erotogenic zones fit themselves into the new arrangement. They have to play an important part in introducing sexual excitation. The eye is perhaps the zone most remote from the sexual object, but it is the one which, in the situation of wooing an object, is liable to be the most frequently stimulated by the particular quality of excitation whose cause, when it occurs in a sexual object, we describe as beauty. (For the same reason the merits of a sexual object are described as 'attractions'.) This stimulation is on the one hand already accompanied by pleasure, while on the other hand it leads to an increase of sexual excitement or produces it if it is not yet present. If the excitation now spreads to another erotogenic zone – to the hand, for instance, through tactile sensations – the effect is the same: a feeling of pleasure on the one side, which is quickly intensified by pleasure arising from the preparatory changes [in the genitals], and on the other side an increase of sexual tension, which soon passes over into the most obvious unpleasure if it cannot be met by a further accession of pleasure. Another instance will perhaps make this even clearer. If an erotogenic zone in a person who is not sexually excited (e.g. the skin of a woman's breast) is stimulated by touch, the contact produces a pleasurable feeling; but it is at the same time better calculated than anything to arouse a sexual excitation that demands an increase of pleasure. The problem is how it can come about that an experience of pleasure can give rise to a need for greater pleasure.

The Mechanism of Fore-Pleasure

The part played in this by the erotogenic zones, however, is clear. What is true of one of them is true of all. They are all used to provide a certain amount of pleasure by being stimulated in the way appropriate to them. This pleasure then leads to an increase in tension which in its turn is responsible for producing the necessary motor energy for the conclusion of the sexual act. The penultimate stage of that act is once again the appropriate stimulation of an erotogenic zone (the

---

[1] [Footnote added 1924:] I have made an attempt at solving this problem in the first part of my paper on 'The Economic Problem of Masochism' (1924c).

genital zone itself, in the glans penis) by the appropriate object (the mucous membrane of the vagina); and from the pleasure yielded by this excitation the motor energy is obtained, this time by a reflex path, which brings about the discharge of the sexual substances. This last pleasure is the highest in intensity, and its mechanism differs from that of the earlier pleasure. It is brought about entirely by discharge: it is wholly a pleasure of satisfaction and with it the tension of the libido is for the time being extinguished.

This distinction between the one kind of pleasure due to the excitation of erotogenic zones and the other kind due to the discharge of the sexual substances deserves, I think, to be made more concrete by a difference in nomenclature. The former may be suitably described as 'fore-pleasure' in contrast to the 'end-pleasure' or pleasure of satisfaction derived from the sexual act. Fore-pleasure is thus the same pleasure that has already been produced, although on a smaller scale, by the infantile sexual instinct; end-pleasure is something new and is thus probably conditioned by circumstances that do not arise till puberty. The formula for the new function of the erotogenic zones runs therefore: they are used to make possible, through the medium of the fore-pleasure which can be derived from them (as it was during infantile life), the production of the greater pleasure of satisfaction.

I was able recently to throw light upon another instance, in a quite different department of mental life, of a slight feeling of pleasure similarly making possible the attainment of a greater resultant pleasure, and thus operating as an 'incentive bonus'. In the same connection I was also able to go more deeply into the nature of pleasure.[1]

Dangers of Fore-Pleasure

The connection between fore-pleasure and infantile sexual life is, however, made clearer by the pathogenic part which it can come to play. The attainment of the normal sexual aim can clearly be endangered by the mechanism in which fore-pleasure is involved. This danger arises if at any point in the preparatory sexual processes the fore-pleasure turns out to be too great and the element of tension too small. The motive for proceeding further with the sexual process then disappears, the whole path is cut short, and the preparatory act in question takes the place of the normal sexual aim. Experience has

[1] See my volume on *Jokes and their Relation to the Unconscious* which appeared in 1905.

shown that the precondition for this damaging event is that the erotogenic zone concerned or the corresponding component instinct shall already during childhood have contributed an unusual amount of pleasure. If further factors then come into play, tending to bring about a fixation, a compulsion may easily arise in later life which resists the incorporation of this particular fore-pleasure into a new context. Such is in fact the mechanism of many perversions, which consist in a lingering over the preparatory acts of the sexual process.

This failure of the function of the sexual mechanism owing to fore-pleasure is best avoided if the primacy of the genitals too is adumbrated in childhood; and indeed things seem actually arranged to bring this about in the second half of childhood (from the age of eight to puberty). During these years the genital zones already behave in much the same way as in maturity; they become the seat of sensations of excitation and of preparatory changes whenever any pleasure is felt from the satisfaction of other erotogenic zones, though this result is still without a purpose – that is to say, contributes nothing to a continuation of the sexual process. Already in childhood, therefore, alongside of the pleasure of satisfaction there is a certain amount of sexual tension, although it is less constant and less in quantity. We can now understand why, in discussing the sources of sexuality, we were equally justified in saying of a given process that it was sexually satisfying or sexually exciting. It will be noticed that in the course of our enquiry we began by exaggerating the distinction between infantile and mature sexual life, and that we are now setting this right. Not only the deviations from normal sexual life but its normal form as well are determined by the infantile manifestations of sexuality.

[2] THE PROBLEM OF SEXUAL EXCITATION

We remain in complete ignorance both of the origin and of the nature of the sexual tension which arises simultaneously with the pleasure when erotogenic zones are satisfied.[1] The most obvious explanation, that this tension arises in some way out of the pleasure itself, is not

---

[1] It is a highly instructive fact that the German language in its use of the word '*Lust*' takes into account the part played by the preparatory sexual excitations which, as has been explained above, simultaneously produce an element of satisfaction and a contribution to sexual tension. '*Lust*' has two meanings, and is used to describe the sensation of sexual tension ('*Ich habe Lust*' = 'I should like to', 'I feel an impulse to') as well as the feeling of satisfaction.

only extremely improbable in itself but becomes untenable when we consider that in connection with the greatest pleasure of all, that which accompanies the discharge of the sexual products, no tension is produced, but on the contrary all tension is removed. Thus pleasure and sexual tension can only be connected in an indirect manner.

Part Played by the Sexual Substances

Apart from the fact that normally it is only the discharge of the sexual substances that brings sexual excitation to an end, there are other points of contact between sexual tension and the sexual products. In the case of a man living a continent life, the sexual apparatus, at varying intervals, which, however, are not ungoverned by rules, discharges the sexual substances during the night, to the accompaniment of a pleasurable feeling and in the course of a dream which hallucinates a sexual act. And in regard to this process (nocturnal emission) it is difficult to avoid the conclusion that the sexual tension, which succeeds in making use of the short cut of hallucination as a substitute for the act itself, is a function of the accumulation of semen in the vesicles containing the sexual products. Our experience in connection with the exhaustibility of the sexual mechanism argues in the same sense. If the store of semen is exhausted, not only is it impossible to carry out the sexual act, but the susceptibility of the erotogenic zones to stimulus ceases, and their appropriate excitation no longer gives rise to any pleasure. We thus learn incidentally that a certain degree of sexual tension is required even for the excitability of the erotogenic zones.

This would seem to lead to what is, if I am not mistaken, the fairly wide-spread hypothesis that the accumulation of the sexual substances creates and maintains sexual tension; the pressure of these products upon the walls of the vesicles containing them might be supposed to act as a stimulus upon a spinal centre, the condition of which would be perceived by higher centres and would then give rise in consciousness to the familiar sensation of tension. If the excitation of the erotogenic zones increases sexual tension, this could only come about on the supposition that the zones in question are in an anatomical connection that has already been laid down with these centres, that they increase the tonus of the excitation in them, and, if the sexual tension is sufficient, set the sexual act in motion or, if it is insufficient, stimulate the production of the sexual substances.[1]

The weakness of this theory, which we find accepted, for instance, in Krafft-Ebing's account of the sexual processes, lies in the fact that, having been designed to account for the sexual activity of adult males, it takes too little account of three sets of conditions which it should also be able to explain. These are the conditions in children, in females and in castrated males. In none of these three cases can there be any question of an accumulation of sexual products in the same sense as in males, and this makes a smooth application of the theory difficult. Nevertheless it may at once be admitted that it is possible to find means by which the theory may be made to cover these cases as well. In any case we are warned not to lay more weight on the factor of the accumulation of the sexual products than it is able to bear.

Importance of the Internal Sexual Organs

Observations on castrated males seem to show that sexual excitation can occur to a considerable degree independently of the production of the sexual substances. The operation of castration occasionally fails to bring about a limitation of libido, although such limitation, which provides the motive for the operation, is the usual outcome. Moreover, it has long been known that diseases which abolish the production of the masculine sex-cells leave the patient, though he is now sterile, with his libido and potency undamaged. It is therefore by no means as astonishing as Rieger [1900] represents it to be that the loss of the masculine sex-glands in an adult may have no further effect upon his mental behaviour.[2] It is true that if castration is performed at a tender age, before puberty, it approximates in its effect to the aim of obliterating the sexual characters; but here too it is possible that what is in question is, besides the actual loss of the sex-glands, an inhibition (connected with that loss) in the development of other factors.

---

[1] [This hypothesis had been discussed by Freud earlier: in Section III of his first paper on anxiety neurosis (1895*b*).]

[2] [The following sentence occurs at this point in editions before 1920, when it was omitted: 'For the sex-glands do not constitute sexuality, and the observations on castrated males merely confirm what had been shown long before by removal of the ovaries – namely that it is impossible to obliterate the sexual characters by removing the sex-glands.' Before 1920, too, the second half of the next sentence began: 'but it seems that what is in question here is not the actual loss of the sex-glands but an inhibition . . .']

Chemical Theory

Experiments in the removal of the sex-glands (testes and ovaries) of animals, and in the grafting into vertebrates of sex-glands from other individuals of the opposite sex,[1] have at last thrown a partial light on the origin of sexual excitation, and have at the same time still further reduced the significance of a possible accumulation of cellular sexual products. It has become experimentally possible (E. Steinach) to transform a male into a female, and conversely a female into a male. In this process the psychosexual behaviour of the animal alters in accordance with the somatic sexual characters and simultaneously with them. It seems, however, that this sex-determining influence is not an attribute of that part of the sex-glands which gives rise to the specific sex-cells (spermatozoa and ovum) but of their interstitial tissue, upon which special emphasis is laid by being described in the literature as the 'puberty-gland'. It is quite possible that further investigation will show that this puberty-gland has normally a her-maphrodite disposition. If this were so, the theory of the bisexuality of the higher animals would be given anatomical foundation. It is already probable that the puberty-gland is not the only organ con-cerned with the production of sexual excitation and sexual characters. In any case, what we already know of the part played by the thyroid gland in sexuality fits in with this new biological discovery. It seems probable, then, that special chemical substances are produced in the interstitial portion of the sex-glands; these are then taken up in the blood stream and cause particular parts of the central nervous system to be charged with sexual tension. (We are already familiar with the fact that other toxic substances, introduced into the body from outside, can bring about a similar transformation of a toxic condition into a stimulus acting on a particular organ.) The question of how sexual excitation arises from the stimulation of erotogenic zones, when the central apparatus has been previously charged, and the question of what interplay arises in the course of these sexual pro-cesses between the effects of purely toxic stimuli and of physiological ones – none of this can be treated, even hypothetically, in the present state of our knowledge. It must suffice us to hold firmly to what is essential in this view of the sexual processes: the assumption that substances of a peculiar kind arise from the sexual metabolism. For this apparently arbitrary supposition is supported by a fact which has

[1] Cf. Lipschütz's work (1919), referred to on p. 292 *n*.

received little attention but deserves the closest consideration. The neuroses, which can be derived only from disturbances of sexual life, show the greatest clinical similarity to the phenomena of intoxication and abstinence that arise from the habitual use of toxic, pleasure-producing substances (alkaloids).

[3] THE LIBIDO THEORY

The conceptual scaffolding which we have set up to help us in dealing with the psychical manifestations of sexual life tallies well with these hypotheses as to the chemical basis of sexual excitation. We have defined the concept of libido as a quantitatively variable force which could serve as a measure of processes and transformations occurring in the field of sexual excitation. We distinguish this libido in respect of its special origin from the energy which must be supposed to underlie mental processes in general, and we thus also attribute a *qualitative* character to it. In thus distinguishing between libidinal and other forms of psychical energy we are giving expression to the presumption that the sexual processes occurring in the organism are distinguished from the nutritive processes by a special chemistry. The analysis of the perversions and psychoneuroses has shown us that this sexual excitation is derived not from the so-called sexual parts alone, but from all the bodily organs. We thus reach the idea of a quantity of libido, to the mental representation of which we give the name of 'ego-libido', and whose production, increase or diminution, distribution and displacement should afford us possibilities for explaining the psychosexual phenomena observed.

This ego-libido is, however, only conveniently accessible to analytic study when it has been put to the use of cathecting sexual objects, that is, when it has become object-libido. We can then perceive it concentrating upon objects, becoming fixed upon them or abandoning them, moving from one object to another and, from these situations, directing the subject's sexual activity, which leads to the satisfaction, that is, to the partial and temporary extinction, of the libido. The psycho-analysis of what are termed transference neuroses (hysteria and obsessional neurosis) affords us a clear insight at this point.

We can follow the object-libido through still further vicissitudes. When it is withdrawn from objects, it is held in suspense in peculiar conditions of tension and is finally drawn back into the ego, so that it becomes ego-libido once again. In contrast to object-libido, we also describe ego-libido as 'narcissistic' libido. From the vantage-point of psycho-analysis we can look across a frontier, which we may not pass, at the activities of narcissistic libido, and may form some idea of the relation between it and object-libido.[1] Narcissistic or ego-libido seems to be the great reservoir from which the object-cathexes are sent out and into which they are withdrawn once more; the narcissistic libidinal cathexis of the ego is the original state of things, realized in earliest childhood, and is merely covered by the later extrusions of libido, but in essentials persists behind them.

It should be the task of a libido theory of neurotic and psychotic disorders to express all the observed phenomena and inferred processes in terms of the economics of the libido. It is easy to guess that the vicissitudes of the ego-libido will have the major part to play in this connection, especially when it is a question of explaining the deeper psychotic disturbances. We are then faced by the difficulty that our method of research, psycho-analysis, for the moment affords us assured information only on the transformations that take place in the object-libido,[2] but is unable to make any immediate distinction between the ego-libido and the other forms of energy operating in the ego.[3]

For the present, therefore, no further development of the libido theory is possible, except upon speculative lines. It would, however, be sacrificing all that we have gained hitherto from psycho-analytic observation, if we were to follow the example of C. G. Jung and water down the meaning of the concept of libido itself by equating it with psychical instinctual force in general. The distinguishing of the sexual instinctual impulses from the rest and the consequent restriction of the concept of libido to the former receives strong support from the assumption which I have already discussed that there is a special chemistry of the sexual function.

[4] THE DIFFERENTIATION BETWEEN MEN AND WOMEN

As we all know, it is not until puberty that the sharp distinction is established between the masculine and feminine characters. From

---

[1] [*Footnote added* 1924:] Since neuroses other than the transference neuroses have become to a greater extent accessible to psycho-analysis, this limitation has lost its earlier validity.

[2] [*Footnote added* 1924:] See the previous footnote.

[3] [*Footnote added* 1915:] Cf. my paper on narcissism (1914c). [*Added* 1920:] The term 'narcissism' was not introduced, as I erroneously stated in that paper, by Näcke, but by Havelock Ellis. [Ellis himself subsequently (1927) discussed this point in detail and considered that the honours should be divided.]

that time on, this contrast has a more decisive influence than any other upon the shaping of human life. It is true that the masculine and feminine dispositions are already easily recognizable in childhood. The development of the inhibitions of sexuality (shame, disgust, pity, etc.) takes place in little girls earlier and in the face of less resistance than in boys; the tendency to sexual repression seems in general to be greater; and, where the component instincts of sexuality appear, they prefer the passive form. The auto-erotic activity of the erotogenic zones, is however, the same in both sexes, and owing to this uniformity there is no possibility of a distinction between the two sexes such as arises after puberty. So far as the autoerotic and masturbatory manifestations of sexuality are concerned, we might lay it down that the sexuality of little girls is of a wholly masculine character. Indeed, if we were able to give a more definite connotation to the concepts of 'masculine' and 'feminine', it would even be possible to maintain that libido is invariably and necessarily of a masculine nature, whether it occurs in men or in women and irrespectively of whether its object is a man or a woman.[1]

Since I have become acquainted with the notion of bisexuality I have regarded it as the decisive factor, and without taking bisexuality into account I think it would scarcely be possible to arrive at an understanding of the sexual manifestations that are actually to be observed in men and women.

[1] [Footnote added 1915:] It is essential to understand clearly that the concepts of 'masculine' and 'feminine', whose meaning seems so unambiguous to ordinary people, are among the most confused that occur in science. It is possible to distinguish at least three uses. 'Masculine' and 'feminine' are used sometimes in the sense of activity and passivity, sometimes in a biological, and sometimes, again, in a sociological sense. The first of these three meanings is the essential one and the most serviceable in psycho-analysis. When, for instance, libido was described in the text above as being 'masculine', the word was being used in this sense, for an instinct is always active even when it has a passive aim in view. The second, or biological, meaning of 'masculine' and 'feminine' is the one whose applicability can be determined most easily. Here 'masculine' and 'feminine' are characterized by the presence of spermatozoa or ova respectively and by the functions proceeding from them. Activity and its concomitant phenomena (more powerful muscular development, aggressiveness, greater intensity of libido) are as a rule linked with biological masculinity; but they are not necessarily so, for there are animal species in which these qualities are on the contrary assigned to the female. The third, or sociological, meaning receives its connotation from the observation of actually existing masculine and feminine individuals. Such observation shows that in human beings pure masculinity or femininity is not to be found either in a psychological or a biological sense. Every individual on the contrary displays a mixture of the character-traits belonging to his own and to the opposite sex; and he shows a combination of activity and passivity whether or not these last character-traits tally with his biological ones.

Leading Zones in Men and Women

Apart from this I have only the following to add. The leading erotogenic zone in female children is located at the clitoris, and is thus homologous to the masculine genital zone of the glans penis. All my experience concerning masturbation in little girls has related to the clitoris and not to the regions of the external genitalia that are important in later sexual functioning. I am even doubtful whether a female child can be led by the influence of seduction to anything other than clitoridal masturbation. If such a thing occurs, it is quite exceptional. The spontaneous discharges of sexual excitement which occur so often precisely in little girls are expressed in spasms of the clitoris. Frequent erections of that organ make it possible for girls to form a correct judgement, even without any instruction, of the sexual manifestations of the other sex: they merely transfer on to boys the sensations derived from their own sexual processes.

If we are to understand how a little girl turns into a woman, we must follow the further vicissitudes of this excitability of the clitoris. Puberty, which brings about so great an accession of libido in boys, is marked in girls by a fresh wave of *repression*, in which it is precisely clitoridal sexuality that is affected. What is thus overtaken by repression is a piece of masculine sexuality. The intensification of the brake upon sexuality brought about by pubertal repression in women serves as a stimulus to the libido in men and causes an increase of its activity. Along with this heightening of libido there is also an increase of sexual overvaluation which only emerges in full force in relation to a woman who holds herself back and who denies her sexuality. When at last the sexual act is permitted and the clitoris itself becomes excited, it still retains a function: the task, namely, of transmitting the excitation to the adjacent female sexual parts, just as – to use a simile – pine shavings can be kindled in order to set a log of harder wood on fire. Before this transference can be effected, a certain interval of time must often elapse, during which the young woman is anaesthetic. This anaesthesia may become permanent if the clitoridal zone refuses to abandon its excitability, an event for which the way is prepared precisely by an extensive activity of that zone in childhood. Anaesthesia in women, as is well known, is often only apparent and local. They are anaesthetic at the vaginal orifice but are by no means incapable of excitement originating in the clitoris or even in other zones. Alongside these erotogenic determinants of anaesthesia must also be set the psychical determinants, which equally arise from repression.

When erotogenic susceptibility to stimulation has been successfully transferred by a woman from the clitoris to the vaginal orifice, it implies that she has adopted a new leading zone for the purposes of her later sexual activity. A man, on the other hand, retains his leading zone unchanged from childhood. The fact that women change their leading erotogenic zone in this way, together with the wave of repression at puberty, which, as it were, puts aside their childish masculinity, are the chief determinants of the greater proneness of woman to neurosis and especially to hysteria. These determinants, therefore, are intimately related to the essence of femininity.[1]

[5] THE FINDING OF AN OBJECT

The processes at puberty thus establish the primacy of the genital zones; and, in a man, the penis, which has now become capable of erection, presses forward insistently towards the new sexual aim – penetration into a cavity in the body which excites his genital zone. Simultaneously on the psychical side the process of finding an object, for which preparations have been made from earliest childhood, is completed. At a time at which the first beginnings of sexual satisfaction are still linked with the taking of nourishment, the sexual instinct has a sexual object outside the infant's own body in the shape of his mother's breast. It is only later that the instinct loses that object, just at the time, perhaps, when the child is able to form a total idea of the person to whom the organ that is giving him satisfaction belongs. As a rule the sexual instinct then becomes auto-erotic, and not until the period of latency has been passed through is the original relation restored. There are thus good reasons why a child sucking at his mother's breast has become the prototype of every relation of love. The finding of an object is in fact a refinding of it.[2]

[1] [The course of development of sexuality in women was further examined by Freud more particularly on four later occasions: in his case history of a homosexual woman (1920a), in his discussion of the consequences of the anatomical distinction between the sexes (1925j), in his paper on female sexuality (1931b), and in Lecutre 33 of his *New Introductory Lectures* (1933a), p. 412 ff. below.]

[2] [*Footnote added* 1915:] Psycho-analysis informs us that there are two methods of finding an object. The first, described in the text, is the 'anaclitic' or 'attachment' one, based on attachment to early infantile prototypes. The second is the narcissistic one, which seeks for the subject's own ego and finds it again in other people. This latter method is of particularly great importance in cases where the outcome is a pathological one, but it is not relevant to the present context.

The Sexual Object During Early Infancy

But even after sexual activity has become detached from the taking of nourishment, an important part of this first and most significant of all sexual relations is left over, which helps to prepare for the choice of an object and thus to restore the happiness that has been lost. All through the period of latency children learn to feel for other people who help them in their helplessness and satisfy their needs a love which is on the model of, and a continuation of, their relation as sucklings to their nursing mother. There may perhaps be an inclination to dispute the possibility of identifying a child's affection and esteem for those who look after him with sexual love. I think, however, that a closer psychological examination may make it possible to establish this identity beyond any doubt. A child's intercourse with anyone responsible for his care affords him an unending source of sexual excitation and satisfaction from his erotogenic zones. This is especially so since the person in charge of him, who, after all, is as a rule his mother, herself regards him with feelings that are derived from her own sexual life: she strokes him, kisses him, rocks him and quite clearly treats him as a substitute for a complete sexual object.[1] A mother would probably be horrified if she were made aware that all her marks of affection were rousing her child's sexual instinct and preparing for its later intensity. She regards what she does as asexual, 'pure' love, since, after all, she carefully avoids applying more excitations to the child's genitals than are unavoidable in nursery care. As we know, however, the sexual instinct is not aroused only by direct excitation of the genital zone. What we call affection will unfailingly show its effects one day on the genital zones as well. Moreover, if the mother understood more of the high importance of the part played by instinct in mental life as a whole – in all its ethical and psychical achievements – she would spare herself any self-reproaches even after her enlightenment. She is only fulfilling her task in teaching the child to love. After all, he is meant to grow up into a strong and capable person with vigorous sexual needs and to accomplish during his life all the things that human beings are urged to do by their instincts. It is true that an excess of parental affection does harm by causing precocious sexual maturity and also because, by spoiling the child, it makes him incapable in later life of temporarily

[1] Anyone who considers this 'sacrilegious' may be recommended to read Havelock Ellis's views [1903; 2nd ed., 1913, 18] on the relation between mother and child, which agree almost completely with mine.

doing without love or of being content with a smaller amount of it. One of the clearest indications that a child will later become neurotic is to be seen in an insatiable demand for his parents' affection. And on the other hand neuropathic parents, who are inclined as a rule of display excessive affection, are precisely those who are most likely by their caresses to arouse the child's disposition to neurotic illness. Incidentally, this example shows there are ways more direct than inheritance by which neurotic parents can hand their disorder on to their children.

Infantile Anxiety

Children themselves behave from an early age as though their dependence on the people looking after them were in the nature of sexual love. Anxiety in children is originally nothing other than an expression of the fact that they are feeling the loss of the person they love. It is for this reason that they are frightened of every stranger. They are afraid in the dark because in the dark they cannot see the person they love; and their fear is soothed if they can take hold of that person's hand in the dark. To attribute to bogeys and blood-curdling stories told by nurses the responsibility for making children timid is to over-estimate their efficacy. The truth is merely that children who are inclined to be timid are affected by stories which would make no impression whatever upon others, and it is only children with a sexual instinct that is excessive or has developed prematurely or has become vociferous owing to too much petting who are inclined to be timid. In this respect a child, by turning his libido into anxiety when he cannot satisfy it, behaves like an adult. On the other hand an adult who has become neurotic owing to his libido being unsatisfied behaves in his anxiety like a child: he begins to be frightened when he is alone, that is to say when he is away from someone of whose love he had felt secure, and he seeks to assuage this fear by the most childish measures.[1]

[1] For this explanation of the origin of infantile anxiety I have to thank a three-year-old boy whom I once heard calling out of a dark room: 'Auntie, speak to me! I'm frightened because it's so dark.' His aunt answered him: 'What good would that do? You can't see me.' 'That doesn't matter,' replied the child, 'if anyone speaks, it gets light.' Thus what he was afraid of was not the dark, but the absence of someone he loved; and he could feel sure of being soothed as soon as he had evidence of that person's presence. [Added 1920:] One of the most important results of psycho-analytic research is this discovery that neurotic anxiety arises out of libido, that it is the product of a transformation of it, and that it is thus related to it in the same kind of way as vinegar is to wine. A further discussion of this problem will be found in my Introductory Lectures on Psycho-Analysis (1916–17), Lecture 25, though even there, it must be confessed, the question is not finally cleared up. [For Freud's latest views on the subject of anxiety see his Inhibitions, Symptoms and Anxiety (1926d) and his New Introductory Lectures (1933a), Chapter 32.]

The Barrier Against Incest

We see, therefore, that the parents' affection for their child may awaken his sexual instinct prematurely (i.e. before the somatic conditions of puberty are present) to such a degree that the mental excitation breaks through in an unmistakable fashion to the genital system. If, on the other hand, they are fortunate enough to avoid this, then their affection can perform its task of directing the child in his choice of a sexual object when he reaches maturity. No doubt the simplest course for the child would be to choose as his sexual objects the same persons whom, since his childhood, he has loved with what may be described as damped-down libido.[1] But, by the postponing of sexual maturation, time has been gained in which the child can erect, among other restraints on sexuality, the barrier against incest, and can thus take up into himself the moral precepts which expressly exclude from his object-choice, as being blood-relations, the persons whom he has loved in his childhood. Respect for this barrier is essentially a cultural demand made by society. Society must defend itself against the danger that the interests which it needs for the establishment of higher social units may be swallowed up by the family; and for this reason, in the case of every individual, but in particular of adolescent boys, it seeks by all possible means to loosen their connection with their family – a connection which, in their childhood, is the only important one.[2]

It is in the world of ideas, however, that the choice of an object is accomplished at first; and the sexual life of maturing youth is almost entirely restricted to indulging in phantasies, that is, in ideas that are not destined to be carried into effect.[3] In these phantasies the infantile tendencies invariably emerge once more, but this time with inten-

---

[1] [*Footnote added* 1915:] Cf. what has been said on p. 339 about children's object-choice and the 'affectionate current'.

[2] [*Footnote added* 1915:] The barrier against incest is probably among the historical acquisitions of mankind, and, like other moral taboos, has no doubt already become established in many persons by organic inheritance. (Cf. my *Totem and Taboo*, 1912–13.) Psycho-analytic investigation shows, however, how intensely the individual struggles with the temptation to incest during his period of growth and how frequently the barrier is transgressed in phantasies and even in reality.

[3] [*Footnote added* 1920:] The phantasies of the pubertal period have as their starting-point the infantile sexual researches that were abandoned in childhood. No doubt, too, they are also present before the end of the latency period. They may persist wholly, or to a great extent, unconsciously and for that reason it is often impossible to date them accurately. They are of great importance in the origin of many symptoms, since they precisely constitute preliminary stages of these symptoms and thus lay down the forms

sified pressure from somatic sources. Among these tendencies the first place is taken with uniform frequency by the child's sexual impulses towards his parents, which are as a rule already differentiated owing to the attraction of the opposite sex – the son being drawn towards his mother and the daughter towards her father.[1] At the same time as these plainly incestuous phantasies are overcome and repudiated, one of the most significant, but also one of the most painful, psychical achievements of the pubertal period is completed: detachment from parental authority, a process that alone makes possible the opposition, which is so important for the progress of civilization, between the new generation and the old. At every stage in the course of development through which all human beings ought by rights to pass, a certain number are held back; so there are some who have never got over their parent's authority and have withdrawn their affection from them either very incompletely or not at all. They are mostly girls,

---

in which the repressed libidinal components find satisfaction. In the same way, they are the prototypes of the nocturnal phantasies which become conscious as dreams. Dreams are often nothing more than revivals of pubertal phantasies of this kind under the influence of, and in relation to, some stimulus left over from the waking life of the previous day (the 'day's residues'). [See Chapter VI, Section I, of *The Interpretation of Dreams* (1900a); *Standard Ed.*, **5**, 492 f.; *P.F.L.*, **4**, 632 f.] Some among the sexual phantasies of the pubertal period are especially prominent, and are distinguished by their very general occurrence and by being to a great extent independent of individual experience. Such are the adolescent's phantasies of overhearing his parents in sexual intercourse, of having been seduced at an early age by someone he loves and of having been threatened with castration [cf. the discussion of 'primal phantasies' in Lecture 23 of Freud's *Introductory Lectures* (1916–17) in Chapter 9 below]; such, too, are his phantasies of being in the womb, and even of experiences there, and the so-called 'family romance', in which he reacts to the difference between his attitude towards his parents now and in his childhood. The close relations existing between these phantasies and myths has been demonstrated in the case of the last instance by Otto Rank (1909).

It has justly been said that the Oedipus complex is the nuclear complex of the neuroses, and constitutes the essential part of their content. It represents the peak of infantile sexuality, which, through its after-effects, exercises a decisive influence on the sexuality of adults. Every new arrival on this planet is faced by the task of mastering the Oedipus complex; anyone who fails to do so falls a victim to neurosis. With the progress of psycho-analytic studies the importance of the Oedipus complex has became more and more clearly evident; its recognition has become the shibboleth that distinguishes the adherents of psycho-analysis from its opponents.

[*Added* 1924:] In another work (1924), Rank has traced attachment to the mother back to the prehistoric intra-uterine period and has thus indicated the biological foundation of the Oedipus complex. He differs from what has been said above, by deriving the barrier against incest from the traumatic effect of anxiety at birth. [See Chapter X of *Inhibitions, Symptoms and Anxiety* (1926d).]

[1] Cf. my remarks in *The Interpretation of Dreams* (1900a), on the inevitability of Fate in the fable of Oedipus [*Standard Ed.*, **4**, 260 ff.; *P.F.L.*, **4**, 362–6.]

who, to the delight of their parents, have persisted in all their childish love far beyond puberty. It is most instructive to find that it is precisely these girls who in their later marriage lack the capacity to give their husbands what is due to them; they make cold wives and remain sexually anaesthetic. We learn from this that sexual love and what appears to be non-sexual love for parents are fed from the same sources; the latter, that is to say, merely corresponds to an infantile fixation of the libido.

The closer one comes to the deeper disturbances of psycho-sexual development, the more unmistakably the importance of incestuous object-choice emerges. In psychoneurotics a large portion or the whole of their psychosexual activity in finding an object remains in the unconscious as a result of their repudiation of sexuality. Girls with an exaggerated need for affection and an equally exaggerated horror of the real demands made by sexual life have an irresistible temptation on the one hand to realize the ideal of asexual love in their lives and on the other hand to conceal their libido behind an affection which they can express without self-reproaches, by holding fast throughout their lives to their infantile fondness, revived at puberty, for their parents or brothers and sisters. Psycho-analysis has no difficulty in showing persons of this kind that they are *in love*, in the everyday sense of the word, with these blood-relations of theirs; for, with the help of their symptoms and other manifestations of their illness, it traces their unconscious thoughts and translates them into conscious ones. In cases in which someone who has previously been healthy falls ill after an unhappy experience in love it is also possible to show with certainty that the mechanism of his illness consists in a turning-back of his libido on to those whom he preferred in his infancy.

After-effects of Infantile Object-choice

Even a person who has been fortunate enough to avoid an incestuous fixation of his libido does not entirely escape its influence. It often happens that a young man falls in love seriously for the first time with a mature woman, or a girl with an elderly man in a position of authority; this is clearly an echo of the phase of development that we have been discussing, since these figures are able to re-animate pictures of their mother or father.[1] There can be no doubt that every

[1] [*Footnote added* 1920:] Cf. my paper 'A Special Type of Choice of Object made by Men' (1910h).

object-choice whatever is based, though less closely, on these proto-types. A man, especially, looks for someone who can represent his picture of his mother, as it has dominated his mind from his earliest childhood; and accordingly, if his mother is still alive, she may well resent this new version of herself and meet her with hostility. In view of the importance of a child's relations to his parents in determining his later choice of a sexual object, it can easily be understood that any disturbance of those relations will produce the gravest effects upon his adult sexual life. Jealousy in a lover is never without an infantile root or at least an infantile reinforcement. If there are quarrels between the parents or if their marriage is unhappy, the ground will be prepared in their children for the severest predisposition to a disturbance of sexual development or to a neurotic illness.

A child's affection for his parents is no doubt the most important infantile trace which, after being revived at puberty, points the way to his choice of an object; but it is not the only one. Other starting-points with the same early origin enable a man to develop more than one sexual line, based no less upon his childhood, and to lay down very various conditions for his object-choice.[1]

Prevention of Inversion

One of the tasks implicit in object-choice is that it should find its way to the opposite sex. This, as we know, is not accomplished without a certain amount of fumbling. Often enough the first impulses after puberty go astray, though without any permanent harm resulting. Dessoir [1894] has justly remarked upon the regularity with which adolescent boys and girls form sentimental friendships with others of their own sex. No doubt the strongest force working against a permanent inversion of the sexual object is the attraction which the opposing sexual characters exercise upon one another. Nothing can be said within the framework of the present discussion to throw light upon it.[2] This factor is not in itself, however, sufficient to exclude

---

[1] [*Footnote added* 1915:] The innumerable peculiarities of the erotic life of human beings as well as the compulsive character of the process of falling in love itself are quite unintelligible except by reference back to childhood and as being residual effects of childhood.

[2] [*Footnote added* 1924:] This is the place at which to draw attention to Ferenczi's *Versuch einer Genitaltheorie* (1924), a work which, though somewhat fanciful, is neverthe-less of the greatest interest, and in which the sexual life of the higher animals is traced back to their biological evolution.

inversion; there are no doubt a variety of other contributory factors. Chief among these is its authoritative prohibition by society. Where inversion is not regarded as a crime it will be found that it answers fully to the sexual inclinations of no small number of people. It may be presumed, in the next place, that in the case of men a childhood recollection of the affection shown them by their mother and others of the female sex who looked after them when they were children contributes powerfully to directing their choice towards women;[1] on the other hand their early experience of being deterred by their father from sexual activity and their competitive relation with him deflect them from their own sex. Both of these two factors apply equally to girls, whose sexual activity is particularly subject to the watchful guardianship of their mother. They thus acquire a hostile relation to their own sex which influences their object-choice decisively in what is regarded as the normal direction. The education of boys by male persons (by slaves, in antiquity) seems to encourage homosexuality. The frequency of inversion among the present-day aristocracy is made somewhat more intelligible by their employment of menservants, as well as by the fact that their mothers give less personal care to their children. In the case of some hysterics it is found that the early loss of one of their parents, whether by death, divorce or separation, with the result that the remaining parent absorbs the whole of the child's love, determines the sex of the person who is later to be chosen as a sexual object, and may thus open the way to permanent inversion.

Summary

The time has arrived for me to attempt to summarize what I have said. We started out from the aberrations of the sexual instinct in respect of its object and of its aim and we were faced by the question of whether these arise from an innate disposition or are acquired as a result of experiences in life. We arrived at an answer to this question from an understanding, derived from psycho-analytic investigation,

[1] [The rest of this sentence and the two following ones date from 1915. In the editions of 1905 and 1910 the following passage takes their place: 'while in the case of girls, who in any case enter a period of repression at puberty, impulses of rivalry play a part in discouraging them from loving members of their own sex.']

of the workings of the sexual instinct in psychoneurotics, a numerous class of people and one not far removed from the healthy. We found that in them tendencies to every kind of perversion can be shown to exist as unconscious forces and betray their presence as factors leading to the formation of symptoms. It was thus possible to say that neurosis is, as it were, the negative of perversion. In view of what was now seen to be the wide dissemination of tendencies to perversion we were driven to the conclusion that a disposition to perversions is an original and universal disposition of the human sexual instinct and that normal sexual behaviour is developed out of it as a result of organic changes and psychical inhibitions occurring in the course of maturation; we hoped to be able to show the presence of this original disposition in childhood. Among the forces restricting the direction taken by the sexual instinct we laid emphasis upon shame, disgust, pity and the structures of morality and authority erected by society. We were thus led to regard any established aberration from normal sexuality as an instance of developmental inhibition and infantilism. Though it was necessary to place in the foreground the importance of the variations in the original disposition, a co-operative and not an opposing relation was to be assumed as existing between them and the influences of actual life. It appeared, on the other hand, that since the original disposition is necessarily a complex one, the sexual instinct itself must be something put together from various factors, and that in the perversions it falls apart, as it were, into its components. The perversions were thus seen to be on the one hand inhibitions, and on the other hand dissociations, of normal development. Both these aspects were brought together in the supposition that the sexual instinct of adults arises from a combination of a number of impulses of childhood into a unity, an impulsion with a single aim.

After having explained the preponderance of perverse tendencies in psychoneurotics by recognizing it as a collateral filling of subsidiary channels when the main current of the instinctual stream has been blocked by 'represssion',[1] we proceeded to a consideration of sexual life in childhood. We found it a regrettable thing that the existence of the sexual instinct in childhood has been denied and that the sexual

---

[1] [*Footnote added* 1915:] This does not apply only to the 'negative' tendencies to perversion which appear in neuroses but equally to the 'positive', properly so-called, perversions. Thus these latter are to be derived not merely from a fixation of infantile tendencies but also from a regression to those tendencies as a result of other channels of the sexual current being blocked. It is for this reason that the positive perversions also are accessible to psycho-analytic therapy.

manifestations not infrequently to be observed in children have been
described as irregularities. It seemed to us on the contrary that
children bring germs of sexual activity with them into the world, that
they already enjoy sexual satisfaction when they begin to take
nourishment and that they persistently seek to repeat the experience
in the familiar activity of 'thumb-sucking'. The sexual activity of
children, however, does not, it appeared, develop *pari passu* with their
other functions, but, after a short period of efflorescence from the ages
of two to five,[1] enters upon the so-called period of latency. During that
period the production of sexual excitation is not by any means
stopped but continues and produces a store of energy which is
employed to a great extent for purposes other than sexual – namely,
on the one hand in contributing the sexual components to social
feelings and on the other hand (through repression and reaction-
forming) in building up the subsequently developed barriers against
sexuality. On this view, the forces destined to retain the sexual
instinct upon certain lines are built up in childhood chiefly at the cost
of perverse sexual impulses and with the assistance of education. A
certain portion of the infantile sexual impulses would seem to evade
these uses and succeed in expressing itself as sexual activity. We next
found that sexual excitation in children springs from a multiplicity of
forces. Satisfaction arises first and foremost from the appropriate
sensory excitation of what we have described as erotogenic zones. It
seems probable that any part of the skin and any sense-organ –
probably, indeed, *any* organ – can function as an erotogenic zone,
though there are some particularly marked erotogenic zones whose
excitation would seem to be secured from the very first by certain
organic contrivances. It further appears that sexual excitation arises
as a by-product, as it were, of a large number of processes that occur in
the organism, as soon as they reach a certain degree of intensity, and
most especially of any relatively powerful emotion, even though it is of
a distressing nature. The excitations from all these sources are not yet
combined; but each follows its own separate aim, which is merely the
attainment of a certain sort of pleasure. In childhood, therefore, the
sexual instinct is not unified and is at first without an object, that is,
auto-erotic.

The erotogenic zone of the genitals begins to make itself noticeable,

[1] [The last seven words were first inserted in 1915. In the edition of that year,
however, the ages given were 'three to five'. The 'two' was substituted in 1920.]

it seems, even during the years of childhood. This may happen in two ways. Either, like any other erotogenic zone, it yields satisfaction in response to appropriate sensory stimulation; or, in a manner which is not quite understandable, when satisfaction is derived from other sources, a sexual excitation is simultaneously produced which has a special relation to the genital zone. We were reluctantly obliged to admit that we could not satisfactorily explain the relation between sexual satisfaction and sexual excitation, or that between the activity of the genital zone and the activity of the other sources of sexuality.

We found from the study of neurotic disorders that beginnings of an organization of the sexual instinctual components can be detected in the sexual life of children from its very beginning. During a first, very early phase, oral erotism occupies most of the picture. A second of these pregenital organizations is characterized by the predominance of sadism and anal erotism. It is not until a third phase has been reached that the genital zones proper contribute their share in determining sexual life, and in children this last phase is developed only so far as to a primacy of the phallus.

We were then obliged to recognize, as one of our most surprising findings, that this early efflorescence of infantile sexual life (between the ages of two and five) already gives rise to the choice of an object, with all the wealth of mental activities which such a process involves. Thus, in spite of the lack of synthesis between the different instinctual components and the uncertainty of the sexual aim, the phase of development corresponding to that period must be regarded as an important precursor of the subsequent final sexual organization.

The fact that the onset of sexual development in human beings occurs in two phases, i.e. that the development is interrupted by the period of latency, seemed to call for particular notice. This appears to be one of the necessary conditions of the aptitude of men for developing a higher civilization, but also of their tendency to neurosis. So far as we know, nothing analogous is to be found in man's animal relatives. It would seem that the origin of this peculiarity of man must be looked for in the prehistory of the human species.

It was not possible to say what amount of sexual activity can occur in childhood without being described as abnormal or detrimental to further development. The nature of these sexual manifestations was found to be predominantly masturbatory. Experience further showed that the external influences of seduction are capable of provoking interruptions of the latency period or even its cessation, and that in this connection the sexual instinct of children proves in fact to be polymorphously perverse; it seems, moreover, that any such premature sexual activity diminishes a child's educability.

In spite of the gaps in our knowledge of infantile sexual life, we had to proceed to an attempt at examining the alterations brought about in it by the arrival of puberty. We selected two of these as being the decisive ones: the subordination of all the other sources of sexual excitation under the primacy of the genital zones and the process of finding an object. Both of these are already adumbrated in childhood. The first is accomplished by the mechanism of exploiting fore-pleasure: what were formerly self-contained sexual acts, attended by pleasure and excitation, become acts preparatory to the new sexual aim (the discharge of the sexual products), the attainment of which enormously pleasurable, brings the sexual excitation to an end. In this connection we had to take into account the differentiation of sexuality into masculine and feminine; and we found that in order to become a woman a further stage of repression is necessary, which discards a portion of infantile masculinity and prepares the woman for changing her leading genital zone. As regards object-choice, we found that it is given its direction by the childhood hints (revived at puberty) of the child's sexual inclination towards his parents and others in charge of him, but that it is diverted away from them, on to other people who resemble them, owing to the barrier against incest which has meanwhile been erected. Finally it must be added that during the transition period of puberty the processes of somatic and of psychical development continue for a time side by side independently, until the irruption of an intense mental erotic impulse, leading to the innervation of the genitals, brings about the unity of the erotic function which is necessary for normality.

Factors Interfering with Development

Every step on this long path of development can become a point of fixation, every juncture in this involved combination can be an occasion for a dissociation of the sexual instinct, as we have already shown from numerous instances. It remains for us to enumerate the various factors, internal and external, that interfere with development, and to indicate the place in the mechanism on which the disturbance arising from each of them impinges. The factors that we shall enumerate can evidently not be of equal importance, and we must be prepared for difficulties in assigning an appropriate value to each.

Constitution and Heredity

First and foremost we must name the innate variety of sexual constitutions, upon which it is probable that the principal weight falls, but which can clearly only be inferred from their later manifestations and even then not always with great certainty. We picture this variety as a preponderance of one or another of the many sources of sexual excitation, and it is our view that a difference in disposition of this kind is always bound to find expression in the final result, even though that result may not overstep the limits of what is normal. No doubt it is conceivable that there may also be variations in the original disposition of a kind which must necessarily, and without the concurrence of any other factors, lead to the development of an abnormal sexual life. These might be described as 'degenerative' and be regarded as an expression of inherited degeneracy. In this connection I have a remarkable fact to record. In more than half of the severe cases of hysteria, obsessional neurosis, etc., which I have treated psychotherapeutically, I have been able to prove with certainty that the patient's father suffered from syphilis before marriage, whether there was evidence of tabes or general paralysis, or whether the anamnesis indicated in some other way the presence of syphilitic disease. I should like to make it perfectly plain that the children who later became neurotic bore no physical signs of hereditary syphilis, so that it was their abnormal sexual constitution that was to be regarded as the last echo of their syphilitic heritage. Though I am far from wishing to assert that descent from syphilitic parents is an invariable or indispensable aetiological condition of a neuropathic constitution, I am nevertheless of opinion that the coincidence which I have observed is neither accidental nor unimportant.

The hereditary conditions in the case of positive perverts are less well known, for they know how to avoid investigation. Yet there are good reasons to suppose that what is true of the neuroses applies also to the perversions. For it is no rare thing to find perversions and psychoneuroses occurring in the same family, and distributed between the two sexes in such a way that the male members of the family, or one of them, are positive perverts, while the females, true to the tendency of their sex to repression, are negative perverts, that is, hysterics. This is good evidence of the essential connections which we have shown to exist between the two disorders.

Further Modification

On the other hand, it is not possible to adopt the view that the form to be taken by sexual life is unambiguously decided, once and for all, with the inception of the different components of the sexual constitution. On the contrary, the determining process continues, and further possibilities arise according to the vicissitudes of the tributary streams of sexuality springing from their separate sources. This further modification is clearly what brings the decisive outcome, and constitutions which might be described as the same can lead to three different final results:–

[1] If the relation between all the different dispositions – a relation which we will assume to be abnormal – persists and grows stronger at maturity, the result can only be a perverse sexual life. The analysis of abnormal constitutional disposition of this kind has not yet been properly taken in hand. But we already know cases which can easily be explained on such a basis as this. Writers on the subject, for instance, have asserted [see p. 287] that the necessary precondition of a whole number of perverse fixations lies in an innate weakness of the sexual instinct. In this form the view seems to me untenable. It makes sense, however, if what is meant is a constitutional weakness of one particular factor in the sexual instinct, namely the genital zone – a zone which takes over the function of combining the separate sexual activities for the purposes of reproduction. For if the genital zone is weak, this combination, which is required to take place at puberty, is bound to fail, and the strongest of the other components of sexuality will continue its activity as a perversion.[1]

Repression

[2] A different result is brought about if in the course of development some of the components which are of excessive strength in the disposition are submitted to the process of repression (which, it must be insisted, is not equivalent to their being abolished). If this happens, the excitations concerned continue to be generated as before; but they

---

[1] [Footnote added 1915:] In such circumstances one often finds that at puberty a normal sexual current begins to operate at first, but that, as a result of its internal weakness, it breaks down in face of the first external obstacles and is then replaced by regression to the perverse fixation.

are prevented by psychical obstruction from attaining their aim and are diverted into numerous other channels till they find their way to expression as symptoms. The outcome may be an approximately normal sexual life – though usually a restricted one – but there is in addition psychoneurotic illness. These particular cases have become familiar to us from the psycho-analytic investigation of neurotics. Their sexual life begins like that of perverts, and a considerable part of their childhood is occupied with perverse sexual activity which occasionally extends far into maturity. A reversal due to repression then occurs, owing to internal causes (usually before puberty, but now and then even long afterwards), and from that time onwards neurosis takes the place of perversion, without the old impulses being extinguished. We are reminded of the proverb 'Junge Hure, alte Betschwester',[1] only that here youth has lasted all too short a time. The fact that perversion can be replaced by neurosis in the life of the same person, like the fact which we have already mentioned that perversion and neurosis can be distributed among different members of the same family, tallies with the view that neurosis is the negative of perversion.

Sublimation

[3] The third alternative result of an abnormal constitutional disposition is made possible by the process of sublimation. This enables excessively strong excitations arising from particular sources of sexuality to find an outlet and use in other fields, so that a not inconsiderable increase in psychical efficiency results from a disposition which in itself is perilous. Here we have one of the origins of artistic activity; and, according to the completeness or incompleteness of the sublimation, a characterological analysis of a highly gifted individual, and in particular of one which an artistic disposition, may reveal a mixture, in every proportion, of efficiency, perversion and neurosis. A sub-species of sublimation is to be found in suppression by reaction-formation, which, as we have seen, begins during a child's period of latency and continues in favourable cases throughout his whole life. What we describe as a person's 'character' is built up to a considerable extent from the material of sexual excitations and is composed of instincts that have been fixed since childhood, of constructions achieved by means of sublimation, and of other constructions,

[1] ['A young whore makes an old nun.']

employed for effectively holding in check perverse impulses which have been recognized as being unutilizable.[1] The multifariously perverse sexual disposition of childhood can accordingly be regarded as the source of a number of our virtues, in so far as through reaction-formation it stimulates their development.[2]

Accidental Experiences

No other influences on the course of sexual development can compare in importance with releases of sexuality, waves of repression and sublimations – the two latter being processes of which the inner causes are quite unknown to us. It might be possible to include repressions and sublimations as a part of the constitutional disposition, by regarding them as manifestations of it in life; and anyone who does so is justified in asserting that the final shape taken by sexual life is principally the outcome of the innate constitution. No one with perception will, however, dispute that an interplay of factors such as this also leaves room for the modifying effects of accidental events experienced in childhood and later. It is not easy to estimate the relative efficacy of the constitutional and accidental factors. In theory one is always inclined to overestimate the former; therapeutic practice emphasizes the importance of the latter. It should, however, on no account be forgotten that the relation between the two is a co-operative and not a mutually exclusive one. The constitutional factor must await experiences before it can make itself felt; the accidental factor must have a constitutional basis in order to come into operation. To cover the majority of cases we can picture what has been described as a 'complemental series', in which the diminishing intensity of one factor is balanced by the increasing intensity of the other; there is, however, no reason to deny the existence of extreme cases at the two ends of the series.

We shall be in even closer harmony with psycho-analytic research if

[1] [*Footnote added* 1920:] In the case of some character-traits it has even been possible to trace a connection with particular erotogenic components. Thus, obstinacy, thrift and orderliness arise from an exploitation of anal erotism, while ambition is determined by a strong urethral-erotic disposition. [See Freud, 1908*b*, *Standard Ed.*, **9**, 175; *P.F.L.*, **7**, 215.]

[2] Emile Zola, a keen observer of human nature, describes in *La joie de vivre* how a girl, cheerfully and selflessly and without thought of reward, sacrificed to those she loved everything that she possessed or could lay claim to – her money and her hopes. This girl's childhood was dominated by an insatiable thirst for affection, which was transformed into cruelty on an occasion when she found herself slighted in favour of another girl.

we give a place of preference among the accidental factors to the experiences of early childhood. The single aetiological series then falls into two, which may be called the dispositional and the definitive. In the first the constitution and the accidental experiences of childhood interact in the same manner as do the disposition and later traumatic experiences in the second. All the factors that impair sexual development show their effects by bringing about a regression, a return to an earlier phase of development.

Let us now resume our task of enumerating the factors which we have found to exercise an influence on sexual development, whether they are themselves operative forces or merely manifestations of such forces.

Precocity

One such factor is spontaneous sexual precocity, whose presence at least can be demonstrated with certainty in the aetiology of the neuroses though, like other factors, it is not in itself a sufficient cause. It is manifested in the interruption, abbreviation or bringing to an end of the infantile period of latency; and it is a cause of disturbances by occasioning sexual manifestations which, owing on the one hand to the sexual inhibitions being incomplete and on the other hand to the genital system being undeveloped, are bound to be in the nature of perversions. These tendencies to perversion may thereafter either persist as such or, after repressions have set in, become the motive forces of neurotic symptoms. In any case sexual precocity makes more difficult the later control of the sexual instinct by the higher mental agencies which is so desirable, and it increases the impulsive quality which, quite apart from this, characterizes the psychical representations of the instinct. Sexual precocity often runs parallel with premature intellectual development and, linked in this way, is to be found in the childhood history of persons of the greatest eminence and capacity; under such conditions its effects do not seem to be so pathogenic as when it appears in isolation.[1]

Temporal Factors

Other factors which, along with precocity, may be classed as temporal also deserve attention. The order in which the various

---

[1] [Cf. some remarks on this point in the case history of 'Little Hans' (1909b), *Standard Ed.*, **10**, 142 f.; *P.F.L.*, **8**, 298 f. – The paragraph which follows was added in 1915.]

instinctual impulses come into activity seems to be phylogenetically determined; so, too, does the length of time during which they are able to manifest themselves before they succumb to the effects of some freshly emerging instinctual impulse or to some typical repression. Variations, however, seem to occur both in temporal sequence and in duration, and these variations must exercise a determining influence upon the final result. It cannot be a matter of indifference whether a given current makes its appearance earlier or later than a current flowing in the opposite direction, for the effect of a repression cannot be undone. Divergences in the temporal sequence in which the components come together invariably produce a difference in the outcome. One the other hand, instinctual impulses which emerge with special intensity often run a surprisingly short course – as, for instance, the heterosexual attachment of persons who later become manifest homosexuals. There is no justification for the fear that trends which set in with the greatest violence in childhood will permanently dominate the adult character; it is just as likely that they will disappear and make way for an opposite tendency. ('Gestrenge Herren regieren nicht lange.')[1]

We are not in a position to give so much as a hint as to the causes of these temporal disturbances of the process of development. A prospect opens before us at this point upon a whole phalanx of biological and perhaps, too, of historical problems of which we have not even come within striking distance.

Pertinacity of Early Impressions

The importance of all early sexual manifestations is increased by a psychical factor of unknown origin, which at the moment, it must be admitted, can only be brought forward as a provisional psychological concept. I have in mind the fact that, in order to account for the situation, it is necessary to assume that these early impressions of sexual life are characterized by an increased pertinacity or susceptibility to fixation in persons who are later to become neurotics or perverts. For the same premature sexual manifestations, when they occur in other persons, fail to make so deep an impression; they do not tend in a compulsive manner towards repetition nor do they lay down the path to be taken by the sexual instinct for a whole lifetime. Part of the explanation of this pertinacity of early impressions may perhaps

---

[1] ['Harsh rulers have short reigns.']

lie in another psychical factor which we must not overlook in the causation of the neuroses, namely the preponderance attaching in mental life to memory-traces in comparison with recent impressions. This factor is clearly dependent on intellectual education and increases in proportion to the degree of individual culture. The savage has been described in contrast as 'das unglückselige Kind des Augenblickes'.[1] In consequence of the inverse relation holding between civilization and the free development of sexuality, of which the consequences can be followed far into the structure of our existences, the course taken by the sexual life of a child is just as unimportant for later life where the cultural or social level is relatively low as it is important where that level is relatively high.

Fixation

The ground prepared by the psychical factors which have just been enumerated affords a favourable basis for such stimulations of infantile sexuality as are experienced accidentally. The latter (first and foremost, seduction by other children or by adults) provide the material which, with the help of the former, can become fixated as a permanent disorder. A good proportion of the deviations from normal sexual life which are later observed both in neurotics and in perverts are thus established from the very first by the impressions of childhood – a period which is regarded as being devoid of sexuality. The causation is shared between a compliant constitution, precocity, the characteristic of increased pertinacity of early impressions and the chance stimulation of the sexual instinct by extraneous influences.

The unsatisfactory conclusion, however, that emerges from these investigations of the disturbances of sexual life is that we know far too little of the biological processes constituting the essence of sexuality to be able to construct from our fragmentary information a theory adequate to the understanding alike of normal and of pathological conditions.

---

[1] ['The hapless child of the moment.'] Increase in pertinacity may also possibly be the effect of an especially intense somatic manifestation of sexuality in early years. [What Freud here describes as 'pertinacity of early impressions' and 'susceptibility to fixation' was also termed by him elsewhere 'adhesiveness of the libido'. Cf., for example, Lectures 22 and 28 of the *Introductory Lectures* (1916–17). See also *Civilization and its Discontents* (1930a), Chapter V, where Freud refers to the special case of 'inertia of the libido'.]

On the Sexual Theories
of Children

(1908)*

The material on which the following synthesis is based is derived from several sources. Firstly, from the direct observation of what children say and do; secondly, from what adult neurotics consciously remember from their childhood and relate during psycho-analytic treatment; and thirdly from the inferences and constructions, and from the unconscious memories translated into conscious material, which result from the psycho-analysis of neurotics.

That the first of these three sources has not by itself supplied all that is worth knowing on the subject is due to the attitude which the adult adopts towards the sexual life of children. He does not credit them with having any sexual activity and therefore takes no trouble to observe any such thing while, on the other hand, he suppresses any manifestation of such an activity which might claim his attention. Consequently the opportunity of obtaining information from this, the most unequivocal and fertile source of all, is a very restricted one. Whatever comes from the uninfluenced communications made by adults concerning their own conscious childhood memories is at the best subject to the objection that it may have been falsified in retrospect; but, in addition to this, it has to be viewed in the light of the fact that the informants have subsequently become neurotic. The material that comes from the third source is open to all the criticisms which it is the custom to marshal against the trustworthiness of psycho-analysis and the reliability of the conclusions that are drawn from it. Thus I cannot attempt to justify it here; I can only give an assurance that those who know and practise the psycho-analytic technique acquire an extensive confidence in its findings.

I cannot guarantee the completeness of my results, but I can answer for the care taken in arriving at them.

*German original first published in Volume 4 of *Sexual-Probleme*. This English version is included in *Standard Ed.*, 9, 209; *P.F.L.*, 7, 187.

There remains a difficult question to decide. How far may one assume that what is here reported of children generally is true of all children – that is, of every particular child? Pressure of education and varying intensity of the sexual instinct certainly make great individual variations in the sexual behaviour of children possible, and, above all, influence the date at which a child's sexual interest appears. For this reason, I have not divided my presentation of the material according to the successive epochs of childhood, but have combined into a single account things that come into play in different children sometimes earlier and sometimes later. It is my conviction that no child – none, at least, who is mentally normal and still less one who is intellectually gifted – can avoid being occupied with the problems of sex in the years *before* puberty.

I do not think much of the objection that neurotics are a special class of people, marked by an innate disposition that is 'degenerate', from whose childhood life we must not be allowed to infer anything about the childhood of other people. Neurotics are people much like others. They cannot be sharply differentiated from normal people, and in their childhood they are not always easily distinguishable from those who remain healthy in later life. It is one of the most valuable results of our psycho-analytic investigations to have discovered that the neuroses of such people have no special mental content that is peculiar to them, but that, as Jung has expressed it, they fall ill of the same complexes against which we healthy people struggle as well. The only difference is that healthy people know how to overcome those complexes without any gross damage demonstrable in practical life, whereas in nervous cases the suppression of the complexes succeeds only at the price of costly substitutive formations – that is to say, from a practical point of view it is a failure. In childhood neurotic and normal people naturally approximate to each other much more closely than they do in later life, so that I cannot regard it as a methodological error to make use of the communications of neurotics about their childhood for drawing conclusions by analogy about normal childhood life. But since those who later become neurotics very often have in their inborn constitution an especially strong sexual instinct and a tendency to precocity and to a premature expression of that instinct, they make it possible for us to recognize a great deal of infantile activity more sharply and clearly than our capacity for observation (which is in any case a blunted one) would enable us to do in other children. But we shall of course only be able to assess the true value of these communications made by neurotic adults when, follow-ing Havelock Ellis's example, we shall have thought it worth while to collect the childhood memories of *healthy* adults as well.[1]

In consequence of unfavourable circumstances, both of an external and an internal nature, the following observations apply chiefly to the sexual development of one sex only – that is, of males. The value of a compilation such as I am attempting here need not, however, be a purely descriptive one. A knowledge of infantile sexual theories in the shapes they assume in the thoughts of children can be of interest in various ways – even, surprisingly enough, for the elucidation of myths and fairy tales. They are indispensable, moreover, for an understand-ing of the neuroses themselves; for in them these childish theories are still operative and acquire a determining influence upon the form taken by the symptoms.

If we could divest ourselves of our corporeal existence, and could view the things of this earth with a fresh eye as purely thinking beings, from another planet for instance, nothing perhaps would strike our atten-tion more forcibly than the fact of the existence of two sexes among human beings, who, though so much alike in other respects, yet mark the difference between them with such obvious external signs. But it does not seem that children choose this fundamental fact in the same way as the starting-point of their researches into sexual problems. Since they have known a father and mother as far back as they can remember in life, they accept their existence as a reality which needs no further enquiry, and a boy has the same attitude towards a little sister from whom he is separated by only a slight difference of age of one or two years. A child's desire for knowledge on this point does not in fact awaken spontaneously, prompted perhaps by some inborn need for established causes; it is aroused under the goad of the self-seeking instincts that dominate him, when – perhaps after the end of his second year – he is confronted with the arrival of a new baby. And a child whose own nursery has received no such addition is able, from observations made in other homes, to put himself in the same situation. The loss of his parents' care, which he actually experiences or justly fears, and the presentiment that from now on he must for evermore share all his possessions with the newcomer, have the effect

---

[1] [Cf. Havelock Ellis, 1903, Appendix B. Freud had discussed these narratives in a footnote to the second of his *Three Essays* (1905*d*), p. 330 above.]

of awakening his emotions and sharpening his capacities for thought. The elder child expresses unconcealed hostility towards his rival, which finds vent in unfriendly criticisms of it, in wishes that 'the stork should take it away again' and occasionally even in small attacks upon the creature lying helpless in the cradle. A wider difference in age usually softens the expression of this primary hostility. In the same way, at a rather later age, if no small brother or sister has appeared, the child's wish for a playmate, such as he has seen in other families, may gain the upper hand.

At the instigation of these feelings and worries, the child now comes to be occupied with the first, grand problem of life and asks himself the question: '*Where do babies come from?*' – a question which, there can be no doubt, first ran: 'Where did this particular, intruding baby come from?' We seem to hear the echoes of this first riddle in innumerable riddles of myth and legend. The question itself is, like all research, the product of a vital exigency, as though thinking were entrusted with the task of preventing the recurrence of such dreaded events. Let us assume, however, that the child's thinking soon becomes independent of this instigation, and henceforward goes on operating as a self-sustained instinct for research. Where a child is not already too much intimidated, he sooner or later adopts the direct method of demanding an answer from his parents or those in charge of him, who are in his eyes the source of all knowledge. This method, however, fails. The child receives either evasive answers or a rebuke for his curiosity, or he is dismissed with the mythologically significant piece of information which, in German countries, runs: 'The stork brings the babies; it fetches them out of the water.' I have reason to believe that far more children than their parents suspect are dissatisfied with this solution and meet it with energetic doubts, which, however, they do not always openly admit. I know of a three-year-old boy who, after receiving this piece of enlightenment, disappeared – to the terror of his nurse. He was found at the edge of the big pond adjoining the country house, to which he had hurried in order to see the babies in the water. I also know of another boy who could only allow his disbelief to find expression in a hesitant remark that he knew better, that it was not a stork that brought babies but a heron. It seems to me to follow from a great deal of information I have received that children refuse to believe the stork theory and that from the time of this first deception and rebuff they nourish a distrust of adults and have a suspicion of there being something forbidden which is being withheld from them by the 'grown-ups', and that they consequently hide their further researches under a cloak of secrecy. With this, however, the child also experiences the first occasion for a 'psychical conflict', in that views for which he feels an instinctual kind of preference, but which are not 'right' in the eyes of the grown-ups, come into opposition with other views, which are supported by the authority of the grown-ups without being acceptable to him himself. Such a psychical conflict may soon turn into a 'psychical dissociation'. The set of views which are bound up with being 'good', but also with a cessation of reflection, become the dominant and conscious views; while the other set, for which the child's work of research has meanwhile obtained fresh evidence, but which are not supposed to count, become the suppressed and 'unconscious' ones. The nuclear complex[1] of a neurosis is in this way brought into being.

Recently, the analysis of a five-year-old boy,[2] which his father undertook and which he has handed over to me for publication, has given me irrefutable proof of the correctness of a view towards which the psycho-analysis of adults had long been leading me. I now know that the change which takes place in the mother during pregnancy does not escape the child's sharp eyes and that he is very well able before long to establish the true connection between the increase in his mother's stoutness and the appearance of the baby. In the case just mentioned the boy was three and a half years old when his sister was born and four and three quarters when he showed his better knowledge by the most unmistakable allusions. This precocious discovery, however, is always kept secret, and later, in conformity with the further vicissitudes of the child's sexual researches, it is repressed and forgotten.

The 'stork fable', therefore, is not one of the sexual theories of children. On the contrary, it is the child's observation of animals, who hide so little of their sexual life and to whom he feels so closely akin, that strengthens his disbelief in it. With his knowledge, independently obtained, that babies grow inside the mother's body, he would be on the right road to solving the problem on which he first tries out his powers of thinking. But his further progress is inhibited by a piece of

---

[1] [Soon after this, e.g. in the 'Rat Man' case history (1909d), Standard Ed., 10, 208n; P.F.L., 9, 89n, Freud was using this term as equivalent to what a little later (1910h), he called the 'Oedipus complex'. In the present passage, where it first appears, the application is wider.]

[2] [The case history of 'Little Hans' (1909b), which was published shortly after the present paper.]

ignorance which cannot be made good and by false theories which the state of his own sexuality imposes on him.

These false sexual theories, which I shall now discuss, all have one very curious characteristic. Although they go astray in a grotesque fashion, yet each one of them contains a fragment of real truth; and in this they are analogous to the attempts of adults, which are looked at as strokes of genius, at solving the problems of the universe which are too hard for human comprehension. What is correct and hits the mark in such theories is to be explained by their origin from the components of the sexual instinct which are already stirring in the childish organism. For it is not owing to any arbitrary mental act or to chance impressions that those notions arise, but to the necessities of the child's psycho-sexual constitution; and this is why we can speak of sexual theories in children as being typical, and why we find the same mistaken beliefs in every child whose sexual life is accessible to us.

The first of these theories starts out from the neglect of the differences between the sexes on which I laid stress at the beginning of this paper as being characteristic of children. It consists in *attributing to everyone, including females, the possession of a penis*, such as the boy knows from his own body. It is precisely in what we must regard as the 'normal' sexual constitution that already in childhood the penis is the leading erotogenic zone and the chief auto-erotic sexual object; and the boy's estimate of its value is logically reflected in his inability to imagine a person like himself who is without this essential constituent. When a small boy sees his little sister's genitals, what he says shows that his prejudice is already strong enough to falsify his perception.[1] He does not comment on the absence of a penis, but *invariably* says, as though by way of consolation and to put things right: 'Her ——'s still quite small. But when she gets bigger it'll grow all right.' The idea of a woman with a penis returns in later life, in the dreams of adults: the dreamer, in a state of nocturnal sexual excitation, will throw a woman down, strip her and prepare for intercourse – and then, in place of the female genitals, he beholds a well-developed penis and breaks off the dream and the excitation. The numerous hermaphrodites of classical antiquity faithfully reproduce this idea, universally held in childhood; one may observe that to most normal people they cause no offence,

---

[1] [This 'falsified perception', or, as Freud afterwards named it, this 'denial' or 'disavowal', was very much later to become the basis of important theoretical discussions. Cf. in particular the paper on 'Fetishism' (1927e) and Chapter VIII of the posthumous *Outline of Psycho-Analysis* (1940a [1938]).]

while the real hermaphroditic formations of the genitals which are permitted to occur by Nature nearly always excite the greatest abhorrence.

If this idea of a woman with a penis becomes 'fixated' in an individual when he is a child, resisting all the influences of later life and making him as a man unable to do without a penis in his sexual object, then, although in other respects he may lead a normal sexual life, he is bound to become a homosexual, and will seek his sexual object among men who, owing to some other physical and mental characteristics, remind him of women.[1] Real women, when he comes to know them later, remain impossible as sexual objects for him, because they lack the essential sexual attraction; indeed, in connection with another impression of his childhood life, they may even become abhorrent to him. The child, having been mainly dominated by excitations in the penis, will usually have obtained pleasure by stimulating it with his hand; he will have been detected in this by his parents or nurse and terrorized by the threat of having his penis cut off. The effect of this 'threat of castration' is proportionate to the value set upon that organ and is quite extraordinarily deep and persistent. Legends and myths testify to the upheaval in the child's emotional life and to the horror which is linked with the castration complex – a complex which is subsequently remembered by consciousness with corresponding reluctance. The woman's genitalia, when seen later on, are regarded as a mutilated organ and recall this threat, and they therefore arouse horror instead of pleasure in the homosexual. This reaction cannot be altered in any way when the homosexual comes to learn from science that his childish assumption that women had a penis too was not so far wrong after all. Anatomy has recognized the clitoris within the female pudenda as being an organ that is homologous to the penis; and the physiology of the sexual processes has been able to add that this small penis which does not grow any bigger behaves in fact during childhood like a real and genuine penis – that it becomes the seat of excitations which lead to its being touched, that its excitability gives the little girl's sexual activity a masculine character and that a wave of repression in the years of puberty is needed in order for this masculine sexuality to be discarded and the woman to emerge. Since the sexual function of many women is crippled, whether by their

---

[1] [Freud returned to this in his case history of 'Little Hans' (1909b), *Standard Ed.*, **10**, 109; *P.F.L.*, **8**, 267–8.]

obstinate clinging on to this excitability of the clitoris so that they remain anaesthetic in intercourse, or by such excessive repression occurring that its operation is partly replaced by hysterical compensatory formations – all this seems to show that there is some truth in the infantile sexual theory that women, like men, possess a penis.[1]

It is easy to observe that little girls fully share their brother's opinion of it. They develop a great interest in that part of the boy's body. But this interest promptly falls under the sway of envy. They feel themselves unfairly treated. They make attempts to micturate in the posture that is made possible for boys by their possessing a big penis; and when a girl declares that 'she would rather be a boy', we know what deficiency her wish is intended to put right.

If children could follow the hints given by the excitation of the penis they would get a little nearer to the solution of their problem. That the baby grows inside the mother's body is obviously not a sufficient explanation. How does it get inside? What starts its development? That the father has something to do with it seems likely; he says that the baby is *his* baby as well.[2] Again, the penis certainly has a share, too, in these mysterious happenings; the excitation in it which accompanies all these activities of the child's thoughts bears witness to this. Attached to this excitation are impulsions which the child cannot account for – obscure urges to do something violent, to press in, to knock to pieces, to tear open a hole somewhere. But when the child thus seems to be well on the way to postulating the existence of the vagina and to concluding that an incursion of this kind by his father's penis into his mother is the act by means of which the baby is created in his mother's body – at this juncture his enquiry is broken off in helpless perplexity. For standing in its way is his theory that his mother possesses a penis just as a man does, and the existence of the cavity which receives the penis remains undiscovered by him. It is not hard to guess that the lack of success of his intellectual efforts makes it easier for him to reject and forget them. This brooding and doubting, however, becomes the prototype of all later intellectual work directed towards the solution of problems, and the first failure has a crippling effect on the child's whole future.

Their ignorance of the vagina also makes it possible for children to believe in the second of their sexual theories. If the baby grows in the

---

[1] [Cf. *Three Essays* (1905*d*), p. 356 above.]
[2] Cf. the 'Analysis of a Five-Year-Old Boy' (1909*b*) [*Standard Ed.*, **10**, 133–4; *P.F.L.*, **8**, 290 f.]

mother's body and is then removed from it, this can only happen along the one possible pathway – the anal aperture. *The baby must be evacuated like a piece of excrement, like a stool.* When, in later childhood, the same question is the subject of solitary reflection or of a discussion between two children, the explanations probably arrived at are that the baby emerges from the navel, which comes open, or that the abdomen is slit up and the baby taken out – which was what happened to the wolf in the story of Little Red Riding-Hood. These theories are expressed aloud and also consciously remembered later on; they no longer contain anything objectionable. These same children have by then completely forgotten that in earlier years they believed in another theory of birth, which is now obstructed by the repression of the anal sexual components that has meanwhile occurred. At that time a motion was something which could be talked about in the nursery without shame. The child was still not so distant from his constitutional coprophilic inclinations. There was nothing degraded about coming into the world like a heap of faeces, which had not yet been condemned by feelings of disgust. The cloacal theory, which, after all, is valid for so many animals, was the most natural theory, and it alone could obtrude upon the child as being a probable one.

This being so, however, it was only logical that the child should refuse to grant women the painful prerogative of giving birth to children. If babies are born through the anus, then a man can give birth just as well as a woman. It is therefore possible for a boy to imagine that he, too, has children of his own, without there being any need to accuse him on that account of having feminine inclinations.[1] He is merely giving evidence in this of the anal erotism which is still alive in him.

If the cloacal theory of birth is preserved in consciousness during later years of childhood, as occasionally happens, it is accompanied too by a solution – no longer, it is true, a primary one – of the problem of the origin of babies. Here it is like being in a fairy story; one eats some particular thing and gets a child from it. This infantile theory of birth is revived in cases of insanity. A manic woman, for instance, will lead the visiting doctor to a little heap of faeces which she has deposited in a corner of her cell, and say to him with a laugh: 'That's the baby I had to-day.'

[1] Freud later drew attention to the close connection that can exist between anal erotism and a feminine attitude. See, for instance, *Standard Ed.*, **17**, 81; *P.F.L.*, **9**, 318.]

The third of the typical sexual theories arises in children if, through some chance domestic occurrence, they become witnesses of sexual intercourse between their parents. Their perceptions of what is happening are bound, however, to be only very incomplete. Whatever detail it may be that comes under their observation – whether it is the relative positions of the two people, or the noises they make, or some accessory circumstance – children arrive in every case at the same conclusion. They adopt what may be called a *sadistic view of coition*. They see it as something that the stronger participant is forcibly inflicting on the weaker, and they (especially boys) compare it to the romping familiar to them from their childish experience – romping which, incidentally, is not without a dash of sexual excitation. I have not been able to ascertain that children recognize this behaviour which they have witnessed between their parents as the missing link needed for solving the problem of babies; it appears more often that the connection is overlooked by them for the very reason that they have interpreted the act of love as an act of violence. But this view of it itself gives an impression of being a return of the obscure impulse towards cruel behaviour which became attached to the excitations of the child's penis when he first began to think about the problem of where babies came from. The possibility, too, cannot be excluded that this premature sadistic impulse, which might so nearly have led to the discovery of coition, itself first emerged under the influence of extremely obscure memories of parental intercourse, for which the child had obtained the material – though at the time he made no use of it – while he was still in his first years and was sharing his parents' bedroom.[1]

The sadistic theory of coitus which, taken in isolation, is misleading where it might have provided confirmatory evidence, is, once again, the expression of one of the innate components of the sexual instinct, any of which may be strongly marked to a greater or lesser degree in each particular child. For this reason the theory is correct up to a certain point; it has in part divined the nature of the sexual act and the 'sex-battle' that precedes it. Not infrequently, too, the child is in a position to support this view by accidental observations which he understands in part correctly, but also in part incorrectly and indeed in a reversed sense. In many marriages the wife does in fact recoil from

[1] Restif de la Bretonne, in his autobiographical work *Monsieur Nicolas* (1794), tells a story of an impression he received at the age of four, which confirms this sadistic misunderstanding of coitus.

her husband's embraces, which bring her no pleasure, but the risk of a fresh pregnancy. And so the child who is believed to be asleep (or who is pretending to be asleep) may receive an impression from his mother which he can only interpret as meaning that she is defending herself against an act of violence. At other times the whole marriage offers an observant child the spectacle of an unceasing quarrel, expressed in loud words and unfriendly gestures; so that he need not be surprised if the quarrel is carried on at night as well, and finally settled by the same method which he himself is accustomed to use in his relations with his brothers and sisters or playmates.

Moreover, if the child discovers spots of blood in his mother's bed or on her underclothes, he regards it as a confirmation of his view. It proves to him that his father has made another similar assault on his mother during the night (whereas we should rather take the fresh spots of blood to mean that there had been a temporary cessation of sexual intercourse). Much of the otherwise inexplicable 'horror of blood' shown by neurotics finds its explanation from this connection. Once again, however, the child's mistake contains a fragment of truth. For in certain familiar circumstances a trace of blood is in fact judged as a sign that sexual intercourse has been begun.

A question connected somewhat indirectly with the insoluble problem of where babies come from also engages the child – the question as to the nature and content of the state called 'being married'; and he answers the question differently according as his chance perceptions in relation to his parents have coincided with instincts of his own which are still pleasurably coloured. All that these answers seem to have in common is that the child promises himself pleasurable satisfaction from being married and supposes that it involves a disregard of modesty. The notion I have most frequently met with is that *each of the married couple urinates in front of the other*. A variation of this, which sounds as if it was meant to indicate a greater knowledge symbolically, is that *the man urinates into the woman's chamber-pot*. In other instances the meaning of marriage is supposed to be that *the two people show their behinds to each other* (without being ashamed). In one case, in which education had succeeded in postponing sexual knowledge especially late, a fourteen-year-old girl, who had already begun to menstruate, arrived from the books she had read at the idea that being married consisted in a 'mixing of blood'; and since her own sister had not yet started her periods, the lustful girl made an assault on a female visitor who had confessed that she was just then menstruating, so as to force her to take part in this 'blood-mixing'.

Childhood opinions about the nature of marriage, which are not seldom retained by conscious memory, have great significance for the symptomatology of later neurotic illness. At first they find expression in children's games in which each child does with another whatever it is that in his view constitutes being married; and then, later on, the wish to be married may choose the infantile form of expression and so make its appearance in a phobia which is at first sight unrecognizable, or in some corresponding symptom.[1]

These seem to be the most important of the typical sexual theories that children produce spontaneously in early childhood, under the sole influence of the components of the sexual instinct. I know that I have not succeeded in making my material complete or in establishing an unbroken connection between it and the rest of infantile life. But I may add one or two supplementary observations, whose absence would otherwise be noticed by any well-informed person. Thus, for instance, there is the significant theory that a baby is got by a kiss – a theory which obviously betrays the predominance of the erotogenic zone of the mouth. In my experience this theory is exclusively feminine and is sometimes found to be pathogenic in girls whose sexual researches have been subjected to exceedingly strong inhibitions in childhood. Again, through an accidental observation, one of my women patients happened upon the theory of the 'couvade', which, as is well known, is a general custom among some races and is probably intended to contradict the doubts as to paternity which can never be entirely overcome. A rather eccentric uncle of this patient's stayed at home for days after the birth of his child and received visitors in his dressing-gown, from which she concluded that both parents took part in the birth of their children and had to go to bed.

In about their tenth or eleventh year, children get to hear about sexual matters. A child who has grown up in a comparatively uninhibited social atmosphere, or who has found better opportunities for observation, tells other children what he knows, because this makes him feel mature and superior. What children learn in this way is mostly correct – that is, the existence of the vagina and its purpose is

---

[1] The games that are most significant for subsequent neuroses are playing at 'doctor' and at 'father and mother'.

revealed to them; but otherwise the explanations they get from one another are not infrequently mixed with false ideas and burdened with remains of the older infantile sexual theories. They are scarcely ever complete or sufficient to solve the primordial problem. Just as formerly it was ignorance of the vagina which prevented the whole process from being understood, so now is it ignorance of the semen. The child cannot guess that another substance besides urine is excreted from the male sexual organ, and occasionally an 'innocent' girl on her wedding night is still indignant at her husband 'urinating into her'. This information acquired in the years of pre-puberty is followed by a new access of sexual researches by the child. But the theories which he now produces no longer have the typical and original stamp which was characteristic of the primary theories of early childhood as long as the infantile sexual components could find expression in theories in an uninhibited and unmodified fashion. The child's later intellectual efforts at solving the puzzles of sex have not seemed to me worth collecting, nor can they have much claim to a pathogenic significance. Their multiplicity is of course mainly dependent on the nature of the enlightenment which a child receives; but their significance consists rather in the fact that they re-awaken the traces, which have since become unconscious, of his first period of sexual interest; so that it is not infrequent for masturbatory sexual activity and some degree of emotional detachment from his parents to be linked up with them. Hence the condemnatory judgement of teachers that enlightenment of such a kind at this age 'corrupts' children.

Let me give a few examples to show what elements often enter into these late speculations by children about sexual life. A girl had heard from her schoolmates that the husband gives his wife an egg, which she hatches out in her body. A boy, who had also heard of the egg, identified it with the testicle, which [in German] is vulgarly called by the same word [*Ei*]; and he racked his brains to make out how the contents of the scrotum could be constantly renewed. The information given seldom goes far enough to prevent important uncertainties about sexual events. Thus a girl may arrive at an expectation that intercourse occurs on one occasion only, but that it lasts a very long time – twenty-four hours – and that all the successive babies come from this single occasion. One would suppose that this child had got her knowledge of the reproductive process from certain insects; but it turned out that this was not so and that the theory emerged as a spontaneous creation. Other girls are ignorant of the period of gestation, the life in the womb, and assume that the baby appears immediately after the first night of intercourse. Marcel Prévost has turned this girlhood mistake into an amusing story in one of his 'Lettres de femmes'.[1] These later sexual researches of children, or of adolescents who have been retarded at the stage of childhood, offer an almost inexhaustible theme and one which is perhaps not uninteresting in general; but it is more remote from my present interest. I must only lay stress on the fact that in this field children produce many incorrect ideas in order to contradict older and better knowledge which has become unconscious and is repressed.

The way in which children react to the information they are given also has its significance. In some, sexual repression has gone so far that they will not listen to anything; and these succeed in remaining ignorant even in later life – *apparently* ignorant, at least – until, in the psycho-analysis of neurotics, the knowledge that originated in early childhood comes to light. I also know of two boys between ten and thirteen years old who, though it is true that they listened to the sexual information, rejected it with the words: '*Your* father and other people may do something like that, but I know for certain *my* father never would.' But however widely children's later reactions to the satisfaction of their sexual curiosity may vary, we may assume that in the first years of childhood their attitude was absolutely uniform, and we may feel certain that at that time all of them tried most eagerly to discover what it was that their parents did with each other so as to produce babies.

[1] [Cf. Prévost, 'La nuit de Raymonde', *Nouvelles lettres de femmes*.]

The Infantile Genital Organization

(An Interpolation into the Theory of Sexuality)

(1923)*

The difficulty of the work of research in psycho-analysis is clearly shown by the fact of its being possible, in spite of whole decades of unremitting observation, to overlook features that are of general occurrence and situations that are characteristic, until at last they confront one in an unmistakable form. The remarks that follow are intended to make good a neglect of this sort in the field of infantile sexual development.

Readers of my *Three Essays on the Theory of Sexuality* (1905*d*) will be aware that I have never undertaken any thorough remodelling of that work in its later editions, but have retained the original arrangement and have kept abreast of the advances made in our knowledge by means of interpolations and alterations in the text. In doing this, it may often have happened that what was old and what was more recent did not admit of being merged into an entirely uncontradictory whole. Originally, as we know, the accent was on a portrayal of the fundamental difference between the sexual life of children and of adults; later, the *pregenital organizations* of the libido made their way into the foreground, and also the remarkable and momentous fact of the *diphasic onset* of sexual development. Finally, our interest was engaged by the *sexual researches* of children; and from this we were able to recognize the far-reaching *approximation of the final outcome of sexuality in childhood* (in about the fifth year) to the definitive form taken by it in the adult. This is the point at which I left things in the last (1922) edition of my *Three Essays*.

On p. 63 of that volume[1] I wrote that 'the choice of an object, such

---

* First published in *Int. Z. Psychoanal.* The present text is included in *Standard Ed.*, 19, 141; *P.F.L.*, 7, 307.

[1] [This corresponds to p. 338 above, where a footnote added in 1924 summarizes the findings of the present paper.]

as we have shown to be characteristic of the pubertal phase of development, has already frequently or habitually been effected during the years of childhood: that is to say, the whole of the sexual currents have become directed towards a single person in relation to whom they seek to achieve their aims. This then is the closest approximation possible in childhood to the final form taken by sexual life after puberty. The only difference lies in the fact that in childhood the combination of the component instincts and their subordination under the primacy of the genitals have been effected only very incompletely or not at all. Thus the establishment of that primacy in the service of reproduction is the last phase through which the organization of sexuality passes.'

To-day I should no longer be satisfied with the statement that in the early period of childhood the primacy of the genitals has been effected only very incompletely or not at all. The approximation of the child's sexual life to that of the adult goes much further and is not limited solely to the coming into being of the choice of an object. Even if a proper combination of the component instincts under the primacy of the genitals is not effected, nevertheless, at the height of the course of development of infantile sexuality, interest in the genitals and in their activity acquires a dominating significance which falls little short of that reached in maturity. At the same time, the main characteristic of this 'infantile genital organization' is its *difference* from the final genital organization of the adult. This consists in the fact that, for both sexes, only one genital, namely the male one, comes into account. What is present, therefore, is not a primacy of the genitals, but a primacy of the *phallus*.

Unfortunately we can describe this state of things only as it affects the male child; the corresponding processes in the little girl are not known to us. The small boy undoubtedly perceives the distinction between men and women, but to begin with he has no occasion to connect it with a difference in their genitals. It is natural for him to assume that all other living beings, humans and animals, possess a genital like his own; indeed, we know that he looks for an organ analogous to his own in inanimate things as well.[1] This part of the

---

[1] It is, incidentally, remarkable what a small degree of attention the other part of the male genitals, the little sac with its contents, attracts in children. From all one hears in analyses, one would not guess that the male genitals consisted of anything more than the penis.

body, which is easily excitable, prone to changes and so rich in sensations, occupies the boy's interest to a high degree and is constantly setting new tasks to his instinct for research. He wants to see it in other people as well, so as to compare it with his own; and he behaves as though he had a vague idea that this organ could and should be bigger. The driving force which this male portion of the body will develop later at puberty expresses itself at this period of life mainly as an urge to investigate, as sexual curiosity. Many of the acts of exhibitionism and aggression which children commit, and which in later years would be judged without hesitation to be expressions of lust, prove in analysis to be experiments undertaken in the service of sexual research.

In the course of these researches the child arrives at the discovery that the penis is not a possession which is common to all creatures that are like himself. An accidental sight of the genitals of a little sister or playmate provides the occasion for this discovery. In unusually intelligent children, the observation of girls urinating will even earlier have aroused a suspicion that there is something different here. For they will have seen a different posture and heard a different sound, and will have made attempts to repeat their observations so as to obtain enlightenment. We know how children react to their first impressions of the absence of a penis. They disavow the fact[1] and believe that they *do* see a penis, all the same. They gloss over the contradiction between observation and preconception by telling themselves that the penis is still small and will grow bigger presently; and they then slowly come to the emotionally significant conclusion that after all the penis had at least been there before and been taken away afterwards. The lack of a penis is regarded as a result of castration, and so now the child is faced with the task of coming to terms with castration in relation to himself. The further developments are too well known generally to make it necessary to recapitulate them here. But it seems to me that *the significance of the castration complex can*

---

[1] [From now on, the concept of 'disavowal' comes to occupy a more and more important place in Freud's writings. '*Leugnen*' is used here, but is later almost invariably replaced by '*verleugnen*'. It appears in a somewhat different context in 'The Loss of Reality in Neurosis and Psychosis' (p. 569 below), but usually, as here, the topic concerned is the castration complex. In his later paper on fetishism (1927*e*) (*Standard Ed.*, **21**, 153 f.; *P.F.L.*, **7**, 352 f.) Freud differentiates between the correct use of the terms '*Verdrängung*' (repression) and '*Verleugnung*' (disavowal). In the posthumous *Outline* (1940*a*) the term serves as a basis for an addition to metapsychological theory.]

only be rightly appreciated if its origin in the phase of phallic primacy is also taken into account.[1]

We know, too, to what a degree depreciation of women, horror of women, and a disposition to homosexuality are derived from the final conviction that women have no penis. Ferenczi (1923) has recently, with complete justice, traced back the mythological symbol of horror – Medusa's head – to the impression of the female genitals devoid of a penis.[2]

It should not be supposed, however, that the child quickly and readily makes a generalization from his observation that some women have no penis. He is in any case debarred from doing so by his assumption that the lack of a penis is the result of having been castrated as a punishment. On the contrary, the child believes that it is only unworthy female persons that have lost their genitals – females who, in all probability, were guilty of inadmissible impulses similar to his own. Women whom he respects, like his mother, retain a penis for a long time. For him, being a woman is not yet synonymous with being without a penis.[3] It is not till later, when the child takes up the problems of the origin and birth of babies, and when he guesses that only women can give birth to them – it is only then that the mother, too, loses her penis. And, along with this, quite complicated theories are built up to explain the exchange of the penis for a baby. In all this, the female genitals never seem to be discovered. The baby, we know, is supposed to live inside the mother's body (in her bowel) and to be born through the intestinal outlet. These last theories carry us beyond the stretch of time covered by the infantile sexual period.

It is not unimportant to bear in mind what transformations are

[1] It has been quite correctly pointed out that a child gets the idea of a narcissistic injury through a bodily loss from the experience of losing his mother's breast after sucking, from the daily surrender of his faeces and, indeed, even from his separation from the womb at birth. Nevertheless, one ought not to speak of a castration complex until this idea of a loss has become connected with the male genitals. [This point is treated at greater length in a footnote added in 1923 to the 'Little Hans' analysis, *Standard Ed.*, **10**, 8; *P.F.L.*, **8**, 172. It is also mentioned in 'The Dissolution of the Oedipus Complex' (1924*d*), p. 397 below.]

[2] I should like to add that what is indicated in the myth is the *mother's* genitals. Athene, who carries Medusa's head on her armour, becomes in consequence the unapproachable woman, the sight of whom extinguishes all thought of a sexual approach.

[3] I learnt from the analysis of a young married woman who had no father but several aunts that she clung, until quite far on in the latency period, to the belief that her mother and her aunts had a penis. One of her aunts, however, was feeble-minded; and she regarded this aunt as castrated, as she felt herself to be.

undergone, during the sexual development of childhood, by the polarity of sex with which we are familiar. A first antithesis is introduced with the choice of object, which, of course, presupposes a subject and an object. At the stage of the pregenital sadistic-anal organization, there is as yet no question of male and female; the antithesis between *active* and *passive* is the dominant one.[1] At the following stage of infantile genital organization, which we now know about, *maleness* exists, but not femaleness. The antithesis here is between having *a male genital* and being *castrated*. It is not until development has reached its completion at puberty that the sexual polarity coincides with *male* and *female*. Maleness combines [the factors of] subject, activity and possession of the penis; femaleness takes over [those of] object and passivity. The vagina is now valued as a place of shelter for the penis; it enters into the heritage of the womb.

---

[1] Cf. [a passage added in 1915 to] *Three Essays on the Theory of Sexuality*, (1905*d*). [See pp. 337 and 355 *n*. above.]

The Dissolution of the Oedipus Complex

(1924)*

To an ever-increasing extent the Oedipus complex reveals its importance as the central phenomenon of the sexual period of early childhood. After that, its dissolution takes place; it succumbs to repression, as we say, and is followed by the latency period. It has not yet become clear, however, what it is that brings about its destruction. Analyses seem to show that it is the experience of painful disappointments. The little girl likes to regard herself as what her father loves above all else; but the time comes when she has to endure a harsh punishment from him and she is cast out of her fool's paradise. The boy regards his mother as his own property; but he finds one day that she has transferred her love and solicitude to a new arrival. Reflection must deepen our sense of the importance of those influences, for it will emphasize the fact that distressing experiences of this sort, which act in opposition to the content of the complex, are inevitable. Even when no special events occur, like those we have mentioned as examples, the absence of the satisfaction hoped for, the continued denial of the desired baby, must in the end lead the small lover to turn away from his hopeless longing. In this way the Oedipus complex would go to its destruction from its lack of success, from the effects of its internal impossibility.

Another view is that the Oedipus complex must collapse because the time has come for its disintegration, just as the milk-teeth fall out when the permanent ones begin to grow. Although the majority of human beings go through the Oedipus complex as an individual experience, it is nevertheless a phenomenon which is determined and laid down by heredity and which is bound to pass away according to programme when the next pre-ordained phase of development sets in. This being so, it is of no great importance what the occasions are

* First published in *Int. Z. Psychoanal.* The present text is included in *Standard Ed.*, **19**, 173; *P.F.L.*, **7**, 315.

which allow this to happen, or, indeed, whether any such occasions can be discovered at all.

The justice of both these views cannot be disputed. Moreover, they are compatible. There is room for the ontogenetic view side by side with the more far-reaching phylogenetic one. It is also true that even at birth the whole individual is destined to die, and perhaps his organic disposition may already contain the indication of what he is to die from. Nevertheless, it remains of interest to follow out how this innate programme is carried out and in what way accidental noxae exploit his disposition.

We have lately[1] been made more clearly aware than before that a child's sexual development advances to a certain phase at which the genital organ has already taken over the leading role. But this genital is the male one only, or more correctly, the penis; the female genital has remained undiscovered. This phallic phase, which is contemporaneous with the Oedipus complex, does not develop further to the definitive genital organization, but is submerged, and is succeeded by the latency period. Its termination, however, takes place in a typical manner and in conjunction with events that are of regular recurrence.

When the (male) child's interest turns to his genitals he betrays the fact by manipulating them frequently; and he then finds that the adults do not approve of this behaviour. More or less plainly, more or less brutally, a threat is pronounced that this part of him which he values so highly will be taken away from him. Usually it is from women that the threat emanates; very often they seek to strengthen their authority by a reference to the father or the doctor, who, so they say, will carry out the punishment. In a number of cases the women will themselves mitigate the threat in a symbolic manner by telling the child that what is to be removed is not his genital, which actually plays a passive part, but his hand, which is the active culprit. It happens particularly often that the little boy is threatened with castration, not because he plays with his penis with his hand, but because he wets his bed every night and cannot be got to be clean. Those in charge of him behave as if this nocturnal incontinence was the result and the proof of his being unduly concerned with his penis, and they are probably right.[2] In any case, long-continued bed-wetting is to be equated with the emissions of adults. It is an

---

[1] [See 'The Infantile Genital Organization' (1923e), p. 391 f. above.]
[2] [Cf. the second of the *Three Essays* (1905d), p. 329 f. above.]

expression of the same excitation of the genitals which has impelled the child to masturbate at this period.

Now it is my view that what brings about the destruction of the child's phallic genital organization is this threat of castration. Not immediately, it is true, and not without other influences being brought to bear as well. For to begin with the boy does not believe in the threat or obey it in the least. Psycho-analysis has recently attached importance to two experiences which all children go through and which, it is suggested, prepare them for the loss of highly valued parts of the body. These experiences are the withdrawal of the mother's breast – at first intermittently and later for good – and the daily demand on them to give up the contents of the bowel. But there is no evidence to show that, when the threat of castration takes place, those experiences have any effect.[1] It is not until a *fresh* experience comes his way that the child begins to reckon with the possibility of being castrated, and then only hesitatingly and unwillingly, and not without making efforts to depreciate the significance of something he has himself observed.

The observation which finally breaks down his unbelief is the sight of the female genitals. Sooner or later the child, who is so proud of his possession of a penis, has a view of the genital region of a little girl, and cannot help being convinced of the absence of a penis in a creature who is so like himself. With this, the loss of his own penis becomes imaginable, and the threat of castration takes its deferred effect.

We should not be as short-sighted as the person in charge of the child who threatens him with castration, and we must not overlook the fact that at this time masturbation by no means represents the whole of his sexual life. As can be clearly shown, he stands in the Oedipus attitude to his parents; his masturbation is only a genital discharge of the sexual excitation belonging to the complex, and throughout his later years will owe its importance to that relationship. The Oedipus complex offered the child two possibilities of satisfaction, an active and a passive one. He could put himself in his father's place in a masculine fashion and have intercourse with his mother as his father did, in which case he would soon have felt the latter as a hindrance; or he might want to take the place of his mother and be

---

[1] [Cf. a footnote added, at about the time this paper was written, to the case history of 'Little Hans' (1909*b*), *Standard Ed.*, **10**, 8; *P.F.L.*, **8**, 172.]

loved by his father, in which case his mother would become superfluous. The child may have had only very vague notions as to what
constitutes a satisfying erotic intercourse; but certainly the penis must
play a part in it, for the sensations in his own organ were evidence of
that. So far he had had no occasion to doubt that women possessed a
penis. But now his acceptance of the possibility of castration, his
recognition that women were castrated, made an end of both possible
ways of obtaining satisfaction from the Oedipus complex. For both of
them entailed the loss of his penis – the masculine one as a resulting
punishment and the feminine one as a precondition. If the satisfaction
of love in the field of the Oedipus complex is to cost the child his penis,
a conflict is bound to arise between his narcissistic interest in that part
of his body and the libidinal cathexis of his parental objects. In this
conflict the first of these forces normally triumphs: the child's ego
turns away from the Oedipus complex.

I have described elsewhere how this turning away takes place.[1] The
object-cathexes are given up and replaced by identifications. The
authority of the father or the parents is introjected into the ego, and
there it forms the nucleus of the super-ego, which takes over the
severity of the father and perpetuates his prohibition against incest,
and so secures the ego from the return of the libidinal object-cathexis.
The libidinal trends belonging to the Oedipus complex are in part
desexualized and sublimated (a thing which probably happens with
every transformation into an identification) and in part inhibited in
their aim and changed into impulses of affection. The whole process
has, on the one hand, preserved the genital organ – has averted the
danger of its loss – and, on the other, has paralysed it – has removed its
function. This process ushers in the latency period, which now
interrupts the child's sexual development.

I see no reason for denying the name of a 'repression' to the ego's
turning away from the Oedipus complex, although later repressions
come about for the most part with the participation of the super-ego,
which in this case is only just being formed. But the process we have
described is more than a repression. It is equivalent, if it is ideally
carried out, to a destruction and an abolition of the complex. We may
plausibly assume that we have here come upon the borderline – never
a very sharply drawn one – between the normal and the pathological.
If the ego has in fact not achieved much more than a *repression* of the

---

[1] [Cf. *The Ego and the Id*, Chapter 6 below.]

complex, the latter persists in an unconscious state in the id and will later manifest its pathogenic effect.

Analytic observation enables us to recognize or guess these connections between the phallic organization, the Oedipus complex, the threat of castration, the formation of the super-ego and the latency period. These connections justify the statement that the destruction of the Oedipus complex is brought about by the threat of castration. But this does not dispose of the problem; there is room for a theoretical speculation which may upset the results we have come to or put them in a new light. Before we start along this new path, however, we must turn to a question which has arisen in the course of this discussion and has so far been left on one side. The process which has been described refers, as has been expressly said, to male children only. How does the corresponding development take place in little girls?

At this point our material – for some incomprehensible reason[1] – becomes far more obscure and full of gaps. The female sex, too, develops an Oedipus complex, a super-ego and a latency period. May we also attribute a phallic organization and a castration complex to it? The answer is in the affirmative; but these things cannot be the same as they are in boys. Here the feminist demand for equal rights for the sexes does not take us far, for the morphological distinction is bound to find expression in differences of psychical development.[2] 'Anatomy is Destiny', to vary a saying of Napoleon's. The little girls's clitoris behaves just like a penis to begin with; but, when she makes a comparison with a playfellow of the other sex, she perceives that she has 'come off badly'[3] and she feels this as a wrong done to her and as a ground for inferiority. For a while still she consoles herself with the expectation that later on, when she grows older, she will acquire just as big an appendage as the boy's. Here the masculinity complex[4] of women branches off. A female child, however, does not understand her lack of a penis as being a sex character; she explains it by assuming that at some earlier date she had possessed an equally large organ and had then lost it by castration. She seems not to extend this inference from herself to other, adult females, but, entirely on the lines of the

[1] [Freud suggested some explanation for this in Section I of his paper on 'Female Sexuality' (1931*b*).]

[2] [See the next paper, 'Some Psychical Consequences of the Anatomical Distinction between the Sexes' (1925*j*). Much of what follows is elaborated there.]

[3] [Literally, 'come off too short'.]

[4] [Cf. p. 406 n. 3 below.]

phallic phase, to regard them as possessing large and complete – that is to say, male – genitals. The essential difference thus comes about that the girl accepts castration as an accomplished fact, whereas the boy fears the possibility of its occurrence.

The fear of castration being thus excluded in the little girl, a powerful motive also drops out for the setting-up of a super-ego and for the breaking-off of the infantile genital organization. In her, far more than in the boy, these changes seem to be the result of upbringing and of intimidation from outside which threatens her with a loss of love. The girl's Oedipus complex is much simpler than that of the small bearer of the penis; in my experience, it seldom goes beyond the taking of her mother's place and the adopting of a feminine attitude towards her father. Renunciation of the penis is not tolerated by the girl without some attempt at compensation. She slips – along the line of a symbolic equation, one might say – from the penis to a baby. Her Oedipus complex culminates in a desire, which is long retained, to receive a baby from her father as a gift – to bear him a child.[1] One has an impression that the Oedipus complex is then gradually given up because this wish is never fulfilled. The two wishes – to possess a penis and a child – remain strongly cathected in the unconscious and help to prepare the female creature for her later sexual role. The comparatively lesser strength of the sadistic contribution to her sexual instinct, which we may no doubt connect with the stunted growth of her penis, makes it easier in her case for the direct sexual trends to be transformed into aim-inhibited trends of an affectionate kind. It must be admitted, however, that in general our insight into these developmental processes in girls is unsatisfactory, incomplete and vague.[2]

I have no doubt that the chronological and causal realtions described here between the Oedipus complex, sexual intimidation (the threat of castration), the formation of a super-ego and the beginning of the latency period are of a typical kind; but I do not wish to assert that this type is the only possible one. Variations in the chronological order and in the linking-up of these events are bound to have a very important bearing on the development of the individual.

[1] [Cf. Freud's paper on 'Transformations of Instinct' (1917c), *Standard Ed.*, **17**, 128 ff.; *P.F.L.*, **7**, 295 ff.]
[2] [Freud discussed this topic much more fully in his papers on the anatomical distinction between the sexes (1925j), see below, and on female sexuality (1931b), in both of which he gave a very different account of the girl's Oedipus complex from the present one.]

Since the publication of Otto Rank's interesting study, *The Trauma of Birth* [1924], even the conclusion arrived at by this modest investigation, to the effect that the boy's Oedipus complex is destroyed by the fear of castration, cannot be accepted without further discussion. Nevertheless, it seems to me premature to enter into such a discussion at the present time, and perhaps inadvisable to begin a criticism or an appreciation of Rank's view at this juncture.[1]

----

[1] [The question was taken up by Freud soon afterwards in *Inhibitions, Symptoms and Anxiety* (1926*d*). Cf. Section (*e*) of the Editor's Introduction to that work, *Standard Ed.*, **20**, 83 ff.; *P.F.L.*, **10**, 234.]

Some Psychical Consequences of the Anatomical Distinction between the Sexes

(1925)*

In my own writings and in those of my followers more and more stress is laid on the necessity that the analyses of neurotics shall deal thoroughly with the remotest period of their childhood, the time of the early efflorescence of sexual life. It is only by examining the first manifestations of the patient's innate instinctual constitution and the effects of his earliest experiences that we can accurately gauge the motive forces that have led to his neurosis and can be secure against the errors into which we might be tempted by the degree to which things have become remodelled and overlaid in adult life. This requirement is not only of theoretical but also of practical importance, for it distinguishes our efforts from the work of those physicians whose interests are focused exclusively on therapeutic results and who employ analytic methods, but only up to a certain point. An analysis of early childhood such as we are considering is tedious and laborious and makes demands both upon the physician and upon the patient which cannot always be met. Moreover, it leads us into dark regions where there are as yet no sign-posts. Indeed, analysts may feel reassured, I think, that there is no risk of their work becoming mechanical, and so of losing its interest, during the next few decades.

In the following pages I bring forward some findings of analytic research which would be of great importance if they could be proved to apply universally. Why do I not postpone publication of them until further experience has given me the necessary proof, if such proof is obtainable? Because the conditions under which I work have undergone a change, with implications which I cannot disguise. Formerly, I was not one of those who are unable to hold back what seems to be a new discovery until it has been either confirmed or corrected. My

* First published in *Int. Z. Psychoanal.* The present text is included in *Standard Ed.*, **19**, 248; *P.F.L.*, **7**, 331.

Interpretation of Dreams (1900*a*) and my 'Fragment of an Analysis of a Case of Hysteria' (1905*e*) (the case of Dora) were suppressed by me – if not for the nine years enjoined by Horace – at all events for four or five years before I allowed them to be published. But in those days I had unlimited time before me – 'oceans of time'[1] as an amiable author puts it – and material poured in upon me in such quantities that fresh experiences were hardly to be escaped. Moreover, I was the only worker in a new field, so that my reticence involved no danger to myself and no loss to others.

But now everything has changed. The time before me is limited. The whole of it is no longer spent in working, so that my opportunities for making fresh observations are not so numerous. If I think I see something new, I am uncertain whether I can wait for it to be confirmed. And further, everything that is to be seen upon the surface has already been exhausted; what remains has to be slowly and laboriously dragged up from the depths. Finally, I am no longer alone. An eager crowd of fellow-workers is ready to make use of what is unfinished or doubtful, and I can leave to them that part of the work which I should otherwise have done myself. On this occasion, therefore, I feel justified in publishing something which stands in urgent need of confirmation before its value or lack of value can be decided.

In examining the earliest mental shapes assumed by the sexual life of children we have been in the habit of taking as the subject of our investigations the male child, the little boy. With little girls, so we have supposed, things must be similar, though in some way or other they must nevertheless be different. The point in development at which this difference lay could not be clearly determined.

In boys the situation of the Oedipus complex is the first stage that can be recognized with certainty. It is easy to understand, because at that stage a child retains the same object which he previously cathected with his libido – not as yet a genital one – during the preceding period while he was being suckled and nursed. The fact, too, that in this situation he regards his father as a disturbing rival and would like to get rid of him and take his place is a straightforward consequence of the actual state of affairs. I have shown elsewhere[2] how the Oedipus attitude in little boys belongs to the phallic phase,

---

[1] [In English in the original. It is not clear what author Freud had in mind. – The reference to Horace is to his *Ars Poetica*, 388.]

[2] 'The Dissolution of the Oedipus Complex' (1924*d*) [see preceding paper].

and how its destruction is brought about by the fear of castration – that is, by narcissistic interest in their genitals. The matter is made more difficult to grasp by the complicating circumstance that even in boys the Oedipus complex has a double orientation, active and passive, in accordance with their bisexual constitution; a boy also wants to take his *mother's* place as the love-object of his *father* – a fact which we describe as the feminine attitude.

As regards the prehistory of the Oedipus complex in boys we are far from complete clarity. We know that that period includes an identification of an affectionate sort with the boy's father, an identification which is still free from any sense of rivalry in regard to his mother. Another element of that stage is invariably, I believe, a masturbatory activity in connection with the genitals, the masturbation of early childhood, the more or less violent suppression of which by those in charge of the child sets the castration complex in action. It is to be assumed that this masturbation is attached to the Oedipus complex and serves as a discharge for the sexual excitation belonging to it. It is, however, uncertain whether the masturbation has this character from the first, or whether on the contrary it makes its first appearance spontaneously as an activity of a bodily organ and is only brought into relation with the Oedipus complex at some later date; this second possibility is by far the more probable. Another doubtful question is the part played by bed-wetting and by the breaking of that habit through the intervention of training measures. We are inclined to make the simple connection that continued bed-wetting is a result of masturbation and that its suppression is regraded by boys as an inhibition of their genital activity – that is, as having the meaning of a threat of castration; but whether we are always right in supposing this remains to be seen. Finally, analysis shows us in a shadowy way how the fact of a child at a very early age listening to his parents copulating may set up his first sexual excitation, and how that event may, owing to its after-effects, act as a starting-point for the child's whole sexual development. Masturbation, as well as the two attitudes in the Oedipus complex, later on become attached to this early experience, the child having subsequently interpreted its meaning. It is impossible, however, to suppose that these observations of coitus are of universal occurrence, so that at this point we are faced with the problem of 'primal phantasies'.[1] Thus the prehistory of the Oedipus

[1] [Cf. the 'Wolf Man' analysis (1918b) (*Standard Ed.*, **17**, 48–60; *P.F.L.*, **9**, 281–95) and Lecture 23 of the *Introductory Lectures* (1916–17) in Chapter 9 below.]

complex, even in boys, raises all of these questions for sifting and explanation; and there is the further problem of whether we are to suppose that the process invariably follows the same course, or whether a great variety of different preliminary stages may not converge upon the same terminal situation.

In little girls the Oedipus complex raises one problem more than in boys. In both cases the mother is the original object; and there is no cause for surprise that boys retain that object in the Oedipus complex. But how does it happen that girls abandon it and instead take their father as an object? In pursuing this question I have been able to reach some conclusions which may throw light precisely on the prehistory of the Oedipus relation in girls.

Every analyst has come across certain women who cling with especial intensity and tenacity to the bond with their father and to the wish in which it culminates of having a child by him. We have good reason to suppose that the same wishful phantasy was also the motive force of their infantile masturbation, and it is easy to form an impression that at this point we have been brought up against an elementary and unanalysable fact of infantile sexual life. But a thorough analysis of these very cases brings something different to light – namely, that here the Oedipus complex has a long prehistory and is in some respects a secondary formation.

The old paediatrician Lindner [1879] once remarked that a child discovers the genital zones (the penis or the clitoris) as a source of pleasure while indulging in sensual sucking (thumb-sucking.)[1] I shall leave it an open question whether it is really true that the child takes the newly found source of pleasure in exchange for the recent loss of the mother's nipple – a possibility to which later phantasies (fellatio) seem to point. Be that as it may, the genital zone is discovered at some time or other, and there seems no justification for attributing any psychical content to the first activities in connection with it. But the first step in the phallic phase which begins in this way is not the linking-up of the masturbation with the object-cathexes of the Oedipus complex, but a momentous discovery which little girls are destined to make. They notice the penis of a brother or playmate, strikingly visible and of large proportions, at once recognize it as the superior counterpart of their own small and

[1] Cf. *Three Essays on the Theory of Sexuality* [(1905d), pp. 320–21 above.]

inconspicuous organ, and from that time forward fall a victim to envy for the penis.

There is an interesting contrast between the behaviour of the two sexes. In the analogous situation, when a little boy first catches sight of a girl's genital region, he begins by showing irresolution and lack of interest; he sees nothing or disavows[1] what he has seen, he softens it down or looks about for expedients for bringing it into line with his expectations. It is not until later, when some threat of castration has obtained a hold upon him, that the observation becomes important to him: if he then recollects or repeats it, it arouses a terrible storm of emotion in him and forces him to believe in the reality of the threat which he has hitherto laughed at. This combination of circumstances leads to two reactions, which may become fixed and will in that case, whether separately or together or in conjunction with other factors, permanently determine the boy's relations to women: horror of the mutilated creature or triumphant contempt for her. These developments, however, belong to the future, though not to a very remote one.

A little girl behaves differently. She makes her judgement and her decision in a flash. She has seen it and knows that she is without it and wants to have it.[2]

Here what has been named the masculinity complex of women branches off.[3] It may put great difficulties in the way of their regular development towards femininity, if it cannot be got over soon enough. The hope of some day obtaining a penis in spite of everything and so of becoming like a man may persist to an incredibly late age and may become a motive for strange and otherwise unaccountable actions. Or again, a process may set in which I should like to call a 'disavowal',[4] a process which in the mental life of children seems neither uncommon nor very dangerous but which in an adult would mean the beginning of a psychosis. Thus a girl may refuse to accept the fact of being castrated, may harden herself in the conviction that she *does* possess a

---

[1] [See Editor's footnote to 'The Infantile Genital Organization', p. 392 above.]

[2] This is an opportunity for correcting a statement which I made many years ago. I believed that the sexual interest of children, unlike that of pubescents, was aroused, not by the difference between the sexes, but by the problem of where babies come from. We now see that, at all events with girls, this is certainly not the case. With boys it may no doubt happen sometimes one way and sometimes the other; or with both sexes chance experiences may determine the event.

[3] [This term seems to have been introduced by Van Ophuijsen (1917).]

[4] [For the parallel process in boys, see 'The Infantile Genital Organization' (1923e), above.]

penis, and may subsequently be compelled to behave as though she were a man.

The psychical consequences of envy for the penis, in so far as it does not become absorbed in the reaction-formation of the masculinity complex, are various and far-reaching. After a woman has become aware of the wound to her narcissism, she develops, like a scar, a sense of inferiority. When she has passed beyond her first attempt at explaining her lack of a penis as being a punishment personal to herself and has realized that that sexual character is a universal one, she begins to share the contempt felt by men for a sex which is the lesser in so important a respect, and, at least in holding that opinion, insists on being like a man.[1]

Even after penis-envy has abandoned its true object, it continues to exist: by an easy displacement it persists in the character-trait of *jealousy*. Of course, jealousy is not limited to one sex and has a wider foundation than this, but I am of opinion that it plays a far larger part in the mental life of women than of men and that that is because it is enormously reinforced from the direction of displaced penis-envy. While I was still unaware of this source of jealousy and was considering the phantasy 'a child is being beaten', which occurs so commonly in girls, I constructed a first phase for it in which its meaning was that another child, a rival of whom the subject was jealous, was to be beaten.[2] This phantasy seems to be a relic of the phallic period in girls. The peculiar rigidity which struck me so much in the monotonous formula 'a child is being beaten' can probably be interpreted in a special way. The child which is being beaten (or caressed) may ultimately be nothing more nor less than the clitoris itself, so that at its very lowest level the statement will contain a confession of

---

[1] In my first critical account of the 'History of the Psycho-Analytic Movement' (1914*d*), I recognized that this fact represents the core of truth contained in Adler's theory. That theory has no hesitation in explaining the whole world by this single point ('organ-inferiority', the 'masculine protest', 'breaking away from the feminine line') and prides itself upon having in this way robbed sexuality of its importance and put the desire for power in its place! Thus the only organ which could claim to be called 'inferior' without any ambiguity would be the clitoris. On the other hand, one hears of analysts who boast that, though they have worked for dozens of years, they have never found a sign of the existence of a castration complex. We must bow our heads in recognition of the greatness of this achievement, even though it is only a negative one, a piece of virtuousity in the art of overlooking and mistaking. The two theories form an interesting pair of opposites: in the latter not a trace of a castration complex, in the former nothing else than its consequences.

[2] '"A Child is Being Beaten"' [(1919*e*); Standard Ed., **17**, 184 f.; *P.F.L.*, **10**, 169 f.]

masturbation, which has remained attached to the content of the formula from its beginning in the phallic phase till later life.

A third consequence of penis-envy seems to be a loosening of the girl's relation with her mother as a love-object. The situation as a whole is not very clear, but it can be seen that in the end the girl's mother, who sent her into the world so insufficiently equipped, is almost always held responsible for her lack of a penis. The way in which this comes about historically is often that soon after the girl has discovered that her genitals are unsatisfactory she begins to show jealousy of another child on the ground that her mother is fonder of it than of her, which serves as a reason for her giving up her affectionate relation to her mother. It will fit in with this if the child which has been preferred by her mother is made into the first object of the beating-phantasy which ends in masturbation.

There is yet another surprising effect of penis-envy, or of the discovery of the inferiority of the clitoris, which is undoubtedly the most important of all. In the past I had often formed an impression that in general women tolerate masturbation worse than men, that they more frequently fight against it and that they are unable to make use of it in circumstances in which a man would seize upon it as a way of escape without any hesitation. Experience would no doubt elicit innumerable exceptions to this statement, if we attempted to turn it into a rule. The reactions of human individuals of both sexes are of course made up of masculine and feminine traits. But it appeared to me nevertheless as though masturbation were further removed from the nature of women than of men, and the solution of the problem could be assisted by the reflection that masturbation, at all events of the clitoris, is a masculine activity and that the elimination of clitoridal sexuality is a necessary precondition for the development of femininity.[1] Analyses of the remote phallic period have now taught me that in girls, soon after the first signs of penis-envy, an intense current of feeling against masturbation makes its appearance, which cannot be attributed exclusively to the educational influence of those in charge of the child. This impulse is clearly a forerunner of the wave of repression which at puberty will do away with a large amount of the girl's masculine sexuality in order to make room for the development of her femininity. It may happen that this first opposition to auto-erotic activity fails to attain its end. And this was in fact the case in

[1] [Cf. *Three Essays* (1905d).]

the instances which I analysed. The conflict continued, and both then and later the girl did everything she could to free herself from the compulsion to masturbate. Many of the later manifestations of sexual life in women remain unintelligible unless this powerful motive is recognized.

I cannot explain the opposition which is raised in this way by little girls to phallic masturbation except by supposing that there is some concurrent factor which turns her violently against that pleasurable activity. Such a factor lies close at hand. It cannot be anything else than her narcissistic sense of humiliation which is bound up with penis-envy, the reminder that after all this is a point on which she cannot compete with boys and that it would therefore be best for her to give up the idea of doing so. Thus the little girl's recognition of the anatomical distinction between the sexes forces her away from masculinity and masculine masturbation on to new lines which lead to the development of femininity.

So far there has been no question of the Oedipus complex, nor has it up to this point played any part. But now the girl's libido slips into a new position along the line – there is no other way of putting it – of the equation 'penis-child'. She gives up her wish for a penis and puts in place of it a wish for a child: and *with that purpose in view* she takes her father as a love-object.[1] Her mother becomes the object of her jealousy. The girl has turned into a little woman. If I am to credit a single analytic instance, this new situation can give rise to physical sensations which would have to be regarded as a premature awakening of the female genital apparatus. When the girl's attachment to her father comes to grief later on and has to be abandoned, it may give place to an identification with him and the girl may thus return to her masculinity complex and perhaps remain fixated in it.

I have now said the essence of what I had to say: I will stop, therefore, and cast an eye over our findings. We have gained some insight into the prehistory of the Oedipus complex in girls. The corresponding period in boys is more or less unknown. In girls the Oedipus complex is a secondary formation. The operations of the castration complex precede it and prepare for it. As regards the relation between the Oedipus and castration complexes there is a fundamental contrast between the two sexes. *Whereas in boys the Oedipus complex is destroyed by*

1 [Cf. 'The Dissolution of the Oedipus Complex', p. 400 above.]

the castration complex, in girls it is made possible and led up to by the castration complex. This contradiction is cleared up if we reflect that the castration complex always operates in the sense implied in its subject-matter: it inhibits and limits masculinity and encourages femininity. The difference between the sexual development of males and females at the stage we have been considering is an intelligible consequence of the anatomical distinction between their genitals and of the psychical situation involved in it; it corresponds to the difference between a castration that has been carried out and one that has merely been threatened. In their essentials, therefore, our findings are self-evident and it should have been possible to foresee them.

The Oedipus complex, however, is such an important thing that the manner in which one enters and leaves it cannot be without its effects. In boys (as I have shown at length in the paper to which I have just referred [1924*d*] and to which all of my present remarks are closely related) the complex is not simply repressed, it is literally smashed to pieces by the shock of threatened castration. Its libidinal cathexes are abandoned, desexualized and in part sublimated; its objects are incorporated into the ego, where they form the nucleus of the super-ego and give that new structure its characteristic qualities. In normal, or, it is better to say, in ideal cases, the Oedipus complex exists no longer, even in the unconscious; the super-ego has become its heir. Since the penis (to follow Ferenczi [1924]) owes its extraordinarily high narcissistic cathexis to its organic significance for the propagation of the species, the catastrophe to the Oedipus complex (the abandonment of incest and the institution of conscience and morality) may be regarded as a victory of the race over the individual. This is an interesting point of view when one considers that neurosis is based upon a struggle of the ego against the demands of the sexual function. But to leave the standpoint of individual psychology is not of any immediate help in clarifying this complicated situation.

In girls the motive for the demolition of the Oedipus complex is lacking. Castration has already had its effect, which was to force the child into the situation of the Oedipus complex. Thus the Oedipus complex escapes the fate which it meets with in boys: it may be slowly abandoned or dealt with by repression, or its effects may persist far into women's normal mental life. I cannot evade the notion (though I hesitate to give it expression) that for women the level of what is ethically normal is different from what it is in men. Their super-ego is never so inexorable, so impersonal, so independent of its emotional origins as we require it to be in men. Character-traits which critics of every epoch have brought up against women – that they show less sense of justice than men, that they are less ready to submit to the great exigencies of life, that they are more often influenced in their judgements by feelings of affection or hostility – all these would be amply accounted for by the modification in the formation of their super-ego which we have inferred above. We must not allow ourselves to be deflected from such conclusions by the denials of the feminists, who are anxious to force us to regard the two sexes as completely equal in position and worth; but we shall, of course, willingly agree that the majority of men are also far behind the masculine ideal and that all human individuals, as a result of their bisexual disposition and of cross-inheritance, combine in themselves both masculine and feminine characteristics, so that pure masculinity and femininity remain theoretical constructions of uncertain content.

I am inclined to set some value on the considerations I have brought forward upon the psychical consequences of the anatomical distinction between the sexes. I am aware, however, that this opinion can only be maintained if my findings, which are based on a handful of cases, turn out to have general validity and to be typical. If not, they would remain no more than a contribution to our knowledge of the different paths along which sexual life develops.

In the valuable and comprehensive studies on the masculinity and castration complexes in women by Abraham (1921), Horney (1923) and Helene Deutsch (1925) there is much that touches closely on what I have written but nothing that coincides with it completely, so that here again I feel justified in publishing this paper.

Femininity

(1933)*

Ladies and Gentlemen – All the while I am preparing to talk to you I am struggling with an internal difficulty. I feel uncertain, so to speak, of the extent of my licence. It is true that in the course of fifteen years of work psycho-analysis has changed and grown richer; but, in spite of that, an introduction to psycho-analysis might have been left without alteration or supplement. It is constantly in my mind that these lectures are without a *raison d'être*. For analysts I am saying too little and nothing at all that is new; but for you I am saying too much and saying things which you are not equipped to understand and which are not in your province. I have looked around for excuses and I have tried to justify each separate lecture on different grounds. The first one, on the theory of dreams, was supposed to put you back again at one blow into the analytic atmosphere and to show you how durable our views have turned out to be. I was led on to the second one, which followed the paths from dreams to what is called occultism, by the opportunity of speaking my mind without constraint on a department of work in which prejudiced expectations are fighting to-day against passionate resistances, and I could hope that your judgement, educated to tolerance on the example of psycho-analysis, would not refuse to accompany me on the excursion. The third lecture, on the dissection of the personality, certainly made the hardest demands upon you with its unfamiliar subject-matter; but it was impossible for me to keep this first beginning of an ego-psychology back from you, and if we had possessed it fifteen years ago I should have had to mention it to you then. My last lecture, finally, which you were probably able to follow only by great exertions, brought forward necessary corrections – fresh attempts at solving the most important conundrums; and my

---

* First published by Internationaler Psychoanalytischer Verlag (Vienna). The present text is included in *Standard Ed.*, **22**, 112; *P.F.L.*, **2**, 145.

introduction would have been leading you astray if I had been silent about them. As you see, when one starts making excuses it turns out in the end that it was all inevitable, all the work of destiny. I submit to it, and I beg you to do the same.

To-day's lecture, too, should have no place in an introduction; but it may serve to give you an example of a detailed piece of analytic work, and I can say two things to recommend it. It brings forward nothing but observed facts, almost without any speculative additions, and it deals with a subject which has a claim on your interest second almost to no other. Throughout history people have knocked their heads against the riddle of the nature of femininity –

> Häupter in Hieroglyphenmützen,
> Häupter in Turban und schwarzem Barett,
> Perückenhäupter und tausend andre
> Arme, schwitzende Menschenhäupter. . . .[1]

Nor will *you* have escaped worrying over this problem – those of you who are men; to those of you who are women this will not apply – you are yourselves the problem. When you meet a human being, the first distinction you make is 'male or female?' and you are accustomed to make the distinction with unhesitating certainty. Anatomical science shares your certainty at one point and not much further. The male sexual product, the spermatozoon, and its vehicle are male; the ovum and the organism that harbours it are female. In both sexes organs have been formed which serve exclusively for the sexual functions; they were probably developed from the same [innate] disposition into two different forms. Besides this, in both sexes the other organs, the bodily shapes and tissues, show the influence of the individual's sex, but this is inconstant and its amount variable; these are what are known as the secondary sexual characters. Science next tells you something that runs counter to your expectations and is probably calculated to confuse your feelings. It draws your attention to the fact that portions of the male sexual apparatus also appear in women's bodies, though in an atrophied state, and vice versa in the alternative case. It regards their occurrence as indications of *bisexuality*,[2] as

---

[1] Heads in hieroglyphic bonnets,
Heads in turbans and black birettas,
Heads in wigs and thousand other
Wretched, sweating heads of humans. . . .

(Heine, *Nordsee*, Second Cycle, VII, 'Fragen'.)

[2] [Bisexuality was discussed by Freud in the first edition of his *Three Essays on the Theory of Sexuality* (1905*d*), pp. 286–9 above.]

though an individual is not a man or a woman but always both –
merely a certain amount more the one than the other. You will then be
asked to make yourselves familiar with the idea that the proportion in
which masculine and feminine are mixed in an individual is subject to
quite considerable fluctuations. Since, however, apart from the very
rarest cases, only one kind of sexual product – ova or semen – is
nevertheless present in one person, you are bound to have doubts as to
the decisive significance of those elements and must conclude that
what constitutes masculinity or femininity is an unknown characteristic which anatomy cannot lay hold of.

Can psychology do so perhaps? We are accustomed to employ
'masculine' and 'feminine' as mental qualities as well, and have in the
same way transferred the notion of bisexuality to mental life. Thus we
speak of a person, whether male or female, as behaving in a masculine
way in one connection and in a feminine way in another. But you will
soon perceive that this is only giving way to anatomy or to convention.
You cannot give the concepts of 'masculine' and 'feminine' *any* new
connotation. The distinction is not a psychological one; when you say
'masculine', you usually mean 'active', and when you say 'feminine',
you usually mean 'passive'. Now it is true that a relation of the kind
exists. The male sex-cell is actively mobile and searches out the female
one, and the latter, the ovum, is immobile and waits passively. This
behaviour of the elementary sexual organisms is indeed a model for
the conduct of sexual individuals during intercourse. The male
pursues the female for the purpose of sexual union, seizes hold of her
and penetrates into her. But by this you have precisely reduced the
characteristic of masculinity to the factor of aggressiveness so far as
psychology is concerned. You may well doubt whether you have
gained any real advantage from this when you reflect that in some
classes of animals the females are the stronger and more aggressive
and the male is active only in the single act of sexual union. This is so,
for instance, with the spiders. Even the functions of rearing and caring
for the young, which strike us as feminine *par excellence*, are not
invariably attached to the female sex in animals. In quite high species
we find that the sexes share the task of caring for the young between
them or even that the male alone devotes himself to it. Even in the
sphere of human sexual life you soon see how inadequate it is to make
masculine behaviour coincide with activity and feminine with passivity. A mother is active in every sense towards her child; the act of

lactation itself may equally be described as the mother suckling the baby or as her being sucked by it. The further you go from the narow sexual sphere the more obvious will the 'error of superimposition'[1] become. Women can display great activity in various directions, men are not able to live in company with their own kind unless they develop a large amount of passive adaptability. If you now tell me that these facts go to prove precisely that both men and women are bisexual in the psychological sense, I shall conclude that you have decided in your own minds to make 'active' coincide with 'masculine' and 'passive' with 'feminine'. But I advise you against it. It seems to me to serve no useful purpose and adds nothing to our knowledge.

One might consider characterizing femininity psychologically as giving preference to passive aims. This is not, of course, the same thing as passivity; to achieve a passive aim may call for a large amount of activity. It is perhaps the case that in a woman, on the basis of her share in the sexual function, a preference for passive behaviour and passive aims is carried over into her life to a greater or lesser extent, in proportion to the limits, restricted or far-reaching, within which her sexual life thus serves as a model. But we must beware in this of underestimating the influence of social customs, which similarly force women into passive situations. All this is still far from being cleared up. There is one particularly constant relation between femininity and instinctual life which we do not want to overlook. The suppression of women's aggressiveness which is prescribed for them constitutionally and imposed on them socially favours the development of powerful masochistic impulses, which succeed, as we know, in binding erotically the destructive trends which have been diverted inwards. Thus masochism, as people say, is truly feminine. But if, as happens so often, you meet with masochism in men, what is left to you but to say that these men exhibit very plain feminine traits?

And now you are already prepared to hear that psychology too is unable to solve the riddle of femininity. The explanation must no doubt come from elsewhere, and cannot come till we have learnt how in general the differentiation of living organisms into two sexes came about. We know nothing about it, yet the existence of two sexes is a most striking characteristic of organic life which distinguishes it sharply from inanimate nature. However, we find enough to study in those human individuals who, through the possession of female

---

[1] [The term is explained in *Introductory Lectures, Standard Ed.*, **16**, 304; *P.F.L.*, **1**, 345.]

genitals, are characterized as manifestly or predominantly feminine. In conformity with its peculiar nature, psycho-analysis does not try to describe what a woman is – that would be a task it could scarcely perform – but sets about enquiring how she comes into being, how a woman develops out of a child with a bisexual disposition. In recent times we have begun to learn a little about this, thanks to the circumstance that several of our excellent women colleagues in analysis have begun to work at the question. The discussion of this has gained special attractiveness from the distinction between the sexes. For the ladies, whenever some comparison seemed to turn out unfavourable to their sex, were able to utter a suspicion that we, the male analysts, had been unable to overcome certain deeply-rooted prejudices against what was feminine, and that this was being paid for in the partiality of our researches. We, on the other hand, standing on the ground of bisexuality, had no difficulty in avoiding impoliteness. We had only to say: 'This doesn't apply to *you*. You're the exception; on this point you're more masculine than feminine.'

We approach the investigation of the sexual development of women with two expectations. The first is that here once more the constitution will not adapt itself to its function without a struggle. The second is that the decisive turning-points will already have been prepared for or completed before puberty. Both expectations are promptly confirmed. Furthermore, a comparison with what happens with boys tells us that the development of a little girl into a normal woman is more difficult and more complicated, since it includes two extra tasks, to which there is nothing corresponding in the development of a man. Let us follow the parallel lines from their beginning. Undoubtedly the material is different to start with in boys and girls: it did not need psycho-analysis to establish that. The difference in the structure of the genitals is accompanied by other bodily differences which are too well known to call for mention. Differences emerge too in the instinctual disposition which give a glimpse of the later nature of women. A little girl is as a rule less aggressive, defiant and self-sufficient; she seems to have a greater need for being shown affection and on that account to be more dependent and pliant. It is probably only as a result of this pliancy that she can be taught more easily and quicker to control her excretions: urine and faeces are the first gifts that children make to those who look after them, and controlling them is the first concession to which the instinctual life of children can be induced. One gets an impression, too, that little girls are more intelligent and livelier than boys of the same age; they go out more to meet the external world and at the same time form stronger object-cathexes. I cannot say whether this lead in development has been confirmed by exact observations, but in any case there is no question that girls cannot be described as intellectually backward. These sexual differences are not, however, of great consequence: they can be outweighed by individual variations. For our immediate purpose they can be disregarded.

Both sexes seem to pass through the early phases of libidinal development in the same manner. It might have been expected that in girls there would already have been some lag in aggressiveness in the sadistic-anal phase, but such is not the case. Analysis of children's play has shown our women analysts that the aggressive impulses of little girls leave nothing to be desired in the way of abundance and violence. With their entry into the phallic phase the differences between the sexes are completely eclipsed by their agreements. We are now obliged to recognize that the little girl is a little man. In boys, as we know, this phase is marked by the fact that they have learned how to derive pleasurable sensations from their small penis and connect its excited state with their ideas of sexual intercourse. Little girls do the same thing with their still smaller clitoris. It seems that with them all their masturbatory acts are carried out on this penis-equivalent, and that the truly feminine vagina is still undiscovered by both sexes. It is true that there are a few isolated reports of early vaginal sensations as well, but it could not be easy to distinguish these from sensations in the anus or vestibulum; in any case they cannot play a great part. We are entitled to keep our view that in the phallic phase of girls the clitoris is the leading erotogenic zone. But it is not, of course, going to remain so. With the change to femininity the clitoris should wholly or in part hand over its sensitivity, and at the same time its importance, to the vagina. This would be one of the two tasks which a woman has to perform in the course of her development, whereas the more fortunate man has only to continue at the time of his sexual maturity the activity that he has previously carried out at the period of the early efflorescence of his sexuality.

We shall return to the part played by the clitoris; let us now turn to the second task with which a girl's development is burdened. A boy's mother is the first object of his love, and she remains so too during the formation of his Oedipus complex and, in essence, all through his life. For a girl too her first object must be her mother (and the figures of wet-nurses and foster-mothers that merge into her). The first object-cathexes occur in attachment to the satisfaction of the major and simple vital needs,[1] and the circumstances of the care of children are the same for both sexes. But in the Oedipus situation the girl's father has become her love-object, and we expect that in the normal course of development she will find her way from this paternal object to her final choice of an object. In the course of time, therefore, a girl has to change her erotogenic zone and her object – both of which a boy retains. The question then arises of how this happens: in particular, how does a girl pass from her mother to an attachment to her father? or, in other words, how does she pass from her masculine phase to the feminine one to which she is biologically destined?

It would be a solution of ideal simplicity if we could suppose that from a particular age onwards the elementary influence of the mutual attraction between the sexes makes itself felt and impels the small woman towards men, while the same law allows the boy to continue with his mother. We might suppose in addition that in this the children are following the pointer given them by the sexual preference of their parents. But we are not going to find things so easy; we scarcely know whether we are to believe seriously in the power of which poets talk so much and with such enthusiasm but which cannot be further dissected analytically. We have found an answer of quite another sort by means of laborious investigations, the material for which at least was easy to arrive at. For you must know that the number of women who remain till a late age tenderly dependent on a paternal object, or indeed on their real father, is very great. We have established some surprising facts about these women with an intense attachment of long duration to their father. We knew, of course, that there had been a preliminary stage of attachment to the mother, but we did not know that it could be so rich in content and so long-lasting, and could leave behind so many opportunities for fixations and dispositions. During this time the girl's father is only a troublesome rival; in some cases the attachment to her mother lasts beyond the fourth year of life. Almost everything that we find later in her relation to her father was already present in this earlier attachment and has been transferred subsequently on to her father. In short, we get an impression that we cannot understand women unless we appreciate this phase of their pre-Oedipus attachment to their mother.

[1] [Cf. *Introductory Lectures*, Lecture 21, *Standard Ed.*, **16**, 328–9; *P.F.L.*, **1**, 371 f.]

We shall be glad, then, to know the nature of the girl's libidinal relations to her mother. The answer is that they are of very many different kinds. Since they persist through all three phases of infantile sexuality, they also take on the characteristics of the different phases and express themselves by oral, sadistic-anal and phallic wishes. These wishes represent active as well as passive impulses; if we relate them to the differentiation of the sexes which is to appear later – though we should avoid doing so as far as possible – we may call them masculine and feminine. Besides this, they are completely ambivalent, both affectionate and of a hostile and aggressive nature. The latter often only come to light after being changed into anxiety ideas. It is not always easy to point a formulation of these early sexual wishes; what is most clearly expressed is a wish to get the mother with child and the corresponding wish to bear her a child – both belonging to the phallic period and sufficiently surprising, but established beyond doubt by analytic observation. The attractiveness of these investigations lies in the surprising detailed findings which they bring us. Thus, for instance, we discover the fear of being murdered or poisoned, which may later form the core of a paranoic illness, already present in this pre-Oedipus period, in relation to the mother. Or another case: you will recall an interesting episode in the history of analytic research which caused me many distressing hours. In the period in which the main interest was directed to discovering infantile sexual traumas, almost all my women patients told me that they had been seduced by their father. I was driven to recognize in the end that these reports were untrue and so came to understand that hysterical symptoms are derived from phantasies and not from real occurrences. It was only later that I was able to recognize in this phantasy of being seduced by the father the expression of the typical Oedipus complex in women. And now we find the phantasy of seduction once more in the pre-Oedipus prehistory of girls; but the seducer is regularly the mother. Here, however, the phantasy touches the ground of reality, for it was really the mother who by her activities over the child's bodily hygiene inevitably stimulated, and perhaps even roused for the first time, pleasurable sensations in her genitals.[1]

[1] [In his early discussions of the aetiology of hysteria Freud often mentioned seduction by adults as among its commonest causes. But nowhere in these early publications did he specifically inculpate the girl's father. Indeed, in some additional footnotes written in 1924 for the *Gesammelte Schriften* reprint of *Studies on Hysteria*, he admitted to having on two occasions suppressed the fact of the father's responsibility.

I have no doubt you are ready to suspect that this portrayal of the abundance and strength of a little girl's sexual relations with her mother is very much overdrawn. After all, one has opportunities of seeing little girls and notices nothing of the sort. But the objection is not to the point. Enough can be seen in the children if one knows how to look. And besides, you should consider how little of its sexual wishes a child can bring to preconscious expression or communicate at all. Accordingly we are only within our rights if we study the residues and consequences of this emotional world in retrospect, in people in whom these processes of development had attained a specially clear and even excessive degree of expansion. Pathology has always done us the service of making discernible by isolation and exaggeration conditions which would remain concealed in a normal state. And since our investigations have been carried out on people who were by no means seriously abnormal, I think we should regard their outcome as deserving belief.

We will now turn our interest on to the single question of what it is that brings this powerful attachment of the girl to her mother to an end. This, as we know, is its usual fate: it is destined to make room for an attachment to her father. Here we come upon a fact which is a pointer to our further advance. This step in development does not involve only a simple change of object. The turning away from the mother is accompanied by hostility; the attachment to the mother ends in hate. A hate of that kind may become very striking and last all through life; it may be carefully overcompensated later on; as a rule one part of it is overcome while another part persists. Events of later years naturally influence this greatly. We will restrict ourselves, however, to studying it at the time at which the girl turns to her father and to enquiring into the motives for it. We are then given a long list of accusations and grievances against the mother which are supposed to justify the child's hostile feelings; they are of varying validity which we shall not fail to examine. A number of them are obvious rationalizations and the true sources of enmity remain to be found. I hope you

---

footnote continued

He made this quite clear, however, in the letter to Fliess of September 21, 1897 (Freud, 1950a, Letter 69), in which he first expressed his scepticism about these stories told by his patients. His first published admission of his mistake was given several years later in a hint in the second of the *Three Essays* (1905d),p. 330 above, but a much fuller account of the position followed in his contribution on the aetiology of the neuroses to a volume by Löwenfeld (Freud, 1906a).]

will be interested if on this occasion I take you through all the details of a psycho-analytic investigation.

The reproach against the mother which goes back furthest is that she gave the child too little milk – which is construed against her as lack of love. Now there is some justification for this reproach in our families. Mothers often have insufficient nourishment to give their children and are content to suckle them for a few months, for half or three-quarters of a year. Among primitive peoples children are fed at their mother's breast for two or three years. The figure of the wet-nurse who suckles the child is as a rule merged into the mother; when this has not happened, the reproach is turned into another one – that the nurse, who fed the child so willingly, was sent away by the mother too early. But whatever the true state of affairs may have been, it is impossible that the child's reproach can be justified as often as it is met with. It seems, rather, that the child's avidity for its earliest nourishment is altogether insatiable, that it never gets over the pain of losing its mother's breast. I should not be surprised if the analysis of a primitive child, who could still suck at its mother's breast when it was already able to run about and talk, were to bring the same reproach to light. The fear of being poisoned is also probably connected with the withdrawal of the breast. Poison is nourishment that makes one ill. Perhaps children trace back their early illnesses too to this frustration. A fair amount of intellectual education is a prerequisite for believing in chance; primitive people and uneducated ones, and no doubt children as well, are able to assign a ground for everything that happens. Perhaps originally it was a reason on animistic lines. Even to-day in some strata of our population no one can die without having been killed by someone else – preferably by the doctor. And the regular reaction of a neurotic to the death of someone closely connected with him is to put the blame on himself for having caused the death.

The next accusation against the child's mother flares up when the next baby appears in the nursery. If possible the connection with oral frustration is preserved: the mother could not or would not give the child any more milk because she needed the nourishment for the new arrival. In cases in which the two children are so close in age that lactation is prejudiced by the second pregnancy, this reproach acquires a real basis, and it is a remarkable fact that a child, even with an age difference of only 11 months, is not too young to take notice of what is happening. But what the child grudges the unwanted intruder and rival is not only the suckling but all the other signs of maternal care. It feels that it has been dethroned, despoiled, prejudiced in its rights; it casts a jealous hatred upon the new baby and develops a grievance against the faithless mother which often finds expression in a disagreeable change in its behaviour. It becomes 'naughty', perhaps, irritable and disobedient and goes back on the advances it has made towards controlling its excretions. All of this has been very long familiar and is accepted as self-evident; but we rarely form a correct idea of the strength of these jealous impulses, of the tenacity with which they persist and of the magnitude of their influence on later development. Especially as this jealousy is constantly receiving fresh nourishment in the later years of childhood and the whole shock is repeated with the birth of each new brother or sister. Nor does it make much difference if the child happens to remain the mother's preferred favourite. A child's demands for love are immoderate, they make exclusive claims and tolerate no sharing.

An abundant source of a child's hostility to its mother is provided by its multifarious sexual wishes, which alter according to the phase of the libido and which cannot for the most part be satisfied. The strongest of these frustrations occur at the phallic period, if the mother forbids pleasurable activity with the genitals – often with severe threats and every sign of displeasure – activity to which, after all, she herself had introduced the child. One would think these were reasons enough to account for a girl's turning away from her mother. One would judge, if so, that the estrangement follows inevitably from the nature of children's sexuality, from the immoderate character of their demand for love and the impossibility of fulfilling their sexual wishes. It might be thought indeed that this first love-relation of the child's is doomed to dissolution for the very reason that it is the first, for these early object-cathexes are regularly ambivalent to a high degree. A powerful tendency to aggressiveness is always present beside a powerful love, and the more passionately a child loves its object the more sensitive does it become to disappointments and frustrations from that object; and in the end the love must succumb to the accumulated hostility. Or the idea that there is an original ambivalence such as this in erotic cathexes may be rejected, and it may be pointed out that it is the special nature of the mother-child relation that leads, with equal inevitability, to the destruction of the child's love; for even the mildest upbringing cannot avoid using compulsion and introducing restrictions, and any such intervention in the child's liberty must provoke as a reaction an inclination to rebelliousness and aggressiveness. A discussion of these possibilities might, I think, be most interesting; but an objection suddenly emerges which forces our interest in another direction. All these factors – the slights, the disappointments in love, the jealousy, the seduction followed by prohibition – are, after all, also in operation in the relation of a *boy* to his mother and are yet unable to alienate him from the maternal object. Unless we can find something that is specific for girls and is not present or not in the same way present in boys, we shall not have explained the termination of the attachment of girls to their mother.

I believe we have found this specific factor, and indeed where we expected to find it, even though in a surprising form. Where we expected to find it, I say, for it lies in the castration complex. After all, the anatomical distinction [between the sexes] must express itself in psychical consequences. It was, however, a surprise to learn from analyses that girls hold their mother responsible for their lack of a penis and do not forgive her for their being thus put at a disadvantage.

As you hear, then, we ascribe a castration complex to women as well. And for good reasons, though its content cannot be the same as with boys. In the latter the castration complex arises after they have learnt from the sight of the female genitals that the organ which they value so highly need not necessarily accompany the body. At this the boy recalls to mind the threats he brought on himself by his doings with that organ, he begins to give credence to them and falls under the influence of fear of castration, which will be the most powerful motive force in his subsequent development. The castration complex of girls is also started by the sight of the genitals of the other sex. They at once notice the difference and, it must be admitted, its significance too. They feel seriously wronged, often declare that they want to 'have something like it too', and fall a victim to 'envy for the penis', which will leave ineradicable traces on their development and the formation of their character and which will not be surmounted in even the most favourable cases without a severe expenditure of psychical energy. The girl's recognition of the fact of her being without a penis does not by any means imply that she submits to the fact easily. On the contrary, she continues to hold on for a long time to the wish to get something like it herself and she believes in that possibility for improbably long years; and analysis can show that, at a period when knowledge of reality has long since rejected the fulfilment of the wish as unattainable, it persists in the unconscious and retains a considerable cathexis of energy. The wish to get the longed-for penis eventually in spite of everything may contribute to the motives that drive a mature woman to analysis, and what she may reasonably expect from analysis – a capacity, for instance, to carry on an intellectual profession – may often be recognized as a sublimated modification of this repressed wish.

One cannot very well doubt the importance of envy for the penis. You may take it as an instance of male injustice if I assert that envy and jealousy play an even greater part in the mental life of women than of men. It is not that I think these characteristics are absent in men or that I think they have no other roots in women than envy for the penis; but I am inclined to attribute their greater amount in women to this latter influence. Some analysts, however, have shown an inclination to depreciate the importance of this first instalment of penis-envy in the phallic phase. They are of opinion that what we find of this attitude in women is in the main a secondary structure which has come about on the occasion of later conflicts by regression to this early infantile impulse. This, however, is a general problem of depth psychology. In many pathological – or even unusual – instinctual attitudes (for instance, in all sexual perversions) the question arises of how much of their strength is to be attributed to early infantile fixations and how much to the influence of later experiences and developments. In such cases it is almost always a matter of complemental series such as we put forward in our discussion of the aetiology of the neuroses.[1] Both factors play a part in varying amounts in the causation; a less on the one side is balanced by a more on the other. The infantile factor sets the pattern in all cases but does not always determine the issue, though it often does. Precisely in the case of penis-envy I should argue decidedly in favour of the preponderance of the infantile factor.

The discovery that she is castrated is a turning-point in a girl's growth. Three possible lines of development start from it: one leads to sexual inhibition or to neurosis, the second to change of character in the sense of a masculinity complex, the third, finally, to normal femininity. We have learnt a fair amount, though not everything, about all three.

---

[1] [See *Introductory Lectures*, 22 and 23, *Standard Ed.*, **16**, 347, 362 and 364; *P.F.L.*, **1**, 392, 409 and 411.]

The essential content of the first is as follows: the little girl has hitherto lived in a masculine way, has been able to get pleasure by the excitation of her clitoris and has brought this activity into relation with her sexual wishes directed towards her mother, which are often active ones; now, owing to the influence of her penis-envy, she loses her enjoyment in her phallic sexuality. Her self-love is mortified by the comparison with the boy's far superior equipment and in consequence she renounces her masturbatory satisfaction from her clitoris, repudiates her love for her mother and at the same time not infrequently represses a good part of her sexual trends in general. No doubt her turning away from her mother does not occur all at once, for to begin with the girl regards her castration as an individual misfortune, and only gradually extends it to other females and finally to her mother as well. Her love was directed to her *phallic* mother; with the discovery that her mother is castrated it becomes possible to drop her as an object, so that the motives for hostility, which have long been accumulating, gain the upper hand. This means, therefore, that as a result of the discovery of women's lack of a penis they are debased in value for girls just as they are for boys and later perhaps for men.

You all know the immense aetiological importance attributed by our neurotic patients to their masturbation. They make it responsible for all their troubles and we have the greatest difficulty in persuading them that they are mistaken. In fact, however, we ought to admit to them that they are right, for masturbation is the executive agent of infantile sexuality, from the faulty development of which they are indeed suffering. But what neurotics mostly blame is the masturbation of the period of puberty; they have mostly forgotten that of early infancy, which is what is really in question. I wish I might have an opportunity some time of explaining to you at length how important all the factual details of early masturbation become for the individual's subsequent neurosis or character: whether or not it was discovered, how the parents struggled against it or permitted it, or whether he succeeded in suppressing it himself. All of this leaves permanent traces on his development. But I am on the whole glad that I need not do this. It would be a hard and tedious task and at the end of it you would put me in an embarrassing situation by quite certainly asking me to give you some practical advice as to have a parent or educator should deal with the masturbation of small children. From the development of girls, which is what my present lecture is concerned with, I can give you the example of a child herself trying to get free from masturbating. She does not always succeed in this. If envy for the penis has provoked a powerful impulse against clitoridal masturbation but this nevertheless refuses to give way, a violent struggle for liberation ensues in which the girl, as it were, herself takes over the role of her deposed mother and gives expression to her entire dissatisfaction with her inferior clitoris in her efforts against obtaining satisfaction from it. Many years later, when her masturbatory activity has long since been suppressed, an interest still persists which we must interpret as a defence against a temptation that is still dreaded. It manifests inself in the emergence of sympathy for those to whom similar difficulties are attributed, it plays a part as a motive in contracting a marriage and, indeed, it may determine the choice of a husband or lover. Disposing of early infantile masturbation is truly no easy or indifferent business.

Along with the abandonment of clitoridal masturbation a certain amount of activity is renounced. Passivity now has the upper hand, and the girl's turning to her father is accomplished principally with the help of passive instinctual impulses. You can see that a wave of development like this, which clears the phallic activity out of the way, smooths the ground for femininity. If too much is not lost in the course of it through repression, this femininity may turn out to be normal. The wish with which the girl turns to her father is no doubt originally the wish for the penis which her mother has refused her and which she now expects from her father. The feminine situation is only established, however, if the wish for a penis is replaced by one for a baby, if, that is, a baby takes the place of a penis in accordance with an ancient symbolic equivalence. It has not escaped us that the girl has wished for a baby earlier, in the undisturbed phallic phase: that, of course, was the meaning of her playing with dolls. But that play was not in fact an expression of her femininity; it served as an identification with her mother with the intention of substituting activity for passivity. *She* was playing the part of her mother and the doll was herself: now she could do with the baby everything that her mother used to do with her. Not until the emergence of the wish for a penis does the doll-baby become a baby from the girl's father, and thereafter the aim of the most powerful feminine wish. Her happiness is great if later on this wish for a baby finds fulfilment in reality, and quite especially so if the baby is a little boy who brings the longed-for penis with him. Often enough in her combined picture of 'a baby from her father' the emphasis is laid on the baby and her father left unstressed. In this way the ancient masculine wish for the possession of a penis is still faintly visible through the femininity now achieved. But perhaps we ought rather to recognize this wish for a penis as being *par excellence* a feminine one.

With the transference of the wish for a penis-baby on to her father, the girl has entered the situation of the Oedipus complex. Her hostility to her mother, which did not need to be freshly created, is now greatly intensified, for she becomes the girl's rival, who receives from her father everything that she desires from him. For a long time the girl's Oedipus complex concealed her pre-Oedipus attachment to her mother from our view, though it is nevertheless so important and leaves such lasting fixations behind it. For girls the Oedipus situation is the outcome of a long and difficult development; it is a kind of preliminary solution, a position of rest which is not soon abandoned, especially as the beginning of the latency period is not far distant. And we are now struck by a difference between the two sexes, which is probably momentous, in regard to the relation of the Oedipus complex to the castration complex. In a boy the Oedipus complex, in which he desires his mother and would like to get rid of his father as being a rival, develops naturally from the phase of his phallic sexuality. The threat of castration compels him, however, to give up that attitude. Under the impression of the danger of losing his penis, the Oedipus complex is abandoned, repressed and, in the most normal cases, entirely destroyed, and a severe super-ego is set up as its heir. What happens with a girl is almost the opposite. The castration complex prepares for the Oedipus complex instead of destroying it; the girl is driven out of her attachment to her mother through the influence of her envy for the penis and she enters the Oedipus situation as though into a haven of refuge. In the absence of fear of castration the chief motive is lacking which leads boys to surmount the Oedipus complex. Girls remain in it for an indeterminate length of time; they demolish it late and, even so, incompletely. In these circumstances the formation of the super-ego must suffer; it cannot attain the strength and independence which give it its cultural significance, and feminists are not pleased when we point out to them the effects of this factor upon the average feminine character.

To go back a little. We mentioned as the second possible reaction to the discovery of female castration the development of a powerful masculinity complex. By this we mean that the girl refuses, as it were, to recognize the unwelcome fact and, defiantly rebellious, even exaggerates her previous masculinity, clings to her clitoridal activity and takes refuge in an identification with her phallic mother or her father. What can it be that decides in favour of this outcome? We can only suppose that it is a constitutional factor, a greater amount of activity, such as is ordinarily characteristic of a male. However that may be, the essence of this process is that at this point in development the wave of passivity is avoided which opens the way to the turn towards femininity. The extreme achievement of such a masculinity complex would appear to be the influencing of the choice of an object in the sense of manifest homosexuality. Analytic experience teaches us, to be sure, that female homosexuality is seldom or never a direct continuation of infantile masculinity. Even for a girl of this kind it seems necessary that she should take her father as an object for some time and enter the Oedipus situation. But afterwards, as a result of her inevitable disappointments from her father, she is driven to regress into her early masculinity complex. The significance of these disappointments must not be exaggerated; a girl who is destined to become feminine is not spared them, though they do not have the same effect. The predominance of the constitutional factor seems indisputable; but the two phases in the development of female homosexuality are well mirrored in the practices of homosexuals, who play the parts of mother and baby with each other as often and as clearly as those of husband and wife.

What I have been telling you here may be described as the prehistory of women. It is a product of the very last few years and may have been of interest to you as an example of detailed analytic work. Since its subject is woman, I will venture on this occasion to mention by name a few of the women who have made valuable contributions to this investigation. Dr Ruth Mack Brunswick [1928] was the first to describe a case of neurosis which went back to a fixation in the pre-Oedipus stage and had never reached the Oedipus situation at all. The case took the form of jealous paranoia and proved accessible to therapy. Dr Jeanne Lampl-de Groot [1927] has established the incredible phallic activity of girls towards their mother by some assured observations, and Dr Helene Deutsch [1932] has shown that the erotic actions of homosexual women reproduce the relations between mother and baby.

It is not my intention to pursue the further behaviour of femininity through puberty to the period of maturity. Our knowledge, moreover, would be insufficient for the purpose. But I will bring a few features together in what follows. Taking its prehistory as a starting-point, I will only emphasize here that the development of femininity remains exposed to disturbance by the residual phenomena of the early masculine period. Regressions to the fixations of the pre-Oedipus phases very frequently occur; in the course of some women's lives there is a repeated alternation between periods in which masculinity or femininity gains the upper hand. Some portion of what we men call 'the enigma of women' may perhaps be derived from this expression of bisexuality in women's lives. But another question seems to have become ripe for judgement in the course of these researches. We have called the motive force of sexual life 'the libido'. Sexual life is dominated by the polarity of masculine–feminine; thus the notion suggests itself of considering the relation of the libido to this antithesis. It would not be surprising if it were to turn out that each sexuality had its own special libido appropriated to it, so that one sort of libido would pursue the aims of a masculine sexual life and another sort those of a feminine one. But nothing of the kind is true. There is only one libido, which serves both the masculine and the feminine sexual functions. To it itself we cannot assign any sex; if, following the conventional equation of activity and masculinity, we are inclined to describe it as masculine, we must not forget that it also covers trends with a passive aim. Nevertheless the juxtaposition 'feminine libido' is without any justification. Furthermore, it is our impression that more constraint has been applied to the libido when it is pressed into the service of the feminine function, and that – to speak teleologically – Nature takes less careful account of its [that function's] demands than in the case of masculinity. And the reason for this may lie – thinking once again teleologically – in the fact that the accomplishment of the aim of biology has been entrusted to the aggressiveness of men and has been made to some extent independent of women's consent.

The sexual frigidity of women, the frequency of which appears to confirm this disregard, is a phenomenon that is still insufficiently understood. Sometimes it is psychogenic and in that case accessible to influence; but in other cases it suggests the hypothesis of its being constitutionally determined and even of there being a contributory anatomical factor.

I have promised to tell you of a few more psychical peculiarities of mature femininity, as we come across them in analytic observation. We do not lay claim to more than an average validity for these assertions; nor is it always easy to distinguish what should be ascribed to the influence of the sexual function and what to social breeding. Thus, we attribute a larger amount of narcissism to femininity, which also affects women's choice of object, so that to be loved is a stronger need for them than to love. The effect of penis-envy has a share, further, in the physical vanity of women, since they are bound to value their charms more highly as a late compensation for their original sexual inferiority.[1] Shame, which is considered to be a feminine characteristic *par excellence* but is far more a matter of convention than might be supposed, has as its purpose, we believe, concealment of genital deficiency. We are not forgetting that at a later time shame takes on other functions. It seems that women have made few contributions to the discoveries and inventions in the history of civilization; there is, however, one technique which they may have invented – that of plaiting and weaving. If that is so, we should be tempted to guess the unconscious motive for the achievement. Nature herself would seem to have given the model which this achievement imitates by causing the growth at maturity of the pubic hair that conceals the genitals. The step that remained to be taken lay in making the threads adhere to one another, while on the body they stick into the skin and are only matted together. If you reject this idea as fantastic and regard my belief in the influence of lack of a penis on the configuration of femininity as an *idée fixe*, I am of course defenceless.

The determinants of women's choice of an object are often made unrecognizable by social conditions. Where the choice is able to show itself freely, it is often made in accordance with the narcissistic ideal of the man whom the girl had wished to become. If the girl has remained in her attachment to her father – that is, in the Oedipus complex – her choice is made according to the paternal type. Since, when she turned from her mother to her father, the hostility of her ambivalent relation remained with her mother, a choice of this kind should guarantee a happy marriage. But very often the outcome is of a kind that presents a general threat to such a settlement of the conflict due to ambivalence. The hostility that has been left behind follows in the train of the positive attachment and spreads over on to the new object. The woman's husband, who to begin with inherited from her father, becomes after a time her mother's heir as well. So it may easily happen

---

[1] [Cf. 'On Narcissism' (1914*c*), *Standard Ed.*, 14, 88–9; *P.F.L.*, 11, 82 f.]

that the second half of a woman's life may be filled by the struggle against her husband, just as the shorter first half was filled by her rebellion against her mother. When this reaction has been lived through, a second marriage may easily turn out very much more satisfying. Another alteration in a woman's nature, for which lovers are unprepared, may occur in a marriage after the first child is born. Under the influence of a woman's becoming a mother herself, an identification with her own mother may be revived, against which she had striven up till the time of her marriage, and this may attract all the available libido to itself, so that the compulsion to repeat reproduces an unhappy marriage between her parents. The difference in a mother's reaction to the birth of a son or a daughter shows that the old factor of lack of a penis has even now not lost its strength. A mother is only brought unlimited satisfaction by her relation to a son; this is altogether the most perfect, the most free from ambivalence of all human relationships.[1] A mother can transfer to her son the ambition which she has been obliged to suppress in herself, and she can expect from him the satisfaction of all that has been left over in her of her masculinity complex. Even a marriage is not made secure until the wife has succeeded in making her husband her child as well and in acting as a mother to him.

A woman's identification with her mother allows us to distinguish two strata: the pre-Oedipus one which rests on her affectionate attachment to her mother and takes her as a model, and the later one from the Oedipus complex which seeks to get rid of her mother and take her place with her father. We are no doubt justified in saying that much of both of them is left over for the future and that neither of them is adequately surmounted in the course of development. But the phase of the affectionate pre-Oedipus attachment is the decisive one for a woman's future: during it preparations are made for the acquisition of the characteristics with which she will later fulfil her role in the sexual function and perform her invaluable social tasks. It is in this identification too that she acquires her attractiveness to a man, whose Oedipus attachment to his mother it kindles into passion. How often it happens, however, that it is only his son who obtains what he himself aspired to! One gets an impression that a man's love and a woman's are a phase apart psychologically.

[1] [This point was made in *Introductory Lectures*, Lecture 13. That exceptions may occur is shown by the example given in Lecture 31 (p. 492 below).]

The fact that women must be regarded as having little sense of justice is no doubt related to the predominance of envy in their mental life; for the demand for justice is a modification of envy and lays down the condition subject to which one can put envy aside. We also regard women as weaker in their social interests and as having less capacity for sublimating their instincts than men. The former is no doubt derived from the dissocial quality which unquestionably characterizes all sexual relations. Lovers find sufficiency in each other, and families too resist inclusion in more comprehensive associations. The aptitude for sublimation is subject to the greatest individual variations. On the other hand I cannot help mentioning an impression that we are constantly receiving during analytic practice. A man of about thirty strikes us as a youthful, somewhat unformed individual, whom we expect to make powerful use of the possibilities for development opened up to him by analysis. A woman of the same age, however, oftens frightens us by her psychical rigidity and unchangeability. Her libido has taken up final positions and seems incapable of exchanging them for others. There are no paths open to further development; it is as though the whole process had already run its course and remains thenceforward insusceptible to influence – as though, indeed, the difficult development to femininity had exhausted the possibilities of the person concerned. As therapists we lament this state of things, even if we succeed in putting an end to our patient's ailment by doing away with her neurotic conflict.

That is all I had to say to you about femininity. It is certainly incomplete and fragmentary and does not always sound friendly. But do not forget that I have only been describing women in so far as their nature is determined by their sexual function. It is true that that influence extends very far; but we do not overlook the fact that an individual woman may be a human being in other respects as well. If you want to know more about femininity, enquire from your own experiences of life, or turn to the poets, or wait until science can give you deeper and more coherent information.

Six

THE STRUCTURE
OF THE PSYCHIC
PERSONALITY

Introduction

Freud's readiness to change his theories as soon as they no longer met his requirements occasionally posed some problems for his followers and pupils. Those who had just begun to familiarize themselves with the theory of the unconscious and to evaluate all psychic processes in terms of their relationship to conscious perception must have found it difficult to give up this point of view again and to exchange it for a new one. And those of Freud's collaborators who were wholly committed to depth psychology were scarcely inclined to turn at least part of their interest once more to the surface of consciousness and to the influences of the external world.

Freud himself, however, had no such misgivings. In the 1920s he was concerned with integrating into his theory two new insights gained in his analytic treatments. The ego which until then had in its entirety coincided with the system conscious now appeared to have distinct unconscious parts; the system unconscious, on the other hand, seemed to contain more than the repressed that Freud had assigned to it. Both observations contradicted the previously adopted simple division of psychic life into spatially separated systems (unconscious, preconscious, conscious) that were clearly demarcated from each other. This classification, then, did not do justice to the newly observed facts and therefore had to be replaced by another one.

In his new formulation which he presented at length for the first time in *The Ego and the Id* (1923b), Freud restricted the concept of unconscious to a quality of psychic processes, i.e., to a characteristic of mental activity that can be found in every part of the psychic apparatus. The psychic apparatus itself was now conceived as a structure consisting of several agencies or institutions. In short, the earlier topographic model of psychic life was superseded by the structural model.

Freud's opponents repeatedly reproached him with proceeding unscientifically because he gave these newly postulated agencies names of their own (viz., ego, id and super-ego); they disparagingly compared this terminological characterization with a description of mythological figures. Nevertheless, it was precisely this obvious personification of theoretical constructs which for the analyst as well as the lay reader brought into focus the contradictions contained in his own person and perhaps made them clearly visible for the first time. That no human individual is a unity, that inner disharmonies are unavoidable, becomes intelligible only when we can clearly discern the different origins, the different contents, the different mechanisms and aims of each single agency. Freud set himself this task of clarification in *The Ego and the Id*, and subsequently once again summarized his solution in his lecture on 'The Dissection of the Psychical Personality' (1933*a*) (which should both be assigned).

According to the new concept, the inner collisions and conflicts are no longer simply between conscious and unconscious elements; rather, other, no less serious contrasts are decisive. The blind search for satisfaction by the drives, which are given at birth and determine the nature of the id, is not compatible with the nature of the ego whose task it is to register conditions, requirements and dangers in the outer world and to take them into consideration. The ego agencies in their turn are naturally, as it were, divided according to their double origin. For the ego itself is nothing other than a remodelled part which, having split off from the id, is adapted to the external world; the super-ego, again, is a precipitate of the child's prolonged dependency on his parents and their demands with regard to drive restriction and socialization.[1] Thus, in every individual, the search for pleasure, for adaptation, and for morality clash with each other and over and over confront each of us with the task of reconciling the irreconcilable and, all contradictions notwithstanding, to strive for inner harmony. When these efforts succeed, psychic health is assured; when they fail, we see inhibitions, symptoms, and morbidly increased anxiety – pathological manifestations.

These introductory words stress the important advances in the formation of Freud's theories. At the same time, however, students should also be warned that the new structural model of the psychic apparatus does not neglect the old classification conscious/un-

[1] The significance and the genesis of the super-ego, and especially the role played by identifications in its development, also are discussed by Freud in *Group Psychology and the Analysis of the Ego* (1921*c*) and *Civilization and Its Discontents* (1930*a*), both of which are assigned reading in the section on the applications of psycho-analysis.

conscious. Modern analytic authors easily forget that Freud's own estimation of the significance of the unconscious mental life did not decisively change with the introduction of the structural model. He was and always remained convinced, as he himself said, that the 'division of the psychical into what is conscious and what is unconscious is the fundamental premise of psycho-analysis' (1923b, p. 13), 'our own beacon-light in the darkness of depth-psychology' (p. 18). The practising analyst is in fact frequently tempted, now as ever, to understand his efforts in terms of the old topographic theory. Again and again he is made to realize that the psychic contents that shun the light of the conscious surface must laboriously be coaxed out of the dark room of the unconscious and furnished with word-presentations, as is the case with the preconscious, before they can take their place in consciousness. In descriptions of this sort, all theoretical advances notwithstanding, the concepts of unconscious and id, and of conscious and ego, obviously coincide once again.

The Ego and the Id

(1923)*

[PREFACE]

The present discussions are a further development of some trains of
thought which I opened up in *Beyond the Pleasure Principle* (1920g), and
to which, as I remarked there, my attitude was one of a kind of
benevolent curiosity. In the following pages these thoughts are linked
to various facts of analytic observation and an attempt is made to
arrive at new conclusions from this conjunction; in the present work,
however, there are no fresh borrowings from biology, and on that
account it stands closer to psycho-analysis than does *Beyond the
Pleasure Principle*. It is more in the nature of a synthesis than of a
speculation and seems to have had an ambitious aim in view. I am
conscious, however, that it does not go beyond the roughest outline
and with that limitation I am perfectly content.

In these pages things are touched on which have not yet been the
subject of psycho-analytic consideration, and it has not been possible
to avoid trenching upon some theories which have been put forward
by non-analysts or by former analysts on their retreat from analysis. I
have elsewhere always been ready to acknowledge what I owe to other
workers; but in this instance I feel burdened by no such debt of
gratitude. If psycho-analysis has not hitherto shown its appreciation
of certain things, this has never been because it overlooked their
achievement or sought to deny their importance, but because it
followed a particular path, which had not yet led so far. And finally,
when it has reached them, things have a different look to it from what
they have to others.

I. CONSCIOUSNESS AND WHAT IS UNCONSCIOUS

In this introductory chapter there is nothing new to be said and it will
not be possible to avoid repeating what has often been said before.

* First published by Internationaler Psychoanalytischer Verlag (Leipzig, Vienna,
Zurich). The present text is included in *Standard Ed.*, **19**, 12; *P.F.L.*, **11**, 350.

The division of the psychical into what is conscious and what is unconscious is the fundamental premiss of psycho-analysis; and it alone makes it possible for psycho-analysis to understand the patho-logical processes in mental life, which are as common as they are important, and to find a place for them in the framework of science. To put it once more, in a different way: psycho-analysis cannot situate the essence of the psychical in consciousness, but is obliged to regard consciousness as a quality of the psychical, which may be present in addition to other qualities or may be absent.

If I could suppose that everyone interested in psychology would read this book, I should also be prepared to find that at this point some of my readers would already stop short and would go no further; for here we have the first shibboleth of psycho-analysis. To most people who have been educated in philosophy the idea of anything psychical which is not also conscious is so inconceivable that it seems to them absurd and refutable simply by logic. I believe this is only because they have never studied the relevant phenomena of hypnosis and dreams, which – quite apart from pathological manifestations – necessitate this view. Their psychology of consciousness is incapable of solving the problems of dreams and hypnosis.

'Being conscious'[1] is in the first place a purely descriptive term, resting on perception of the most immediate and certain character. Experience goes on to show that a psychical element (for instance, an idea) is not as a rule conscious for a protracted length of time. On the contrary, a state of consciousness is characteristically very transitory; an idea that is conscious now is no longer so a moment later, although it can become so again under certain conditions that are easily brought about. In the interval the idea was – we do not know what. We can say that it was *latent*, and by this we mean that it was *capable of becoming conscious* at any time. Or, if we say that it was *unconscious*, we shall also be giving a correct description of it. Here 'unconscious' coincides with 'latent and capable of becoming conscious'. The philosophers would no doubt object: 'No, the term "unconscious" is not applicable here; so long as the idea was in a state of latency it was not anything psychical at all.' To contradict them at this point would lead to nothing more profitable than a verbal dispute.

But we have arrived at the term or concept of the unconscious along another path, by considering certain experiences in which mental

[1] [Cf. editorial note on p. 18 above.]

dynamics play a part. We have found – that is, we have been obliged to assume – that very powerful mental processes or ideas exist (and here a quantitative or *economic* factor comes into question for the first time) which can produce all the effects in mental life that ordinary ideas do (including effects that can in their turn become conscious as ideas), though they themselves do not become conscious. It is unnecessary to repeat in detail here what has been explained so often before.[1] It is enough to say that at this point psycho-analytic theory steps in and asserts that the reason why such ideas cannot become conscious is that a certain force opposes them, that otherwise they could become conscious, and that it would then be apparent how little they differ from other elements which are admittedly psychical. The fact that in the technique of psycho-analysis a means has been found by which the opposing force can be removed and the ideas in question made conscious renders this theory irrefutable. The state in which the ideas existed before being made conscious is called by us *repression*, and we assert that the force which instituted the repression and maintains it is perceived as *resistance* during the work of analysis.

Thus we obtain our concept of the unconscious from the theory of repression. The repressed is the prototype of the unconscious for us. We see, however, that we have two kinds of unconscious – the one which is latent but capable of becoming conscious, and the one which is repressed and which is not, in itself and without more ado, capable of becoming conscious. This piece of insight into psychical dynamics cannot fail to affect terminology and description. The latent, which is unconscious only descriptively, not in the dynamic sense, we call *preconscious*; we restrict the term *unconscious* to the dynamically unconscious repressed; so that now we have three terms, conscious (*Cs.*), preconscious (*Pcs.*), and unconscious (*Ucs.*), whose sense is no longer purely descriptive. The *Pcs.* is presumably a great deal closer to the *Cs.* than is the *Ucs.*, and since we have called the *Ucs.* psychical we shall with even less hesitation call the latent *Pcs.* psychical. But why do we not rather, instead of this, remain in agreement with the philosophers and, in a consistent way, distinguish the *Pcs.* as well as the *Ucs.* from the conscious psychical? The philosophers would then propose that the *Pcs.* and the *Ucs.* should be described as two species or stages of the 'psychoid', and harmony would be established. But endless difficulties in exposition would follow; and the one important

---

[1] [See, for instance, 'A Note on the Unconscious' (1912*g*), pp. 137, 139 above.]

fact, that these two kinds of 'psychoid' coincide in almost every other respect with what is admittedly psychical, would be forced into the background in the interests of a prejudice dating from a period in which these psychoids, or the most important part of them, were still unknown.

We can now play about comfortably with our three terms, *Cs.*, *Pcs.*, and *Ucs.*, so long as we do not forget that in the descriptive sense there are two kinds of unconscious, but in the dynamic sense only one.[1] For purposes of exposition this distinction can in some cases be ignored, but in others it is of course indispensable. At the same time, we have become more or less accustomed to this ambiguity of the unconscious and have managed pretty well with it. As far as I can see, it is impossible to avoid this ambiguity; the distinction between conscious and unconscious is in the last resort a question of perception, which must be answered 'yes' or 'no', and the act of perception itself tells us nothing of the reason why a thing is or is not perceived. No one has a right to complain because the actual phenomenon expresses the dynamic factor ambiguously.[2]

---

[1] [Some comments on this sentence will be found in Appendix A.]

[2] This may be compared so far with my 'Note on the Unconscious in Psycho-Analysis' (1912g). [Cf. also Sections I and II of the metapsychological paper on 'The Unconscious' (1915e); Chapter 3 above.] A new turn taken by criticisms of the unconscious deserves consideration at this point. Some investigators, who do not refuse to recognize the facts of psycho-analysis but who are unwilling to accept the unconscious, find a way out of the difficulty in the fact, which no one contests, that in consciousness (regarded as a phenomenon) it is possible to distinguish a great variety of gradations in intensity or clarity. Just as there are processes which are very vividly, glaringly, and tangibly conscious, so we also experience others which are only faintly, hardly even noticeably conscious; those that are most faintly conscious are, it is argued, the ones to which psycho-analysis wishes to apply the unsuitable name 'unconscious'. These too, however (the argument proceeds), are conscious or 'in consciousness', and can be made fully and intensely conscious if sufficient attention is paid to them.

In so far as it is possible to influence by arguments the decision of a question of this kind which depends either on convention or on emotional factors, we may make the following comments. The reference to gradations of clarity in consciousness is in no way conclusive and has no more evidential value than such analogous statements as: 'There are so very many gradations in illumination – from the most glaring and dazzling light to the dimmest glimmer – therefore there is no such thing as darkness at all'; or, 'There are varying degrees of vitality, therefore there is no such thing as death.' Such statements may in a certain way have a meaning, but for practical purposes they are worthless. This will be seen if one tries to draw particular conclusions from them, such as, 'there is therefore no need to strike a light', or, 'therefore all organisms are immortal'. Further, to include 'what is unnoticeable' under the concept of 'what is conscious' is simply to play havoc with the one and only piece of direct and certain knowledge that we have about the mind. And after all, a consciousness of which one

In the further course of psycho-analytic work, however, even these distinctions have proved to be inadequate and, for practical purposes, insufficient. This has become clear in more ways than one; but the decisive instance is as follows. We have formed the idea that in each individual there is a coherent organization of mental processes; and we call this his *ego*. It is to this ego that consciousness is attached; the ego controls the approaches to motility – that is, to the discharge of excitations into the external world; it is the mental agency which supervises all its own constituent processes, and which goes to sleep at night, though even then it exercises the censorship on dreams. From this ego proceed the repressions, too, by means of which it is sought to exclude certain trends in the mind not merely from consciousness but also from other forms of effectiveness and activity. In analysis these trends which have been shut out stand in opposition to the ego, and the analysis is faced with the task of removing the resistances which the ego displays against concerning itself with the repressed. Now we find during analysis that, when we put certain tasks before the patient, he gets into difficulties; his associations fail when they should be coming near the repressed. We then tell him that he is dominated by a resistance; but he is quite unaware of the fact, and, even if he guesses from his unpleasurable feelings that a resistance is now at work in him, he does not know what it is or how to describe it. Since, however, there can be no question but that this resistance emanates from his ego and belongs to it, we find ourselves in an unforeseen situation. We have come upon something in the ego itself which is also unconscious, which behaves exactly like the repressed – that is, which produces powerful effects without itself being conscious and which requires special work before it can be made conscious. From the point of view of analytic practice, the consequence of this discovery is that we land in endless obscurities and difficulties if we keep to our

---

knows nothing seems to me a good deal more absurd than something mental that is unconscious. Finally, this attempt to equate what is unnoticed with what is unconscious is obviously made without taking into account the dynamic conditions involved, which were the decisive factors in forming the psycho-analytic view. For it ignores two facts: first, that it is exceedingly difficult and requires very great effort to concentrate enough attention on something unnoticed of this kind; and secondly, that when this has been achieved the thought which was previously unnoticed is not recognized by consciousness, but often seems entirely alien and opposed to it and is promptly disavowed by it. Thus, seeking refuge from the unconscious in what is scarcely noticed or unnoticed is after all only a derivative of the preconceived belief which regards the identity of the psychical and the conscious as settled once and for all.

habitual forms of expression and try, for instance, to derive neuroses from a conflict between the conscious and the unconscious. We shall have to substitute for this antithesis another, taken from our insight into the structural conditions of the mind – the antithesis between the coherent ego and the repressed which is split off from it.[1]

For our conception of the unconscious, however, the consequences of our discovery are even more important. Dynamic considerations caused us to make our first correction; our insight into the structure of the mind leads to the second. We recognize that the *Ucs.* does not coincide with the repressed; it is still true that all that is repressed is *Ucs.*, but not all that is *Ucs.* is repressed. A part of the ego, too – and Heaven knows how important a part – may be *Ucs.*, undoubtedly is *Ucs.* And this *Ucs.* belonging to the ego is not latent like the *Pcs.*; for if it were, it could not be activated without becoming *Cs.*, and the process of making it conscious would not encounter such great difficulties. When we find ourselves thus confronted by the necessity of postulating a third *Ucs.*, which is not repressed, we must admit that the characteristic of being unconscious begins to lose significance for us. It becomes a quality which can have many meanings, a quality which we are unable to make, as we should have hoped to do, the basis of far-reaching and inevitable conclusions. Nevertheless we must beware of ignoring this characteristic, for the property of being conscious or not is in the last resort our one beacon-light in the darkness of depth-psychology.

II. THE EGO AND THE ID

Pathological research has directed our interest too exclusively to the repressed. We should like to learn more about the ego, now that we know that it, too, can be unconscious in the proper sense of the word. Hitherto the only guide we have had during our investigations has been the distinguishing mark of being conscious or unconscious; we have finally come to see how ambiguous this can be.

Now all our knowledge is invariably bound up with consciousness. We can come to know even the *Ucs.* only by making it conscious. But stop, how is that possible? What does it mean when we say 'making something conscious'? How can that come about?

---

[1] Cf. *Beyond the Pleasure Principle* (1920g) [in Chapter 4 above].

We already know the point from which we have to start in this connection. We have said that consciousness is the *surface* of the mental apparatus; that is, we have ascribed it as a function to a system which is spatially the first one reached from the external world – and spatially not only in the functional sense but, on this occasion, also in the sense of anatomical dissection.[1] Our investigations too must take this perceiving surface as a starting-point.

All perceptions which are received from without (sense-perceptions) and from within – what we call sensations and feelings – are *Cs.* from the start. But what about those internal processes which we may – roughly and inexactly – sum up under the name of thought-processes? They represent displacements of mental energy which are effected somewhere in the interior of the apparatus as this energy proceeds on its way towards action. Do they advance to the surface, which causes consciousness to be generated? Or does consciousness make its way to them? This is clearly one of the difficulties that arise when one begins to take the spatial or 'topographical' idea of mental life seriously. Both these possibilities are equally unimaginable, there must be a third alternative.[2]

I have already, in another place,[3] suggested that the real difference between a *Ucs.* and a *Pcs.* idea (thought) consists in this: that the former is carried out on some material which remains unknown, whereas the latter (the *Pcs.*) is in addition brought into connection with word-presentations. This is the first attempt to indicate distinguishing marks for the two systems, the *Pcs.* and the *Ucs.*, other than their relation to consciousness. The question, 'How does a thing become conscious?' would thus be more advantageously stated: 'How does a thing become preconscious?' And the answer would be: 'Through becoming connected with the word-presentations corresponding to it.'

These word-presentations are residues of memories; they were at one time perceptions, and like all mnemic residues they can become conscious again. Before we concern ourselves further with their nature, it dawns upon us like a new discovery that only something which has once been a *Cs.* perception can become conscious, and that anything arising from within (apart from feelings) that seeks to

---

[1] *Beyond the Pleasure Principle* [p. 234 f. above].

[2] [This had been discussed at greater length in the second section of 'The Unconscious' (Chapter 3 above).]

[3] 'The Unconscious' [Chapter 3, pp. 171–3 above].

become conscious must try to transform itself into external perceptions: this becomes possible by means of memory-traces.

We think of the mnemic residues as being contained in systems which are directly adjacent to the system *Pcpt.-Cs.*, so that the cathexes of those residues can readily extend from within on to the elements of the latter system.[1] We immediately think here of hallucinations, and of the fact that the most vivid memory is always distinguishable both from a hallucination and from an external perception;[2] but it will also occur to us at once that when a memory is revived the cathexis remains in the mnemic system, whereas a hallucination, which is not distinguishable from a perception, can arise when the cathexis does not merely spread over from the memory-trace on to the *Pcpt.* element, but passes over to it *entirely.*

Verbal residues are derived primarily from auditory perceptions,[3] so that the system *Pcs.* has, as it were, a special sensory source. The visual components of word-presentations are secondary, acquired through reading, and may to begin with be left on one side; so may the motor images of words, which, except with deaf-mutes, play the part of auxiliary indications. In essence a word is after all the mnemic residue of a word that has been heard.

We must not be led, in the interests of simplification perhaps, to forget the importance of optical mnemic residues, when they are of *things*, or to deny that it is possible for thought-processes to become conscious through a reversion to visual residues, and that in many people this seems to be the favoured method. The study of dreams and of preconscious phantasies as shown in Varendonck's observations[4] can give us an idea of the special character of this visual thinking. We learn that what becomes conscious in it is as a rule only the concrete subject-matter of the thought, and that the relations between the various elements of this subject-matter, which is what specially characterizes thoughts, cannot be given visual expression. Thinking in pictures is, therefore, only a very incomplete form of becoming conscious. In some way, too, it stands nearer to unconscious processes

[1] [Cf. Chapter VII (B) of *The Interpretation of Dreams* (1900a), *Standard Ed.*, 5, 538; *P.F.L.*, 4, 687.]

[2] [This view had been expressed by Breuer in his theoretical contribution to *Studies on Hysteria* (1895d), *Standard Ed.*, 2, 188; *P.F.L.*, 3, 263.]

[3] [Freud had arrived at this conclusion in his monograph on aphasia (1891b) on the basis of pathological findings (ibid., 92–4). The point is represented in the diagram reproduced from that work in Appendix C to the paper on 'The Unconscious' (Chapter 3 above).]

[4] [Cf. Varendonck (1921).]

than does thinking in words, and it is unquestionably older than the latter both ontogenetically and phylogenetically.

To return to our argument: if, therefore, this is the way in which something that is in itself unconscious becomes preconscious, the question how we make something that is repressed (pre)conscious would be answered as follows. It is done by supplying *Pcs.* intermediate links through the work of analysis. Consciousness remains where it is, therefore; but, on the other hand, the *Ucs.* does not rise into the *Cs.*

Whereas the relation of *external* perceptions to the ego is quite perspicuous, that of *internal* perceptions to the ego requires special investigation. It gives rise once more to a doubt whether we are really right in referring the whole of consciousness to the single superficial system *Pcpt.-Cs.*

Internal perceptions yield sensations of processes arising in the most diverse and certainly also in the deepest strata of the mental apparatus. Very little is known about these sensations and feelings; those belonging to the pleasure-unpleasure series may still be regarded as the best examples of them. They are more primordial, more elementary, than perceptions arising externally and they can come about even when consciousness is clouded. I have elsewhere[1] expressed my views about their greater economic significance and the metapsychological reasons for this. These sensations are multilocular, like external perceptions; they may come from different places simultaneously and may thus have different or even opposite qualities.

Sensations of a pleasurable nature have not anything inherently impelling about them, whereas unpleasurable ones have it in the highest degree. The latter impel towards change, towards discharge, and that is why we interpret unpleasure as implying a heightening and pleasure a lowering of energic cathexis. Let us call what becomes conscious as pleasure and unpleasure a quantitative and qualitative 'something' in the course of mental events; the question then is whether this 'something' can become conscious in the place where it is, or whether it must first be transmitted to the system *Pcpt.*

Clinical experience decides for the latter. It shows us that this 'something' behaves like a repressed impulse. It can exert driving force without the ego noticing the compulsion. Not until there is

<hr>

[1] [*Beyond the Pleasure Principle* (1920g), Section IV in Chapter 4 above.]

resistance to the compulsion, a hold-up in the discharge-reaction, does the 'something' at once become conscious as unpleasure. In the same way that tensions arising from physical needs can remain unconscious, so also can pain – a thing intermediate between external and internal perception, which behaves like an internal perception even when its source is in the external world. It remains true, therefore, that sensations and feelings, too, only become conscious through reaching the system *Pcpt.*; if the way forward is barred, they do not come into being as sensations, although the 'something' that corresponds to them in the course of excitation is the same as if they did. We then come to speak, in a condensed and not entirely correct manner, of 'unconscious feelings', keeping up an analogy with unconscious ideas which is not altogether justifiable. Actually the difference is that, whereas with *Ucs. ideas* connecting links must be created before they can be brought into the *Cs.*, with *feelings*, which are themselves transmitted directly, this does not occur. In other words: the distinction between *Cs.* and *Pcs.* has no meaning where feelings are concerned; the *Pcs.* here drops out – and feelings are either conscious or unconscious. Even when they are attached to word-presentations, their becoming conscious is not due to that circumstance, but they become so directly.[1]

The part played by word-presentations now becomes perfectly clear. By their interposition internal thought-processes are made into perceptions. It is like a demonstration of the theorem that all knowledge has its origin in external perception. When a hypercathexis of the process of thinking takes place, thoughts are *actually* perceived – as if they came from without – and are consequently held to be true.

After this clarifying of the relations between external and internal perception and the superficial system *Pcpt.-Cs.*, we can go on to work out our idea of the ego. It starts out, as we see, from the system *Pcpt.*, which is its nucleus, and begins by embracing the *Pcs.*, which is adjacent to the mnemic residues. But, as we have learnt, the ego is also unconscious.

Now I think we shall gain a great deal by following the suggestion of a writer who, from personal motives, vainly asserts that he has nothing to do with the rigours of pure science. I am speaking of Georg Groddeck, who is never tired of insisting that what we call our ego behaves essentially passively in life, and that, as he expresses it, we are

---

[1] [Cf. Section III of 'The Unconscious' (1915*e*), in Chapter 3 above.]

'lived' by unknown and uncontrollable forces. [Groddeck (1923).] We have all had impressions of the same kind, even though they may not have overwhelmed us to the exclusion of all others, and we need feel no hesitation in finding a place for Groddeck's discovery in the structure of science. I propose to take it into account by calling the entity which starts out from the system *Pcpt.* and begins by being *Pcs.* the 'ego', and by following Groddeck in calling the other part of the mind, into which this entity extends and which behaves as though it were *Ucs.*, the 'id'.[1]

We shall soon see whether we can derive any advantage from this view for purposes either of description or of understanding. We shall now look upon an individual as a psychical id, unknown and unconscious, upon whose surface rests the ego, developed from its nucleus the *Pcpt.* system. If we make an effort to represent this pictorially, we may add that the ego does not completely envelop the id, but only does so to the extent to which the system *Pcpt.* forms its [the ego's] surface, more or less as the germinal disc rests upon the ovum. The ego is not sharply separated from the id; its lower portion merges into it.

But the repressed merges into the id as well, and is merely a part of it. The repressed is only cut off sharply from the ego by the resistances of repression; it can communicate with the ego through the id. We at once realize that almost all the lines of demarcation we have drawn at the instigation of pathology relate only to the superficial strata of the mental apparatus – the only ones known to us. The state of things which we have been describing can be represented diagrammatically (Fig. 1);[2] though it must be remarked that the form chosen has no pretensions to any special applicability, but is merely intended to serve for purposes of exposition.

We might add, perhaps, that the ego wears a 'cap of hearing'[3] – on one side only, as we learn from cerebral anatomy. It might be said to wear it awry.

It is easy to see that the ego is that part of the id which has been modified by the direct influence of the external world through the medium of the *Pcpt.-Cs.*; in a sense it is an extension of the surface-

[1] Groddeck himself no doubt followed the example of Nietzsche, who habitually used this grammatical term for whatever in our nature is impersonal and, so to speak, subject to natural law.

[2] [Compare the slightly different diagram in Lecture 31, *New Introductory Lectures* (1933*a*), on p. 503 below.]

[3] ['*Hörkappe.*' I.e. the auditory lobe.]

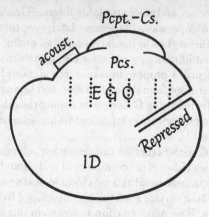

FIG. I

differentiation. Moreover, the ego seeks to bring the influence of the external world to bear upon the id and its tendencies, and endeavours to substitute the reality principle for the pleasure principle which reigns unrestrictedly in the id. For the ego, perception plays the part which in the id falls to instinct. The ego represents what may be called reason and common sense, in contrast to the id, which contains the passions. All this falls into line with popular distinctions which we are all familiar with; at the same time, however, it is only to be regarded as holding good on the average or 'ideally'.

The functional importance of the ego is manifested in the fact that normally control over the approaches to motility devolves upon it. Thus in its relation to the id it is like a man on horseback, who has to hold in check the superior strength of the horse; with this difference, that the rider tries to do so with his own strength while the ego uses borrowed forces. The analogy may be carried a little further. Often a rider, if he is not to be parted from his horse, is obliged to guide it where it wants to go; so in the same way the ego is in the habit of transforming the id's will into action as if it were its own.

Another factor, besides the influence of the system *Pcpt.*, seems to have played a part in bringing about the formation of the ego and its differentiation from the id. A person's own body, and above all its surface, is a place from which both external and internal perceptions may spring. It is *seen* like any other object, but to the *touch* it yields two kinds of sensations, one of which may be equivalent to an internal perception. Psychophysiology has fully discussed the manner in which a person's own body attains its special position among other objects in the world of perception. Pain, too, seems to play a part in the process, and the way in which we gain new knowledge of our organs during painful illnesses is perhaps a model of the way by which in general we arrive at the idea of our body.

The ego is first and foremost a bodily ego; it is not merely a surface entity, but is itself the projection of a surface.[1] If we wish to find an anatomical analogy for it we can best identify it with the 'cortical homunculus' of the anatomists, which stands on its head in the cortex, sticks up its heels, faces backwards and, as we know, has its speech-area on the left-hand side.

The relation of the ego to consciousness has been entered into repeatedly; yet there are some important facts in this connection which remain to be described here. Accustomed as we are to taking our social or ethical scale of values along with us wherever we go, we feel no surprise at hearing that the scene of the activities of the lower passions is in the unconscious; we expect, moreover, that the higher any mental function ranks in our scale of values the more easily it will find access to consciousness assured to it. Here, however, psycho-analytic experience disappoints us. On the one hand, we have evidence that even subtle and difficult intellectual operations which ordinarily require strenuous reflection can equally be carried out preconsciously and without coming into consciousness. Instances of this are quite incontestable; they may occur, for example, during the state of sleep, as is shown when someone finds, immediately after waking, that he knows the solution to a difficult mathematical or other problem with which he had been wrestling in vain the day before.[2]

There is another phenomenon, however, which is far stranger. In our analyses we discover that there are people in whom the faculties of self-criticism and conscience – mental activities, that is, that rank as extremely high ones – are unconscious and unconsciously produce effects of the greatest importance; the example of resistance remaining unconscious during analysis is therefore by no means unique. But this new discovery, which compels us, in spite of our better critical

[1] [I.e. the ego is ultimately derived from bodily sensations, chiefly from those springing from the surface of the body. It may thus be regarded as a mental projection of the surface of the body, besides, as we have seen above, representing the superficies of the mental apparatus.]

[2] I was quite recently told an instance of this which was, in fact, brought up as an objection against my description of the 'dream-work'.

judgment, to speak of an 'unconscious sense of guilt',[1] bewilders us far more than the other and sets us fresh problems, especially when we gradually come to see that in a great number of neuroses an unconscious sense of guilt of this kind plays a decisive economic part and puts the most powerful obstacles in the way of recovery. If we come back once more to our scale of values, we shall have to say that not only what is lowest but also what is highest in the ego can be unconscious. It is as if we were thus supplied with a proof of what we have just asserted of the conscious ego: that it is first and foremost a body-ego.

III. THE EGO AND THE SUPER-EGO (EGO IDEAL)

If the ego were merely the part of the id modified by the influence of the perceptual system, the representative in the mind of the real external world, we should have a simple state of things to deal with. But there is a further complication.

The considerations that led us to assume the existence of a grade in the ego, a differentiation within the ego, which may be called the 'ego ideal' or 'super-ego', have been stated elsewhere.[2] They still hold good.[3] The fact that this part of the ego is less firmly connected with consciousness is the novelty which calls for explanation.

At this point we must widen our range a little. We succeeded in explaining the painful disorder of melancholia by supposing that [in those suffering from it] an object which was lost has been set up again inside the ego – that is, that an object-cathexis has been replaced by an identification.[4] At that time, however, we did not appreciate the full significance of this process and did not know how common and how typical it is. Since then we have come to understand that this kind

---

[1] [Cf. footnote on p. 470 below.]

[2] Cf. 'On Narcissism: an Introduction' (1914c), and *Group Psychology and the Analysis of the Ego* (1921c).

[3] Except that I seem to have been mistaken in ascribing the function of 'reality-testing' to this super-ego – a point which needs correction. [See *Group Psychology* (1921c), *Standard Ed.*, **18**, 114 and *n.* 2, and the Editor's Note to the metapsychological paper on dreams (1917d), **14**, 220.] It would fit in perfectly with the relations of the ego to the world of perception if reality-testing remained a task of the ego itself. Some earlier suggestions about a 'nucleus of the ego', never very definitely formulated, also require to be put right, since the system *Pcpt.-Cs.* alone can be regarded as the nucleus of the ego. [In *Beyond the Pleasure Principle* Freud had spoken of the unconscious part of the ego as its nucleus (p. 229 above), and in his later paper on 'Humour' (1927d) he referred to the super-ego as the nucleus of the ego.]

[4] 'Mourning and Melancholia' (1917e).

of substitution has a great share in determining the form taken by the ego and that it makes an essential contribution towards building up what is called its 'character'.

At the very beginning, in the individual's primitive oral phase, object-cathexis and identification are no doubt indistinguishable from each other.[1] We can only suppose that later on object-cathexes proceed from the id, which feels erotic trends as needs. The ego, which to begin with is still feeble, becomes aware of the object-cathexes, and either acquiesces in them or tries to fend them off by the process of repression.[2]

When it happens that a person has to give up a sexual object, there quite often ensues an alteration of his ego which can only be described as a setting up of the object inside the ego, as it occurs in melancholia; the exact nature of this substitution is as yet unknown to us. It may be that by this introjection, which is a kind of regression to the mechanism of the oral phase, the ego makes it easier for the object to be given up or renders that process possible. It may be that this identification is the sole condition under which the id can give up its objects. At any rate the process, especially in the early phases of development, is a very frequent one, and it makes it possible to suppose that the character of the ego is a precipitate of abandoned object-cathexes and that it contains the history of those object-choices. It must, of course, be admitted from the outset that there are varying degrees of capacity for resistance, which decide the extent to which a person's character fends off or accepts the influences of the history of his erotic object-choices. In women who have had many experiences in love there seems to be no difficulty in finding vestiges of their object-cathexes in the traits of their character. We must also take into consideration cases of simultaneous object-cathexis and identification – cases, that is, in which the alteration in character occurs before the object has been given up. In such cases the alteration in character has been able to survive the object-relation and in a certain sense to conserve it.

[1] [Cf. Chapter VII of *Group Psychology* (1921c).]

[2] An interesting parallel to the replacement of object-choice by identification is to be found in the belief of primitive peoples, and in the prohibitions based upon it, that the attributes of animals which are incorporated as nourishment persist as part of the character of those who eat them. As is well known, this belief is one of the roots of cannibalism and its effects have continued through the series of usages of the totem meal down to Holy Communion. [Cf. *Totem and Taboo* (1912–13).] The consequences ascribed by this belief to oral mastery of the object do in fact follow in the case of the later sexual object-choice.

From another point of view it may be said that this transformation of an erotic object-choice into an alteration of the ego is also a method by which the ego can obtain control over the id and deepen its relations with it – at the cost, it is true, of acquiescing to a large extent in the id's experiences. When the ego assumes the features of the object, it is forcing itself, so to speak, upon the id as a love-object and is trying to make good the id's loss by saying: 'Look, you can love me too – I am so like the object.'

The transformation of object-libido into narcissistic libido which thus takes place obviously implies an abandonment of sexual aims, a desexualization – a kind of sublimation, therefore. Indeed, the question arises, and deserves careful consideration, whether this is not the universal road to sublimation, whether all sublimation does not take place through the mediation of the ego, which begins by changing sexual object-libido into narcissistic libido and then, perhaps, goes on to give it another aim.[1] We shall later on have to consider whether other instinctual vicissitudes may not also result from this transformation, whether, for instance, it may not bring about a defusion of the various instincts that are fused together.[2]

Although it is a digression from our aim, we cannot avoid giving our attention for a moment longer to the ego's object-identifications. If they obtain the upper hand and become too numerous, unduly powerful and incompatible with one another, a pathological outcome will not be far off. It may come to a disruption of the ego in consequence of the different identifications becoming cut off from one another by resistances; perhaps the secret of the cases of what is described as 'multiple personality' is that the different identifications seize hold of consciousness in turn. Even when things do not go so far as this, there remains the question of conflicts between the various identifications into which the ego comes apart, conflicts which cannot after all be described as entirely pathological.

But, whatever the character's later capacity for resisting the influences of abandoned object-cathexes may turn out to be, the effects of the first identifications made in earliest childhood will be general and lasting. This leads us back to the origin of the ego ideal; for behind

---

[1] Now that we have distinguished between the ego and the id, we must recognize the id as the great reservoir of libido indicated in my paper on narcissism (1914c). The libido which flows into the ego owing to the identifications described above brings about its 'secondary narcissism'.

[2] [Freud returns to the subject of this paragraph in Sections IV and V below.]

it there lies hidden an individual's first and most important identification, his identification with the father in his own personal prehistory.[1] This is apparently not in the first instance the consequence or outcome of an object-cathexis; it is a direct and immediate identification and takes place earlier than any object-cathexis.[2] But the object-choices belonging to the first sexual period and relating to the father and mother seem normally to find their outcome in an identification of this kind, and would thus reinforce the primary one.

The whole subject, however, is so complicated that it will be necessary to go into it in greater detail. The intricacy of the problem is due to two factors: the triangular character of the Oedipus situation and the constitutional bisexuality of each individual.

In its simplified form the case of a male child may be described as follows. At a very early age the little boy develops an object-cathexis for his mother, which originally related to the mother's breast and is the prototype of an object-choice on the anaclitic model;[3] the boy deals with his father by identifying himself with him. For a time these two relationships proceed side by side, until the boy's sexual wishes in regard to his mother become more intense and his father is perceived as an obstacle to them; from this the Oedipus complex originates.[4] His identification with his father then takes on a hostile colouring and changes into a wish to get rid of his father in order to take his place with his mother. Henceforward his relation to his father is ambivalent; it seems as if the ambivalence inherent in the identification from the beginning had become manifest. An ambivalent attitude to his father and an object-relation of a solely affectionate kind to his mother make up the content of the simple positive Oedipus complex in a boy.

Along with the demolition of the Oedipus complex, the boy's object-cathexis of his mother must be given up. Its place may be filled by one of two things: either an identification with his mother or an intensification of his identification with his father. We are accustomed to regard the latter outcome as the more normal; it permits the

[1] Perhaps it would be safer to say 'with the parents'; for before a child has arrived at definite knowledge of the difference between the sexes, the lack of a penis, it does not distinguish in value between its father and its mother. I recently came across the instance of a young married woman whose story showed that, after noticing the lack of a penis in herself, she had supposed it to be absent not in all women, but only in those whom she regarded as inferior, and had still supposed that her mother possessed one. In order to simplify my presentation I shall discuss only identification with the father.

[2] [See the beginning of Chapter VII of *Group Psychology* (1921c).]

[3] [See the paper on narcissism (1914c), *Standard Ed.*, **14**, 87 ff.; *P.F.L.*, **11**, 81 ff.]

[4] Cf. *Group Psychology* (1921c), loc. cit.

affectionate relation to the mother to be in a measure retained. In this way the dissolution of the Oedipus complex[1] would consolidate the masculinity in a boy's character. In a precisely analogous way,[2] the outcome of the Oedipus attitude in a little girl may be an intensification of her identification with her mother (or the setting up of such an identification for the first time) – a result which will fix the child's feminine character.

These identifications are not what we should have expected [from the previous account (p. 453)], since they do not introduce the abandoned object into the ego; but this alternative outcome may also occur, and is easier to observe in girls than in boys. Analysis very often shows that a little girl, after she has had to relinquish her father as a love-object, will bring her masculinity into prominence and identify herself with her father (that is, with the object which has been lost), instead of with her mother. This will clearly depend on whether the masculinity in her disposition – whatever that may consist in – is strong enough.

It would appear, therefore, that in both sexes the relative strength of the masculine and feminine sexual dispositions is what determines whether the outcome of the Oedipus situation shall be an identification with the father or with the mother. This is one of the ways in which bisexuality takes a hand in the subsequent vicissitudes of the Oedipus complex. The other way is even more important. For one gets an impression that the simple Oedipus complex is by no means its commonest form, but rather represents a simplification or schematization which, to be sure, is often enough justified for practical purposes. Closer study usually discloses the more complete Oedipus complex, which is twofold, positive and negative, and is due to the bisexuality originally present in children: that is to say, a boy has not merely an ambivalent attitude towards his father and an affectionate object-choice towards his mother, but at the same time he also behaves like a girl and displays an affectionate feminine attitude to his father and a corresponding jealousy and hostility towards his mother. It is this complicating element introduced by bisexuality that makes it so difficult to obtain a clear view of the facts in connection with the

[1] [Cf. the paper bearing this title (1924d) in Chapter 5 above.]
[2] [The idea that the outcome of the Oedipus complex was 'precisely analogous' in girls and boys was abandoned by Freud not long after this. See 'Some Psychical Consequences of the Anatomical Distinction between the Sexes' (1925j), in Chapter 5 above.]

earliest object-choices and identifications, and still more difficult to describe them intelligibly. It may even be that the ambivalence displayed in the relations to the parents should be attributed entirely to bisexuality and that it is not, as I have represented above, developed out of identification in consequence of rivalry.[1]

In my opinion it is advisable in general, and quite especially where neurotics are concerned, to assume the existence of the complete Oedipus complex. Analytic experience then shows that in a number of cases one or the other constituent disappears, except for barely distinguishable traces; so that the result is a series with the normal positive Oedipus complex at one end and the inverted negative one at the other, while its intermediate members exhibit the complete form with one or other of its two components preponderating. At the dissolution of the Oedipus complex the four trends of which it consists will group themselves in such a way as to produce a father-identification and a mother-identification. The father-identification will preserve the object-relation to the mother which belonged to the positive complex and will at the same time replace the object-relation to the father which belonged to the inverted complex: and the same will be true, *mutatis mutandis*, of the mother-identification. The relative intensity of the two identifications in any individual will reflect the preponderance in him of one or other of the two sexual dispositions.

The broad general outcome of the sexual phase dominated by the Oedipus complex may, therefore, be taken to be the forming of a precipitate in the ego, consisting of these two identifications in some way united with each other. This modification of the ego retains its special position; it confronts the other contents of the ego as an ego ideal or super-ego.

The super-ego is, however, not simply a residue of the earliest object-choices of the id; it also represents an energetic reaction-formation against those choices. Its relation to the ego is not exhausted by the precept: 'You *ought to be* like this (like your father).' It also comprises the prohibition: 'You *may not be* like this (like your father) – that is, you may not do all that he does; some things are his prerogative.' This double aspect of the ego ideal derives from the fact that the ego ideal had the task of repressing the Oedipus complex;

[1] [Freud's belief in the importance of bisexuality went back a very long way. Cf. the *Three Essays* (1905*d*), p. 355 above. But still earlier we find a passage in a letter to Fliess (who influenced him greatly on this subject) which seems almost to foreshadow the present paragraph (Freud, 1950*a*, Letter 113, of August 1, 1899): 'Bisexuality! I am sure you are right about it. And I am accustoming myself to regarding every sexual act as an event between four individuals.']

indeed, it is to that revolutionary event that it owes its existence. Clearly the repression of the Oedipus complex was no easy task. The child's parents, and especially his father, were perceived as the obstacle to a realization of his Oedipus wishes; so his infantile ego fortified itself for the carrying out of the repression by erecting this same obstacle within itself. It borrowed strength to do this, so to speak, from the father, and this loan was an extraordinarily momentous act. The super-ego retains the character of the father, while the more powerful the Oedipus complex was and the more rapidly it succumbed to repression (under the influence of authority, religious teaching, schooling and reading), the stricter will be the domination of the super-ego over the ego later on – in the form of conscience or perhaps of an unconscious sense of guilt. I shall presently bring forward a suggestion about the source of its power to dominate in this way – the source, that is, of its compulsive character which manifests itself in the form of a categorical imperative.

If we consider once more the origin of the super-ego as we have described it, we shall recognize that it is the outcome of two highly important factors, one of a biological and the other of a historical nature: namely, the lengthy duration in man of his childhood helplessness and dependence, and the fact of his Oedipus complex, the repression of which we have shown to be connected with the interruption of libidinal development by the latency period and so with the diphasic onset of man's sexual life. According to one psycho-analytic hypothesis,[1] the last-mentioned phenomenon, which seems to be peculiar to man, is a heritage of the cultural development necessitated by the glacial epoch. We see, then, that the differentiation of the super-ego from the ego is no matter of chance; it represents the most important characteristics of the development both of the individual and of the species; indeed, by giving permanent expression to the influence of the parents it perpetuates the existence of the factors to which it owes its origin.

Psycho-analysis has been reproached time after time with ignoring the higher, moral, supra-personal side of human nature. The reproach is doubly unjust, both historically and methodologically. For, in the first place, we have from the very beginning attributed the function of instigating repression to the moral and aesthetic trends in

[1] [The idea was put forward by Ferenczi (1913). Freud seems to accept it rather more definitely near the end of Chapter X of *Inhibitions, Symptoms and Anxiety* (1926d), *Standard Ed.*, **20**, 155; *P.F.L.*, **10**, 314.]

the ego, and secondly, there has been a general refusal to recognize that psycho-analytic research could not, like a philosophical system, produce a complete and ready-made theoretical structure, but had to find its way step by step along the path towards understanding the intricacies of the mind by making an analytic dissection of both normal and abnormal phenomena. So long as we had to concern ourselves with the study of what is repressed in mental life, there was no need for us to share in any agitated apprehensions as to the whereabouts of the higher side of man. But now that we have embarked upon the analysis of the ego we can give an answer to all those whose moral sense has been shocked and who have complained that there must surely be a higher nature in man: 'Very true,' we can say, 'and here we have that higher nature, in this ego ideal or super-ego, the representative of our relation to our parents. When we were little children we knew these higher natures, we admired them and feared them; and later we took them into ourselves.'

The ego ideal is therefore the heir of the Oedipus complex, and thus it is also the expression of the most powerful impulses and most important libidinal vicissitudes of the id. By setting up this ego ideal, the ego has mastered the Oedipus complex and at the same time placed itself in subjection to the id. Whereas the ego is essentially the representative of the external world, of reality, the super-ego stands in contrast to it as the representative of the internal world, of the id. Conflicts between the ego and the ideal will, as we are now prepared to find, ultimately reflect the contrast between what is real and what is psychical, between the external world and the internal world.

Through the forming of the ideal, what biology and the vicissitudes of the human species have created in the id and left behind in it is taken over by the ego and re-experienced in relation to itself as an individual. Owing to the way in which the ego ideal is formed, it has the most abundant links with the phylogenetic acquisition of each individual – his archaic heritage. What has belonged to the lowest part of the mental life of each of us is changed, through the formation of the ideal, into what is highest in the human mind by our scale of values. It would be vain, however, to attempt to localize the ego ideal, even in the sense in which we have localized the ego, or to work it into any of the analogies with the help of which we have tried to picture the relation between the ego and the id.

It is easy to show that the ego ideal answers to everything that is expected of the higher nature of man. As a substitute for a longing for the father, it contains the germ from which all religions have evolved. The self-judgement which declares that the ego falls short of its ideal produces the religious sense of humility to which the believer appeals in his longing. As a child grows up, the role of father is carried on by teachers and others in authority; their injunctions and prohibitions remain powerful in the ego ideal and continue, in the form of conscience, to exercise the moral censorship. The tension between the demands of conscience and the actual performances of the ego is experienced as a sense of guilt. Socil feelings rest on identifications with other people, on the basis of having the same ego ideal.

Religion, morality, and a social sense – the chief elements in the higher side of man[1] – were originally one and the same thing. According to the hypothesis which I put forward in *Totem and Taboo* (1912–13) they were acquired phylogenetically out of the father-complex: religion and moral restraint through the process of mastering the Oedipus complex itself, and social feeling through the necessity for overcoming the rivalry that then remained between the members of the younger generation. The male sex seems to have taken the lead in all these moral acquisitions; and they seem to have then been transmitted to women by cross-inheritance. Even to-day the social feelings arise in the individual as a superstructure built upon impulses of jealous rivalry against his brothers and sisters. Since the hostility cannot be satisfied, an identification with the former rival develops. The study of mild cases of homosexuality confirms the suspicion that in this instance, too, the identification is a substitute for an affectionate object-choice which has taken the place of the aggressive, hostile attitude.[2]

With the mention of phylogenesis, however, fresh problems arise, from which one is tempted to draw cautiously back. But there is no help for it, the attempt must be made – in spite of a fear that it will lay bare the inadequacy of our whole effort. The question is: which was it, the ego of primitive man or his id, that acquired religion and morality in those early days out of the father-complex? If it was his ego, why do we not speak simply of these things being inherited by the ego? If it was the id, how does that agree with the character of the id? Or are we wrong in carrying the differentiation between ego, super ego, and id back into such early times? Or should we not honestly confess that our

---

[1] I am at the moment putting science and art on one side.
[2] Cf. *Group Psychology* (1921*c*) and 'Some Neurotic Mechanisms in Jealousy, Paranoia and Homosexuality' (1922*b*).

whole conception of the processes in the ego is of no help in under-standing phylogenesis and cannot be applied to it?

Let us answer first what is easiest to answer. The differentiation between ego and id must be attributed not only to primitive man but even to much simpler organisms, for it is the inevitable expression of the influence of the external world. The super-ego, according to our hypothesis, actually originated from the experiences that led to totemism. The question whether it was the ego or the id that experienced and acquired these things soon comes to nothing. Reflec-tion at once shows us that no external vicissitudes can be experienced or undergone by the id, except by way of the ego, which is the representative of the external world to the id. Nevertheless it is not possible to speak of direct inheritance in the ego. It is here that the gulf between an actual individual and the concept of a species becomes evident. Moreover, one must not take the difference between ego and id in too hard-and-fast a sense, nor forget that the ego is a specially differentiated part of the id. The experiences of the ego seem at first to be lost for inheritance; but, when they have been repeated often enough and with sufficient strength in many individuals in successive generations, they transform themselves, so to say, into experiences of the id, the impressions of which are preserved by heredity. Thus in the id, which is capable of being inherited, are harboured residues of the existences of countless egos; and, when the ego forms its super-ego out of the id, it may perhaps only be reviving shapes of former egos and be bringing them to resurrection.

The way in which the super-ego came into being explains how it is that the early conflicts of the ego with the object-cathexes of the id can be continued in conflicts with their heir, the super-ego. If the ego has not succeeded in properly mastering the Oedipus complex, the energic cathexis of the latter, springing from the id, will come into operation once more in the reaction-formation of the ego ideal. The abundant communication between the ideal and these *Ucs*. Instinctual impulses solves the puzzle of how it is that the ideal itself can to a great extent remain unconscious and inaccessible to the ego. The struggle which once raged in the deepest strata of the mind, and was not brought to an end by rapid sublimation and identifica-tion, is now continued in a higher region, like the Battle of the Huns in Kaulbach's painting.

IV. THE TWO CLASSES OF INSTINCTS

We have already said that, if the differentiation we have made of the mind into an id, an ego, and a super-ego represents any advance in our knowledge, it ought to enable us to understand more thoroughly the dynamic relations within the mind and to describe them more clearly. We have also already concluded that the ego is especially under the influence of perception, and that, speaking broadly, perceptions may be said to have the same significance for the ego as instincts have for the id. At the same time the ego is subject to the influence of the instincts, too, like the id, of which it is, as we know, only a specially modified part.

I have lately developed a view of the instincts[1] which I shall here hold to and take as the basis of my further discussions. According to this view we have to distinguish two classes of instincts, one of which, the sexual instincts or Eros, is by far the more conspicuous and accessible to study. It comprises not merely the uninhibited sexual instinct proper and the instinctual impulses of an aim-inhibited or sublimated nature derived from it, but also the self-preservative instinct, which must be assigned to the ego and which at the beginning of our analytic work we had good reason for contrasting with the sexual object-instincts. The second class of instincts was not so easy to point to; in the end we came to recognize sadism as its representative. On the basis of theoretical considerations, supported by biology, we put forward the hypothesis of a death instinct, the task of which is to lead organic life back into the inanimate state; on the other hand, we supposed that Eros, by bringing about a more and more far-reaching combination of the particles into which living substance is dispersed, aims at complicating life and at the same time, of course, at preserving it. Acting in this way, both the instincts would be conservative in the strictest sense of the word, since both would be endeavouring to re-establish a state of things that was disturbed by the emergence of life. The emergence of life would thus be the cause of the continuance of life and also at the same time of the striving towards death; and life itself would be a conflict and compromise between these two trends. The problem of the origin of life would remain a cosmological one; and the problem of the goal and purpose of life would be answered dualistically.

---

[1] *Beyond the Pleasure Principle* [(1920g) in Chapter 4 above].

On this view, a special physiological process (of anabolism or catabolism) would be associated with each of the two classes of instincts; both kinds of instinct would be active in every particle of living substance, though in unequal proportions, so that some one substance might be the principal representative of Eros.

This hypothesis throws no light whatever upon the manner in which the two classes of instincts are fused, blended, and alloyed with each other; but that this takes place regularly and very extensively is an assumption indispensable to our conception. It appears that, as a result of the combination of unicellular organisms into multicellular forms of life, the death instinct of the single cell can successfully be neutralized and the destructive impulses be diverted on to the external world through the instrumentality of a special organ. This special organ would seem to be the muscular apparatus; and the death instinct would thus seem to express itself – though probably only in part – as an instinct of destruction directed against the external world and other organisms.

Once we have admitted the idea of a fusion of the two classes of instincts with each other, the possibility of a – more or less complete – 'defusion' of them forces itself upon us. The sadistic component of the sexual instinct would be a classical example of a serviceable instinctual fusion; and the sadism which has made itself independent as a perversion would be typical of a defusion, though not of one carried to extremes. From this point we obtain a view of a great domain of facts which has not before been considered in this light. We perceive that for purposes of discharge the instinct of destruction is habitually brought into the service of Eros; we suspect that the epileptic fit is a product and indication of an instinctual defusion; and we come to understand that instinctual defusion and the marked emergence of the death instinct call for particular consideration among the effects of some severe neuroses – for instance, the obsessional neuroses. Making a swift generalization, we might conjecture that the essence of a regression of libido (e.g. from the genital to the sadistic-anal phase) lies in a defusion of instincts, just as, conversely, the advance from the earlier phase to the definitive genital one would be conditioned by an accession of erotic components. The question also arises whether ordinary ambivalence, which is so often unusually strong in the constitutional disposition to neurosis, should not be regarded as the product of a defusion; ambivalence, however, is such a fundamental phenomenon that it more probably represents an instinctual fusion that has not be completed.

It is natural that we should turn with interest to enquire whether there may not be instructive connections to be traced between the structures we have assumed to exist – the ego, the super-ego and the id – on the one hand and the two classes of instincts on the other; and, further, whether the pleasure principle which dominates mental processes can be shown to have any constant relation both to the two classes of instincts and to these differentiations which we have drawn in the mind. But before we discuss this, we must clear away a doubt which arises concerning the terms in which the problem itself is stated. There is, it is true, no doubt about the pleasure principle, and the differentiation within the ego has good clinical justification; but the distinction between the two classes of instincts does not seem sufficiently assured and it is possible that facts of clinical analysis may be found which will do away with its pretension.

One such fact there appears to be. For the opposition between the two classes of instincts we may put the polarity of love and hate.[1] There is no difficulty in finding a representative of Eros; but we must be grateful that we can find a representative of the elusive death instinct in the instinct of destruction, to which hate points the way. Now, clinical observation shows not only that love is with unexpected regularity accompanied by hate (ambivalence), and not only that in human relationships hate is frequently a forerunner of love, but also that in a number of circumstances hate changes into love and love into hate. If this change is more than a mere succession in time – if, that is, one of them actually turns into the other – then clearly the ground is cut away from under a distinction so fundamental as that between erotic instincts and death instincts, one which presupposes physiological processes running in opposite directions.

Now the case in which someone first loves and then hates the same person (or the reverse) because that person has given him cause for doing so, has obviously nothing to do with our problem. Nor has the other case, in which feelings of love that have not yet become manifest express themselves to begin with by hostility and aggressive tendencies; for it may be that here the destructive component in the object-cathexis has hurried on ahead and is only later on joined by the

---

[1] [For what follows, see the earlier discussion of the relation between love and hate in 'Instincts and their Vicissitudes' (in Chapter 4 above), as well as the later one in Chapters V and VI of *Civilization and its Discontents* (1930a).]

erotic one. But we know of several instances in the psychology of the neuroses in which it is more plausible to suppose that a transformation does take place. In persecutory paranoia the patient fends off an excessively strong homosexual attachment to some particular person in a special way; and as a result this person whom he loved most becomes a persecutor, against whom the patient directs an often dangerous aggressiveness. Here we have a right to interpolate a previous phase which has transformed the love into hate. In the case of the origin of homosexuality, and of desexualized social feelings as well, analytic investigation has only recently taught us to recognize that violent feelings of rivalry are present which lead to aggressive inclinations, and that it is only after these have been surmounted that the formerly hated object becomes the loved one or gives rise to an identification. The question arises whether in these instances we are to assume a direct transformation of hate into love. It is clear that here the changes are purely internal and an alteration in the behaviour of the object plays no part in them.

There is another possible mechanism, however, which we have come to know of by analytic investigation of the processes concerned in the change in paranoia. An ambivalent attitude is present from the outset and the transformation is effected by means of a reactive displacement of cathexis, energy being withdrawn from the erotic impulse and added to the hostile one.

Not quite the same thing but something like it happens when the hostile rivalry leading to homosexuality is overcome. The hostile attitude has no prospect of satisfaction; consequently – for economic reasons, that is – it is replaced by a loving attitude for which there is more prospect of satisfaction – that is, possibility of discharge. So we see that we are not obliged in any of these cases to assume a direct transformation of hate into love, which would be incompatible with the qualitative distinction between the two classes of instincts.

It will be noticed, however, that by introducing this other mechanism of changing love into hate, we have tacitly made another assumption which deserves to be stated explicitly. We have reckoned as though there existed in the mind – whether in the ego or in the id – a displaceable energy, which, indifferent in itself, can be added to a qualitatively differentiated erotic or destructive impulse, and augment its total cathexis. Without assuming the existence of a displaceable energy of this kind we can make no headway. The only question is where it comes from, what it belongs to, and what it signifies.

The problem of the quality of instinctual impulses and of its persistence throughout their various vicissitudes is still very obscure and has hardly.been attacked up to the present. In the sexual component instincts, which are especially accessible to observation, it is possible to perceive a few processes which are in the same category as what we are discussing. We see, for instance, that some degree of communication exists between the component instincts, that an instinct deriving from one particular erotogenic source can make over its intensity to reinforce another component instinct originating from another source, that the satisfaction of on instinct can take the place of the satisfaction of another, and more facts of the same nature – which must encourage us to venture upon certain hypotheses.

In the present discussion, moreover, I am only putting forward a hypothesis; I have no proof to offer. It seems a plausible view that this displaceable and indifferent energy, which is no doubt active in both the ego and id, proceeds from the narcissistic store of libido – that it is desexualized Eros. (The erotic instincts appear to be altogether more plastic, more readily diverted and displaced than the destructive instincts.) From this we can easily go on to assume that this displaceable libido is employed in the service of the pleasure principle to obviate blockages and to facilitate discharge. In this connection it is easy to observe a certain indifference as to the path along which the discharge takes place, so long as it takes place somehow. We know this trait; it is characteristic of the cathectic processes in the id. It is found in erotic cathexes, where a peculiar indifference in regard to the object displays itself; and it is especially evident in the transferences arising in analysis, which develop inevitably, irrespective of the persons who are their object. Not long ago Rank [1913] published some good examples of the way in which neurotic acts of revenge can be directed against the wrong people. Such behaviour on the part of the unconscious reminds one of the comic story of the three village tailors, one of whom had to be hanged because the only village blacksmith had committed a capital offence. Punishment must be exacted even if it does not fall upon the guilty. It was in studying the dream-work that we first came upon this kind of looseness in the displacements brought about by the primary process. In that case it was the objects that were thus relegated to a position of no more than secondary importance, just as in the case we are now discussing it is the paths of discharge. It would be characteristic of the ego to be more particular about the choice both of an object and of a path of discharge.

If this displaceable energy is desexualized libido, it may also be described as *sublimated* energy; for it would still retain the main purpose of Eros – that of uniting and binding – in so far as it helps towards establishing the unity, or tendency to unity, which is particularly characteristic of the ego. If thought-processes in the wider sense are to be included among these displacements, then the activity of thinking is also supplied from the sublimation of erotic motive forces.

Here we arrive again at the possibility which has already been discussed that sublimation may take place regularly through the mediation of the ego. The other case will be recollected, in which the ego deals with the first object-cathexes of the id (and certainly with later ones too) by taking over the libido from them into itself and binding it to the alteration of the ego produced by means of identification. The transformation [of erotic libido] into ego-libido of course involves an abandonment of sexual aims, a desexualization. In any case this throws light upon an important function of the ego in its relation to Eros. By thus getting hold of the libido from the object-cathexes, setting itself up as sole love-object, and desexualizing or sublimating the libido of the id, the ego is working in opposition to the purposes of Eros and placing itself at the service of the opposing instinctual impulses. It has to acquiesce in some of the other object-cathexes of the id; it has, so to speak, to participate in them. We shall come back later to another possible consequence of this activity of the ego.

This would seem to imply an important amplification of the theory of narcissism. At the very beginning, all the libido is accumulated in the id, while the ego is still in process of formation or is still feeble. The id sends part of this libido out into erotic object-cathexes, whereupon the ego, now grown stronger, tries to get hold of this object-libido and to force itself on the id as a love-object. The narcissism of the ego is thus a secondary one, which has been withdrawn from objects.[1]

Over and over again we find, when we are able to trace instinctual impulses back, that they reveal themselves as derivatives of Eros. If it were not for the considerations put forward in *Beyond the Pleasure Principle*, and ultimately for the sadistic constituents which have attached themselves to Eros, we should have difficulty in holding to

[1] [See Appendix B below for a discussion of this.]

our fundamental dualistic point of view.[1] But since we cannot escape that view, we are driven to conclude that the death instincts are by their nature mute and that the clamour of life proceeds for the most part from Eros.[2]

And from the struggle against Eros! It can hardly be doubted that the pleasure principle serves the id as a compass in its struggle against the libido – the force that introduces disturbances into the process of life. If it is true that Fechner's principle of constancy[3] governs life, which thus consists of a continuous descent towards death, it is the claims of Eros, of the sexual instincts, which, in the form of instinctual needs, hold up the falling level and introduce fresh tensions. The id, guided by the pleasure principle – that is, by the perception of unpleasure – fends off these tensions in various ways. It does so in the first place by complying as swiftly as possible with the demands of the non-desexualized libido – by striving for the satisfaction of the directly sexual trends. But it does so in a far more comprehensive fashion in relation to one particular form of satisfaction in which all component demands converge – by discharge of the sexual substances, which are saturated vehicles, so to speak, of the eortic tensions.[4] The ejection of the sexual substances in the sexual act corresponds in a sense to the separation of soma and germ-plasm. This accounts for the likeness of the condition that follows complete sexual satisfaction to dying, and for the fact that death coincides with the act of copulation in some of the lower animals. These creatures die in the act of reproduction because, after Eros has been eliminated through the process of satisfaction, the death instinct has a free hand for accomplishing its purposes. Finally, as we have seen, the ego, by sublimating some of the libido for itself and its purposes, assists the id in its work of mastering the tensions.

V. THE DEPENDENT RELATIONSHIPS OF THE EGO

The complexity of our subject-matter must be an excuse for the fact that none of the chapter-headings of this book quite correspond to

[1] [The consistency with which Freud held to a dualistic classification of the instincts will be seen from his long footnote at the end of Section VI of *Beyond the Pleasure Principle* in Chapter 4 above.]

[2] In fact, on our view it is through the agency of Eros that the destructive instincts that are directed towards the external world have been diverted from the self.

[3] [Cf. pp. 219–20 above.]

[4] [Freud's views on the part played by the 'sexual substances' will be found in Section 2 of the third of his *Three Essays* (1905d), in Chapter 5 above.]

their contents, and that in turning to new aspects of the topic we are constantly harking back to matters that have already been dealt with.

Thus we have said repeatedly that the ego is formed to a great extent out of identifications which take the place of abandoned cathexes by the id; that the first of these identifications always behave as a special agency in the ego and stand apart from the ego in the form of a super-ego, while later on, as it grows stronger, the ego may become more resistant to the influences of such identifications. The super-ego owes its special position in the ego, or in relation to the ego, to a factor which must be considered from two sides: on the one hand it was the first identification and one which took place while the ego was still feeble, and on the other hand it is the heir to the Oedipus complex and has thus introduced the most momentous objects into the ego. The super-ego's relation to the later alterations of the ego is roughly similar to that of the primary sexual phase of childhood to later sexual life after puberty. Although it is accessible to all later influences, it nevertheless preserves throughout life the character given to it by its derivation from the father-complex – namely, the capacity to stand apart from the ego and to master it. It is a memorial of the former weakness and dependence of the ego, and the mature ego remains subject to its domination. As the child was once under a compulsion to obey its parents, so the ego submits to the categorical imperative of its super-ego.

But the derivation of the super-ego from the first object-cathexes of the id, from the Oedipus complex, signifies even more for it. This derivation, as we have already shown, brings it into relation with the phylogenetic acquisitions of the id and makes it a reincarnation of former ego-structures which have left their precipitates behind in the id. Thus the super-ego is always close to the id and can act as its representative *vis-à-vis* the ego. It reaches deep down into the id and for that reason is farther from consciousness than the ego is.[1]

We shall best appreciate these relations by turning to certain clinical facts, which have long since lost their novelty but which still await theoretical discussion.

There are certain people who behave in a quite peculiar fashion during the work of analysis. When one speaks hopefully to them or expresses satisfaction with the progress of the treatment, they show

[1] It may be said that the psycho-analytic or metapsychological ego stands on its head no less than the anatomical ego – the 'cortical homunculus'.

signs of discontent and their condition invariably becomes worse. One begins by regarding this as defiance and as an attempt to prove their superiority to the physician, but later one comes to take a deeper and juster view. One becomes convinced, not only that such people cannot endure any praise or appreciation, but that they react inversely to the progress of the treatment. Every partial solution that ought to result, and in other people does result, in an improvement or a temporary suspension of symptoms produces in them for the time being an exacerbation of their illness; they get worse during the treatment instead of getting better. They exhibit what is known as a 'negative therapeutic reaction'.

There is no doubt that there is something in these people that sets itself against their recovery, and its approach is dreaded as though it were a danger. We are accustomed to say that the need for illness has got the upper hand in them over the desire for recovery. If we analyse this resistance in the usual way – then, even after allowance has been made for an attitude of defiance towards the physician and for fixation to the various forms of gain from illness, the greater part of it is still left over; and this reveals itself as the most powerful of all obstacles to recovery, more powerful than the familiar ones of narcissistic inaccessibility, a negative attitude towards the physician and clinging to the gain from illness.

In the end we come to see that we are dealing with what may be called a 'moral' factor, a sense of guilt, which is finding its satisfaction in the illness and refuses to give up the punishment of suffering. We shall be right in regarding this disheartening explanation as final. But as far as the patient is concerned this sense of guilt is dumb; it does not tell him he is guilty; he does not feel guilty, he feels ill. This sense of guilt expresses itself only as a resistance to recovery which it is extremely difficult to overcome. It is also particularly difficult to convince the patient that this motive lies behind his continuing to be ill; he holds fast to the more obvious explanation that treatment by analysis is not the right remedy for his case.[1]

---

[1] The battle with the obstacle of an unconscious sense of guilt is not made easy for the analyst. Nothing can be done against it directly, and nothing indirectly but the slow procedure of unmasking its unconscious repressed roots, and of thus gradually changing it into a *conscious* sense of guilt. One has a special opportunity for influencing it when this *Ucs.* sense of guilt is a 'borrowed' one – when it is the product of an identification with some other person who was once the object of an erotic cathexis. A sense of guilt that has been adopted in this way is often the sole remaining trace of the

The description we have given applies to the most extreme instances of this state of affairs, but in a lesser measure this factor has to be reckoned with in very many cases, perhaps in all comparatively severe cases of neurosis. In fact it may be precisely this element in the situation, the attitude of the ego ideal, that determines the severity of a neurotic illness. We shall not hesitate, therefore, to discuss rather more fully the way in which the sense of guilt expresses itself under different conditions.

An interpretation of the normal, conscious sense of guilt (conscience) presents no difficulties; it is based on the tension between the ego and the ego ideal and is the expression of a condemnation of the ego by its critical agency. The feelings of inferiority so well known in neurotics are presumably not far removed from it. In two very familiar maladies the sense of guilt is over-strongly conscious; in them the ego ideal displays particular severity and often rages against the ego in a cruel fashion. The attitude of the ego ideal in these two conditions, obsessional neurosis and melancholia, presents, alongside of this similarity, differences that are no less significant.

In certain forms of obsessional neurosis the sense of guilt is over-noisy but cannot justify itself to the ego. Consequently the patient's ego rebels against the imputation of guilt and seeks the physician's support in repudiating it. It would be folly to acquiesce in this, for to do so would have no effect. Analysis eventually shows that the super-ego is being influenced by processes that have remained unknown to the ego. It is possible to discover the repressed impulses which are really at the bottom of the sense of guilt. Thus in this case the super-ego knew more than the ego about the unconscious id.

---

abandoned love-relation and not at all easy to recognize as such. (The likeness between this process and what happens in melancholia is unmistakable.) If one can unmask this former object-cathexis behind the *Ucs.* sense of guilt, the therapeutic success is often brilliant, but otherwise the outcome of one's efforts is by no means certain. It depends principally on the intensity of the sense of guilt; there is often no counteracting force of a similar order of strength which the treatment can oppose to it. Perhaps it may depend, too, on whether the personality of the analyst allows of the patient's putting him in the place of his ego ideal, and this involves a temptation for the analyst to play the part of prophet, saviour and redeemer to the patient. Since the rules of analysis are diametrically opposed to the physician's making use of his personality in any such manner, it must be honestly confessed that here we have another limitation to the effectiveness of analysis; after all, analysis does not set out to make pathological reactions impossible, but to give the patient's ego *freedom* to decide one way or the other. – [Freud returned to this topic in his paper on 'The Economic Problem of Masochism' (1924c), where he discussed the distinction between the unconscious sense of guilt and moral masochism. See also Chapters VII and VIII of *Civilization and its Discontents* (1930a).]

In melancholia the impression that the super-ego has obtained a hold upon consciousness is even stronger. But here the ego ventures no objection; it admits its guilt and submits to the punishment. We understand the difference. In obsessional neurosis what were in question were objectionable impulses which remained outside the ego, while in melancholia the object to which the super-ego's wrath applies has been taken into the ego through identification.

It is certainly not clear why the sense of guilt reaches such an extraordinary strength in these two neurotic disorders; but the main problem presented in this state of affairs lies in another direction. We shall postpone discussion of it until we have dealt with the other cases in which the sense of guilt remains unconscious.

It is essentially in hysteria and in states of a hysterical type that this is found. Here the mechanism by which the sense of guilt remains unconscious is easy to discover. The hysterical ego fends off a distressing perception with which the criticisms of its super-ego threaten it, in the same way in which it is in the habit of fending off an unendurable object-cathexis – by an act of repression. It is the ego, therefore, that is responsible for the sense of guilt remaining unconscious. We know that as a rule the ego carries out repressions in the service and at the behest of its super-ego; but this is a case in which it has turned the same weapon against its harsh taskmaster. In obsessional neurosis, as we know, the phenomena of reaction-formation predominate; but here [in hysteria] the ego succeeds only in keeping at a distance the material to which the sense of guilt refers.

One may go further and venture the hypothesis that a great part of the sense of guilt must normally remain unconscious, because the origin of conscience is intimately connected with the Oedipus complex, which belongs to the unconscious. If anyone were inclined to put forward the paradoxical proposition that the normal man is not only far more immoral than he believes but also far more moral than he knows, psycho-analysis, on whose findings the first half of the assertion rests, would have no objection to raise against the second half.[1]

It was a surprise to find that an increase in this *Ucs.* sense of guilt can turn people into criminals. But it is undoubtedly a fact. In many criminals, especially youthful ones, it is possible to detect a very powerful sense of guilt which existed before the crime, and is therefore

---

[1] This proposition is only apparently a paradox; it simply states that human nature has a far greater extent, both for good and for evil, than it thinks it has – i.e. than its ego is aware of through conscious perception.

not its result but its motive. It is as if it was a relief to be able to fasten this unconscious sense of guilt on to something real and immediate.[1]

In all these situations the super-ego displays its independence of the conscious ego and its intimate relations with the unconscious id. Having regard, now, to the importance we have ascribed to preconscious verbal residues in the ego, the question arises whether it can be the case that the super-ego, in so far as it is *Ucs.*, consists in such word-presentations and, if it does not, what else it consists in. Our tentative answer will be that it is as impossible for the super-ego as for the ego to disclaim its origin from things heard; for it is a part of the ego and remains accessible to consciousness by way of these word-presentations (concepts, abstractions). But the *cathectic energy* does not reach these contents of the super-ego from auditory perception (instruction or reading) but from sources in the id.

The question which we put off answering [see p. 472] runs as follows: How is it that the super-ego manifests itself essentially as a sense of guilt (or rather, as criticism – for the sense of guilt is the perception in the ego answering to this criticism) and moreover develops such extraordinary harshness and severity towards the ego? If we turn to melancholia first, we find that the excessively strong super-ego which has obtained a hold upon consciousness rages against the ego with merciless violence, as if it had taken possession of the whole of the sadism available in the person concerned. Following our view of sadism, we should say that the destructive component had entrenched itself in the super-ego and turned against the ego. What is now holding sway in the super-ego is, as it were, a pure culture of the death instinct, and in fact it often enough succeeds in driving the ego into death, if the latter does not fend off its tyrant in time by the change round into mania.

The reproaches of conscience in certain forms of obsessional neurosis are as distressing and tormenting, but here the situation is less perspicuous. It is noteworthy that the obsessional neurotic, in contrast to the malancholic, never in fact takes the step of self-destruction; it is as though he were immune against the danger of suicide, and he is far better protected from it than the hysteric. We can see that what guarantees the safety of the ego is the fact that the object has been retained. In obsessional neurosis it has become possible, through a regression to the pregenital organization, for the love-

---

[1] [This is discussed more fully in Freud's paper on 'Some Character-Types' (1916*d*).]

impulses to transform themselves into impulses of aggression against the object. Here again the instinct of destruction has been set free and it seeks to destroy the object, or at least it appears to have that intention. These purposes have not been adopted by the ego and it struggles against them with reaction-formations and precautionary measures; they remain in the id. The super-ego, however, behaves as if the ego were responsible for them and shows at the same time by the seriousness with which it chastises these destructive intentions that they are no mere semblance evoked by regression but an actual substitution of hate for love. Helpless in both directions, the ego defends itself vainly, alike against the instigations of the murderous id and against the reproaches of the punishing conscience. It succeeds in holding in check at least the most brutal actions of both sides; the first outcome is interminable self-torment, and eventually there follows a systematic torturing of the object, in so far as it is within reach.

The dangerous death instincts are dealt with in the individual in various ways: in part they are rendered harmless by being fused with erotic components, in part they are diverted towards the external world in the form of aggression, while to a large extent they un-doubtedly continue their internal work unhindered. How is it then that in melancholia the super-ego can become a kind of gathering-place for the death instincts?

From the point of view of instinctual control, of morality, it may be said of the id that it is totally non-moral, of the ego that it strives to be moral, and of the super-ego that it can be super-moral and then become as cruel as only the id can be. It is remarkable that the more a man checks his aggressiveness towards the exterior the more severe – that is aggressive – he becomes in his ego ideal. The ordinary view sees the situation the other way round: the standard set up by the ego ideal seems to be the motive for the suppression of aggressiveness. The fact remains, however, as we have stated it: the more a man controls his aggressiveness, the more intense becomes his ideal's inclination to aggressiveness against his ego.[1] It is like a displacement, a turning round upon his own ego. But even ordinary normal morality has a harshly restraining, cruelly prohibiting quality. It is from this, in-deed, that the conception arises of a higher being who deals out punishment inexorably.

[1] [Freud returned to this paradox in Chapter VII of *Civilization and its Discontents* (1930a), *Standard Ed.*, **21**, 123 f.; *P.F.L.*, **12**, 315 f.]

I cannot go further in my consideration of these questions without introducing a fresh hypothesis. The super-ego arises, as we know, from an identification with the father taken as a model. Every such identification is in the nature of a desexualization or even of a sublimation. It now seems as though when a transformation of this kind takes place, an instinctual defusion occurs at the same time. After sublimation the erotic component no longer has the power to bind the whole of the destructiveness that was combined with it, and this is released in the form of an inclination to aggression and destruction. This defusion would be the source of the general character of harshness and cruelty exhibited by the ideal – its dictatorial 'Thou shalt'.

Let us again consider obsessional neurosis for a moment. The state of affairs is different here. The defusion of love into aggressiveness has not been effected by the work of the ego, but is the result of a regression which has come about in the id. But this process has extended beyond the id to the super-ego, which now increases its severity towards the innocent ego. It would seem, however, that in this case, no less than in that of melancholia, the ego, having gained control over the libido by means of identification, is punished for doing so by the super-ego through the instrumentality of the aggressiveness which was mixed with the libido.

Our ideas about the ego are beginning to clear, and its various relationships are gaining distinctness. We now see the ego in its strength and in its weaknesses. It is entrusted with important functions. By virtue of its relation to the perceptual system it gives mental processes an order in time and submits them to 'reality-testing'.[1] By interposing the processes of thinking, it secures a postponement of motor discharges and controls the access to motility.[2] This last power is, to be sure, a question more of form than of fact; in the matter of action the ego's position is like that of a constitutional monarch, without whose sanction no law can be passed but who hesitates long before imposing his veto on any measure put forward by Parliament. All the experiences of life that originate from without enrich the ego; the id, however, is its second external world, which it strives to bring into subjection to itself. It withdraws libido from the id and transforms the object-cathexes of the id into ego-structures. With the aid of

[1] [Cf. 'The Unconscious', p. 161 above.]
[2] [Cf. 'Formulations on the Two Principles of Mental Functioning', in Chapter 7 below.]

the super-ego, in a manner that is still obscure to us, it draws upon the experiences of past ages stored in the id.

There are two paths by which the contents of the id can penetrate into the ego. The one is direct, the other leads by way of the ego ideal; which of these two paths they take may, for some mental activities, be of decisive importance. The ego develops from perceiving instincts of controlling them, from obeying instincts to inhibiting them. In this achievement a large share is taken by the ego ideal, which indeed is partly a reaction-formation against the instinctual processes of the id. Psycho-analysis is an instrument to enable the ego to achieve a progressive conquest of the id.

From the other point of view, however, we see this same ego as a poor creature owing service to three masters and consequently menaced by three dangers: from the external world, from the libido of the id, and from the severity of the super-ego. Three kinds of anxiety correspond to these three dangers, since anxiety is the expression of a retreat from danger. As a frontier-creature, the ego tries to mediate between the world and the id, to make the id pliable to the world and, by means of its muscular activity, to make the world fall in with the wishes of the id. In point of fact it behaves like the physician during an analytic treatment: it offers itself, with the attention it pays to the real world, as a libidinal object to the id, and aims at attaching the id's libido to itself. It is not only a helper to the id; it is also a submissive slave who courts his master's love. Whenever possible, it tries to remain on good terms with the id; it clothes the id's *Ucs.* commands with its *Pcs.* rationalizations; it pretends that the id is showing obedience to the admonitions of reality, even when in fact it is remaining obstinate and unyielding; it disguises the id's conflicts with reality and, if possible, its conflicts with the super-ego too. In its position midway between the id and reality, it only too often yields to the temptation to become sycophantic, opportunist and lying, like a politician who sees the truth but wants to keep his place in popular favour.

Towards the two classes of instincts the ego's attitude is not impartial. Through its work of identification and sublimation it gives the death instincts in the id assistance in gaining control over the libido, but in so doing it runs the risk of becoming the object of the death instincts and of itself perishing. In order to be able to help in this way it has had itself to become filled with libido; it thus itself becomes the representative of Eros and thenceforward desires to live and to be loved.

But since the ego's work of sublimation results in a defusion of the instincts and a liberation of the aggressive instincts in the super-ego, its struggle against the libido exposes it to the danger of maltreatment and death. In suffering under the attacks of the super-ego or perhaps even succumbing to them, the ego is meeting with a fate like that of the protista which are destroyed by the products of decomposition that they themselves have created. From the economic point of view the morality that functions in the super-ego seems to be a similar product of decomposition.

Among the dependent relationships in which the ego stands, that to the super-ego is perhaps the most interesting.

The ego is the actual seat of anxiety.[1] Threatened by dangers from three directions, it develops the flight-reflex by withdrawing its own cathexis from the menacing perception or from the similarly regarded process in the id, and emitting it as anxiety. This primitive reaction is later replaced by the carrying-out of protective cathexes (the mechanism of the phobias). What it is that the ego fears from the external and from the libidinal dangers cannot be specified; we know that the fear is of being overwhelmed or annihilated, but it cannot be grasped analytically. The ego is simply obeying the warning of the pleasure principle. On the other hand, we can tell what is hidden behind the ego's dread of the super-ego, the fear of conscience. The superior being, which turned into the ego ideal, once threatened castration, and this dread of castration is probably the nucleus round which the subsequent fear of conscience has gathered; it is this dread that persists as the ear of conscience.

The high-sounding phrase, 'every fear is ultimately the fear of death', has hardly any meaning, and at any rate cannot be justified. [Cf. Stekel (1908, 5).] It seems to me, on the contrary, perfectly correct to distinguish the fear of death from dread of an object (realistic anxiety) and from neurotic libidinal anxiety. It presents a difficult problem to psycho-analysis, for death is an abstract concept with a negative content for which no unconscious correlative can be found. It would seem that the mechanism of the fear of death can only be that the ego relinquishes its narcissistic libidinal cathexis in a very large measure – that is, that it gives up itself, just as it gives up some *external* object in other cases in which it feels anxiety. I believe that the

[1] [What follows on the subject of anxiety must be read in connection with Freud's revised views as stated in *Inhibitions, Symptoms and Anxiety* (1926*d*), where most of the points raised here are further discussed.]

fear of death is something that occurs between the ego and the super-ego.

We know that the fear of death makes its appearance under two conditions (which, moreover, are entirely analogous to situations in which other kinds of anxiety develop), namely, as a reaction to an external danger and as an internal process, as for instance in melancholia. Once again a neurotic manifestation may help us to understand a normal one.

The fear of death in melancholia only admits of one explanation: that the ego gives itself up because it feels itself hated and persecuted by the super-ego, instead of loved. To the ego, therefore, living means the same as being loved – being loved by the super-ego, which here again appears as the representative of the id. The super-ego fulfils the same function of protecting and saving that was fulfilled in earlier days by the father and later by Providence or Destiny. But, when the ego finds itself in an excessive real danger which it believes itself unable to overcome by its own strength, it is bound to draw the same conclusion. It sees itself deserted by all protecting forces and lets itself die. Here, moreover, is once again the same situation as that which underlay the first great anxiety-state of birth and the infantile anxiety of longing – the anxiety due to separation from the protecting mother.[1]

These considerations make it possible to regard the fear of death, like the fear of conscience, as a development of the fear of castration. The great significance which the sense of guilt has in the neuroses makes it conceivable that common neurotic anxiety is reinforced in severe cases by the generating of anxiety between the ego and the super-ego (fear of castration, of conscience, of death).

The id, to which we finally come back, has no means of showing the ego either love or hate. It cannot say what it wants; it has achieved no unified will. Eros and the death instinct struggle within it; we have seen with what weapons the one group of instincts defends itself against the other. It would be possible to picture the id as under the domination of the mute but powerful death instincts, which desire to be at peace and (prompted by the pleasure principle) to put Eros, the mischief-maker, to rest; but perhaps that might be to undervalue the part played by Eros.

---

[1] [This foreshadows the 'separation anxiety' discussed in *Inhibitions, Symptoms and Anxiety* (1926d) *Standard Ed.*, **20**, 85–6, 151; *P.F.L.*, **10**, 234–6, 309.]

APPENDIX A

The Descriptive and the Dynamic Unconscious

A curious point arises out of two sentences which appear on pp. 441–2 above. The Editor's attention was drawn to it in a private communication from Dr Ernest Jones, who had come across it in the course of examining Freud's correspondence.

On October 28, 1923, a few months after this work appeared, Ferenczi wrote to Freud in these terms: '. . . Nevertheless I venture to put a question to you . . . since there is a passage in *The Ego and the Id* which, without your solution, I do not understand . . . On p. 13[1] I find the following: ". . . that in the descriptive sense there are two kinds of unconscious, but in the dynamic sense only one." Since, however, you write on p. 12 that the latent unconscious is unconscious only descriptively, not in the dynamic sense, I had thought that it was precisely the dynamic line of approach that called for the hypothesis of there being two sorts of *Ucs.*, while description knows only *Cs.* and *Ucs.*'

On inspection, however, the two statements do not contradict each other: the fact that the latent unconscious is only descriptively unconscious does not in the least imply that it is the only thing that is descriptively unconscious.

There is, indeed, a passage in Lecture 31 of Freud's *New Introductory Lectures* (1933a),[2] written some ten years later than the present work, in which the whole of this argument is repeated in very similar terms. In that passage it is explained more than once that in the descriptive sense both the preconscious and the repressed are unconscious, but that in the dynamic sense the term is restricted to the repressed.

It seems likely that on reflection Freud realized that Ferenczi's discovery was a mare's nest, for the passage was never altered in the later editions of the book.

---

[1] Of the German edition.
[2] [See the next paper.]

APPENDIX B

APPENDIX B
The Great Reservoir of Libido

There is considerable difficulty over this matter, which is mentioned on p. 454 *n.* 1 and discussed at greater length on p. 467.

The analogy seems to have made its first appearance in a new section added to the third edition of the *Three Essays* (1905*d*), which was published in 1915 but had been prepared by Freud in the autumn of 1914. The passage runs as follows (*Standard Ed.*, **7**, 218): 'Narcissistic or ego libido seems to be the great reservoir from which the object-cathexes are sent out and into which they are withdrawn once more; the narcissistic libidinal cathexis of the ego is the original state of things, realized in earliest childhood, and is merely covered by the later extrusions of libido, but in essentials persists behind them.'

The same notion had, however, been expressed earlier in another favourite analogy of Freud's, which appears sometimes as an alternative and sometimes alongside the 'great reservoir'. This earlier passage is in the paper on narcissism itself (1914*c*), which was written by Freud in the early part of the same year, 1914 (*Standard Ed.*, **14**, 75): 'Thus we form the idea of there being an original libidinal cathexis of the ego, from which some is later given off to objects, but which fundamentally persists and is related to the object-cathexis much as the body of an amoeba is related to the pseudopodia which it puts out.'

The two analogies appear together in a semi-popular paper written at the end of 1916 for a Hungarian periodical ('A Difficulty in the Path of Psycho-Analysis', 1917*a*, *Standard Ed.*, **17**, 139): 'The ego is a great reservoir from which the libido that is destined for objects flows out and into which it flows back from those objects . . . As an illustration of this state of things we may think of an amoeba, whose viscous substance puts out pseudopodia . . .'

The amoeba appears once more in Lecture 26 of the *Introductory Lectures* (1916–17), dating from 1917, and the reservoir in *Beyond the Pleasure Principle* (1920*g*), *Standard Ed.*, **18**, 51: 'Psycho-analysis . . . came to the conclusion that the ego is the true and original reservoir of libido, and that it is only from that reservoir that libido is extended on to objects.'

Freud included a very similar passage in an encyclopaedia article which he wrote in the summer of 1922 (1923*a*, *Standard Ed.*, **18**, 257), and then almost immediately afterwards came the announcement of the id, and what appears like a drastic correction of the earlier statements: 'Now that we have distinguished between the ego and the id, we must recognize the id as the great reservoir of libido . . .' And again: 'At the very beginning, all the libido is accumulated in the id, while the ego is still in process of formation or is still feeble. The id sends part of this libido out into erotic object-cathexes, whereupon the ego, now grown stronger, tries to get hold of this object-libido and to force itself on the id as a love-object. The narcissism of the ego is thus a secondary one, which has been withdrawn from objects.'

This new position seems quite clearly intelligible, and it is therefore a little disturbing to come upon the following sentences, written only a year or so after *The Ego and the Id*, in the *Autobiographical Study* (1925*d* [1924]), *Standard Ed.*, **20**, 56: 'All through the subject's life his ego remains the great reservoir of his libido, from which object-cathexes are sent out and into which the libido can stream back again from the objects'.[1]

The sentence, it is true, occurs in the course of a historical sketch of the development of psycho-analytic theory; but there is no indication of the change of view announced in *The Ego and the Id*. And, finally, we find this passage in one of Freud's very last writings, in Chapter II of the *Outline of Psycho-Analysis* (1940*a*), written in 1938: 'It is hard to say anything of the behaviour of the libido in the id and in the super-ego. All that we know about it relates to the ego, in which at first the whole available quota of libido is stored up. We call this state the absolute primary narcissism. It lasts till the ego begins to cathect the ideas of objects with libido, to transform narcissistic libido into object-libido. Throughout the whole of life the ego remains the great reservoir, from which libidinal cathexes are sent out to objects and into which they are also once more withdrawn, just as an amoeba behaves with its pseudopodia.'

Do these later passages imply that Freud had retracted the opinions he expressed in the present work? It seems difficult to believe it, and there are two points that may help towards a reconciliation of the apparently conflicting views. The first is a very small one. The analogy of the 'reservoir' is from its very nature an ambiguous one: a

---

[1] An almost identical statement is made in Lecture 32 of the *New Introductory Lectures* (1933*a*), but there is also the sentence: 'The object-cathexes spring from the instinctual demands of the id.'

reservoir can be regarded either as a water storage tank or as a source of water supply. There is no great difficulty in applying the image in both senses both to the ego and to the id, and it would certainly have clarified the various passages that have been quoted – and in particular the footnote on p. 30 – if Freud had shown more precisely which picture was in his mind.

The second point is of greater importance. In the *New Introductory Lectures*, only a few pages after the passage referred to in the footnote above, in the course of a discussion of masochism, Freud writes: 'If it is true of the destructive instinct as well that the ego – but what we have in mind here is rather the id, the whole person – originally includes all the instinctual impulses . . .' The parenthesis points, of course, to a primitive state of things in which the id and the ego are still undifferentiated.[1] And there is a similar, but more definite, remark in the *Outline*, this time two paragraphs before the passage already quoted: 'We may picture an initial state as one in which the total available energy of Eros, which henceforward we shall speak of as "libido", is present in the still undifferentiated ego-id . . .' If we take this as being the true essence of Freud's theory, the apparent contradiction in his expression of it is diminished. This 'ego-id' was originally the 'great reservoir of libido' in the sense of being a storage tank. After differentiation had occurred, the id would continue as a storage tank but, when it began sending out cathexes (whether to objects or to the now differentiated ego) it would in addition be a source of supply. But the same would be true of the ego as well, for it would be a storage tank of narcissistic libido as well as, on one view, a source of supply for object-cathexes.

This last point leads us, however, to a further question, on which it seems inevitable to suppose that Freud held different views at different times. In *The Ego and the Id*, 'at the very beginning, all the libido is accumulated in the id'; then 'the id sends part of this libido out into erotic object-cathexes', which the ego tries to get control of by forcing itself on the id as a love-object: 'the narcissism of the ego is thus a secondary one.' But in the *Outline*, 'at first the whole available quota of libido is stored up in the ego', 'we call this state the absolutely primary narcissism' and 'it lasts until the ego begins to cathect the ideas of objects with libido'. Two different processes seem to be envisaged in these two accounts. In the first the original object-

[1] This is, of course, a familiar view of Freud's.

cathexes are thought of as going out direct from the id, and only reaching the ego indirectly; in the second the whole of the libido is thought of as going from the id to the ego and only reaching the objects indirectly. The two processes do not seem incompatible, and it is possible that both may occur; but on this question Freud is silent.

The Dissection of
the Psychical Personality

(1933)*

Ladies and Gentlemen – I know you are aware in regard to your own
relations, whether with people or things, of the importance of your
starting-point. This was also the case with psycho-analysis. It has not
been a matter of indifference for the course of its developments or for
the reception it met with that it began its work on what is, of all the
contents of the mind, most foreign to the ego – on symptoms.
Symptoms are derived from the repressed, they are, as it were, its
representatives before the ego; but the repressed is foreign territory to
the ego – internal foreign territory – just as reality (if you will forgive
the unusual expression) is external foreign territory. The path led
from symptoms to the unconscious, to the life of the instincts, to
sexuality; and it was then that psycho-analysis was met by the
brilliant objection that human beings are not merely sexual creatures
but have nobler and higher impulses as well. It might have been
added that, exalted by their consciousness of these higher impulses,
they often assume the right to think nonsense and to neglect facts.

You know better. From the very first we have said that human
beings fall ill of a conflict between the claims of instinctual life and the
resistance which arises within them against it; and not for a moment
have we forgotten this resisting, repelling, repressing agency, which
we thought of as equipped with its special forces, the ego instincts, and
which coincides with the ego of popular psychology. The truth was
merely that, in view of the laborious nature of the progress made by

* First published by Internationaler Psychoanalytischer Verlag (Vienna). The
present text is included in *Standard Ed.*, 22, 57; *P.F.L.*, 2, 88.

scientific work, even psycho-analysis was not able to study every field simultaneously and to express its views on every problem in a single breath. But at last the point was reached when it was possible for us to divert our attention from the repressed to the repressing forces, and we faced this ego, which had seemed so self-evident, with the secure expectation that here once again we should find things for which we could not have been prepared. It was not easy, however, to find a first approach; and that is what I intend to talk to you about to-day.

I must, however, let you know of my suspicion that this account of mine of ego psychology will affect you differently from the introduction into the psychical underworld which preceded it. I cannot say with certainty why this should be so. I thought first that you would discover that whereas what I reported to you previously were, in the main, facts, however strange and peculiar, now you will be listening principally to opinions – that is, to speculations. But that does not meet the position. After further consideration I must maintain that the amount of intellectual working-over of the factual material in our ego psychology is not much greater than it was in the psychology of the neuroses. I have been obliged to reject other explanations as well of the result I anticipate: I now believe that it is somehow a question of the nature of the material itself and of our being unaccustomed to dealing with it. In any case, I shall not be surprised if you show yourselves even more reserved and cautious in your judgement than hitherto.

The situation in which we find ourselves at the beginning of our enquiry may be expected itself to point the way for us. We wish to make the ego the matter of our enquiry, our very own ego. But is that possible? After all, the ego is in its very essence a subject; how can it be made into an object? Well, there is no doubt that it can be. The ego can take itself as an object, can treat itself like other objects, can observe itself, criticize itself, and do Heaven knows what with itself. In this, one part of the ego is setting itself over against the rest. So the ego can be split; it splits itself during a number of its functions – temporarily at least. Its parts can come together again afterwards. That is not exactly a novelty, though it may perhaps be putting an unusual emphasis on what is generally known. On the other hand, we are familiar with the notion that pathology, by making things larger and coarser, can draw our attention to normal conditions which would otherwise have escaped us. Where it points to a breach or a rent, there may normally be an articulation present. If we throw a crystal to the floor, it breaks; but not into haphazard pieces. It comes apart along its lines of cleavage into fragments whose boundaries, though they were invisible, were predetermined by the crystal's structure. Mental patients are split and broken structures of this same kind. Even we cannot withhold from them something of the reverential awe which peoples of the past felt for the insane. They have turned away from external reality, but for that very reason they know more about internal, psychical reality and can reveal a number of things to us that would otherwise be inaccessible to us.

We describe one group of these patients as suffering from delusions of being observed. They complain to us that perpetually, and down to their most intimate actions, they are being molested by the observation of unknown powers – presumably persons – and that in hallucinations they hear these persons reporting the outcome of their observation: 'now he's going to say this, now he's dressing to go out' and so on. Observation of this sort is not yet the same thing as persecution, but it is not far from it; it presupposes that people distrust them, and expect to catch them carrying out forbidden actions for which they would be punished. How would it be if these insane people were right, if in each of us there is present in his ego an agency like this which observes and threatens to punish, and which in them has merely become sharply divided from their ego and mistakenly displaced into external reality?

I cannot tell whether the same thing will happen to you as to me. Ever since, under the powerful impression of this clinical picture, I formed the idea that the separation of the observing agency from the rest of the ego might be a regular feature of the ego's structure, that idea has never left me, and I was driven to investigate the further characteristics and connections of the agency which was thus separated off. The next step is quickly taken. The content of the delusions of being observed already suggests that the observing is only a preparation for judging and punishing, and we accordingly guess that another function of this agency must be what we call our conscience. There is scarcely anything else in us that we so regularly separate from our ego and so easily set over against it as precisely our conscience. I feel an inclination to do something that I think will give me pleasure, but I abandon it on the ground that my conscience does not allow it. Or I have let myself be persuaded by too great an expectation of pleasure into doing something to which the voice of conscience has objected and after the deed my conscience punishes me with distressing reproaches and causes me to feel remorse for the deed. I might simply say that the special agency which I am beginning to distinguish in the ego is conscience. But it is more prudent to keep the agency as something independent and to suppose that conscience is one of its functions and that self-observation, which is an essential preliminary to the judging activity of conscience, is another of them. And since when we recognize that something has a separate existence we give it a name of its own, from this time forward I will describe this agency in the ego as the 'super-ego'.

I am now prepared to hear you ask me scornfully whether our ego psychology comes down to nothing more than taking commonly used abstractions literally and in a crude sense, and transforming them from concepts into things – by which not much would be gained. To this I would reply that in ego-psychology it will be difficult to escape what is universally known; it will rather be a question of new ways of looking at things and new ways of arranging them than of new discoveries. So hold to your contemptuous criticism for the time being and await further explanations. The facts of pathology give our efforts a background that you would look for in vain in popular psychology. So I will proceed.

Hardly have we familiarized ourselves with the idea of a super-ego like this which enjoys a certain degree of autonomy, follows its own intentions and is independent of the ego for its supply of energy, than a clinical picture forces itself on our notice which throws a striking light on the severity of this agency and indeed its cruelty, and on its changing relations to the ego. I am thinking of the condition of melancholia,[1] or, more precisely, of melancholic attacks, which you too will have heard plenty about, even if you are not psychiatrists. The most striking feature of this illness, of whose causation and mechanism we know much too little, is the way in which the super-ego – 'conscience', you may call it, quietly – treats the ego. While a melancholic can, like other people, show a greater or lesser degree of severity to himself in his healthy periods, during a melancholic attack his super-ego becomes over-severe, abuses the poor ego, humiliates it and ill-treats it, threatens it with the direst punishments, reproaches it for actions in the remotest past which had been taken lightly at the time – as though it had spent the whole interval in collecting

[1] [Modern terminology would probably speak of 'depression'.]

accusations and had only been waiting for its present access of strength in order to bring them up and make a condemnatory judgement on their basis. The super-ego applies the strictest moral standard to the helpless ego which is at its mercy; in general it represents the claims of morality, and we realize all at once that our moral sense of guilt is the expression of the tension between the ego and the super-ego. It is a most remarkable experience to see morality, which is supposed to have been given us by God and thus deeply implanted in us, functioning [in these patients] as a periodic phenomenon. For after a certain number of months the whole moral fuss is over, the criticism of the super-ego is silent, the ego is rehabilitated and again enjoys all the rights of man till the next attack. In some forms of the disease, indeed, something of a contrary sort occurs in the intervals; the ego finds itself in a blissful state of intoxication, it celebrates a triumph, as though the super-ego had lost all its strength or had melted into the ego; and this liberated, manic ego permits itself a truly uninhibited satisfaction of all its appetites. Here are happenings rich in unsolved riddles!

No doubt you will expect me to give you more than a mere illustration when I inform you that we have found out all kinds of things about the formation of the super-ego – that is to say, about the origin of conscience. Following a well-known pronouncement of Kant's which couples the conscience within us with the starry Heavens, a pious man might well be tempted to honour these two things as the masterpieces of creation. The stars are indeed magnificent, but as regards conscience God has done an uneven and careless piece of work, for a large majority of men have brought along with them only a modest amount of it or scarcely enough to be worth mentioning. We are far from overlooking the portion of psychological truth that is contained in the assertion that conscience is of divine origin; but the thesis needs interpretation. Even if conscience is something 'within us', yet it is not so from the first. In this it is a real contrast to sexual life, which is in fact there from the beginning of life and not only a later addition. But, as is well known, young children are amoral and possess no internal inhibitions against their impulses striving for pleasure. The part which is later taken on by the super-ego is played to begin with by an external power, by parental authority. Parental influence governs the child by offering proofs of love and by threatening punishments which are signs to the child of loss of love and are bound to be feared on their own account. This realistic anxiety is the precursor of the later moral anxiety.[1] So long as it is dominant there is no need to talk of a super-ego and of a conscience. It is only subsequently that the secondary situation develops (which we are all too ready to regard as the normal one), where the external restraint is internalized and the super-ego takes the place of the parental agency and observes, directs and threatens the ego in exactly the same way as earlier the parents did with the child.

The super-ego, which thus takes over the power, function and even the methods of the parental agency, is however not merely its successor but actually the legitimate heir of its body. It proceeds directly out of it, we shall learn presently by what process. First, however, we must dwell upon a discrepancy between the two. The super-ego seems to have made a one-sided choice and to have picked out only the parents' strictness and severity, their prohibiting and punitive function, whereas their loving care seems not to have been taken over and maintained. If the parents have really enforced their authority with severity we can easily understand the child's in turn developing a severe super-ego. But, contrary to our expectation, experience shows that the super-ego can acquire the same character-istic of relentless severity even if the upbringing had been mild and kindly and had so far as possible avoided threats and punishments. We shall come back later to this contradiction when we deal with the transformations of instinct during the formation of the super-ego.

I cannot tell you as much as I should like about the metamorphosis of the parental relationship into the super-ego, partly because that process is so complicated that an account of it will not fit into the framework of an introductory course of lectures such as I am trying to give you, but partly also because we ourselves do not feel sure that we understand it completely. So you must be content with the sketch that follows.

The basis of the process is what is called an 'identification' – that is to say, the assimilation of one ego to another one,[2] as a result of which the first ego behaves like the second in certain respects, imitates it and in a sense takes it up into itself. Identification has been not unsuitably compared with the oral, cannibalistic incorporation of the other person. It is a very important form of attachment to someone else, probably the very first, and not the same thing as the choice of an

[1] [Literally 'conscience anxiety'.]
[2] [I.e. one ego coming to resemble another one.]

object. The difference between the two can be expressed in some such way as this. If a boy identifies himself with his father, he wants to *be like* his father; if he makes him the object of his choice, he wants to *have* him, to possess him. In the first case his ego is altered on the model of his father; in the second case that is not necessary. Identification and object-choice are to a large extent independent of each other; it is however possible to identify oneself with someone whom, for instance, one has taken as a sexual object, and to alter one's ego on his model. It is said that the influencing of the ego by the sexual object occurs particularly often with women and is characteristic of femininity. I must already have spoken to you in my earlier lectures of what is by far the most instructive relation between identification and object-choice. It can be observed equally easily in children and adults, in normal as in sick people. If one has lost an object or has been obliged to give it up, one often compensates oneself by identifying oneself with it and by setting it up once more in one's ego, so that here object-choice regresses, as it were, to identification.[1]

I myself am far from satisfied with these remarks on identification; but it will be enough if you can grant me that the installation of the super-ego can be described as a successful instance of identification with the parental agency. The fact that speaks decisively for this view is that this new creation of a superior agency within the ego is most intimately linked with the destiny of the Oedipus complex, so that the super-ego appears as the heir of that emotional attachment which is of such importance for childhood. With his abandonment of the Oedipus complex a child must, as we can see, renounce the intense object-cathexes which he has deposited with his parents, and it is as a compensation for this loss of objects that there is such a strong intensification of the identifications with his parents which have probably long been present in his ego. Identifications of this kind as precipitates of object-cathexes that have been given up will be repeated often enough later in the child's life; but it is entirely in accordance with the emotional importance of this first instance of such a transformation that a special place in the ego should be found for its outcome. Close investigation has shown us, too, that the super-ego is stunted in its strength and growth if the surmounting of the Oedipus complex is only incompletely successful. In the course of

---

[1] [Identification was the subject of Chapter VII of *Group Psychology* (1912c). The formation of the super-ego was discussed at length in Section III of *The Ego and the Id* above.]

development the super-ego also takes on the influences of those who have stepped into the place of parents – educators, teachers, people chosen as ideal models. Normally it departs more and more from the original parental figures; it becomes, so to say, more impersonal. Nor must it be forgotten that a child has a different estimate of its parents at different periods of its life. At the time at which the Oedipus complex gives place to the super-ego they are something quite magnificent; but later they lose much of this. Identifications then come about with these later parents as well, and indeed they regularly make important contributions to the formation of character; but in that case they only affect the ego, they no longer influence the super-ego, which has been determined by the earliest parental imagos.[1]

I hope you have already formed an impression that the hypothesis of the super-ego really describes a structural relation and is not merely a personification of some such abstraction as that of conscience. One more important function remains to be mentioned which we attribute to this super-ego. It is also the vehicle of the ego ideal by which the ego measures itself, which it emulates, and whose demand for ever greater perfection it strives to fulfil. There is no doubt that this ego ideal is the precipitate of the old picture of the parents, the expression of admiration for the perfection which the child then attributed to them.[2]

I am sure you have heard a great deal of the sense of inferiority which is supposed particularly to characterize neurotics. It especially haunts the pages of what are known as *belles lettres*. An author who uses the term 'inferiority complex' thinks that by so doing he has fulfilled all the demands of psycho-analysis and has raised his composition to a higher psychological plane. In fact 'inferiority complex' is a technical term that is scarcely used in psycho-analysis. For us it does not bear the meaning of anything simple, let alone elementary. To trace it back to the self-perception of possible organic defects, as the school of what are known as 'Individual Psychologists'[3] likes to do, seems to us a short-sighted error. The sense of inferiority has strong erotic roots. A child feels inferior if he notices that he is not loved, and so does an

---

[1] [This point was discussed by Freud in a paper on 'The Economic Problem of Masochism' (1924c).]

[2] [Freud is here drawing a distinction between the 'super-ego' and the 'ego ideal'. Section III of *The Ego and the Id*, in contrast, treats the two terms as synonymous.]

[3] [Their views are discussed in Lecture 34 of the *New Introductory Lectures* (1933a).]

adult. The only bodily organ which is really regarded as inferior is the atrophied penis, a girl's clitoris.[1] But the major part of the sense of inferiority derives from the ego's relation to its super-ego; like the sense of guilt it is an expression of the tension between them. Altogether, it is hard to separate the sense of inferiority and the sense of guilt. It would perhaps be right to regard the former as the erotic complement to the moral sense of inferiority. Little attention has been given in psycho-analysis to the question of the delimitation of the two concepts.

If only because the inferiority complex has become so popular, I will venture to entertain you here with a short digression. A historical personality of our own days, who is still alive though at the moment he has retired into the background, suffers from a defect in one of his limbs owing to an injury at the time of his birth. A very well-known contemporary writer who is particularly fond of compiling the biographies of celebrities has dealt, among others, with the life of the man I am speaking of.[2] Now in writing a biography it may well be difficult to suppress a need to plumb the psychological depths. For this reason our author has ventured on an attempt to erect the whole of the development of his hero's character on the sense of inferiority which must have been called up by his physical defect. In doing so, he has overlooked one small but not insignificant fact. It is usual for mothers whom Fate has presented with a child who is sickly or otherwise at a disadvantage to try to compensate him for his unfair handicap by a superabundance of love. In the instance before us, the proud mother behaved otherwise; she withdrew her love from the child on account of his infirmity. When he had grown up into a man of great power, he proved unambiguously by his actions that he had never forgiven his mother. When you consider the importance of a mother's love for the mental life of a child, you will no doubt make a tacit correction of the biographer's inferiority theory.

But let us return to the super-ego. We have allotted it the functions of self-observation, of conscience and of [maintaining] the ideal. It follows from what we have said about its origin that it presupposes an immensely important biological fact and a fateful psychological one:

---

[1] [Cf. a footnote of Freud's to his paper on the anatomical distinction between the sexes in Chapter 5 above.]

[2] [*Wilhelm II*, by Emil Ludwig (1926).]

namely, the human child's long dependence on its parents and the Oedipus complex, both of which, again, are intimately interconnected. The super-ego is the representative for us of every moral restriction, the advocate of a striving towards perfection – it is, in short, as much as we have been able to grasp psychologically of what is described as the higher side of human life. Since it itself goes back to the influence of parents, educators and so on, we learn still more of its significance if we turn to those who are its sources. As a rule parents and authorities analogous to them follow the precepts of their own super-egos in educating children. Whatever understanding their ego may have come to with their super-ego, they are severe and exacting in educating children. They have forgotten the difficulties of their own childhood and they are glad to be able now to identify themselves fully with their own parents who in the past laid such severe restrictions upon them. Thus a child's super-ego is in fact constructed on the model not of its parents but of its parents' super-ego; the contents which fill it are the same and it becomes the vehicle of tradition and of all the time-resisting judgements of value which have propagated themselves in this manner from generation to generation. You may easily guess what important assistance taking the super-ego into account will give us in our understanding of the social behaviour of mankind – in the problem of delinquency, for instance – and perhaps even what practical hints on education. It seems likely that what are known as materialistic views of history sin in under-estimating this factor. They brush it aside with the remark that human 'ideologies' are nothing other than the product and superstructure of their contemporary economic conditions. That is true, but very probably not the whole truth. Mankind never lives entirely in the present. The past, the tradition of the race and of the people, lives on in the ideologies of the super-ego, and yields only slowly to the influences of the present and to new changes; and so long as it operates through the super-ego it plays a powerful part in human life, independently of economic conditions.

In 1921 I endeavoured to make use of the differentiation between the ego and the super-ego in a study of group psychology. I arrived at a formula such as this: a psychological group is a collection of individuals who have introduced the same person into their super-ego and, on the basis of this common element, have identified themselves with one another in their ego.[1] This applies, of course, only to groups

1 [*Group Psychology* (1921*c*), *Standard Ed.*, **18**, 116; *P.F.L.*, **12**, 147.]

that have a leader. If we possessed more applications of this kind, the hypothesis of the super-ego would lose its last touch of strangeness for us, and we should become completely free of the embarrassment that still comes over us when, accustomed as we are to the atmosphere of the underworld, we move in the more superficial, higher strata of the mental apparatus. We do not suppose, of course, that with the separation off of the super-ego we have said the last word on the psychology of the ego. It is rather a first step; but in this case it is not only the first step that is hard.

Now, however, another problem awaits us – at the opposite end of the ego, as we might put it. It is presented to us by an observation during the work of analysis, an observation which is actually a very old one. As not infrequently happens, it has taken a long time to come to the point of appreciating its importance. The whole theory of psycho-analysis is, as you know, in fact built up on the perception of the resistance offered to us by the patient when we attempt to make his unconscious conscious to him. The objective sign of this resistance is that his associations fail or depart widely from the topic that is being dealt with. He may also recognize the resistance *subjectively* by the fact that he has distressing feelings when he approaches the topic. But this last sign may also be absent. We then say to the patient that we infer from his behaviour that he is now in a state of resistance; and he replies that he knows nothing of that, and is only aware that his associations have become more difficult. It turns out that we were right; but in that case his resistance was unconscious too, just as unconscious as the repressed, at the lifting of which we were working. We should long ago have asked the question: from what part of his mind does an unconscious resistance like this arise? The beginner in psycho-analysis will be ready at once with the answer: it is, of course, the resistance of the unconscious. An ambiguous and unserviceable answer! If it means that the resistance arises from the repressed, we must rejoin: certainly not! We must rather attribute to the repressed a strong upward drive, an impulsion to break through into conscious-ness. The resistance can only be a manifestation of the ego, which originally put the repression into force and now wishes to maintain it. That, moreover, is the view we always took. Since we have come to assume a special agency in the ego, the super-ego, which represents demands of a restrictive and rejecting character, we may say that repression is the work of this super-ego and that it is carried out either by itself or by the ego in obedience to its orders. If then we are met by the case of the resistance in analysis not being conscious to the patient, this means either that in quite important situations the super-ego and the ego can operate unconsciously, or – and this would be still more important – that portions of both of them, the ego and the super-ego themselves, are unconscious. In both cases we have to reckon with the disagreeable discovery that on the one hand (super-) ego and conscious and on the other hand repressed and unconscious are far from coinciding.

And here, Ladies and Gentlemen, I feel that I must make a pause to take breath – which you too will welcome as a relief – and, before I go on, to apologize to you. My intention is to give you some addenda to the introductory lectures on psycho-analysis which I began fifteen years ago, and I am obliged to behave as though you as well as I had in the interval done nothing but practise psycho-analysis. I know that that assumption is out of place; but I am helpless, I cannot do otherwise. This is no doubt related to the fact that it is in general so hard to give anyone who is not himself a psycho-analyst an insight into psycho-analysis. You can believe me when I tell you that we do not enjoy giving an impression of being members of a secret society and of practising a mystical science. Yet we have been obliged to recognize and express as our conviction that no one has a right to join in a discussion of psycho-analysis who has not had particular experiences which can only be obtained by being analysed oneself. When I gave you my lectures fifteen years ago I tried to spare you certain speculative portions of our theory; but it is precisely from them that are derived the new acquisitions of which I must speak to you to-day.

I return now to our topic. In face of the doubt whether the ego and super-ego are themselves unconscious or merely produce unconscious effects, we have, for good reasons, decided in favour of the former possibility. And it is indeed the case that large portions of the ego and super-ego can remain unconscious and are normally unconscious. That is to say, the individual knows nothing of their contents and it requires an expenditure of effort to make them conscious. It is a fact that ego and conscious, repressed and unconscious do not coincide. We feel a need to make a fundamental revision of our attitude to the problem of conscious-unconscious. At first we are inclined greatly to reduce the value of the criterion of being conscious since it has shown itself so untrustworthy. But we should be doing it an injustice. As may be said of our life, it is not worth much, but it is all we have. Without the illumination thrown by the quality of consciousness, we should be lost in the obscurity of depth psychology; but we must attempt to find our bearings afresh.

There is no need to discuss what is to be called conscious: it is removed from all doubt. The oldest and best meaning of the word 'unconscious' is the descriptive one; we call a psychical process unconscious whose existence we are obliged to assume – for some such reason as that we infer it from its effects –, but of which we know nothing. In that case we have the same relation to it as we have to a psychical process in another person, except that it is in fact one of our own. If we want to be still more correct, we shall modify our assertion by saying that we call a process unconscious if we are obliged to assume that it is being activated *at the moment*, though *at the moment* we know nothing about it. This qualification makes us reflect that the majority of conscious processes are conscious only for a short time; very soon they become *latent*, but can easily become conscious again. We might also say that they had become unconscious, if it were at all certain that in the condition of latency they are still something psychical. So far we should have learnt nothing new; nor should we have acquired the right to introduce the concept of an unconscious into psychology. But then comes the new observation that we were already able to make in parapraxes. In order to explain a slip of the tongue, for instance, we find ourselves obliged to assume that the intention to make a particular remark was present in the subject. We infer it with certainty from the interference with his remark which has occurred; but the intention did no put itself through and was thus unconscious. If, when we subsequently put it before the speaker, he recognizes it as one familiar to him, then it was only temporarily unconscious to him; but if he repudiates it as something foreign to him, then it was permanently unconscious.[1] From this experience we retrospectively obtain the right also to pronounce as something unconscious what had been described as latent. A consideration of these dynamic relations permits us now to distinguish two kinds of unconscious – one which is easily, under frequently occurring circumstances, transformed into something conscious, and another with which this transformation is difficult and takes place only subject to a

---

[1] [Cf. *Introductory Lectures*, Lecture 4, *Standard Ed.*, 15, 64; *P.F.L.*, 1, 91–2.]

considerable expenditure of effort or possibly never at all. In order to escape the ambiguity as to whether we mean the one or the other unconscious, whether we are using the word in the descriptive or in the dynamic sense, we make use of a permissible and simple way out. We call the unconscious which is only latent, and thus easily becomes conscious, the 'preconscious' and retain the term 'unconscious' for the other. We now have three terms, 'conscious', 'preconscious' and 'unconscious', with which we can get along in our description of mental phenomena. Once again: the proconscious is also unconscious in the purely descriptive sense, but we do not give it that name, except in talking loosely or when we have to make a defence of the existence in mental life of unconscious processes in general.

You will admit, I hope, that so far that is not too bad and allows of convenient handling. Yes, but unluckily the work of psycho-analysis has found itself compelled to use the word 'unconscious' in yet another, third, sense, and this may, to be sure, have led to confusion. Under the new and powerful impression of there being an extensive and important field of mental life which is normally withdrawn from the ego's knowledge so that the processes occurring in it have to be regarded as unconscious in the truly dynamic sense, we have come to understand the term 'unconscious' in a topographical or systematic sense as well; we have come to speak of a 'system' of the preconscious and a 'system' of the unconscious, of a conflict between the ego and the system *Ucs.*, and have used the word more and more to denote a mental province rather than a quality of what is mental. The discovery, actually an inconvenient one, that portions of the ego and super-ego as well are unconscious in the dynamic sense, operates at this point as a relief – it makes possible the removal of a complication. We perceive that we have no right to name the mental region that is foreign to the ego 'the system *Ucs.*', since the characteristic of being unconscious is not restricted to it. Very well; we will no longer use the term 'unconscious' in the systematic sense and we will give what we have hitherto so described a better name and one no longer open to misunderstanding. Following a verbal usage of Nietzsche's and taking up a suggestion by Georg Groddeck [1923],[1] we will in future call it the 'id'.[2] This impersonal pronoun seems particularly well suited for expressing the main characteristic of this province of the mind –

---

[1] [A German physician by whose unconventional ideas Freud was much attracted. See pp. 448–9 above.]

[2] [In German '*Es*', the ordinary word for 'it'.]

the fact of its being alien to the ego. The super-ego, the ego and the id – these, then, are the three realms, regions, provinces, into which we divide an individual's mental apparatus, and with the mutual relations of which we shall be concerned in what follows.

But first a short interpolation. I suspect that you feel dissatisfied because the three qualities of the characteristic of consciousness and the three provinces of the mental apparatus do not fall together into three peaceable couples, and you may regard this as in some sense obscuring our findings. I do not think, however, that we should regret it, and we should tell ourselves that we had no right to expect any such smooth arrangement. Let me give you an analogy; analogies, it is true, decide nothing, but they can make one feel more at home. I am imagining a country with a landscape of varying configuration – hill-country, plains, and chains of lakes –, and with a mixed population: it is inhabited by Germans, Magyars and Slovaks, who carry on different activities. Now things might be partitioned in such a way that the Germans, who breed cattle, live in the hill-country, the Magyars, who grow cereals and wine, live in the plains, and the Slovaks, who catch fish and plait reeds, live by the lakes. If the partitioning could be neat and clear-cut like this, a Woodrow Wilson would be delighted by it; it would also be convenient for a lecture in a geography lesson. The probability is, however, that you will find less orderliness and more mixing, if you travel through the region. Germans, Magyars and Slovaks live interspersed all over it; in the hill-country there is agricultural land as well, cattle are bred in the plains too. A few things are naturally as you expected, for fish cannot be caught in the mountains and wine does not grow in the water. Indeed, the picture of the region that you brought with you may on the whole fit the facts; but you will have to put up with deviations in the details.

You will not expect me to have much to tell you that is new about the id apart from its new name. It is the dark, inaccessible part of our personality; what little we know of it we have learnt from our study of the dream-work and of the construction of neurotic symptoms, and most of that is of a negative character and can be described only as a contrast to the ego. We approach the id with analogies: we call it a chaos, a cauldron full of seething excitations. We picture it as being open at its end to somatic influences, and as there taking up into itself instinctual needs which find their psychical expression in it,[1] but we cannot say in what substratum. It is filled with energy reaching it from the instincts, but it has no organization, produces no collective will, but only a striving to bring about the satisfaction of the instinctual needs subject to the observance of the pleasure principle. The logical laws of thought do not apply in the id, and this is true above all of the law of contradiction. Contrary impulses exist side by side, without cancelling each other out or diminishing each other: at the most they may converge to form compromises under the dominating economic pressure towards the discharge of energy. There is nothing in the id that could be compared with negation; and we perceive with surprise an exception to the philosophical theorem that space and time are necessary forms of our mental acts.[2] There is nothing in the id that corresponds to the idea of time; there is no recognition of the passage of time, and – a thing that is most remarkable and awaits consideration in philosophical thought – no alteration in its mental processes is produced by the passage of time. Wishful impulses which have never passed beyond the id, but impressions, too, which have been sunk into the id by repression, are virtually immortal; after the passage of decades they behave as though they had just occurred. They can only be recognized as belonging to the past, can only lose their importance and be deprived of their cathexis of energy, when they have been made conscious by the work of analysis, and it is on this that the therapeutic effect of analytic treatment rests to no small extent.

Again and again I have had the impression that we have made too little theoretical use of this fact, established beyond any doubt, of the unalterability by time of the repressed. This seems to offer an approach to the most profound discoveries. Nor, unfortunately, have I myself made any progress here.

The id of course knows no judgements of value: no good and evil, no morality. The economic or, if you prefer, the quantitative factor, which is intimately linked to the pleasure principle, dominates all its processes. Instinctual cathexes seeking discharge – that, in our view, is all there is in the id. It even seems that the energy of these instinctual impulses is in a state different from that in the other

---

[1] [Freud is here regarding instincts as something physical, of which mental processes are the representatives.]

[2] [The reference is to Kant.]

regions of the mind, far more mobile and capable of discharge;[1] otherwise the displacements and condensations would not occur which are characteristic of the id and which so completely disregard the *quality* of what is cathected – what in the ego we should call an idea. We would give much to understand more about these things! You can see, incidentally, that we are in a position to attribute to the id characteristics other than that of its being unconscious, and you can recognize the possibility of portions of the ego and super-ego being unconscious without possessing the same primitive and irrational characteristics.[2]

We can best arrive at the characteristic of the actual ego, in so far as it can be distinguished from the id and from the super-ego, by examining its relation to the outermost superficial portion of the mental apparatus, which we describe as the system *Pept.-Cs.*[3] This system is turned towards the external world, it is the medium for the perceptions arising thence, and during its functioning the phenom-enon of consciousness arises in it. It is the sense-organ of the entire apparatus; moreover it is receptive not only to excitation from outside but also to those arising from the interior of the mind. We need scarcely look for a justification of the view that the ego is that portion of the id which was modified by the proximity and influence of the external world, which is adapted for the reception of stimuli and as a protective shield against stimuli, comparable to the cortical layer by which a small piece of living substance is surrounded. The relation to the external world has become the decisive factor for the ego; it has taken on the task of representing the external world to the id – fortunately for the id, which could not escape destruction if, in its blind efforts for the satisfaction of its instincts, it disregarded that supreme external power. In accomplishing this function, the ego must observe the external world, must lay down an accurate picture of it in the memory-traces of its perceptions, and by its exercise of the function of 'reality-testing'[4] must put aside whatever in this picture of

[1] [This difference was referred to by Freud in many passages. See, in particular, Section V of the metapsychological paper on 'The Unconscious' (Chapter 3 above), where Freud attributes the distinction to Breuer and where he remarks that in his opinion this distinction represents the deepest insight we have gained up to the present into the nature of nervous energy.]

[2] [This account of the id is in the main based on Section V of 'The Unconscious' in Chapter 3 above.]

[3] [Perceptual-conscious.]

[4] [Cf. Freud (1917d); *Standard Ed.*, 14, 231–4; *P.F.L.*, 11, 239–42.]

the external world is an addition derived from internal sources of excitation. The ego controls the approaches to motility under the id's orders; but between a need and an action it has interposed a postponement in the form of the activity of thought,[1] during which it makes use of the mnemic residues of experience. In that way it has dethroned the pleasure principle which dominates the course of events in the id without any restriction and has replaced it by the reality principle, which promises more certainty and greater success.

The relation to time, which is so hard to describe, is also introduced into the ego by the perceptual system; it can scarcely be doubted that the mode of operation of that system is what provides the origin of the idea of time.[2] But what distinguishes the ego from the id quite especially is a tendency to synthesis in its contents, to a combination and unification in its mental processes which are totally lacking in the id. When presently we come to deal with the instincts in mental life we shall, I hope, succeed in tracing this essential characteristic of the ego back to its source.[3] It alone produces the high degree of organization which the ego needs for its best achievements. The ego develops from perceiving the instincts to controlling them; but this last is only achieved by the [psychical] representative of the instinct[4] being allotted its proper place in a considerable assemblage, by its being taken up into a coherent context. To adopt a popular mode of speaking, we might say that the ego stands for reason and good sense while the id stands for the untamed passions.

So far we have allowed ourselves to be impressed by the merits and capabilities of the ego; it is now time to consider the other side as well. The ego is after all only a portion of the id, a portion that has been expediently modified by the proximity of the external world with its threat of danger. From a dynamic point of view it is weak, it has borrowed its energies from the id, and we are not entirely without insight into the methods – we might call them dodges – by which it extracts further amounts of energy from the id. One such method, for instance, is by identifying itself with actual or abandoned objects. The object-cathexes spring from the instinctual demands of the id. The

---

[1] [Cf. *Standard Ed.*, **22**, 89; *P.F.L.*, **2**, 122.]

[2] [Freud gave some indication of what he had in mind by this in his paper on the 'Mystic Writing-Pad' (1925*a*).]

[3] [Freud does not seem, in fact, to have returned to the subject in these lectures. – He had discussed this characteristic of the ego at length in Chapter III of *Inhibitions, Symptoms and Anxiety* (1926*d*).]

[4] [See footnote 1, p. 499 above.]

ego has in the first instance to take note of them. But by identifying itself with the object it recommends itself to the id in place of the object and seeks to divert the id's libido on to itself. We have already seen that in the course of its life the ego takes into itself a large number of precipitates like this of former object-cathexes. The ego must on the whole carry out the id's intentions, it fulfils its task by finding out the circumstances in which those intentions can best be achieved. The ego's relation to the id might be compared with that of a rider to his horse. The horse supplies the locomotive energy, while the rider has the privilege of deciding on the goal and of guiding the powerful animal's movement. But only too often there arises between the ego and the id the not precisely ideal situation of the rider being obliged to guide the horse along the path by which it itself wants to go.

There is one portion of the id from which the ego has separated itself by resistances due to repression. But the repression is not carried over into the id: the repressed merges into the remainder of the id.

We are warned by a proverb against serving two masters at the same time. The poor ego has things even worse: it serves three severe masters and does what it can to bring their claims and demands into harmony with one another. These claims are always divergent and often seem incompatible. No wonder that the ego so often fails in its task. Its three tyrannical masters are the external world, the super-ego and the id. When we follow the ego's efforts to satisfy them simultaneously – or rather, to obey them simultaneously – we cannot feel any regret at having personified this ego and having set it up as a separate organism. It feels hemmed in on three sides, threatened by three kinds of danger, to which, if it is hard pressed, it reacts by generating anxiety. Owing to its origin from the experiences of the perceptual system, it is earmarked for representing the demands of the external world, but it strives too to be a loyal servant of the id, to remain on good terms with it, to recommend itself to it as an object and to attract its libido to itself. In its attempts to mediate between the id and reality, it is often obliged to cloak the *Ucs.* commands of the id with its own *Pcs.* rationalizations, to conceal the id's conflicts with reality, to profess, with diplomatic disingenuousness, to be taking notice of reality even when the id has remained rigid and unyielding. On the other hand it is observed at every step it takes by the strict super-ego, which lays down definite standards for its conduct, without taking any account of its difficulties from the direction of the id and the external world, and which, if those standards are not obeyed, punishes it with tense feelings of inferiority and of guilt. Thus the ego, driven by the id, confined by the super-ego, repulsed by reality, struggles to master its economic task of bringing about harmony among the forces and influences working in and upon it; and we can understand how it is that so often we cannot suppress a cry: 'Life is not easy!' If the ego is obliged to admit its weakness, it breaks out in axiety – realistic anxiety regarding the external world, moral anxiety regarding the super-ego and neurotic anxiety regarding the strength of the passions in the id.

I should like to portray the structural relations of the mental personality, as I have described them to you, in the unassuming sketch which I now present you with:

As you see here, the super-ego merges into the id; indeed, as heir to the Oedipus complex it has intimate relations with the id; it is more remote than the ego from the perceptual system.[1] The id has intercourse with the external world only through the ego – at least, according to this diagram. It is certainly hard to say to-day how far the drawing is correct. In one respect it is undoubtedly not. The space occupied by the unconscious id ought to have been incomparably greater than that of the ego or the preconscious. I must ask you to correct it in your thoughts.

[1] [This diagram differs principally from the one given in *The Ego and the Id*, p. 450 above, in the fact that the super-ego was not indicated in the earlier diagram.]

And here is another warning, to conclude these remarks, which have certainly been exacting and not, perhaps, very illuminating. In thinking of this division of the personality into an ego, a super-ego and an id, you will not, of course, have pictured sharp frontiers like the artificial ones drawn in political geography. We cannot do justice to the characteristics of the mind by linear outlines like those in a drawing or in primitive painting, but rather by areas of colour melting into one another as they are presented by modern artists. After making the separation we must allow what we have separated to merge together once more. You must not judge too harshly a first attempt at giving a pictorial representation of something so intangible as psychical processes. It is highly probable that the development of these divisions is subject to great variations in different individuals; it is possible that in the course of actual functioning they may change and go through a temporary phase of involution. Particularly in the case of what is phylogenetically the last and most delicate of these divisions – the differentiation between the ego and the super-ego – something of the sort seems to be true. There is no question but that the same thing results from psychical illness. It is easy to imagine, too, that certain mystical practices may succeed in upsetting the normal relations between the different regions of the mind, so that, for instance, perception may be able to graps happenings in the depths of the ego and in the id which were otherwise inaccessible to it. It may safely be doubted, however, whether this road weill lead us to the ultimate truths from which salvation is to be expected. Nevertheless it may be admitted that the therapeutic efforts of psycho-analysis have chosen a similar line of approach. Its intention is, indeed, to strengthen the ego, to make it more independent of the super-ego, to widen its field of perception and enlarge its organization, so that it can appropriate fresh portions of the id. Where id was, there ego shall be. It is a work of culture – not unlike the draining of the Zuider Zee.

Seven

THE PLEASURE PRINCIPLE
AND THE REALITY
PRINCIPLE

Introduction

It is one of the premises of psycho-analysis that psychic processes are subject to laws and that the regulatory laws governing them undergo development. Freud described one such progressive regulatory step in 'Formulations on the Two Principles of Mental Functioning', a brief but fundamental paper which was written in 1911, long before he introduced the structural model discussed above. Stated simply, this paper deals with mankind's advance from the blind search for pleasure and instinctual satisfaction to the capacities to recognize the conditions in the external world and to take reality factors into account – an advance that in the childhood of each individual must be repeated and newly accomplished. Freud assigns the primary search for pleasure of the earliest times to the hallucinatory thinking of the system unconscious, and the subsequent phase of reality observation and evaluation to an adaptation of the psychic apparatus, i.e., to the equipment of the system conscious with such functions as attention, noting, passing of judgement, and action. The progression from the pleasure principle to the reality principle is described as a transformation of the ego: from pleasure ego to reality ego.

It is important for the student to recognize that this highly condensed work forms a bridge between Freud's early conceptions and his later formulations. The initial postulate that the mastering of stimuli is the task of the psychic apparatus, 'which has the function of getting rid of the stimuli that reach it, or of reducing them to the lowest possible level' (1915c), belongs to the early phase of Freud's thinking, as does the notion that phylogenetic acquisitions must be attained anew, in abbreviated form, in ontogenesis. On the other hand, 'Formulations on the Two Principles of Mental Functioning' already contains the first hints of his subsequent division of the psychic personality into distinct agencies.

The pleasure principle which, according to the topographic point of view, originates in the system unconscious but extends its influence to the conscious ego, obviously is, in the later structural theory, the regulatory principle which dominates the id and to which the instinctual id contents are subject. Thus, the pleasure principle is coordinated not only with hallucinatory thinking but with the entire primitive mode of thought characteristic of the id – the so-called primary process which operates with thing- rather than word-presentations; without knowledge of the conditions in the external world, indeed, without access to them; without understanding of causal relationships; and, insofar as the access to the motoric sphere is open to it, purely impulsively in action; and, finally, without the capability to evaluate the consequences of actions and to anticipate dangers. The reality principle, in contrast, reigns, according to the structural viewpoint, in the ego, and the functions that enable it to operate are those of the so-called secondary process – perception, thinking in word-presentations, memory, reality-testing, control of motility, etc.

In 'Formulations on the Two Principles of Mental Functioning' as well as on other occasions, Freud emphasized that 'the substitution of the reality principle for the pleasure principle implies no deposing of the pleasure principle, but only a safeguarding of it. A momentary pleasure, uncertain in its results, is given up, but only in order to gain along the new path an assured pleasure at a later time' (1911b). Seen from this vantage point, the aim-inhibiting activity of the reality ego is friendly to the instinctual drives. As every practising analyst knows, this objective assessment does not always coincide with the judgement of the individual in whose inner life these processes are enacted. In the case of the derivatives of the sexual instinct, in particular, the restrictions required by the reality principle are experienced as inimical to the drives. Here lie the causes of the individual's conflicts between the id's adherence to the instinctual aims appropriate to it and the postponement, inhibition and transformation of the instinctual impulses which the ego considers to be necessary.

Formulations on the Two Principles
of Mental Functioning
(1911)*

We have long observed that every neurosis has as its result, and probably therefore as its purpose, a forcing of the patient out of real life, an alienating of him from reality.[1] Nor could a fact such as this escape the observation of Pierre Janet; he spoke of a loss of 'the function of reality' as being a special characteristic of neurotics, but without discovering the connection of this disturbance with the fundamental determinants of neurosis. [Janet, 1909] By introducing the process of repression into the genesis of the neuroses we have been able to gain some insight into this connection. Neurotics turn away from reality because they find it unbearable – either the whole or parts of it. The most extreme type of this turning away from reality is shown by certain cases of hallucinatory psychosis which seek to deny the particular event that occasioned the outbreak of their insanity (Griesinger).[2] But in fact every neurotic does the same with some fragment of reality.[3] And we are now confronted with the task of investigating the development of the relation of neurotics and of mankind in general to reality, and in this way of bringing the psychological significance of the real external world into the structure of our theories.

In the psychology which is founded on psycho-analysis we have

---

* First published in *Jb. psychoanalyt. psychopathol. Forsch.* The present text is included in *Standard Ed.*, **12**, 218; *P.F.L.*, **11**, 35.

[1] [The idea, with the phrase 'flight into psychosis', is already to be found in Section III of Freud's first paper on 'The Neuro-Psychoses of Defence' (1894a). The actual phrase 'flight into illness' occurs in Section B of his paper on hysterical attacks (1909a).]

[2] [W. Griesinger (1817–1868) was a well-known Berlin psychiatrist of an earlier generation, much admired by Freud's teacher, Meynert. In this passage Griesinger (1845, 89) drew attention to the wish-fulfilling character of both psychoses and dreams.]

[3] Otto Rank (1910) has recently drawn attention to a remarkably clear prevision of this causation shown in Schopenhauer's *The World as Will and Idea* [Volume II (Supplements), Chapter 32].

become accustomed to taking as our starting-point the unconscious mental processes, with the peculiarities of which we have become acquainted through analysis. We consider these to be the older, primary processes, the residues of a phase of development in which they were the only kind of mental process. The governing purpose obeyed by these primary processes is easy to recognize; it is described as the pleasure-unpleasure principle, or more shortly the pleasure principle. These processes strive towards gaining pleasure; psychical activity draws back from any event which might arouse unpleasure. (Here we have repression.) Our dreams at night and our waking tendency to tear ourselves away from distressing impressions are remnants of the dominance of this principle and proofs of its power.

I shall be returning to lines of thought which I have developed elsewhere[1] when I suggest that the state of psychical rest was originally disturbed by the peremptory demands of internal needs. When this happened, whatever was thought of (wished for) was simply presented in a hallucinatory manner, just as still happens to-day with our dream-thoughts every night.[2] It was only the non-occurrence of the expected satisfaction, the disappointment experienced, that led to the abandonment of this attempt at satisfaction by means of hallucination. Instead of it, the psychical apparatus had to decide to form a conception of the real circumstances in the external world and to endeavour to make a real alteration in them. A new principle of mental functioning was thus introduced; what was presented in the mind was no longer what was agreeable but what was real, even if it happened to be disagreeable.[3] This setting-up of the *reality principle* proved to be a momentous step.

[1] In the General Section of *The Interpretation of Dreams*. [I.e. in Chapter VII. See in particular *Standard Ed.*, 5, 565–7 and 598 ff.; *P.F.L.*, 4, 718–21 and 757 ff.]

[2] The state of sleep is able to re-establish the likeness of mental life as it was before the recognition of reality, because a prerequisite of sleep is a deliberate rejection of reality (the wish to sleep).

[3] I will try to amplify the above schematic account with some further details. It will rightly be objected that an organization which was a slave to the pleasure principle and neglected the reality of the external world could not maintain itself alive for the shortest time, so that it could not have come into existence at all. The employment of a fiction like this is, however, justified when one considers that the infant – provided one includes with it the care it receives from its mother – does almost realize a psychical system of this kind. It probably hallucinates the fulfilment of its internal needs; it betrays its unpleasure, when there is an increase of stimulus and an absence of satisfaction, by the motor discharge of screaming and beating about with its arms and legs, and it then experiences the satisfaction it has hallucinated. Later, as an older child, it learns to employ these manifestations of discharge intentionally as methods of

(1) In the first place, the new demands made a succession of adaptations necessary in the psychical apparatus, which, owing to our insufficient or uncertain knowledge, we can only retail very cursorily.

The increased significance of external reality heightened the importance, too, of the sense-organs that are directed towards that external world, and of the *consciousness* attached to them. Consciousness now learned to comprehend sensory qualities in addition to the qualities of pleasure and unpleasure which hitherto had alone been of interest to it. A special function was instituted which had periodically to search the external world, in order that its data might be familiar already if an urgent internal need should arise – the function of *attention*. Its activity meets the sense-impressions half way, instead of awaiting their appearance. At the same time, probably, a system of *notation* was introduced, whose task it was to lay down the results of this periodical activity of consciousness – a part of what we call *memory*.

The place of repression, which excluded from cathexis as productive of unpleasure some of the emerging ideas, was taken by an *impartial passing of judgement*,[1] which had to decide whether a given idea was true or false – that is, whether it was in agreement with reality or not – the decision being determined by making a comparison with the memory-traces of reality.

A new function was now allotted to motor discharge, which, under the dominance of the pleasure principle, had served as a means of unburdening the mental apparatus of accretions of stimuli, and which had carried out this task by sending innervations into the interior of

---

expressing its feelings. Since the later care of children is modelled on the care of infants, the dominance of the pleasure principle can really come to an end only when a child has achieved complete psychical detachment from its parents. – A neat example of a psychical system shut off from the stimuli of the external world, and able to satisfy even its nutritional requirements autistically (to use Bleuler's term [1912]), is afforded by a bird's egg with its food supply enclosed in its shell; for it, the care provided by its mother is limited to the provision of warmth. – I shall not regard it as a correction, but as an amplification of the schematic picture under discussion, if it is insisted that a system living according to the pleasure principle must have devices to enable it to withdraw from the stimuli of reality. Such devices are merely the correlative of 'repression', which treats internal unpleasurable stimuli as if they were external – that is to say, pushes them into the external world.

[1] [This notion, often repeated by Freud, appears in his book on jokes (1905c), *Standard Ed.*, **8**, 175; *P.F.L.*, **6**, 233. It is examined more deeply in the paper on 'Negation' (1925h), *Standard Ed.*, **19**, 236; *P.F.L.*, **11**, 438.]

the body (leading to expressive movements and the play of features and to manifestations of affect). Motor discharge was now employed in the appropriate alteration of reality; it was converted into *action*.

Restraint upon motor discharge (upon action), which then became necessary, was provided by means of the process of *thinking*, which was developed from the presentation of ideas. Thinking was endowed with characteristics which made it possible for the mental apparatus to tolerate an increased tension of stimulus while the process of discharge was postponed. It is essentially an experimental kind of acting, accompanied by displacement of relatively small quantities of cathexis together with less expenditure (discharge) of them.[1] For this purpose the conversion of freely displaceable cathexes into 'bound' cathexes was necessary, and this was brought about by means of raising the level of the whole cathectic process. It is probable that thinking was originally unconscious, in so far as it went beyond mere ideational presentations and was directed to the relations between impressions of objects, and that it did not acquire further qualities, perceptible to consciousness, until it became bound to verbal residues.[2]

(2) A general tendency of our mental apparatus, which can be traced back to the economic principle of saving expenditure [of energy], seems to find expression in the tenacity with which we hold on to the sources of pleasure at our disposal, and in the difficulty with which we renounce them. With the introduction of the reality principle one species of thought-activity was split off; it was kept free from reality-testing and remained subordinated to the pleasure principle alone.[3] This activity is *phantasying*, which begins already in children's play, and later, continued as *day-dreaming*, abandons dependence on real objects.

(3) The supersession of the pleasure principle by the reality principle, with all the psychical consequences involved, which is here schematically condensed into a single sentence, is not in fact accom-

---

[1] [This important principle had been put forward by Freud in *The Interpretation of Dreams* (Standard Ed., 5, 599 f.; *P.F.L.*, 4, 758 f.) and more clearly in the book on jokes (1905c), Standard Ed., 8, 192; *P.F.L.*, 6, 251.]

[2] [Cf. *The Interpretation of Dreams* (Standard Ed., 5, 574 and 617; *P.F.L.*, 4, 729 f. and 779). This is further developed in Section VII of 'The Unconscious' in Chapter 3 above.]

[3] In the same way, a nation whose wealth rests on the exploitation of the produce of its soil will yet set aside certain areas for reservation in their original state and for protection from the changes brought about by civilization. (E.g. Yellowstone Park.) [Cf. the discussions of phantasies in 'Creative Writers and Day-Dreaming' (1908e) and in 'Hysterical Phantasies and their Relation to Bisexuality' (1908a).]

plished all at once; nor does it take place stimultaneously all along the line. For while this development is going on in the ego instincts, the sexual instincts become detached from them in a very significant way. The sexual instincts behave auto-erotically at first; they obtain their satisfaction in the subject's own body and therefore do not find themselves in the situation of frustration which was what necessitated the institution of the reality principle; and when, later on, the process of finding an object begins, it is soon interrupted by the long period of latency, which delays sexual development until puberty. These two factors – auto-erotism and the latency period – have as their result that the sexual instinct is held up in its psychical development and remains far longer under the dominance of the pleasure principle, from which in many people it is never able to withdraw.

In consequence of these conditions, a closer connection arises, on the one hand, between the sexual instinct and phantasy and, on the other hand, between the ego instincts and the activities of consciousness. Both in healthy and in neurotic people this connection strikes us as very intimate, although the considerations of genetic psychology which have just been put forward lead us to recognize it as a *secondary* one. The continuance of auto-erotism is what makes it possible to retain for so long the easier momentary and imaginary satisfaction in relation to the sexual object in place of real satisfaction, which calls for effort and postponement. In the realm of phantasy, repression remains all-powerful; it brings about the inhibition of ideas *in statu nascendi* before they can be noticed by consciousness, if their cathexis is likely to occasion a release of unpleasure. This is the weak spot in our psychical organization; and it can be employed to bring back under the dominance of the pleasure principle thought-processes which had already become rational. An essential part of the psychical disposition to neurosis thus lies in the delay in educating the sexual instincts to pay regard to reality and, as a corollary, in the conditions which make this delay possible.

(4) Just as the pleasure-ego can do nothing but *wish*, work for a yield of pleasure, and avoid unpleasure, so the reality-ego need do nothing but strive for what is *useful* and guard itself against damage.[1]

---

[1] The superiority of the reality-ego over the pleasure-ego has been aptly expressed by Bernard Shaw in these words: 'To be able to choose the line of greatest advantage instead of yielding in the direction of least resistance.' (*Man and Superman.*) [A much more elaborate account of the relations between the 'pleasure-ego' and the 'reality-ego' is given in 'Instincts and their Vicissitudes' (1915c), in Chapter 4 above.]

Actually the substitution of the reality principle for the pleasure principle implies no deposing of the pleasure principle, but only a safeguarding of it. A momentary pleasure, uncertain in its results, is given up, but only in order to gain along the new path an assured pleasure at a later time. But the endopsychic impression made by this substitution has been so powerful that it is reflected in a special religious myth. The doctrine of reward in the after-life for the – voluntary or enforced – renunciation of earthly pleasures is nothing other than a mythical projection of this revolution in the mind. Following consistently along these lines, *religions* have been able to effect absolute renunciation of pleasure in this life by means of the promise of compensation in a future existence; but they have not by this means achieved a conquest of the pleasure principle. It is *science* which comes nearest to succeeding in that conquest; science too, however, offers intellectual pleasure during its work and promises practical gain in the end.

(5) *Education* can be described without more ado as an incitement to the conquest of the pleasure principle, and to its replacement by the reality principle; it seeks, that is, to lend its help to the developmental process which affects the ego. To this end it makes use of an offer of love as a reward from the educators; and it therefore fails if a spoilt child thinks that it possesses that love in any case and cannot lose it whatever happens.

(6) *Art* brings about a reconciliation between the two principles in a peculiar way. An artist is originally a man who turns away from reality because he cannot come to terms with the renunciation of instinctual satisfaction which it at first demands, and who allows his erotic and ambitious wishes full play in the life of phantasy. He finds the way back the reality, however, from this world of phantasy by making use of special gifts to mould his phantasies into truths of a new kind, which are valued by men as precious reflections of reality. Thus in a certain fashion he actually becomes the hero, the king, the creator, or the favourite he desired to be, without following the long roundabout path of making real alterations in the external world. But he can only achieve this because other men feel the same dissatisfaction as he does with the renunciation demanded by reality, and because that dissatisfaction, which results from the replacement of the pleasure principle by the reality principle, is itself a part of reality.[1]

[1] Cf. the similar position taken by Otto Rank (1907). [See also 'Creative Writers and Day-Dreaming' (1908*e*).]

(7) While the ego goes through its transformation from a *pleasure-ego* into a *reality-ego*, the sexual instincts undergo the changes that lead them from their original auto-erotism through various intermediate phases to object-love in the service of procreation. If we are right in thinking that each step in these two courses of development may become the site of a disposition to later neurotic illness, it is plausible to suppose that the form taken by the subsequent illness (the *choice of neurosis*) will depend on the particular phase of the development of the ego and of the libido in which the dispositional inhibition of development has occurred. Thus unexpected sigificance attaches to the chronological features of the two developments (which have not yet been studied), and to possible variations in their synchronization.[1]

(8) The strangest characteristic of unconscious (repressed) processes, to which no investigator can become accustomed without the exercise of great self-discipline, is due to their entire disregard of reality-testing; they equate reality of thought with external actuality, and wishes with their fulfilment – with the event – just as happens automatically under the dominance of the ancient pleasure principle. Hence also the difficulty of distinguishing unconscious phantasies from memories which have become unconscious.[2] But one must never allow oneself to be misled into applying the standards of reality to repressed psychical structures, and on that account, perhaps, into undervaluing the importance of phantasies in the formation of symptoms on the ground that they are not actualities, or into tracing a neurotic sense of guilt back to some other source because there is no evidence that any actual crime has been committed. One is bound to employ the currency that is in use in the country one is exploring – in our case a neurotic currency. Suppose, for instance, that one is trying to solve a dream such as this. A man who had once nursed his father through a long and painful mortal illness, told me that in the months following his father's death he had repeatedly dreamt that *his father was alive once more and that he was talking to him in his usual way. But he felt it exceedingly painful that his father had really died, only without knowing it.* The only way of understanding this apparently nonsensical dream is by adding 'as the dreamer wished' or 'in consequence of his wish' after the words 'that his father had really died', and by further adding 'that

---

[1] [This theme is developed in 'The Disposition to Obsessional Neurosis' (1913*i*); *Standard Ed.*, **12**, 324 ff.; *P.F.L.*, **10**, 142 ff.]

[2] [This difficulty is discussed at length in the later part of Lecture 23 in Chapter 9 below.]

he [the dreamer] wished it' to the last words. The dream-thought then runs: it was a painful memory for him that he had been obliged to wish for his father's death (as a release) while he was still alive, and how terrible it would have been if his father had had any suspicion of it! What we have here is thus the familiar case of self-reproaches after the loss of someone loved, and in this instance the self-reproach went back to the infantile significance of death-wishes against the father.

The deficiencies of this short paper, which is preparatory rather than expository, will perhaps be excused only in small part if I plead that they are unavoidable. In these few remarks on the psychical consequences of adaptation to the reality principle I have been obliged to adumbrate views which I should have preferred for the present to withhold and whose justification will certainly require no small effort. But I hope it will not escape the notice of the benevolent reader how in these pages too the dominance of the reality principle is beginning.

Eight

THE CONCEPT OF
REPRESSION

Introduction

For Freud, repression was the fundamental problem from which 'the study of the neurotic processes took its whole start' (1937c, p. 236); the 'theory of repression became the cornerstone of our understanding of the neuroses' (1925d). Throughout his working'life Freud persisted in his attempts to explain the phenomenon that there are psychic processes capable of excluding other psychic processes from consciousness. What he described in the later-abandoned 'Project for a Scientific Psychology' of 1895 (1950a) as a failure in the translation of an earlier mode into a subsequently superimposed mode of psychic expression appeared, in the topographic theory, as hindering the passage from the system unconscious to the systems preconscious and conscious – specifically, as the withdrawal of the quantity of cathexis which alone would make the emergence into conscious perception possible; and finally, in the structural model of the psychic apparatus, as the result of the dynamic interplay between the psychic agencies. The element which in these successive attempts remains constant is the motive of repression, namely, the prevention of the arousal of anxiety or unpleasure in the system conscious and conscious ego, respectively.

Where these purely theoretical expositions may perplex the student or lay reader, Freud's allegorical descriptions come to his aid. In the topographical model, Freud uses the picture of the censor who guards the border between unconscious and conscious, severs the connections between the forbidden drive derivatives and the feelings accompanying them or the thoughts and images representing them, and thereby prevents their rising into the higher systems. In the structural model, it is the picture of the ego which is hard pressed by the instinctual claims of the id, the conditions in the external world, and the moral demands of the super-ego, and which takes refuge by resorting to the defence mechanism of repression. These lively descriptions reflect something of the individual's actual and immediate experience: a dim intimation of pressing impulses at work; a sense of being at odds with oneself; in short, the distress connected with an internal conflictual state.

As is usually the case in psycho-analytic investigations, the study of repression started not with the successful but with the miscarried defence. Where repression achieves the desired aim, namely, to keep the unwelcome psychic elements more or less permanently away from consciousness, there are on the surface of consciousness no visible indications of what has occurred; at best, there are breaks in the psychic connections and such gaps are frequently enough disregarded. On the other hand, where repression does not succeed or succeeds only partially, symptoms are formed and the conflict between impulse and defence, between the upsurge of the repressed material and the repressing forces, continues before the eyes of the observer; this makes it possible for us to gain an understanding of all the stages, forms and mechanisms of the defensive struggle, beginning with the extensive withdrawal of cathexis from the conscious representatives to the return of the repressed in its original or distorted form.

Repression is not the only possible form of defence; there exist other mechanisms of defence which support and augment and also succeed it. Freud only hinted at this in the paper we shall study next, namely, 'Repression' (1915d), a relatively early work (written before the introduction of the structural model), but he elaborated on it in later publications. In 1926 Freud speaks of defence as 'a general designation for all the techniques which the ego makes use of in conflicts which may lead to a neurosis, while we retain the word "repression" for the special method of defence which the line of approach taken by our investigation made us better acquainted with in the first instance' (1926d, p. 163).

It will be obvious to every reader of Freud's case histories what Freud means by 'the line of approach taken by our investigation'. In the early *Studies on Hysteria* (1893–95), it is the defensive device of repression followed by conversion of the repressed into somatic innervation which is convincingly demonstrated. In the later 'Notes upon a Case of Obsessional Neurosis' (1909d), the same occurs with regard to the mechanisms of defence characteristic of this illness: obsessional thinking, compulsive actions, doubts, indecision, undoing, isolation of affect and ideas, turning into the opposite, reaction-formations. 'Analysis of a Phobia in a Five-Year-Old Boy' (1909b) throws light on psychic displacement and flight, and 'Psycho-Analytic Notes on an Autobiographical Account of a Case of Paranoia' (1911c) primarily on the defence mechanism of projection.

The avoidance of anxiety and unpleasure is the overriding principle that dominates the individual's life from the very beginning; accordingly, the development of a reliable chronology of defensive processes is a task of psycho-analytic theory which has high priority but which, for the time being, has not yet been solved. It is obvious that there can be no repressions in the period of complete immaturity, i.e., prior to the division of the psychic apparatus into the systems conscious and unconscious, ego and id. The defensive devices commonly used in this early period are primitive – flight, denial, reversal into the opposite, turning against the self. As soon as psychic differentiation between the self and the surrounding world, between inner and outer, has taken place, unpleasant elements of the inner life can be displaced into the outer world. When later on genuine repressions are accomplished but remain unreliable, they are reinforced by the cathexis, in the realm of the conscious ego, of representatives of the opposite of the repudiated elements (e.g., compassion instead of cruelty, disgust instead of pleasure in soiling, etc.). Finally, under the influence of the super-ego, primitive impulses are transformed, inhibited in their aims, and the drive energies belonging to them deflected to moral, ethical or socially higher aims.

The fact that such defence mechanisms as denial, reversal into the opposite, turning against the self, projection, reaction-formation and sublimation develop and are used does not diminish the outstanding position of repression in psychic life. Repression is and remains 'something quite peculiar and is more sharply differentiated from the other mechanisms than they are from one another' (1937c, p. 236). Although these other mechanisms may bring about deflections, changes in direction, and transformations of drive derivatives, only repression succeeds in completely obliterating their appearance in the conscious material. For this reason, repression is the most stable and highly developed defence.

Repression

(1915)*

One of the vicissitudes an instinctual impulse may undergo is to meet with resistances which seek to make it inoperative. Under certain conditions, which we shall presently investigate more closely, the impulse then passes into the state of 'repression'. If what was in question was the operation of an external stimulus, the appropriate method to adopt would obviously be flight; with an instinct, flight is of no avail, for the ego cannot escape from itself. At some later period, rejection based on judgement (*condemnation*) will be found to be a good method to adopt against an instinctual impulse. Repression is a preliminary stage of condemnation, something between flight and condemnation; it is a concept which could not have been formulated before the time of psycho-analytic studies.

It is not easy in theory to deduce the possibility of such a thing as repression. Why should an instinctual impulse undergo a vicissitude like this? A necessary condition of its happening must clearly be that the instinct's attainment of its aim should produce unpleasure instead of pleasure. But we cannot well imagine such a contingency. There are no such instincts: satisfaction of an instinct is always pleasurable. We should have to assume certain peculiar circumstances, some sort of process by which the pleasure of satisfaction is changed into unpleasure.

In order the better to delimit repression, let us discuss some other instinctual situations. It may happen that an external stimulus becomes internalized – for example, by eating into and destroying some bodily organ – so that a new source of constant excitation and increase of tension arises. The stimulus thereby acquires a far-reaching similarity to an instinct. We know that a case of this sort is experienced by us as *pain*. The aim of this pseudo-instinct, however, is

* First published in *Int. Z. ärztl. Psychoanal.* The present text is included in *Standard Ed.*, **14**, 146; *P.F.L.*, **11**, 145.

simply the cessation of the change in the organ and of the unpleasure accompanying it. There is no other direct pleasure to be attained by cessation of pain. Further, pain is imperative; the only things to which it can yield are removal by some toxic agent or the influence of mental distraction.

The case of pain is too obscure to give us any help in our purpose.[1] Let us take the case in which an instinctual stimulus such as hunger remains unsatisfied. It then becomes imperative and can be allayed by nothing but the action that satisfies it; it keeps up a constant tension of need. Nothing in the nature of a repression seems in this case to come remotely into question.

Thus repression certainly does not arise in cases where the tension produced by lack of satisfaction of an instinctual impulse is raised to an unbearable degree. The methods of defence which are open to the organism against that situation must be discussed in another connection.

Let us rather confine ourselves to clinical experience, as we meet with it in psycho-analytic practice. We then learn that the satisfaction of an instinct which is under repression would be quite possible, and further, that in every instance such a satisfaction would be pleasurable in itself; but it would be irreconcilable with other claims and intentions. It would, therefore, cause pleasure in one place and unpleasure in another. It has consequently become a condition for repression that the motive force of unpleasure shall have acquired more strength than the pleasure obtained from satisfaction. Psychoanalytic observation of the transference neuroses, moreover, leads us to conclude that repression is not a defensive mechanism which is present from the very beginning, and that it cannot arise until a sharp cleavage has occurred between conscious and unconscious mental activity – that *the essence of repression lies simply in turning something away, and keeping it at a distance, from the conscious.*[2] This view of repression would be made more complete by assuming that, before the mental organization reaches this stage, the task of fending off instinctual impulses is dealt with by the other vicissitudes which instincts may undergo – e.g. reversal into the opposite or turning round upon the subject's own self.[3]

---

[1] [Pain and the organism's method of dealing with it are discussed in Section IV of *Beyond the Pleasure Principle* in Chapter 4 above.]

[2] [See p. 173 above.]

[3] [See p. 205 above.]

It seems to us now that, in view of the very great extent to which repression and what is unconscious are correlated, we must defer probing more deeply into the nature of repression until we have learnt more about the structure of the succession of psychical agencies and about the differentiation between what is unconscious and conscious.[1] Till then, all we can do is to put together in a purely descriptive fashion a few characteristics of repression that have been observed clinically, even though we run the risk of having to repeat unchanged much that has been said elsewhere.

We have reason to assume that there is a *primal repression*, a first phase of repression, which consists in the psychical (ideational) representative of the instinct being denied entrance into the conscious. With this a *fixation* is established; the representative in question persists unaltered from then onwards and the instinct remains attached to it. This is due to the properties of unconscious processes of which we shall speak later [p. 160].

The second stage of repression, *repression proper*, affects mental derivatives of the repressed representative, or such trains of thought as, originating elsewhere, have come into associative connection with it. On account of this association, these ideas experience the same fate as what was primally repressed. Repression proper, therefore, is actually an after-pressure. Moreover, it is a mistake to emphasize only the repulsion which operates from the direction of the conscious upon what is to be repressed; quite as important is the attraction exercised by what was primally repressed upon everything with which it can establish a connection. Probably the trend towards repression would fail in its purpose if these two forces did not co-operate, if there were not something previously repressed ready to receive what is repelled by the conscious.[2]

Under the influence of the study of the psychoneuroses, which brings before us the important effects of repression, we are inclined to overvalue their psychological bearing and to forget too readily that repression does not hinder the instinctual representative from continuing to exist in the unconscious, from organizing itself further, putting out derivatives and establishing connections. Repression in

---

[1] [See Section IV of 'The Unconscious' in Chapter 3 above.]
[2] [The two stages of repression described in the last two paragraphs had been anticipated by Freud in his Schreber analysis (1911c), *Standard Ed.*, **12**, 67; *P.F.L.*, **9**, 205. See also *Standard Ed.*, **5**, 547 *n*; *P.F.L.*, **4**, 698 *n.2*.]

fact interferes only with the relation of the instinctual representative to *one* psychical system, namely, to that of the conscious.

Psycho-analysis is able to show us other things as well which are important for understanding the effects of repression in the psychoneuroses. It shows us, for instance, that the instinctual representative develops with less interference and more profusely if it is withdrawn by repression from conscious influence. It proliferates in the dark, as it were, and takes on extreme forms of expression, which when they are translated and presented to the neurotic are not only bound to seem alien to him, but frighten him by giving him the picture of an extraordinary and dangerous strength of instinct. This deceptive strength of instinct is the result of an uninhibited development in phantasy and of the damming-up consequent on frustrated satisfaction. The fact that this last result is bound up with repression points the direction in which the true significance of repression has to be looked for.

Reverting once more, however, to the opposite aspect of repression, let us make it clear that it is not even correct to suppose that repression withholds from the conscious *all* the derivatives of what was primally repressed.[1] If these derivatives have become sufficiently far removed from the repressed representative, whether owing to the adoption of distortions or by reason of the number of intermediate links inserted, they have free access to the conscious. It is as though the resistance of the conscious against them was a function of their distance from what was originally repressed. In carrying out the technique of psycho-analysis, we continually require the patient to produce such derivatives of the repressed as, in consequence either of their remoteness or of their distortion, can pass the censorship of the conscious. Indeed, the associations which we require him to give without being influenced by any conscious purposive idea and without any criticism, and from which we reconstitute a conscious translation of the repressed representative – these associations are nothing else than remote and distorted derivatives of this kind. During this process we observe that the patient can go on spinning a thread of such associations, till he is brought up against some thought, the relation of which to what is repressed becomes so obvious that he is compelled to repeat his attempt at repression. Neurotic symptoms, too, must have fulfilled

[1] [What follows in this paragraph is discussed at greater length in Section VI of 'The Unconscious' in Chapter 3 above.]

this same condition, for they are derivatives of the repressed, which has, by their means, finally won the access to consciousness which was previously denied to it.

We can lay down no general rule as to what degree of distortion and remoteness is necessary before the resistance on the part of the conscious is removed. A delicate balancing is here taking place, the play of which is hidden from us; its mode of operation, however, enables us to infer that it is a question of calling a halt when the cathexis of the unconscious reaches a certain intensity – an intensity beyond which the unconscious would break through to satisfaction. Repression acts, therefore, in a *highly individual* manner. Each single derivative of the repressed may have its own special vicissitude; a little more or a little less distortion alters the whole outcome. In this connection we can understand how it is that the objects to which men give most preference, their ideals, proceed from the same perceptions and experiences as the objects which they most abhor, and that they were originally only distinguished from one another through slight modifications. Indeed, as we found in tracing the origin of the fetish,[1] it is possible for the original instinctual representative to be split in two, one part undergoing repression, while the remainder, precisely on account of this intimate connection, undergoes idealization.

The same result as follows from an increase or a decrease in the degree of distortion may also be achieved at the other end of the apparatus, so to speak, by a modification in the condition for the production of pleasure and unpleasure. Special techniques have been evolved, with the purpose of bringing about such changes in the play of mental forces that what would otherwise give rise to unpleasure may on this occasion result in pleasure; and, whenever a technical device of this sort comes into operation, the repression of an instinctual representative which would otherwise be repudiated is lifted. These techniques have till now only been studied in any detail in jokes.[2] As a rule the repression is only temporarily lifted and is promptly reinstated.

Observations like this, however, enable us to note some further characteristics of repression. Not only is it, as we have just shown, *individual* in its operation, but it is also exceedingly *mobile*. The process of repression is not to be regarded as an event which takes place *once*,

---

[1] [Cf. Section 2 (A) of the first of Freud's *Three Essays* (1905*d*), in Chapter 5 above.]
[2] [See Chapter II of Freud's book on jokes (1905*c*).]

the results of which are permanent, as when some living thing has been killed and from that time onward is dead; repression demands a persistent expenditure of force, and if this were to cease the success of the repression would be jeopardized, so that a fresh act of repression would be necessary. We may suppose that the repressed exercises a continuous pressure in the direction of the conscious, so that this pressure must be balanced by an unceasing counter-pressure.[1] Thus the maintenance of a repression involves an uninterrupted expenditure of force, while its removal results in a saving from an economic point of view. The mobility of repression, incidentally, also finds expression in the psychical characteristics of the state of sleep, which alone renders possible the formation of dreams.[2] With a return to waking life the repressive cathexes which have been drawn in are once more sent out.

Finally, we must not forget that after all we have said very little about an instinctual impulse when we have established that it is repressed. Without prejudice to its repression, such an impulse may be in widely different states. It may be inactive, i.e. only very slightly cathected with mental energy; or it may be cathected in varying degrees, and so enabled to be active. True, its activation will not result in a direct lifting of the repression, but it will set in motion all the processes which end in a penetration by the impulse into consciousness along circuitous paths. With unrepressed derivatives of the unconscious the fate of a particular idea is often decided by the degree of its activity or cathexis. It is an everyday occurrence that such a derivative remains unrepressed so long as it represents only a small amount of energy, although its content would be calculated to give rise to a conflict with what is dominant in consciousness. The quantitative factor proves decisive for this conflict: as soon as the basically obnoxious idea exceeds a certain degree of strength, the conflict becomes a real one, and it is precisely this activation that leads to repression. So that, where repression is concerned, an increase of energic cathexis operates in the same sense as an approach to the unconscious, while a decrease of that cathexis operates in the same sense as remoteness from the unconscious or distortion. We see that the repressive trends may find a substitute for repression in a weakening of what is distasteful.

---

[1] [This is discussed further in Section IV of 'The Unconscious' in Chapter 3 above.]
[2] [Cf. *The Interpretation of Dreams*, Standard Ed., 5, 567 f.; P.F.L., 4, 721 f.]

In our discussion so far we have dealt with the repression of an instinctual representative, and by the latter we have understood an idea[1] or group of ideas which is cathected with a definite quota of psychical energy (libido or interest) coming from an instinct. Clinical observation now obliges us to divide up what we have hitherto regarded as a single entity; for it shows us that besides the idea, some other element representing the instinct has to be taken into account, and that this other element undergoes vicissitudes of repression which may be quite different from those undergone by the idea. For this other element of the psychical representative the term *quota of affect* has been generally adopted. It corresponds to the instinct in so far as the latter has become detached from the idea and finds expression, proportionate to its quantity, in processes which are sensed as affects. From this point on, in describing a case of repression, we shall have to follow up separately what, as the result of repression, becomes of the *idea*, and what becomes of the instinctual energy linked to it.

We should be glad to be able to say something general about the vicissitudes of both; and having taken our bearings a little we shall in fact be able to do so. The general vicissitude which overtakes the *idea* that represents the instinct can hardly be anything else than that it should vanish from the conscious if it was previously conscious, or that it should be held back from consciousness if it was about to become conscious. The difference is not important; it amounts to much the same thing as the difference between my ordering an undesirable guest out of my drawing-room (or out of my front hall), and my refusing, after recognizing him, to let him cross my threshold at all.[2] The *quantitative* factor of the instinctual representative has three possible vicissitudes, as we can see from a cursory survey of the observations made by psycho-analysis: either the instinct is altogether suppressed, so that no trace of it is found, or it appears as an affect which is in some way or other qualitatively coloured, or it is changed into anxiety.[3] The two latter possibilities set us the task of taking into account, as a further instinctual vicissitude, the

---

[1] ['*Vorstellung.*' See footnote 2, p. 149.]

[2] This simile, which is thus applicable to the process of repression, may also be extended to a characteristic of it which has been mentioned earlier: I have merely to add that I must set a permanent guard over the door which I have forbidden this guest to enter, since he would otherwise burst it open. (See above.)

[3] [Freud's altered views on this last point were stated by him in *Inhibitions, Symptoms and Anxiety* (1926*d*), especially at the end of Chapter IV and in Chapter XI, Section A (*b*).]

transformation into *affects*, and especially into *anxiety*, of the psychical energies of *instincts*.

We recall the fact that the motive and purpose of repression was nothing else than the avoidance of unpleasure. It follows that the vicissitude of the quota of affect belonging to the representative is far more important than the vicissitude of the idea, and this fact is decisive for our assessment of the process of repression. If a repression does not succeed in preventing feelings of unpleasure or anxiety from arising, we may say that it has failed, even though it may have achieved its purpose as far as the ideational portion is concerned. Repressions that have failed will of course have more claim on our interest than any that may have been successful; for the latter will for the most part escape our examination.

We must now try to obtain some insight into the *mechanism* of the process of repression. In particular we want to know whether there is a single mechanism only, or more than one, and whether perhaps each of the psychoneuroses is distinguished by a mechanism of repression peculiar to it. At the outset of this enquiry, however, we are met by complications. The mechanism of a repression becomes accessible to us only by our deducing that mechanism from the *outcome* of the repression. Confining our observations to the effect of repression on the ideational portion of the representative, we discover that as a rule it creates a *substitutive formation*. What is the mechanism by which such a substitute is formed? Or should we distinguish several mechanisms here as well? Further, we know that repression leaves *symptoms* behind it. May we then suppose that the forming of substitutes and the forming of symptoms coincide, and, if this is so on the whole, is the mechanism of forming symptoms the same as that of repression? The general probability would seem to be that the two are widely different, and that it is not the repression itself which produces substitutive formations and symptoms, but that these latter are indications of a *return of the repressed* and owe their existence to quite other processes. It would also seem advisable to examine the mechanisms by which substitutes and symptoms are formed before considering the mechanisms of repression.

Obviously this is no subject for further speculation. The place of speculation must be taken by a careful analysis of the results of repression observable in the different neuroses. I must, however, suggest that we should postpone this task, too, until we have formed reliable conceptions of the relation of the conscious to the

unconscious.[1] But, in order that the present discussion may not be
entirely unfruitful, I will say in advance that (1) the mechanism of
repression does not in fact coincide with the mechanism or mechanisms of forming substitutes, (2) there are a great many different
mechanisms of forming substitutes and (3) the mechanisms of repression have at least this one thing in common: a *withdrawal of the cathexis
of energy* (or of *libido*, where we are dealing with sexual instincts).

Further, restricting myself to the three best-known forms of
psychoneurosis, I will show by means of some examples how the
concepts here introduced find application to the study of repression.

From the field of *anxiety hysteria* I will choose a well-analysed
example of an animal phobia.[2] The instinctual impulse subjected to
repression here is a libidinal attitude towards the father, coupled with
fear of him. After repression, this impulse vanishes out of consciousness: the father does not appear in it as an object of libido. As a
substitute for him we find in a corresponding place some animal
which is more or less fitted to be an object of anxiety. The formation of
the substitute for the ideational portion [of the instinctual representa-
tive] has come about by *displacement* along a chain of connections
which is determined in a particular way. The quantitative portion has
not vanished, but has been transformed into anxiety. The result is fear
of a wolf, instead of a demand for love from the father. The categories
here employed are of course not enough to supply an adequate
explanation of even the simplest case of psychoneurosis: there are
always other considerations to be taken into account. A repression
such as occurs in an animal phobia must be described as radically
unsuccessful. All that it has done is to remove and replace the idea; it
has failed altogether in sparing unpleasure. And for this reason, too,
the work of the neurosis does not cease. It proceeds to a second phase,
in order to attain its immediate and more important purpose. What
follows is an attempt at flight – the formation of the *phobia proper*, of a
number of avoidances which are intended to prevent a release of the
anxiety. More specialized investigation enables us to understand the
mechanism by which the phobia achieves its aim.

We are obliged to take quite another view of the process of
repression when we consider the picture of a true *conversion hysteria*.
Here the salient point is that it is possible to bring about a total

[1] [Cf. Section IV of 'The Unconscious' in Chapter 3 above.]
[2] [This is, of course, a reference to the case history of the 'Wolf Man' (1918b).]

disappearance of the quota of affect. When this is so, the patient displays towards his symptoms what Charcot called '*la belle indifférence des hystériques*'. In other cases this suppression is not so completely successful: some distressing sensations may attach to the symptoms themselves, or it may prove impossible to prevent some release of anxiety, which in turn sets to work the mechanism of forming a phobia. The ideational content of the instinctual representative is completely withdrawn from consciousness; as a substitute – and at the same time as a symptom – we have an over-strong innervation (in typical cases, a somatic one), sometimes of a sensory, sometimes of a motor character, either as an excitation or an inhibition. The over-innervated area proves on a closer view to be a part of the repressed instinctual representative itself – a part which, as though by a process of *condensation*, has drawn the whole cathexis on to itself. These remarks do not of course bring to light the whole mechanism of a conversion hysteria; in especial the factor of *regression*, which will be considered in another connection, has also to be taken into account. In so far as repression in [conversion] hysteria is made possible only by the extensive formation of substitutes, it may be judged to be entirely unsuccessful; as regards dealing with the quota of affect, however, which is the true task of repression, it generally signifies a total success. In conversion hysteria the process of repression is completed with the formation of the symptom and does not, as in anxiety hysteria, need to continue to a second phase – or rather, strictly speaking, to continue endlessly.

A totally different picture of repression is shown, once more, in the third disorder which we shall consider to the purposes of our illustration – in *obsessional neurosis*. Here we are at first in doubt what it is that we have to regard as the instinctual representative that is subjected to repression – whether it is a libidinal or a hostile trend. This uncertainty arises because obsessional neurosis has as its basis a regression owing to which a sadistic trend has been substituted for an affectionate one. It is this hostile impulsion against someone who is loved which is subjected to repression. The effect at an early stage of the work of repression is quite different from what it is at a later one. At first the repression is completely successful; the ideational content is rejected and the affect made to disappear. As a substitutive formation there arises an alteration in the ego in the shape of an increased conscientiousness, and this can hardly be called a symptom. Here, substitute and symptom do not coincide. From this we learn something, too, about the mechanism of repression. In this instance, as in all others, repression has brought about a withdrawal of libido; but here it has made use of *reaction-formation* for this purpose, by intensifying an opposite. Thus in this case the formation of a substitute has the same mechanism as repression and at bottom coincides with it, while chronologically, as well as conceptually, it is distinct from the formation of a symptom. It is very probable that the whole process is made possible by the ambivalent relationship into which the sadistic impulsion that has to be repressed has been introduced. But the repression, which was at first successful, does not hold firm; in the further course of things its failure becomes increasingly marked. The ambivalence which has enabled repression through reaction-formation to take place is also the point at which the repressed succeeds in returning. The vanished affect comes back in its transformed shape as social anxiety, moral anxiety and unlimited self-reproaches; the rejected idea is replaced by a *substitute by displacement*, often a displacement on to something very small or indifferent.[1] A tendency to a complete re-establishment of the repressed idea is as a rule unmistakably present. The failure in the repression of the quantitative, affective factor brings into play the same mechanism of flight, by means of avoidance and prohibitions, as we have seen at work in the formation of hysterical phobias. The rejection of the *idea* from the conscious is, however, obstinately maintained, because it entails abstention from action, a motor fettering of the impulse. Thus in obsessional neurosis the work of repression is prolonged in a sterile and interminable struggle.

The short series of comparisons presented here may easily convince us that more comprehensive investigations are necessary before we can hope thoroughly to understand the processes connected with repression and the formation of neurotic symptoms. The extraordinary intricacy of all the factors to be taken into consideration leaves only one way of presenting them open to us. We must select first one and then another point of view, and follow it up through the material as long as the application of it seems to yield results. Each separate treatment of the subject will be incomplete in itself, and there cannot fail to be obscurities where it touches upon material that has not yet been treated; but we may hope that a final synthesis will lead to a proper understanding.

[1] [Cf. Section II (*c*) of the 'Rat Man' analysis, *Standard Ed.*, 10, 241; *P.F.L.*, 9, 120.]

Nine

SYMPTOM-FORMATION

Introduction

Those who have studied the preceding material (especially 1915e, 1905d) will not find it difficult to understand the complicated ways of symptom-formation and their end-products. Drastic changes in the course of psychic processes, such as those enforced by repression and the other mechanism of defence, cannot remain without serious consequences. What starts out as seemingly harmless, namely, in the service of avoiding unpleasure, ends more or less intractably in ego alterations, character distortions and pathological manifestations.

The student who has followed us thus far must by now have gained a clear notion of the conflict between drive satisfaction and defence against the drives. At this point he needs to be introduced to two new concepts – regression and fixation.

An individual who finds the path to an instinctual aim of adulthood blocked by internal or external obstacles can respond to such a frustration by reverting to childhood forms of satisfaction; i.e., he regresses in his search for pleasure. Which one of the old forms of satisfaction will in this way be revived depends upon the real or phantasied occurrences of his own repressed early childhood, i.e., on the quantity of libidinal energy attached to or fixated at specific developmental phases. The larger the quantity is, the stronger is the pull exerted by the phase involved and by the forms of satisfaction in question. But that which in childhood was a legitimate part of the infantile drive constitution is for the adult, non-regressed ego a piece of perversion and as such inadmissible and unpleasure-provoking. A defensive struggle ensues and comes to an end only when a compromise between instinctual drive and defence has been found. The compromise solution is the neurotic symptom, which is two-faced. On the one hand, it represents a partial success of the defensive forces which contrived to prevent the instinctual drives from attaining their aim; on the other hand, it serves as a substitute for the instinctual satisfaction, though in a 'very much reduced, displaced and inhibited' form (1926d, p. 95).

The path to the neurotic symptom thus proceeds via several steps: from the demands of the instinctual impulses to their frustration; from the frustration of satisfaction to regression to the fixation point in infancy; from the infantile phantasied satisfaction to anxiety and unpleasure; from anxiety and unpleasure to defence; finally, from defensive struggle to compromise formation. It is impossible to over-estimate the role played by anxiety in this context. Where the individual's ego acquiesces to the infantile satisfactions and does not object to them, that is, where no anxiety arises, neither defence nor symptom-formation comes about. Instead the individual's entire behaviour reverts to an earlier level.

As the main work illustrating these formulations I would select Freud's lecture on 'The Paths to the Formation of Symptoms' (1916–17). The processes involved are further illustrated in Freud's case histories (1905e, 1909b, 1909d, 1911c, 1918b), which, according to his own account, 'read like short stories' (1893–95, p. 160). As mentioned in the paper on repression, different combinations of defensive processes are at work in each of the different neuroses described by Freud. It is the choice and mixture of mechanisms which in hysteria (repression, conversion), phobia (flight, displacement, avoidance), obsessional neurosis (repression, reaction-formation, isolation, undoing), paranoia (projection) determine the form of symptom-formation.

The Paths to the Formation of Symptoms

(1916–17)*

Ladies and Gentlemen, – For laymen the symptoms constitute the essence of a disease and its cure consists in the removal of the symptoms. Physicians attach importance to distinguishing the symptoms from the disease and declare that getting rid of the symptoms does not amount to curing the disease. But the only tangible thing left of the disease after the symptoms have been got rid of is the capacity to form new symptoms. For that reason we will for the moment adopt the layman's position and assume that to unravel the symptoms means the same thing as to understand the disease.

Symptoms – and of course we are dealing now with psychical (or psychogenic) symptoms and psychical illness – are acts detrimental, or at least useless, to the subject's life as a whole, often complained of by him as unwelcome and bringing unpleasure or suffering to him. The main damage they do resides in the mental expenditure which they themselves involve and in the further expenditure that becomes necessary for fighting against them. Where there is an extensive formation of symptoms, these two sorts of expenditure can result in an extraordinary impoverishment of the subject in regard to the mental energy available to him and so in paralysing him for all the important tasks of life. Since this outcome depends mainly on the *quantity* of the energy which is thus absorbed, you will easily see that 'being ill' is in its essence a practical concept. But if you take up a theoretical point of view and disregard this matter of quantity, you may quite well say that we are *all* ill – that is, neurotic – since the preconditions for the formation of symptoms can also be observed in normal people.

* First published by Heller (Vienna). The present text is included in *Standard Ed.*, **16**, 358; *P.F.L.*, **1**, 404.

We already know that neurotic symptoms are the outcome of a conflict which arises over a new method of satisfying the libido. The two forces which have fallen out meet once again in the symptom and are reconciled, as it were, by the compromise of the symptom that has been constructed. It is for that reason, too, that the symptom is so resistant: it is supported from both sides. We also know that one of the two partners to the conflict is the unsatisfied libido which has been repulsed by reality and must now seek for other paths to its satisfaction. If reality remains relentless even though the libido is ready to take another object in place of the one that has been refused to it, then it will finally be compelled to take the path of regression and strive to find satisfaction either in one of the organizations which it has already outgrown or from one of the objects which it has earlier abandoned. The libido is lured into the path of regression by the fixation which it has left behind it at these points in its development.

The path to perversion branches off sharply from that to neurosis. If these regressions rouse no objection from the ego, no neurosis will come about either; and the libido will arrive at some real, even though no longer normal, satisfaction. But if the ego, which has under its control not only consciousness but also the approaches to motor innervation and accordingly to the realization of mental desires, does not agree with these regressions, conflict will follow. The libido is, as it were, cut off and must try to escape in some direction where, in accordance with the requirements of the pleasure principle, it can find a discharge for its cathexis of energy. It must withdraw from the ego. An escape of this kind is offered it by the fixations on the path of its development which it has now entered on regressively – fixations from which the ego had protected itself in the past by repressions. By cathecting these repressed positions as it flows backward, the libido has withdrawn from the ego and its laws, and has at the same time renounced all the education it has acquired under the ego's influence. It was docile so long as satisfaction beckoned to it; but under the double pressure of external and internal frustration it becomes refractory, and recalls earlier and better times. Such is the libido's fundamentally unchangeable character. The ideas to which it now transfers its energy as a cathexis belong to the system of the unconscious and are subject to the processes which are possible there, particularly to condensation and displacement. In this way conditions are established which completely resemble those in dream-construction. The dream proper, which has been completed in the unconscious and is the fulfilment of an unconscious wishful phantasy, is brought up against a portion of (pre)conscious activity which exercises the office of censorship and which, when it has been indemnified, permits the formation of the manifest dream as a compromise. In the same way, what represents[1] the libido in the unconscious has to reckon with the power of the preconscious ego. The opposition which had been raised against it in the ego pursues it as an 'anticathexis'[2] and compels it to choose a form of expression which can at the same time become an expression of the opposition itself. Thus the symptom emerges as a many-times-distorted derivative of the unconscious libidinal wish-fulfilment, an ingeniously chosen piece of ambiguity with two meanings in complete mutual contradiction. In this last respect, however, there is a distinction between the construction of a dream and of a symptom. For in dream-formation the preconscious purpose is merely concerned to preserve sleep, to allow nothing that would disturb it to make its way into consciousness; it does not insist upon calling out sharply 'No! on the contrary!' to the unconscious wishful impulse. It can afford to be more tolerant because the situations of someone sleeping is less perilous. The state of sleep in itself bars any outlet into reality.

You see, then, that the libido's escape under conditions of conflict is made possible by the presence of fixations. The regressive cathexis of these fixations leads to the circumvention of the repression and to a discharge (or satisfaction) of the libido, subject to the conditions of a compromise being observed. By the roundabout path *viâ* the unconscious and the old fixations, the libido finally succeeds in forcing its way through to real satisfaction – though to one which is extremely restricted and scarcely recognizable as such. Let me add two comments to this conclusion. First, I should like you to notice how closely here the libido and the unconscious on one side and the ego, consciousness and reality on the other are shown to be inter-linked, although to begin with they did not belong together at all. And secondly, I must ask you to bear in mind that everything I have said about this and what is still to follow relates only to the formation of symptoms in the neurosis of hysteria.

[1] [I.e. the representative in psychical terms of the libido regarded as something somatic.]

[2] [That is, a force acting in a sense contrary to the primary instinctual energy.]

Where, then, does the libido find the fixations which it requires in order to break through the repressions? In the activities and experiences of infantile sexuality, in the abandoned component trends, in the objects of childhood which have been given up. It is to them, accordingly, that the libido returns. The significance of this period of childhood is twofold: on the one hand, during it the instinctual trends which the child has inherited with his innate disposition first become manifest, and secondly, others of his instincts are for the first time awakened and made active by external impressions and accidental experiences. There is no doubt, I think, that we are justified in making this twofold division. The manifestation of the innate disposition is indeed not open to any critical doubts, but analytic experience actually compels us to assume that purely chance experiences in childhood are able to leave fixations of the libido behind them. Nor do I see my theoretical difficulty in this. Constitutional dispositions are also undoubtedly after-effects of experiences by ancestors in the past; they too were once acquired. Without such acquisition there would be no heredity. And is it conceivable that acquisitions such as this, leading to inheritance, would come to an end precisely with the generation we are considering? The significance of infantile experiences should not be totally neglected, as people like doing, in comparison with the experiences of the subject's ancestors and of his own maturity; on the contrary, they call for particular consideration. They are all the more momentous because they occur in times of incomplete development and are for that very reason liable to have traumatic effects. The studies on developmental mechanics by Roux[1] and others have shown that the prick of a needle into an embryonic germinal layer in the act of cell-division results in a severe disturbance of development. The same injury inflicted on a larval or fully grown animal would do no damage.

Thus fixation of the libido in the adult, which we introduced into the aetiological equation of neurosis as representing the constitutional factor, now falls, for our purposes, into two further parts: the inherited constitution and the disposition acquired in early childhood. As we all know, a diagram is certain of a sympathetic reception from students. So I will summarize the position diagrammatically:[1]

[1] [Wilhelm Roux (1850–1924) was one of the founders of experimental embryology.]

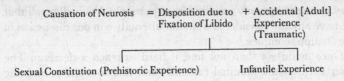

The hereditary sexual constitution presents us with a great variety of dispositions, according as one component instinct or another, alone or in combination with others, is inherited in particular strength. The sexual constitution forms once again, together with the factor of infantile experience, a 'complemental series' exactly similar to the one we first came to know between disposition and the accidental experience of the adult. In both of them we find the same extreme cases and the same relations between the two factors concerned. And here the question suggests itself of whether the most striking kinds of libidinal regressions – those to earlier stages of the sexual organization – may not be predominantly determined by the hereditary constitutional factor. But it is best to postpone answering this question till we have been able to take a wider range of forms of neurotic illness into account.

Let us dwell now on the fact that analytic research shows the libido of neurotics tied to their infantile sexual experiences. It thus lends these the appearance of an enormous importance for the life and illness of human beings. They retain this importance undiminished so far as the work of therapeutics is concerned. But if we turn away from that task we can nevertheless easily see that there is a danger here of a misunderstanding which might mislead us into basing our view of life too one-sidedly on the neurotic situation. We must after all subtract from the importance of infantile experiences the fact that the libido has returned to them *regressively*, after being driven out of its later positions. In that case the contrary conclusion becomes very tempting – that these libidinal experiences had no importance at all at the time

[1] [Readers may find this diagram easier to follow in the form of a genealogical tree:

Sexual Constitution   + Infantile Experience
(Prehistoric Experience)
                        |

        Disposition due to   + Accidental [Adult]
        Fixation of Libido   Experience (Traumatic)
                            |

                        Neurosis]

they occurred but only acquired its regressively. You will recall that we have already considered a similar alternative in our discussion of the Oedipus complex.[1]

Once again we shall not find it hard to reach a decision. The assertion that the libidinal cathexis (and therefore the pathogenic significance) of the infantile experiences has been largely intensified by the regression of the libido is undoubtedly correct, but it would lead to error if we were to regard it alone as decisive. Other considerations must be allowed weight as well.

In the first place observation shows, in a manner that excludes all doubt, that the infantile experiences have an importance of their own and give evidence of it already in childhood. Children too have their neuroses, in which the factor of displacement backwards in time is necessarily very much reduced or is even completely absent, since the onset of the illness follows the traumatic experiences immediately. The study of these infantile neuroses protects us from more than one dangerous misunderstanding of the neuroses of adults, just as the dreams of children gave us the key to an understanding of adult dreams.[2] Children's neuroses are very common, much commoner than is supposed. They are often overlooked, regarded as signs of a bad or naughty child, often, too, kept under by the nursery authorities; but they can always be easily recognized in retrospect. They usually appear in the form of *anxiety hysteria*. We shall learn on a later occasion what that means. If a neurosis breaks out in later life, analysis regularly reveals it as a direct continuation of the infantile illness which may have emerged as no more than a veiled hint. As I have said, however, there are cases in which these signs of neurosis in childhood proceed uninterruptedly into a lifelong illness. We have been able to analyse a few examples of these children's neuroses in childhood itself – when they were actually present;[3] but far more often we have had to be content with someone who has fallen ill in adult life enabling us to obtain a deferred insight into his childhood neurosis. In such cases we must not fail to make certain corrections and take certain precautions.

In the second place, we must reflect that it would be inconceivable for the libido to regress so regularly to the period of childhood unless

---

[1] [See Lecture 21, *Introductory Lectures* (*Standard Ed.*, **16**, 336; *P.F.L.*, **1**, 380).]

[2] [See Lecture 8, *ibid.* Freud was no doubt thinking here of his 'Wolf Man' analysis (1918*b*).]

[3] [Cf. the case history of 'Little Hans' (1909*b*).]

there were something there to exercise an attraction on it. The fixation which we have supposed to be present at particular points in the course of development can only have a meaning if we regard it as consisting in the retention of a certain quota of libidinal energy. And finally I may point out to you that between the intensity and pathogenic importance of infantile and of later experiences a complemental relationship exists similar to the series we have already discussed. There are cases in which the whole weight of causation falls on the sexual experiences of childhood, cases in which those impressions exert a definitely traumatic effect and call for no other support than can be afforded them by an average sexual constitution and the fact of its incomplete development. Alongside of these cases there are others in which the whole accent lies on the later conflicts and the emphasis we find in the analysis laid on the impressions of childhood appears entirely as the work of regression. Thus we have extremes of 'developmental inhibition' and 'regression' and between them every degree of co-operation between the two factors.

These facts have a certain interest from the point of view of education, which plans the prevention of neuroses by intervening at an early stage in children's sexual development. So long as one focuses attention principally on infantile sexual experiences, one must suppose that one has done everything for the prophylaxis of nervous illnesses by taking care that the child's development is delayed and that it is spared experiences of the sort. We already know, however, that the preconditions for the causation of neuroses are complex and cannot be influenced in general if we take account of only a single factor. Strict protection of the young loses value because it is powerless against the constitutional factor. Besides, it is more difficult to carry out than educationists imagine and it brings with it two fresh dangers which must not be underestimated: the fact that it may achieve too much – that it may encourage an excess of sexual repression, with damaging results, and the fact that it may send the child out into life without any defence against the onrush of sexual demands that is to be looked for at puberty.[1] Thus it remains extremely doubtful how far prophylaxis in childhood can be carried with advantage and whether an altered attitude to the immediate situation may not offer a better angle of approach for the prevention of neuroses.

[1] [Freud elaborated this difficulty in Lecture 34 of the *New Introductory Lectures* (*Standard Ed.*, **22**, 149; *P.F.L.*, **2**, 184).]

Let us now go back to the symptoms. They create a substitute, then, for the frustrated satisfaction by means of a regression of the libido to earlier times, with which a return to earlier stages of object-choice or of the organization is inseparably bound up. We discovered some time ago that neurotics are anchored somewhere in their past;[1] we know now that it is at a period of their past in which their libido did not lack satisfaction, in which they were happy. They search about in the history of their life till they find a period of that sort, even if they have to go back as far as the time when they were infants in arms – as they remember it or as they imagine it from later hints. In some way the symptom repeats this early infantile kind of satisfaction, distorted by the censorship arising from the conflict, turned as a rule to a feeling of suffering, and mingled with elements from the precipitating cause of the illness. The kind of satisfaction which the symptom brings has much that is strange about it.

We may disregard the fact that it is unrecognizable to the subject, who, on the contrary, feels the alleged satisfaction as suffering and complains of it. This transformation is a function of the psychical conflict under pressure of which the symptom had to be formed. What was once a satisfaction to the subject is, indeed, bound to arouse his resistance or his disgust to-day. We are familar with a trivial but instructive model of this change of mind. The same child who once eagerly sucked the milk from his mother's breast is likely a few years later to display a strong dislike to drinking milk, which his upbringing has difficulties in overcoming. This dislike increases to disgust if a skin forms on the milk or the drink containing it. We cannot exclude the possibility, perhaps, that the skin conjures up a memory of the mother's breast, once so ardently desired. Between the two situations, however, there lies the experience of weaning, with its traumatic effects.

It is something else besides that makes symptoms seem strange to us and incomprehensible as a means of libidinal satisfaction. They do not remind us in the very least of anything from which we are in the habit of normally expecting satisfaction. Usually they disregard objects and in so doing abandon their relation to external reality. We can see that this is a consequence of turning away from the reality principle and of returning to the pleasure principle. But it is also a return to a kind of extended auto-erotism, of the sort that offered the

[1] [See, for instance, Lecture 18 of the *Introductory Lectures* (*Standard Ed.*, **16**, 273; *P.F.L.*, **1**, 313).]

sexual instinct its first satisfactions. In place of a change in the external world these substitute a change in the subject's own body: they set an internal act in place of an external one, an adaptation in place of an action – once again, something that corresponds, phylogenetically, to a highly significant regression. We shall only understand this in connection with something new that we have still to learn from the analytic researches into the formation of symptoms. We must further remember that the same processes belonging to the unconscious play a part in the formation of symptoms as in the formation of dreams – namely, condensation and displacement. A symptom, like a dream, represents something as fulfilled: a satisfaction in the infantile manner. But by means of extreme condensation that satisfaction can be comparessed into a single sensation or innervation, and by means of extreme displacement it can be restricted to one small detail of the entire libidinal complex. It is not to be wondered at if we, too, often have difficulty in recognizing in a symptom the libidinal satisfaction whose presence we suspect and which is invariably confirmed.

I have warned you that we still have something new to learn; it is indeed something surprising and perplexing. By means of analysis, as you know, starting from the symptoms, we arrive at a knowledge of the infantile experiences to which the libido is fixated and out of which the symptoms are made. Well, the surprise lies in the fact that these scenes from infancy are not always true. Indeed, they are not true in the majority of cases, and in a few of them they are the direct opposite of the historical truth. As you will see, this discovery is calculated more than any other to discredit either analysis, which has led to this result, or the patients, on whose statements the analysis and our whole understanding of the neuroses are founded. But there is something else remarkably perplexing about it. If the infantile experiences brought to light by analysis were invariably real, we should feel that we were standing on firm ground; if they were regularly falsified and revealed as inventions, as phantasies of the patient, we should be obliged to abandon this shaky ground and look for salvation elsewhere. But neither of these things is the case: the position can be shown to be that the childhood experiences constructed or remembered in analysis are sometimes indisputably false and sometimes equally certainly correct, and in most cases compounded of truth and falsehood. Sometimes, then, symptoms represent events which really took place and to which we may attribute an influence on the fixation of the libido, and sometimes they represent phantasies of the patient's which are not, of course, suited to playing an aetiological role. It is difficult to find one's way about in this. We can make a first start, perhaps, with a similar discovery – namely, that the isolated childhood memories that people have possessed consciously from time immemorial and before there was any such thing as analysis may equally be falsified or at least may combine truth and falsehood in plenty. In their case there is seldom any difficulty in showing their incorrectness; so we at least have the reassurance of knowing that the responsibility for this unexpected disappointment lies, not with analysis, but in some way with the patients.

After a little reflection we shall easily understand what it is about this state of things that perplexes us so much. It is the low valuation of reality, the neglect of the distinction between it and phantasy. We are tempted to feel offended at the patient's having taken up our time with invented stories. Reality seems to us something worlds apart from invention, and we set a very different value on it. Moreover the patient, too, looks at things in this light in his normal thinking. When he brings up the material which leads from behind his symptoms to the wishful situations modelled on his infantile experiences, we are in doubt to begin with whether we are dealing with reality or phantasies. Later, we are enabled by certain indications to come to a decision and we are faced by the task of conveying it to the patient. This, however, invariably gives rise to difficulties. If we begin by telling him straight away that he is now engaged in bringing to light the phantasies with which he has disguised the history of his childhood (just as every nation disguises its forgotten prehistory by constructing legends), we observe that his interest in pursuing the subject further suddenly diminishes in an undesirable fashion. He too wants to experience realities and despises everything that is merely 'imaginary'. If, however, we leave him, till this piece of work is finished, in the belief that we are occupied in investigating the real events of his childhood, we run the risk of his later on accusing us of being mistaken and laughing at us for our apparent credulity. It will be a long time before he can take in our proposal that we should equate phantasy and reality and not bother to begin with whether the childhood experiences under examination are the one or the other. Yet this is clearly the only correct attitude to adopt towards these mental productions. They too possess a reality of a sort. It remains a fact that the patient has created these phantasies for himself, and this fact is of scarcely less importance for his neurosis than if he had really experienced what the phantasies contain. The phantasies possess *psychical* as contrasted with *material* reality, and we gradually learn to understand that *in the world of the neuroses it is psychical reality which is the decisive kind*.

Among the occurrences which recur again and again in the youthful history of neurotics – which are scarcely ever absent – there are a few of particular importance, which also deserve on that account, I think, to be brought into greater prominence than the rest. As specimens of this class I will enumerate these: observation of parental intercourse, seduction by an adult and threat of being castrated. It would be a mistake to suppose that they are never characterized by material reality; on the contrary, this is often established incontestably through enquiries from older members of the patient's family. It is by no means a rare thing, for instance, for a little boy, who is beginning to play with his penis in a naughty way and is not yet aware that one must conceal such activities, to be threatened by a parent or nurse with having his penis or his sinful hand cut off. Parents will often admit this when they are asked, since they think they have done something useful in making such a threat; a number of people have a correct conscious memory of such a threat, especially if it was made at a somewhat later period. If the threat is delivered by the mother or some other female she usually shifts its performance on to the father – or the doctor. In *Struwwelpeter*, the famous work of the Frankfurt paediatrician Hoffmann (which owes its popularity precisely to an understanding of the sexual and other complexes of childhood), you will find castration softened into a cutting-off of the thumbs as a punishment for obstinate sucking. But it is highly improbable that children are threatened with castration as often as it appears in the analyses of neurotics. We shall be satisfied by realizing that the child puts a threat of this kind together in his imagination on the basis of hints, helped out by a knowledge that auto-erotic satisfaction is forbidden and under the impression of his discovery of the female genitals. Nor is it only in proletarian families that it is perfectly possible for a child, while he is not yet credited with possessing an understanding or a memory, to be witness of the sexual act between his parents or other grown-up people; and the possibility cannot be rejected that he will be able to understand and react to the impression *in retrospect*. If, however, the intercourse is described with the most minute details, which would be difficult to observe, or if, as happens most frequently, it turns out to have been intercourse from behind, *more ferarum* [in the manner of animals], there can be no remaining doubt that the phantasy is based on an observation of intercourse between animals (such as dogs) and that its motive was the child's unsatisfied scopophilia during puberty. The extreme achievement on these lines is a phantasy of observing parental intercourse while one is still an unborn baby in the womb. Phantasies of being seduced are of particular interest, because so often they are not phantasies but real memories. Fortunately, however, they are nevertheless not real as often as seemed at first to be shown by the findings of analysis. Seduction by an older child or by one of the same age is even more frequent than by an adult; and if in the case of girls who produce such an event in the story of their childhood their father figures fairly regularly as the seducer, there can be no doubt either of the imaginary nature of the accusation or of the motive that has led to it.[1] A phantasy of being seduced when no seduction has occurred is usually employed by a child to screen the autoerotic period of his sexual activity. He spares himself shame about masturbation by retrospectively phantasying a desired object into these earliest times. You must not suppose, however, that sexual abuse of a child by its nearest male relatives belongs entirely to the realm of phantasy. Most analysts will have treated cases in which such events were real and could be unimpeachably established; but even so they related to the later years of childhood and had been transposed into earlier times.

The only impression we gain is that these events of childhood are somehow demanded as a necessity, that they are among the essential elements of a neurosis. If they have occurred in reality, so much to the good; but if they have been withheld by reality, they are put together from hints and supplemented by phantasy. The outcome is the same, and up to the present we have not succeeded in pointing to any difference in the consequences, whether phantasy or reality has had the greater share in these events of childhood. Here we simply have once again one of the complemental relations that I have so often mentioned; moreover it is the strangest of all we have met with. Whence comes the need for these phantasies and the material for them? There can be no doubt that their sources lie in the instincts; but

---

[1] [Freud has more to say on this subject in Lecture 33 in the *New Introductory Lectures* (1933*a*), p. 419 above.]

it has still to be explained why the same phantasies with the same content are created on every occasion. I am prepared with an answer which I know will seem daring to you. I believe these *primal phantasies*, as I should like to call them, and no doubt a few others as well, are a phylogenetic endowment. In them the individual reaches beyond his own experience into primaeval experience at points where his own experience has been too rudimentary. It seems to me quite possible that all the things that are told to us to-day in analysis as phantasy – the seduction of children, the inflaming of sexual excitement by observing parental intercourse, the threat of castration (or rather castration itself) – were once real occurrences in the primaeval times of the human family, and that children in their phantasies are simply filling in the gaps in individual truth with prehistoric truth. I have repeatedly been led to suspect that the psychology of the neuroses has stored up in it more of the antiquities of human development than any other source.[1]

The things I have just been discussing, Gentlemen, compel me to enter more closely into the origin and significance of the mental activity which is described as 'phantasy' [or 'imagination'].[2] As you are aware, it enjoys a universally high reputation, without its position in mental life having become clear. I have the following remarks to make about it. The human ego is, as you know, slowly educated by the pressure of external necessity to appreciate reality and obey the reality principle; in the course of this process it is obliged to renounce, temporarily or permanently, a variety of the objects and aims at which its striving for pleasure, and not only for sexual pleasure, is directed. But men have always found it hard to renounce pleasure; they cannot bring themselves to do it without some kind of compensation. They have therefore retained a mental activity in which all these abandoned sources of pleasure and methods of achieving pleasure are granted a further existence – a form of existence in which they are left free from the claims of reality and of what we call 'reality-testing'.[3] Every desire takes before long the form of picturing

---

[1] [This discussion of 'primal phantasies' and the possibility of their being inherited was based to a considerable extent on Freud's findings in his 'Wolf Man' case history (1918b).]

[2] Freud's main earlier discussion of phantasy was in 'Creative Writers and Day-Dreaming' (1908e), *Standard Ed.*, 9, 143 ff.; *P.F.L.*., 14, 127 ff. Cf. also 'Hysterical Phantasies and their Relation to Bisexuality', *Standard Ed.*, 9, 159 ff.; *P.F.L.*, 10, 83 ff.]

[3] [I.e. the process of judging whether things are real or not.]

its own fulfilment; there is no doubt that dwelling upon imaginary wish-fulfilments brings satisfaction with it, although it does not interfere with a knowledge that what is concerned is not real. Thus in the activity of phantasy human beings continue to enjoy the freedom from external compulsion which they have long since renounced in reality. They have contrived to alternate between remaining an animal of pleasure and being once more a creature of reason. Indeed, they cannot subsist on the scanty satisfaction which they can extort from reality. 'We cannot do without auxiliary constructions', as Theodor Fontane once said. The creation of the mental realm of phantasy finds a perfect parallel in the establishment of 'reservations' or 'nature reserves' in places where the requirements of agriculture, communications and industry threaten to bring about changes in the original face of the earth which will quickly make it unrecognizable. A nature reserve preserves its original state which everywhere else has to our regret been sacrified to necessity. Everything, including what is useless and even what is noxious, can grow and proliferate there as it pleases. The mental realm of phantasy is just such a reservation withdrawn from the reality principle.

The best-known productions of phantasy are the so-called 'day-dreams', which we have already come across, imagined satisfactions of ambitious, megalomanic, erotic wishes, which flourish all the more exuberantly the more reality counsels modesty and restraint. The essence of the happiness of phantasy – making the obtaining of pleasure free once more from the assent of reality – is shown in them unmistakably. We know that such day-dreams are the nucleus and prototype of night-dreams. A night-dream is at bottom nothing other than a day-dream that has been made utilizable owing to the liberation of the instinctual impulses at night, and that has been distorted by the form assumed by mental activity at night. We have already become familiar with the idea that even a day-dream is not necessarily conscious – that there are unconscious day-dreams, as well. Such unconscious day-dreams are thus the source not only of night-dreams but also of neurotic symptoms.

The importance of the part played by phantasy in the formation of symptoms will be made clear to you by what I have to tell you. I have explained how in the case of frustration the libido cathects regressively the positions which it has given up but to which some quotas of it have remained adhering. I shall not withdraw this or correct it, but I have to insert a connecting link. How does the libido find its way to these points of fixation? All the objects and trends which the libido has given up have not yet been given up in every sense. They or their derivatives are still retained with a certain intensity in phantasies. Thus the libido need only withdraw on to phantasies in order to find the path open to every repressed fixation. These phantasies have enjoyed a certain amount of toleration: they have not come into conflict with the ego, however sharp the contrast between them may have been, so long as a particular condition is observed. This condition is of a *quantitative* nature and it is now upset by the backward flow of libido on to the phantasies. As a result of this surplus, the energic cathexis of the phantasies is so much increased that they begin to raise claims, that they develop a pressure in the direction of becoming realized. But this makes a conflict between them and the ego inevitable. Whether they were previously preconscious or conscious, they are now subjected to repression from the direction of the ego and are at the mercy of attraction from the direction of the unconscious. From what are now unconscious phantasies the libido travels back to their origins in the unconscious – to its own points of fixation.

The libido's retreat to phantasy is an intermediate stage on the path to the formation of symptoms and it seems to call for a special name. C. G. Jung coined the very appropriate one of 'introversion', but then most inexpediently gave it another meaning as well.[1] We will continue to take it that introversion denotes the turning away of the libido from the possibilities of real satisfaction and the hypercathexis[2] of phantasies which have hitherto been tolerated as innocent. An introvert is not yet a neurotic, but he is in an unstable situation: he is sure to develop symptoms of the next shift of forces, unless he finds some other outlets for his dammed-up libido. The unreal character of neurotic satisfaction and the neglect of the distinction between phantasy and reality are on the other hand already determined by the fact of lingering at the stage of introversion.

You will no doubt have observed that in these last discussions I have introduced a fresh factor into the structure of the aetiological chain – namely the quantity, the magnitude, of the energies concerned. We have still to take this factor into account everywhere. A purely qualitative analysis of the aetiological determinants is not

---

[1] [Jung, who introduced the term in 1910, at one stage applied it exclusively to dementia praecox. (Cf. Jung, 1911–12.)]

[2] [I.e., charging with an extra amount of psychical energy.]

enough. Or, to put it another way, a merely *dynamic* view of these mental processes is insufficient; an *economic* line of approach is also needed. We must tell ourselves that the conflict between two trends does not break out till certain intensities of cathexis have been reached, even though the determinants for it have long been present so far as their subject-matter is concerned. In the same way, the pathogenic significance of the constitutional factors must be weighed according to how much *more* of one component instinct than of another is present in the inherited disposition. It may even be supposed that the disposition of all human beings is qualitatively alike and that they differ only owing to these quantitative conditions. The quantitative factor is no less decisive as regards capacity to resist neurotic illness. It is a matter of *what quota* of unemployed libido a person is able to hold in suspension and of *how large a fraction* of his libido he is able to divert from sexual to sublimated aims. The ultimate aim of mental activity, which may be described qualitatively as an endeavour to obtain pleasure and avoid unpleasure, emerges, looked at from the economic point of view, as the task of mastering the amounts of excitation (mass of stimuli) operating in the mental apparatus and of keeping down their accumulation which creates unpleasure.[1]

This, then, is what I wanted to tell you about the formation of symptoms in the neuroses. But I must not fail to lay emphasis expressly once again on the fact that everything I have said here applies only to the formation of symptoms in hysteria. Even in obsessional neurosis there is much – apart from fundamentals, which remain unaltered – that will be found different. The anticathexes opposing the demands of the instincts (which we have already spoken of in the case of hysteria as well) become prominent in obsessional neurosis and dominate the clinical picture in the form of what are known as 'reaction-formations'. We discover similar and even more far-reaching divergences in the other neuroses, where our researches into the mechanisms of symptom-formation are not yet concluded at any point.

Before I let you go to-day, however, I should like to direct your attention a little longe to a side of the life of phantasy which deserves

[1] [Here Freud appears to be equating the 'pleasure principle' and 'the principle of constancy'. At a later date he drew a clear distinction between the two (see Freud, 1924c, *Standard Ed.*, **19**, 159–61; *P.F.L.*, **11**, 413–15.]

the most general interest. For there is a path that leads back from phantasy to reality – the path, that is, of art. An artist is once more in rudiments an introvert, not far removed from neurosis. He is oppressed by excessively powerful instinctual needs. He desires to win honour, power, wealth, fame and the love of women; but he lacks the means for achieving these satisfactions. Consequently, like any other unsatisfied man, he turns away from reality and transfers all his interest, and his libido too, to the wishful constructions of his life of phantasy, whence the path might lead to neurosis. There must be, no doubt, a convergence of all kinds of things if this is not to be the complete outcome of his development; it is well known, indeed, how often artists in particular suffer from a partial inhibition of their efficiency owing to neurosis. Their constitution probably includes a strong capacity for sublimation and a certain degree of laxity in the repressions which are decisive for a conflict. An artist, however, finds a path back to reality in the following manner. To be sure, he is not the only one who leads a life of phantasy. Access to the half-way region of phantasy is permitted by the universal assent of mankind, and everyone suffering from privation expects to derive alleviation and consolation from it. But for those who are not artists the yield of pleasure to be derived from the sources of phantasy is very limited. The ruthlessness of their repressions forces them to be content with such meagre day-dreams as are allowed to become conscious. A man who is a true artist has more at his disposal. In the first place, he understands how to work over his day-dreams in such a way as to make them lose what is too personal about them and repels strangers, and to make it possible for others to share in the enjoyment of them. He understands, too, how to tone them down so that they do not easily betray their origin from proscribed sources. Furthermore, he possesses the mysterious power of shaping some particular material until it has become a faithful image of his phantasy; and he knows, moreover, how to link so large a yield of pleasure to this representation of his unconscious phantasy that, for the time being at least, repressions are outweighed and lifted by it. If he is able to accomplish all this, he makes it possible for other people once more to derive consolation and alleviation from their own sources of pleasure in their unconscious which have come inaccessible to them; he earns their gratitude and admiration and he has thus achieved *through* his phantasy what originally he had achieved only *in* his phantasy – honour, power and the love of women.

Ten

NEUROSIS AND PSYCHOSIS

Introduction

Freud's field of work was the neuroses, his observational material being limited by the conditions of his medical practice. For this reason, his ventures into the area of psychosis were few, instigated by the occasional psychotic episodes of his patients or the intensive study of publications such as Daniel Paul Schreber's *Denkwürdigkeiten eines Nervenkranken* (1903). Freud explores, on the one hand, the common factors and, on the other, the considerable differences between these two forms of illness (1924*b*, 1924*e*). In his opinion, both have their onset in the frustration of a vital instinctual wish. Their difference lies in the nature of what is substituted for the frustrated wish.

As was demonstrated in the previous section, the neurotic's relationship to reality is important to Freud's theory of the neuroses, though he had stressed that 'in the world of the neuroses it is psychical reality which is . . . decisive' (1916–17, p. 368). Or, put differently, he does not discriminate whether 'the infantile experiences to which the libido is fixated and out of which the symptoms are made' (p. 367) actually happened or whether they belonged to the patient's phantasies; the pathogenic effect is the same in both cases. In 'The Loss of Reality in Neurosis and Psychosis' (1924*e*), on the other hand, Freud explicitly emphasizes that it would be wrong to conclude from this finding that he believed neurotics to be incapable of clearly distinguishing between phantasy and reality, between inner and outer reality. On the contrary, it is in fact a defining characteristic of the neuroses that the ego function of reality-testing has for all practical purposes remained intact and that the equivalence and equality of inner and outer reality are confined to the processes of symptom-formation. The neurotic, e.g., in obsessional neurosis, behaves as though he truly believed in the omnipotence of his death wishes; or he may believe that some harmless everyday utensils contain dangerous substances which might pass over to him and from which he must protect himself by avoiding contact with them. At the same time he knows that these apprehensions are only a product of his phantasies; and it is precisely this reality-adequate knowledge which forces him to fashion his symptomatic substitute formations in such a way that they simultaneously take into account the pressure of the instinctual wishes and the demands by the external world represented by the super-ego which has adopted them.

As 'Neurosis and Psychosis' (1924b) shows, Freud sees the significant difference of the psychoses in the circumstance that the frustration of the instinctual wish is from the very beginning experienced as intolerable and therefore leads to a rupture in the relations to the external world which is held to be responsible for the non-fulfilment. Depending upon the form of the psychotic illness, the cathexes are withdrawn from the real perception, the real persons, and even the real memories, as a result of which the external world no longer has any influence on psychic processes. Unlike the neurotic, the psychotic then is free to evolve symptoms and substitute formations that need to be adequate only to the demands of the id and no longer to those of reality.

In his paper on the Schreber case (1911c), Freud demonstrated that psycho-analysis can reach beyond the area of neurosis and illuminate diverse psychic mechanisms and their ways of operating and unravel such pathological forms as amentia, schizophrenia and paranoia. On the other hand, he did not base any therapeutic claims on this understanding. He was convinced that psychotics lack the fundamental prerequisite that makes a patient suitable for psycho-analytic therapy: a more or less normal ego that has retained the capacities of reality-testing, self-observation, and insight into the illness; the libidinal cathexis of real persons, which makes the emotional transference to the analyst possible; the readiness of the inner world to perceive, acknowledge, and at least partially to subject itself to external influences. Since these functions are not at the disposal of the psychotic, he was, in Freud's opinion, not amenable to psycho-analysis and at best accessible only in periods of remission between psychotic episodes.

Freud's pupils and followers who in general uphold his views do not share this one, which they regard as therapeutic nihilism. Today the therapeutic ambitions of many analysts extend far beyond the frame of the symptom neuroses and character disturbances to the so-called borderline cases that lead over to the psychoses and to the psychoses themselves. It is difficult to decide how much of this is to be ascribed to general human interest in the bizarre phenomena of psychosis, how much to the thorough psychiatric training of medical analysts, and how much simply to the desire to advance beyond the frontiers of what has already been explored to new territories. In any event, preoccupation with the psychoses now constitutes a special field of interest in the psycho-analytic literature dealing with problems of theory and technique of therapy. In view of certain technical considerations, many believe that it is possible to arouse in the psychotic enough of the still-present remnants of object libido so that a transference relationship from the patient to the therapist can be established; to compensate temporarily for the patient's ego defects by means of the analyst's putting his own intact psychic apparatus at the disposal of the patient; and in general to enter together with the patient into the primary thought processes and phantasies of his id before the patient is gradually urged toward and made capable of replacing id processes by ego processes, in the tradition of psycho-analytic therapy.

Whether the treatment of psychotics by psycho-analytic means can be successful is still a matter of debate in psycho-analysis. It remains a task for the future to find a middle course between therapeutic pessimism and therapeutic optimism in this area.

Freud's work on the psychoses had serious consequences for a central aspect of psycho-analytic theory, namely, libido theory, i.e., the theory of the vicissitudes of the psychic energy emanating from the sexual drives. What Freud previously conceived of as an antithesis between sexual instinct and ego instincts (1915c) became, in the new conceptualization (1914c), the different deployment of one and the same sexual energy, on the one hand for the cathexis of real or phantasied persons in the external world (object libido) and, on the other, for the cathexis of one's own somatic and psychic person (narcissistic libido).

The introduction of the theory of narcissism in 1914 led to the explanation of many previously ununderstood phenomena. In this new conception, the paranoiac's megalomania, for example, is understood as caused by the withdrawal of cathexis from objects and the hypercathexis of his own person and its functions; the same process also is held responsible for the 'end of the world' anxieties of these patients because, for them, the external world is devoid of libidinal cathexis. Hypochondriasis, on the other hand, is thought to develop when all libido is concentrated on the body or a specific part of the body or a specific body organ. A complete counterpart to this is the impoverishment of a person in the state of being in love in which all libido is withdrawn from narcissistic purposes and transferred to the love object that as a consequence is overvalued. The love life of adults also is thought, in many respects, especially in the choice of a partner, to be determined by the difference between object-libidinal and narcissistic impulses.

In his explanation of this phenomenon, Freud goes back to childhood, i.e., to 'the idea of there being an original libidinal cathexis of the ego, from which some of it is later given off to objects, but which fundamentally persists and is related to the object-cathexes much as the body of an amoeba is related to the pseudopodia which it puts out' (1914c, p. 75). The intense ego cathexis which the child and the psychotic (as well as primitive peoples) have in common also explains their own 'over-estimation of the power of their wishes and mental acts', the so-called grandiose 'omnipotence of thought' (1914c, p. 75). The hypothesis that the same libido is capable of object-libidinal as well as narcissistic deployment – i.e., is mobile – is one that can no longer be dispensed with in Freud's theory. As valuable as the more recent studies of narcissism may be for the theory and practice of psycho-analysis, the assumption of an autonomous narcissistic libido independent of object libido cannot be reconciled with the conceptualization described above.

Neurosis and Psychosis

(1924)*

In my recently published work, *The Ego and the Id* (1923*b*), I have proposed a differentiation of the mental apparatus, on the basis of which a number of relationships can be represented in a simple and perspicuous manner. As regards other points – for instance, in what concerns the origin and role of the super-ego – enough remains obscure and unelucidated. Now one may reasonably expect that a hypothesis of this kind should prove useful and helpful in other directions as well, if only to enable us to see what we already know from another angle, to group it differently and to describe it more convincingly. Such an application of the hypothesis might also bring with it a profitable return from grey theory to the perpetual green of experience.[1]

In the work I have mentioned I described the numerous dependent relationships of the ego, its intermediate position between the external world and the id and its efforts to humour all its masters at once. In connection with a train of thought raised in other quarters, which was concerned with the origin and prevention of the psychoses, a simple formula has now occurred to me which deals with what is perhaps the most important genetic difference between a neurosis and a psychosis: *neurosis is the result of a conflict between the ego and its id, whereas psychosis is the analogous outcome of a similar disturbance in the relations between the ego and the external world.*

There are certainly good grounds for being suspicious of such simple solutions of a problem. Moreover, the most that we may expect is that this formula will turn out to be correct in the roughest outline. But even that would be something. One recalls at once, too, a whole number of discoveries and findings which seem to support our thesis. All our analyses go to show that the transference neuroses originate

---

* First published in *Int. Z. Psychoanal.* The present text is included in *Standard Ed.*, **19**, 149; *P.F.L.*, **10**, 213.
[1] [A quotation from Goethe's *Faust*.]

from the ego's refusing to accept a powerful instinctual impulse in the id or to help it to find a motor outlet, or from the ego's forbidding that impulse the object at which it is aiming. In such a case the ego defends itself against the instinctual impulse by the mechanism of repression. The repressed material struggles against this fate. It creates for itself, along paths over which the ego has no power, a substitutive representation (which forces itself upon the ego by way of a compromise) – the symptom. The ego finds its unity threatened and impaired by this intruder, and it continues to struggle against the symptom, just as it fended off the original instinctual impulse. All this produces the picture of a neurosis. It is no contradiction to this that, in undertaking the repression, the ego is at bottom following the commands of its super-ego – commands which, in their turn, originate from influences in the external world that have found representation in the super-ego. The fact remains that the ego *has* taken sides with those powers, that in it their demands have more strength than the instinctual demands of the id, and that the ego is the power which sets the repression in motion against the portion of the id concerned and which fortifies the repression by means of the anticathexis of resistance. The ego has come into conflict with the id in the service of the super-ego and of reality; and this is the state of affairs in every transference neurosis.

On the other side, it is equally easy, from the knowledge we have so far gained of the mechanism of the psychoses, to adduce examples which point to a disturbance in the relationship between the ego and the external world. In Meynert's amentia – an acute hallucinatory confusion which is perhaps the most extreme and striking form of psychosis – either the external world is not perceived at all, or the perception of it has no effect whatever.[1] Normally, the external world governs the ego in two ways: firstly, by current, present perceptions which are always renewable, and secondly, by the store of memories of earlier perceptions which, in the shape of an 'internal world', form a possession of the ego and a constituent part of it. In amentia, not only is the acceptance of new perceptions refused, but the internal world, too, which, as a copy of the external world, has up till now represented it, loses its significance (its cathexis). The ego creates, autocratically, a new external and internal world; and there can be no doubt of two facts – that this new world is constructed in accordance with the id's wishful impulses, and that the motive of this dissociation from the

[1] [A passage in Chapter VIII of Freud's posthumous *Outline of Psycho-Analysis* (1940a [1938]) qualifies this statement.]

external world is some very serious frustration by reality of a wish – a frustration which seems intolerable. The close affinity of this psychosis to normal dreams is unmistakable. A precondition of dreaming, moreover, is a state of sleep, and one of the features of sleep is a complete turning away from perception and the external world.[1]

We know that other forms of psychosis, the schizophrenias, are inclined to end in affective hebetude – that is, in a loss of all participation in the external world. In regard to the genesis of delusions, a fair number of analyses have taught us that the delusion is found applied like a patch over the place where originally a rent had appeared in the ego's relation to the external world. If this precondition of a conflict with the external world is not much more noticeable to us than it now is, that is because, in the clinical picture of the psychosis, the manifestations of the pathogenic process are often overlaid by manifestations of an attempt at a cure or a reconstruction.[2]

The aetiology common to the onset of a psychoneurosis and of a psychosis always remains the same. It consists in a frustration, a non-fulfilment, of one of those childhood wishes which are for ever undefeated and which are so deeply rooted in our phylogenetically determined organization. This frustration is in the last resort always an external one;[3] but in the individual case it may proceed from the internal agency (in the super-ego) which has taken over the representation of the demands of reality. The pathogenic effect depends on whether, in a conflictual tension of this kind, the ego remains true to its dependence on the external world and attempts to silence the id, or whether it lets itself be overcome by the id and thus torn away from reality. A complication is introduced into this apparently simple situation, however, by the existence of the super-ego, which, through a link that is not yet clear to us, unites in itself influences coming from the id as well as from the external world, and is to some extent an ideal model of what the whole endeavour of the ego is aiming at – a reconciliation between its various dependent relationships.[4] The attitude of the super-ego should be taken into account – which has not hitherto been done – in every form of psychical illness. We may

---

[1] [Cf. the metapsychological paper on dreams (1917d).]

[2] [Cf. the Schreber analysis (1911c), *Standard Ed.*, **12**, 71; *P.F.L.*, **9**, 209.]

[3] [See some remarks in the discussion of frustration in 'Types of Onset of Neurosis' (1912c), *Standard Ed.*, **12**, 234; *P.F.L.*, **10**, 123.]

[4] [Cf. 'The Economic Problem of Masochism' (1924c).]

provisionally assume that there must also be illnesses which are based on a conflict between the ego and the super-ego. Analysis gives us a right to suppose that melancholia is a typical example of this group; and we would set aside the name of 'narcissistic psychoneuroses' for disorders of that kind. Nor will it clash with our impressions if we find reasons for separating states like melancholia from the other psychoses. We now see that we have been able to make our simple genetic formula more complete, without dropping it. Transference neuroses correspond to a conflict between the ego and the id; narcissistic neuroses, to a conflict between the ego and the super-ego; and psychoses, to one between the ego and the external world. It is true that we cannot tell at once whether we have really gained any new knowledge by this, or have only enriched our store of formulas; but I think that this possible application of the proposed differentiation of the mental apparatus into an ego, a super-ego and an id cannot fail to give us courage to keep that hypothesis steadily in view.

The thesis that neuroses and psychoses originate in the ego's conflicts with its various ruling agencies – that is, therefore, that they reflect a failure in the functioning of the ego, which is at pains to reconcile all the various demands made on it – this thesis needs to be supplemented in one further point. One would like to know in what circumstances and by what means the ego can succeed in emerging from such conflicts, which are certainly always present, without falling ill. This is a new field of research, in which no doubt the most varied factors will come up for examination. Two of them, however, can be stressed at once. In the first place, the outcome of all such situations will undoubtedly depend on economic considerations – on the relative magnitude of the trends which are struggling with one another. In the second place, it will be possible for the ego to avoid a rupture in any direction by deforming itself, by submitting to encroachments on its own unity and even perhaps by effecting a cleavage or division of itself.[1] In this way the inconsistencies, eccentricities and follies of men would appear in a similar light to their sexual perversions, through the acceptance of which they spare themselves repressions.

In conclusion, there remains to be considered the question of what

[1] [This is an early hint at a problem that was to occupy Freud in his later years. It was first discussed at length in the paper on 'Fetishism' (1927e) and afterwards in two unfinished works, in 'Splitting of the Ego in the Process of Defence' (1940e [1938]) and in Chapter VIII of the Outline (1940a [1938]).]

the mechanism, analogous to repression, can be by means of which the ego detaches itself from the external world. This cannot, I think, be answered without fresh investigations; but such a mechanism, it would seem, must, like repression, comprise a withdrawal of the cathexis sent out by the ego.[1]

---

[1] [This problem, too – the nature of what Freud later called '*Verleugnung*', 'disavowal' – was discussed in the later papers mentioned in the previous footnote. See an Editor's footnote to 'The Infantile Genital Organization', on p. 392 above, for a fuller discussion of the question.]

The Loss of Reality in Neurosis and Psychosis

(1924)*

I have recently[1] indicated as one of the features which differentiate a neurosis from a psychosis the fact that in a neurosis the ego, in its dependence on reality, suppresses a piece of the id (of instinctual life), whereas in a psychosis, this same ego, in the service of the id, withdraws from a piece of reality. Thus for a neurosis the decisive factor would be the predominance of the influence of reality, whereas for a psychosis it would be the predominance of the id. In a psychosis, a loss of reality would necessarily be present, whereas in a neurosis, it would seem, this loss would be avoided.

But this does not at all agree with the observation which all of us can make that every neurosis disturbs the patient's relation to reality in some way, that it serves him as a means of withdrawing from reality, and that, in its severe forms, it actually signifies a flight from real life. This contradiction seems a serious one; but it is easily resolved, and the explanation of it will in fact help us to understand neuroses.

For the contradiction exists only as long as we keep our eyes fixed on the situation at the *beginning* of the neurosis, in which the ego, in the service of reality, sets about the repression of an instinctual impulse. This, however, is not yet the neurosis itself. The neurosis consists rather in the processes which provide a compensation for the portion of the id that has been damaged – that is to say, in the reaction against the repression and in the failure of the repression. The loosening of the relation to reality is a consequence of this second step in the formation of a neurosis, and it ought not to surprise us if a detailed examination shows that the loss of reality affects precisely that piece of reality as a result of whose demands the instinctual repression ensued.

There is nothing new in our characterization of neurosis as the

* First published in *Int. Z. Psychoanal.* The present text is included in *Standard Ed.*, **19**, 183; *P.F.L.*, **10**, 221.

[1] 'Neurosis and Psychosis' (1924*b*). [See the preceding paper in this volume.]

result of a repression that has failed. We have said this all along,[1] and it is only because of the new context in which we are viewing the subject that it has been necessary to repeat it.

Incidentally, the same objection arises in a specially marked manner when we are dealing with a neurosis in which the exciting cause (the 'traumatic scene') is known, and in which one can see how the person concerned turns away from the experience and consigns it to amnesia. Let me go back by way of example to a case analysed a great many years ago,[2] in which the patient, a young woman, was in love with her brother-in-law. Standing beside her sister's death-bed, she was horrified at having the thought: 'Now he is free and can marry me.' This scene was instantly forgotten, and thus the process of regression, which led to her hysterical pains, was set in motion. It is instructive precisely in this case, moreover, to learn along with path the neurosis attempted to solve the conflict. It took away from the value of the change that had occurred in reality, by repressing the instinctual demand which had emerged – that is, her love for her brother-in-law. The *psychotic* reaction would have been a disavowal[3] of the fact of her sister's death.

We might expect that when a psychosis comes into being, something analogous to the process in a neurosis occurs, though, of course, between different agencies of the mind; thus we might expect that in a psychosis, too, two steps could be discerned, of which the first would drag the ego away, this time from reality, while the second would try to make good the damage done and re-establish the subject's relations to reality at the expense of the id. And, in fact, some analogy of the sort can be observed in a psychosis. Here, too, there are two steps, the second of which has the character of a reparation. But beyond that the analogy gives way to a far more extensive similarity between the two processes. The second step of the psychosis is indeed intended to make good the loss of reality, not, however, at the expense of a restriction of the id – as happens in neurosis at the expense of the relation to reality – but in another, more autocratic manner, by the creation of a new reality which no longer raises the same objections as the old one that

[1] [The notion that the 'return of the repressed' constitutes 'the illness proper' is already stated in Draft K of the Fliess correspondence, of January 1, 1896 (Freud, 1950a). A little later Freud restated this, using the actual words 'failure of defence' as equivalent to 'return of the repressed', in Section II of the second paper on 'The Neuro-Psychoses of Defence' (1896b).]

[2] In *Studies on Hysteria* (1895d). [*Standard Ed.*, **2**, 156 and 167; *P.F.L.*, **3**, 226 and 238.]

[3] [See a footnote to 'The Infantile Genital Organization' in Chapter 3, p. 392 above.]

has been given up. The second step, therefore, both in neurosis and psychosis, is supported by the same trends. In both cases it serves the desire for power of the id, which will not allow itself to be dictated to by reality. Both neurosis and psychosis are thus the expression of a rebellion on the part of the id against the external world, of its unwillingness – or, if one prefers, its incapacity – to adapt itself to the exigencies of reality, to Ἀνάγκη [Necessity].[1] Neurosis and psychosis differ from each other far more in their first, introductory, reaction than in the attempt at reparation which follows it.

Accordingly, the initial difference is expressed thus in the final outcome: in neurosis a piece of reality is avoided by a sort of flight, whereas in psychosis it is remodelled. Or we might say: in psychosis, the initial flight is succeeded by an active phase of remodelling; in neurosis, the initial obedience is succeeded by a deferred attempt at flight. Or again, expressed in yet another way: neurosis does not disavow the reality, it only ignores it; psychosis disavows it and tries to replace it. We call behaviour 'normal' or 'healthy', if it combines certain features of both reactions – if it disavows the reality as little as does a neurosis, but if it then exerts itself, as does a psychosis, to effect an alteration of that reality. Of course, this expedient, normal, behaviour leads to work being carried out on the external world; it does not stop, as in psychosis, at effecting internal changes. It is no longer *autoplastic* but *alloplastic*.[2]

In a psychosis, the transforming of reality is carried out upon the psychical precipitates of former relations to it – that is, upon the memory-traces, ideas and judgements which have been previously derived from reality and by which reality was represented in the mind. But this relation was never a closed one; it was continually being enriched and altered by fresh perceptions. Thus the psychosis is also faced with the task of procuring for itself perceptions of a kind which shall correspond to the new reality; and this is most radically effected by means of hallucination. The fact that, in so many forms and cases of psychosis, the paramnesias, the delusions and the hallucinations that occur are of a most distressing character and are bound up with a generation of anxiety – this fact is without doubt a

---

[1] [See 'The Economic Problem of Masochism' (1924c).]

[2] [These terms are possibly due to Ferenczi, who used them in a paper on 'The Phenomena of Hysterical Materialization' (1919, 24; English trans., 1926, 97). But he there appears to attribute them to Freud, who, however, does not seem to have used them elsewhere than in this passage.]

sign that the whole process of remodelling is carried through against forces which oppose it violently. We may construct the process on the model of a neurosis, with which we are more familiar. There we see that a reaction of anxiety sets in whenever the repressed instinct makes a thrust forward, and that the outcome of the conflict is only a compromise and does not provide complete satisfaction. Probably in a psychosis the rejected piece of reality constantly forces itself upon the mind, just as the repressed instinct does in a neurosis, and that is why in both cases the consequences too are the same. The elucidation of the various mechanisms which are designed, in the psychoses, to turn the subject away from reality and to reconstruct reality – this is a task for specialized psychiatric study which has not yet been taken in hand.[1]

There is, therefore, a further analogy between a neurosis and a psychosis, in that in both of them the task which is undertaken in the second step is partly unsuccessful. For the repressed instinct is unable to procure a full substitute (in neurosis); and the representation of reality cannot be remoulded into satisfying forms (not, at least, in every species of mental illness). But the emphasis is different in the two cases. In a psychosis it falls entirely on the first step, which is pathological in itself and cannot but lead to illness. In a neurosis, on the other hand, it falls on the second step, on the failure of the repression, whereas the first step may succeed, and does succeed in innumerable instances without overstepping the bounds of health – even though it does so at a certain price and not without leaving behind traces of the psychical expenditure it has called for. These distinctions, and perhaps many others as well, are a result of the topographical difference in the initial situation of the pathogenic conflict – namely whether in it the ego yielded to its allegiance to the real world or to its dependence on the id.

A neurosis usually contents itself with avoiding the piece of reality in question and protecting itself against coming into contact with it. The sharp distinction between neurosis and psychosis, however, is weakened by the circumstance that in neurosis, too, there is no lack of attempts to replace a disagreeable reality by one which is more in keeping with the subject's wishes. This is made possible by the

---

[1] [Cf., however, some beginnings made by Freud himself as regards paranoia in the Schreber analysis (1911*c*) (*Standard Ed.*, **12**, 69–71; *P.F.L.*, **9**, 208–10), and paraphrenia, in his papers on 'Narcissism' (1914*c*), the metapsychology of dreams (1917*d*) and 'The Unconscious' (Chapter 3 above).]

existence of a *world of phantasy*, of a domain which became separated from the real external world at the time of the introduction of the reality principle. This domain has since been kept free from the demands of the exigencies of life, like a kind of 'reservation'; it is not inaccessible to the ego, but is only loosely attached to it. It is from this world of phantasy that the neurosis draws the material for its new wishful constructions, and it usually finds that material along the path of regression to a more satisfying real past.

It can hardly be doubted that the world of phantasy plays the same part in psychosis and that there, too, it is the storehouse from which the materials or the pattern for building the new reality are derived. But whereas the new, imaginary external world of a psychosis attempts to put itself in the place of external reality, that of a neurosis, on the contrary, is apt, like the play of children, to attach itself to a piece of reality – a different piece from the one against which it has to defend itself – and to lend that piece a special importance and a secret meaning which we (not always quite appropriately) call a *symbolic* one. Thus we see that both in neurosis and psychosis there comes into consideration the question not only of a *loss of reality* but also of a *substitute for reality*.

Chronological Table of Freud's Life and Work

This table traces very roughly some of the main turning-points in Freud's intellectual development and opinions. A few of the chief events in his external life are also included in it.

1856. 6 May. Birth at Freiberg in Moravia.

1860. Family settles in Vienna.

1865. Enters Gymnasium (secondary school).

1873. Enters Vienna University as medical student.

1876–82. Works under Brücke at the Institute of Physiology in Vienna.

1877. First publications: papers on anatomy and physiology.

1881. Graduates as Doctor of Medicine.

1882. Engagement to Martha Bernays.

1882–5. Works in Vienna General Hospital, concentrating on cerebral anatomy: numerous publications.

1884–7. Researches into the clinical uses of cocaine.

1885. Appointed *Privatdozent* (University Lecturer) in Neuropathology.

1885. (October)–1886 (February). Studies under Charcot at the Salpêtrière (hospital for nervous diseases) in Paris. Interest first turns to hysteria and hypnosis.

1886. Marriage to Martha Bernays. Sets up private practice in nervous diseases in Vienna.

1886–93. Continues work on neurology, especially on the cerebral palsies of children at the Kassowitz Institute in Vienna, with numerous publications. Gradual shift of interest from neurology to psychopathology.

1887. Birth of eldest child (Mathilde).

1887–1902. Friendship and correspondence with Wilhelm Fliess in Berlin. Freud's letters to him during this period, published posthumously in 1950, throw much light on the development of his views.

1887. Begins the use of hypnotic suggestion in his practice.

c. 1888. Begins to follow Breuer in using hypnosis for cathartic treatment of hysteria. Gradually drops hypnosis and substitutes free association.

1889. Visits Bernheim at Nancy to study his suggestion technique.

1889. Birth of eldest son (Martin).

1891. Monograph on Aphasia.
Birth of second son (Oliver).

1892. Birth of youngest son (Ernst).

1893. Publication of Breuer and Freud 'Preliminary Communication': exposition of trauma theory of hysteria and of cathartic treatment.
Birth of second daughter (Sophie).

1893–8. Researches and short papers on hysteria, obsessions, and anxiety.

1895. Jointly with Breuer, *Studies on Hysteria*: case histories and description by Freud of his technique, including first account of transference.

1893–6. Gradual divergence of views between Freud and Breuer. Freud introduces concepts of defence and repression and of neurosis being a result of a conflict between the ego and the libido.

1895. *Project for a Scientific Psychology*: included in Freud's letters to Fliess and first published in 1950. An abortive attempt to state psychology in neurological terms; but foreshadows much of Freud's later theories.
Birth of youngest child (Anna).

1896. Introduces the term 'psycho-analysis'.
Death of father (aged 80).

1897. Freud's self-analysis, leading to the abandonment of the trauma theory and the recognition of infantile sexuality and the Oedipus complex.

1900. *The Interpretation of Dreams*, with final chapter giving first full account of Freud's dynamic view of mental processes, of the unconscious, and of the dominance of the 'pleasure principle'.

1901. *The Psychopathology of Everyday Life*. This, together with the book on dreams, made it plain that Freud's theories applied not only to pathological states but also to normal mental life.

1902. Appointed Professor Extraordinarius.

1905. *Three Essays on the Theory of Sexuality*: tracing for the first time the course of development of the sexual instinct in human beings from infancy to maturity.

c. 1906. Jung becomes an adherent of psycho-analysis.

1908. First international meeting of psycho-analysts (at Salzburg).

1909. Freud and Jung invited to the USA to lecture.
Case history of the first analysis of a child (Little Hans, aged five): confirming inferences previously made from adult analyses, especially as to infantile sexuality and the Oedipus and castration complexes.

c. 1910. First emergence of the theory of 'narcissism'.

1911–15. Papers on the technique of psycho-analysis.

1911. Secession of Adler.
Application of psycho-analytic theories to a psychotic case: the autobiography of Dr Schreber.

1913–14. *Totem and Taboo*: application of psycho-analysis to anthropological material.

1914. Secession of Jung.
'On the History of the Psycho-Analytic Movement'. Includes a polemical section on Adler and Jung.
Writes his last major case history, of the 'Wolf Man' (not published till 1918).

1915. Writes a series of twelve 'metapsychological' papers on basic theoretical questions, of which only five have survived.

1915–17. *Introductory Lectures*: giving an extensive general account of the state of Freud's views up to the time of the First World War.

1919. Application of the theory of narcissism to the war neuroses.

1920. Death of second daughter.

Beyond the Pleasure Principle: the first explicit introduction of the concept of the 'compulsion to repeat' and of the theory of the 'death instinct'.

1921. *Group Psychology*. Beginnings of a systematic analytic study of the ego.

1923. *The Ego and the Id*. Largely revised account of the structure and functioning of the mind with the division into an id, an ego, and a super-ego.

1923. First onset of cancer.

1925. Revised views on the sexual development of women.

1926. *Inhibitions, Symptoms, and Anxiety*. Revised views on the problem of anxiety.

1927. *The Future of an Illusion*. A discussion of religion: the first of a number of sociological works to which Freud devoted most of his remaining years.

1930. *Civilization and its Discontents*. This includes Freud's first extensive study of the destructive instinct (regarded as a manifestation of the 'death instinct').

Freud awarded the Goethe Prize by the City of Frankfurt.

Death of mother (aged 95).

1933. Hitler seizes power in Germany: Freud's books publicly burned in Berlin.

1934–8. *Moses and Monotheism*: the last of Freud's works to appear during his lifetime.

1936. Eightieth birthday. Election as Corresponding Member of Royal Society.

1938. Hitler's invasion of Austria. Freud leaves Vienna for London. *An Outline of Psycho-Analysis*. A final, unfinished but profound, exposition of psycho-analysis.

1939. 23 September. Death in London.

JAMES STRACHEY

Bibliography

Titles of books and periodicals are in italics, titles of papers are in inverted commas. Abbreviations are in accordance with the *World List of Scientific Periodicals* (London, 1963–5). Numerals in bold type refer to volumes, ordinary numerals refer to pages.

In the case of the Freud entries, only English translations are given. The initial dates are those of the German original publications. (The date of writing is added in square brackets where it differs from the latter.) The letters attached to the dates of publication are in accordance with the corresponding entries in the complete bibliography of Freud's writings included in Volume 24 of the *Standard Edition*. Details of the original publication, including the original German title, are given in the editorial introduction to each work in the *Standard Edition* and in the *Pelican Freud Library*.

ABRAHAM, K. (1908) 'Die psychosexuellen Differenzen der Hysterie und der Dementia praecox', *Zentbl. Nervenheilk.*, N.F., **19**, 521.
[*Trans.*: 'The Psychosexual Differences Between Hysteria and Dementia Praecox', *Selected Papers*, London, 1927, Chap. II.]
(1916) 'Untersuchungen über die früheste prägenitale Entwicklungsstufe der Libido', *Int. Z. (ärztl.) Psychoanal.*, **4**, 71.
[*Trans.*: 'The First Pregenital Stage of the Libido', *Selected Papers*, London, 1927, Chap. XII.]
(1921) 'Äusserungsformen des weiblichen Kastrationskomplexes', *Int. Z. Psychoanal.*, **7**, 422.
[*Trans.*: 'Manifestations of the Female Castration Complex', *Selected Papers*, London, 1927, Chap. XXII.]
(1924) *Versuch einer Entwicklungsgeschichte der Libido*, Leipzig, Vienna, Zurich.
[*Trans.*: 'A Short Study of the Development of the Libido', *Selected Papers*, London, 1927, Chap. XXVI.]

ADLER, A. (1907) *Studie über Minderwertigkeit der Organen*, Berlin and Vienna. [*Trans.: Study of Organ-Inferiority*, New York, 1917.]

(1908) 'Aggressionstrieb im Leben und in der Neurose', *Fortschr. Med.*, **26**, 677.

ANDREAS-SALOMÉ, L. (1916) ' "Anal" and "Sexual" ', *Imago*, **4**, 249.

ARDUIN (1900) 'Die Frauenfrage und die sexuellen Zwischenstufen', *Jb. sex. Zwischenst.*, **2**, 211.

ARTEMIDORUS OF DALDIS. *Oneirocritica.*

AZAM, E. (1876) 'Amnésie périodique ou dédoublement de la vie', *Ann. méd.-psychol.* (5ᵉ série), **16**, 5.

(1887) *Hypnotisme, double conscience et altérations de la personnalité*, Paris.

BALDWIN, J. M. (1895) *Mental Development in the Child and the Race*, New York.

BAYER, H. (1902) 'Zur Entwicklungsgeschichte der Gebärmutter', *Dtsch. Arch. klin. Med.*, **73**, 422.

BELL, J. S. (1902) 'A Preliminary Study of the Emotion of Love between the Sexes', *Amer. J. Psychol.*, **13**, 325.

BERNHEIM, H. (1886) *De la suggestion et de ses applications à la thérapeutique*, Paris.

(1891) *Hypnotisme, suggestion, psychothérapie*, Paris.

BINET, A. (1888) *Études de psychologie expérimentale: le fétichisme dans l'amour*, Paris.

BINZ, C. (1878) *Über den Traum*, Bonn.

BLEULER, E. (1908) 'Sexuelle Abnormitäten der Kinder', *Jb. schweiz. Ges. SchulgesundPfl.*, **9**, 623.

(1910) 'Vortrag über Ambivalenz' (Berne), Report in *Zentbl. Psychoanal.*, **1**, 266.

(1911) *Dementia Praecox, oder Gruppe der Schizophrenien*, Leipzig and Vienna. [*Trans.: Dementia Praecox, or the Group of Schizophrenias*, New York, 1950.]

(1912) *Das autistische Denken*, Leipzig and Vienna.

(1913) 'Der Sexualwiderstand', *Jb. psychoanal. psychopath. Forsch.*, **5**, 442.

(1914) 'Die Kritiken der Schizophrenien', *Z. ges. Neurol. Psychiat.*, **22**, 19.

BLOCH, I. (1902–3) *Beiträge zur Ätiologie der Psychopathologia sexualis*, Dresden.

BRENNER, C. (1957, 2nd ed. 1973) *An Elementary Textbook of Psychoanalysis*, New York.

BREUER, J., and FREUD, S. *See* FREUD, S. (1893a)

(1895) *See* FREUD, S. (1895d)

BRUNSWICK, R. M. (1928) 'Die Analyse eines Eifersuchtswahnes', *Int. Z. Psychoanal.*, **14**, 458.

BURDACH, K. F. (1838) *Die Physiologie als Erfahrungswissenschaft*, Berlin.

BUTLER, S. (1880) *Unconscious Memory*, London.

CALKINS, G. N. (1902) 'Studies on the Life-History of Protozoa', *Arch. Env. Mech. Org.*, **15**, 139.

CHEVALIER, J. (1893) *L'inversion sexuelle*, Lyon.

CLARK, D. STAFFORD- (1967) *What Freud Really Said*, London.

DESSOIR, M. (1894) 'Zur Psychologie der Vita sexualis', *Allg. Z. Psychiat.*, **50**, 941.

DEUTSCH, H. (1925) *Psychoanalyse der weiblichen Sexualfunktionen*, Vienna.

(1932) 'Über die weibliche Homosexualität', *Int. Z. Psychoanal.*, **18**, 219.
[*Trans.*: 'Homosexuality in Women', *Int. J. Psycho-Anal.*, **14** (1933), 34.]

DISKUSSIONEN DER WIENER PSYCHOANALYTISCHER VEREINIGUNG, **2**, *Die Onanie*, Wiesbaden, 1912.

DOFLEIN, F. (1919) *Das Problem des Todes und der Unsterblichkeit bei den Pflanzen und Tieren*, Jena.

ELLIS, HAVELOCK (1897) *Studies in the Psychology of Sex*, Vol. II. Philadelphia.

(1898) 'Auto-Erotism: a Psychological Study', *Alien & Neurol.*, **19**, 260.

(1903) *Studies in the Psychology of Sex*, Vol. III: *Analysis of the Sexual Impulse; Love and Pain; the Sexual Impulse in Women*, Philadelphia.

(1927) 'The Conception of Narcissism', *Studies in the Psychology of Sex*, Vol. VII, Philadelphia, Chap. VI.

FECHNER, G. T. (1873) *Einige Ideen zur Schöpfungs- und Entwicklungsgeschichte der Organismen*, Leipzig.

FEDERN, P. (1913) 'Beiträge zur Analyse des Sadismus und Masochismus, I: Die Quellen des männlichen Sadismus', *Int. Z. (ärztl.) Psychoanal.*, **1**, 29.

FERENCZI, S. (1909) 'Introjektion und Übertragung', *Jb. psychoanal. psychopath. Forsch.*, **1**, 422.
[*Trans.*: 'Introjection and Transference', *First Contributions to Psycho-Analysis*, London, 1952, Chap. II.]

(1913) 'Entwicklungsstufen des Wirklichkeitssinnes', *Int. Z. (ärztl.) Psychoanal.*, **1**, 124.
[*Trans.*: 'Stages in the Development of a Sense of Reality', *First Contributions to Psycho-Analysis*, London, 1952, Chap. VIII.]

(1914) 'Zur Nosologie der männlichen Homosexualität (Homoërotik)', *Int. Z. (ärztl.) Psychoanal.*, **2**, 131.
[*Trans.*: 'The Nosology of Male Homosexuality (Homoerotism)', *First Contributions to Psycho-Analysis*, London, 1952, Chap. XII.]

(1919) *Hysterie und Pathoneurosen*, Leipzig and Vienna.
[*Trans.*: In *Further Contributions to the Theory and Technique of Psycho-Analysis*, London, 1926, Chaps. V, VI, IX, X, XI, XV.]

(1920) Review of Lipschütz, *Die Pubertätsdrüse*, *Int. Z. Psychoanal.*, **6**, 84.
[*Trans.*: *Int. J. Psycho-Anal.*, **2**, (1921), 143.]

(1924) *Versuch einer Genitaltheorie*, Leipzig and Vienna.
[*Trans.*: *Thalassa: a Theory of Genitality*, New York, 1938.]

FERENCZI, S. *et al.* (1919) *Zur Psychoanalyse der Kriegsneurosen*, Leipzig and Vienna.
[*Trans.*: *Psycho-Analysis and the War Neuroses*, London, Vienna and New York, 1921.]

FINKELNBURG, F. (1870) Niederrheinische Gesellschaft, Sitzung vom 21. März 1870 in Bonn. *Berlin. klin. Wschr.*, **7**, 449, 460.

FLIESS, W. (1892) *Neue Beiträge zur Klinik und Therapie der nasalen Reflexneurose*, Vienna.

(1906) *Der Ablauf des Lebens*, Vienna.

FREUD, A. (1922) 'Beating Fantasies and Daydreams', in *Introduction to Psychoanalysis: Lectures for Child Analysts and Teachers, 1922–1935*, New York and London, 1974.

FREUD, S. (1891b) *On Aphasia*, London and New York, 1953.

— (1893a) with BREUER, J., 'On the Psychical Mechanism of Hysterical Phenomena: Preliminary Communication', *Standard Ed.*, **2**, 3; *P.F.L.*, **3**, 51.

— (1893c) 'Some Points for a Comparative Study of Organic and Hysterical Motor Paralyses', *Standard Ed.*, **1**, 157.

— (1893h) 'Lecture "On the Psychical Mechanism of Hysterical Phenomena"', *Standard Ed.*, **3**, 27.

— (1894a) 'The Neuro-Psychoses of Defence', *Standard Ed.*, **3**, 43.

— (1895b) 'On the Grounds for Detaching a Particular Syndrome from Neurasthenia under the Description "Anxiety Neurosis"', *Standard Ed.*, **3**, 87; *P.F.L.*, **10**, 31.

— (1895d) With BREUER, J., *Studies on Hysteria*, London, 1956; *Standard Ed.*, **2**; *P.F.L.*, **3**.

— (1896b) 'Further Remarks on the Neuro-Psychoses of Defence', *Standard Ed.*, **3**, 159.

— (1896c) 'The Aetiology of Hysteria', *Standard Ed.*, **3**, 189.

— (1898a) 'Sexuality in the Aetiology of the Neuroses', *Standard Ed.*, **3**, 261.

— (1899a) 'Screen Memories', *Standard Ed.*, **3**, 301.

— (1900a) *The Interpretation of Dreams*, London and New York, 1955; *Standard Ed.*, **4–5**; *P.F.L.*, **4**.

— (1901a) *On Dreams*, London and New York, 1951; *Standard Ed.*, **5**, 633.

— (1901b) *The Psychopathology of Everyday Life*, *Standard Ed.*, **6**; *P.F.L.*, **5**.

— (1904a) 'Freud's Psycho-Analytic Procedure', *Standard Ed.*, **7**, 249.

— (1905c) *Jokes and their Relation to the Unconscious*, London, 1960; *Standard Ed.*, **8**; *P.F.L.*, **6**.

— (1905d) *Three Essays on the Theory of Sexuality*, London, 1962; *Standard Ed.*, **7**, 125; *P.F.L.*, **7**, 31.

— (1905e) 'Fragment of an Analysis of a Case of Hysteria', *Standard Ed.*, **7**, 3; *P.F.L.*, **8**, 29.

— (1906a [1905]) 'My Views on the Part played by Sexuality in the Aetiology of the Neuroses', *Standard Ed.*, **7**, 271; *P.F.L.*, **10**, 71.

— (1907a) *Delusions and Dreams in Jensen's 'Gradiva'*, *Standard Ed.*, **9**, 3; *P.F.L.*, **14**, 27.

— (1908a) 'Hysterical Phantasies and their Relation to Bisexuality', *Standard Ed.*, **9**, 157; *P.F.L.*, **10**, 83.

— (1908b) 'Character and Anal Erotism', *Standard Ed.*, **9**, 169; *P.F.L.*, **7**, 205.

— (1908c) 'On the Sexual Theories of Children', *Standard Ed.*, **9**, 207; *P.F.L.*, **7**, 183.

— (1908e [1907]) 'Creative Writers and Day-Dreaming', *Standard Ed.*, **9**, 143; *P.F.L.*, **14**, 131.

— (1909a [1908]) 'Some General Remarks on Hysterical Attacks', *Standard Ed.*, **9**, 229; *P.F.L.*, **10**, 95.

— (1909b) 'Analysis of a Phobia in a Five-Year-Old Boy', *Standard Ed.*, **10**, 3; *P.F.L.*, **8**, 165.

— (1909d) 'Notes upon a Case of Obsessional Neurosis', *Standard Ed.*, **10**, 155; *P.F.L.*, **9**, 31.

— (1910e) 'The Antithetical Meaning of Primal Words', *Standard Ed.*, **11**, 155.

(1910*h*) 'A Special Type of Object Choice made by Men', *Standard Ed.*, 11, 165; *P.F.L.*, 7, 227.

(1911*b*) 'Formulations on the two Two Principles of Mental Functioning', *Standard Ed.*, 12, 215; *P.F.L.*, 11, 31.

(1911*c*) 'Psycho-Analytic Notes on an Autobiographical Account of a Case of Paranoia (Dementia Paranoides)', *Standard Ed.*, 12, 3; *P.F.L.*, 9, 129.

(1912*c*) 'Types of Onset of Neurosis', *Standard Ed.*, 12, 229; *P.F.L.*, 10, 115.

(1912*f*) 'Contributions to a Discussion on Masturbation', *Standard Ed.*, 12, 243.

(1912*g*) 'A Note on the Unconscious in Psycho-Analysis', *Standard Ed.*, 12, 257; *P.F.L.*, 11, 45.

(1912–13) *Totem and Taboo*, London, 1950; New York, 1952; *Standard Ed.*, 13, 1; *P.F.L.*, 13, 43.

(1913*i*) 'The Disposition to Obsessional Neurosis', *Standard Ed.*, 12, 313; *P.F.L.*, 10, 131.

(1913*j*) 'The Claims of Psycho-Analysis to Scientific Interest', *Standard Ed.*, 13, 165; *P.F.L.*, 15.

(1914*c*) 'On Narcissism: An Introduction', *Standard Ed.*, 14, 69; *P.F.L.*, 11, 59.

(1914*d*) 'On the History of the Psycho-Analytic Movement', *Standard Ed.*, 14, 3; *P.F.L.*, 15.

(1914*g*) 'Remembering, Repeating and Working Through', *Standard Ed.*, 12, 147.

(1915*b*) 'Thoughts for the Times on War and Death', *Standard Ed.*, 14, 275; *P.F.L.*, 12, 57.

(1915*c*) 'Instincts and their Vicissitudes', *Standard Ed.*, 14, 111; *P.F.L.*, 11, 105.

(1915*d*) 'Repression', *Standard Ed.*, 14, 143; *P.F.L.*, 11, 139.

(1915*e*) 'The Unconscious', *Standard Ed.*, 14, 161; *P.F.L.*, 11, 159.

(1916*d*) 'Some Character-Types Met with in Psycho-Analytic Work', *Standard Ed.*, 14, 311; *P.F.L.*, 14, 291.

(1916–17) *Introductory Lectures on Psycho-Analysis*, New York, 1966; London, 1971; *Standard Ed.*, 15–16; *P.F.L.*, 1.

(1917*a*) 'A Difficulty in the Path of Psycho-Analysis', *Standard Ed.*, 17, 137.

(1917*b*) 'A Childhood Recollection from *Dichtung und Wahrheit*', *Standard Ed.*, 17, 147; *P.F.L.*, 14, 321.

(1917*c*) 'On Transformations of Instinct as Exemplified in Anal Erotism', *Standard Ed.*, 17, 127; *P.F.L.*, 7, 295.

(1917*d* [1915]) 'A Metapsychological Supplement to the Theory of Dreams', *Standard Ed.*, 14, 219; *P.F.L.*, 11, 223.

(1917*e* [1915]) 'Mourning and Melancholia', *Standard Ed.*, 14, 239; *P.F.L.*, 11, 245.

(1918*b* [1914]) 'From the History of an Infantile Neurosis', *Standard Ed.*, 17, 3; *P.F.L.*, 9, 225.

(1919*d*) Introduction to *Psycho-Analysis and the War Neuroses*, London and New York, 1921; *Standard Ed.*, 17, 207.

(1919*e*) 'A Child is Being Beaten', *Standard Ed.*, 17, 177; *P.F.L.*, 10, 159.

(1920a) 'The Psychogenesis of a Case of Homosexuality in a Woman', *Standard Ed.*, **18**, 147; *P.F.L.*, **9**, 367.

(1920g) *Beyond the Pleasure Principle*, London, 1961; *Standard Ed.*, **18**, 7; *P.F.L.*, **11**, 269.

(1921c) *Group Psychology and the Analysis of the Ego*, London and New York, 1959; *Standard Ed.*, **18**, 69; *P.F.L.*, **12**, 91.

(1922b [1921]) 'Some Neurotic Mechanisms in Jealousy, Paranoia and Homosexuality', *Standard Ed.*, **18**, 223; *P.F.L.*, **10**, 195.

(1923a [1922]) 'Two Encyclopaedia Articles', *Standard Ed.*, **18**, 235; *P.F.L.*, **15**.

(1923b) *The Ego and the Id*, London and New York, 1962; *Standard Ed.*, **19**, 3; *P.F.L.*, **11**, 339.

(1923c [1922]) 'Remarks on the Theory and Practice of Dream-Interpretation', *Standard Ed.*, **19**, 109.

(1923e) 'The Infantile Genital Organization', *Standard Ed.*, **19**, 141; *P.F.L.*, **7**, 303.

(1924b [1923]) 'Neurosis and Psychosis', *Standard Ed.*, **19**, 149; *P.F.L.*, **10**, 209.

(1924c) 'The Economic Problem of Masochism', *Standard Ed.*, **19**, 157; *P.F.L.*, **11**, 409.

(1924d) 'The Dissolution of the Oedipus Complex', *Standard Ed.*, **19**, 173; *P.F.L.*, **7**, 313.

(1924e) 'The Loss of Reality in Neurosis and Psychosis', *Standard Ed.*, **19**, 183; *P.F.L.*, **10**, 219.

(1924f [1923]) 'A Short Account of Psycho-Analysis', *Standard Ed.*, **19**, 191.

(1925a) 'A Note on the "Mystic Writing-Pad"', *Standard Ed.*, **19**, 227; *P.F.L.*, **11**, 427.

(1925d [1924]) *An Autobiographical Study*, *Standard Ed.*, **20**, 3; *P.F.L.*, **15**.

(1925e [1924]) 'The Resistances to Psycho-Analysis', *Standard Ed.*, **19**, 213; *P.F.L.*, **15**.

(1925h) 'Negation', *Standard Ed.*, **19**, 235; *P.F.L.*, **11**, 435.

(1925j) 'Some Psychical Consequences of the Anatomical Distinction between the Sexes', *Standard Ed.*, **19**, 243; *P.F.L.*, **7**, 323.

(1926d [1925]) *Inhibitions, Symptoms and Anxiety*, London, 1960; *Standard Ed.*, **20**, 77; *P.F.L.*, **10**, 227.

(1926e) *The Question of Lay Analysis*, *Standard Ed.*, **20**, 179; *P.F.L.*, **15**.

(1926f) 'Psycho-Analysis: Freudian School', *Encyclopaedia Britannica*, 13th ed., vol. 3, 253; *Standard Ed.*, **20**, 261.

(1927a) 'Postscript to *The Question of Lay Analysis*', *Standard Ed.*, **20**, 251; *P.F.L.*, **15**.

(1927c) *The Future of an Illusion*, London, 1962; *Standard Ed.*, **21**, 3; *P.F.L.*, **12**, 179.

(1927d) 'Humour', *Standard Ed.*, **21**, 159; *P.F.L.*, **14**, 425.

(1927e) 'Fetishism', *Standard Ed.*, **21**, 149; *P.F.L.*, **7**, 345.

(1930a) *Civilization and its Discontents*, New York and London, 1963; *Standard Ed.*, **21**, 59; *P.F.L..*, **12**, 243.

(1931b) 'Female Sexuality', *Standard Ed.*, **21**, 223; *P.F.L.*, **7**, 367.

(1933*a* [1932]) *New Introductory Lectures on Psycho-Analysis*, New York, 1966; London, 1971; *Standard Ed.*, **22**; *P.F.L.*, **2**.

(1937*c*) 'Analysis Terminable and Interminable', *Standard Ed.*, **23**, 211.

(1937*d*) 'Constructions in Analysis', *Standard Ed.*, **23**, 257.

(1940*a* [1938]) *An Outline of Psycho-Analysis*, New York, 1968; London, 1969; *Standard Ed.*., **23**, 141; *P.F.L.*, **15**.

(1940*b* [1938]) 'Some Elementary Lessons in Psycho-Analysis', *Standard Ed.*, **23**, 281.

(1940*e* [1938]) 'Splitting of the Ego in the Process of Defence', *Standard Ed.*, **23**, 273; *P.F.L.*, **11**, 459.

(1942*a* [1905–6]) 'Psychopathic Characters on the Stage', *Standard Ed.*, **7**, 305; *P.F.L.*, **14**, 119.

(1950*a* [1887–1902]) *The Origins of Psycho-Analysis*, London and New York, 1954. (Partly, including 'A Project for a Scientific Psychology', in *Standard Ed.*, **1**, 175.)

(1960*a*) *Letters 1873–1939* (ed. E. L. Freud) (trans. T. and J. Stern), New York, 1960; London, 1961.

GALANT, S. (1919) 'Sexualleben im Sauglings- und Kindersalter', *Neurol. Zentbl.*, **38**, 652.

GLEY, E. (1884) 'Les aberrations de l'instinct sexuel', *Rev. phil.*, **17**, 66.

GOETTE, A. (1883) *Über den Ursprung des Todes*, Hamburg.

GRIESINGER, W. (1845) *Pathologie und Therapie der psychischen Krankheiten*, Stuttgart.

GRODDECK, G. (1923) *Das Buch vom Es*, Vienna.
 [*Trans.: The Book of the It*, New York, 1950.]

GROOS, C. (1899) *Die Spiele der Menschen*, Jena.

(1904) *Das Seelenleben des Kindes*, Berlin.

HALBAN, J. (1903) 'Die Entstehung der Geschlechtscharaktere', *Arch. Gynaek.*, **70**, 205.

(1904) 'Schwangerschaftsreaktion der fötalen Organe und ihre puerperale Involution', *Z. Geburtsh. Gynäk.*, **53**, 191.

HALL, G. S. (1904) *Adolescence* (2 vols.), New York.

HARTMANN, M. (1906) *Tod und Fortpflanzung*, Munich.

HELLER, T. (1904) *Grundriss der Heilpädagogik*, Leipzig.

HERING, E. (1870) 'Über das Gedächtnis als eine allgemeine Funktion der organisierten Materie', Lecture to Imperial Academy of Sciences, Vienna.

(1878) *Zur Lehre vom Lichtsinne*, Vienna.

HERMAN, G. (1903) *'Genesis', das Gesetz der Zeugung*, Bd. 5, Leipzig.

HIRSCHFELD, M. (1899) 'Die objektive Diagnose der Homosexualität', *Jb. sex. Zwischenst.*, **1**, 4.

(1904) 'Statistische Untersuchungen über den Prozentsatz der Homosexuellen', *Jb. sex. Zwischenst.*, **6**.

HORNEY, K. (1923) 'On the Genesis of the Castration Complex in Women', *Int. J. Psycho-Anal.*, **5** (1924), 50.

HUG-HELLMUTH, H. VON (1913) *Aus dem Seelenleben des Kindes*, Leipzig and Vienna.
 [*Trans.: A Study of the Mental Life of the Child*, New York, 1919.]

JACKSON, J. HUGHLINGS (1878) 'On Affections of Speech from Disease of
    the Brain', *Brain*, **1**, 304.
JANET, P. (1909) *Les névroses*, Paris.
JEKELS, L. (1913) 'Einige Bemerkungen zur Trieblehre', *Int. Z. (ärztl.)
    Psychoanal.*, **1**, 439.
JONES, E. (1953–57) *Sigmund Freud: Life and Work* (3 vols.), London and New
    York.
JUNG, C. G. (1909) 'Die Bedeutung des Vaters für das Schicksal des
    Einzelnen', *Jb. psychoanalyt. psychopath. Forsch.*, **1**, 155.
    (1911–12) 'Wandlungen und Symbole der Libido', *Jb. psychoanalyt. psycho-
    path. Forsch.*, **3**, 120 and **4**, 162; in book form, Leipzig and Vienna, 1912.
KIERNAN, J. G. (1888) 'Sexual Perversion and the Whitechapel Murders',
    Med. Standard Chicago, **4**, 170.
KRAFFT-EBING, R. VON (1892) 'Bemerkungen über 'geschlechtliche Hörig-
    keit" und Masochismus', *Jb. Psychiat.*, **10**, 199.
    (1895) 'Zur Erklärung der konträren Sexualempfindung', *Jb. Psychiat.
    Neurol.*, **13**, 1.
KRIS, E. (1956) 'Freud in the History of Science', *The Listener*, **55**, No. 1416
    (May 17), 631.
LAMPL-DE GROOT, J. (1927) 'Zur Entwicklungsgeschichte des Ödipus-
    komplexes der Frau', *Int. Z. Psychoanal.*, **13**, 269.
LEVINE, I. (1923) *The Unconscious*, London.
    [*German trans.: Das Unbewusste*, Vienna, 1926.]
LINDNER, S. (1879) 'Das Säugen an den Fingern, Lippen, etc., bei den
    Kindern (Ludeln)', *Jb. Kinderheilk*, N.F., **14**, 68.
LIPSCHÜTZ, A. (1914) *Warum wir sterben*, Stuttgart.
    (1919) *Die Pubertätsdrüse und ihre Wirkungen*, Berne.
LOEB, J. (1909) *Die chemische Entwicklungserrugung des tierischen Eies*, Paris.
LOW, B. (1920) *Psycho-Analysis*, London.
LYDSTON, G. F. (1889) 'A Lecture on Sexual Perversion, Satyriasis and
    Nymphomania', *Med. Surg. Reporter, Philadelphia*, **61**.
MARCINOWSKI, J. (1918) 'Erotische Quellen der Minderwertigkeits-
    gefühle', *Z. Sexualwiss.*, Bonn, **4**, 313.
MASTERS, W. H., and JOHNSON, V. E. (1970) *Human Sexual Inadequacy*,
    Boston.
MAUPAS, E. (1888) 'Recherches expérimentales sur la multiplication des
    infusoires ciliés', *Arch. Zool. exp. gén.* (sér. 2), **6**, 165.
MILL, J. S. (1843) *A System of Logic*, London.
    (1865) *An Examination of Sir William Hamilton's Philosophy*, London.
MOEBIUS, P. J. (1900) 'Über Entartung', *Grenzfr. Nerv.- und Seelenlebens*,
    No. 3, 95, Wiesbaden.
MOLL, A. (1898) *Untersuchungen über die Libido sexualis*, Berlin.
    (1909) *Das Sexualleben des Kindes*, Berlin.
NACHMANSOHN, M. (1915) 'Freuds Libidotheorie verglichen mit der Eros-
    lehre Platos', *Int. Z. (ärztl.) Psychoanal.*, **3**, 65.
OPHUIJSEN, J. H. W. VAN (1917) 'Beiträge zum Männlichkeitskomplex
    der Frau', *Int. Z. (ärztl.) Psychoanal.*, **4**, 241.
PÉREZ, B. (1886) *L'enfant de trois à sept ans*, Paris.

PFEIFER, S. (1919) 'Äusserungen infantil-erotischer Triebe im Spiele', *Imago*, 5, 243.

PREYER, W. (1882) *Die Seele des Kindes*, Leipzig.

RANK, O. (1907) *Der Künstler*, Leipzig and Vienna.

(1909) *Der Mythus der Geburt des Helden*, Leipzig and Vienna.

[*Trans.: The Myth of the Birth of the Hero*, New York, 1914.]

(1910) 'Ein Traum, der sich selbst deutet', *Jb. psychoanalyt. psychopath. Forsch.*, 2, 465.

(1913) 'Eine noch nicht beschriebene Form des Ödipus-Traumes', *Int. Z. (ärztl.) Psychoanal.*, 1, 151.

(1924) *Das Trauma der Geburt*, Vienna.

[*Trans.: The Trauma of Birth*, London, 1929.]

RICKMAN, J. (ed.) (1937), *A General Selection from the Works of Sigmund Freud*, London.

RIEGER, C. (1900) *Die Castration*, Jena.

ROHLEDER, H. (1899) *Die Masturbation*, Berlin.

SADGER, I. (1908) 'Fragment der Psychoanalyse eines Homosexuellen', *Jb. sex. Zwischenst.*, 9, 339.

SANCTIS, SANTE DE (1899) *I sogni*, Turin.

[*German trans.: Die Träume* (trans. O. Schmidt), Halle, 1901.]

SCHERNER, K. A. (1861) *Das Leben des Traumes*, Berlin.

SCHOPENHAUER, A. (1819) *Die Welt als Wille und Vorstellung*, Leipzig.

(1851) 'Über die anscheinende Absichtlichkeit im Schicksale des Einzelnen', *Parerga und Paralipomena* (Essay IV), Vol. 1, Leipzig.

SCHREBER, D. P. (1903) *Denkwürdigkeiten eines Nervenkranken*, Leipzig.

SCHRENCK-NOTZING, A. VON (1899) 'Literaturzusammenstellung über die Psychologie und Psychopathologie der Vita sexualis', *Z. Hypnot.*, 9, 98.

SCHUBERT, G. H. VON (1814) *Die Symbolik des Traumes*, Bamberg.

SPAMER, C. (1876) 'Über Aphasie und Asymbolie', *Arch. Psychiat. Nervenkr.*, 6, 496.

SPIELREIN, S. (1912) 'Die Destruktion als Ursache des Werdens', *Jb. psychoanalyt. psychopath. Forsch.*, 4, 465.

STÄRCKE, A. (1914) Introduction to Dutch translation of Freud's '"Civilized" Sexual Morality and Modern Nervous Illness', Leyden.

(1921) 'Der Kastrationskomplex', *Int. Z. Psychoanal.*, 7, 9.

STEKEL, W. (1908) *Nervöse Angstzustände und ihre Behandlung*, Berlin and Vienna.

(1911) *Die Sprache des Traumes*, Wiesbaden.

STOUT, G. F. (1938) *A Manual of Psychology* (5th ed.), London.

STRÜMPELL, L. (1877) *Die Natur und Entstehung der Träume*, Leipzig.

(1899) *Die pädagogische Pathologie*, Leipzig.

SULLY, J. (1895) *Studies of Childhood*, London.

TARUFFI, C. (1903) *Hermaphroditismus und Zeugungsunfähigkeit*, Berlin.

VAIHINGER, H. (1911) *Die Philosphie des Als Ob*, Berlin.

[*Trans.: The Philosophy of 'As If'*, London, 1924.]

VARENDONCK, J. (1921) *The Psychology of Day-Dreams*, London and New York.

VOLKELT, J. (1875) *Die Traum-Phantasie*, Stuttgart.

WEININGER, O. (1903) *Geschlecht und Charakter*, Vienna.
[*Trans.: Sex and Character*, London, 1906.]

WEISMANN, A. (1882) *Über die Dauer des Lebens*, Jena.
(1884) *Über Leben und Tod*, Jena.
(1892) *Das Keimplasma*, Jena.
[*Trans.: The Germ-Plasm*, London, 1893.]

WOODRUFF, L. L. (1914) 'A Five-Year Pedigreed Race of *Paramecium* without Conjugation', *Proc. Soc. exp. Biol.*, **9**, 129.

ZIEGLER, K. (1913) 'Menschen- und Weltwerden', *Neue Jb. klass. Altertums*, **31**, 529.

Subject Index

Compiled by Diana LeCore

Conscious: definition, 135; latent, 164; and *Pcs.*, 164, 441; and the psychical, 186; relation with conscious and preconscious, 133; and unconscious, distinction between, 77, 136, 442

Conscious system (*Cs.*,), 133, 148, 149, 150, 153, 154, 156–9 *passim*, 161, 163–6 *passim*, 174, 233, 234, 235, 237–242, 441, 442, 445, 447, 448, 479, 519, 521

Consciousness, 165, 175, 187, 193, 204, 306, 442*n*, 447; assumption of, 145; conceptions latent in, 135; conceptions present in, 135; content of, 193; development of, 246; and dreams, 83, 114, 115, 125, 140; and ego, 19, 22, 119, 443, 451, 540; and ego-instincts, 513; gradations of clarity, 442*n*; nature of, 130; "official", 77; origin of, 234, 235, 500; and psychic activity, 131, 139; and psychical processes, 163; and preconscious system, 160; quality of, 496; and reality, 541; relationships of, 168; and repression, 153, 173, 317, 513; and sense-organs, 511; splitting, or shifting of, 138, 146; and substitutive formations, 163; and super-ego, 473; and system *Pcpt-Cs.*, 447, 500; and tension, 267; and thought-constructing agencies, 117

Cruelty, 301, 302, 309, 311, 332, 333, 471, 474, 475, 487, 521

Death, 50, 246, 247, 248, 250–53 *passim*, 261, 477
Delusion, 83, 113, 486, 565, 570
Dementia praecox, 167, 173, 242, 306
Depth-psychology, 26, 39, 46, 62, 63, 149, 185, 265, 424, 437, 444, 496
Desexualization, 454, 466, 467, 475
Disavowal, 381*n*, 392, 406, 567*n*, 569, 570
Disgust, 30, 296, 300, 301, 302, 304,

305, 318, 319, 323, 331, 355, 365, 521, 546
Displacement, 99–104 *passim*, 110, 111, 113, 116, 125, 156, 157, 159, 170, 242, 273, 301, 353, 407, 466, 500, 531, 533, 538, 540, 544, 547
Distortion, 164, 526, 527, 528
Dream-content, 82, 86–9 *passim*, 92, 94, 96–105 *passim*, 107, 109, 110, 111, 114, 118, 121
Dream-life, 130, 167; conflicting views of, 89; and memory, 82; and psychical illness, 82
Dream-thoughts, 89, 94, 95, 96, 98–106 *passim*, 108, 110, 112, 113, 114, 125, 170, 516
Dream-work, 89, 94, 95, 96, 98, 99, 102–5 *passim*, 108–14 *passim*, 116, 117, 125, 170*n*, 242, 451*n*, 498
Dreams, dreaming, 77–125, 143, 440; absurdity in, 106–8; anxiety-, 116, 120, 240; bewildering, 89–90; and censorship, 117, 118, 443; children's, 90–92, 118–19; compromise, 102; and condensation, 94–9; and day-dreams, 552; and dissociated cerebral activity, 89, 90; distortion, 114–15, 116, 118, 121; and dramatization, 99; and ego, 107; elements of, 85–7, 95–6, 98; formation, 113, 140, 163, 528, 541, 547; function of, 78, 118, 241; as guardians of sleep, 118–21; instigators of, 89, 100, 101–2; intelligible, 89, 100, 109, 115; interpretation of, 15–16, 25–6, 81, 82, 84–125, 131, 139, 194; latent content, 88, 89, 90, 94, 99; manifest content, 88, 89, 90, 94, 99, 103, 122, 133, 242; and pleasure principle, 510; punishment, 240–41; regression in, 104; relation to sleep, 79; relation to waking mental life, 81, 100; repression, 114–16; as sensory and somatic stimuli, 82; sexual, 122, 350; significance of, 81–3; theory of, 412; transitory character, 81; traumatic, 232; and

256, 258, 259, 262, 265, 266n, 268; mastery, 247; object of, 202; origin of, 263; pressure of, 201; primal, 203; and primal phantasies, 550; quality of, 203; regressive character, 264; repression, 205, 249, 524, 571; reversal of, 205, 208; sadistic, 259; scopophilic, 208, 209, 210, 299n, 309, 339; self-assertion, 247; sexual (see Sexual instincts); source of, 202, 203, 310; sublimation, 205; towards perfection, 249–50; transformation, 205–6, 207, 208

Instinctual impulses, 151, 221, 481; affective, 151, 152; emotional, 152; hunger as, 524; and id, 499; repression of, 38, 151, 221, 230, 267, 528, 531, 564; and resistances, 523; in Ucs. system, 163; unconscious, 151, 152; wishful aim of, 158

Interpretation, 15–16, 25–6, 38, 42, 46

Introjection, 213, 398, 453

Introversion, 169, 553

Intuition, 264

Inversion, 282–92, 296, 303, 308–9, 363–4

Lay analysis, 7–73

Libido, 30, 256–60, 292n, 431; and achievement of satisfaction, 541; aggressive factor in, 302; and castration, 351; children's, 333, 360, 362, 403, 409, 422; concept of, 257, 276; damming-up of, 312, 553; and disgust, 296; and ego, 540; and Eros, 256, 258; fixation of, 362, 542, 547, 548, 561; and hypnotism, 295n; and id, 468, 481, 482, 483; and inverts, 283, 285, 292n; Jung's concept of, 258–9; masculine nature of, 355, 429; narcissistic, 257–8, 265–6, 354, 454, 466, 480, 481, 482, 561, 562; and neurotic anxiety, 359n; and Nirvana principle, 201n; and physical illness, 241; in puberty,

356; quantitative factor, 554; and reality, 540; regression of, 463, 540, 542–6 passim; and sexual object, 259–60, 283, 308; and unconscious, 541; withdrawal, 154, 155, 167, 257

Libido theory, 68, 242, 256, 353–4, 561

Love, 211; and aggressiveness, 475; analytic, 43–6; children for parents, 32, 46, 272, 358, 362; and ego, 212–13, 214; genesis of, 215–16; narcissistic, 215

Love-hate antithesis, 205, 211, 212, 213–16, 260, 464, 465

Love-object, 467, 481; father as, 409, 418

Masculine-feminine antithesis, 212, 354–7

Masculinity complex, 399, 409, 424, 427–8, 431

Masochism, 205, 206, 207, 210, 260, 301–2, 309, 333, 471n, 482

Masturbation, 36, 170, 272, 273, 286, 291, 296, 314, 321, 322n, 328–30, 332, 356, 397, 404, 405, 408, 409, 425, 426, 550

Melancholia, 222, 242, 452, 453, 471–5 passim, 478, 487, 566

Memory, 136, 137, 138, 185, 508, 511, 515, 560; childhood, 315, 316, 329, 376, 549, 550; and conceptions, 135; conscious, 161; and dream-life, 82; foundation of, 233; and inverts, 283, 285; latent, 143, 176; and pathogenic manifestations, 271; and repressed ideas, 150, 151, 228; and word-presentations, 445

Memory-traces, 151, 153, 161, 172, 234, 244, 316, 375, 446, 500, 570

Meynert's amentia, 564–5

Mnemic images, 176, 178

Mnemic residues, 445, 446, 448

Morality, 305n, 307, 319, 331, 365, 460, 474, 477, 488

Mother: child's libidinal relations with, 419; and child's object-choice, 362, 363, 455; and